Volume One

PROBLEMS IN
ANCIENT HISTORY
*The Ancient Near East
and Greece*

PROBLEMS IN ANCIENT HISTORY

Second Edition

VOLUME ONE

The Ancient Near East and Greece

DONALD KAGAN
Yale University

MACMILLAN PUBLISHING CO., INC.
New York

COLLIER MACMILLAN PUBLISHERS
London

Macmillan Publishing Co., Inc.
866 Third Avenue, New York, New York 10022

Collier-Macmillan Canada, Ltd.

Library of Congress Cataloging in Publication Data

Kagan, Donald, comp.
  Problems in ancient history.

  CONTENTS: v. 1. The ancient Near East and Greece.—
v. 2. The Roman World.
  1. History, Ancient—Addresses, essays, lectures.
1. Title.
DS3. A2K3   1975   930   73-20995
ISBN 0-02-361820-5 (v. 1.)

Printing: 12 13 14 15 16   Year: 0 1 2 3 4 5 6 7

ISBN   0-02-361820-5

PREFACE

THIS ANTHOLOGY is an attempt to meet several problems facing the college student beginning the study of ancient history. It is meant to be used in conjunction with a narrative history or some suitable substitute. Together with such a narrative account it provides the material for instructive and, I hope, exciting discussions. Each section is a self-contained unit that presents a problem of continuing interest to historians. In almost every case there is a selection of the pertinent sources in translation, with a number of modern viewpoints also presented. In this way the beginning student may experience immediately the nature of the historian's craft: the excitement of weighing and evaluating sources, the problem of posing meaningful and enlightening questions, the need to change hypotheses in the light of new evidence or new insights, the necessity in some cases of suspending judgment. This method aims at reproducing in some small measure the actual conditions of historical investigation and making the results available to the neophyte.

The problems have been selected on the basis of several criteria: first, they attempt to span the chronological period usually covered by courses in ancient history in a reasonably representative way; second, they are all real problems that continue to excite interest among scholars, and in almost every case they have been the subject of relatively recent study; finally, they are meant to be sufficiently varied in topic and approach to expose the student to a variety of historical methods and techniques. Each problem, along with an accompanying narrative text, is sufficient for a week's work, but teachers will be able to assign the material to meet their own needs. It is hoped that the sampling of the ancient authors offered here will provide an irresistible stimulus for the student to read them in their entirety.

The changes I have introduced in this edition are intended to incorporate the results of recent scholarship and to reflect my own experience and that of others in teaching the material in it. Sections IV, VI, and VIII have been changed fundamentally to emphasize a new aspect of the general problem dealt with as well as to include more recent points of view. Each, in effect, is a new section rather than a revised one. The remaining sections are unchanged.

D. K.

CONTENTS

VOLUME ONE   The Ancient Near East and Greece

SECTION I

Government in Mesopotamia

THE FIRST CIVILIZATIONS arose in the valleys of the Nile and of the Tigris and Euphrates. In each, a complex urban society developed based on specialization of function, a written language, and a relatively centralized form of government. Egyptian government was put into the hands of a single ruler very early. The king was also god, and problems of his relation to law and restraints upon his powers do not arise. In Mesopotamia, however, the picture is different. Here, for some time, the city-state was the unit of government; only late and gradually did a single empire emerge from the confusion of independent states. There is evidence of popular assemblies at a very early date, and written law codes are known from the earliest times. These facts have given rise to much speculation and some disagreement as to the earliest development of government in Mesopotamia. Although the problem is difficult because of the scarcity and ambiguity of the evidence, it is well worth our attention. It is intrinsically rewarding as a means for shedding light on the society of ancient Mesopotamia; and, as well, Mesopotamian government can be interestingly compared with the development of Greek and Roman institutions.

1. THE SUMERIAN KING LIST*

This document seems to date from the time of Utukhegal of Erech (*ca.* 2125 B.C.). It is an attempt to demonstrate the continuous unity of Sumer under a single monarch from the very beginning of human society. It is not altogether reliable historically, but it gives us the view held by the Sumerians and a valuable insight into their mode of thinking about the past.

After kingship had descended from heaven, Eridu became (the seat) of kingship. In Eridu Alulim reigned 28,800 years as king; Alalgar reigned 36,000 years—two kings reigned 64,800 years. Eridu was abandoned, (and) its kingship was carried off to Badtibira.

In Badtibira, Enmenluanna reigned 43,200 years; Enmengalanna reigned 28,800 years; Dumuzi, the shepherd,

* Reprinted from *The Sumerians* by Samuel Noah Kramer by permission of the University of Chicago Press (Copyright 1963 by University of Chicago Press), pp. 328–331.

1

reigned 36,000 years—three kings reigned 108,000 years. Badtibira was abandoned, (and) its kingship was carried off to Larak.

In Larak, Ensipazianna reigned 28,800 years—one king reigned 28,800 years. Larak was abandoned, (and) its kingship was carried off to Sippar.

In Sippar, Enmeduranna reigned 21,000 years as king—one king reigned 21,000 years. Sippar was abandoned, (and) its kingship was carried off to Shuruppak.

In Shuruppak, Ubartutu reigned 18,600 years as king—one king reigned 18,600 years.

(Total) five cities, eight kings reigned 241,200 years.

The Flood then swept over (the land). After the Flood had swept over (the land) and kingship had descended from heaven (a second time), Kish became (the seat) of kingship. In Kish, Gaur reigned 1,200 years as king; Gulla-Nidaba-annapad reigned 960 years; Palakinatim reigned 900 years; Nangishlishma reigned . . . . years; Bahina reigned . . . . years; Buanum reigned 840 years; Kalibum reigned 960 years; Galumum reigned 840 years; Zukakip reigned 900 years; Atab reigned 600 years; Mashda, the son of Atab, reigned 840 years; Arurim, the son of Mashda, reigned 720 years; Etana, the shepherd, he who ascended to heaven, who made firm all the lands, reigned 1,560 years as king; Balih, the son of Etana, reigned 400 years; Enmenunna reigned 660 years; Melam-Kish, the son of Enmenunna, reigned 900 years; Barsalnunna, the son of Enmenunna, reigned 1,200 years; Mesza-mug, the son of Barsalnunna, reigned 140 years; Tizkar, the son of Meszamug, reigned 305 years; Ilku reigned 900 years; Iltasadum reigned 1,200 years; Enmeba-raggesi, he who smote the weapons of the land Elam, reigned 900 years as king; Agga, the son of Enmebaraggesi, reigned 625 years. (Total) twenty-three kings reigned 24,510 years, 3 months, 3½ days. Kish was defeated (in battle), (and) its kingship was carried off to Eanna.

In Eanna, Meskiaggasher, the son of (the sun-god) Utu reigned (both) as *en* (and) king 324 years—Meskiaggasher entered the sea (and) ascended the mountains; Enmerkar, the son of Meskiaggasher, the king of Erech who had built Erech, reigned 420 years as king; Lugalbanda, the shepherd, reigned 1,200 years; Dumuzi, the fisherman, whose city was Kua, reigned 100 years; Gilgamesh, whose father was a nomad(?), reigned 126 years; Urnungal, the son of Gilgamesh, reigned 30 years; Udulkalamma, the son of Urnungal, reigned 15 years; Labasher reigned 9 years; Ennundaranna reigned 8 years; Meshede reigned 36 years; Melamanna reigned 6 years; Lugalkidul reigned 36 years. (Total) twelve kings reigned 2,310 years. Erech was defeated (in battle), (and) its kingship was carried off to Ur.

In Ur, Mesannepadda reigned 80 years as king; Meskiagnunna, the son of Mesannepadda, reigned 36 years as king; Elulu reigned 25 years; Balulu reigned 36 years. (Total) four kings reigned 177 years. Ur was defeated (in battle), (and) its kingship was carried off to Awan.

(In Awan, there were three kings who reigned 356 years, but their names are destroyed in large part; the text then continues:) Awan was defeated (in battle), (and) its kingship was carried off to Kish.

In Kish . . . . reigned (more than) 201 years as king; Dadasig reigned . . . . years; Mamagal reigned 420 years; Kalbum, the son of Mamagal, reigned 132 years; Tuge reigned 360 years; Mennumna reigned 180 years; Lugalmu reigned 420 years; Ibbi-Ea reigned 290 (?) years. (Total) eight kings reigned 3,195 years. Kish was defeated (in battle), (and) its kingship was carried off to Hamazi.

In Hamazi, Hadanish reigned 360 years. (Total) one king reigned 360 years. Hamazi was defeated, (and) its kingship was carried off to Erech.

In Erech . . . . reigned 60 years as king; Lugalure reigned 120 years; Argandea reigned 7 years. (Total) three kings reigned

187 years. Erech was defeated, (and) its kingship was carried off to Ur.

In Ur (the names of the rulers of the Second Dynasty of Ur, who were four in number and probably reigned 116 years, are destroyed). Ur was defeated, (and) its kingship was carried off to Adab.

In Adab, Lugalannemundu reigned 90 years as king. (Total) one king reigned 90 years. Adab was defeated, (and) its kingship was carried off to Mari.

In Mari, Ilshu reigned 30 years as king; ... the son of Ilshu, reigned 17 years .... reigned 30 years; .. reigned 20 years; .. reigned 30 years; .. reigned 9 years. (Total) six kings reigned 136 years. Mari was defeated, (and) its kingship was carried off to Kish.

In Kish, Ku-Bau, the innkeeper, she who made firm the foundations of Kish, reigned 100 years as "king." (Total) one king reigned 100 years. Kish was defeated, (and) its kingship was carried off to Akshak.

In Akshak, Unzi reigned 30 years as king; Undalulu reigned 12 years; Urur (perhaps to be read, Zuzu) reigned 6 years; Puzur-Nirah reigned 20 years; Ishu-Il reigned 24 years; Shu-Sin, the son of Ishu-Il, reigned 7 years. (Total) six kings reigned 99 years. Akshak was defeated, (and) its kingship was carried off to Kish.

In Kish, Puzur-Sin, son of Ku-Bau, reigned 25 years as king; Ur-Zababa, the son of Puzur-Sin, reigned 400 years. Simudarra reigned 30 years; Usiwatar, the son of Simudarra, reigned 7 years; Ishtar-muti reigned 11 years; Ishme-Shamash reigned 11 years; Nannia, the stone-worker, reigned 7 years. (Total) seven kings reigned 491 years. Kish was defeated, (and) its kingship was carried off to Erech.

In Erech, Lugalzaggesi reigned 25 years as king. (Total) one king reigned 25 years. Erech was defeated, (and) its kingship was carried off to Agade.

In Agade, Sargon, whose father (?) was a gardener, the cupbearer of Ur-Zababa, the king of Agade who built Agade, reigned 56 years as king; Rimush, the son of Sargon, reigned 9 years; Manishtushu, the older brother of Rimush, son of Sargon, ruled 15 years; Naram-Sin, the son of Manishtushu, reigned 56 years; Sharkali-sharri, the son of Naram-Sin, reigned 25 years. Who was king? Who was not king? (that is, a period of anarchy). Igigi, the king; Nanum, the king; Imi, the king; Elulu, the king—the four of them were kings (but) reigned (only) 3 years. Dudu reigned 21 years; Shudurul, the son of Dudu, reigned 15 years. (Total) eleven kings reigned 197 years. Agade was defeated, (and) its kingship was carried off to Erech.

In Erech, Urnigin reigned 7 years as king; Urgigir, the son of Urnigin, reigned 6 years; Kudda reigned 6 years; Puzur-ili reigned 5 years; Ur-Utu reigned 6 years. (Total) five kings reigned 30 years. Erech was smitten with weapons, (and) its kingship was carried off to the Gutium hordes.

In the Gutium hordes, (first reigned) a nameless king; (then) Imta reigned 3 years as king; Inkishush reigned 6 years; Sarlagab reigned 6 years; Shulme reigned 6 years; Elulumesh reigned 6 years; Inimbakesh reigned 5 years; Igeshaush reigned 6 years; Iarlagab reigned 15 years; Ibate reigned 3 years; ... reigned 3 years, Kurum reigned 1 year; ... reigned 3 years; ... reigned 2 years; Irarum reigned 2 years; Ibranum reigned 1 year; Hablum reigned 2 years; Puzur-Sin, the son of Hablum, reigned 7 years; Iarlaganda reigned 7 years; ... reigned 7 years; ... reigned 40 days. (Total) twenty-one kings reigned 91 years, 40 days. The Gutium hordes were defeated, (and) their kingship was carried off to Erech.

In Erech, Utuhegal reigned 7 years, 6 months, 15 days as king. (Total) one king reigned 7 years, 6 months, 15 days. Erech was smitten with weapons, (and) its kingship carried off to Ur.

In Ur, Ur-Nammu reigned 18 years as king; Shulgi, the son of Ur-Nammu, reigned 48 years; Amar-Sin, the son of Shulgi, reigned 9 years; Shu-Sin, the son of Amar-Sin (an error for "the son of Shulgi"), reigned 9 years; Ibbi-Sin, the son of Shu-Sin, reigned 24 years. (Total) five kings reigned 108 years. Ur was defeated, (and) its kingship was carried off to Isin.

In Isin, Ishbi-Erra reigned 33 years as king; Shuilishu, the son of Ishbi-Erra, reigned 10 years; Idin-Dagan, the son of Shuilishu, reigned 21 years; Ishme-Dagan, the son of Idin-Dagan, reigned 20 years; Lipit-Ishtar, the son of Ishme-Dagan, reigned 11 years; Ur-Ninurta reigned 28 years; Bur-Sin, the son of Ur-Ninurta, reigned 21 years; Lipit-Enlil, the son of Bur-Sin, reigned 5 years; Erraimitti reigned 8 years; Enlilbani reigned 24 years; Zambia reigned 3 years; Iterpisha reigned 4 years; Urdukuga reigned 4 years; Sinmagir reigned 11 years. (Total) fourteen kings reigned 203 years.

2. GILGAMESH AND AGGA*

One of the most important documents for the earliest government of Mesopotamia is the Sumerian epic poem "Gilgamesh and Agga." It tells of a conflict between two city-states of Sumer—Kish, ruled by Agga, and Erech, whose king is Gilgamesh. As a result of one of the many conflicts between city-states, Agga issued an ultimatum demanding submission. The poem tells of the response it received.

The envoys of Agga, the son of Enmeba-raggesi
Proceeded from Kish to Gilgamesh in Erech,
The lord Gilgamesh before the elders of his city
Put the matter, seeks out their word:

"To complete the wells, to complete all the wells of the land,
To complete the wells, the small bowls of the land,
To dig the wells, to complete the fastening ropes—
Let us not submit to the house of Kish, let us smite it with weapons."

The convened assembly of the elders of his city
Answer Gilgamesh:
"To complete the wells, to complete all the wells of the land,
To complete the wells, the small bowls of the land,

To dig the wells, to complete the fastening ropes—
Let us submit to the house of Kish, let us not smite it with weapons."

Gilgamesh, the lord of Kullab,
Who performs heroic deeds for Inanna,
Took not the word of the elders of his city to heart.

A second time Gilgamesh, the lord of Kullab,
Before the "men" of his city, put the matter, seeks out their word:
"To complete the wells, to complete all the wells of the land,
To complete the wells, the small bowls of the land,
To dig the wells, to complete the fastening ropes,
Do not submit to the house of Kish, let us smite it with weapons."

The convened assembly of the "men" of his city answer Gilgamesh:
"Of those who stand, those who sit,
Of those who have been raised with the sons of kings,

* Translated by S. N. Kramer, *The Sumerians* (Copyright 1963 by University of Chicago Press), pp. 187–190.

Of those who press the donkey's thigh,
Who has their spirit!
Do not submit to the house of Kish, let us smite it with weapons,
Erech, the handiwork of the Gods,
Eanna, the house ascending from heaven—
It is the great gods who have fashioned its parts—
Its great walls touching the clouds,
Its lofty dwelling place established by An,
You have cared for—you, king and hero.
Conqueror, prince beloved of An,
How should you fear his coming!
That army is small, its rear totters,
Its men hold not high their eyes."

Then, Gilgamesh, the lord of Kullab,
At the words of the "men" of his city his heart rejoiced, his spirit brightened,
He says to his servant Enkidu:
"Now, then, let the (peaceful) tool be put aside for the violence of battle,
Let the battle weapons return to your side,
Let them bring about fear and terror,
He, when he comes—my great fear will fall upon him,
His judgment will be confounded, his counsel will be dissipated."

The days were not five, the days were not ten,
Agga, the son of Enmebaraggesi besieged Erech,
Erech—its judgment was confounded.

Gilgamesh, the lord of Kullab,
Says to its heroes:
"My heroes with darkened faces,
Who has heart, let him arise, I would have him go to Agga."

Birhurturre, the head man, to his king,
To his king, utters praise:
"I shall go to Agga,
His judgment will be confounded, his counsel will be dissipated."

Birhurturre went out through the city gate—

When Birhurturre had gone out through the city gate,
They seized him at the doors of the city gate,
Birhurturre—they crush his flesh,
Bring him before Agga,
Agga speaks to him.

He had not finished his words, when Zabardibunugga ascended the wall.
Agga saw him,
Says to Birhurturre:
"Slave, is that man your king?"

"That man is not my king,
Would that that man were my king,
That it were his strong forehead,
That it were his bison-like face,
That it were his lapis-like beard,
That it were his gracious fingers,"

The multitude rose not, the multitude left not,
The multitude rolled not in the dust,
The foreigners, the lot of them, felt not overwhelmed,
The natives bit not the dust,
The prows of the longboats were not cut down,
Agga, the king of Kish, restrained not his troops,
They strike him, they beat him,
Birhurturre—they crush his flesh.

Following Zabardibunugga, Gilgamesh ascends the wall,
Terror fell upon the young and old of Kullab,
The doors of the city gate—they stationed themselves at their approaches,
Enkidu went out through the city gate,
Gilgamesh peered over the wall,
Agga saw him:
"Slave, is that man your king?"
"That man is indeed my king."

No sooner had he said this,
The multitude rose, the multitude left,
The multitude rolled in the dust.

The foreigners, the lot of them, felt over-
whelmed,
The natives bit the dust,
The prows of the longboats were cut down,
Agga, the king of Kish, restrained his troops.

Gilgamesh, the lord of Kullab,
Says to Agga:
"Agga, my lieutenant, Agga, my captain,
Agga, my army general,
Agga, you have filled with grain the fleeing
bird,
Agga, you have given me breath, you have
given me life,

Agga, you have brought the fugitive to
your lap."

Erech, the handiwork of the god,
The great walls touching the sky,
The lofty dwelling established by An,
You have cared for, you, king and hero,
Conqueror, prince beloved of An,
Agga has set you free for the sake of
Kish,
Before Utu, he has returned you the favor
of former days,
Gilgamesh, lord of Kullab,
Your praise is good.

3. PRIMITIVE DEMOCRACY IN ANCIENT MESOPOTAMIA*

By far the most influential study of early Mesopotamian government is this account
by Thorkild Jacobsen of the University of Chicago.

Words which embody the hopes, the
fears, and the values of generations are
likely to lose in clarity what they gain in
depth. One such word is "democracy,"
which denoted a form of government and
now stands for a way of life. It may not be
amiss, therefore, first to make clear in what
sense we intend to use the word before we
plunge *in medias res.*

We shall use "democracy" in its classical
rather than in its modern sense as denoting
a form of government in which internal
sovereignty resides in a large proportion of
the governed, namely in all free, adult,
male citizens without distinction of fortune
or class. That sovereignty resides in these
citizens implies that major decisions—such
as the decision to undertake a war—are
made with their consent, that these citizens
constitute the supreme judicial authority in
the state, and also that rulers and magistrates obtain their positions with and
ultimately derive their power from that
same consent.

By "primitive democracy," furthermore,

we understand forms of government which,
though they may be considered as falling
within the definition of democracy just
given, differ from the classical democracies
by their more primitive character: the
various functions of government are as yet
little specialized, the power structure is
loose, and the machinery for social co-
ordination by means of power is as yet
imperfectly developed.

We should perhaps add that the contrast
with which we are primarily concerned is
the one between "democracy" as defined
above, on the one hand, and "autocracy,"
used as a general term for forms which
tend to concentrate the major political
powers in the hands of a single individual,
on the other. "Oligarchy," which so subtly
merges into democracy and which so often
functions in forms similar to it, can hardly,
at the present stage of our knowledge of
ancient Mesopotamia, be profitably distinguished.

AUTOCRATIC ORIENTATION IN
HISTORICAL TIMES

The political development in early historical times seems to lie under the spell

* Thorkild Jacobsen, "Primitive Democracy in
Ancient Mesopotamia," reprinted from *Journal of
Near Eastern Studies*, 2 (Copyright 1943 by Univer-
sity of Chicago Press), pp. 159–172.

of one controlling idea: concentration of political power in as few hands as possible.

Within small areas, in town and township, this principle had been realized—or was being realized—to a very substantial degree during the first centuries of Mesopotamian history. The country formed a mosaic of diminutive, self-sufficient, autonomous city-states, and in each such state one individual, the ruler, united in his hands the chief political powers: legislative, judiciary, and executive. Only he could promulgate and carry into effect new law; he alone was personally responsible by contract with the city-god for upholding justice and righteousness; as supreme commander of all armed forces, he led the state in battle; and, as administrator of the main temple complex, he controlled the most powerful single economic unit within the state.

But the momentum of the autocratic idea was still far from spent with the realization of this idea within small separate areas. It drove Mesopotamia forward relentlessly toward the more distant aim: centralization of power within one large area. Each ruler of a city-state was forever striving to subdue his neighbors, striving to become the one who would unite all of southern Mesopotamia into a single centralized state under a single ruling hand—his own. From before the dawn of history through the soldier-kingdoms of Lugalzagesi and the early Sargonids to the highly organized bureaucratic state of the Third Dynasty of Ur, we watch these efforts toward ultimate centralization steadily grow in power, in intensity, and in efficiency.

DEMOCRATIC INSTITUTIONS IN THE JUDICIARY IN POST-IMPERIAL TIMES

To find in a world so singularly autocratic in outlook, propelled in its domestic and foreign policies by the one urge for concentration of power, institutions based on diametrically opposite concepts is somewhat unexpected. Yet in the judiciary branch of government, as a heterogeneous, unassimilated block, appear, even in the latest period of Sumero-Akkadian civilization, features of a distinct and democratic character.

ASSYRIA. As a particularly striking example may serve the Assyrian merchant colonies in Asia Minor on the border of our cultural province. Here in early post-Imperial times (Isin-Larsa period) the highest judicial authority was not vested in any one individual but resided in a general assembly of all colonists: "the colony, young and old," as it is called. This general assembly was called into session by a clerk at the bidding of a majority of its senior members. Characteristically the clerk was not permitted to act at the bidding of any single individual and was severely punished if he did so.

The general assembly tried and decided lawsuits which arose in the colony, and even commissaries sent by the legal authorities of the mother-city Assur could not proceed, if they met with resistance on the part of a colonist, except by authority of this local assembly.

BABYLONIA. Turning from the "republican" Assyrian colonies to the Babylonia of Hammurabi as it is revealed some generations later in documents of the Old Babylonian Kingdom, we are very naturally struck first of all by the degree to which royal power is there in evidence. Anybody can turn to the king with complaints; he looks into the matter and delegates the case to a suitable court for decision. At his service stands a corps of royal officials and "judges of the king," dealing out justice according to the "legal practice of the king."

But it is worth noting that alongside of, and integrated with, this judiciary organization centered in the king stands another having its center in the Babylonian city. The city as such deals out justice according to its own local ideas of right and wrong. Town mayor and town elders settle minor local disputes; other cases—perhaps the more especially difficult or especially important ones—are brought before the town as a whole, the "assembly," for decision. Our sources furnish a vivid and interesting picture of the workings of this assembly; we shall comment, however, on two significant points only—its composition and its competence.

That the Old Babylonian assembly comprises, as already mentioned, the citizens of a given town or village is apparent from the use of "town" and "assembly" as alternatives in our documents. In the text *VAS*, VII, 149, for instance, after a report has been made "in the assembly of (the town) Dilbat," the ensuing actions are carried out "as Dilbat commanded." The assembly of Dilbat is thus equivalent to the town itself. Similar evidence is given by the letter *TCL*, XVII, 30. The writer of this letter needed a tribunal before which to compose a legal dispute; so he "assembled the town" (*a-lam ú-pa-ḫi-ir-ma*). His phrase—since the act *puḫḫurum*, "to assemble," produces a *puḫrum*, "assembly"—shows again that the town constitutes the assembly.

In interpreting this evidence, there is naturally some danger of going too far. Though citizens and therefore part of the *ālum*, "the town," women are not likely to have participated in the assembly. Even the men may not always have put in an appearance in numbers which we should consider adequate representation of the citizenry. One inference, however, may be drawn from the fact that *puḫrum* can alternate with the highly comprehensive term *ālum*: participation in the *puḫrum* and in the judicial functions which it exercised did not constitute the prerogative of some small favored class or group; it must have been open to the citizenry at large. And this is borne out by a Babylonian proverb which prudently, though with conspicuous lack of public spirit, warns:

Do not go to stand in the assembly;
Do not stray to the very place of strife.

It is precisely in strife that fate may overtake you;
Besides, you may be made a witness for them
So that they take you along to testify in a lawsuit not your own.

As will be readily seen, this proverb presupposes that anybody who happened along and had a mind to could "stand"— that is, participate—in the *puḫrum*.

The competence of the Old Babylonian assembly is in general that of a court of law. A plaintiff may himself "notify the assembly" (*puḫram lummudum*), or the case may be delegated to the assembly by the king or other high authority. The assembly investigates the case (inim-inimma igi-du$_8$), hears testimony, and may send one of the parties and his witness to some temple to prove their testimony by oath. Finally, it renders its decision (e or du$_{11}$ and *qabû*).

The cases tried by the assembly were, as shown by the records which have come down to us, both civil cases and criminal cases. The assembly had, as proved by one such record dealing with a case of murder, power to pronounce sentence of death. Occasional infliction of punishment in the assembly may represent a survival from times when the people met in assembly as both judge and executioner at the same time. The Code of Hammurabi decrees in paragraph 202 that "if a man has smitten the cheek of a man who is his superior (or "his senior"?) he shall be given sixty lashes with an ox whip in the assembly." It is also worth noting that if a judge has committed fraud in the carrying-out of his duties he shall make twelve-fold restitution, and "in the assembly they shall make him get up from his judge's seat not to return (ever) to sit in judgment with judges."

Of particular interest for the light it throws on the relation between these popular tribunals and the royal power is an Old Babylonian letter which shows that a man who had been arrested by a royal official for seditious utterances was placed before the assembly, where the charges were proved against him before he was committed to prison. Note also that the king, as already mentioned, may delegate cases to the assembly.

As will be readily perceived, the judiciary organization here outlined is democratic in essence. Judicial powers are vested in the community as a whole, in an assembly open to all citizens. Such institutions are manifestly not of a piece with the period in which they are found—a period dominated by the very opposite principle: that of concentration of powers in the hands of one single individual. The question then arises whether these institutions represent new ideas which are just beginning to gain momentum or something old which has been retained from earlier times.

The first alternative seems not very plausible, since the entire drift of Mesopotamian political life and thought in the historical periods is wholeheartedly in the other direction. Throughout we find no signs of growing democratic ideas. The second alternative, therefore, seems the more likely: these judiciary institutions represent a last stronghold, a stubborn survival, of ideas rooted in earlier ages.

WIDER SCOPE OF ASSEMBLY IN OLDER TIMES

This inference is confirmed when we turn to the material which bears on earlier periods, for as we go back in time the competence and influence of the "assembly" appear to grow and to extend from judiciary functions to other, even more vital, aspects of government.

Tradition relating to times no farther back than those of the kings of Akkad already shows that the assembly deemed it within its authority to choose a king:

In the "Common of Enlil," a field
belonging to Esabad, the temple of Gula,
Kish assembled
and Iphurkish, a man of Kish,

.   .   .   .

they raised to kingship.

When we consult still older tradition, tradition concerning Uruk in the time of Gilgamesh, beyond the border line of history proper, we find the ruler scrupulously refraining from action in the matter of peace or war until he obtains the consent of the assembly, in which, therefore, internal sovereignty of the state would seem to be vested.

The tradition in question relates that King Agga of Kish sent messengers to Uruk. Gilgamesh, lord of Uruk, is bent on resistance; but the decision apparently does not rest with him. He first approaches the senate, the elders of Uruk, to lay his proposal before them:

Gilgamesh before the elders of his town
spoke up . . . . .

His address—urging reasons which are not yet entirely clear—ends in the plea:

Let us not bow to the palace of Kish;
let us smite (it) with weapons!

The elders consider the proposal in their assembly:

After an assembly had been established, the elders of his town
gave answer unto Gilgamesh concerning it.

This answer is in the affirmative, exactly repeating Gilgamesh's words and ending in the same exhortation. It greatly pleases Gilgamesh:

(As for) Gilgamesh, lord of Kullab,
.   .   .   .
at the word of the elders of his town his heart rejoiced, his liver was made bright.

But he is not yet through; the men of the town must be heard on the issue:

Next Gilgamesh before the men of his town
spoke up . . . . .

His plea here is a word-for-word repetition of the plea before the elders, and the "men of his town," "after an assembly had been established," answer it. With differently worded reasons they urge the same course of action: "May you not bow to the palace of Kish; let us smite it with weapons." They add a declaration of confidence and faith, and Gilgamesh is again highly pleased:

On that day (as for) Gilgamesh, lord of Kullab,
   at the word of the men of his town his heart
   rejoiced, his liver was made bright.

Now the road is clear before him, and he immediately sets about arming for the coming conflict.

Here, then, we seem to have portrayed a state in which the ruler must lay his proposals before the people, first the elders, then the assembly of the townsmen, and obtain their consent, before he can act. In other words, the assembly appears to be the ultimate political authority.

PROJECTIONS OF THE OLD ASSEMBLY INTO THE WORLD OF THE GODS

Since the traces of this older, democratic form of political organization in Mesopotamia all point back to a time before the earliest historical inscriptions, it would normally be impossible to gain closer insight into its details and workings simply because we lack sources for the time when it was flourishing. A peculiar circumstance, however, comes to our aid.

The Sumerians and Akkadians pictured their gods as human in form, governed by human emotions, and living in the same type of world as did men. In almost every particular the world of the gods is therefore a projection of terrestrial conditions. Since this process began relatively early, and since man is by nature conservative in religious matters, early features would, as a matter of course, be retained in the world of the gods after the terrestrial counterpart had disappeared. The gods, to mention only one example, were pictured as clad in a characteristic tufted (sheepskin?) garment long after that material was no longer

in use among men. In similar fashion must we explain the fact that the gods are organized politically along democratic lines, essentially different from the autocratic terrestrial states which we find in Mesopotamia in the historical periods. Thus in the domain of the gods we have a reflection of older forms, of the terrestrial Mesopotamian state as it was in pre-historic times.

The assembly which we find in the world of the gods rested on a broad democratic basis; it was, according to the Adad myth in *CT*, XV, 3, an "assembly of all the gods." Nor was participation limited by sex: goddesses as well as gods played an active part in its deliberations.

The assembly was usually held in a large court called Ubshuukkinna. As the gods arrived, they met friends and relatives who had similarly come from afar to participate in the assembly, and there was general embracing. In the sheltered court the gods then sat down to a sumptuous meal; wine and strong drink soon put them in a happy and carefree mood, fears and worries vanished, and the meeting was ready to settle down to more serious affairs.

They set (their) tongues (in readiness) [and sat
   down] to the banquet;
They ate bread (and) drank(?) [wine].
The sweet drink dispelled their fears;
(So that) they sang for joy as they drank the
   strong drink.
Exceedingly carefree were they, their heart was
   exalted;
For Marduk, their champion, they decreed the
   destiny.

The description is psychologically interesting. Here, as so often in Mesopotamian mythology, the important decisions originate when the gods are in their cups. In the toilsome earthbound life of the primitive Sumerians wine and beer were evidently necessary to lift the spirit out of the humdrum existence of everyday cares to original thought and perspective.

The leadership of the assembly belonged by right, it would seem, to An, god of heaven and "father of the gods"; but with him or alone appears also Enlil, god of the storm. An or Enlil usually broached the matters to be considered; and we may assume—our evidence does not allow us to decide the point—that the discussion which followed would be largely in the hands of the so-called *ilū rabiūtum*, the "great gods" or, perhaps better, "the senior gods," whose number is said to have been fifty. In this discussion it was the intrinsic merit of a proposal which gave it weight: wise counsel, testifying to "intelligence, profundity, and knowledge," is much admired; and ability to make the others listen to one's words is a prized gift. Through such general discussion—"asking one another," as the Babylonians expressed it—the issues were clarified and the various gods had opportunity to voice their opinions for or against, at times espousing proposals which they later bitterly regretted. Such regrets befell Ishtar, who had supported the proposal to wipe out mankind with a flood, when she saw the results of the decision:

Ishtar shrieks like a woman in birth-pangs,
The lovely-voiced lady of the gods yells aloud:
"The times before are indeed turned to earth,
Because I myself in the gods' assembly
Gave the ill counsel!
How could I in the gods' assembly
Give such ill counsel,
To decree the fight
For the destruction of my mankind?
I alone give birth to my mankind
Now they fill, like the spawn of fishes, the
    sea!"

A group of seven powerful gods, "the seven gods who determine destinies"—that is, whose word is decisive—had, it would seem, the final say, and when an agreement had at last been reached in this manner—voting is a technique of much later origin—it was announced by An and Enlil as "the verdict, the word of the assembly of the gods, the command of An and Enlil." The executive duties, carrying into effect the decisions of the assembly, seem to have rested with Enlil.

The functions of this divine assembly were in part those of a court of law. Here the crime of a man who destroys an inscription is taken up, and the deity to whom the inscription was dedicated speaks against him and "makes bad his case." Here sentence was once passed on all humanity because the constant noise which they made was obnoxious to divine ears. Another *cause célèbre* was against Enlil in his youth, when he was ostracized by "the fifty senior gods and the seven gods who determine destiny" for raping young Ninlil.

But the functions of the divine assembly which go beyond those of a court of law are the ones that command our greatest attention: the assembly is the authority which grants kingship. Once, we are told, great danger threatened: Tiʾāmat, the primeval waters, and her host of monsters planned war against the gods. The gods learned that

They are angry, they are plotting, they rest
    not night and day;
they have taken up the fight, they fume, they
    rage like lions;
they have established an assembly and are
    planning the combat.
Mother Hubur, who fashions all things,
has added (thereunto) irresistible weapons, has
    borne monster serpents
sharp of tooth, with unsparing fang;
she has filled their bodies with poison for blood.
Dragons grim she has clothed with terror,
has crowned them with glory and made them
    like gods,
so that he who looks upon them shall perish
    from terror
so that their bodies shall rear up and their
    breasts not be turned back.

In this emergency young Marduk proved willing to champion the cause of the gods, but he demanded absolute authority:

If I am to be your champion,
vanquish Tiʾāmat, and keep you alive;
then establish an assembly and proclaim my
    lot supreme.
Seat yourselves together gladly in Ubshuuk-
    kinna,

and let me when I open my mouth (have
power to) determine destiny even as you,
(so that) whatever I frame shall not be altered
(and) the command of my lips shall not return
(void), shall not be changed.

So the call to assembly went out, the gods
gathered in Ubshuukkinna, and there, to
meet the exigencies of the situation, they
gave Marduk supreme authority:

Thou carriest weight among the senior gods,
thy status is unequaled, thy command is (like
that of) Anu.
Marduk, thou carriest weight among the senior
gods,
thy status is unequaled, thy command is (like
that of) Anu.
From this day onward thy order(s) shall not
be altered;
to exalt and to abase—this shall be thy power.
True shall be what(ever) thou dost utter, nor
shall thy word prove vain (ever);
none among the gods shall encroach upon thy
rights.

They acclaimed him king and invested him
with the insignia of royalty:

They rejoiced (and) did homage, (saying:)
"Marduk is king!"
They bestowed upon him the scepter, the
throne, and the *palû*;
They gave him an unrivaled weapon to smite
the enemy, (saying:)
"Go and cut off the life of Ti'āmat
May the winds carry her blood to out-of-the-
way places."

Then, having armed himself, Marduk led
the gods to battle with Ti'āmat.

As the assembly is the authority which
grants kingship, it can also take it back.
The Sumerians counted kingship as a *bala*,
an office to be held by each incumbent for
a limited period. Similarly kingship would
be given for a time to one city and its god;
then it would be transferred to another
city and god. The period—to mention an
example—during which Inanna's two
cities, Kish and Akkad, held sway over
Mesopotamia was "the term (*bala*) of
Inanna."

The authority which determines when
such a royal *bala* is to end is the assembly,
as may be seen most clearly in a group of
texts dealing with the fall of Ur. Under
its famous Third Dynasty, Ur had dominated all of southern Mesopotamia. Its
rule ended tragically in a savage attack by
invading Elamites which all but wiped out
the city. Among the texts which deal with
this catastrophe we may first quote one in
which the god of Ur, Nanna, is complaining to his father Enlil about what has
happened. His complaint, however, evokes
only a cool response:

Enlil [answere]d his son Sîn concerning it:
"The deserted city, its heart, sobbing, wee[ps
bitterly];
in it [thou passest] in sobs the day.
(But), Nanna, through thy own 'submission'
[thou didst accept(?)] the 'Let it be!'
By verdict, by the word [of] the assembly [of
the] g[ods],
by command of An and Enlil [. . . .]
[was the] k[ing]ship of Ur [. . . . carried away].
Since olden days when the country was founded [. . . .]
[are] the terms of kingship [constantly
changed];
(as for) its (i.e., Ur's) kingship; [its] term [has
(now) been changed for a different term]."

Though the text here quoted has suffered
considerable damage, the view which it
takes of the fall of Ur stands out, fortunately, quite clearly: it was the normal end
of Ur's—and of Nanna's—term of kingship;
and it was brought about in the proper
fashion, by a decision of the assembly of
the gods.

This same view, that Ur's fall was a
normal end to its term of reign, decided
upon beforehand by the gods, underlies
also the lament *BE*, XXXI, 3. It finds,
however, its most vivid expression in the
long *Lamentation over the Destruction of Ur*,
composed only a few generations after the
disaster. There, toward the end of the
fourth song, we are taken to the very
assembly of the gods in which the decision
was made and witness the passionate plea

of Ningal, Nanna's consort, for mercy for the doomed city:

Next unto the assembly, where the people were still (tarrying) on the ground,
the Anunnakki gods being still seated after they had given the binding promise,
did I verily drag (my) legs, did I verily stretch out (my) arms.
I verily poured out my tears before An;
verily I myself mourned before Enlil.
"May my city not be destroyed!" I said indeed to them;
"May Ur not be destroyed!" I said indeed to them;
"May its people not be killed!" I said indeed to them.
But An the while never bent toward that word;
Enlil with a "It is pleasing; let it be!" never soothed my heart.
The destruction of my city they verily gave in commission;
the destruction of Ur they verily gave in commision;
that its people be killed, as its fate they verily determined.

There can thus be no doubt that the assembly had power to revoke, as it had power to grant, kingship.

CONCLUSIONS

Our material seems to preserve indications that pre-historic Mesopotamia was organized politically along democratic lines, not, as was historic Mesopotamia, along autocratic. The indications which we have, point to a form of government in which the normal run of public affairs was handled by a council of elders but ultimate sovereignty resided in a general assembly comprising all members—or, perhaps better, all adult free men—of the community. This assembly settled conflicts arising in the community, decided on such major issues as war and peace, and could, if need arose, especially in a situation of war, grant supreme authority, kingship, to one of its members for a limited period.

Such a form of government is, it may be added, in no way unique but can be abundantly paralleled from elsewhere. We call attention especially to the early European material, for which we may quote two summaries by W. J. Shepard.

Among all the primitive peoples of the West there seems to have been some kind of popular assembly which shared with the tribal chief or king and with a council of lesser chieftains the powers of social control.

Again, still more striking:

The significant political institutions of the primitive Teutonic tribes who overran Western Europe were a folkmoot, or meeting of all the adult males bearing arms; a council of elders; and in time of war a war leader or chieftain; All important questions, such as peace and war, were decided by the folkmoot. The council of elders prepared questions to be submitted to the folkmoot and decided minor matters. It was a rude form of democracy in which government was not differentiated nor law clearly distinguished from religious or social custom.

It need hardly be stressed that the existence of such close parallels in other societies lends strong support to the correctness of the reconstruction here proposed and promises valuable help in the interpretation of the fragmentary Mesopotamian data.

4. THE "REFORM TEXTS" OF URUKAGINA OF LAGASH*

Urukagina ruled the Sumerian city-state of Lagash from about 2415 to 2400 B.C. The following text describes the reforms he enacted, revealing the social and economic conditions of his time.

* Translated by S. N. Kramer, *The Sumerians* (Chicago: University of Chicago Press, 1963), pp. 317–319.

For Ningirsu, the foremost warrior of
Enlil, Urukagina, the king of Lagash, built
the palace Tirash; built the Antasurra for
him; built the house of Bau for her (Bau);
built the Bursag, his *sadug*-house, for him
(Ningirsu); built the sheep-shearing shed
in the "Holy City" for her (Bau); dug for
Nanshe the Idninadu ("the-canal-going-
to-Nina"), her beloved canal, (and) made
its reservoir like unto the mid-ocean for
her; built the wall of Girsu for him
(Ningirsu).

Formerly, from days of yore, from (the
day) the seed (of man) came forth, the man
in charge of the boatmen seized the boats.
The head shepherd seized the donkeys.
The head shepherd seized the sheep. The
man in charge of the fisheries seized the
fisheries. The barley rations of the *guda*-
priests were measured out (to their disadvantage) in the Ashte (presumably the
storehouse of the *ensi*). The shepherds of
the wool-bearing sheep had to pay silver
(to the *ensi*) for (the shearing of) the white
sheep. The man in charge of field surveyors,
the head *gala*, the *agrig*, the man in charge
of brewing, (and) all of the *ugula*'s had to
pay silver for the shearing of the *gaba*-
lambs. The oxen of the gods plowed the
onion patches of the *ensi*, (and) the onion
(and) cucumber fields of the *ensi* were
located in the god's best fields. The *birra*-
donkeys (and) the prize oxen of the *sanga*'s
were bundled off (presumably as taxes for
the *ensi*). The attendants of the *ensi*
divided the barley of the *sanga*'s (to the
disadvantage of the *sanga*'s). The wearing
apparel (here follows a list of fifteen
objects, principally garments, most of
which are unidentifiable) of the *sanga*'s
were carried off as a tax (to the palace of
the *ensi*). The *sanga* (in charge) of the
food (supplies) felled the trees in the garden
of the indigent mother and bundled off
the fruit.

He who brought the dead man to the
cemetery (for burial)—his beer (that is, the
beer he received in return) was 7 pitchers
(and) his (loaves of) bread were 420. The ..

(an unidentifiable official) received 2 *ul*
hazi-barley, 1 garment, 1 head-support,
(and) 1 bed. The *ludimma* received 1 (*ul*)
barley.

He who brought a citizen to rest among
the reeds of Enki—his beer was 7 pitchers
(and) his (loaves of) bread were 420. The ..
(an unidentifiable official) received 2 *ul* of
barley, 1 bed, (and) 1 chair. The *ludimma*
received 1 (*ul*) of barley.

The artisans had to beg for their bread
(literally, "took bread of supplication").
The apprentices had to take the food
leavings (?) of the great gate.

The houses of the *ensi* (and) the fields of
the *ensi*, the houses of the (palace) harem
(and) the fields of the (palace) harem, the
houses of the (palace) nursery (and) the
fields of the (palace) nursery crowded each
other side by side. From the borders of
Ningirsu to the sea, there was the tax
collector.

If the king's retainer dug a well in the
highest part of his field, he seized a blind
man (to draw water and presumably did not
provide him with adequate food and drink).
He (the king's retainer) seized a blind man
for the *mushdu*-water which is in the field
(presumably to drain it off if necessary and
did not provide him with adequate food
and drink).

These were the (social) practices of
former days.

(But) when Ningirsu, the foremost
warrior of Enlil, gave the kingship of
Lagash to Urukagina, (and) his (Ningirsu's)
hand had grasped him out of the multitude
(literally, "36,000 men"); then he (Ningirsu) enjoined upon (literally, "set up
for") him the (divine) decrees of former
days.

He (Urukagina) held close to the word
which his king (Ningirsu) spoke to him.
He banned (literally, "threw off") the man
in charge of the boatmen from (seizing)
the boats. He banned the head shepherds
from (seizing) the donkeys and sheep. He
banned the man in charge of the fisheries
from (seizing) the fisheries. He banned the

man in charge of the storehouse from (measuring out) the barley ration of the *guda*-priests. He banned the bailiff from (receiving) the silver (paid for the shearing) of the white sheep and of the *gaba*-lambs. He banned the bailiffs from the tax of (that is, levied on) the *sanga*'s which (used to be) carried off (to the palace).

He made Ningirsu king of the houses of the *ensi* (and) of the fields of the *ensi*. He made Bau queen of the houses of the (palace) harem (and) of the fields of the (palace) harem. He made Shulshaggana king of the houses of the (palace) nursery (and) of the fields of the (palace) nursery. From the borders of Ningirsu to the sea, there was no tax collector.

He who brought the dead to the cemetery (for burial)—his beer was (only) 3 pitchers (and) his (loaves of) bread were (only) 80. The . . (an unidentifiable official) received (only) 1 bed (and) 1 head-suport. The *ludimma* received (only) 3 *ban* ($\frac{1}{2}$ of an *ul*) of barley. He who brought a citizen (to rest) among the reeds of Enki—his beer was (only) 4 pitchers and his (loaves of) bread were (only) 240. The . . (an unidentifiable official) received (only) 1 *ul* of barley. The *ludimma* received (only) 3 *ban* of barley. The *nindingir* received 1 woman's headband and 1 *sila* of butter.

(At this point the text records a reform which seems to be an innovation rather than a rectification of an earlier abuse: various amounts and kinds of bread and beer were to be given as a permanent ration to such peoples as the *gala*-priest of Girsu and the *gala*-priest of Lagash as well as to the other *gala*-priests, the craftsmen's guilds, unidentifiable officials from the city of Nina, certain blind laborers, and other workers. Following this, the text continues with the reforms of former abuses:)

He did away with (the necessity of) the apprentices (to take) the food leavings (?) of the gate. He did away with (the necessity of) the artisans to beg for their bread. The *sanga* (in charge) of the food (supplies) did not (dare) enter the garden of the indigent mother (for the purpose of felling the trees and carrying off the fruit).

He (Urukagina) (also) promulgated (these two ordinances): (1) When a good donkey is born to a king's retainer, (and) his supervisor says to him, "I want to buy it from you," and when he (the supervisor) is about to buy it from him, he (the king's retainer) says to him (the supervisor), "Pay me as much as I think fair" (literally, "Weigh out for me the silver pleasing to my heart"), then when he refuses to sell it (literally, "does not let it be bought from him"), the supervisor must not coerce him to do so (literally, "he must not strike him" in order to compel his assent to it). (2) When the house of a king's retainer is next to the house of a "big man" (and) that "big man" says to him, "I want to buy it from you," and if when he (the "big man") is about to buy it from him, he (the king's retainer) says, "Pay me as much as I think fair" or "Pay me in barley equivalent to my house," then when he refuses to sell it, that "big man" must not coerce him to do so.

He (Urukagina) amnestied the "citizens" (literally, "the sons") of Lagash who (were imprisoned because of) the debts (which they) had incurred, (or because of) the amounts (of grain claimed by the palace as its) due, (or because of) the barley (claimed by the palace for its) stores, (or because of) theft (or) murder, and set them free.

(Finally) Urukagina made a covenant with Ningirsu that a man of power must not commit an (injustice) against an orphan or widow.

During this year he (Urukagina) dug for Ningirsu the little canal belonging (?) to Girsu (literally, perhaps, "which Girsu has"); gave it its former name (or perhaps conversely, set aside its former name), calling it "Ningirsu-who-is-powerful-out-of-Nippur." He joined it to the Ninadu canal, (saying) "May the pure canal, whose 'heart' is bright, bring clear water to Nanshe."

5. THE KING OF THE SUMERIAN CITY-STATE*

The following selection discussing the changes in early Mesopotamian kingship is based on texts like the "Reforms of Urukagina" as well as epics and legends like "Gilgamesh and Agga," just as is the essay of Jacobsen. The interpretation here, however, is quite different, emphasizing the sovereign power of the king throughout Sumerian history.

THE KING (PRINCE OF THE CITY)

The position of the king in the system of the Sumerian city-temple underwent important changes in the course of historical evolution. We know, according to the "reform texts" of Urukagina, that the kings who preceded him had formed personal domains for themselves in the process of secularizing the temples. But since the economic texts from Lagash only begin a short time before the reign of Urukagina, the oldest order and the details of change cannot be reconstituted with complete certainty. The normal designation of the chief of a city-state is *ensi*. According to an interpretation, sometimes disputed, it defines him as "the lord who established the foundation (of a temple)." On the other hand, the princes were often called *lugal*, that is, "great man" or "king," which implies by definition the claim to extend their domination over a territory beyond the limits of the city-state. Thus one may say simply "King of Kish," since in the period of the earliest dynasties the domination of Kish was equivalent to supreme power over all Babylonia, or again "King of Sumer" (*lugal-kalam-ma*), whereas the word *ensi* is used almost exclusively before the name of a city. But since Urukagina himself, although seriously threatened by the neighboring city of Umma, sometimes calls himself *ensi* and sometimes "King," we may deduce a gradual depreciation of the royal title. There exists a denomination still more ancient, if we admit that the epic tradition of the Sumerians has on this particular point transmitted to us the memory of a distant past. It is the title of *en*, the complete meaning of which is not conveyed by the current translation of "lord," since the word indicates a sacerdotal quality of a special character. In the historical period we actually come across priestesses—*en*, regularly recruited among the members of the ruling house. A priest —*en* and a priestess—*en* were considered to be the husband or wife of the deity of whom they were the servants. They lived in a special sector of the temple quarter called *gi6-par*. In the epic cycle dedicated to the rulers of Uruk—Enmerkar, Gilgamesh, and Lugalbanda—they bore the title, "Lord of Uruk, Lord of Kullab"; the adversary of Enmerkar is equally called "Lord of Aratta." A similar title which clearly indicates the functions exercised by the sovereign in the realm of religion is perfectly in accord with the essential evidence of the Sumerian political order, permitting a close connection between the chief of a city and the world of the gods. In the monuments of the protohistoric period we often see the king exercising the functions of a priest. The epic poems of the Sumerians make of their royal heroes the sons of the gods, and this notion is confirmed by the sovereigns themselves, to whom we owe the oldest inscriptions on dedications or constructions. They call themselves "children of the gods"; the gods raised them, called them to royal power, and lend them aid and counsel. Eannatum, the most remarkable of the princes of Lagash, writes:

* A. Falkenstein, "La Cité-temple sumérienne". Prepared for the International Commission for a History of the Scientific and Cultural Development of Mankind, and originally issued in French in the *Journal of World History*, I, 4 (1954). Translated by Donald Kagan.

Innana took him in her arms, called his name: He who was carried into the Eanna of Innana from the sanctuary of Ebgal and then placed on the sacred knees of the goddess Ninhursag. Ninhursag made him drink of her holy bosom. In the person of Eannatum, pro-created by Ningirsu, Ningirsu delighted. Ningursu measured him with his span—he was five cubits—, he measured him with his fore-arm; five cubits and a span did Ningursu give him, to him, to his king, in his great joy.

The protodynastic period, nevertheless, although some of its characters (among them Eannatum) were admitted into the Sumerian pantheon, did not take the leap which would transform the chiefs of cities, sons of the gods, into deified sovereigns.

It was the duty of the prince of the city, called to his functions by the divine will, to serve the principal god of the city-state and to administer the city in his name. This priestly quality that belonged to the prince of the city and that is expressed with sufficient clarity in the names of *en* and *ensi* appears quite natural in a govern-mental system which, by definition, attri-butes all landed property to the temples, the landed property which was the base of all the Babylonian political forms. In these conditions the success of a usurper, so long as he was not a foreigner, was only possible, in all likelihood, if he could plead exception from his role as priest. When the prince of the city of Umma was killed in combat by Entmena of Lagash, "He, the priest of Innana, took possession of the principate of the city." In the beginning Lugalzaggesi of Umma was, like his father, a seer in the service of the principal goddess of the city. When he made Uruk the center of his empire he placed himself as "purifying priest" of the god of heaven, in the com-munity of the priests of Uruk.

But if we see Lugalzaggesi as satisfied with a relatively modest position, this could only be permitted in a period when royalty was somewhat detached from the priesthood, not only at Lagash (where we can follow the evolution, based on the

"reform texts" of Urukagina) but every-where else. In reconstructing the primitive period of the Sumerian city-temple we must exclude the possibility of a prince of the city who will not have combined his functions with that of the supreme priest of the principal god, the true master of the city. It is uniquely in this role that he could pretend to the direction of the priests of the other sanctuaries, for in order to make this direction effective he had to dispose of the largest part of the arable lands and of the majority of the lesser priests of the temples. His powers as chief extended to all the tasks which the temple commonly carried out: the creation, main-tenance, and renewal of the irrigation system; the construction of shops and temples; the construction and maintenance of fortifications; and finally, defense against foreign enemies. Internally he had, above all, to defend the juridical rights of the citizens. It was he who was supreme judge and it was in this role that he must apply himself to the maintenance of social justice. The sentence of the "reform texts" where it is said of Urukagina that "he did not hand over the orphan and the widow to the powerful" represents one of the first affirmations of an idea which was deeply anchored in the Sumerian city-temple and which is found again, formulated in a like manner, in all the law codes up to that of Hammurabi of Babylon.

The direction of the work of deepening the canals was considered particularly im-portant. It is mentioned in the oldest royal inscriptions, where it is attributed, as in the dedication of statues and the recon-struction or repair of temples, uniquely to the prince of the city. In reality, as emerges from the economic texts, the prince only indicated to the various temples the part they must take in the common labor, while permitting them to distribute the burden among their underlings. Ur-Nanshe of Lagash is represented on a votive plaque as builder of the temple of Ningursu; we see him carrying on his head the basket in which he carries earth gathered during the work of foundation. From all evidence it was at this point only a symbolic gesture, for the work of embankment, etc., was considered especially afflicting: Gudea emphasizes expressly that he assigns it only to strong men, and never to a woman.

In his role as military leader the prince of the city already appears to us on the seals of the protohistoric period, where his enemies are presented to him vanquished and stripped of all clothing. On the "Stele of the Vultures" Eannatum leads his warriors fighting from a heavy chariot, and with his lance he strikes the head of his adversary. The inscriptions attribute to him alone all the exploits and all the successes, mentioning only the divine assistance. Although this role of supreme warleader gradually separated from his functions as priest, it nevertheless had belonged to him from the beginning, for it made up a part of the concerns belonging to the terrestrial lieutenant of the divinity. We learn through a letter of Luenna, priest of the goddess Ninmara, that he repulsed an attack of six hundred Elamites against the territory of Lagash and that he put the enemy to flight. When a campaign was crowned with success the booty, or more probably a part of that booty, was turned back to the principal god, the master of the state. Gudea tells us again, "With these arms he defeated Anshan and Elam. The booty that he took on this occasion he brought to Ningursu in the temple of Enninu." The God of the Sumerian empire, Enlil of Nippur, in the same way received offerings taken from the booty. . . .

Some important changes in the relations between the prince of the city in his role as chief of the state and temples and the priests who directed the latter can be deduced from texts from Lagash, which, however, come only from the end of the protodynastic period. In this order of ideas it is necessary above all to emphasize that there was in the time of Entemena a "(special) priest of Ningursu." At the end of certain of his inscriptions (reports of constructions or dedications) we read the following notice: "At this time Dudu was priest of Ningirsu," while in a dedicatory inscription Dudu is designated as "supreme priest of Ningirsu." A bill of sale contains as an indication of date this passage: "At this time Entemena was prince of the city of Lagash (and) Enentarzi priest of Ningursu." From all evidence this innovation is due to the initiative of the prince of the city; if not, it would certainly not have been mentioned in the official inscriptions. The problem now is to know what was the exact role of the priest of Ningursu. We may exclude the possibility that he had taken upon himself the complete direction and administration of the economic affairs of the sanctuary of Ningursu, because such a measure would have deprived the prince of the city of his essential support and his most important revenues. But even if we admit that in designating a priest of Ningursu the intention was only to delegate to him the obligations incumbent upon the sovereign in the domain of religion, that would already represent an important innovation, since up to then the claim of the prince to direct the city-state was based in the first place on the fact that he was priest and steward of the principal god.

The "reform texts" of Urukagina . . . mention other changes in the primitive situation. . . . In so far as these texts concern the situation of the prince of the city they insist in the first place on the fact that the sovereign had appropriated the landed property of the temples of Ningursu, Baba, and the children of those divinities; that he had used the temple oxen to work the lands which he had seized contrary to law; that he taken from the priests the best packasses and oxen; that he had distributed to his men the wheat which belonged to the priests. The texts inform us in detail of the control established by the sovereign and of the disorder which resulted from the many abuses of power of which the royal functionaries were guilty in respect to the humble. The priests themselves were sometimes guilty, for example, of making too great demands for the performance of religious rites such as funerals. The functions of supreme judge represented another source of revenue for the prince of the city. For example, he collected for the indictment, the trial, and the court journal of a divorce the significant sum of five shekels of silver and did not oppose the supplementary collection of one silver shekel by the grand vizier. All this indicates the same tendency: it is a matter of affirming the independence of the power of the sovereign in regard to the temples and permits the formation of a class of palace functionaries, called to exercise in the name of the sovereign a control unknown up to then. . . .

Economic texts from Lagash which come in large part from the period preceding the reign of Urukagina furnish us with the following picture of the economic activity of the prince of the city: The prince administers the goods of the temple of the supreme god; those of his wife; those of the temple of Baba; and, simultaneously, in the name of his children, those of the children of Ningursu and of Baba. The prince receives, just like the other servants of the temple, "land for his subsistence," which was, however, taken from the ni-en-na domain, the temple domain proper. But beside the land furnished by the landed wealth of the temple of Ningursu, he had supplementary revenues coming from the domains of different sanctuaries. According to a document, the temple of Baba furnished one hundred and twenty-three acres, that is, about five per cent of the cultivated land of this sanctuary. . . .

A similar measure was taken to assure to the prince of the city an economic predominance over the priests of other sanctuaries. The exploitation of the land naturally fell to the employees of the temple. On the occasion of great holidays the prince received from his subjects offerings which consisted originally of goats. . . . After some time these offerings consisted of oxen, different victuals, and also, on rare occasions, objects of current use. On the other hand, certain categories of workers (shepherds, boatmen, fishermen) paid their dues in silver. All these revenues assured to the prince of the city a situation which rendered him almost unassailable in the eyes of the priests of the sanctuaries which he did not administer himself or by the members of his family, even if all these priests were leagued against him. Also the functions of the prince of the city became hereditary, being passed on regularly from father to son.

Although he had little to fear from the rivalry of the clergy, the prince of the city was not what we may properly call an "oriental despot." We must not forget that the Sumerian city-temple made him primarily an administrator of the earthly possessions of the gods. On the other hand I believe that we must not exaggerate the importance of the "assembly" of the free citizens ("unkem," later called "pu-uh-rum," a term borrowed from the Akkadian). That was an institution which was scarcely an organ of control and still less of command but which probably exercised consultative functions. In this "assembly of the elders of the city," things must have happened in much the same way as in the council of the gods, whose description certainly inspired the terrestrial model: when the supreme gods, masters of destiny, had pronounced their sentence, all the other divinities present immediately answered, "So be it." The fact that in the epic poem of the struggle of Gilgamesh against Agga of Kish "the assembly of the elders of the city" opposes to the fatal appeal of Gilgamesh for war a proposal to submit hardly contradicts our opinion. For Gilgamesh took no heed of the council's advice. He immediately appealed to the youth of the city and received its support.

6. ANCIENT MESOPOTAMIAN ASSEMBLIES*

The stimulation provided by Jacobsen's pioneer article led to strong support by some scholars, to disagreement by others such as Falkenstein, and, in the following selection, to more detailed investigation and refinement by Geoffrey Evans of the University of Sydney, Australia. The result is not the final resolution of the problem, but rather a deeper and more meaningful discussion.

Well over ten years have passed since the publication of Professor Thorkild Jacobsen's important study "Primitive Democracy in Ancient Mesopotamia." During that time, all works touching upon this aspect of ancient civilisation have cited it as the standard discussion of the subject. Speaking generally, there has been surprisingly little attempt to pursue the matter further, and Professor Jacobsen's position has gone largely uncriticised. In the remarks which follow, an attempt has been made to examine his conclusions from two main points of view, firstly his general approach, and secondly the character and organisation of some of the assemblies. In addition to the article already named, two texts are fundamental for what follows, Professor S. N. Kramer's edition of the short epic "Gilgamesh and Agga," together with Professor Jacobsen's additional comments thereon, and the Old Assyrian Laws from Kaneš.

At the very beginning of his article, Jacobsen makes use of an interesting expression. He writes: "The political development in early historical times seems to lie under the spell of one controlling idea: concentration of political power in as few hands as possible," and later "the momentum of the autocratic idea was still far from spent with the realisation of this idea within separate areas. It drove Mesopotamia forward relentlessly toward the more distant aim: centralisation of power within one large area." This is a good summary of the constitutional development of Mesopotamia seen from the vantage point of the present day, and since Jacobsen himself has proved that early Sumerian society was anything but autocratic, the question inevitably arises, why did it become so? The discussion of this problem was only lightly touched upon in the article, to which it was of tangential significance, so a short discussion may not be out of place here. One point may be made at once: "the autocratic idea," while perfectly justifiable in the context of the statement quoted, must not be taken to imply the existence in remote antiquity of precise political concepts, which were not developed until Hellenic times. Even today, a sharp distinction must be drawn between the strict definitions of political theory, and such portmanteau expressions as "democracy" and "colonialism" as they are used in popular speech and propaganda. Since the content of the latter is so vague and all-inclusive, their use often gives rise to confusions, which are sometimes deliberately contrived. We may acquit the Mesopotamians of any desire to deceive, but were they any more advanced in the use or understanding of political concepts than the modern propagandist? They were certainly incapable of formulating such categories as autocracy and democracy. Kingship was probably their most developed political institution, yet its religious and secular aspects seem to have become inextricably united in their minds; this mixture of functions is perhaps already suggested in the formula "kingship descended from the gods." The primitive nature of Sumerian political thought was not without its practical consequences: it is probable that it rendered the subversion

* Geoffrey Evans, "Ancient Mesopotamian Assemblies," *Journal of the American Oriental Society*, 78 (1958), pp. 1–11.

of democratic institutions more easy in a Sumerian community than it was in a more sophisticated and politically self-conscious Greek city-state. If this inference is correct, it provides us with one factor—a negative factor—which aided the establishment of autocracy in Mesopotamia.

In the early stages of the evolution of Mesopotamia towards a centralised, autocratically governed empire, it is important to distinguish between two processes, that towards the destruction of democracy within each city, and that towards the destruction of the independence of the individual cities, however governed internally. The discussion of these issues also fell outside the scope of Jacobsen's article, but they deserve a short examination, slight as the evidence we have upon them may be. It is a safe initial assumption that individual settlements came into existence before the creation of the first empire, and from what we know of the organisation of the earliest cities, it is clear that there were various paths open by which an individual or a group might gain disproportionate power in the community. We may conclude, then, that the assault upon democracy came first from forces within the cities, and that it was prosecuted more unremittingly from within than without; the existence of empires in early times seems to have been intermittent. We should anticipate that internal and external forces sometimes worked in association, acting as the upper and nether millstones between which democratic institutions were ground almost out of existence. The presence of an external threat is always a good excuse for the abridgement of liberty. In like manner, the possession of an empire must have had subversive effects upon the democratic institutions of the imperial city, though this probably acted more insidiously. The loss of internal democracy does not seem to have resulted in the disappearance of local loyalties; indeed, "parish-pump patriotism" retained great strength in Sumer long after the rise of the empires, and was one of the most serious obstacles which they had to overcome. Such sentiments are essentially popular, and though they may be made use of by ambitious despots, are not necessarily shared by them—as witness the removal of Lugalzaggesi from Umma to Uruk. The reasons for the survival of such feelings were partly political: in a sense, the struggle by imperial despots to master local dynasts was anti-democratic, since, from the point of view of the citizens, a native autocracy was preferable to one exercised from a distance, if only because it was obliged to pay more heed to public feeling. Such local sentiments must have been a factor in enabling some ensis to retain considerable powers to a surprisingly late period.

PROCEDURE IN THE ASSEMBLIES, AND THEIR INTER-RELATIONS

Professor Kramer has remarked upon the paucity of our information about the procedures followed in the Mesopotamian assemblies; Jacobsen did not treat of this topic, beyond remarking that the practice of voting is to be excluded as anachronistic. The members seem to have reached a decision by "asking one another." Although he nowhere expressly says so, he naturally assumes that the elders met first to discuss business, and that only thereafter was the full assembly called. At Kaneš this was certainly so, for the full assembly was summoned only in certain circumstances, in some cases at any rate only after the elders had failed to agree, or with their consent. By comparison with the assemblies at Uruk in earlier times, the competence of both groups at Kaneš seems to have been restricted to judicial matters. It would not be safe to assume a similar relation between the assemblies of Uruk, under the very different conditions prevailing in the older city; this very difficult problem has now been somewhat clarified by the alternative version of certain lines in "Gilgamesh and Agga" used by Kramer in his complete edition. In that offered by Jacobsen in his article, Gilgamesh went first to the assembly of elders, and sought their support for resistance to the demands of Agga. They gave their approval, whereupon he took the same proposal before the general assembly, who also approved. In the alternative version the elders refuse his request and counsel surrender; then, as before, Gilgamesh referred the matter to the full assembly which supported his policy.

Then Gilgamesh—the lord of Kullab—
at the word of the men of his city, his heart
  rejoiced, his spirits brightened;
He says to his servant Enkidu:
Therefore let the šukara implement be put
  aside for the violence of battle . . .

In short, he had gained his point, since the decision of the assembly over-rode the contrary opinion of the elders. Jacobsen has already suggested that the functions of the elders were advisory. The new version shows that the assembly was fully sovereign and able to set aside such advice. This is in marked contrast to the position at Kaneš, where "small and great" were only to be called together if the "great" failed to reach a decision.

In discussing the nature of procedure in the Mesopotamian assemblies, it may be of assistance, with all due caution, to make comparisons with those at Sparta and Rome in Classical antiquity. At Sparta, while the popular assembly was theoretically sovereign, the elders, a council of twenty-eight men over sixty years of age, enjoyed the right to set aside any "crooked decree" which it might pass. This was in effect a power of veto. In neither the Spartan nor the Roman assembly might a person other than a magistrate address the gathering or propose a motion. At Rome, the electors voted in groups, while at Sparta, proposals were carried only by acclamation. Assuming that voting was unknown in the earliest Mesopotamian assemblies, it may further be assumed that

something in the nature of carrying a motion by acclamation must have existed in them also. Since procedure was almost certainly of a primitive nature, the practice of moving a formal motion from the floor must have been unknown, even if we suppose that discussion and the shouting of suggestions was freer than at Rome or Sparta. Now we know that in the Classical cities this state of affairs prevented the development of effective democratic institutions, and it seems likely that the consequences were similar in Mesopotamia. A comparison of the assemblies of Uruk with those of Kaneš shows clearly how far the sector of public affairs under popular control had shrunk in the interval: what had once been sovereign bodies had shrunk into law courts, while the full assembly had lost ground to that of the elders.

Despite this reduction in competence, the assemblies of Kaneš remain of the first importance historically. They possess features similar to the earlier ones, and we possess a little more information about the manner in which they operated. On the other hand, their difference in function and that between a city and a trading colony should warn us against pressing parallels too far. The first point to be noted is the use in connexion with each of the assemblies at Kaneš of a word which has been translated "majority"—a thoroughly democratic concept. The word used of the full assembly is *madudum*, that applied to the "great" on their own is *namedum*; perhaps the use of *namedum* in this sense is more dubious than that of the other term. Unfortunately, procedures used to determine the majority are not defined: the phrase *i pi-ì ša ma-du-dim*, being idiomatic, carries no necessary connotation of voting by acclamation—as witness *i pi-ì we-dim* in the second tablet—but it remains possible that the full assembly did express its views in this way. The manner in which the majority among the "great" was determined in the second tablet, if majority is the correct translation, is even more obscure.

There remains the question of the procedure envisaged in the assembly of the "great" in the first tablet. It is clear that a different procedure prevailed in this case, since the clerk was enjoined to divide them into three and "they shall give judgement." What may have been the character and origin of the three groups into which this assembly was divided, and what was their function? These are questions more easy to pose than answer, and in our present state of knowledge it is possible that no final answer can be given; nevertheless, the issues raised are so important that a discussion must be attempted. Several explanations suggest themselves immediately:

1) The most tempting, and the most open to attack on the ground that it is anachronistic, is that the three groups consisted of those for, those against, and those undecided upon some course of action. This process of voting by division can be matched in many more modern assemblies, among them the House of Commons: a parallel closer in time would be the Roman Senate which also voted in this fashion. Indeed, the lesser members of that body were called "*pedarii,*" since they never had an opportunity to open their mouths to express an opinion, but "voted with their feet." It would not, on this hypothesis, be necessary to suppose that there was a counting of heads at Kaneš; the numbers would be small enough to make the position clear at a glance, and in the event of doubt, it was expressly provided that the clerk should assemble "small and great." This theory is open to a number of objections. The procedure of voting by division would render the discussion of alternative penalties difficult, so that the assembly may have been reduced to passing a verdict. To this it is possible to reply that it is not nearly so difficult to admit the restriction of the functions of a judicial body to passing a verdict as would be the case with a political assembly; moreover, if the procedure followed in "Gilgamesh and Agga"

can be taken literally, the g u r u š there did no more than decide for or against a proposal placed before them. Again, it is quite possible that all that was required of the "great" at Kaneš was a verdict as to the facts, punishments being prescribed by custom or statute; if the exercise of discretion was felt to be necessary, this could have been left to the GAL *alim,* who was required to be present. In any event, a similar difficulty had to be faced in the event of a decision being referred to "small and great." We know that there the matter was decided "at the mouth of the majority," and since the numbers present must have been considerably larger, any detailed discussion must have been more difficult still. But other explanations are possible:

2) The three groups referred to may have been purely *ad hoc* bodies, possessing no significance nor even existence outside the session at which they were called into being. In this case, their purpose may have been to render discussion of the case easier, and each group must have declared its decision in some way when the time came, rather as a modern jury delivers its verdict. Since disagreement is envisaged, it seems that there was no question of the view of two groups together prevailing over that of the third. This theory presupposes something in the nature of reaching a group decision, which is really a primitive form of voting. While this procedure is not very common, it may be pointed out that all three Roman assemblies employed a very highly developed form of it.

3) Alternatively, it is possible that these three groups within the assembly corresponded to some bodies within the community outside. It is not easy to suggest what these may have been: perhaps they were tribal or familial, as in a Greek city-state, or territorial. An obvious objection to this suggestion is that an outpost like Kaneš is hardly the place where we should expect to find such divisions. The community of colonists must have been small and relatively homogeneous. A possible

solution is that the three divisions, like both assemblies, are only a reflection of originals outside the colony, probably in the mother city. Jacobsen has shown that there are considerable similarities between these assemblies and those at Uruk so long before, and if such institutions persisted so long in time, there should be no difficulty in admitting that they could be transmitted from a mother city to its commercial colonies. A curious feature about these divisions is that they occur only within the assembly of the "great." How can this be reconciled with a theory that they corresponded to some institution within the city as a whole? There is one such institution known to us from sources of about the same period which would fit, though it can of course only be suggested very hesitantly on such slight evidence, the *bâbtum*, or "ward." However this may be, once again some form of group deliberation and decision would appear to be called for. This discussion has necessarily been inconclusive because of the nature of the evidence, but it does not follow that it has been without result. Leaving aside all possible views as to the origin of the three groups, their existence and their relevance in some way to the task of reaching a decision is certain. The most natural interpretation of the text seems to me to be that after the groups had formed, they each arrived at a decision upon which its members were agreed, probably by discussion. This decision would be in the form of an answer to a simple question, and once it had been reached it must have been communicated to the other two, perhaps through the agency of a "foreman." If all three groups were in agreement, the case was settled; if not, we know that it had to be referred to a meeting of the full assembly. As already suggested, it is difficult to resist the conclusion that such a procedure implies the existence of group-voting in some form. It does not in the least follow that we must suppose that this method of procedure existed in the period

of "primitive democracy." We know that the assemblies of Kaneš differed in function from those at Uruk, and it is unlikely that their forms of procedure were completely unchanged. The restriction of the competence of the later assemblies to law may in itself have caused changes. Meanwhile, political control had passed into the hands of the kings, so that even the most promising advances in political technique would have been rendered fruitless.

THE COMPOSITION OF THE ASSEMBLIES

A question which remains to be discussed is that of the composition of the assembly of elders (the term is used without prejudice) in the two cities. Here Jacobsen seems to take the view that the basis of choice of the upper assembly differed in the two communities. At Uruk, he writes "the elders were, to judge from the Sumerian term a b b a, literally 'father,' and a b b a   u r u, 'town fathers,' originally the heads of the various large families which made up the population of the town. Assembled, they would therefore represent an aggregate of the *patria potestas* in the community. Their relation to the king appears to have been that of counselors." He then proceeds to give examples of their exercising this function. The whole picture, the title "town fathers," the term "*patria potestas*," the advice which these "heads of large families" were privileged to give their king, inescapably suggests something similar in character to the Senate of regal Rome, whose members were likewise called "*Patres*." These expressions show clearly that he had something of the kind in mind. This would place the town fathers in precisely the same position as the early Greek and Roman aristocrats, who originally held their positions as heads of their *genos* or gens. This view has a great deal to recommend it. Assemblies of the kind have had an almost worldwide distribution at different times, and membership of them has usually had little to do with age as such. In Classical examples, while very young men were often ineligible, the true qualification was social position, and men of advanced years but low status were excluded.

This is in contrast with his views upon the composition of the assemblies at Kaneš. Here he has abandoned the idea of a division based upon differences of class, as described above, in favour of one determined solely by considerations of age. Hence he translates ṣaḫir rabi as "young and old" and not "small and great." There is, of course, no doubt that the Babylonians used ṣiḫrum to mean both young and small, and rabûm both old and great, so that the words themselves do not enable us to reach a decision. Since however it is clear that in the texts with which we are concerned they are employed in a legal, perhaps a technical sense, it may be worth while to see what they signify in legal phraseology of about the same period.

Section 202 of the Code of Hammurabi contains an interesting example of the use of rabûm: šum-ma a-wi-lum a-wi-lim ša e-li-šu ra-bu-ú im-ta-ḫa-aṣ ... In view of the words me-iḫ-ri-šu in section 200, which clearly means "of rank equal to his own," and ki-ma šu-a-ti in section 203, meaning "like unto himself," there can be no doubt that here šâ elišu rabû means "of a rank superior to his own," and not "older than he is." Indeed, Driver and Miles observe that this law may indicate the existence of different grades of freemen at Babylon. There is also a number of legal documents from Larsa, in the reign of Rim-Sin, which mention persons described as rabium. They are agreements by which someone went surety for the good conduct and continued services of a citizen enslaved for debt. If the debt-slave decamped or became unfit, the guarantor became liable to pay a forfeit, usually of some specified sum, to the owner-creditor. Among the conditions listed as making the forfeit payable are fleeing the country, being eaten by lions, and gaining asylum with or at the ekallum, kabtum, rabium or bît sinništim. Szlechter translates rabium in general terms as "puissant." This may be as close as present knowledge allows, but the meaning was probably more precise, for while the Code of Hammurabi provides against the abandonment of a rēdûm to "a strong man" in a lawsuit, the word employed is dannum, which may be more informal, deliberately. It seems unlikely that the creditor, or more especially the guarantor, would wish to concede the right of asylum to a class so loosely defined, and most of the other provisions in the penal clause seem clear enough. For our present purpose, it is evident that whoever the rabium may have been, he was a person of superior rank and status, capable of protecting a runaway debtor against the wrath of his creditor, and not simply an old man.

The uses of ṣiḫrum in the Code are more numerous; the term seems always to refer to small children, and G. R. Driver translates it as "infant" in several places. In one clause, a child so described is too young to succeed to his father's ilku-land, since he is unable to perform the duties arising from its possession; in another, he is too young to be married before his father's death, and his brothers are directed to set aside a part of the paternal estate to provide his future bride-gift. The clearest example of all is the law which lays down the conditions under which a widow with young children may re-marry: the paternal estate of the children of the first marriage is safeguarded, and the woman and her second husband are required to "rear the infants." The element common to all these uses would seem to be that the person described as ṣiḫrum was not merely young, but incapable of protecting his own interests on the one hand, or of undertaking the rights and responsibilities of a full member of society upon the other. While this was the consequence of his tender years, it is important to note that it was not simple youth which was in question, but legal minority; in Babylonia a person remained young for many years after attaining his majority. It is possible that the two senses of small, young, and consequently weak, remained unseparated in the minds of the Babylonians in such cases. To return to Kaneš, it is at least clear that no member of the full assembly can have been young in the sense required by these laws, but we do know that the ṣiḫrū enjoyed powers which were far more restricted than those of the rabū, and this may have provided the connexion. The ṣiḫrū were probably the "little men" of the colony in more senses than one. If we look again at the expression ṣaḫir rabi in the light of this evidence, it may seem more natural to translate it as "small and great" than "young and old."

This view is supported by the argument from analogy. Professor Jacobsen has demonstrated some remarkable resemblances between the institutions of Uruk and Kaneš, and since, as he has argued, the upper assembly at Uruk was aristocratic in character, we might reasonably expect to find that the "great" at Kaneš were likewise drawn from the most influential section of the community. However, such arguments can be hazardous, and it may be that one of the reasons which led him to take a different view was the great contrast in the characters of the two cities. A less obvious danger of the same kind arises from the terminology which we employ. The use of "elders" to describe the members of this body at Uruk must not be allowed to blind us to their true character. If they were not simply old men, it is fallacious to argue from analogy with them that their counter parts at Kaneš were; if an analogy is permissible at all, it is much more probable that they were men prominent in the settlement, officials and merchants.

The picture of Kaneš as a tiny trading colony outside the native city has recently been seriously challenged; it would appear that it was, on the contrary, of a respectable size, and that a number of Assyrians settled there for long periods, owning land. Such a community is likely to have been organised upon the model of the metropolis, while, on the other hand, we should not expect to find clan patriarchs there, even supposing they still existed elsewhere. The natural criteria for prominence in such a place would be wealth and official position rather than age. We have to choose in what respect the upper assembly there resembled that at Uruk; it must either have contained all the older men of the settlement, as Jacobsen holds, or it contained the more prominent members of the community. In the first case it was less selective than that at Uruk, for which age was only a partial qualification; in the second an age qualification was largely irrelevant under the prevailing conditions. The available evidence and the probabilities surely favour the latter alternative.

The attempt to draw a parallel between ṣaḫir rabi and the Latin terms minor and maior can be misleading, if these expressions are taken in a political sense. The Romans certainly used them to mean younger and older even in cases where no question of size can have arisen, as it does among brothers; for example they were applied to two men of the same name even when they belonged to widely separated generations. This usage has a special sense, the same as that found in English in such expressions as "the younger Pitt" or "the elder Pitt." We may take a single Roman example, that of the famous Publius Cornelius Scipio Africanus Maior and his adopted son Scipio Aemilianus Africanus Minor: the older man would never have been called Maior if his son had not also earned the title Africanus. What matters most in this connexion is that these terms are not used in Latin when any distinction in political rights based upon age is in point. When this was so, in the Comitia Centuriata, the Centuries were called iuniores and seniores, the division falling at 46, the age at which a man ceased to be liable for military service.

We may now turn to the question of the membership of the general assembly, a rather easier matter. If we leave out the upper classes, women, minors and slaves, we are left with the free adult male population of the city. This simple definition is no doubt correct, though it leaves unsolved the knotty problem how citizenship was defined and established. The issue is complicated by the question of the nature of the gurus̆, a term which though it came eventually to mean simply "workman" had a much wider significance in earlier times. Jacobsen expresses the view that, at Uruk, its membership was more or less identical with that of the popular assembly. Beside the elders he sets the gurus̆, "members of the apparently identical labor and military organisation of the city-state," and adds "and since the assembly has been convened to consider a line of action which will almost certainly lead to war, it is not unlikely that we should view it as essentially a gathering of the male population bearing arms." Later, in 1949, he took the opportunity offered by the invitation to comment upon Kramer's edition of "Gilgamesh and Agga" to make a further remark: "whereas the older men will be used for agricultural tasks, the gurus̆ will be used for raids and campaigns in military service." This is in explanation of the situation which faced the men of Uruk as a result of Agga's demand that they should recognise him as their overlord. The immediate consequence would have been, apparently, that they would have had to provide labour for irrigation works (?), the corvée upon which the maintenance of life depended. In this second quotation he is clearly trying to draw a distinction between the gurus̆ as weapon-bearing men, and older citizens, still liable for agricultural tasks though no longer members of the gurus̆; in that case, however, the gurus̆ could no longer be termed "the apparently identical labor and military organisation of the city-state." The germ of this inconsistency, as between the views expressed in 1943 and 1949, can

perhaps be traced to the remark that the assembly should be regarded as essentially a gathering of the male population bearing arms. A possible way out of this dilemma is to suppose that the older citizens liable for land work are none other than the members of the assembly of elders. This would help to account for the fact that they stress the labour service to which they would be liable, while the young men seize upon the conscription to fight in the wars of Kish which would fall to their lot—if the interpretation given of a very difficult passage is correct. We should thus arrive at the same view of the membership of the assembly of elders at Uruk as Jacobsen has postulated for that at Kanes̆. Unfortunately, this would be in conflict with the views he has expressed as to its essentially aristocratic character.

It seems probable that, if the gurus̆ consisted of the weapon-bearing men only, it cannot have been identical with the popular assembly. Even if it also included those fit only for work on the land, it seems highly improbable that there was any regulation forbidding the attendance of men too old even for that. On the whole, the most likely interpretation of the evidence we possess, slight as this is, would seem to be that the popular assembly consisted of all the ordinary male citizens of Uruk, regardless of age, and that the type of service demanded of its members was determined by their capacities. Under ancient conditions of life expectancy, youngish men in their prime would be in a large majority without doubt, but perhaps we could define the relationship of the assembly to the gurus̆ by saying that it consisted of its present and past members.

The attempt to buttress this view of the gurus̆ as essentially an assembly of warriors by invoking the analogy of the Roman comitia, "parallels for the 'male population bearing arms' as the original nucleus of legislative assemblies are many: we may mention the Roman comitia as an example" deserves close examination. There were three Roman *comitia*, the Curiata, Centuriata and Tributa. The earliest of these was the Comitia Curiata, only a survival in historical times, membership of which seems to have depended upon a mixture of local and family associations—i.e. a *curia* was probably drawn from the households of a single district. Each *curia* voted as a single unit, the majority decision within each deciding its vote. This method of voting in groups was very characteristic of Roman practice, and applied in all three assemblies. If the *Comitia* ever had a military function or origin, it had certainly disappeared already in regal times, and we hear nothing of it. The Comitia Tributa may be passed over here, for it was a later development, based upon the reformed Roman tribal system, and did not play a military role. This leaves the Comitia Centuriata. This does seem to have been military in its inception, but any possible connexion between its Centuries and those of the army vanished very rapidly. With typical conservatism, the Romans continued to employ some of the military trappings of the assembly—for example, it was summoned by a bugle and met in the Campus Martius—but these were merely picturesque survivals, as a closer examination of the assembly soon shows. Its Centuries were divided up into those of *iuniores* and those of *seniores*, the *seniores* all being men of above military age; in view of life expectancy, the Centuries of *seniores* were certainly much smaller in numbers, but they enjoyed equal voting rights. Thus the assembly was weighted in favour of age. Nor had the number of men in each Century any bearing upon the number required to provide a century of troops. The distribution of Centuries was based upon a property census, the wealthy being given an entirely disproportionate degree of representation. How disproportionate this was may be judged from the fact that the eighteen Centuries of Knights together with the eighty allotted to the first of the five classes made up more than half the 193

Centuries into which the whole assembly was formed. Since voting was by classes, and went on only until a majority of Centuries was obtained for or against a proposal, it is obvious that this assembly in its developed form—which totally overshadows its brief military functioning—had little in common with "the male population bearing arms," or for that matter with democracy of any kind, whether primitive or otherwise.

No doubt the assembly at Uruk in the time of Gilgamesh was more primitive than any of those at Rome, and nearer to the days when armed tribesmen congregated to form the folk moot. Nevertheless, it did form part of a true urban civilisation with a considerable period of settled life behind it, so that it is reasonable to suppose that it had advanced some distance from its original form, just as society had done. The example given above shows clearly how even an assembly which on the surface may appear to preserve its original military character can in fact have evolved into something quite different.

CONCLUSIONS

This discussion has been both long and discursive. It may be of value therefore to summarise the conclusions which have been drawn tentative though some of these may be:

The assemblies of Uruk in the time of Gilgamesh consisted of a body of elders with advisory powers, recruited from the heads of the powerful family groupings which made up the state; many of them may have been in fact elderly men, but age was not of itself a qualification for membership; and an assembly of all the freemen of the city, young and old, which enjoyed ultimate sovereignty. This popular assembly may have been handicapped by an inadequate procedural technique, especially in the era of inter-city rivalry then setting in.

The assemblies at Kaneš shortly after the beginning of the second millennium

B.C. show a great decline in power and a shift of the balance of the legal powers which were left from the full assembly to that of the "great." The latter were chosen not on the basis of age—which was not the main criterion in the assembly of elders even at Uruk—but probably because of their commercial and official importance within the colony. In cases where they failed to agree, a matter might be referred for decision to the full assembly of the colony. There are indications of the use of a more advanced form of procedure within the assembly of the "great" than in the popular assembly. This may have involved a form of voting or reaching a decision in groups, but the decline in the importance of the assemblies for political purposes deprived this development—if it was an innovation—of the significance which it might otherwise have possessed for political development.

7. THE LIPIT-ISHTAR LAW CODE*

A key factor in our judgment of any political system is the relationship between the sovereign and the law. Lipit-Ishtar (1934–1924 B.C.) of Isin promulgated a law code which was by no means the first such code in Mesopotamia. It is, however, quite typical, and a shorter forerunner of the more famous Code of Hammurabi.

PROLOGUE

When the great An, the father of the gods, (and) Enlil, the king of all the lands, the lord who determines ordinances, had . . . to Ninisinna, the daughter of An, the . . . for her . . . (and) the rejoicing . . . for her bright forehead; when they had given her the kingship of Sumer (and) Akkad (and) a favorable reign in her (city) Isin, the . . . established by An; when An (and) Enlil had called Lipit-Ishtar—Lipit-Ishtar, the wise shepherd, whose name had been pronounced by the Nunamnir—to the princeship of the land in order to establish justice in the land, to banish complaints, to turn back enmity (and) rebellion by the force of arms, (and) to bring well-being to the Sumerians and Akkadians, then I, Lipit-Ishtar, the humble shepherd of Nippur, the stalwart farmer of Ur, who abandons not Eridu, the suitable lord of Erech, king of Isin, king of Sumer and Akkad, who am fit for the heart of Inanna, established justice in Sumer and Akkad in accordance with the word of Enlil. Verily, in those days I procured . . . the freedom of the sons and daughters of Nippur, the sons and daughters of Ur, the sons and daughters of Isin, the sons and daughters of Sumer and Akkad upon whom . . . slaveship . . . had been imposed. Verily, in accordance with . . . , I made the father support his children, (and) I made the children support their father; I made the father stand by his children, (and) I made the children stand by their father; in the father's house (and) in the brother's house, I . . . . Verily, I, Lipit-Ishtar, the son of Enlil, brought seventy into the father's house (and) the brother's house; into the bachelor's house, I brought . . . for ten months . . . . the wife of a man, ... the child of a man . . . . .

THE LAWS

1 . . . which had been set up . . . . .
2 . . . the property of the father's house from its . . . . .
3 . . . the son of the state official, the son of the palace official, the son of the supervisor . . . . .
4 . . . a boat . . . a boat he shall . . . . .
5 If a man hired a boat (and) set it on a . . . journey for him . . . . .

---

* Translated by S. N. Kramer in *The Sumerians* (Chicago: University of Chicago Press, 1963), pp. 336–340.

6 ... the gift ... he shall .....

7 If he gave his orchard to a gardener to raise ... (and) the gardener ... to the owner of the garden .....

8 If a man gave bare ground to (another) man to set out an orchard (and the latter) did not complete setting out that bare ground as an orchard, he shall give to the man who set out the orchard the bare ground which he neglected, as part of his share.

9 If a man entered the orchard of (another) man (and) was seized there for stealing, he shall pay 10 shekels of silver.

10 If a man cut down a tree in the garden of (another) man, he shall pay $\frac{1}{2}$ mina of silver.

11 If adjacent to the house of a man the bare ground of (another) man has been neglected and the owner of the house has said to the owner of the bare ground, "Because your ground has been neglected someone may break into my house; strengthen your house," (and) this agreement has been confirmed by him, the owner of the bare ground shall restore to the owner of the house any of his property that is lost.

12 If a slave girl or slave of a man has fled into the heart of the city (and) it has been confirmed that he (or she) dwelt in the house of (another) man for one month, he shall give slave for slave.

13 If he has no slave, he shall pay 15 shekels of silver.

14 If a man's slave has compensated his slaveship to his master (and) it is confirmed (that he has compensated) his master twofold, that slave shall be freed.

15 If a *miqtum* is a grant of the king, he shall not be taken away.

16 If a *miqtum* went to a man of his own free will, that man shall not hold him; he (the *miqtum*) may go where he desires.

17 If a man without authorization bound (another) man to a matter to which he (the latter) had no knowledge, that man

is not affirmed; he (the first man) shall bear the penalty in regard to the matter to which he has bound him.

18 If the master of an estate or the mistress of an estate has defaulted on the tax of the estate (and) a stranger has borne it, for three years he (the owner) may not be evicted. (Afterward) the man who bore the tax of the estate shall possess that estate, and the (former) owner of the estate shall not raise any claim.

19 If the master of an estate .....

20 If a man from the heir(s) seized .....

21 [If] .... the house of the father ... he married, the gift of the house of her father which was presented to her as her heir he shall take.

22 If the father (is) living, his daughter whether she be a *nindingir*, a *lukur*, or a hierodule shall dwell in the house like an heir.

23 If the daughter in the house of (her) living father ....

24 If the second wife whom he had married bore him children, the dowry which she brought from her father's house belongs to her children; (but) the the children of (his) first wife and the children of (his) second wife shall divide equally the property of their father.

25 If a man married a wife (and) she bore him children (and) those children are living, and a slave also bore children for her master (but) the father granted freedom to the slave and her children, the children of the slave shall not divide the estate with the children of their (former) master.

26 If his first wife dies (and) after her (death) he takes his slave as a wife, the children of his first wife are his heirs; the children which the slave bore for her master shall be like ..., his house they shall .....

27 If a man's wife has not borne him children (but) a harlot (from) the public square has borne him children, he shall provide grain, oil, and clothing for that

harlot; the children which the harlot has borne him shall be his heirs, and as long as his wife lives the harlot shall not live in the house with his wife.

28 If a man turned his face away from his first wife . . . (but) she has not gone out of the house, his wife which he married as his favorite is a second wife; he shall continue to support his first wife.

29 If a (prospective) son-in-law has entered the house of his father-in-law (and if) he made his betrothal (but) afterward they made him go out (of the house) and gave his wife to his companion, they shall present to him the betrothal gifts which he brought (and) that wife may not marry his companion.

30 If a young man married a harlot (from) the public square (and) the judges have ordered him not to visit her, (but) afterward he divorced his wife, money . . . . .

31 [If] . . . . he has given him, after their father's death the heirs shall divide the estate of their father, (but) the inheritance of the estate they shall not divide; they shall not "cook their father's word in water."

32 If the father while living has set aside a betrothal gift for his eldest son (and) in the presence of the father who was still alive he (the son) married a wife, after the father's (death) the heir . . . . .

33 If it has been confirmed that the . . . had not divided the estate, he shall pay 10 shekels of silver.

34 If a man rented an ox (and) injured the flesh at the nose-ring, he shall pay one-third of (its) price.

35 If a man rented an ox (and) damaged its eye, he shall pay one-half of (its) price.

36 If a man rented an ox (and) broke its horn, he shall pay one-fourth of (its) price.

37 If a man rented an ox (and) damaged its tail, he shall pay one-fourth of (its) price.

38 [If] . . . . he shall pay.

EPILOGUE

Verily, in accordance with the true word of Utu, I caused Sumer and Akkad to hold to true justice. Verily, in accordance with the pronouncement of Enlil, I, Lipit-Ishtar, the son of Enlil, abolished enmity and rebellion; made weeping, lamentations, outcries . . . taboo; caused righteousness and truth to exist; brought well-being to the Sumerians and the Akkadians . . . .

Verily, when I had established the wealth of Sumer and Akkad, I erected this stele. May he who will not commit any evil deed with regard to it, who will not damage my handiwork, who will not erase its inscription, who will not write his own name upon it—be presented with life and breath of long days; may he rise high in the Ekur; may Enlil's bright forehead look down upon him. (On the other hand) he who will commit some evil deed with regard to it, who will damage my handiwork, who will enter the storeroom (and) change its pedestal, who will erase its inscription, who will write his own name upon it, (or) who, because of this curse, will substitute someone else for himself—that man, whether he be a . . . , whether he be a . . . , may he take away from him . . (and) bring to him . . . in his . . . his . . . whoever; may Ashnan and Sumugan, the lords of abundance, take away from him . . . his . . . may he abolish . . . . May Utu, the judge of heaven and earth . . . take away . . . his . . . its foundation . . . as . . . may he be counted; let not the foundation of his land be firm; its king, whoever he may be, may Ninurta, the mighty hero, the son of Enlil . . . .

8. AUTHORITY AND LAW IN MESOPOTAMIA*

On the basis of codes such as that of Lipit-Ishtar, E. A. Speiser of the University of Pennsylvania comments on the crucial question of the place of the king and the law in Mesopotamia.

I

The outstanding feature of kingship in ancient Mesopotamia is the ruler's subservience to the gods throughout the long recorded history of that composite civilization. Thus in the Sumerian myth of cultural norms the attributes of kingship are listed in fourth place, after three separate divine groupings. Old Assyrian inscriptions state explicitly that the real king was the god Ashur, whereas the mortal ruler was merely the god's agent (iššakku). Other times and places likewise provide abundant evidence of similar recognition of the gods' overriding authority.

Such a climate is clearly unfavorable to persistent deification of the temporal ruler. In point of fact, this practice, although often alleged, has never been established beyond dispute. It is true that some of the kings of Akkad, in common with those of the Third Dynasty of Ur and of sundry other places and periods, appear to boast certain aspects of divinity. The actual import of these instances is not altogether clear. They are, in any event, scattered and sporadic. The practice was limited and atypical at best. While it does embrace a Naram-Sin or an Ibbi-Sin, it is precisely these kings on whom tradition, so far from extolling them as gods, fastened the stigma of ill-fated rulers. Moreover, the Mesopotamian king remains at all times subject to the tyranny of the omens. A god incarnate would not be normally expected to take his cue from the liver of a sheep.

There are other significant details of the Mesopotamian pattern which point uniformly to the conclusion that the very concept of a deified ruler would be incompatible with the whole spirit of the underlying civilization. In the area of government, e.g., ultimate authority resided not in the given individual incumbent, but in the corporate assembly. The proemium to the Etana Epic recalls a barbarous stage when mankind had not as yet had the benefit of consultative government (mitluku). It was presumably in order to put an end to such chaos that kingship, as a constructive civilizing factor, came down from heaven. Etana himself, incidentally, as the traditional shepherd, personifies the abiding cultural stereotype whereby the Mesopotamian king is the "shepherd of the great people," and hence responsible to his own master for the welfare of the flock. Kingship, in other words, was limited here from the start by the twin checks of state and religion.

The assembly (Sum. ukkin, Akk. puḫrum) is shown to operate as a safeguard against autocracy already in the penumbral stage that separates prehistory from history. Before he can embark on a fateful campaign against his rival Agga, Gilgamesh must obtain, according to a Sumerian poem, the approval of the elders as well as the townsmen of Uruk. The Akkadian Epic of Gilgamesh retrojects the same condition to the days preceding the Flood; for Utnapishtim cannot start the construction of his ark until he has broached the subject to the elders and the people of Shuruppak. What is more, the assembly is not just a fanciful motif appropriate to myth and legend. Its reality is vouched for by the practical and sober discipline of omens. An Old Babylonian specimen informs us that in certain circumstances "the

* E. A. Speiser, "Authority and Law in Mesopotamia," *Journal of the American Oriental Society*, Supplement 17 (1954), pp. 8–15.

assembly has failed to reach an agreement." Other instances tell repeatedly of elders gathering to advise the ruler on matters of moment. Evidently, this was a right and a privilege cherished not only by the nobles but by the people at large.

It is, however, the evidence of religion that speaks most eloquently of the vital place of government by assembly in the total pattern of Mesopotamian civilization. In the Sumerian world view, which became normative for the land as a whole, divine and human societies interfused. Things on earth were but an echo of cosmic conditions and, conversely, divine doings reflected mortal pursuits. The fact, then, that the assembly was also the ultimate source of authority among the gods lends added emphasis to the enormous significance of that institution in human affairs.

All the gods, even the highest ones in the hierarchy, were subject to the decisions of the cosmic body. That group alone was competent to name the head of the pantheon, to determine destinies, to regulate the length of reigns. Even the grant of immortality to a human, an Utnapishtim for example, required formal approval by the divine council.

This concept of collective authority as the supreme authority is basic to our present theme. None of the gods of Mesopotamia enjoyed absolute power individually. By the same token, no mortal had a warrant for unchecked power on earth. On the one hand, the king had to satisfy the proper councils of his realm; and on the other hand, he must answer to the gods for the management of the affairs which they had entrusted to him.

To interpret the pleasure of the gods and to act all times in accordance with their wishes was an ever more complex task. Only experts were competent to pass upon it. To that extent, therefore, the king was subject to the discretion of the priests. The priests imposed upon him various expiatory rituals, often to his intense discomfort and even distaste. All sorts of phenomena were to the priests the means for a prognosis of the ruler's every move. Small wonder, then, that in the solemn commemoration of the New Year there was an elaborate ceremony in which the high priest administered tangible and painful proof of the king's essential unworthiness. This would seem to be the utmost in constitutional safeguards.

State and religion, then, through the elders and the priests, were the instruments whereby the power of the Mesopotamian ruler was curbed. In all their essentials these two institutions are as old as the historic Mesopotamian civilization itself. They were inevitably among the most distinctive features of that civilization. Together with a third such feature they comprise the foundation of the Mesopotamian way of life. That third basic component is law.

II

Legal systems both implement and reflect the underlying concepts of state. The two are closely interrelated. All advanced societies, of course, whatever their system of government may be, have their laws. But the status of the law in each instance depends on the nature of the parent society.

Mesopotamia has furnished a prodigious body of material pertaining to legal practice, but very little that bears on the theory. Such directly relevant terms as *dīnu* and *ṣimdatu* are confined to the practice in that they refer to 'decision' and to 'the process and the results of due judicial procedure.' The theory has to be reconstructed on the basis of the two general terms *kittum* and *mēšarum*, which may roughly be rendered 'truth' and 'justice.' Yet any unqualified translation of such intimate cultural rubrics is likely to fall flat, for these rubrics embody the stratification of the culture as a whole.

In essence, *mēšarum* is the process whereby law is made to function equitably.

This is one of the ruler's principal duties. It involves supervision, adjustment, amendments. An able administrator may find it necessary to make up-to-date compilations of normative provisions. Hammurapi did that, and so before him did Lipit-Ishtar and Bilalama, Ur-nammu and apparently also Urukagina. The ruler who has fulfilled these obligations, or claims to have done so, is described as *šar mēšarim* 'the just king.'

The Mesopotamian king, however, for all his extensive judicial activity, was not the source of the law but only its agent. He was merely the faithful shepherd who tended the flock on behalf of his master. The cosmos was founded on certain eternal truths which the laws strove to safeguard. These truths applied to the ruler no less than to his subjects. The king, more than anyone else, must be ever watchful to maintain them.

The sum of such cosmic and immutable truths was called *kittum*. A king might seek to 'establish' (*šakānum*) the *kittum* just as he was bound to institute *mēšarum*. Yet the final source of *kittum* was divine, not human. Shamash, the sun-god, was the prime heavenly authority in the matter, the *bēl kitti(m) u mēšari(m)*. The mortal ruler could at best claim that he merited the title of *šarru(m)-kēn* 'the king is legitimate,' if his office was in conformance with divine norms. The fundamental distinction between *kittum* and *mēšarum*—a distinction that has not received adequate notice—is observed neatly by Hammurapi who speaks of himself as 'the just king (*šar mīšarim*) to whom Shamash committed the truths (*kīnātim*). The king, in short, was a trustee, not an autocrat. Total law (*kittum u mēšarum*) was impersonal and above the crown. The ruler was no more exempt from the legal provisions than any average citizen.

Since the law was not subject to a ruler's whims, its proper application had to be guided by collected statutes reflecting both the established tradition and the necessary topical amendments. Enough such compilations are now extant—they are not codes in the fullest technical sense of the term—to indicate that the underlying legislative process reaches back to the late third millennium, and to suggest that even older instances may be assumed with confidence. The arrangement into a prologue, a legal corpus, and an epilogue was itself apparently a matter of tradition. Expedience dictated that the text be available for consultation in the administrative centers of the realm; hence the number of copies in which Hammurapi's revision has come down to us.

The fact should be stressed that, although state and church interpenetrated throughout the ancient Near East, Mesopotamian law, as we know it from many sources that span scores of centuries, was strictly secular. It concerns itself with private and public property, trade and commerce, agriculture and land tenure, professions and wages, and the general administration of justice. It is not a religious pronouncement. However closely the law may blend with the total cultural fabric, it enjoys nevertheless the dignity of an independent discipline. This is perhaps one of the main reasons for its great influence and appeal. Basically, of course, the law is always *kittum* and hence an aspect of the cosmic order and an object of zealous care on the part of the meritorious king. The enforcement was the task of the governors, judges, and various other officials. As the chief steward, however—the trusted shepherd—the king bore the final responsibility and acted as the human court of the last instance. Royal correspondence abounds in examples of this particular activity.

III

Government and law comprise the means whereby civilization attempts to solve the problem of the individual's relation to society. The kind of solution employed brings out, in turn, the essential character of the civilization which evolved it.

The Mesopotamian answer, which has just been sketched in barest outline, featured a ruler who must account for his acts, first, to an assembly of his fellow-mortals and, second, to the gods, who were often unpredictable and even capricious. The supporting law concentrated on earthly security and steered clear of the doubts and anxieties which beset religion. Judging by the results, this particular solution of the societal problem enjoyed extraordinary success.

Such success is signalized in several ways. For one, we are obliged to speak of a Mesopotamian civilization rather than of separate Sumerian, Babylonian, or Assyrian cultures, precisely because the existing unifying factors outweighed the normally divisive differences of language, geography, and political boundaries; and foremost among these unifying factors were the law and the concept of state. For another, the influence of Mesopotamian society spreads far beyond the limits marked out by the Euphrates and the Tigris. The Elamites and the Hurrians, the Hittites and the Syrians—these and others show close affinities with Mesopotamia proper in regard to law and government. In law, especially, generic relationship is assured by the prevailing use of the Akkadian language, the cuneiform script, and the legal document, three outstanding features common to what has come to be called "cuneiform law." For yet another, the dynamism of Mesopotamian civilization, largely through the medium of the same two factors, eventually influences also neighboring areas in matters of religion and literature, arts and sciences, and in various other aspects of society. International correspondence is conducted in Akkadian. Mesopotamia's myths and the products of its wisdom literature travel far afield. In spite of unceasing political unrest and disruption, much of Western Asia comes to reflect a community of basic cultural interests. Finally, the overwhelming importance of law as the key to a cherished way of life does not diminish with the end of the historic states of ancient Mesopotamia. The old tradition survives in part in the very name of the Babylonian Talmud and in the Islamic legal schools which flourished on Mesopotamian soil.

There is, in these circumstances, the danger of overstating the whole achievement. It is in order, therefore, to add that Mesopotamian ideas of the cosmos were not conducive to notable ethical progress; that related cultures made independent contributions which in many respects went far beyond any comparable Mesopotamian results; and that contemporary civilizations which lived by opposing faiths were highly productive in their own way.

This inquiry, however, serves to underscore one thing in particular: material remains in themselves are not the decisive criteria of ancient civilizations that they are usually believed to be. However great may be the difference between the pyramids and the siqqurrats, and however spectacular, the principal features of the parent cultures reach deeper and loom larger. It is the societal features, and especially the respective concepts of state and of law, that afford a truly distinctive picture of a given civilization all the way back to the beginning of recorded history. Indeed, in the final analysis, it is these features that proved to make history.

SECTION II

The Religious Reform of Ikhnaton:
The Great Man in History

THE EIGHTEENTH DYNASTY of Egypt was a vital and active one which had liberated the land from the Hyksos invaders. Under Thutmose III it had pushed Egypt's boundaries further than they had ever been and made of her a great imperial power. The accession of Amenhotep IV, however, radically changed its nature. Warfare was avoided, the empire neglected, secular concerns apparently abandoned to a new religious concern. The chief god of the kingdom, Amon-Re, was replaced by Aton; the king changed his name to Ikhnaton; the capital was moved to the newly built holy city of Akhetaton. In the space of a few years a major revolution had taken place among a people noted for conservatism. Scholars have not ceased to be fascinated by the problems presented by these events. What was the nature of the religion of Aton? Was it monotheistic? Was it related to the religion of the Hebrews? Was the revolution's purpose solely or even mainly religious? Most recently scholars have fixed on the career of Ikhnaton to illustrate one of the favorite arguments among historians: Is history made by great men or by objective forces? It may be especially pleasant to confront this ever-contemporary problem in the person of an Egyptian pharaoh who passed from the scene over five millennia ago.

1. THE GREAT MAN *vs.* THE CULTURAL PROCESS*

Lawgivers, statesmen, religious leaders, discoverers, inventors, therefore only seem to shape civilization. The deep-seated, blind, and intricate forces that shape culture, also mold the so-called creative leaders of society as essentially as they mold the mass of humanity. Progress, so far as it can objectively be considered to be such, is something that makes itself. We do not make it.—A. L. Kroeber.

* * *

In Egypt in the fourteenth century before the Christian era some remarkable

* Leslie A. White, "Ikhnaton: The Great Man *vs.* the Cultural Process," *Journal of the American Oriental Society*, 68 (1948), pp. 91–103.

events took place. Monotheism came to the fore and waged war on the old polytheism. All gods were abolished save one, and he was made Lord of all. Temples were closed, their priests driven out, their lands and revenues confiscated. A new capital was built. The government was reorganized. A marked change in art occurred. The whole regime of Egypt changed its aspect, and, it has been claimed, the events which took place then have profoundly affected our lives today. How did all this come about? What caused this upheaval that shook Egypt to its foundations and extended its influence even to us today? One of the answers has been: Ikhnaton. This genius, through his vision and insight, caught a glimpse of a new philosophy and a new way of life, and through sheer will and determination transformed the nation at his feet. At least, so we have been told.

Needless to say, not all students of Egyptian history have relied upon so simple an explanation. There are many, especially in recent years, who have a live appreciation of the significance of cultural forces in the historic process. We shall take note of their work later.

Social science is frequently absolved from its sins of sterility and impotence by sympathetic friends who point out that the scientist in the social field does not have laboratories at his command like the physicist and hence cannot be expected to produce theories that can withstand the tests these techniques can administer. But this exoneration is fallacious and misleading. It is true of course that the social scientist does not have laboratories—*like the physicist*. But he does have laboratories in another, and in a very real, sense. History and ethnography provide the social scientist with the equivalent of the laboratories of the physicist. How does the human organism respond to polyandry, to mothers-in-law, money, spectroscopes, holy water, governmental regulation of prices; how will men live in desert, tundra, or jungle; what will be the effect of technological advance on social life and philosophy? Answers to these and thousands of similar questions may be obtained by studies of the infinitely varied circumstances and conditions under which man has lived on this planet during the last million years. If the social scientist could set up his experiments as the physicist or rat psychologist does, it would be difficult to imagine a requirement that has not been met by some tribe, some culture, at some time and place. The meager yield of social science is not due to lack of laboratories but rather from not knowing how to use the resources at its disposal.

Ancient Egypt is an excellent laboratory in which the social scientist can test many theories. It was quite isolated, being cut off from its neighbors by deserts, mountains, and the sea. It was therefore relatively undisturbed by outside influence. We have a fairly good record, both archeologic and documentary, of history and cultural development of Egypt for tens of centuries. The land was richly endowed—as contrasted, let us say, with Australia—and so we can observe the growth of culture from a fairly primitive level to one of the greatest civilizations of the ancient world. Here we have laid out before us, on a stage of adequate size and against a background of millennia, a culture process at work. We can take note of the materials employed, the resources both natural and cultural. We can follow the changes one by one. We can trace the development step by step. We can see how one factor influenced others. We can count and evaluate. In short, we can do about all that a physical scientist can do in his laboratory—except repeat the experiment. We have, then, in Egypt a proving ground in which to test many theories of social science.

We may distinguish two main types of historical interpretation: the *psychological* and the *culturological*. Especially prominent in the psychological interpretation is the explanation of historic events in terms of the personalities of outstanding individuals, but it resorts also to the "temperaments" of peoples or races, and even to such things as "the spirit of the times." The culturo-logical type of interpretation explains history in terms of *cultural* forces and processes, in terms of the behavior, not of the human psyche, but of technologies, institutions, and philosophies. Let us then go to our laboratory and use it to evaluate the theories which undertake to explain the great philosophic and political events that took place during the life of Ikhnaton. We shall examine first the psychological interpretation.

The great religious and political revolution which gripped Egypt about 1380 B.C. has been pictured as the work of *one man*: Ikhnaton. "Until Ikhnaton," says Breasted, "the history of the world had been but the irresistible drift of tradition. All men had been but drops of water in the great current. *Ikhnaton was the first individual in history*." And, says Breasted, Ikhnaton accomplished this revolution by imposing his own ideas, ideas born in his own mind, upon the external world: "*Consciously and deliberately, by intellectual process* he gained his position, and then placed himself squarely in the face of tradition and swept it aside" (emphasis ours).

But ideas alone were not enough; will power and energy were required too. Ikhnaton possessed these qualities also, we are told. "He possessed unlimited personal force of character." He "was fully convinced that he might entirely recast the world of religion, thought, art, and life by the invincible purpose he held. . . . Everything bears the stamp of his individuality. The men about him must have been irresistibly swayed by his unbending will. . . . The court officials blindly followed their young king, and to every word which he spoke they listened attentively." H. R. Hall interprets Egyptian history in terms of the waxing and waning of intelligence which reached its "acme under the supremely intelligent" Ikhnaton. "His

reign was the earliest age of the rule of ideas, irrespective of the condition and willingness of the people" (Breasted). The revolution of Ikhnaton "can only be ascribed to the individual genius of a very exceptional man" (Gardiner). Alexandre Moret asserts that "Amenophis IV [Ikhnaton] was the man who turned aside the natural course of events."

To E. A. Wallis Budge Ikhnaton was "a religious fanatic, intolerant, arrogant and obstinate, but earnest and sincere." No one, he says, "but a half-insane man would have been so blind to facts as to attempt to overthrow Amen and his worship." James Baikie saw him as a man with a "remorselessly clear mind," but exceedingly intolerant. "Seeing clearly," he writes, "that the universality of his god meant monotheism, he saw also that with his rigid devotion to truth there could be no room for tolerance of the easy-going old cults of the other gods." In short, the great upheaval in Egypt was brought about by a man's passion for truth and his devotion to logic. Geo. Steindorff and K. C. Seele regard Ikhnaton as "probably the most fascinating personality who ever sat on the throne of the pharaohs." He had a "mystical temperament" and "an extraordinary single-minded character." When once "embarked on a purpose he held to it with tenacity and carried it through unwaveringly with nothing short of fanaticism." J. D. S. Pendlebury who rejects Breasted's view that Ikhnaton was "the first individual in history," regards him, nevertheless, as an "extraordinary character," the "first rebel . . . whom we know, the first man with *ideas of his own* . . ." (emphasis ours).

Ikhnaton revolutionized not only theology but art as well, we are told. The new era in painting and sculpture that is associated with his reign was initiated and directed by Ikhnaton himself: "It is evident that the artists of Ikhnaton's court were taught by him to make the chisel and the brush tell the story of what they actually saw." Breasted believes that the remarkable hymn to Aton "was probably written by the king himself."

So remarkable a person does Ikhnaton appear to some observers that they cannot believe him to be a normal man. "Ikhnaton pursued his aims with [such] fatuous blindness and feverish fanaticism" that Breasted feels that "there is something hectic and abnormal in this extraordinary man, suggesting a mind which may even have been diseased." Weigall believes that Ikhnaton was an epileptic, subject to hallucinations.

There is of course some evidence to support the theory that Ikhnaton was abnormal. In the art of the day, which is said to be characterized by naturalism and realism, he is not infrequently depicted as misshapen and abnormal.

"The King preaches the return to nature, makes the artist work from the living model, and allows a plaster cast of his face to be taken (specimens have been found), to make sure that his features are correctly reproduced. . . . The sculptors faithfully reproduce the prominent lower jaw and the long, bulging skull, even when these deformities have been further aggravated by disease."

In his later years, Ikhnaton is depicted, according to Moret, as "rounded and effeminate—a hermaphrodite figure, with prominent breasts, wide hips, and thighs too much curved, which makes one suspect a morbid nature, with some pathological flaw."

Some writers have attempted to account for the remarkable and unusual character of Ikhnaton in terms of *race* as well as of psychology; they have maintained that he was not a full-blooded Egyptian. Thus, Weigall reminds us that "it must always be remembered that the king had much foreign blood in his veins." This helped him to stand out amongst the "superstitious Egyptians [who were] ever lacking in originality." Moret, too, comments on "the mixture of Aryan blood . . . further

complicated by the Syrian descent of Tii" in Ikhnaton's racial background.

Here, then, we have an explanation of Egyptian history for this period. A phenomenal person appears on the scene, a man with so much genius and power of will as to go beyond the boundaries of the normal, and by himself to transform the religion, social organization, and the art of a great nation. Here we have a theory to be tested in our "laboratory."

Before turning to our laboratory proper, namely, the culture history of Egypt as we knew it through archeological research and documentary studies, let us consider briefly what we know about the evolution of culture in general and the nature of societies like that of ancient Egypt in particular.

Man began his career as an anthropoid who was just learning to talk. He was distinguished from all other animal species by the faculty of articulate speech. It was this faculty which transformed the discontinuous, non-accumulative, non-progressive process of tool-using among the anthropoids into a continuous, cumulative and progressive process in the human species. Articulate speech transformed, also, the social organization of this gifted primate, and by the inauguration of cooperation as a way of life and security, opened the door to virtually unlimited social evolution. And, finally, language and speech made it possible for man to accumulate experience and knowledge in a form that made easy transmission and maximum use possible.

It was the ability to use symbols—of which articulate speech is the most important and characteristic form of expression—that made the origin and subsequent growth of culture possible. But symbols did not provide the motive power for cultural advance. This could only come from energy, energy in the sense in which the physicist uses this term. All life is a matter of energy transformations. Organisms enable themselves to live by capturing free energy from non-living systems and by incorporating it into their own living systems. Culture is man's peculiar means of harnessing energy and of putting it to work in order to make human life secure. Culture grows and develops as ways of harnessing more energy per capita per year are found and as the means of making the expenditure of this energy more effective are improved. Animal husbandry, agriculture, water power, and the use of fuels in engines, together with countless inventions and improvements of tools and mechanical devices mark the growth of culture as it is carried forward by technological advance.

The evolution of society is marked by two great stages: primitive or tribal, and civil or national. The tribe and clan are characteristics of primitive society (although the clan is by no means universal); the political state characterizes *civil* society. Primitive society is based upon kinship ties; civil society upon property relationships and territorial distinctions. Primitive society was relatively homogeneous structurally; civil society, more diversified.

The transition from primitive to civil society was brought about by technological advance, specifically, by the development of agriculture, supplemented—though not everywhere—by the domestication of animals. The maturation of the agricultural arts produced the following chain of sequences: increased food supply, increase in population, increase in population density and in size of political groupings, diversion of human labor from food-producing to specialized arts and crafts, a new type of exchange and distribution of goods, money and markets, economic classes, and so on.

The differentiation of structure, the specialization of function, of civil society required a special mechanism to co-ordinate the various segments and classes of society and to integrate them into a coherent and effective whole. Such an integrative mechanism was produced. It was the "State-Church," i.e., a mechanism having temporal and ecclesiastical aspects.

The function of the state-church is to preserve the integrity of society against dissolution from within and against destruction from outside forces. In other words, this integrative mechanism must co-ordinate the various elements of society —occupational groups, social strata and classes—and relate them to one another harmoniously, on the one hand; and on the other, the life of the society must be made secure against the aggression of its neighbors. This integrative mechanism has a variety of forms. Church and state, priest and king, may be distinct or they may be one, structurally. And, of course, there are many degrees of overlapping or distinction. But everywhere in civil society—whether it be among the Maya or Inca of the New World, or in Mesopotamia, India, or China in the Old—we find this fundamental mechanism of co-ordination, integration, and regulation. And it always presents these two aspects: temporal and ecclesiastical. Thus we find it in ancient Egypt.

But one further observation before we turn to the culture history of Egypt itself: In civil societies where the temporal and ecclesiastical aspects of the integrative mechanism are structurally distinct there is always rivalry, a rivalry which not infrequently becomes a bitter struggle for power. This is not surprising, of course. Both church and state are engaged in the same tasks, both have the same function so far as the social organism is concerned, namely, integration, co-ordination, regulation.

* * *

Let us turn now to the culture history of Egypt and trace the relationship between Church and State, priest and king, through the centuries.

In the Old Kingdom (2800–2250 B.C.) we find the state, the Pharaoh, playing the leading role. To quote Breasted:

". . . there arose at the beginning of the nation's history a state form of religion, in which the Pharaoh played the supreme role. In theory, therefore, it was he alone who worshipped the gods; in fact, however, he was of necessity represented in each of the many temples of the land by a high priest."

The various temples and their respective priesthoods were supported by the produce from their endowments in land and by contributions from the royal revenues. It was the business of the priests, in addition to their religious and ceremonial duties, to administer these lands and to collect revenue from them upon which they lived.

A few centuries later, during the Middle Kingdom, or the Feudal Age, we find that although the temples had increased somewhat in size, "the official cult was not materially altered, and there was still no large class of priests."

But the basis for a rise to power of the priesthoods had long existed in their possession of lands which were under their control and whose produce was appropriated by them. In addition to this they received frequent contributions from the royal treasury. The temples were, of course, not subject to taxation. They were, therefore, in a favorable position to increase their wealth through accumulation and expansion, and to grow in political power as their wealth accumulated.

Under the Empire, First Period (beginning with Ahmose I, who completed the expulsion of the Hyksos about 1546 B.C.), the priesthoods had grown to considerable power and affluence. Says Breasted:

"As a natural consequence of the great wealth of the temples under the Empire, the priesthood becomes a profession, no longer merely an incidental office held by a layman, as in the Old and Middle Kingdoms. As the priests increase in numbers they gain more and more political power; while the growing wealth of the temples demands for its proper administration a veritable army of temple officials of all sorts, who were unknown to the old days of simplicity."

Not only were the temples becoming wealthier and the priesthoods more powerful, they were becoming unified as well:

"Heretofore the priests of the various sanctuaries had never been united by any official ties, but existed only in individual and entirely separated communities without interrelation. All these priestly bodies were now united in a great sacerdotal organization embracing the whole land. The head of the state temple at Thebes, the High Priest of Amon, was the supreme head of this greater body also and his power was thereby increased far beyond that of his older rivals . . ."

Thus we find the priesthoods becoming wealthy, powerful, and organized. They are approaching the time when they will be able to threaten the supremacy of the Pharaoh himself, as we shall see.

We get some notion of the growing political power of the priesthoods from an incident that occurred during the feud of the Thutmosids. During the declining years of Thutmose I, one of his sons, born to the King by an obscure concubine, Thutmose III, was put upon the throne "by a highly dramatic coup d'état" of the priests of Amon and in the temple of that god. In the struggles for the throne which followed, between Thutmose III and his half-brother Thutmose II, and between Thutmose III and his half-sister wife, Hatshepsut, the priests played an important part. Originally kept in the background by Thutmose III, Hatshepsut was eventually elevated to a position of supremacy by a group the most powerful member of which was Hapuseneb, who was both High Priest of Amon and vizier. "He thus united in his person all the power of the administrative government with that of the strong priestly party."

These events took place about a century before the time of Ikhnaton. During the reign of Amenhotep III, the father of

Ikhnaton, one of the High Priests of Amon, Ptahmose by name, was also one of the two grand viziers of the kingdom. Another held the office of chief treasurer. During this reign also the priests of Amon acquired some, if not complete control over the gold produced in the Sudan. In the use of spells used in mortuary rites (hike), the priests "were provided with a means of acquiring wealth and influence which they did not fail to utilize to the utmost."

Thus we observe the growing power of the priesthoods. They held the most important offices in the realm next to that of the king himself. To have been chief treasurer of the kingdom must have placed great power in the hands of the High Priests of Amon, a power that was augmented by control over the gold supply from the Sudanese mines. These priests could make and unmake kings. They had but one more step to take: to seize the throne for themselves. Breasted believes that Ikhnaton's father "had evidently made some attempt to shake off the priestly hand that lay so heavily on the sceptre, for he had succeeded Ptahmose by a vizier who was not a High Priest of Amon." And Peet feels that "it is not impossible that the increased power of the priesthood . . . was a circumstance which precipitated, if it did not actually cause, the religious revolution of Ikhnaton." It was upon this stage that Amenhotep IV was thrust at birth.

Amenhotep IV was born about 1409 B.C., the son of Amenhotep III and his Queen Tiy. Estimates of his age at the time he ascended the throne as coregent with his father vary from nine to twenty-four years. For the first years of his reign, according to those who believe he ascended to the throne as a child, the affairs of state were managed by his mother. "To all intents and purposes, Ti ruled Egypt for several years after her husband's death," according to Wallis Budge, "and the boy king did for a time at least what his mother told him." Glanville also believes that "Tiy clearly

controlled him to some extent until he left Thebes." Although Amenhotep III did not die until about the tenth year of Ikhnaton's reign, he was in bad health during this period and seems to have had little to do with the government. The fact that his name was chiselled out of inscriptions in the sixth year of Ikhnaton's reign would seem to support this view.

Very early in the reign of Amenhotep IV the worship of a supreme god, Aton, was inaugurated. Aton was none other than the old sun-god, Re, in a new role. Other gods were tolerated for a while, but with the growing resentment of the priesthoods, particularly that of Amon, Amenhotep IV built a new city-capital, Akhetaton, for his god, changed his name to Ikhnaton, closed the temples of the other gods, dispossessed the priesthoods, confiscated their lands and revenues, and set to work to establish his new regime, both religious and political. All this had taken place by the sixth year of his reign.

Ikhnaton's reign was full of troubles, as may well be imagined. Not only did he have a bitter struggle with powerful priesthoods on his hands, but by closing the temples he incurred the resentment and opposition of numerous other classes as well, such as tradesmen, artisans, actors, scribes, and even shepherds and peasants, who had a vested occupational interest in the old order. To be sure, the Heretic King had a group of loyal followers, whom he rewarded handsomely for their loyalty and support. Occupied as he was with a revolution at home, Ikhnaton had little or no time for affairs abroad. As a consequence, revolts flared up among Egypt's vassals in Asia, the Hittites in particular becoming defiant and aggressive. In the twelfth year of his reign, Ikhnaton's mother, Tiy, who resided in Thebes, visited Akhetaten, at which time she may have urged action against the revolting vassals and a moderation of policy at home, perhaps even a compromise with the priests of Aton. At any rate, we find Ikhnaton making a feeble gesture against the rebels abroad and initiating conciliatory measures at home. Smenkhkare, the "beloved" of Ikhnaton and now coregent with him, was sent to Thebes to effect a reconciliation with the priests of Amon. But dissension now broke out in the king's own household. Although Ikhnaton seems to have been willing to compromise, Nefertiti, his wife, was not. At any rate, she fell into disgrace, or was estranged from her husband, and retired with some powerful followers to the north end of the city where she built a palace for herself. The political structure was disintegrating at home and abroad.

Ikhnaton died about 1369 B.C. at Akhetaten; Smenkhkare, the coregent, died at almost the same time in Thebes. Tutankhaten, a boy of nine, ascended the throne. By now the priestly party was growing rapidly in strength. The new king soon realized that he could stay on the throne only if he "came to terms with the supporters of the traditional faith," i.e., the priests. He was obliged to abandon his capital at Akhetaten and move his court to Thebes. He was compelled to abandon the heresy of Ikhnaton and to "acknowledge himself officially as an adherent of . . . Amun." Accordingly, he changed his name to Tutankhamun, "Beautiful in Life is Amun." In a manifesto he tells of his devotion to "his father Amun" and of his benefactions to his priests. He "made monuments for all the gods, fashioning their statues of pure *djam*-gold, restoring their sanctuaries . . . providing them with perpetual endowments, investing them with divine offerings for the daily service, and supplying their provisions on earth." The triumph of the priests was virtually complete.

Tutenkhamon reigned but nine years and was followed by Eye, a member of Ikhnaton's court. He too lasted but a short time. Egypt was now in a state of anarchy. Even Thebes became a prey to plundering bands. Thus ended the Eighteenth Dynasty.

Out of this chaos and confusion law and order eventually emerged organized around a man who had been an important figure in Egyptian government for years. This man was Harmhab. He had been commander in chief of the army under Ikhnaton and Tutankhamun, and as deputy of the king he had attained a position in the empire second only to the king himself. Despite this fact, however, Harmhab was never converted to the Aton religion. He did not go to Akhetaten with his king but remained in Memphis where he had his residence. "He remained loyal to the old gods, especially to the patron divinity of his native city and to Amun." He was thus acceptable to the priests of Amon. With their backing and that of the army which was already under his control he ascended the throne. The ceremony of installation was in fact carried out by the priests of Amon themselves. Some writers assert that he legalized his new position by marrying the sister of Nefertiti, but Alexander Scharff says that it "is certain" that this was not the case, that this assumption was born of an error of translation.

Having come into power with priestly backing it is not surprising to see Harmhab busying himself with the restoration begun by Tutankhamun. As a matter of fact, as soon as his government was in working order he set about energetically to restore the temples and their priesthoods to their former condition of wealth and power:

"He restored the temples from the pools of the Delta marshes to Nubia. He shaped all their images in number more than before, increasing the beauty in that which he made. . . . He raised up their temples; he fashioned a hundred images with all their bodies correct and with all splendid costly stones. He sought the precincts of the gods which were in the districts in this land; he furnished them as they had been since the time of the first beginning. He established for them daily offerings every day. All the vessels of their temples were wrought of silver and gold. He equipped them with priests and with ritual priests and with the choicest of the army. He transferred to them lands and cattle, supplied with all equipment."

Harmhab attempted to obliterate all traces of the era of heresy. He had the names of Ikhnaton, Tutankhamun, and Eye hacked from the monuments and his own put in their place. He considered himself the direct successor to Amenhotep III, as if Ikhnaton and his followers had never existed.

At Thebes, Harmhab razed the temple of Aton and used the materials to enlarge the temple of Amon. Aton's temple at Akhetaton was likewise despoiled to obtain building materials. Ikhnaton's "tomb was wrecked and its reliefs chiselled out; while the tombs of his nobles there were violated in the same way. Every effort was made to annihilate all trace of the reign of such a man; and when in legal procedure it was necessary to cite documents or enactments from his reign he was designated as 'that criminal of Akhetaton'." The prosperity and power of the priesthoods under Harmhab is well indicated by the words of Neferhotep, the priest of Amon:

"How bountiful are the possessions of him who knows the gifts of that god (Amon), the king of gods. Wise is he who knows him, favoured is he who serves him, there is protection for him who follows him." Neferhotep "was at the moment receiving the richest tokens of the king's favour."

As Breasted observes, the triumph of Amon was now complete.

We may now follow the course of the relationship between church and state in Egypt for a few more centuries.

The Nineteenth Dynasty began with wars of reconquest in Asia, followed by campaigns in Israel and against the Libyans. With the death of Merenptah, son of Ramesses II, the land fell again into virtual anarchy from which it emerged in 1200 B.C. under Sethnakt, founder of the Twentieth Dynasty. Sethnakt came to the throne backed by the priesthoods, "these wealthiest and most powerful communities in Egypt." Ramesses III, Sethnakt's successor, was completely in the grip of the priests. The temples, says Breasted, "were fast becoming a grave political and economic menace." But Ramesses could do naught else but pour the wealth of the royal house into the sacred coffers with the most lavish liberality.

We get a fair notion of the wealth and power of the priesthoods of the time of Ramesses III (1198–1167 B.C.) from an inventory in the Papyrus Harris which covers almost all of the temples of Egypt:

". . . they possessed over one hundred and seven thousand slaves; . . . in all likelihood one person in every fifty was a slave of some temple. The temples thus owned two percent of the population. In lands we find the sacred endowments amounting to nearly three quarters of a million acres, that is, nearly one seventh, or over fourteen and a half percent of the cultivable land of the country . . . They owned nearly a half million head of . . . cattle; their combined fleets numbered eighty eight vessels, some fifty three workshops and shipyards . . . while in Syria, Kush and Egypt they owned in all one hundred and sixty nine towns. When we remember that all this vast property in a land of less than ten thousand square miles and some five or six million inhabitants was entirely exempt from taxation it will be seen that the economic equilibrium of the state was endangered."

Among the priesthoods, that of the god of Amon stood out as by far the richest and most powerful of all. Their estates and revenues were second only to those of the king. "The political power wielded by a community of priests who controlled such vast wealth," says Breasted, "was from now on a force which no Pharaoh could ignore. Without compromising with it and continually conciliating it, no Pharaoh could have ruled long."

Sometimes the royal treasury stood

empty while the temples were loaded down with wealth. We read of workmen during the reign of Ramesses III starving as they labored on some public works until in desperation they gather before the office of their master demanding their rations of grain. "Thus while the poor in the employ of the state were starving at the door of an empty treasury, the store-houses of the gods were groaning with plenty."

At the coronation of Ramesses IV, a "detailed list of all the benefactions conferred . . . [by Ramesses III] on each and every large and small temple of the land" was published. "In this manner the new king contrived to confirm the clergy in their holdings of property and to gain their influential good will for his own reign . . . As the authority of the state grew weaker . . . the power and prestige of Amun and his priesthood expanded proportionately. All important public and private affairs were regulated and decided either by the priesthood or by an oracle which operated . . . in the imperial temple . . ." As Breasted puts it, "the state was rapidly moving toward a condition in which its chief function should be religious and sacerdotal, and the assumption of royal power by the High Priest of Amon but a very natural and easy transition."

It was not long until this transition did indeed take place. In the reign of Ramesses XI, a man named Hrihor was appointed high priest of Amon at Karnak. Next he became viceroy of Nubia and commander in chief of the army. A little later he assumed the vizierate of Upper Egypt. He now "had united under his personal control all the highest spiritual, military, and civil functions of the state. It was but a single step more to put aside the impotent Ramesses XI and ascend the throne in his place. By this act of usurpation (1085 B.C.), the secular state of the pharaonic empire was ushered to its grave and an ecclesiastical state was erected in its place, in which the chief god of Thebes exercised the authority through the medium of his

priesthood." The triumph of the priests was now complete.

No matter how individualistic Ikhnaton might have been, no matter how enormous his intellect and indomitable his will, he had his setting in a great nation, in a rich and mature culture, and we may assume that it affected his life as he is supposed to have so profoundly changed the world about him. Let us, therefore, turn to an examination of the relationship between Ikhnaton and the culture history of Egypt.

It is plain at the outset that the events which mark the reign of Ikhnaton are not novel by any means. Far from it, they are merely part of a process that had been going on for centuries before Ikhnaton was born, namely, the philosophic trend toward monotheism and the age-old rivalry between king and priest. This culture process receives more emphatic and dramatic expression during the lifetime of Ikhnaton, no doubt, but there is nothing original in it whatever.

Religious philosophy in Egypt had been moving in the direction of monotheism for centuries before Ikhnaton was born. We find in religious philosophy a reflection of the real world; the theology of a people will echo a dominant note in their terrestrial mode of life. A pastoral culture may find its image in a Good Shepherd and his flock; an era of cathedral building sees God as a Great Architect; an age of commerce finds Him with a ledger, jotting down moral debits and credits; emphasis upon the profit system and the high-pressure salesmanship that is required to make it function, picture Jesus as a super-salesman; and, in an age of science, God "is a god of law and order" (Millikan), a Great Scientist moving about in his cosmic laboratory, his experiments to perform.

In ancient Egypt, theological thinking was, as Breasted has so well said, "brought into close and sensitive relationship with political conditions." In the very early period, there were numerous deities, many of which were *local* gods, or patrons of little kingdoms. As the political unification of Egypt progressed, a few of the greater gods emerged as *national* deities. As the nation became more and more integrated under the rule of a powerful single head, there was a tendency for one god to become supreme. The ascendancy of Re, the sun-god, became marked during the Fifth Dynasty and by the rise of the Twelfth Dynasty his supremacy was unquestioned. Other priesthoods, "desirous of securing for their own, perhaps purely local deity, a share of the sun-god's glory, gradually discovered that their god was but a form and name of Re; and some of them went so far that their theologizing found practical expression in the god's name. Thus, for example, the priests of Sobk, a crocodile god, who had no connectio.1 with the sun-god in the beginning, now called him Sobk-Re. In like manner, Amon, hitherto an obscure local god of Thebes, who had attained some prominence by the political rise of the city, was from now on a solar god, and was commonly called by his priest Amon-Re. There were in this movement the beginnings of a tendency toward a pantheistic solar monotheism, which we shall yet trace to its remarkable culmination."

The concept of Maat was developed from the designation of personal qualities, or something practised by individuals, to something of national dimensions—a "spirit and method of a *national* guidance and control of human affairs . . . suffused with moral conviction. There was thus created for the first time a realm of universal values, and in conceiving the divine ruler of such a realm the Egyptians were moving on the road towards monotheism."

But the conception of a supreme deity whose rule extended to the farthest reaches of the earth and embraced all lands and peoples was impossible so long as Egypt's power remained confined to the Nile valley. In the Pyramid Age the Sun-god ruled only Egypt, and in the hymns of

the day we find him standing guard at her frontiers, "where he builds the gates which restrain all outsiders from entering his inviolable domain." It is otherwise after Egypt's conquests abroad and the era of empire. Then the supreme god of Egypt became the Lord of the Universe. As Breasted has so succinctly put it: "Monotheism is but imperialism in religion."

Thus we see that for centuries on end before the reign of Ikhnaton, religious philosophy in Egypt had been developing in the direction of monotheism as the political unification and imperial expansion of Egypt proceeded. And, as we have already seen, the rivalry between church and state, between priest and king, was already old before Amenhotep IV was born.

What then did Ikhnaton originate? The answer must be, "Virtually nothing." The trend toward monotheism was already there, and it was not until the latter years of his reign that Ikhnaton took the last logical step and attempted to abolish all other gods but Aton. As Breasted says, "this whole monotheistic movement is the culmination of the ancient recognition of a moral order by the Egyptian thinkers of the Pyramid Age and their creation of a realm of universal ethical values." Aton, the Disk god, was of sufficient importance during the reign of Ikhnaton's father to have a temple erected in his honor at Thebes. Even "the full name of the new deity, 'Re-Horus-of-the-Horizon who rejoices in his name of Shu who is the Disk' is to be ascribed not to Akhenaten but to his father or even to some earlier king." Indeed, the "most striking fact" pertaining to the various names of the new deity "is that they embody a distinct attempt at continuity with the sun worship of past ages." The Hymn to Aton, which was composed by Ikhnaton himself, according to the belief of many authors (who, however, may know full well that the addresses of modern heads of state are frequently written by others), was remarkable but unoriginal, according to Peet. Two architects of Amenhotep III, he writes, had already dedicated a hymn to the sun-god which was "a very close anticipation of Ikhnaton's hymn to the disk . . .; the ideas . . . [expressed in the latter] are not at all new, nor indeed are the phrases in which these ideas are embodied." Nor was Ikhnaton the first to erase the names of his rivals from public monuments; this was done freely in the feud of the Thutmosids.

The struggle with the priesthoods was also acute when Ikhnaton ascended the throne. We have already seen that the priests of Amon held powerful offices under his father, Amenhotep III, threatening the security of the throne. And Breasted says of them: They were rich and powerful when Ikhnaton ascended the throne. "They had installed Thutmose III as king, and could they have supplanted with one of their own tools the young dreamer [Ikhnaton] who now held the throne they would of course have done so at the first opportunity." Moret, too, sees the drastic steps taken by Ikhnaton as an attempt to "break the power of the priests of Amon lest they should dethrone the kings."

With the throne in danger of being captured by the priests, is it necessary to assume that it was a new philosophy germinating in the mind of an adolescent genius that precipitated the move against the priests and temples—especially when this philosophy was not new? Would it not be more reasonable to assume that it was a bold and drastic step taken by the temporal government in self-defense, in self-preservation? To close the temples and confiscate their lands and revenues would be a doubly effective political move: it would strengthen the throne at the same time that it weakened its rivals. It is significant to note that it was not a *priesthood* of the new god Aton who succeeded to the estates of Amon. Ikhnaton was himself the First Prophet of Aton, and as such assumed control of the vast wealth of his god. "This appropriation of the property of the temples," observes Moret, "shows us what lay beneath the religious revolution, the economic and political objects of the rupture." It was probably not the first time that struggles for terrestrial power were carried on in terms of celestial ideology; it certainly has not been the last. The break between Ikhnaton and the priests was therefore but the culmination of centuries of rivalry and competition between palace and temple. With the growing power of the priests a drastic move was necessary if the king was to retain his independence. For the temporal government it was do or die. The maturing philosophy of monotheism provided an excellent pretext and a weapon. But it was merely the means employed; it was not the cause.

2. THE FIRST INDIVIDUAL IN HISTORY*

A detached attitude, especially toward the remote and partially unknown, can bar from sight those many vistas glimpsed by the historian who approaches the task of reconstructing an era with sympathy, affection and imagination. In recording the

* Fred Gladstone Bratton, *The First Heretic: The Life and Times of Ikhnaton the King* (Boston: Beacon Press, 1961), pp. vii–x, 178–186. Reprinted by permission of the Beacon Press, copyright © 1961 by Fred Gladstone Bratton.

life of Ikhnaton, I have eulogized him. The strength and warmth of his intellect require a similar warmth in its depiction; and neither the accuracy nor the equilibrium of scholarship are upset by controlled imagination and honest praise.

Though eulogy need not conflict with scholarship, it must conflict with theories of historical inevitability, which deny that a single great man can profoundly alter the course of events. I have written this book as a protest against such deterministic philosophies of history. Protest is needed, since at mid-century this de-emphasis of the individual and his influence has passed from historiography into our culture at large. Too much of our current literature and thought rejects the role of the hero in history, denies the importance of individual genius in social change, refuses to recognize superiority, and fears eccentricity and dissent. This determinism has its immediate historical origin in the debunking period of the 1920s. Debunking was then a salutary corrective in American biography, lowering the Victorian pedestal of the haloed hero and making possible an improved synthesis of fine journalistic style with critical scholarship in the biographical writing of the 1930s. But at mid-century, debunking has reappeared in the form of a systematic and dulling determinism, which threatens to sap the vitality from all serious biography of significant lives.

Historical fatalism has received increasingly influential support, while it has appeared in increasingly varied guises: Calvin's "theological determinism," Hegel's "world spirit," Marx's "inevitable dialectic," Tolstoi's "Things happen because they were bound to happen," Spengler's and later Toynbee's "cyclic theory of cultures," Sorokin's "irresistible socio-cultural currents" and A. L. Kroeber's "deep-seated, blind, and intricate forces that shape culture." The deterministic prevails over the purposive and the social prevails over the individual. The historical fatalists tell us that history is shaped by economic laws, social forces or divine will, and that these inexorable necessities go their way uninfluenced by individual geniuses. The hero is a particle caught in the drift of history, a mere by-product. What happened *had* to happen. Great men only *seem* to shape civilization, since progress—if it occurs at all—is its own creator. The great man is the "slave of history"; human will, choice and innovation are in reality non-existent. So say the fatalists.

The fact is that social change, critical events and new movements in history are produced as much by the originality and power of great men as by blind social forces grinding along on their inevitable courses. Confucius, Michelangelo, Shakespeare, Spinoza, Newton, Beethoven and others like them achieved creative expressions which were far more than reflections of the times or by-products of irresistible social forces. The titans of history have not supplied needs of the moment; rather they have run counter to their times, generating forces that changed history. It is still true that every significant movement in history is "the lengthened shadow of a great man."

Men can and do determine their own destiny. Whether for good or for evil, individual genius has made civilization. Fatalism is not a philosophical and historical truth, but an escape from responsibility and possibility. Historical inevitability is an excuse for the denial of freedom. The rejection of the hero is an excuse for mediocrity. The churlish refusal to acknowledge excellence is a last refuge of the small man.

I am portraying Ikhnaton's life and thought not in order to worship a hero, but to recognize a hero. Ikhnaton took his stand against two thousand years of tradition, "drift of history" and preconditioning. He brought to life an idea new under the sun and lived by it. A hero of thought, he influenced world history more than most heroes of action. His life and teachings make him different in kind from all other kings and thinkers of the ancient world. The unique position of Ikhnaton was recognized by Emil Ludwig in his book, *The Nile*, when he wrote: "Only once in the history of Egypt was a revolution created from above (royalty, upper class); this was the achievement of Ikhnaton, the only Pharaoh whose life would be worth writing"—a judgment which provided ample justification for me—if such were needed—for writing this book.

Ikhnaton has become a controversial

figure in recent historical researches and discussion; but all the facts are not yet in. Historians have attempted to strip him of his reputation for originality and genius by maintaining that his doctrines of universalism and monotheism were either not new or not revolutionary. They have called attention to his deformed appearance and possibly epileptic condition and have claimed that he was unsophisticated in private life and naive in political life. Historians have called him "an unprincipled idealist," have insisted that "the trend of events would have been the same had Ikhnaton been but a sack of sawdust." One writer has called him "the mad Pharaoh, an inbred neurotic," whose doctrine of the sun cult was prompted by an obsessive fear of darkness. On the other hand, Ikhnaton's personality evokes unbridled admiration from other historians.

Whatever the true judgment of Ikhnaton's personality may be, his reign as pharaoh was the great divide in the history of Egypt, as well as in the history of the entire ancient world of the Middle East. The long story of Egyptian culture reached its most brilliant chapter in the Amarna Age. Cultural and political forces had built up a critical world situation, but the reaction to the world crisis was primarily the result of one man's personality. Ikhnaton shaped his times as much as Alexander or Caesar shaped theirs, but in another fashion. The first historically prominent individual to oppose the established order and the first thinker who both created and put into action original ideas, he was in fact the only prophetic voice in four thousand years of Egyptian history.

* * *

Ikhnaton might have been the founder of a lasting religious movement—the first monotheistic religion—but the times were not ripe. The man was ready for history but history was not ready for the man. The world was seething with unrest. The founding of a new religion requires a kind of situation that did not exist in the fourteenth century B.C. Furthermore, there were no great disciples of Atonism to carry it to the world. As for Egypt itself, it is unreasonable to expect that a country steeped in animistic polytheism for two thousand years would learn overnight to embrace an abstract monotheism. Also, a tolerance of the past and a conciliatory attitude toward the present—so necessary for the effective spread and continuation of any new movement—were both lacking in Ikhnaton. The revolution of Ikhnaton was too hurried and precipitous to last. It was a sweeping reform but premature. The stream of tradition was dammed up for a moment in history but the unstable construction of the Amarna ideal was suddenly broken down and drowned by the flood of tradition that flowed over it. And it might be added that the king's deliberate attempt to erase all mystery and official dignity from his person was not conducive to the maintenance of his authority and prestige, especially among the common people. He encouraged his artists in their exaggerated candor so that they had no hesitation in caricaturing him in all his public appearances. Atonism never became more than the religion of Amarna, and it died with its originator.

Ikhnaton, therefore, remains a prophet, the first prophet in history and, in some respects, one of the greatest. Like all later prophets of the first order, he failed, at least in the eyes of his contemporaries. But a prophet appeals to the ages rather than the age. Like the Hebrew prophets, he subordinated the political destiny of his country to a spiritual ideal, trusting to the survival of the ideal in spite of political downfall. In the Amarna revolution we can observe the power of an idea to hold sway in the face of tradition, environment and the desires of the people. In an age of militarism Ikhnaton was the first to teach the doctrine of peace. He was the first to preach the gospel of the simple life. Only an inspired prophet could oppose custom and tradition, and, by the force of his personality, found a new religion. In Egypt, as in the later Hebrew culture, the validity of an idea depended upon its claim to antiquity. Kings and wise men appealed to the sacred tradition to gain sanction for their writings. Ikhnaton appealed to no ancient legend or law, to no myths sanctified by time. His religion was of the eternal present, the evidences of which were open for all to see.

From our vantage point of three millennia we are able to appraise the greatness of Ikhnaton with true perspective and deep appreciation. Consider his unique situation in the history of religion. The lives of all other religious geniuses of antiquity are legendary, little more than unreliable traditions. There is, in fact, great doubt about the historicity of some of the founders of ancient religions. Their original teachings are not extant, but exist only in the manuscripts of a much later date—manuscripts that were the product of so much editing and changing over the centuries that we cannot be sure that later transcriptions are at all faithful to the original message. Both lives and teachings are obscured by ecclesiastical and theological accretions so that no one can be sure of the facts.

No such conditions obtain in the case of Ikhnaton. His original writings on the walls of the Amarna tombs can be read today just as when they were originally inscribed. No manuscripts, copies or conjectures are necessary here. The evidence of his career and home life is faithfully preserved in stone for all to see. The disclosures at Tell-el-Amarna today after thirty-three hundred years, including the wall paintings, the numerous busts of the royal family, the death mask of Ikhnaton and the mummy itself, give to the life and teachings of the heretic king a ring of authenticity not discernible anywhere else in the history of religion.

Most prophets are an integral part of the flow of history; that is, they are dependent to some extent upon both antecedent and environmental influences. There has to be a fertilization of the soil before the flower of their genius blooms. They stand upon the shoulders of previous and less important precursors, any one of whom might have gone down in history as equally great had the times been right. The situation produces the great man but he in turn transcends the time and turns the world into a new channel. Such geniuses were original, to be sure, but not profoundly independent of their age. Such was the case of a Jesus, a Luther or a Newton. But Ikhnaton was a mutation, quite isolated from both historical background and contemporary influences, except for the existence of the sun cult of Ra and the use of the term Aton by his father. Herein lies his genius. In the evolution of religious ideas, societies, as a rule, undergo a gradual growth through primitive magic, the worship of local spirits, national deities, anthropomorphic gods and finally monotheism. With Ikhnaton, a direct leap was made over all this evolutionary process to a cosmic theism that is not unlike that of Spinoza or Wordsworth. Ikhnaton's religion was not simply the worship of the sun. It recognized the vast creative force of the sun and the spiritual being of which the sun was a symbol. He called this invisible force "Heat which is in Aton," thus representing God as a dynamic, vital reality, creator of the sun and all forms of life. Aton was the source of all energy, the primal power behind all things, a formless essence, an intelligence permeating the universe. In fact, Ikhnaton intuited—as did Wordsworth—that God is one "whose dwelling is the light of setting suns." This was man's first attempt to define God in intangible terms and idealistic qualities. Ikhnaton's god was both transcendent and immanent, original causation and continuous presence. Such a philosophical conception could mean nothing to a people whose gods were tangible and whose worship was prescribed in a specific formula.

In fact, such a naturalistic, nonceremonial type of religion has unfortunately had difficulty in making headway in any age, so it is not surprising that Ikhnaton had no following. His was a voice crying in the wilderness, a harbinger of things to come. Thus, against the black night of Egyptian anthropomorphic religion this brilliant comet flashed for a moment, a prototype of the best modern theistic thought.

In the midst of the stilted, standardized living of our day and of social and religious conformity, the personality of this heretic of Amarna is a fresh breeze of originality and courage. In the casuistry and dishonesty of public life today, it shames us to contemplate the integrity and utter frankness of this lone individual. The example of his sincere family life is a rebuke to the decadence of contemporary culture. In a world of war he preached and practised the life of peace. Surrounded by superstition and ignorance, he pursued the life of reason. His was the success of failure, reminding all liberals today of the inertia of the status quo. But it also confirms the necessity of paying the price for one's reasoned convictions.

While the reform of Ikhnaton failed and was replaced by the powerful cult of Amonism, the idea of the fatherhood of God, the inner experience of God's presence and the love of natural beauty were deposited in the cultural soil of the world. True, the reform of Ikhnaton left little impression on the total civilization of Egypt; but if it was negligible in the history of Egypt, it looms large in the history of humanity. Seldom has a voice sung such praises that were worthy of God, the universal Providence and Father of all creatures. To have stood alone against tradition and to have given expression to these universal truths is Ikhnaton's claim to greatness. His pacifism caused the collapse of the Egyptian empire; but that was the price of his idealism, and it is perhaps doubtful, for that matter, that Egypt would have retained her supremacy anyway in the face of the successive periods of ascendancy of Babylonia, Persia and Greece.

Ikhnaton's importance in the final analysis is in the field of religion. His thinking is especially relevant for us today because he saw religion as a qualitative attitude toward the universe, an attitude that, in his case, at least, resulted in an ethical way of life. Popular religion today is just about what it always was: a quantitative, prescribed code based on the doctrine of penalties and rewards. Ikhnaton's distinction lies in his devotion to ends rather than means, universal principles rather than petty dogma, a total attitude toward life rather than a specific formula of sacramental works.

Too often religion is conceived as a segregated compartment, divorced from the so-called "secular" life. The segment of life called religion has little or nothing to do with the other phases of life. This religious-secular distinction is a false one, a construction in which religion is merely a nominal function. If religion, instead of being merely one innocuous division of life, can be experienced as the very core of existence, the central harmonizing factor, the determining influence, then all of life can be religious.

Religion has always been defined by its instrumentalities or means. These means— the Torah, the Mass, the Church, the Bible, the Sacraments, the Creeds, the Rituals—are purely incidental to the culture of any given individual. As such, they are important as helps to the good life. But more often than not these man-made instruments are regarded as ends in themselves, and religion becomes concerned with times and seasons, feasts and fasts, do's and don'ts, calendars, rites and taboos. Evidently, there is a vast difference, as John Dewey pointed out, between *having a religion and being religious*.

Religion consistently tends to reduce itself to a specific code. The prophet gives way to the priest, and the original spiritual ideal turns into a legalistic and ritualistic cult. By following a prescribed formula, the devotee is assured of salvation; but he must keep in line.

So it was with all primitive tribes. The medicine man decreed what the people should do and they conformed. They were told what to wear, when and how to plant or hunt, what to avoid eating, touching or saying. These tribal customs have survived in most modern cultures. Every religion has experienced this institutionalizing process, which seems necessary for the protection and propagation of the ideal, but which in turn kills the ideal. The cultus, with its tangible and visible apparatus, misses the very point of pure religion. It does not plumb the depths of the soul; it does not offer the challenge of the unattainable, for it prescribes a routine of duties which can be done and done easily.

There have been a few individuals in history who have seen religion as a dedication to ideal ends and ultimate principles, as a progressive realization of divine truth rather than as a closed system of revelation, as a high way of living rather than as an orthodox way of believing. One of these was Ikhnaton.

The criterion for prophetic genius is timelessness or contemporaneousness. Ikhnaton's religion of cosmic theism is more challenging and more imperative in the shrunken world of the space age than it was in the fourteenth century B.C., because the present demands such a world outlook for survival. Only a cosmic and universalistic faith can raise mankind above the particularisms of the cults which divide men into rival religious camps. Only a common faith in the fatherhood of God and its moral imperative can unite people on a supra-sectarian level. To stay below that level is to rest content with the shibboleths and intolerance of tribal religion.

The cosmic religion of Ikhnaton has much to say to a generation that lives between two worlds, the one dead and the other unable to be born, a generation that reaches for the moon but has not learned to live in a civilized manner on the earth. Indeed, with the advance of the space age and new knowledge about other worlds, one should expect some theological revision in the near future. The issue boils down to this: Is God the God of this planet only or is He a cosmic consciousness? Is He a tribal deity or a universal reality? Is He interested in revealing Himself only at a certain point in time at a certain place through a certain man; is He concerned only with Christian history? The theologians must enlarge their ideas of God, man and history if they take seriously the findings of comparative religion, the history of religions, the facts of history and human reason. The present age will force us to reappraise the theological pattern of the Christian church and to re-evaluate our place in the cosmos. Christian theology, ignoring the implications of the Copernican theory, continues to maintain that the earth is the focal center of creation and the sole object of God's concern. The heliocentric theory, for that matter, is no longer an adequate statement of our knowledge of the multiverse, in which the solar system is a mere speck of dust. Our ideology still includes the ancient Semitic myth of the origin of life and the fall of man. It may well be that the earth is not the only planet that sustains life. It is entirely possible that many solar systems have the same or similar conditions found on our earth. Can we therefore consider ourselves unique? Perhaps the recognition of the cosmic immensities will force us to outgrow our provincialism and suicidal national rivalries.

The fact is that we can no longer find God by clinging to a primitive cosmology or to an anthropomorphic deity who deliberately intervenes in the process of earthly history, or, more specifically, the history of one section of the earth. No longer can we hold to our theological views as a special and unique revelation when the same views are held in every other religion. We are struggling toward a world civilization and some day chauvinistic sectarianism will be as anachronistic as chauvinistic nationalism. The world is rapidly shrinking, and we can no longer rub shoulders with other cultures and still claim to have the final or only religion. We shall have to unite with others on a supra-sectarian plane—the plane of spiritual and moral values—rather than insist on our theological particularisms.

The prophet-king Ikhnaton was still a child of his age and could not escape all the restrictions of the ancient world, but in his dream of universalism he was born for this time. The cosmic or naturalistic theism, suggested in his universal moral order of *maat*, appears today to be the most adequate philosophical formulation for the coming space age.

Ikhnaton's reign was the most interesting in Egyptian history, a period in which human values came first, a period in which at least one man lived "in truth." For the first time in history a king defied tradition, transcended convention and insisted that his people regard him as a man, not a god. And so he lived—as a man—in truth and simplicity among his people, a man with a sense of humor, sympathy and courage. When Ikhnaton died, his contemporaries called him the "criminal of Akhetaton." Today, some thirty-three hundred years later, he is recognized as a prophet and genius, "the first individual in history."

3. THE RELIGION OF IKHNATON*

The most important observation about Amarna religion is that there were two gods central to the faith, and not one. Akh-en-Aton and his family worshipped the Aton, and everybody else worshipped Akh-en-Aton *as a god*. In addition to his formal names and titles, the pharaoh was referred to as "the good god," and he asserted that he was the physical son of the Aton. The abundant scenes in the Amarna tombs show him serving the living sun-disk, while all of his courtiers bow in adoration to him. Their prayers were not addressed to the Aton, but directly to Akh-en-Aton. The courtier Eye, who was later to become pharaoh, asked Akh-en-Aton for mortuary benefits: "Mayest thou grant to me a good old age as thy favorite; mayest thou grant to me a goodly burial by the command of thy *ka* in my house. . . . May (I) hear thy sweet voice in the sanctuary when thou performest that which pleases thy father, the living Aton." Another noble did pray to the Aton, but prayed only on behalf of

Akh-en-Aton, with his petition for himself addressed to the pharaoh: "Mayest thou make thy beloved son Akh-en-Aton to live with thee forever, [to do] what thy heart [wishes], and to behold what thou dost every day, for he rejoices in the sight of thy beauty. . . . Let him (remain) here, until the swan turns black, until the raven turns white, until the mountains stand up to walk, and until the sea runs up the river. And may I continue in service of the good god (Akh-en-Aton), until he assigns (to me) the burial that he gives." This is a stated acknowledgement of the centrality of the pharaoh in the worship of the Aton and of the dependence of the noble upon his god-king.

Akh-en-Aton himself in his famous hymn to the Aton asserted that this was his personal god. The hymn is entitled "the worship of the Aton . . . by the King Akh-en-Aton and the Queen Nefert-iti," and pharaoh says explicitly: "Thou art in my heart, and there is no other that knows thee except thy son (Akh-en-Aton), whom thou hast initiated into thy plans and into thy power." It must be emphasized that the Aton faith had no penetration below the

* Reprinted from *The Burden of Egypt* by John A. Wilson by permission of The University of Chicago Press (Chicago, The University of Chicago Press, 1951), pp. 223-229.

level of the royal family as an effective religious expression; it was stated to be the exclusive faith of the god-king and his divine family, and the god-king welcomed and encouraged his subjects' worship of his divine being as the source of all the benefits which they might desire.

The self-centered nature of Akh-en-Aton's faith, the fact that only the royal family had a trained and reasoned loyalty to the Aton, and the fact that all of pharaoh's adherents were forced to give their entire devotion to him as a god-king explain why the new religion collapsed after Akh-en-Aton's death. Political and economic factors were also important, but the observation that the Amarna courtiers had contact with the Aton only through their worship of Akh-en-Aton shows the fleeting and superficial nature of the religion. We cannot believe that they cherished within their bosoms the teaching about a benevolent and sustaining sole god, the Aton, when all of their religious exercise was exhausted in worship of Akh-en-Aton. When that pharaoh died and the movement collapsed, they must have scrambled penitently back into the traditional faith, which they could understand and in which they were allowed wider devotion.

Two important questions face us. Was this monotheism? If so, was it the world's first ancestral monotheism, and did it come down to us through the Hebrews? Our own answer to each question is in the negative, even though such an answer may rest upon definitions of the terms, and such definitions must necessarily be those of modern distinctions.

Our modern Jewish, Christian, and Moslem faiths express the doctrine that there is one—and only one—God and that all ethical and religious values derive from that God. In the application of this definition to the Amarna religion, we see that there were at least two gods, that the Aton was concerned strictly with creating and maintaining life, and that ethics and religion derived from the pharaoh Akh-en-Aton.

It is true that the Amarna texts call the Aton the "sole god, like whom there is no other." This, however, was nothing new in Egyptian religious address. The form of expression was a fervid exaggeration or concentration, which went back to the earliest religious literature, more than a thousand years before Akh-en-Aton's time. In the period before the Amarna revolution, Amon, Re, Atum, Har-akhti, and Min were severally called "the sole god." Sometimes this term recalled the creation, when the one existent god was going to bring other gods into being. Sometimes it was a flattering exaggeration meaning the only important god, *like whom* there was no other. Often it was a focusing of the worshipper's attention upon one god, to the exclusion of others—what is called henotheism or monolatry. In no sense does it imply the absolute unity carried by the Moslem: "There is no god but God."

In ancient times a man's name was a vital part of his being: the effacing of his name from his tomb destroyed his continued existence in the next world; the expunging of an official's name from the records ended that earthly success which was so important to his survival. The same psychology applies to Akh-en-Aton's attack upon Amon and topically upon other gods. If the philosophy of the new religion was that only the Aton was a god and that, therefore, Amon did not and could not exist, why was there so virulent an attack upon Amon, and why was his name systematically hacked out of the records? In those ancient terms he had still some kind of existence as long as his name was effectively a part of a single record.

We are conscious that we are arguing in modern terms and that Atonism was at one and the same time native to Egyptian religion and unique within that religion. It was native because the Egyptian state was built upon the dogma that pharaoh was a god and stood between the people and the other gods; thus the double relationship at Amarna retained the past essentials. It was unique because the gods other than pharaoh were made one god, by a process of exclusion rather than syncretism, if we ignore that limited syncretism present in the official names of the Aton. It is immaterial to that argument that there was still personification in the texts, by which the Aton was described as "satisfied with the goddess Maᶜat" and Akh-en-Aton was praised as being "the god Fate," because personification was also native to Egyptian thought. Much more important was the elimination of Osiris from the mortuary faith, with the ascription of all mortuary benefits to the pharaoh. One could say that it was the closest approach to monotheism possible within the thought of the day. That would still fall short of making it a belief in and worship of only one god.

The question as to whether Atonism was ancestral to Hebrew monotheism and thus to modern expressions of religion is also difficult. However, it may be stated flatly that the mechanism of transmission from the faith of Akh-en-Aton to the monotheism of Moses is not apparent. This was the personal religion of a pharaoh who later became a heretic within one generation. It was not accessible to Egyptians at large. Their subsequent reaction in a fervent return to the older forms, particularly the Osirian faith and the cherishing care of little personal gods, shows how little penetration Atonism had below the royal family. Even assuming that there were Israelite slave troops in Egypt in Amarna times, there was no way by which they could learn the teaching of Atonism, that there was a single, universal god, who made and continued life, toward whom the worshipper felt a warm sense of gratitude. Atonism taught that the pharaoh of Egypt was essential as the only intermediary between god and people.

There is another discontinuity between Atonism and Hebrew monotheism as the latter developed, and that is the marked lack of ethical content in the hymns directed to the Aton. Akh-en-Aton's faith was intellectual rather than ethical; its strong emotional content derived from the fervor of the discoverer and convert, who rejected past forms and preached new forms. The conviction of right and wrong was not ethical, but was a passionate reiteration that the new was right and the old was wrong. Aton's blessings were primarily physical; he made and sustained life. The worshipper was called upon to render gratitude for that life, but was in no text called upon to render to the god an upright and ethically correct life in his social relations or in his innermost heart. The universalism of the Aton could have carried the implication that all men are equal under the god and should be so treated, but such a logical conclusion is strikingly absent from the texts.

The one point of question against this description of Atonism as nature worship lies in the understanding of *maᶜat* emphasized by this faith. Akh-en-Aton lived on *maᶜat* as his food, and the Aton was satisfied with *maᶜat* as his offering. If this meant "righteousness" or "justice," it would carry an ethical weight. When, however, we see in scenes and texts the emphasis on candid relations, on the open air, and on adoration of the sun-disk, we can only translate it as "truth" and understand it as the worship of the forces of nature, in contradistinction to the remote and artificial activity of the older gods. Nowhere do we find that rigorous insistence upon law which was central in Hebrew monotheism.

There is a more important consideration about the transmission of monotheism from one culture to another, and that is whether any great intellectual, spiritual, or ethical concept can be passed from one culture to quite a different culture. We have argued that the Egyptians were "civilized" in a sense of the word which has both strength and weakness. Much of the importance of the Hebrews to world history lies in the fact that they avoided some of the weakening and distracting phases of civilization. A concept which was imperfectly articulated and understood at pharaoh's court at Amarna would have been quite foreign to Asiatic tribes wandering in the desert. When the Children of Israel penetrated Canaan and settled down to work out a new way of life, their progressive religious steps were achieved through their own national religious experience as their own God-given discoveries, without derivation from any foreign source. Such precious and inner expressions of religion can never be borrowed, but must be experienced. When they have been experienced, the *forms* in which they are uttered may be borrowed from others, but never the innermost spirit.

This brings us to a main argument for the contact between Atonism and Hebrew religion: the extraordinary parallelism in thought and structure between Akh-en-Aton's hymn to the Aton and the 104th Psalm. Three selected passages will illustrate the striking similarity:

The Aton Hymn	*Psalm 104*
When thou settest in the western horizon, The land is in darkness like death. . . . Every lion comes forth from his den; All creeping things, they sting.	Thou makest darkness and it is night, Wherein all the beasts of the forest creep forth. The young lions roar after their prey.
At daybreak, when thou arisest in the horizon . . . Thou drivest away the darkness . . . Men awake and stand upon their feet . . . All the world, they do their labor.	The sun ariseth, they get them away . . . Man goeth forth unto his work, And to his labor until the evening.
How manifold are thy works! They are hidden from man's sight. O sole god, like whom there is no other, Thou hast made the earth according to thy desire.	O Jahweh, how manifold are thy works! In wisdom hast thou made them all; The earth is full of thy riches.

It has been claimed that such correspondences must show derivative connection and that Hebrew psalmists must have known the Egyptian sun-hymn. Since the obliteration of Atonism was complete some six or seven centuries before the psalm was written, it is argued that the Aton hymn must have passed into Asia when Akh-en-Aton was still in power and escaped destruction by translation into some Semitic dialect.

So ingenious a mechanism of transmission is not necessary. We have already seen that the several ideas and modes of expression visible in Atonism were present in Egypt before Atonism and independent of Atonism. Since these were current forms in Egypt, not invented by the Amarna priests or scribes, it is not surprising to find them still in use after the fall of Atonism and without relation to the fact that the specific cult had been proclaimed a heresy.

A papyrus in Leyden dates from the Nineteenth Dynasty and has passages which have been called monotheistic, but which we, with a narrower definition, prefer to call syncretistic. These hymns treat the god ₋Amon as the summation of all other important gods, without rejecting the separate existence of those other gods.

"Mysterious of form, glistening of appearance, the marvelous god of many forms. All gods boast of him, to magnify themselves through his beauty, according as he is divine. Re himself is united with his body, and he is the great one who is in Heliopolis. He is called Ta-tenen (of Memphis) and Amon who came forth from Nun. . . . Another of his forms is the Eight (primeval gods of Hermopolis). . . . His soul, they say, is that which is in heaven, but it is he who is in the underworld and presides over the east. His soul is in heaven, his body is in the west, and his statue is in Hermonthis, heralding his appearances (to mankind). . . . One is Amon, hiding himself from them, concealing himself from (other) gods, so that his (very) color is unknown. He is far from heaven, he is absent from (?) the underworld, and no (other) god knows his true form. . . . All gods are three: Amon, Re, and Ptah, and there is no second to them. 'Hidden' is his name as Amon, he is Re in face, and his body is Ptah. . . . Only he is: Amon, with Re, [and with Ptah]—together three."

Another set of hymns dating from the late Nineteenth or the Twentieth Dynasty treats Amon as a universal god, who again achieves unity by borrowing the forms of other gods. As the creator-god, he is Amon-Re-Atum-Har-akhti, four in one, or is Ptah, the fashioner of men. He delights in assuming functional roles. "His love is (to play the role of) the moon, as a child to whom everybody dances. . . . His love is (to play the role of) Har-akhti shining in the horizon of heaven." He is both the son and father of *ma͑at*, the "truth" which destroys deceit: "Thy mother is Ma͑at, O Amon! She belongs uniquely to thee, and she came forth from thee (already) inclined to rage and burn up them that attack thee. Ma͑at is more unique, O Amon, than anyone that exists." He is the universal creator, "who spoke with his mouth and there came into existence all men, gods,

large and small cattle in their entirety, and all that which flies and lights." He is the warmer and sustainer of all nature: "Green plants turn about in his direction, that they may be beautiful, and lotuses are gay because of him." He is the good shepherd: "Thou art valiant as a herdsman tending them forever and ever. . . . Their hearts turn about to thee, good at all times. Everybody lives through the sight of thee."

We shall see that artistic forms and themes survived the condemnation of the Amarna movement, and it is equally true that religious concepts and forms of expression continued after Atonism had been made a heresy. This is an adequate explanation of the similarity between the Aton hymn and the 104th Psalm. Hymns of this kind were current long after the fall of Akh-en-Aton, so that when Hebrew religion had reached a point where it needed a certain mode of expression it could find in another literature phrases and thoughts which would meet the need.

The negative statement which we have made about the Aton religion has been argumentative and fails to do justice to the elements of supreme importance in that faith. To be sure, it was intellectual and lacking in full ethical value. At the same time, it expressed beautifully the concept of a god who was creative, nurturing, and kindly and who gave his gifts to all mankind and to all living things everywhere and not to the Egyptians alone. For such bounty the worshipper returned gratitude and devotion to the god. Atonism further brought religion out into the open and tried to end the remoteness and secrecy of the old cults of the powerful and wealthy gods. It was a major tragedy that a religion of such broad intellectual scope lacked the inner moral warmth to give it permanency. The fuller realization of the meaning of God's cherishing care was to be made by other and later peoples.

4. EGYPTIAN "MONOTHEISM" BEFORE AND AFTER IKHNATON*

A HYMN TO AMON-RE

Egypt's world position under her Empire produced strong tendencies toward centralization and unification of Egyptian religion, with universalism and with syncretism of the gods. The following hymn antedates the Amarna Revolution. The imperial god Amon-Re is here viewed as supreme and as the force which creates and sustains life.

Adoration of Amon-Re, the Bull Residing in Heliopolis, chief of all gods, the good god, the beloved, who gives life to all that is warm and to all good cattle.

Hail to thee, Amon-Re,
Lord of the Thrones of the Two Lands,
    Presiding over Karnak,
Bull of His Mother, Presiding over His Fields!
Far-reaching of stride, presiding over Upper Egypt,
Lord of the Madjoi and ruler of Punt,
Eldest of heaven, first-born of earth,
Lord of what is, enduring in all things, enduring in all things.
UNIQUE IN HIS NATURE LIKE THE *FLUID* of the gods,
The goodly bull of the Ennead, chief of all gods.
The lord of truth and father of the gods.
Who made mankind and created the beasts,
Lord of what is, who created the fruit tree,
Made herbage, and gave life to cattle.
The goodly daemon whom Ptah made,

(ii)

The goodly beloved youth to whom the gods give praise,
Who made what is below and what is above,
Who illuminates the Two Lands

And crosses the heavens in peace:
The King of Upper and Lower Egypt: Re, the triumphant,
Chief of the Two Lands,
Great of strength, lord of reverence,
The chief one, who made the entire earth.
MORE DISTINGUISHED IN NATURE THAN any (other) god,
In whose beauty the gods rejoice,
To whom is given jubilation in the Per-wer,
Who is given ceremonial appearance in the Per-nezer.
Whose fragrance the gods love, when he comes from Punt,
Rich in perfume, when he comes down (from) Madjoi,
The Beautiful of Face who comes (from) God's Land.
The gods FAWN (at) his feet,
According as they recognize his majesty as their lord,
The lord of fear, great of dread,
Rich in might, terrible of appearances,
Flourishing in offerings and making provisions.
Jubilation to thee who made the gods,
Raised the heavens and laid down the ground!

(iii)

THE END.

He who awakes in health, Min-Amon,
Lord of eternity, who made everlastingness,
Lord of praise, presiding over [the Ennead],
Firm of horns, beautiful of face,
Lord of the uraeus-serpent, lofty of plumes,
Beautiful of diadem, and lofty of White Crown.
The serpent-coil and the Double Crown, *these are before him,*
The aromatic gum which is in the palace,
The Double Crown, the head-cloth, and the Blue Crown.

* Translations and commentaries by John A. Wilson in *Ancient Near Eastern Texts Relating to the Old Testament*, ed. James B. Pritchard (Princeton: Princeton University Press, 1950), pp. 365–368.

Beautiful of face, when he receives the *atef*-crown,

He whom the crowns of Upper and Lower Egypt love,

Lord of the Double Crown, when he receives the *ames*-staff,

Lord of the *mekes*-scepter, holding the flail.

THE GOODLY ruler, CROWNED WITH THE WHITE CROWN,

The lord of rays, who makes brilliance,

To whom the gods give thanksgiving,

Who extends his arms to him whom he loves,

(But) his enemy is consumed by a flame.

It is his Eye that overthrows the rebels,

That sends its spear into him that sucks up Nun,

(iv)

And makes the fiend disgorge what he has swallowed.

HAIL TO THEE, O Re, lord of truth!

Whose shrine is hidden, the lord of the gods,

Khepri in the midst of his barque,

Who gave commands, and the gods came into being.

Atum, who made the people,

Distinguished their nature, made their life,

And separated colors, one from another.

Who hears the prayer of him who is in captivity,

Gracious of heart in the face of an appeal to him.

SAVING THE FEARFUL FROM THE TERRIBLE OF HEART,

Judging the weak and the injured.

Lord of Perception, in whose mouth Command is placed,

For love of whom the Nile has come,

Possessor of sweetness, greatly beloved;

When he comes, the people live.

He who gives scope to every eye that may be made in Nun,

Whose loveliness has created the light,

(v)

In whose beauty the gods rejoice;

Their hearts live when they see him.

THE END.

O Re, ADORED IN KARNAK,

Great of appearances in the House of the *Benben*,

The Heliopolitan, lord of the New Moon Feast,

For whom the Sixth-Day and Quarter Month feasts are celebrated.

The Sovereign—life, prosperity, health!— lord of all gods;

[They] behold him in the midst of the horizon,

The overlord of men *of the silent land*,

Whose name is hidden from his children,

In this his name of Amon.

HAIL TO THEE, WHO ART IN PEACE!

Lord of joy, terrible of appearances,

Lord of the uraeus-serpent, lofty of plumes,

Beautiful of diadem, and lofty of White Crown.

The gods love to see thee

With the Double Crown fixed upon thy brow.

The love of thee is spread throughout the Two Lands,

When thy rays shine forth in the eyes.

The good of the people is thy arising;

The cattle grow languid when thou shinest.

The love of thee is in the southern sky;

(vi)

The sweetness of thee is in the northern sky.

The beauty of thee carries away hearts;

The love of thee makes arms languid;

Thy beautiful form relaxes the hands;

And hearts are forgetful at the sight of thee.

THOU ART the sole one, WHO MADE [ALL] THAT IS,

[The] solitary sole [one], who made what exists,

From whose eyes mankind came forth,

And upon whose mouth the gods came into being.

He who made herbage [for] the cattle,

And the fruit tree for mankind,

Who made that (on which) the fish in the
river may live,
And the birds *soaring in* the sky.
He who gives breath to that which is in the
egg,
Gives life to the son of the slug,
And makes that on which gnats may live,
And worms and flies in like manner;
Who supplies the needs of the mice in
their holes,
And gives life to flying things in every tree.
HAIL TO THEE, WHO DID ALL THIS!
Solitary sole one, with many hands,

(vii)

Who spends the night wakeful, while all
men are asleep,
Seeking benefit for his creatures.
Amon, enduring in all things, Atum and
Har-akhti—
Praises are thine, when they all say:
"Jubilation to thee, because thou weariest
thyself with us!
Salaams to thee, because thou didst create
us!"
HAIL TO THEE FOR ALL BEASTS!
Jubilation to thee for every foreign
country—
To the height of heaven, to the width of
earth,
To the depth of the Great Green Sea!
The gods are bowing down to thy majesty
And exalting the might of him who created
them,
Rejoicing at the approach of him who begot
them.
They say to thee: "Welcome in peace!
Father of the fathers of all the gods,
Who raised the heavens and laid down the
ground,
WHO MADE WHAT IS AND CREATED WHAT
EXISTS;
Sovereign—life, prosperity, health!—and
chief of the gods!

(viii)

We praise thy might, according as thou
didst make us.

Let (*us*) *act* for thee, because thou
brought us forth.
We give thee thanksgiving because thou
hast wearied thyself with us!"
HAIL TO THEE, WHO MADE ALL THAT IS!
Lord of truth and father of the gods,
Who made mortals and created beasts,
Lord of the grain,
Who made (also) the living of the beasts of
the desert.
Amon, the bull beautiful of countenance,
The beloved in Karnak,
Great of appearances in the House of the
Benben,
Taking again the diadem in Heliopolis,
Who judges the Two in the great broad
hall,
The chief of the Great Ennead.
THE SOLITARY SOLE ONE, WITHOUT HIS
PEER,
Presiding over Karnak,
The Heliopolitan, presiding over his
Ennead,
And living on truth every day.
The horizon-dweller, Horus of the east,
From whom the desert creates silver and
gold,
Genuine lapis lazuli for love of him,

(ix)

Benzoin and various incenses from Madjoi,
And fresh myrrh for thy nostrils—
Beautiful of face when coming (from)
Madjoi!
Amon-Re, Lord of the Thrones of the
Two Lands,
Presiding over Karnak,
The Heliopolitan, presiding over his
harem!
THE END.

The sole king, like the *fluid* of the gods,
With many names, unknown in number,
Rising in the eastern horizon,
And going to rest in the western horizon;
Who overthrows his enemies,
(RE)BORN EARLY EVERY DAY.

Thoth lifts up his two eyes,
And satisfies him with his effective deeds.
The gods rejoice in his beauty,
He whom his apes exalt.
Lord of the evening barque and the morning barque;
They cross Nun in peace for thee.
Thy CREW IS IN JOY,
When they see the overthrow of the rebel,
His body licked up by the knife.

(x)

Fire has devoured him;
His soul is more consumed than his body.
That dragon, his (power of) motion is taken away.
The gods are in joy,
The crew of Re is in satisfaction,
Heliopolis is in joy,
For the enemies of Atum are overthrown.
Karnak is in satisfaction, Heliopolis is in joy,
The heart of the Lady of Life is glad,
For the enemy of her lord is overthrown.
The gods of Babylon are in jubilation,
They who are in the shrines are salaaming,
WHEN THEY SEE HIM RICH IN HIS MIGHT.
The daemon of the gods,
The righteous one, Lord of Karnak,
In this thy name of Maker of Righteousness;
The lord of provisions, bull of *offerings*,
In this thy name of Amon, Bull of His Mother;
Maker of all mankind,
Creator and maker of all that is,

(xi)

In this thy name of Atum-Khepri,
Great falcon, festive of bosom,
Beautiful of face, festive of breast,
Pleasing of form, lofty of plume,
On whose brow the two uraei *flutter*.
To whom the hearts of mankind make approach,
To whom the people turn about;
Who makes festive the Two Lands with his comings forth.

Hail to thee, Amon-Re, Lord of the Thrones of the Two Lands,
Whose city loves his rising!
IT HAS COME (TO ITS END) . . .

A UNIVERSALIST HYMN TO THE SUN

The forces of empire and of international contacts were moving Egypt toward universalism and a partial approach to monotheism, even before the Amarna Revolution. One of the clearest expressions of the new spirit comes from a hymn to the sun-god on behalf of two brothers named Seth and Horus.

Praising Amon, when he rises as Harakhti, by the Overseer of the Works of Amon, Seth, and the Overseer of the Works of Amon, Horus. They say:
Hail to thee, beautiful Re of every day, who rises at dawn without ceasing, Khepri wearying (himself) with labor! Thy rays are in (one's) face, without one knowing it. Fine gold is not like the radiance of thee. Thou who hast constructed thyself, thou didst fashion thy body, a shaper who was (himself) not shaped; unique in his nature, passing eternity above, (so that) the ways by millions carry thy image, according as thy radiance is like the radiance of heaven and thy color glistens more than its surface.
When thou crossest the sky, all faces behold thee, (but) when thou departest, thou art hidden from their faces. Thou presentest thyself daily at dawn. Steadfast is thy sailing which carries thy majesty. A brief day—and thou racest a course of millions and hundred-thousands of leagues. Every day under thee is an instant, and when it passes, thou settest. So also thou hast completed the hours of the night: thou hast regulated it without a pause coming in thy labors.
All eyes see through thee, and they have no fulfillment when thy majesty sets. Thou bestirrest thyself early to rise at dawn. Thy rays open the wakeful eyes. When thou

settest in *Manu*, then they sleep in the manner of death.

Hail to thee, sun disc of the daytime, creator of all and maker of their living! Great falcon, bright of plumage, who came into being to elevate himself, self-created, who was not born! Horus, the first-born in the midst of the sky-goddess, for whom they make jubilation at rising, as well as at his setting! The fashioner of that which the soil produces, the Khnum and Amon of mankind. He who seizes upon the Two Lands, (from) great to small. A mother of profit to gods and men; a patient craftsman, greatly wearying (himself) as their maker, without number; valiant herdsman, driving his cattle, their refuge and the maker of their living.

Runner, racer, courser! Khepri, whose birth was distinct, whose beauty was upraised in the body of the sky-goddess. He who illuminates the Two Lands with his disc, the primordial one of the Two Lands, who made himself and who beheld what he would make.

The sole lord, who reaches the ends of the lands every day, being (thus) one who sees them that tread thereon. He who rises in heaven, (his) form being the sun. He makes the seasons by months, heat when he wishes, and cold when he wishes. He makes the body lax, or he gathers it together. Every land chatters at his rising every day, in order to praise him. . . .

AMON AS THE SOLE GOD

The following hymns have been characterized as monotheistic in spirit. They come from the Nineteenth Dynasty, subsequent to the Amarna Revolution. They are extracts from a long document in praise of the imperial god Amon-Re of Thebes and treat that deity as the sole god, or, perhaps, as the first principle and the sole god of immediate attention.

HUNDREDTH STANZA

The first to come into being in the earliest times, Amon, who came into being at the beginning, so that his mysterious nature is unknown. No god came into being before him; there was no other god with him, so that he might tell his form. He had no mother, after whom his name might have been made. He had no father who had begotten him and who might have said: "This is I!" Building his own egg, a daemon mysterious of birth, who created his (own) beauty, the divine god who came into being by himself. All (other) gods came into being after he began himself.

TWO-HUNDREDTH STANZA

Mysterious of form, glistening of appearance, the marvelous god of many forms. All (other) gods boast of him, to magnify themselves through his beauty, according as he is divine. Re himself is united with his body. He is the great one who is in Heliopolis. He is called Ta-tenen, and Amon who came forth from Nun, *for he leads the people.* Another of his forms is the Ogdoad. The procreator of the primeval gods, who brought Re to birth; he completed himself as Atum, a single body with him. He is the All-Lord, the beginning of that which is. His soul, they say, is that which is in heaven. It is he who is in the underworld and presides over the East; his soul is in heaven, his body is in the West, and his statue is in Hermonthis, heralding his appearances.

One is Amon, hiding himself from them, concealing himself from the (other) gods, so that his (very) color is unknown. He is far from heaven, he is *absent from* the Underworld, (so that) no gods know his true form. His image is not *displayed* in writings. No one bears witness to him . . . He is too mysterious that his majesty might be disclosed, he is too great that (men) should ask about him, too powerful that he might be known. Instantly (one) falls in a death of violence at the utterance of his mysterious name, unwittingly or wittingly. No (other) god knows how to *call him* by it, the Soul who hides his name, according as he is mysterious.

5. HYMNS TO ATON*

UNIVERSAL SPLENDOUR AND POWER OF ATON

"Thou dawnest beautifully in the horizon of the sky,
O living Aton who wast the Beginning of life!
When thou didst rise in the eastern horizon,
Thou didst fill every land with thy beauty.
Thou art beautiful, great, glittering, high over every land,
Thy rays, they encompass the lands, even to the end of all that thou hast made.
Thou art Re, and thou penetratest to the very end of them;
Thou bindest them for thy beloved son (the Pharaoh).
Though thou art far away, thy rays are upon earth;
Though thou art in the faces of men, thy footsteps are unseen.

NIGHT AND MAN

"When thou settest in the western horizon of the sky,
The earth is in darkness like death.
They sleep in their chambers,
Their heads are wrapped up,
Their nostrils are stopped,
And none seeth the other,
While all their things are stolen,
Which are under their heads,
And they know it not.
Thou makest darkness, and it is night,
Wherein all the beasts of the forest creep forth.
(Psalm 104:20.)

NIGHT AND ANIMALS

"Every lion cometh forth from his den,
All serpents, they sting.
Darkness broods,
The world is in silence,
He that made them resteth in his horizon.
The young lions roar after their prey,
And seek their food from God.
(Psalm 104:21.)

DAY AND MAN

"Bright is the earth when thou risest in the horizon;
When thou shinest as Aton by day
Thou drivest away the darkness.
When thou sendest forth thy rays,
The Two Lands (Egypt) are in daily festivity.
Men waken and stand upon their feet
When thou hast raised them up.
Their limbs bathed, they take their clothing,
Their arms uplifted in adoration to thy dawning.
Then in all the world they do their work.
The sun ariseth, they get them away,
And lay them down in their dens.
Man goeth forth unto his work
And to his labour until the evening.
(Psalm 104:22–23.)

DAY AND THE ANIMALS AND PLANTS

"All cattle rest upon their pasturage,
The trees and the plants flourish,
The birds flutter in their marshes,
Their wings uplifted in adoration to thee.
All the antelopes dance upon their feet,
All creatures that fly or alight,
They live when thou hast shone upon them.

*Reprinted with the permission of Charles Scribner's Sons from *The Dawn of Conscience* by James H. Breasted. Copyright 1933 James Henry Breasted; renewal copyright © 1961 Charles Breasted, James Breasted, Jr. & Astrid Breasted Hormann.

DAY AND THE WATERS

"The barques sail up-stream and down-
stream alike.
Every highway is open because thou
dawnest.
The fish in the river leap up before thee.
Thy rays are in the midst of the great green
sea.
Yonder is the sea, great and wide,
Wherein are things creeping innumerable,
Both small and great beasts.
There go the ships;
There is leviathan, whom thou hast formed
to play therein.

(Psalm 104:25-26.)

CREATION OF MAN

"Creator of the germ in woman,
Who makest seed into men,
Making alive the son in the body of his
mother,
Soothing him that he may not weep,
Nurse even in the womb,
Giver of breath to sustain alive every one
that he maketh!
When he descendeth from the body (of his
mother) on the day of his birth,
Thou openest his mouth altogether,
Thou suppliest his necessities.

CREATION OF ANIMALS

"When the fledgling in the egg chirps in
the shell,
Thou givest him breath in the midst of it to
preserve him alive.
Thou hast made for him his term in the
egg, for breaking it.
He cometh forth from the egg to chirp at
his term;

. . . .

He goeth about upon his two feet
When he cometh forth therefrom.

UNIVERSAL CREATION

"How manifold are thy works!
They are hidden before men
O sole God, beside whom there is no other.

Thou didst create the earth according to
thy heart.
O lord, how manifold are thy works!
In wisdom hast thou made them all:
The earth is full of thy riches.

(Psalm 104:24.)

While thou wast alone:
Even men, all herds of cattle and the
antelopes;
All that are upon the earth,
That go about upon their feet;
They that are on high,
That fly with their wings.
The highland countries, Syria and Kush,
And the land of Egypt;
Thou settest every man into his place,
Thou suppliest their necessities,
Every one has his food,
And his days are reckoned.
The tongues are divers in speech,
Their forms likewise and their skins are
distinguished,
For thou makest different the strangers.

WATERING THE EARTH IN EGYPT
AND ABROAD

"Thou makest the Nile in the Nether
World,
Thou bringest it as thou desirest,
To preserve alive the people of Egypt
For thou hast made them for thyself,
Thou lord of them all, who weariest thy-
self for them;
Thou lord of every land, who risest for
them,
Thou Sun of day, great in glory,
All the distant highland countries,
Thou makest also their life,
Thou didst set a Nile in the sky.
When it falleth for them,
It maketh waves upon the mountains,
Like the great green sea,
Watering their fields in their towns.

How benevolent are thy designs, O lord of
eternity!
There is a Nile in the sky for the strangers

And for the antelopes of all the highlands
that go about upon their feet.
But the Nile, it cometh from the Nether
World for Egypt.

THE SEASONS

"Thy rays nourish every garden;
When thou risest they live,
They grow by thee.
Thou makest the seasons
In order to make develop all that thou hast
made.
Winter to bring them coolness,
And heat that they may taste thee.

UNIVERSAL DOMINION

"Thou didst make the distant sky in order
to rise therein,
In order to behold all that thou hast made,
While thou wast yet alone
Shining in thy form as living Aton,
Dawning, glittering, going afar and return-
ing.
Thou makest millions of forms
Through thyself alone;
Cities, villages, and fields, highways and
rivers.
All eyes see thee before them,
For thou art Aton of the day over the earth,
When thou hast gone away,
And all men, whose faces thou hast
fashioned
In order that thou mightest no longer see
thyself alone,
[Have fallen asleep, so that not] one [seeth]
that which thou hast made,
Yet art thou still in my heart.

REVELATION TO THE KING

. . . .
"There is no other that knoweth thee
Save thy son Ikhnaton.
Thou hast made him wise
In thy designs and in thy might.

UNIVERSAL MAINTENANCE

"The world subsists in thy hand,
Even as thou hast made them.
When thou hast risen they live,
When thou settest they die;
For thou art length of life of thyself,
Men live through thee.

The eyes of men see beauty
Until thou settest.
All labour is put away
When thou settest in the west.
When thou risest again
[Thou] makest ⌐every hand⌐ to flourish for
the king
And ⌐prosperity⌐ is in every foot,
Since thou didst establish the world,
And raise them up for thy son,
Who came forth from thy flesh,
The king of Upper and Lower Egypt,
Living in Truth, Lord of the Two Lands,
Nefer-khepru-Re, Wan-Re (Ikhnaton),
Son of Re, living in Truth, lord of diadems,
Ikhnaton, whose life is long;
(And for) the chief royal wife, his beloved,
Mistress of the Two Lands, Nefer-nefru-
Aton, Nofretete,
Living and flourishing for ever and ever."

THE SHORTER HYMN

"Thou risest beautifully, O living Aton,
Lord of Eternity;
Thou art glittering, beautiful, strong;
Thy love is great and mighty,
Thy rays furnish vision to every one of thy
creatures,
Thy glowing hue brings life to the hearts
of men,
When thou hast filled the Two Lands with
thy love.
O God, who himself fashioned himself,
Maker of every land,
Creator of that which is upon it:
Even men, all herds of cattle and the
antelopes,
All trees that grow in the soil,
They live when thou dawnest for them,

Thou art the mother and the father of all that thou hast made.
As for their eyes, when thou dawnest,
They see by means of thee.
Thy rays illuminate the whole earth,
And every heart rejoices because of seeing thee,
When thou dawnest as their lord.

"When thou settest in the western horizon of the sky,
They sleep after the manner of the dead,
Their heads are wrapped up,
Their nostrils are stopped,
Until thy rising comes in the morning,
In the eastern horizon of the sky.
Then their arms are uplifted in adoration of thee,
Thou makest the hearts of men to live by thy beauty,
For men live when thou sendest forth thy rays,
Every land is in festivity:
Singing, music, and shouting of joy
Are in the hall of the Benben-house,
Thy temple in Akhetaton, the seat of Truth (Maat),
Wherewith thou art satisfied.
Food and provision are offered therein;
Thy pure son performs thy pleasing ceremonies,

O living Aton, at his festal processions.
All that thou hast made dance before thee,
Thy august son rejoices, his heart is joyous,
O living Aton, born in the sky every day.
He begets his august son Wanre (Ikhnaton)
Like himself without ceasing,
Son of Re, wearing his beauty, Nefer-khepru-Re, Wan-Re (Ikhnaton),
Even me, thy son, in whom thou art satisfied,
Who bears thy name.
Thy strength and thy might abide in my heart,
Even thine, O Aton, living forever . . .
Thou hast made the distant sky to rise therein,
In order to behold all that thou didst make,
While thou wast yet alone.
Myriads of life are in thee to sustain them alive,
For it is the breath of life in the nostrils to behold thy radiance.
All flowers live and what grows in the soil
Is made to grow because thou dawnest.
They are drunken before thee.
All cattle skip upon their feet;
The birds in the marsh fly with joy,
Their wings that were folded are spread,
Uplifted in adoration to the living Aton,
Thou maker. . . ."

6. THE FAITH OF IKHNATON*

The faith of Ikhnaton, as revealed in these hymns, contained many qualities usually attributed to later thinkers. One is the concept of constraining love. Aton binds all people and all nations together in his tender love. A second "modern" idea is Ikhnaton's doctrine of immanence. Although Aton is transcendent, his power pervades all life on the earth.

Though thou art far away,
Thy rays are upon the earth;
Though thou are on high,
Thy footprints are the day.

The idea of the god bestowing his blessings upon his creatures is most graphically represented in the Amarna paintings and reliefs which portray the solar disc, from which long rays descend terminating in human hands which hold the Ankh, or sign of life. Such a symbol suggests the power of deity in the affairs of men through the life-giving rays of the disc.

* F. G. Bratton, *The Life and Times of Ikhnaton the King* (Boston: Beacon Press, 1961), pp. 126–131. Reprinted by permission of the Beacon Press, copyright © 1961 by Fred Gladstone Bratton.

Here we note one of the most distinctive features of Ikhnaton's religion. In every Amarna relief, the rays are given the most prominent place as the source of radiant energy. In so picturing the deity, Ikhnaton broke from the anthropomorphic, as well as from the totally transcendent conception of deity, to formulate the more profound idea of God's immanence. For the first time in history, God was conceived as a formless being. The God of Genesis walked about "in the garden in the cool of the day" and talked to Adam and Eve. The Yahweh of Moses was a god of wrath and vengeance. Ikhnaton's god was the Lord of Peace, an intangible essence, the energetic force that acted through the sun, the creator who held all things in his hands. It was hundreds of years before any thinker again referred to God as compassionate, merciful and tender—a beneficent creator, loving all creatures, great and small.

One of the most conspicuous elements in the religion of Ikhnaton is the joy of life, the sheer delight in God's creation. Here was a poet finding God in the contemplation of nature, in the enjoyment of sunshine, and in the simple life. God is the loving Father who caused the birds to flutter in their marshes, the sheep to dance in the fields and the fish to leap in the river. Such a naive appreciation of nature —if one may use the expression—has characterized all creative periods in history —the Golden Age of Greece, the Italian Renaissance, the Romantic Era in England and the Concord Period in American letters. The feeling of ecstasy and rapture in being a part of life, the *joie de vivre* so prominent in these hymns, recalls a line of Browning: "How good is man's life, the mere living!"

A final noteworthy aspect is that God was thought to be the sole creator. "While he was still alone" Aton created all things and his creativity was everlasting. "Thou makest millions of forms through thyself alone." With surprising sensitivity and almost childlike wonder, the God-intoxi-

cated prophet wonders at the creative capacity of Aton in calling forth life even from such a small thing as an egg.

When the fledgling in the egg chirps in the shell,
Thou givest him breath therein to preserve him alive.

The joy of being alive pervades the picture of the chick emerging from the shell and chirping with delight:

He cometh forth from the egg
To chirp with all his might.
He goeth about upon his two feet
When he hath come forth therefrom.

Ikhnaton taught not only the universality of God but his eternal duration. Aton, the author of his own being, was "the reminder of eternity," without beginning or end. This thought is reminiscent of Spinoza's idea of God as "creative nature existing in infinite attributes and endless time."

The Egyptian's traditional exaltation of the Nile as a source of life has already been discussed. The river was identified with Osiris, the god of life and immortality. The heresy of Ikhnaton's religion is more apparent when we perceive his total rejection of the deification of the Nile as identified with Osiris. Ignoring all mythological traditions, he attributes the annual overflow to natural forces created by Aton —an unmistakable expression of the naturalistic or rational point of view. Osiris, in fact, is not mentioned anywhere in the Amarna literature. But while Ikhnaton sees the phenomenon of the Nile's inundation as natural, he goes beyond the materialistic explanation to the ultimate divine source. In fact, his conception of God as the author of the universe, omnipresent and immanent, revealing himself in the visible world, was not only an iconoclastic idea for his day, but it also anticipated much of what usually goes under the name of modern religious philosophy. The philosopher-king addressed his God as "the father and mother of all that thou hast made." To him the earth was "filled with the glory of God." All living creatures rejoiced in the beauty of the earth and exulted in the radiant presence of God.

All creatures that fly or alight,
They live when thou hast shone upon them.

The presence of God was identified with light itself. Even after Aton had "gone to rest in the horizon," he was present in the hearts of men.

Ikhnaton's ecstatic exaltation of light may be compared to the feelings of Ruskin in his contemplation of "the breathing, animated exulting light, which feels and receives and rejoices and acts . . . leaping from rock to rock, from leaf to leaf, from wave to wave. It is the living light which sleeps but never dies." In this teaching of the beneficence of the natural order and sheer delight in its manifestations, we discern an anticipation of the nineteenth century "return-to-nature" movement.

Such was the genius of Ikhnaton's religious reform. It is not enough to say that it was materialistic. His ecstatic delight in the earth as a manifestation of God's benevolent and continued presence is an expression of spiritual monism unsurpassed in religious literature.

Much has been made of the absence of ethics in the religion of Amarna. Admittedly the two hymns contain no explicit teaching about righteousness or integrity, but the argument of silence is never conclusive. Furthermore, the surviving literature is only fragmentary and there may well have been other documents more directly concerned with morality. The solar theology of Heliopolis was concerned with moral values and, dependent as it was on the religion of Ra, it is hard to understand why Atonism should have neglected the earlier emphasis on ethics. It is improbable that the two hymns found on the walls of the nobles' tombs constitute Ikhnaton's entire system of thought. Repeated references to the "teaching" of Ikhnaton found in the tombs indicate that he had

composed some formal doctrine which was later destroyed by his enemies. He must have subscribed to the earlier ethical principles of the Heliopolitan solar faith, for his use of the phrase "Living in Truth" in all official documents bearing his name clearly implies that he followed the doctrine of *maat*.

Regardless of the presence or absence of moral values in the surviving literature, the fact is that Ikhnaton's actions were those of a person with a high moral standard of living. He was convinced that hatred, conquest and war were inconsistent with the universal love of God, and he acted on that belief. If God has good will toward all men, it must follow that his children should have good will toward each other. This meant outright pacifism, a pacifism to which he adhered even though it ultimately meant his political ruin.

The two hymns, together with whatever other inscriptions remained, testify to the king's personal integrity and devotion to truth. The following statements, for example, appear in the tomb of Ay: "The king put truth in my body and my abomination is lying. I know that Ikhnaton rejoices in the truth." The sun-god is one whose "heart is satisfied with truth, whose abomination is falsehood."

The reform of Ikhnaton has been relegated to a purely political category by several historians. This ignores the impact of these two great hymns of universalism. There is something fresh and original in them, a new spirit, something with a sweep that had never been known before. Here was a genius who anticipated the "one world, one god" idea of our own day. God is the creator of the natural world and all that is in it. God's beneficence includes all peoples regardless of race or clime. True, Ikhnaton's conception of God, as far as we know, does not contain the quality of righteousness so characteristic of the Hebrew prophets; but his is the God of truth and integrity, principles which the king applied in both public and private life.

SECTION III

The Hebrews and the Origin of Monotheism

THE GREAT CONTRIBUTION of the Hebrews to the history of the world was their monotheistic religion. Christianity and Islam no less than Judaism find their roots in the worship of the single deity of the Hebrews and in the union of ethics and theology which came from it. It has been an occupation of modern scholarship to question whether monotheism really first arose in Israel, or whether it may have existed earlier in Mesopotamia, Egypt, or elsewhere. Among those who agree on a Hebrew origin there is still another dispute: Did monotheism originate with Moses or did its origin come in the time of the prophets?

1. THE MESOPOTAMIAN ORIGINS OF MONOTHEISM*

The complicated Sumerian pantheon was obviously the work of theologians and of gradual growth. Almost all the names of deities express some aspect of nature worship, some personification of natural powers, ethical or cultural functions, perfectly intelligible to the Sumerologist. The names of their oldest trinity, An, "Heaven-god," Enlil, "Earth-god," and Enki, "Water-god," are not lost in the mysteries of folk-lore. They are names given to definite mythological conceptions by clear thinking theologians and accepted in popular religion. Whether they were called by other unintelligible popular names in the prehistoric period, when they wandered on the Iranian plateau long

before 5000 B.C., is a question for which we have no answer. As it was evolved after their occupation of Mesopotamia, the pantheon is the product of theology and not of natural religion. The earliest written records from which any information concerning the Sumerian deities can be obtained is found twenty-five feet below modern plain level at Kish and at a prehistoric site, modern Jemdet Nasr, seventeen miles north-east of Kish, and from a period *circa* 4000 B.C. On the prehistoric tablets only the trinity An, Enlil, Enki is found, possibly Babbar the Sun-god also. Since in their mythology all the gods descended from An, the Sky-god, it is extremely probable that the priests who constructed this pantheon were monotheists at an earlier stage, having only the god An, a word which actually means "high." This is to be expected, for we

* Stephen Herbert Langdon, *Semites*, Vol. 5 of *The Mythology of All Races*, published for the Archaeological Institute of America (Boston: Marshall Jones Co., 1931), pp. 89–93.

69

have here not a mythology springing from primitive religion, but speculation based upon nature, spiritual, and ethical values. The tablets are frequently covered with curious seals, but it is difficult to discover any mythology on them; wild and tame animals are frequent, especially the serpent, and some fantastic monsters, and in one case there is a man holding a long serpent. On one seal there is a design of a tower rising by five stages to a smaller but higher top stage on only one side, which may possibly prove that they had already begun to build towers of this kind as symbols of the earth and sacred to the Earth-god. It is obvious that the serpent was already regarded as symbolic of the generative powers of the earth in this very early period, but the Earth-mother goddess, whose primitive pictograph apparently represents a serpent winding around a staff, does not appear on the pictographic inscriptions which have been recovered. On seals of the primitive period the Grain-goddess appears with a minor male deity, who is also a deity of vegetation. The latter may be Tammuz; he is here represented with a beard, but Tammuz is invariably described as a child or youth. Very primitive seals represent a male deity whose upper parts are human, but whose lower parts are a long coiled serpent, undoubtedly the serpent deity Mush, whose Accadian names Sherah, "grain," "vegetation," and Shahan, "fire," clearly reveal his connection with the generative powers of the earth and the heat of the sun. However, one of the parasite Tammuz forms was Ningishzida, a tree deity, who is invariably represented with a mythical serpent springing from each shoulder, and he too always appears bearded. The cult of the Earth-goddess and her son, the young god of vegetation, belongs to the early period. By giving special names to the diverse functions of each deity the theologians obtained an enormous pantheon, and by assigning special functions of the three great gods

to their sons, and again giving special names to their functions, the parent tree became a forest of gods and minor deities. In addition to this, at an early period the constellations, fixed stars, and planets were identified with various deities. Astral names were, therefore, invented for each deity, which added a very large number of names to the pantheon. As soon as any given deity became patron of a special religious or intellectual activity, they received additional names for these activities. For example, the Earth-goddess, as female principle of An, received the title Ninanna, Nininni, Innini, but, as goddess of childbirth, Nintud, Aruru, Ninhursag, Ninkarraka, and as the planet Venus, Nina-nasianna, Ninsianna, Ninsinna, Ninisinna, "Heavenly lady, light of heaven"; as patroness of medicine she was Gula. These are all regarded as separate goddesses in the cults and literature. Each of the great deities received as many as fifty to a hundred different names, and they had their attendants and courts in Heaven or in the lower world, wherever mythological fancy placed their abode. They had their musicians, messengers, counsellors, bakers, butlers, barbers, gardeners, throne-bearers, priests of sacrifices, watchmen, shepherds, commissioners, envoys, boatmen, sword-bearers, wizards, gate-keepers, charioteers, etc.

Anu was the first of the gods of civilized man, descended through a line of divine beings, beginning with Apsu, the nether sea of fresh water, and Tiamat, the dragon of the ocean. This late theological speculation by which the gods and all things were created from water was certainly no part of the original system, which apparently was monotheistic to begin with, at least in the Sumerian religion as it has come down to us. The later speculative system is set forth at the beginning of the Accadian or Babylonian Epic of Creation.

"When on high the Heavens were not named,
And below a home existed not,

Apsû, the primeval, their engenderer,
And the 'Form' Tiamat, bearer of all of them,
Mingled their waters together;
The secret chambers were not constructed and marsh-lands were not seen;
When none of the gods had been brought into being,
And they were not named, and had not been assigned (their) destinies,
Then were created the gods in the midst thereof.
Lahmu and Lahamu were brought into being and they were named.
For ages they grew up and became lofty.
Anshar and Kishar were created more excellent than they.
The days lengthened and the years increased.
Anu their son, the rival of his fathers—
Anshar made Anu his first-born equal (to himself).
And as to Anu, he begat Nudimmud,
Nudimmud, begetter of his fathers was he.''

In these seventeen opening lines the Epic on the origin of the gods according to later theories makes Anu the first actual personal deity; for Anshar and Kishar mean simply "host of Heaven," "host of Earth," or male and female creative spirits of what is above and beneath. From Anu descended the water deity Enki, latterly called Ea, "god óf the house of the waters," who as creator of mankind received the title Nudimmud, "creator of the form of man." The Earth-god Enlil is nowhere described as the son of Anu. His name means literally, "Lord of the wind"; for the winds were supposed to issue from the caverns of his vast abode in the nether world.

The texts which first contain the fully developed early pantheon come from Shuruppak in southern Sumer, and from a period more than 500 years later than the pictographic tablets of Kish. Not until this period does the Moon-god appear under the title EN-ZU, i.e., ZU-EN, latterly Sin, but his principal title is Nanna, which means "lord of Heaven," the same word as Ninanna, Innini. Here the Moon-god has already received the title, "Lord of wisdom," as a god of divination, Sin. The

scribes of this early period place An, Enlil, Innini, Enki, Nanna, Utu, in that order at the head of the pantheon, that is Heaven, Earth, Earth-goddess as female principle of Heaven, Water-god, Moon-god, Sun-god. The two sons of the Earth-god, Ninurta and Nergal, who figure so largely in later Sumerian and Babylonian mythology, do not yet appear by name; earlier titles of Ninurta, god of the spring sun, are already here, as Ningirsu and Ninsubur; while Lugalmeslam, "King of Meslam," i.e., of the underworld, and Gir, prove that the mythology concerning the terrible deity of summer heat and winter's cold, Nergal, was already part of their religion.

Above I concluded that the Semitic word for "god" meant originally, "he who is high," a Sky-god; and here also I believe that their religion began with monotheism; they probably worshipped El, Ilāh, as their first deity, a Sky-god, corresponding to the Babylonian Anu, and the Greek Zeus. In Sumerian, the word for "god," *dingir*, also means "shining," "bright," and the sign used for writing *dingir* also stands for An, the Sky-god; the word also means "high," "Heaven." An is the only Sumerian deity whose ideogram is never preceded by the determinative for "god." They write *dingir* Enlil, "god Enlil," *dingir* Sin, "god Sin," etc., but never *dingir* An. Surely this means that An (Anu) is not only older than other deities, but An was in the beginning "god," "the Sky-god." The ideogram for writing "god," "high," "Heaven," "bright," and for the god An, was the picture of a star. In the minds of the earliest Sumerians *dingir* Enlil, *dingir* Enki, etc., really mean An-Enlil, An-Enki, etc.; that is Enlil, Enki, etc., are only aspects of the father Anu. On seals of the pictographic tablets and on painted pots of that prehistoric period, the picture of a star constantly occurs. This star sign is almost the only religious symbol in this primitive age. These facts cannot be explained without assuming monotheism in the beginning.

2. AGAINST THE NON-HEBREW ORIGINS OF MONOTHEISM*

So many students of religion today are being led astray by the widely publicized claims of primitive monotheism that it has become a veritable menace to clear thinking and a challenge to real scholarship. When its advocates assert that their methodology is absolutely objective and scientific, reaching results that are completely authoritative and final, although contradicting all previous results, it behooves us to take notice of the theory; and when a writer like Marston berates critical scholarship in the words, "It is surely time that distinguished scholars gave up the habit of representing exploded theories as historical facts," it is time to turn the tables on him.

Sir Charles Marston may not be a writer to whom scholars give serious attention, but he is, nevertheless, a writer whose books sell in thousands where theirs sell in hundreds, and his case is symptomatic of the impression that is being made by the theory of primitive monotheism. In his latest book, *The Bible Comes Alive*, he makes this astounding statement: "In the year 1931 these two Sciences [viz., archeology and anthropology] simultaneously reached the conclusion that the evidence in their possession pointed to the fact that Monotheism was the original Religion of Man" (p. 24). That is a sweeping statement, and it becomes still more sweeping and extravagant when we discover that one man is made to speak for the whole science of archeology and one man for that of anthropology. The man who is to be accepted as the sole and final authority in archeology, the most inexact of all the sciences, is one who himself never professed to be an archeologist, but an Assyriologist, and who in all his work was

notoriously inexact, the late Professor S. H. Langdon of Oxford; while the authority who is to speak for the whole of anthropology, even though the most eminent anthropologists repudiate his theories, is the Catholic ethnologist, Wilhelm Schmidt, until recently Professor in Vienna. Let us examine these two men to see how strongly they can speak for themselves, not to mention the two sciences which they supposedly represent.

Of all the advocates of primitive monotheism Schmidt is the one who makes the most extravagant claims for his method and its results. His most elaborate work, *Der Ursprung der Gottesidee* (1926-1937), already runs to six large volumes, each comprising over 1000 pages, but his theories are most succinctly presented in his *Origin and Growth of Religion*. Schmidt is harshly critical of all methods but his own, and particularly so of any method connected with evolution, as being totally subjective, quite innocent of historical research (p. 158), and leading to "cloud-castles lacking positive, exact, and concrete support" (p. 156). In contrast, his own method, the ethnological, or historical, as he often calls it, is absolutely objective, scientific, and authoritative—so he says.

According to Schmidt the true origin and original character of religion is to be discovered from the study of the aborigines still found in remote corners of the world, and that study, he states dogmatically, shows that the further back one carries his ethnological investigation the less of magic he finds and the more of monotheism, proving that man's original religion was absolute monotheism, untainted by magic. The tools and weapons of prehistoric man, and those of the ethnologically oldest peoples of today, viz., the Pygmies, show primitive man to have been of a high order: "His mental powers made their way through nature and analysed her phenom-

* Theophile James Meek, "Primitive Monotheism and the Religion of Moses," *Review of Religion*, Vol. IV, No. 3, pp. 286-298. Copyright 1940 by Columbia University Press.

ena; his synthetic activities mastered her by forming generalizing and classificatory ideas; he grasped the conception of cause and effect, and then adapted that to the relationship of means to end" (p. 136). The desire to find a cause, combined with the tendency to personify, led man to the recognition of a Supreme Being back of all and the Cause of all, a personal, morally perfect, loving God, the father of all, omniscient and omnipotent, filling and dominating all time and hence eternal, filling and dominating all space and hence leaving room for no other, so great that by himself he sufficed for all needs (pp. 136, 262-283).

However, despite the high intelligence that Schmidt attributes to his primitives, which gave them a religion satisfying the sum total of human needs that should have made them the masters of the world and not its slaves (p. 283), he recognizes that they lost out in the struggle for existence. Squeezed into unattractive and remote corners of the earth (pp. 252 ff.), these peoples, once vigorous and intelligent (p. 136), were socially and economically backward (pp. 254, 256), and hence lapsed into a condition of stagnation, poverty, and insignificance (pp. 255 f., 289 f.), overcome by peoples more advanced and self-confident and with keener intellects (pp. 159, 256). Thus the primitives never played any important part in the world (p. 256), but were succeeded by peoples of higher culture. The peoples of higher culture, however, developed from the primitives, perhaps indeed from a common Asiatic home (p. 234), and whatever elements of monotheism are found with them are to be accounted for solely as the survival of primitive monotheism, and not as an independent achievement (pp. 254 ff., 261, 285, 288). They were better fitted to live than the primitives, but their religion represents a decadence of the old, with many gods and much of magic (pp. 140, 203, 289). Where the primitives resorted to prayer alone (pp. 154 f., 279, 282), the later cultures, with their larger knowledge and greater self-confidence, introduced magic (pp. 152, 155, 158 ff.).

To Schmidt's contentions there are many objections. He unquestionably idealizes and overrates primitive man, and attributes to him an intelligence, an imagination, and a universal outlook that even modern man has not reached. The god of most moderns is a Hindu god, or a Muslim god, or a Christian god, or even a Catholic or a Protestant god; and the Great War showed us that with most peoples God is still a German god, or a French god, or an English god—scarcely a universal god, but one narrowly provincial. What man has always wanted, and still insists on having, is a god to meet his immediate needs, a god near at hand, a local god. When a Muslim finds himself in very great trouble, it is not to almighty Allah that he appeals, but to the local Weli, even as the Catholic in similar circumstances prays to his patron saint or the Virgin Mary. When modern man finds it so difficult to reach out beyond his environment and find satisfaction in a great High God, it must have been quite impossible to primitive man. With all peoples everywhere it has been to the friendly little spirits, near at hand and approachable, that man has looked for protection, and not to the great gods of the Pantheon or to the great High God when there was one. The great gods were never of much use in daily life, but belonged to the cultus of the state. They were too far away to be trusted by the common people, or to be meaningful or useful.

What primitive man was first conscious of was, not the universe as a whole, but his immediate environment, the things at hand among which he lived and moved and had his being. He could not possibly know or think of the universe as a whole, and he assuredly had no occasion and no urge to think back of that universe to the First Cause and Creator of all. Primitive man was practical, not speculative, and the category of cause and effect simply did not exist in his psychology, as psychologists have long since recognized. What he had to do was to live, and to live he had to come to terms with his environment, and in doing this he introduced religion, because "religion is man's belief that there is that in his environment which is greater than himself and upon which he feels to some degree dependent and with which he accordingly attempts to establish a relationship of mutual interest and good-will." If this is a correct definition of religion, and it agrees with that of Schmidt himself (p. 2), man's first religion could not possibly have been monotheistic. Primitive man had no occasion to feel a sense of dependence upon an omnipotent, omniscient, universal god, the creator of the world, but upon the many mysterious phenomena that constituted his immediate environment, phenomena which, he believed, did things to him with intent and purpose and may roughly be called powers. Primitive man had no conception of the regularity of nature (he had not lived long enough); he had no conception of forces and laws; the only activities of nature that he knew were these powers round about him that did things to him, and it was with these powers that he felt the necessity of establishing friendly relations, and not with Schmidt's hypothetical and impossible transcendent god, all-powerful, all-righteous, all-wise, the creator and ruler of all. That kind of god could only come after long centuries of profoundest thought and experience, as is demonstrated in the great historical religions, such as Judaism, Islam, and Hinduism.

It is true of course that most, perhaps all the aboriginal peoples known to us today have a belief in a Supreme Being, but it is not so clear that nowhere is the Supreme Being to be found in so clear, so definite, vivid, and direct a form as among peoples who are ethnologically the most primitive, as Schmidt contends. Nor is it at all certain that this belief with them is a survival from primitive monotheism rather than an achievement on their own part or an acquisition from others. As all anthropologists have long since recognized, there is no such thing as a racially pure stock anywhere in the world, and there never has been since the appearance of mankind on the earth. From the very beginning there was intermixture of blood and ideas, so that it is utterly impossible that anywhere on the earth, no matter how remote or inaccessible the spot, peoples survive today who are untainted by alien blood and thought. As Schmidt himself recognizes, the primitives that survive today survive as such because they lacked the capacity of their neighbors, got shunted off into the remote corners of the earth, and there became stagnant, with the result that their religion ceased to grow and underwent "that fossilization and loss of inner vitality which is inseparately connected with such a state of rest, and is especially fatal to anything so essentially spiritual as religion," to quote Schmidt's own words (p. 255; cf. also pp. 289 f.). But man does not stand still; he must either go forward or back, and in the case of the primitives he has manifestly deteriorated, so that his religion may well be the survival of a religion developed in a higher stage of culture than the present food-gathering stage. The peoples who became the primitives of today are primitives because they were unequipped to grapple successfully with life, and hence must be decadent in physique, intellect, religion, and everything else. It is scarcely fair to take them, the dregs of mankind, as representative of the species *homo sapiens* in his first virility. The modern aborigine can never be a guide for primitive man because he is not primitive man, or at best he is primitive man at his worst, defeated and decadent. Schmidt himself recognizes this when he says that "the religious forms of the primitive cultures now available do not immediately and without more ado show us the primitive form of religion" (p. 255; cf. also pp. 285, 290).

And yet he would argue back from the religion of these decadent primitives of to-day to the religion of primitive man—a most precarious line of argument, as speculative, subjective, and unscientific as anything which he condemns so scathingly in his opponents. Up to the present we have discovered no method whereby we can determine with absolute certainty what primitive man was and what he thought.

Furthermore, the religion of surviving primitives is not nearly so monotheistic as Schmidt affirms. In fact, it is strictly not monotheistic at all. Besides the Supreme Being, who is "without exception un-alterably righteous," Schmidt finds another being who is the source of evil, but he re-fuses to call this belief in two powers dualism, because "the good Supreme Being is represented as far the stronger and more important" (p. 271). Indeed, he goes further and asserts that the primitives are monotheists even though they have a plurality of gods, because there is one Supreme Being dominating all the others (p. 264). But this is begging the whole question. Schmidt and all others of his kind give to the word "monotheism" a meaning that it cannot and should not bear. According to the dictionaries mono-theism is "the doctrine that there is but one god," and that means the worship of one god, and one god alone, and the denial of all other gods. The primitives of today may show a tendency in the direction of monotheism; at best they are henotheists, but not monotheists; and if Schmidt and his school insist upon calling monotheism what I and others call henotheism, then there is no difference between us on that particular point. If by "white" he means "black," then we mean exactly the same thing, but it is unfortunate that our nomenclature is so different. Schmidt and his followers profess to be objective and scientific, but their use of the word "monotheism" is anything but scientific and accurate, because it includes under a single term ideas that are disparate. As

Barton has well said in his review of Shryock's *Desire and the Universe:*

A primitive tribe was not monotheistic because, in order to give unity to its world, it believed in a supreme god. There is inherent in real monotheism an element of hostility to other beliefs. Genuine monotheism differs from this kind of primitive belief as positive virtue differs from the innocence of childhood. It is something that has been won by struggle. The intelligent leaders of a monotheistic com-munity are conscious of its cost, of its worth, and of its difference from polytheism. The real monotheist denies that other gods have juris-diction at all or that they exist. . . . Whenever real monotheism has existed it is militant and hostile to the worship of any god but one.

To call the religion of primitives mono-theism may save the face of Christian dogma and hoodwink the uncritical, but to call something monotheism that is not monotheism can never make it mono-theism.

Marston's second supreme authority, Professor Langdon, reaches conclusions like those of Schmidt, but by a different method. He writes as an Assyriologist, although Marston makes him an archeol-ogist. Langdon's argument, as presented in his *Semitic Mythology* (pp. 89, 93), is that An is the only Sumerian deity whose ideogram in the cuneiform script, origin-ally the picture of a star, is never preceded by the determinative for "god," that ideo-gram itself being the determinative for "god" used with all other god names. Hence the Sumerian wrote [d]Enlil, [d]Enki, etc., but never [d]An. From this he argues that An, the sky god, was originally the only god that the Sumerians had, and that then, as they fell away from monotheism into polytheism, they thought of the several new gods as simply forms or aspects or manifestations of An, and so in writing their names they used the ideogram for An as the determinative of deity. The same argument was used many years ago by M.-J. Lagrange, and more recently by Langdon himself, in the effort to prove that the Semites as a whole were originally monotheists, having as their one god El, also interpreted as a sky god. From being a proper name originally, it is argued, El came to be used as a common noun to mean god in general, and hence the several gods, as they were introduced, were regarded as forms or manifestations of the original El and so each in turn was called an El.

In these arguments, however, Langdon fails to take account of two facts: (1) when the Semites and Sumerians began to write, they had by that time advanced far along the road to knowledge, and theology was already hard at work on the riddle of the universe; and (2) the Sumerians and Babylonians did not at first use the determinatives before god names, the usage being only gradually introduced for the easier identification of the names as god names. When the Sumerians first appear on the pages of history, they are worshipers of many gods, and on this point all scholars are agreed. Out of the early welter of gods, goddesses, and spirits, the Sumerian theologians tried to develop some kind of order, and so in the Creation Myth they traced all the gods back to the father-god An, since he was the sky god and hence god over all, the god *par excellence*. What was more natural, then, than that the sign which represented the sky god, when a system of writing came to be invented, should be used as the ideogram of god in general, and the determinative of "god," when a determinative came to be written before god names; and what was more natural than that El, the sky god of the Semites, should likewise come to be the designation of god in general? Instead of seeing in the phenomenon a reminiscence of an earlier, prehistoric monotheism, we are rather to see in it the work of early theologians trying to bring cosmos out of chaos, order out of disorder.

To his earlier argument Langdon more recently added another (in the *Evangelical Quarterly* for April, 1937). This argument

runs as follows. The Sumerian religion in its latest development contains about 5000 gods; the inscriptions of c. 3000 B.C. show only 750; the 300 tablets from Kish (strictly Jemdet Nasr) contain only three gods, Enlil, the sky god, Enki, the earth god, and Babbar, the sun god; while the 575 tablets from Uruk, which he dates c. 4000 B.C. (fully 500 years too early), contain the names of only two deities, An, the sky god, and Innini, the mother-goddess. In this statement, however, Langdon is no more accurate than he usually is. In the Jemdet Nasr texts there are more gods than three; he himself speaks of four a little later in his article; in the introduction to the publication of his own texts from Jemdet Nasr he lists the names of five gods, An, Enlil, Enki, Babbar, and Lamma, with the last-named somewhat doubtful; and in some additional texts (published in the *Journal of the Royal Asiatic Society*, 1931, pp. 837 ff.) he has discovered still another god, Shara, to make six in all according to his own count; while Falkenstein in the study of his Jemdet Nasr texts indicates the probability of a seventh, Shume, in the personal name En-dingir-shu-me (var., En-shu-me), and still another god, Enlu, is manifestly to be found in the personal name En-lu-ti. Since the archaic texts from Jemdet Nasr and Uruk are as yet very imperfectly understood and the god names are written without determinatives, there are doubtless a number of god names in them as yet unrecognized. With the larger understanding of the texts, and with the publication of additional texts of the same kind, the list of gods will unquestionably be extended, but the fact remains that we can never expect the number to be large. Hence Langdon has some right on his side when he says that the numerous pantheon of the late Sumerian period "dwindles down to four and then only two deities," proving, he holds, that earlier there must have been one god alone, the sky god An. To the layman this argument is most impressive and convincing, and particularly so when Langdon goes on to say that "if there really was a larger pantheon at the dawn of history, these numerous tablets, which are all temple records, would have mentioned them." But just there is the weakness of his whole argument. The argument *e silentio* is always a precarious one, and particularly so in the present instance. It is true that the tablets are probably temple records, but they are in no sense religious. With the ancient Sumerians the temple was the centre of business, and all the archaic tablets from Uruk and Jemdet Nasr, with the exception of a few word-lists, are account tablets, listing the quantities of various items (bread, barley, beer, sheep, land, etc.) administered by the temple in its capacity as business agent. In such tablets in the early period, or in any other period, there is seldom any occasion to mention the gods and hence they rarely appear. According to Langdon's line of argument the Old Akkadians of Nuzi had no gods at all, because none of their many tablets so far excavated mentions any gods whatsoever; and yet it is ridiculous to say that they had none, but no more ridiculous than to say that the Sumerians had only four gods in the Jemdet Nasr period and only two in the Uruk period. Outside of texts definitely religious (myths, liturgies, prayers, and the like) the gods of a people are seldom mentioned, and when they do occur in account tablets they are found almost exclusively as elements in the proper names, but it so happens that in the archaic texts from Uruk and Jemdet Nasr there are practically no proper names. The further back we go the fewer are the religious texts, with none from the archaic period; and the earlier the text the fewer are the proper names, with the earliest texts consisting of itemized lists of articles only. Hence the diminution in god names is not at all a reflection of the religious ideas of the Sumerians and has a vastly different explanation from that presented by Langdon. The ancient Sumerians might have been wor-shippers of only one or of a million gods, but neither situation could be reflected in the kind of texts that have been preserved to us from that early period.

Furthermore, these ancient Sumerians were far removed from primitive man, as Langdon himself notes, and he himself recognizes that pictographic writing, no matter how ancient, cannot take us back to the primitive period of religion, to the primitive concept of deity. Even if the ancient Sumerians were monotheists, that does not prove or even suggest that primitive man was monotheistic, because thousands, if not millions, of years lay between them and him, and much can happen both for and against the development of monotheism in a thousand years, not to speak of thousands or millions. There is nothing at all in Langdon's arguments to show that primitive man was monotheistic, and he negatives his whole position when he records, as of course he must, that the antediluvian peoples, who according to the Sumerians themselves antedated them by thousands of years, were polytheists.

Schmidt and Langdon, and their followers, are particularly hostile to anything smacking of evolution, but evolution is not something vicious and obnoxious—if it is not misunderstood, as it is so frequently. For example, Marston is absolutely wrong when he asserts that the theory of evolution is based on the idea of steady, consistent, unbroken progress from barbarism to the present day, and it is not at all correct for him to say that according to evolution the early Israelites should have been illiterates. Like so many others, Marston sets up a man of straw and then proceeds to knock him down. Evolution, as everyone should know, is not a force in itself, and it never runs in a straight line, but has its flows and ebbs, with periods of retrogression as well as progress. In religion there have always been two movements: one toward monotheism, as man rationalized the universe, usually in the person of a religious genius, and one toward polytheism, as experience outran reason. Sometimes one was the stronger, sometimes the other, with the result that all religions, if they lived long enough, became more or less monotheistic in the end, but more monotheistic at some times than at others. Man developed, not piecemeal, but as a unit—physically, mentally, emotionally, and religiously. When he lagged in one field, as he sometimes did, there were maladjustments, and progress stopped or retrogression set in until a readjustment was made. It is utterly impossible to isolate man's religious development and separate it from his general cultural development, from his history, "and that history [to quote Guillaume, *Prophecy and Divination* (1938), pp. 234 f.] —both sacred and profane—speaks with no uncertain voice of the slow and tortuous path which man has taken in his journey from swamp and jungle, hill and plain, to the city and the town." There is absolutely nothing in anthropology or archeology to show that monotheism antedated polytheism, and there is nothing whatsoever to discredit evolution, when evolution is rightly understood.

However, even though we were to grant that the theory of evolution is all wrong and that primitive man was monotheistic, that does not prove that the early Hebrews were monotheists, because they, like the Sumerians, were far removed from primitive man. On the contention of Schmidt the only people in the Old Testament who were primitives were Adam and Eve, and they did not remain primitives long, but ate of the forbidden tree and became agriculturalists, a state of culture far beyond the primitive food-gathering stage, and one that conduces to polytheism, according to Schmidt. The early stories in Genesis are generally considered to represent a monotheistic point of view, and that leads Marston to make another astounding statement to add to the one already quoted, a statement absolutely consistent, however, with the theory of primitive monotheism and the inevitable deduction

from it. He says: "Since Monotheism, or the Belief in one God, antedates polytheism or the belief in many, then it is reasonable to regard the Creation, and other stories in Genesis, as representing the original version; and the polytheistic ones as corruptions of it." That is, the Hebrews are to be regarded as having preserved the original stories, of which the Sumerian stories are a late corruption, even though we have the actual Sumerian tablets containing the stories written long before the Hebrews ever came into existence. This is a preposterous statement, but apart from that, it is not so clear that the Genesis stories are as monotheistic as generally believed. The oldest of these is recognized to be that in Gen. 2, 3, universally assigned to the document J, and dating in its present form from the ninth century or thereabouts. In a story as late as this, one would expect a more or less monotheistic point of view, but as Alfred Guillaume has well said, a close examination of the story shows that the world of Adam and Eve was not a completely religious world at all, "but a state of society in which magic and religion lived uneasily side by side. The knowledge of God which Adam and Eve are said to possess is not what we understand by knowledge. They were not living in a world of innocence and beauty in the immediate consciousness of the presence of God, as Milton would have had us believe; theirs was the dark, semi-heathen world of polytheism and magic, in which Yahweh-Elohim narrowly escaped disaster through leaving a tree with magical properties within the reach of mortals." The wily serpent, the prototype of Satan, was able to frustrate the purpose of Yahweh-Elohim by persuading simple-minded man to eat of one magic tree, and to prevent access to the other, Yahweh had to expel man from the Garden of Eden and station the semi-divine cherubim as guards to keep him out: "Then Yahweh-Elohim said, 'See, man has become like one of us [note the plural], in knowing good from evil; and now, suppose he were to reach out his hand and take the fruit of the tree of life also, and eating it, live forever!' So Yahweh-Elohim expelled him from the Garden of Eden, to till the ground from which he had been taken; he drove man out, and stationed the cherubim east of the Garden of Eden, with the flaming, whirling sword to guard the way to the tree of life" (Gen. 2:22-24). Yahweh was not the sole power in the world, and he had semi-divine helpers to assist him. He was stronger than man and hence was able to prevent his

access to the tree of life, but he was not stronger than the magic inherent in the tree, a co-existent power that could thwart his purpose and endanger his prerogatives. Hence it is not so clear, after all, that the Old Testament teaches the fall of man from a pristine state of perfect religious knowledge and moral perfection; it seems to teach something quite the opposite of this and more in line with modern ideas of evolution. If this were generally recognized, we should have less railings against evolution and less of the theory of primitive monotheism.

3. THE GOD OF MOSES*

19

On the third new moon after the people of Israel had gone forth out of the land of Egypt, on that day they came into the wilderness of Sinai. 2 And when they set out from Reph'idim and came into the wilderness of Sinai, they encamped in the wilderness; and there Israel encamped before the mountain. 3 And Moses went up to God, and the LORD called him out of the mountain, saying, "Thus you shall say to the house of Jacob, and tell the people of Israel: 4 You have seen what I did to the Egyptians, and how I bore you on eagles' wings and brought you to myself. 5 Now therefore, if you will obey my voice and keep my covenant, you shall be my own possession among all peoples; for all the earth is mine, 6 and you shall be to me a kingdom of priests and a holy nation. These are the words which you shall speak to the children of Israel."

7 So Moses came and called the elders of the people, and set before them all these words which the LORD had commanded

him. 8 And all the people answered together and said, "All that the LORD has spoken we will do." And Moses reported the words of the people to the LORD. 9 And the LORD said to Moses, "Lo, I am coming to you in a thick cloud, that the people may hear when I speak with you, and may also believe you for ever."

Then Moses told the words of the people to the LORD. 10 And the LORD said to Moses, "Go to the people and consecrate them today and tomorrow, and let them wash their garments, 11 and be ready by the third day; for on the third day the LORD will come down upon Mount Sinai in the sight of all the people. 12 And you shall set bounds for the people round about, saying, "Take heed that you do not go up into the mountain or touch the border of it; whoever touches the mountain shall be put to death; 13 no hand shall touch him, but he shall be stoned or shot; whether beast or man, he shall not live.' When the trumpet sounds a long blast, they shall come up to the mountain." 14 So Moses went down from the mountain to the people, and consecrated the people; and they washed their garments. 15 And he said to the people, "Be ready by the third day; do not go near a woman."

16 On the morning of the third day

---

* Exodus 19-20; 31.18-34.16, from the *Revised Standard Version of the Bible*, copyright 1946 and 1952 by the Division of Christian Education, National Council of Churches, and used by permission.

there were thunders and lightnings, and a thick cloud upon the mountain, and a very loud trumpet blast, so that all the people who were in the camp trembled. 17 Then Moses brought the people out of the camp to meet God; and they took their stand at the foot of the mountain. 18 And Mount Sinai was wrapped in smoke, because the LORD descended upon it in fire; and the smoke of it went up like the smoke of a kiln, and the whole mountain quaked greatly. 19 And as the sound of the trumpet grew louder and louder, Moses spoke, and God answered him in thunder. 20 And the LORD came down upon Mount Sinai, to the top of the mountain; and the LORD called Moses to the top of the mountain, and Moses went up. 21 And the LORD said to Moses, "Go down and warn the people, lest they break through to the LORD to gaze and many of them perish. 22 And also let the priests who come near to the LORD consecrate themselves, lest the LORD break out upon them." 23 And Moses said to the LORD, "The people cannot come up to Mount Sinai; for thou thyself didst charge us, saying, 'Set bounds about the mountain, and consecrate it.'" 24 And the LORD said to him, "Go down, and come up bringing Aaron with you; but do not let the priests and the people break through to come up to the LORD, lest he break out against them." 25 So Moses went down to the people and told them.

20

And God spoke all these words, saying, 2 "I am the LORD your God, who brought you out of the land of Egypt, out of the house of bondage.
3 "You shall have no other gods before me.
4 "You shall not make yourself a graven image, or any likeness of anything that is in heaven above, or that is in the earth beneath, or that is in the water under the earth; 5 you shall not bow down to them or serve them; for I the LORD your God am a jealous God, visiting the iniquity of the fathers upon the children to the third and the fourth generation of those who hate me, 6 but showing steadfast love to thousands of those who love me and keep my commandments.
7 "You shall not take the name of the LORD your God in vain; for the LORD will not hold him guiltless who takes his name in vain.
8 "Remember the sabbath day, to keep it holy. 9 Six days you shall labor, and do all your work; 10 but the seventh day is a sabbath to the LORD your God; in it you shall not do any work, you, or your son, or your daughter, your manservant, or your maidservant, or your cattle, or the sojourner who is within your gates; 11 for in six days the LORD made heaven and earth, the sea, and all that is in them, and rested the seventh day; therefore the LORD blessed the sabbath day and hallowed it.
12 "Honor your father and your mother, that your days may be long in the land which the LORD your God gives you.
13 "You shall not kill.
14 "You shall not commit adultery.
15 "You shall not steal.
16 "You shall not bear false witness against your neighbor.
17 "You shall not covet your neighbor's house; you shall not covet your neighbor's wife, or his manservant, or his maidservant, or his ox, or his ass, or anything that is your neighbor's."
18 Now when all the people perceived the thunderings and the lightnings and the sound of the trumpet and the mountain smoking, the people were afraid and trembled; and they stood afar off, 19 and said to Moses, "You speak to us, and we will hear; but let not God speak to us, lest we die." 20 And Moses said to the people, "Do not fear; for God has come to prove you, and that the fear of him may be before your eyes, that you may not sin."
21 And the people stood afar off, while Moses drew near to the thick cloud where God was. 22 And the LORD said to Moses,

"Thus you shall say to the people of Israel: 'You have seen for yourselves that I have talked with you from heaven. 23 You shall not make gods of silver to be with me, nor shall you make for yourselves gods of gold. 24 An altar of earth you shall make for me and sacrifice on it your burnt offerings and your peace offerings, your sheep and your oxen; in every place where I cause my name to be remembered I will come to you and bless you. 25 And if you make me an altar of stone, you shall not build it of hewn stones; for if you wield your tool upon it you profane it. 26 And you shall not go up by steps to my altar, that your nakedness be not exposed on it.'"

31

18 And he gave to Moses, when he had made an end of speaking with him upon Mount Sinai, the two tables of the testimony, tables of stone, written with the finger of God.

32

When the people saw that Moses delayed to come down from the mountain, the people gathered themselves together to Aaron, and said to him, "Up, make us gods, who shall go before us; as for this Moses, the man who brought us up out of the land of Egypt, we do not know what has become of him." 2 And Aaron said to them, "Take off the rings of gold which are in the ears of your wives, your sons, and your daughters, and bring them to me." 3 So all the people took off the rings of gold which were in their ears, and brought them to Aaron. 4 And he received the gold at their hand, and fashioned it with a graving tool, and made a molten calf; and they said, "These are your gods, O Israel, who brought you up out of the land of Egypt!" 5 When Aaron saw this, he built an altar before it; and Aaron made proclamation and said, "Tomorrow shall be a feast to the LORD." 6 And they rose up early on the morrow, and offered burnt. offerings and brought peace offerings; and the people sat down to eat and drink, and rose up to play.

7 And the LORD said to Moses, "Go down; for your people, whom you brought up out of the land of Egypt, have corrupted themselves; 8 they have turned aside quickly out of the way which I commanded them; they have made for themselves a molten calf, and have worshiped it and sacrificed to it, and said, 'These are your gods, O Israel, who brought you up out of the land of Egypt!'" 9 And the LORD said to Moses, "I have seen this people, and behold, it is a stiff-necked people; 10 now therefore let me alone, that my wrath may burn hot against them and I may consume them; but of you I will make a great nation."

11 But Moses besought the LORD his God, and said, "O LORD, why does thy wrath burn hot against thy people, whom thou hast brought forth out of the land of Egypt with great power and with a mighty hand? 12 Why should the Egyptians say, 'With evil intent did he bring them forth, to slay them in the mountains, and to consume them from the face of the earth'? Turn from thy fierce wrath, and repent of this evil against thy people. 13 Remember Abraham, Isaac, and Israel, thy servants, to whom thou didst swear by thine own self, and didst say to them, 'I will multiply your descendants as the stars of heaven, and all this land that I have promised I will give to your descendants, and they shall inherit it for ever.'" 14 And the LORD repented of the evil which he thought to do to his people.

15 And Moses turned, and went down from the mountain with the two tables of the testimony in his hands, tables that were written on both sides; on the one side and on the other were they written. 16 And the tables were the work of God, and the writing was the writing of God, graven upon the tables. 17 When Joshua heard the noise of the people as they shouted, he said to

Moses, "There is a noise of war in the camp." 18 But he said, "It is not the sound of shouting for victory, or the sound of the cry of defeat, but the sound of singing that I hear." 19 And as soon as he came near the camp and saw the calf and the dancing, Moses' anger burned hot, and he threw the tables out of his hands and broke them at the foot of the mountain. 20 And he took the calf which they had made, and burnt it with fire, and ground it to powder, and scattered it upon the water, and made the people of Israel drink it.

21 And Moses said to Aaron, "What did this people do to you that you have brought a great sin upon them?" 22 And Aaron said, "Let not the anger of my lord burn hot; you know the people, that they are set on evil. 23 For they said to me, 'Make us gods, who shall go before us; as for this Moses, the man who brought us up out of the land of Egypt, we do not know what has become of him.' 24 And I said to them, 'Let any who have gold take it off'; so they gave it to me, and I threw it into the fire, and there came out this calf."

25 And when Moses saw that the people had broken loose (for Aaron had let them break loose, to their shame among their enemies), 26 then Moses stood in the gate of the camp, and said, "Who is on the LORD's side? Come to me." And all the sons of Levi gathered themselves together to him. 27 And he said to them, "Thus says the LORD God of Israel, 'Put every man his sword on his side, and go to and fro from gate to gate throughout the camp, and slay every man his brother, and every man his companion, and every man his neighbor.' " 28 And the sons of Levi did according to the word of Moses; and there fell of the people that day about three thousand men. 29 And Moses said, "Today you have ordained yourselves for the service of the LORD, each one at the cost of his son and of his brother, that he may bestow a blessing upon you this day."

30 On the morrow Moses said to the people, "You have sinned a great sin. And now I will go up to the LORD; perhaps I can make atonement for your sin." 31 So Moses returned to the LORD and said, "Alas, this people have sinned a great sin; they have made for themselves gods of gold. 32 But now, if thou wilt forgive their sin—and if not, blot me, I pray thee, out of thy book which thou hast written." 33 But the LORD said to Moses, "Whoever has sinned against me, him will I blot out of my book. 34 But now go, lead the people to the place of which I have spoken to you; behold, my angel shall go before you. Nevertheless, in the day when I visit, I will visit their sin upon them."

35 And the LORD sent a plague upon the people, because they made the calf which Aaron made.

33

The LORD said to Moses, "Depart, go up hence, you and the people whom you have brought up out of the land of Egypt, to the land of which I swore to Abraham, Isaac, and Jacob, saying, 'To your descendants I will give it.' 2 And I will send an angel before you, and I will drive out the Canaanites, the Amorites, the Hittites, the Per'izzites, the Hivites, and the Jeb'usites. 3 Go up to a land flowing with milk and honey; but I will not go up among you, lest I consume you in the way, for you are a stiff-necked people."

4 When the people heard these evil tidings, they mourned; and no man put on his ornaments. 5 For the LORD had said to Moses, "Say to the people of Israel, 'You are a stiff-necked people; if for a single moment I should go up among you, I would consume you. So now put off your ornaments from you, that I may know what to do with you.' " 6 Therefore, the people of Israel stripped themselves of their ornaments, from Mount Horeb onward.

7 Now Moses used to take the tent and pitch it outside the camp, far off from the camp; and he called it the tent of meeting. And every one who sought the LORD would

go out to the tent of meeting, which was outside the camp. 8 Whenever Moses went out to the tent, all the people rose up, and every man stood at his tent door, and looked after Moses, until he had gone into the tent. 9 When Moses entered the tent, the pillar of cloud would descend and stand at the door of the tent, and the LORD would speak with Moses. 10 And when all the people saw the pillar of cloud standing at the door of the tent, all the people would rise up and worship, every man at his tent door. 11 Thus the LORD used to speak to Moses face to face, as a man speaks to his friend. When Moses turned again into the camp, his servant Joshua the son of Nun, a young man, did not depart from the tent.

12 Moses said to the LORD, "See, thou sayest to me, 'Bring up this people'; but thou hast not let me know whom thou wilt send with me. Yet thou hast said, 'I know you by name, and you have also found favor in my sight.' 13 Now therefore, I pray thee, if I have found favor in thy sight, show me now thy ways, that I may know thee and find favor in thy sight. Consider too that this nation is thy people." 14 And he said, "My presence will go with you, and I will give you rest." 15 And he said to him, "If thy presence will not go with me, do not carry us up from here. 16 For how shall it be known that I have found favor in thy sight, I and thy people? Is it not in thy going with us, so that we are distinct, I and thy people, from all other people that are upon the face of the earth?"

17 And the LORD said to Moses, "This very thing that you have spoken I will do; for you have found favor in my sight, and I know you by name." 18 Moses said, "I pray thee, show me thy glory." 19 And he said, "I will make all my goodness pass before you, and will proclaim before you my name 'The LORD'; and I will be gracious to whom I will be gracious, and will show mercy on whom I will show mercy. 20 But," he said, "you cannot see my face; for man shall not see me and live." 21 And the LORD said, "Behold, there is a place by me where you shall stand upon the rock; 22 and while my glory passes by I will put you in a cleft of the rock, and I will cover you with my hand until I have passed by; 23 then I will take away my hand, and you shall see my back; but my face shall not be seen."

34

The LORD said to Moses, "Cut two tables of stone like the first; and I will write upon the tables the words that were on the first tables, which you broke. 2 Be ready in the morning, and come up in the morning to Mount Sinai, and present yourself there to me on the top of the mountain. 3 No man shall come up with you, and let no man be seen throughout all the mountain; let no flocks or herds feed before that mountain." 4 So Moses cut two tables of stone like the first; and he rose early in the morning and went up on Mount Sinai, as the LORD had commanded him, and took in his hand two tables of stone. 5 And the LORD descended in the cloud and stood with him there, and proclaimed the name of the LORD. 6 The LORD passed before him, and proclaimed, "The LORD, the LORD, a God merciful and gracious, slow to anger, and abounding in steadfast love and faithfulness, 7 keeping steadfast love for thousands, forgiving iniquity and transgression and sin, but who will by no means clear the guilty, visiting the iniquity of the fathers upon the children and the children's children, to the third and the fourth generation." 8 And Moses made haste to bow his head toward the earth, and worshiped. 9 And he said, "If now I have found favor in thy sight, O LORD, let the LORD, I pray thee, go in the midst of us, although it is a stiff-necked people; and pardon our iniquity and our sin, and take us for thy inheritance."

10 And he said, "Behold, I make a covenant. Before all your people I will do marvels, such as have not been wrought in

all the earth or in any nation; and all the people among whom you are shall see the work of the LORD; for it is a terrible thing that I will do with you.

11 "Observe what I command you this day. Behold, I will drive out before you the Amorites, the Canaanites, the Hittites, the Per'izzites, the Hivites, and the Jeb'usites. 12 Take heed to yourself, lest you make a covenant with the inhabitants of the land whither you go, lest it become a snare in the midst of you. 13 You shall tear down their altars, and break their pillars, and cut down their Ashe'rim 14 (for you shall worship no other god, for the LORD, whose name is Jealous, is a jealous God), 15 lest you make a covenant with the inhabitants of the land, and when they play the harlot after their gods and sacrifice to their gods and one invites you, you eat of his sacrifice, 16 and you take of their daughters for your sons, and their daughters play the harlot after their gods and make your sons play the harlot after their gods."

4. MOSES AND MONOTHEISM*

We are handicapped in dealing with this subject by the fact that all our literary sources are relatively late, as we have seen, and that we must therefore depend upon a tradition which was long transmitted orally. Many scholars go so far as to deny the historian any right to use these sources to determine what the religion of Moses actually was. Under the circumstances we must content ourselves with establishing certain facts and some other probabilities. In the first place, it is absurd to deny that Moses was actually the founder of the Israelite commonwealth and the framer of Israel's religious system. This fact is emphasized so unanimously by tradition that it may be regarded as absolutely certain. Nowhere is there the slightest breath of doubt cast on this irrefragable fact by Israelite tradition. If we regard Zoroaster, Buddha, and Confucius as the founders of nomistic religions we cannot deny this right to Moses. In this case we are no more justified in insisting that the religion introduced by Moses was radically different from that of the Book of Exodus than we should be in trying to divorce the other higher religions which we have named from their founders. The Pentateuch reflects a series of traditions coming from circles in which the "law of Moses" was the ultimate standard. In order to determine the details of this law there had to be priests or scribes whose primary function it was to preserve and transmit them. As has recently been pointed out by S. Gandz (1935), there was a class of priests who are called by Jeremiah (2:8) "holders of the law" (*tôfesê hat-tôrah*), with name and function which remind us of the Moslem "holders" (*ḥuffâz*) of the Qur'an. In many ways the transmission of the Torah must have resembled that of the Tradition (*ḥadîth*) in Islam; the apparent lack of the validating "chain" (*isnâd*) in Israel is presumably due to the anonymity of authors and scholars there (aside from the prophets of the eighth century and later). In the course of time a great many laws and practices which can hardly have been Mosaic were introduced into Israel; their lateness is often established by comparison of the forms which they assume in JE, D, and P, which show a progressive development first adequately emphasized by Wellhausen.

There is absolute unanimity in our sources about the name given his God by Moses. The spelling *YHWH* (pronounced *Yahweh*, as we know from Greek transcriptions) is always found in prose passages in the Hebrew Bible, as well as in the Mesha Stone (ninth century) and the

* William Foxwell Albright, *From the Stone Age to Christianity*, 2nd ed. (Baltimore: Johns Hopkins Press, 1957), pp. 257–272.

Lachish Letters (cir. 589 B.C.). Beside this fuller form there was also a normally abbreviated form *Yahu* (the jussive form of the imperfect causative which appears as *Yahweh*), which is found in all early personal names (shortened in northern Israel to -*yau*- and after the Exile to -*yah*). It has often been maintained in the past thirty years that *Yahu* is more original than *Yahweh*, but all the epigraphic and linguistic facts are utterly opposed to this paradoxical view. It has also been insisted that this or that earlier non-Israelite divine name or element in a personal name shows the existence of the prototype of the Tetragrammaton before Moses. In itself this is not impossible, but every single suggestion has been effectively disproved, including the latest from Ugarit, where Virolleaud suggests that a word *yw* is identical with *Yahweh*. Unfortunately, the context does not lend itself in the least to such an interpretation, and the supposed *yw* should probably be read *yr* "offspring," which suits the context well, so far as it is preserved. It is well known today that the most plausible of the older suggestions, Accadian *yaum* in the name *Yaum-ilu*, means simply "Mine (is the god)." Many different meanings have been attributed to *Yahweh* by scholars who recognized its relative antiquity, but only one yields any suitable sense: "He causes to be." The other suggestions, "He blows, He fells, He loves, He is kindly," etc., are totally without parallel in ancient Near-Eastern onomastics. It is objected that "to cause to be" is too abstract a meaning for so early a period. This again is erroneous, since Egyptian and Accadian texts of pre-Mosaic days swarm with illustrations of this idea, beginning with the Pyramid Texts. Linguistically the form *yahweh* can only be causative, and to judge from many analogies in Babylonia, Egypt, and Canaan, it is an abbreviation of a longer name or litanic formula. A few illustrations must suffice. In Sumerian Babylonia the name *Shagan* (later *Shakkan*), belonging to the

god of animal husbandry, is an abbreviation of *Ama-shagan-gub* "He who Assists Bearing Mothers"; *Dumuzi* (later *Tammuz*) stands for *Dumu-zid-abzu*; *Asari* (a name of Marduk) represents the fuller *Asari-ludug*; *Gish* stands for *Gishbilgamesh* (later *Gilgamesh*), etc. Similar abbreviated formulae are common as divine names in later Accadian and Egyptian religion: cf. Accadian *Ašūshu-namer*, *Uṣur-amatsa*, and Egyptian *Iusas*, etc. It is, indeed, probable that many Egyptian names of gods are just as abbreviated as the names of kings and commoners are known to be in all early periods; e.g., the name *Osiris* is probably an abbreviation of the fuller *Osirisonnophris*. A most remarkable illustration comes from the Canaanite religion of the 15th century B.C., where the standing appellation of the storm-god, Baal, usually given as *Al'iyan*, appears in its full form as "I prevail (*'al'iyu*) over the champions whom I meet in the land of battle." The abbreviated name accordingly means simply "I will surely prevail." The enigmatic formula in Ex. 3:14, which in Biblical Hebrew means "I am what I am," if transposed into the form in the third person required by the causative *Yahweh*, can only become *Yahweh asher yihweh* (later *yihyeh*), "He Causes to be what Comes into Existence." Later this formula was modified, presumably because the old causative was no longer used in later Hebrew. In the dialect of Moses the formula may even have been *Yahweh zê-yihweh*, employing the *zê* which appears as a relative preposition in Canaanite and poetic Hebrew as well as in the appellation of Yahweh in Jud. 5:5, *Zê-Sinai* "the One of Sinai" (as first pointed out by H. Grimme, in accordance with widespread West-Semitic usage). If the restored formula were isolated, one would be justified despite the evidence in suspecting its correctness, but we have it again and again in Egyptian texts of the second millennium B.C.: "(a god) who causes to be (or who creates) what comes into existence" (e.g., repeatedly in the great hymn to Amun from the 15th century B.C.). Even if this view should prove to be wrong, there is ample evidence in the Bible that the Israelites had always regarded Yahweh as Creator of All.

Another original characteristic of the Israelite God was that He stood alone, without any family connections, whether consort, son, or daughter. The nearest approach to attributing a family to Him that we meet before the Exile is the term *benê El* or *benê ha-'elôhîm* "sons of God," employed for the angels, but this expression which was borrowed, as we shall see, from Canaanite does not necessarily have any more concrete meaning than does the frequent reference to the Israelites as children of God; both angels and Israelites were created by God and consequently might be poetically called His "children."

Still another equally original characteristic of Yahweh is that He is not restricted to any special abode. As the lord of all cosmic forces, controlling sun, moon, and storm but not identified with any of them, His normal dwelling-place is in heaven, from which He may come down, either to a lofty mountain like Sinai, to a shrine like the Tabernacle, or to any spot which He may choose. It is very significant that early Israelite poetry refers in only the most general terms to Mount Seir and Edom (Song of Deborah), to Teman and Mount Paran (the hymn imbedded in Habakkuk 3), to Sinai, Seir, and Paran (Deut. 33). The early Israelites laid so little stress on the exact spot that even the name of the mountain varies in our prose sources (Sinai or Horeb). This does not mean that it was not a sacred spot, but that there was no special cult associated with it, so the precise name and location were unimportant. The same situation is found in the early Christian church with reference to the location of the inn where Jesus was born and the tomb in which He was buried. The frequently stated view that Sinai must have been a volcano, a view

popularized by A. Musil and Ed. Meyer, is without any solid basis. J. Morgenstern has effectively shown that the biblical theophany of Yahweh in Ex. 19 must be explained through the Hebrew imagery connected with the Glory of Yahweh (*kebhôdh YHWH*). There is no volcano, active or extinct, in all Sinai or Midian proper. However, in adjacent regions of Hauran and Arabia there are many volcanoes which must have been active within the past few thousands of years. It is, therefore, quite possible that the sublime picture of the theophany in Exodus 19 was ultimately influenced by folk memories of volcanic eruptions (preserved in myth or metaphor), combined with more recent recollections of terrific thunder-storms in the mountains of north-western Arabia or Syria. In other words, the sublime description of the theophany may owe certain features to the two most majestic spectacles vouchsafed to mankind: a sub-tropical thunder-storm and a volcanic eruption. We cannot emphasize too strongly that the principle of skeuomorphism operates even more frequently in the world of ideas than it does in that of objects. Many ideas whose origin cannot be explained from the culture or the environment in which they are found, have been taken over from an entirely different cultural environment where they have a perfectly logical explanation.

Just as there is nothing in the Mosaic tradition which demands a derivation of Yahweh from an original volcanic deity or storm-god, so there is nothing which requires us to explain Him as a modified moon-god. It is improbable that the name *Sînai* is derived from that of Sumerian *Zen* (older *Zu-en*), Accadian *Sin*, the moon-god worshipped at Ur (in his form Nannar) and at Harran, since there is no indication that the name *Sin* was ever employed by the Canaanites or the Semitic nomads of Palestine. It is much more likely that the name *Sînai* is connected with the place-name *Sîn*, which belongs to a desert plain in Sinai as well as to a Canaanite city in Syria and perhaps to a city in the north-eastern Delta of Egypt. It has also long been recognized that it may somehow be connected with *seneh* (Aram. *sanyâ*), the name of a kind of bush where Moses is said to have first witnessed the theophany of Yahweh. The usual aetiological explanation is inadequate, though possible.

Fundamental to early Israelite religion and profoundly rooted in Mosaic tradition is the anthropomorphic conception of Yahweh. Among the Egyptians, Mesopotamians, and Canaanites we find tendencies in this direction, but the concept of deity remained fluid and subject to extraordinary variation. Without considering the primitive dynamistic and corporative elements inherent in the concept of deity in the ancient Near East, we have only to glance at the mythologies, the iconographies, and the litanies to see that Near-Eastern gods shifted in disconcerting fashion from astral form to zoomorphic, dendromorphic, and composite manifestations. Yahweh, on the other hand, is virtually always referred to in the earlier sources in a way which suggests His human form though His body was usually hidden in a refulgent envelope called His Glory (*kabhôdh*). The most drastic and at the same time the clearest and presumably the most archaic illustration is the passage Ex. 33:23, where by special grace Moses sees Yahweh's back but not His face, "for there shall no man see Me and live." In the same way He appears in the early sources as having traits of human psychology, such as capacity for love and hatred, joy and sorrow, revenge and remorse, though always on a heroic plane.

There has been a great deal of futile writing about the anthropomorphism of early Israel. First of all, we must be very cautious in using material from the stories of Genesis 1-11, since most of this goes back to the Patriarchal Age, sometimes perhaps in its very wording (e.g., Gen.

6:1-4). To be sure, some of these stories are more recent and they have nearly all been more or less influenced by later monotheistic conceptions (so for example in the Story of the Flood when compared with the cuneiform version). Similarly, we must be careful not to make uncritical deductions as to Mosaic or later Israelite religion from the narratives of the Patriarchs (Gen. 12-50), most of which come down, as we have seen, in substantially their present form from pre-Mosaic days. Thus the appearances of God in Gen. 18-19 are to be explained from pre-Mosaic polytheism, though the narratives have been revised in such a way as not to offend later Israelite, or for that matter Jewish or Christian readers.

Secondly, it cannot be emphasized too strongly that the anthropomorphic conception of Yahweh was absolutely necessary if the God of Israel was to remain a God of the individual Israelite as well as of the people as a whole. For the limited few who are natural mystics or have learned to employ certain methods to attain ecstatic state, the theological concepts attached to deity matter relatively little; there is a striking parallelism between the psychology of mysticism in Judaism, Islam, Buddhism, and Christianity. For the average worshipper, however, it is very essential that his god be a divinity who can sympathize with his human feelings and emotions, a being whom he can love and fear alternately, and to whom he can transfer the holiest emotions connected with memories of father and mother and friend. In other words, it was precisely the anthropomorphism of Yahweh which was essential to the initial success of Israel's religion. Like man at his noblest the God of Israel might be in form and affective reactions, but there was in Him none of the human frailties that make the Olympian deities of Greece such charming poetic figures and such unedifying examples. All the human characteristics of Israel's deity were exalted; they were projected against a cosmic screen and they served to interpret the cosmic process as the expression of God's creative word and eternally active will.

Equally vital to Mosaic religion was the aniconic character of Yahweh, who could not be represented in any visual or tangible form. In spite of the unanimous testimony of Israelite tradition, scholars have made repeated efforts to prove the existence of representations of deity in early Israel. Every effort of this kind has been based on subjective arguments and on arbitrary assumptions which have won only the most limited acceptance even in friendly circles. Of course, it would be equally unscholarly to deny the *possibility* of such images or portrayals in material form. But the testimony of our written sources, plus the completely negative results of excavation, should be evidence enough to prove that Yahwism was essentially aniconic and that material representations were foreign to its spirit from the beginning. We shall show below that there is no basis whatever for the idea that Yahweh was worshipped in bull form by the northern tribes at Bethel and Dan. The golden calf simply formed the pedestal on which the invisible Yahweh stood, just as in the Temple of Solomon the invisible Glory of God was enthroned above the cherubim; conceptually the two ideas are virtually identical.

After the demonstration by R. Hartmann and especially by H. Lammens of nomadic Arab parallels to the portable Tabernacle and Ark of the Covenant, some of them going far back into pre-Islamic times, it is captious to refuse them Mosaic date, since they were completely foreign to sedentary Canaanite practice and since they are known to have persisted for some time after the Conquest of Palestine. The archaeologist no longer has any difficulty in proving the antiquity of many details in the description which is given in the Priestly Code.

The uniform testimony of our sources with respect to the existence of some kind of sacrificial ritual in earliest Israel can hardly be erroneous, though the constant reaction of the prophets against the formalism and externality of sacrificial cult hardly suggests that undue emphasis was laid upon it in the Mosaic system. The sacrifice of domesticated animals, such as cattle, sheep, goats, and doves, goes back to hoary antiquity and was common to all Western-Asiatic religions from the third millennium B.C. on down; it might thus have passed into Israelite religion in the Mosaic period or later, with numerous other elements borrowed from the sedentary peoples of Palestine. However the part played by animal sacrifice in Semitic religion was so vital that it may be doubted whether Moses could have omitted it from his system without seriously weakening its appeal to worshippers. Among the Semites of antiquity sacrifice was a means of bringing gifts to the deity and of paying him homage which was valid both for a single worshipper and for a group; it served to solemnize every important occasion in the life of a group; and as shown by Bertholet it brought the deity into dynamistic relationship to his worshippers, who became united in flesh and spirit with him by jointly partaking of the sacrificial flesh. Both the substitutional sacrifice, where an animal replaced a more primitive human sacrifice, and the ceremony of the scapegoat (found also in related form in Mesopotamia) emphasized a vital religious concept, that of vicarious atonement for moral transgressions which would otherwise have to be physically expiated by the people.

The problem of the origin of the ethical, civil, and ceremonial laws attributed in later Israel to Moses has been profoundly affected by the appearance of A. Alt's monograph, *Die Ursprünge des israelitischen Rechts* (1934). In this epochal study the gifted Leipzig scholar has distinguished sharply between two main types of pentateuchal legislation: apodictic law and casuistic law. The latter is found primarily in the Book of the Covenant (Ex. 21-23), which is a fragmentary legal code of the same class as the Code of Hammurabi (cir. 1700 B.C.), the Hittite Laws (cir. 14th century B.C.) and the Assyrian laws (12th century B.C.). All these codes go back in their basic formulation (provided that . . . then) to the Sumerian jurisprudence of the third millennium. The Book of the Covenant represents the form which the more-or-less common corpus of older customary laws and court decisions took under the special conditions existing in Canaan, and it may have passed into Israelite hands during the period of the Judges. In the form which it takes in the Book of the Covenant it can hardly be dated before the ninth century. However, it is unlikely that the ninth-century form differed much from its Northwest-Semitic prototype many centuries earlier, in view of numerous archaisms in practice and terminology which have older Mesopotamian parallels. The formulation and spirit of the apodictic laws are unique and original in Israel; those of the casuistic laws are at home throughout Western Asia. Besides the Ten Commandments, which best illustrate the spirit of the apodictic laws, we have many other examples, such as the old list of curses imbedded in Deut. 27 and miscellaneous warnings that certain sins must be punished by death, in different parts of the Pentateuch. The most striking thing about the apodictic laws is their categorical character, which stands in sharp contrast to their nearest extra-Israelite parallels, the Egyptian Negative Confession and the Babylonian *Shurpu*; the Israelites are commanded *not* to commit sin, *because Yahweh so wills*.

Of course, we cannot say how many of the apodictic laws actually emanate directly from Moses, but the fact that they cannot be paralleled in this form outside of Israel and that they were believed by different schools of traditional thought in Israel to go back to the time of Moses is sufficient indication that they are in accord with the movement which bears his name. Again we must stress the fact that oral transmission of tradition is inherently more consistent and logical in its results than written transmission, since it sifts and refines, modifying whatever does not fit into the spirit of the main body of tradition . . . In general it subjects detail to mass scrutiny instead of to the examination of a few who may be mentally superior but who are bound to deviate more frequently from accepted standards. The apodictic law of Israel was not so refined nor so all-inclusive as the Negative Confession of the Egyptians about 1500 B.C., nor did it lay so much stress on social solidarity as the Babylonian *Shurpu* of somewhat later date; on the other hand, it reflects a much more advanced standard of conduct in many respects. Vicious religious customs, such as child sacrifice, necromancy, and sodomy (which formed part of certain religious ceremonies in the ancient Near East), are forbidden; work on the sabbath, which endangered the physical and mental health of workers (as we know from the recent experience of occidental nations), was prohibited; the worship of all gods save Yahweh and the careless use of His name were banned. As Alt has pointed out, there is nothing in this legislation that conflicts with conditions in Israel under Moses. In this respect it is very different from the Book of the Covenant, which presupposes organized sedentary society. As he has shown, an independent and very important testimony to the antiquity of the apodictic code is provided by the fact that it was annually recited in connection with the Feast of Tabernacles at Shechem.

Having sketched the certain or probable content of the Mosaic system, let us consider possible sources of its teaching. That it was a true "teaching" (*doctrina*, in the empirical, not in the philosophical sense, of course) may be considered as virtually certain, in view of its traditional name *tôrah*, its traditional content, and the fact that the slightly earlier system of Akhenaten was also known as the "teaching" (sbâyet). Since Moses bore an Egyptian name and according to tradition had reached a place of considerable social importance in Egypt in his early life, his original tôrah may well have contained Egyptian elements which later disappeared before the impact of native Hebrew conceptions. Some of these elements seem still to persist, though we cannot be absolutely sure of any one case, owing to the absence of direct documentation or of complex borrowings from Egyptian sources. Among such possible Egyptian influences may be mentioned: 1. The concept of the god who is sole creator of everything and the formula from which his name, Yahweh, was derived (cf. Amun-Re' and his litany in the New Empire); 2. The concept of a single god and the establishment of a doctrine based on monotheism (cf. the Aten); 3. Recognition of the necessarily international, cosmic dominion of the reigning deity (cf. Sutekh-Baal under the early Ramessides). On the negative side it is clear that the religion of Israel revolted against virtually every external aspect of Egyptian religion, including the complex and grotesque iconography, the dominion of daily life in the Nineteenth Dynasty by magic, the materialistic absorption in preparing for a selfish existence in the hereafter.

Turning to assess the influence exerted by native Hebrew religion on Moses, we are faced with the difficulty of determining just what the latter accepted and what was introduced into Yahwism after his death from the older Hebrew stock. Leaving the second alternative aside for the moment, since it has been partly stressed above and will be emphasized again in other respects below, we can distinguish a number of clear Hebrew factors—and they are what gave Yahwism much of its vital power over the hearts and minds of Israel: 1. The close association between god and worshipper(s), illustrated by the giving of personal names

and by sacrificial rites; 2. The contractual relationship between the deity of a tribe and his people, as illustrated by the constant use of the word berîth "covenant," in early Israel (specific forms of this contractual relationship may be later); 3. The association of terrestrial manifestations of deity with storms and mountains, and the identification of Yahweh with Shaddai, "The One of the Mountain(s)"; the adoption of the stories of the Fathers as part of Israel's inheritance, and the identification of Yahweh with the God of the Fathers; specific appellations of deity and perhaps the nucleus of the cosmogony of Genesis, though the latter may again have been developed later from the native stock of myths and legends.

There is no clear trace of any West-Semitic influence of characteristically Canaanite type on the earliest religion of Israel. After the occupation of Palestine, however, this influence became more and more significant . . . How remote early Hebrew tradition was from Canaanite influences may be illustrated by the total absence from it of any story of the conflict between the creator and the dragon at the beginning of world-history. After the seventh century B.C. we find such references becoming more and more frequent and the myth of the victory of Yahweh over Leviathan ultimately obtained wide popularity in rabbinic literature.

In bringing this chapter to a close we have yet one question to answer: Was Moses a true monotheist? If by "monotheist" is meant a thinker with views specifically like those of Philo Judaeus or Rabbi Aqiba, of St. Paul or St. Augustine, of Mohammed or Maimonides, of St. Thomas or Calvin, of Mordecai Kaplan or H. N. Wieman, Moses was not one. If, on the other hand, the term "monotheist" means one who teaches the existence of only one God, the creator of everything, the source of justice, who is equally powerful in Egypt, in the desert, and in

Palestine, who has no sexuality and no mythology, who is human in form but cannot be seen by human eye and cannot be represented in any form—then the founder of Yahwism was certainly a monotheist.

5. THE GOD OF THE PROPHETS*

42

5 Thus says God, the LORD,
who created the heavens and stretched them out,
who spread forth the earth and what comes from it,
who gives breath to the people upon it and spirit to those who walk in it:
6 "I am the LORD, I have called you in righteousness,
I have taken you by the hand and kept you;
I have given you as a covenant to the people,
a light to the nations,
7 to open the eyes that are blind,
to bring out the prisoners from the dungeon,
from the prison those who sit in darkness.
8 I am the LORD, that is my name;
my glory I give to no other,
nor my praise to graven images.
9 Behold, the former things have come to pass,
and new things I now declare;
before they spring forth
I tell you of them."

* * *

44

6 Thus says the LORD, the King of Israel and his Redeemer, the LORD of hosts:
"I am the first and I am the last;
besides me there is no god.
7 Who is like me? Let him proclaim it,
let him declare and set it forth before me.

Who has announced from of old the things to come?
Let them tell us what is yet to be.
8 Fear not, nor be afraid;
have I not told you from of old and declared it?
And you are my witnesses!
Is there a God besides me?
There is no Rock; I know not any."

9 All who make idols are nothing, and the things they delight in do not profit; their witnesses neither see nor know, that they may be put to shame. 10 Who fashions a god or casts an image, that is profitable for nothing? 11 Behold, all his fellows shall be put to shame, and the craftsmen are but men; let them all assemble, let them stand forth, they shall be terrified, they shall be put to shame together.

12 The ironsmith fashions it and works it over the coals; he shapes it with hammers and forges it with his strong arm; he becomes hungry and his strength fails, he drinks no water and is faint. 13 The carpenter stretches a line, he marks it out with a pencil; he fashions it with planes, and marks it with a compass; he shapes it into the figure of a man, with the beauty of a man, to dwell in a house. 14 He cuts down cedars; or he chooses a holm tree or an oak and lets it grow strong among the trees of the forest; he plants a cedar and the rain nourishes it. 15 Then it becomes fuel for a man; he takes a part of it and warms himself, he kindles a fire and bakes bread; also he makes a god and worships it, he makes it a graven image and falls down before it. 16 Half of it he burns in the fire; over the half he eats flesh, he roasts meat and is satisfied; also he warms himself and says,

---

* Isaiah 42.5–9; 44.6–20; 45.18–46.11; 49. Revised Standard Version.

"Aha, I am warm, I have seen the fire!"
17 And the rest of it he makes into a god,
his idol; and falls down to it and worships
it; he prays to it and says, "Deliver me, for
thou art my god!"

18 They know not, nor do they discern;
for he has shut their eyes, so that they cannot see, and their minds, so that they
cannot understand. 19 No one considers,
nor is there knowledge or discernment to
say, Half of it I burned in the fire, I also
baked bread on its coals, I roasted flesh
and have eaten; and shall I make the resi-
due of it an abomination? Shall I fall down
before a block of wood? 20 He feeds on
ashes; a deluded mind has led him astray,
and he cannot deliver himself or say, "Is
there not a lie in my right hand?"

*   *   *

45

18 For thus says the LORD,
who created the heavens
(he is God!),
who formed the earth and made it
(he established it;
he did not create it a chaos,
he formed it to be inhabited!):
"I am the LORD, and there is no other.
19 I did not speak in secret,
in a land of darkness;
I did not say to the offspring of Jacob,
'Seek me in chaos.'
I the LORD speak the truth,
I declare what is right.

20 "Assemble yourselves and come,
draw near together,
you survivors of the nations!
They have no knowledge
who carry about their wooden idols,
and keep on praying to a god
that cannot save.
21 Declare and present your case;
let them take counsel together!
Who told this long ago?
Who declared it of old?

Was it not I, the LORD?
And there is no other god besides
me,
a righteous God and a Savior;
there is none besides me.

22 "Turn to me and be saved,
all the ends of the earth!
For I am God, and there is no other.
23 By myself I have sworn,
from my mouth has gone forth in
righteousness
a word that shall not return:
'To me every knee shall bow,
every tongue shall swear.'
24 "Only in the LORD, it shall be said of
me,
are righteousness and strength;
to him shall come and be ashamed,
all who were incensed against him.
25 In the LORD all the offspring of Israel
shall triumph and glory."

46

Bel bows down, Nebo stoops,
their idol are on beasts and cattle;
these things you carry are loaded
as burdens on weary beasts.
2 They stoop, they bow down together,
they cannot save the burden,
but themselves go into captivity.

3 "Hearken to me, O house of Jacob,
all the remnant of the house of Israel,
who have been borne by me from your
birth,
carried from the womb;
4 even to your old age I am He,
and to gray hairs I will carry you.
I have made, and I will bear;
I will carry and will save.

5 "To whom will you liken me and make
me equal,
and compare me, that we may be
alike?
6 Those who lavish gold from the purse,
and weigh out silver in the scales,

hire a goldsmith, and he makes it into
 a god;
then they fall down and worship!
7 They lift it upon their shoulders, they
 carry it,
 they set it in its place, and it stands
 there;
 it cannot move from its place.
If one cries to it, it does not answer
 or save him from his trouble.

8 "Remember this and consider,
 recall it to mind, you transgressors,
9 remember the former things of old;
for I am God, and there is no other,
 I am God, and there is none like me,
10 declaring the end from the beginning
 and from ancient times things not yet
 done,
saying, 'My counsel shall stand,
 and I will accomplish all my purpose,'
11 calling a bird of prey from the east,
 the man of my counsel from a far
 country.
I have spoken, and I will bring it to
 pass;
I have purposed, and I will do it.

* * *

49

Listen to me, O coastlands,
 and hearken, you peoples from afar.
The LORD called me from the womb,
 from the body of my mother he named
 my name.
2 He made my mouth like a sharp sword,
 in the shadow of his hand he hid
 me;
he made me a polished arrow,
 in his quiver he hid me away.
3 And he said to me, "You are my servant,
 Israel, in whom I will be glorified."
4 But I said, "I have labored in vain,
 I have spent my strength for nothing
 and vanity;
yet surely my right is with the LORD,
 and my recompense with my God."

5 And now the LORD says,
 who formed me from the womb to be
 his servant,
to bring Jacob back to him,
 and that Israel might be gathered to
 him,
for I am honored in the eyes of the
 LORD,
 and my God has become my
 strength—
6 he says:
"It is too light a thing that you should be
 my servant
 to raise up the tribes of Jacob
 and to restore the preserved of Israel;
I will give you as a light to the nations,
 that my salvation may reach to the end
 of the earth."

7 Thus says the LORD,
 the Redeemer of Israel and his Holy
 One,
to one deeply despised, abhorred by the
 nations,
 the servant of rulers:
"Kings shall see and arise;
 princes, and they shall prostrate themselves;
because of the LORD, who is faithful,
 the Holy One of Israel, who has
 chosen you."

8 Thus says the LORD:
"In a time of favor I have answered you,
 in a day of salvation I have helped you;
I have kept you and given you
 as a covenant to the people,
to establish the land,
 to apportion the desolate heritages;
9 saying to the prisoners, 'Come forth,'
 to those who are in darkness, 'Appear.'
They shall feed along the ways,
 on all bare heights shall be their pasture;
10 they shall not hunger or thirst,
 neither scorching wind nor sun shall
 smite them,

for he who has pity on them will lead
them,
and by springs of water will guide
them.
11 And I will make all my mountains a way,
and my highways shall be raised up.
12 Lo, these shall come from afar,
and lo, these from the north and from
the west,
and these from the land of Syene."
13 Sing for joy, O heavens, and exult, O
earth;
break forth, O mountains, into singing!
For the LORD has comforted his people,
and will have compassion on his
afflicted.

14 But Zion said, "The LORD has forsaken
me,
my Lord has forgotten me."
15 "Can a woman forget her sucking child,
that she should have no compassion
on the son of her womb?"
Even these may forget,
yet I will not forget you.
16 Behold, I have graven you on the
palms of my hands;
your walls are continually before me.
17 Your builders outstrip your destroyers,
and those who laid you waste go forth
from you.
18 Lift up your eyes round about and see;
they all gather, they come to you.
As I live, says the LORD,
you shall put them all on as an ornament,
you shall bind them on as a bride does.

19 "Surely your waste and your desolate
places
and your devastated land—
surely now you will be too narrow for
your inhabitants,
and those who swallowed you up will
be far away.
20 The children born in the time of your
bereavement

will yet say in your ears:
'The place is too narrow for me;
make room for me to dwell in.'
21 Then you will say in your heart:
'Who has borne me these?
I was bereaved and barren,
exiled and put away,
but who has brought up these?
Behold, I was left alone;
whence then have these come?'"

22 Thus says the Lord GOD:
"Behold, I will lift up my hand to the
nations,
and raise my signal to the peoples;
and they shall bring your sons in their
bosom,
and your daughters shall be carried on
their shoulders.
23 Kings shall be your foster fathers,
and their queens your nursing
mother.
With their faces to the ground they
shall bow down to you,
and lick the dust of your feet.
Then you will know that I am the LORD;
those who wait for me shall not be put
to shame."

24 Can the prey be taken from the mighty,
or the captives of a tyrant be rescued?
25 Surely, thus says the LORD:
"Even the captives of the mighty shall
be taken,
and the prey of the tyrant be rescued,
for I will contend with those who contend with you,
and I will save your children.
26 I will make your oppressors eat their
own flesh,
and they shall be drunk with their
own blood as with wine.
Then all flesh shall know
that I am the LORD your Savior,
and your Redeemer, the Mighty One
of Jacob."

6. The Prophets and Monotheism*

Among critical scholars today there is none who claims real monotheism for anyone earlier than Moses; but there are a number who claim this for Moses, and of these Albright is unquestionably the most outstanding. Unfortunately he has not presented his argument at any length. He discusses the matter briefly in his *Archaeology of Palestine and the Bible* (pp. 163-167), and in a recent article in *The American Scholar* (Spring, 1938, pp. 186 f.), entitled "Archaeology Confronts Biblical Criticism." In that article he says, "The only time in the history of the ancient Near East when we find monotheism in the leading cultural centers, Egypt and Babylonia, is about the fourteenth century B.C.; it is also then that we find the closest approach to monotheism in Syria and Asia Minor. Since it is now an historical commonplace that we find similar ideas emerging simultaneously in different parts of a given cultural continuum, we should expect to find Israelite monotheism somehow emerging about that time"—viz., in the time of Moses, according to Albright. The argument is most unconvincing, and the statement can be challenged at a number of points. There was no great, onrushing movement toward monotheism in the Near East in the fourteenth century, such as Albright affirms. There is no evidence that Syria and Asia Minor were more monotheistic then than at any other period. The texts from Asia Minor do not show this, nor do the Ras Shamra texts, to which Albright apparently has reference. El may have been a great High God to the people of Ras Shamra, but along with him were hosts of other deities, many of them little less important than he. The Babylonians and Assyrians never became real monotheists, and were no more monotheistic in the fourteenth century than they

were later. As a matter of fact they were less so, because the texts over the following centuries show an ever-growing tendency to emphasize one god to the exclusion of the others, or through the absorption of the others, so that the most monotheistic of the texts date considerably after the fourteenth century. The only real monotheist in the ancient Near East was Ikhnaton of Egypt (and some scholars question this), and he had no great following. What following he got was obtained by force, and he made so little impression upon his own people that his religion was stamped out as a vicious heresy immediately following his death after a brief reign of only eighteen years. Instead of helping the cause of monotheism Ikhnaton killed it by bringing the Egyptian movement toward monotheism to a head too soon, by making too great a break with the old religion, by resorting to force to establish his religion, and by dying too soon, leaving no proper successor to carry on his work. If Ikhnaton was not able to impress his own people in his own life-time, it is surely unthinkable that he was able after his death to impress an alien like Moses, particularly so when Moses lived, as Albright believes, in the period of bitter reaction against Ikhnaton.

However, even though Moses and his people were surrounded on every side by the most monotheistic of peoples, it would not follow at all that they would necessarily become monotheistic themselves, nor is there a necessary presumption to that effect. In contrast with the tiny flicker of monotheism which momentarily developed in Egypt's religion in the time of Ikhnaton, is the dominating role of the resurrection idea throughout her whole history, and yet this idea, which had everything in favor of its adoption, made no impression whatsoever on the Hebrews or any others of the ancient Near East. It is one of the enigmas of history that the Hebrews were

* Theophile J. Meek, *op. cit.*, pp. 298–303.

so little affected by the culture of Egypt, when both history and archeology show such intimate contacts between the two. Albright protests that "the history of religion in Israel was not a microcosmic reflection of the evolution of religion in world-history; it was just as homogeneous and as much an organic entity as the history of religion in Egypt, in Babylonia, or in ancient Rome," and yet he would derive Israel's monotheism from a hypothetical world movement instead of having it grow out of its own roots in Israel, in and out of its own environment, influenced no doubt by world thought, but largely independent of it—a monotheism that became the religion, not of a single man or a few religionists, but of a whole people, and a monotheism that was strictly monotheistic, as the others, with the possible exception of Ikhnaton's, were not. Albright protests against giving a unitarian definition to the word "monotheism," but, as we have already indicated, the only acceptable use of the word is in its dictionary sense, and it is Albright and his kind, rather than his opponents, as he affirms, who are "highly misleading" when they read into the word a meaning that it cannot and should not bear.

We heartily endorse Albright's dictum that "the history of Yahwism in Israel, north and south, becomes unintelligible unless we accept the clear evidence of Israelite tradition"; but Israelite tradition nowhere says or indicates that Moses was a monotheist—not even in Albright's sense of the word. Since we have no autobiography of Moses, it is impossible to say with certainty what he did or did not believe. At best the Old Testament account can only be credited with general and not with detailed accuracy, and in that account the most explicit statement on the subject attributed to Moses is the first command in the Decalogue. Even though we grant the Mosaic authorship of this command, the most that we can claim for Moses in it is henotheism. Neither here nor anywhere

else does he deny the existence of gods other than Yahweh. Even Professor E. O. James, who is an anthropologist as well as an Old Testament scholar, and has decided leanings toward the theory of primitive monotheism, has to acknowledge that the command asserts nothing more than monolatry and not pure monotheism, and so conservative a churchman as the late Bishop Gore has to concede that it neither proves nor disproves either monolatry or monotheism. The command reads literally: "Since I, Yahweh, am your god who brought you out of the land of Egypt, out of a state of slavery, there must not be to you any other gods against my face," the last phrase of which, 'al-pānay, "against my face," is most uncertain in meaning. It may mean "in my presence," or "on an equality with me," or "alongside of me," or "to my disadvantage," or "in addition to me," or even "in defiance of me," as most recently suggested, but no meaning that anyone has yet suggested indicates anything other than henotheism or monolatry. As a matter of fact, the meaning of the command is too uncertain to permit its use as a proof-text of monotheism or henotheism or anything else.

Another statement attributed to Moses, but questionably so, is Deut. 6:4, which is usually translated, "Hear, O Israel; Yahweh, our God, is one Yahweh," whatever that may mean. If it makes any sense at all, it seems to mean that there was only one Yahweh and not many, as there were of the Baals; but grammar and syntax both indicate that the popular translation is wrong, the correct rendering being, "Hear, O Israel; Yahweh is our God, Yahweh alone." Again there is nothing to suggest anything more than henotheism.

Albright protests that "it is singularly lacking in historic logic to insist that because we find undoubted indications of henotheism in the traditions of early Israel all Israelites must have been henotheists"; but unless we have evidence that some were monotheists we cannot affirm it. Outside of Deut. 4:35, 39 and 32:39, there is absolutely nothing in all the reputed sayings of Moses to indicate that he was a monotheist, and no modern scholar would regard these passages as genuinely Mosaic. On the other hand, there is much to indicate that Moses was not a monotheist. Over and over again in the records of the work of Moses and his time, late though the records are, the Hebrews are represented as Yahweh's peculiar people, just as the Moabites are represented as the peculiar people of Chemosh. Take, for example, a passage as late as Judges 11:24, "Should you not occupy the territory of those whom Chemosh, your own god, drives out, while we occupy that of all those whom Yahweh, our God, has driven out of our way?" Yahweh and Chemosh are here represented on an absolute equality, and the reality and power of Chemosh here and elsewhere are no more doubted than those of Yahweh himself. Usually, however, inborn pride in one's own, common to all peoples, caused Yahweh to be represented as greater than the other gods, as, for example, in Exod. 15:11:

Who is like thee among the gods, O Yahweh?
Who is there like thee, so glorious in holiness,
So awe-inspiring in renown, such a wonder worker?

Or Deut 3:24:

O lord Yahweh, thou hast only begun to show thy servant thy greatness and thy mighty power; for what god is there in the heavens or on the earth who can do such deeds and mighty acts as thine?

However, this is nothing but flattery, quite after the order of that which we find in all polytheistic literature, as, for example, in the early Vedic or Egyptian hymns.

Once Yahweh is represented as a great High God assigning to the different peoples their deities, viz. in Deut. 4:19:

Beware, when you lift your eyes to the heavens and see all the host of the heavens, the sun, the moon, and the stars, that you do not let yourself be allured into paying homage to them and serving them, whom Yahweh, your God, has allotted to all the peoples everywhere under the heavens.

In another passage, Deut. 32:8 f., Elyon seems to be the great High God, with Yahweh subsidiary to him:

When Elyon gave heritages to the nations,
When he made divisions among mankind,
He assigned the realms of the nations
To the various deities;
And Yahweh's apportionment was his people,
Jacob, the allotment for him to receive.

As I have tried to show in my *Hebrew Origins* (pp. 35, 193), the new thing that came with Moses was not the worship of Yahweh to the exclusion of all other gods, but the exaltation of Yahweh above the other tribal gods and the united allegiance of the several tribes to him as their confederate god, Yahweh being to the confederacy as a whole what the tribal god was to the tribe. Moses organized his followers into a confederacy or amphictyony, and he made the old tribal god Yahweh the god of the amphictyony, and in his name made a covenant with the people. This was henotheism and not monotheism. It was the selection of one god out of many for exclusive worship by a particular group as a group, and such theological particularism, as always, was the inevitable outgrowth and accompaniment of a political particularism, a movement toward nationalism. As Principal Graham has well said in answer to Albright, "Modes of theological thought never establish themselves as disembodied ideologies. They develop along with, and inside of, corresponding institutional structures." In the words of Breasted, "Monotheism is but imperialism in religion," and a world dominion, a world concept is the necessary prerequisite to the idea of a world god. In the time of Moses the Hebrews were just getting their first lessons in nationalism and could not possibly reach up to a world concept or a world god. Moses unquestionably sowed the seeds of monotheism, but the real fruitage did not come until centuries later, in the time of Deuteronomy, Jeremiah, and Second Isaiah, who were the first to claim Yahweh as the one and only god of the world and not of the Hebrews alone (Deut. 4:35, 39; 32:39; Jer. 5:7; 10:2 ff.; 16:20; Isa. 41:21 ff.; 44:9 ff.).

SECTION IV

Greece and the Aegean in the Bronze Age

In 1876 Heinrich Schliemann discovered the grave circle at Mycenae. In 1900 Sir Arthur Evans excavated the palace complex at Cnossus. These two pivotal discoveries marked the beginning of the long, difficult, and as yet uncompleted unravelling of Greek prehistory. One of the most debated questions arising from the archaeological revelations was that of the relationship between Crete and the mainland in the Late Bronze Age (*ca.* 1550–1100 B.C.). Evans postulated a Cretan or Minoan control over the mainland based on a great navy and an unquestioned control of the sea, that is, a thalassocracy. Others, led by A. J. B. Wace, argued that the situation was quite different: that it was the mainland which dominated Crete. The most recent development has been the apparent decipherment of the Linear B script found on clay tablets at Cnossus and on the mainland during this period. There are still many problems connected with the decipherment and some scholars remain unconvinced, but the majority opinion is that Michael Ventris indeed deciphered the script and that its language is Greek. The evidence of the tablets, therefore, has become an element in the debate.

In the last decade the archaeological evidence for the Palace at Cnossus, the cornerstone of Aegean chronology has been called into question, raising new questions and provoking new theories. Most recently excavations on the island of Santorini, ancient Thera, have given evidence of a great earthquake, possibly during the Bronze Age, which may have affected the rise and fall of Aegean civilizations.

1. THESEUS AND MINOS*

The richest source of legendary material about Minos is the story of Theseus and the slaying of the Minotaur. It is fully related by Plutarch, a Greek biographer of the second century of the Christian era.

Not long after arrived the third time from Crete the collectors of the tribute

which the Athenians paid them upon the following occasion. Androgeus having been treacherously murdered in the confines of Attica, not only Minos, his father,

---

* Plutarch, *Theseus*, 15–19, translated by John Dryden.

put the Athenians to extreme distress by a perpetual war, but the gods also laid waste their country; both famine and pestilence lay heavy upon them, and even their rivers were dried up. Being told by the oracle that, if they appeased and reconciled Minos, the anger of the gods would cease and they should enjoy rest from the miseries they laboured under, they sent heralds, and with much supplication were at last reconciled, entering into an agreement to send to Crete every nine years a tribute of seven young men and as many virgins, as most writers agree in stating; and the most poetical story adds, that the Minotaur destroyed them, or that, wandering in the labyrinth, and finding no possible means of getting out, they miserably ended their lives there; and that this Minotaur was (as Euripides hath it)—

"A mingled form where two strange shapes combined,
And different natures, bull and man, were joined."

But Philochorus says that the Cretans will by no means allow the truth of this, but say that the labyrinth was only an ordinary prison, having no other bad quality but that it secured the prisoners from escaping, and that Minos, having instituted games in honour of Androgeus, gave, as a reward to the victors, these youths, who in the meantime were kept in the labyrinth; and that the first that overcame in those games was one of the greatest powers and command among them, named Taurus, a man of no merciful or gentle disposition, who treated the Athenians that were made his prize in a proud and cruel manner. Also Aristotle himself, in the account that he gives of the form of government of the Bottiæans, is manifestly of opinion that the youths were not slain by Minos, but spent the remainder of their days in slavery in Crete; that the Cretans, in former times, to acquit themselves of an ancient vow which they had made, were used to send an offering of the first-fruits of their men to Delphi,

and that some descendants of these Athenian slaves were mingled with them and sent amongst them, and, unable to get their living there, removed from thence, first into Italy, and settled about Japygia; from thence again, that they removed to Thrace, and were named Bottiæans; and that this is the reason why, in a certain sacrifice, the Bottiæan girls sing a hymn beginning *Let us go to Athens*. This may show us how dangerous it is to incur the hostility of a city that is mistress of eloquence and song. For Minos was always ill spoken of, and represented ever as a very wicked man, in the Athenian theatres; neither did Hesiod avail him by calling him "the most royal Minos," nor Homer, who styles him "*Jupiter's familiar friend*;" the tragedians got the better, and from the vantage ground of the stage showered down obloquy upon him, as a man of cruelty and violence; whereas, in fact, he appears to have been a king and a law-giver, and Rhadamanthus, a judge under him, administering the statutes that he ordained.

Now, when the time of the third tribute was come, and the fathers who had any young men for their sons were to proceed by lot to the choice of those that were to be sent, there arose fresh discontents and accusations against Ægeus among the people, who were full of grief and indignation that he who was the cause of all their miseries was the only person exempt from the punishment; adopting and settling his kingdom upon a bastard and foreign son, he took no thought, they said, of their destitution and loss, not of bastards, but lawful children. These things sensibly affected Theseus, who, thinking it but just not to disregard, but rather partake of, the sufferings of his fellow-citizens, offered himself for one without any lot. All else were struck with admiration for the nobleness and with love for the goodness of the act; and Ægeus, after prayers and entreaties, finding him inflexible and not to be persuaded, proceeded to the choosing of the rest by lot. Hellanicus, however, tells us that the Athenians did not send the young men and virgins by lot, but that Minos himself used to come and make his own choice, and pitched upon Theseus before all others; according to the conditions agreed upon between them, namely, that the Athenians should furnish them with a ship and that the young men that were to sail with him should carry no weapons of war; but that if the Minotaur was destroyed, the tribute should cease.

On the two former occasions of the payment of the tribute, entertaining no hopes of safety or return, they sent out the ship with a black sail, as to unavoidable destruction; but now, Theseus encouraging his father, and speaking greatly of himself, as confident that he should kill the Minotaur, he gave the pilot another sail, which was white, commanding him, as he returned, if Theseus were safe, to make use of that; but if not, to sail with the black one, and to hang out that sign of his misfortune. . . .

* * *

When he arrived at Crete, as most of the ancient historians as well as poets tell us, having a clue of thread given him by Ariadne, who had fallen in love with him, and being instructed by her how to use it so as to conduct him through the windings of the labyrinth, he escaped out of it and slew the Minotaur, and sailed back, taking along with him Ariadne and the young Athenian captives. Phercydes adds that he bored holes in the bottom of the Cretan ships to hinder their pursuit. Demon writes that Taurus, the chief captain of Minos, was slain by Theseus at the mouth of the port, in a naval combat as he was sailing out for Athens. But Philochorus gives us the story thus: That at the setting forth of the yearly games by King Minos, Taurus was expected to carry away the prize, as he had done before; and was much grudged the honour. His character and manners made his power hateful, and he was accused moreover of too near familiarity with Pasiphae, for which reason, when Theseus desired the combat, Minos readily complied. And as it was a custom in Crete that the women also should be admitted to the sight of these games, Ariadne, being present, was struck with admiration of the manly beauty of Theseus, and the vigour and address which he showed in the combat, overcoming all that encountered with him. Minos, too, being extremely pleased with him, especially because he had overthrown and disgraced Taurus, voluntarily gave up the young captives to Theseus, and remitted the tribute to the Athenians. Clidemus gives an account peculiar to himself, very ambitiously, and beginning a great way back: That it was a decree consented to by all Greece, that no vessel from any place, containing above five persons, should be permitted to sail, Jason only excepted, who was made captain of the great ship Argo, to sail about and scour the sea of pirates. But Dædalus having escaped from Crete, and flying by sea to Athens, Minos, contrary to this decree, pursued him with his ships of war, was forced by a storm upon Sicily, and there ended his life. After his decease, Deucalion, his son, desiring a quarrel with the Athenians, sent to them, demanding that they should deliver up Dædalus to him, threatening upon their refusal, to put to death all the young Athenians whom his father had received as hostages from the city. To this angry message Theseus returned a very gentle answer excusing himself that he could not deliver up Dædalus, who was nearly related to him, being his cousin-german, his mother being Merope, the daughter of Erechtheus. In the meanwhile he secretly prepared a navy, part of it at home near the village of the Thymœtadæ, a place of no resort, and far from any common roads, the other part by his grandfather Pittheus's means at Trœzen, that so his design might be carried on with the greatest secrecy. As soon as ever his fleet was in readiness, he set sail, having with him Dædalus and other exiles from Crete for his guides; and none of the Cretans having any knowledge of his coming, but imagining when they saw his fleet that they were friends and vessels of their own, he soon made himself master of the port, and immediately making a descent, reached Cnossus before any notice of his coming, and, in a battle before the gates of the labyrinth, put Deucalion and all his guards to the sword. The government by his means falling to Ariadne, he made a league with her, and received the captives of her, and ratified a perpetual friendship between the Athenians and the Cretans, whom he engaged under an oath never again to commence any war with Athens.

* * *

Now Theseus, in his return from Crete, put in at Delos, and having sacrificed to the god of the island, dedicated to the temple the image of Venus which Ariadne had given him, and danced with the young Athenians a dance that, in memory of him, they say is still preserved among the inhabitants of Delos, consisting in certain measured turnings and returnings, imitative of the windings and twistings of the labyrinth. And this dance, as Dicæarchus writes, is called among the Delians the Crane. This he danced around the Ceratonian Altar, so called from its consisting of horns taken from the left side of the head. They say also that the instituted games in Delos, where he was the first that began the custom of giving a palm to the victors.

When they were come near the coast of Attica, so great was the joy for the happy success of their voyage, that neither Theseus himself nor the pilot remembered to hang out the sail which should have been the token of their safety to Ægeus, who, in despair at the sight, threw himself headlong from a rock, and perished in the sea. But Theseus being arrived at the port of Phalerum, paid there the sacrifices which he had vowed to the gods at his setting out to sea, and sent a herald to the city to carry the news of his safe return. At his entrance, the herald found the people for the most part full of grief for the loss of their king; others, as may well be believed, as full of joy for the tidings that he brought, and eager to welcome him and crown him with garlands for his good news, which he indeed accepted of, but hung them upon his herald's staff; and thus returning to the seaside before Theseus had finished his libation to the gods, he stayed apart for fear of disturbing the holy rites; but, as soon as the libation was ended, went up and related the king's death, upon the hearing of which, with great lamentations and a confused tumult of grief, they ran with all haste to the city. And from hence, they say, it comes that at this day, in the feast of Oschophoria, the herald is not crowned, but his staff, and all who are present at the libation cry out *eleleu, iou, iou*, the first of which confused sounds is commonly used by men in haste, or at a triumph, the other is proper to people in consternation or disorder of mind.

2. The Minoan Thalassocracy.

The Account of Aristotle*

Aristotle (384–322 B.C.) was born at Stagira on the Chalcidic peninsula protruding into the northern Aegean. He studied in Plato's Academy and later founded his own school in Athens. The *Politics* seems to consist of the lectures he delivered at his school, the Lyceum. It is based on a good deal of historical research and reflects the information and opinions which were current in the fourth century.

... According to tradition, Lycurgus, when he ceased to be the guardian of King Charillus, went abroad and spent most of his time in Crete. For the two countries are nearly connected; the Lyctians are a colony of the Lacedaemonians, and the colonists, when they came to Crete, adopted the constitution which they found existing among the inhabitants. Even to this day the Perioeci, or subject population of Crete, are governed by the original laws which Minos is supposed to have enacted. The island seems to be intended by nature for dominion in Hellas, and to be well situated; it extends right across the sea, around which nearly all the Hellenes are settled; and while one end is not far from the Peloponnese, the other almost reaches to the region of Asia about Triopium and Rhodes. Hence Minos acquired the empire of the sea, subduing some of the islands and colonizing others; at last he invaded Sicily, where he died near Camicus.

* *Politics*, 1271b, translated by Benjamin Jowett.

The Account of Herodotus*

Herodotus was born in Halicarnassus in Asia Minor shortly after the Persian Wars. His history was composed after the beginning of the Peloponnesian War in 431 and perhaps as late as 425 B.C. It is a mixture of fabulous tales and very reliable information, of credulousness and sharp critical acumen.

... The Carians are a race who came into the mainland from the islands. In ancient times they were subjects of king Minos, and went by the name of Leleges, dwelling among the isles, and, so far as I have been able to push my inquiries, never liable to give tribute to any man. They served on board the ships of king Minos whenever he required; and thus, as he was a great conqueror and prospered in his wars, the Carians were in his day the most famous by far of all the nations of the earth....

... For Polycrates entertained a design which no other Greek, so far as we know, ever formed before him, unless it were Minos the Cnossian, and those (if there were any such) who had the mastery of the Aegean at an earlier time—Polycrates, I say, was the first of mere human birth who conceived the design of gaining the empire of the sea, and aspired to rule over Ionia and the islands....

* 1. 171; 3. 122; translated by George Rawlinson.

THE ACCOUNT OF THUCYDIDES*

Thucydides (*ca.* 460–400 B.C.), son of Olorus, was an Athenian nobleman who wrote a history of the Peloponnesian War, in which he was a participant. His understanding of the scope and significance of that war led him to investigate the history of Greece from the earliest times, and his powerful analytic mind critically examined the myths and legends of ancient times.

Indeed, they [the Greeks] could not unite for this expedition till they had gained increased familiarity with the sea. And the first person known to us by tradition as having established a navy is Minos. He made himself master of what is now called the Hellenic sea, and ruled over the Cyclades, into most of which he sent the first colonies, expelling the Carians and appointing his own sons governors; and thus did his best to put down piracy in those waters, a necessary step to secure the revenues for his own use.

For in early times the Hellenes and the barbarians of the coast and islands, as communication by sea became more common, were tempted to turn pirates, under the conduct of their most powerful men; the motives being to serve their own cupidity and to support the needy. They would fall upon a town unprotected by walls, and consisting of a mere collection of villages, and would plunder it; indeed, this came to be the main source of their livelihood, no disgrace being yet attached to such an achievement, but even some glory. An illustration of this is furnished by the honour with which some of the inhabitants of the continent still regard a successful marauder, and by the question we find the old poets everywhere representing the people as asking of voyagers— 'Are they pirates?'—as if those who are asked the question would have no idea of disclaiming the imputation, or their interrogators of reproaching them for it. The same rapine prevailed also by land.

* * *

With respect to their towns, later on, at an era of increased facilities of navigation and a greater supply of capital, we find the shores becoming the site of walled towns, and the isthmuses being occupied for the purposes of commerce, and defence against a neighbour. But the old towns, on account of the great prevalence of piracy, were built away from the sea, whether on the islands or the continent, and still remain in their old sites. For the pirates used to plunder one another, and indeed all coast populations, whether seafaring or not.

The islanders, too, were great pirates. These islanders were Carians and Phœnicians, by whom most of the islands were colonised, as was proved by the following fact. During the purification of Delos by Athens in this war all the graves in the island were taken up, and it was found that above half their inmates were Carians: they were identified by the fashion of the arms buried with them, and by the method of interment, which was the same as the Carians still follow. But as soon as Minos had formed his navy, communication by sea became easier, as he colonised most of the islands, and thus expelled the malefactors. The coast populations now began to apply themselves more closely to the acquisition of wealth, and their life became more settled; some even began to build themselves walls on the strength of their newly-acquired riches. For the love of gain would reconcile the weaker to the dominion of the stronger, and the possession of capital enabled the more powerful to reduce the smaller towns to subjection. And it was at a somewhat later stage of this development that they went on the expedition against Troy.

---

* Thucydides, 1. 4–8; translated by Richard Crawley.

3. THE THEORY OF MINOAN SUPREMACY*

The theory of Minoan supremacy was first formulated by Evans, but its most compact and sophisticated presentation was made by Pendlebury. The first selection argues for the thalassocracy, the second for Minoan domination of the mainland.

The Late Minoan Period (c. 1600–before 1100 B.C.) is divided into two by the disaster at the end of L.M.I–II. This disaster, however, seems to have had little effect on the density of population, its result being rather to break up the large communities into smaller ones . . . how thickly the towns and villages cluster. The unifying process, which had begun in M.M. times, is now complete. Except for the L.M.II style of pottery, which was exclusively Knossian and which was seldom exported to other sites, it is in very rare cases only that we can tell from what part of the island a particular object comes. There are no gaps now in the map and we can no longer talk about groups of sites except in so far as there will naturally be in every district one site which is the 'county town.'

In L.M.I. a regular network of roads is in evidence with guard-stations at intervals. The impression we get is of an ordered state with a highly centralized bureaucracy, the whole being ruled from the royal city of Knossos, where, as all Greek legends agree, was the seat of Minos, lord of Crete and many overseas dominions. How deep an impression this empire made has been fascinatingly brought forward by J. K. Frost, who pointed out the extraordinary resemblances between Plato's Atlantis as described in the *Critias* and Minoan Crete. Even more interesting is Leaf's suggestion that the Phaiacia of the *Odyssey* is no less than a picture of the Minoan realm trans-

ferred to fairyland, while Miss Lorimer has shown that many of the early elements in the Homeric poems are a reflection of the golden days of L.M.I.–II.

One of the reasons for the depth of this impression was no doubt the fact that for the only time in the history of the Greek world until Alexander's days the civilized parts of the Aegean were under a single ruler. Agamemnon is overlord of the Mycenaean Empire, but he is only *primus inter pares* and at the mercy of his barons. Just as in Egypt the fall of the Old Kingdom, with its strong, bureaucratic government centred on the Pharaoh, was followed by the feudal age of the First Intermediate Period with the local barons technically owing allegiance to the king of the moment, so the destruction of Knossos was followed by the splitting up of its empire into small baronies which might or might not pay lip service to an overlord.

Crete in the sixteenth century became a world power. That she is not mentioned as such in contemporary Egyptian documents must be due solely to the fact that she was in peaceful relationship with that country. Her warlike exploits were confined to the extension of her empire to the North, over the Mainland and islands, and according to legend westwards to Sicily. The acquisition of that empire probably began in very much the same way as the British Empire in India. First of all, come the trading stations. All over the Aegean the name Minoa survived into historical times. There is one in Siphnos, one in Amorgos, an island off Megara, one in Delos, one in Laconia, and others on the coasts of Syria the West and even Arabia. These may have been the names given by the original inhabitants to the station occupied by the traders of Minos or by the traders them-

* J. D. S. Pendlebury, *The Archaeology of Crete* (London: Methuen and Co., Ltd., 1939), pp. 285–287, 225, 228–231. Reprinted from *The Archaeology of Crete, An Introduction*, J. D. S. Pendlebury. By permission of W. W. Norton & Company, Inc., 1965. All rights reserved by W. W. Norton & Co., Inc. Also by permission of the British publishers, Methuen and Co., Ltd., London.

selves. The next stage is when a local prince calls on the traders for help against a neighbour, which is given at a price. And so, gradually and probably peacefully, most of the country comes under the power of the new-comers. Finally comes the stage when further acquisitions becomes necessary owing to the need of putting down piracy or rather of ensuring against other seafarers poaching on their preserves. The peace of the seas is essential to an empire whose wealth is based on trade, and the thalassocracy of Minos is no myth. But that the empire was not obtained by a deliberate policy of fire and sword seems clear from the lack of a general catastrophe on the Mainland at the beginning of the Late Bronze Age.

* * *

In its relations with Mainland Greece and the islands, the influence of Crete is overwhelming. So Minoanized does the rest of the Aegean become that it is impossible for the present writer at least to avoid the conclusion that it was dominated politically by Crete. Athenian tradition, always the most vocal, remembered the tyranny of Minos over the Saronic gulf. We cannot separate the legend of the youths and maidens, sent to be devoured by the Minotaur, from the bull-sports of Late Minoan Crete. Indeed, it would be an extremely good way of keeping down the old noble families of the Mainland if their best was taken and had the honour of being trained for the bull-ring. Many a king and country has been known by its badge, and as Lord Hastings was 'gored by the White Boar', so the Mainland hostages might well be said to be devoured by the Bull of Minos.

* * *

The catastrophe which overtook the Cretan cities at the end of L.M.i*b* (or L.M.II at Knossos) was practically universal. Knossos, Phaistos, Agia Triadha, Gournia, Mokhlos, Mallia, and Zakros all show traces of violent destruction accompanied by burning. At Palaikastro, Pseira, Nirou Khani, Tylissos, and Plate there is a distinct break in the habitation, though no trace of burning was found.

This overwhelming disaster must have taken place at one and the same time and it has been attributed to a severe earthquake. Earthquakes, however, in ancient times are not liable to cause fires; these are the result of gas and electricity. It has been seen, too, that woodwork was more sparingly used at this time than before, and that previous earthquakes, which were strong enough to fling great blocks of the Palace at Knossos into the houses below, had neither caused fires, though the woodwork was more extensive, nor had they caused such a complete break and set-back in the culture. Rather they had acted as a spur to fresh endeavours. Furthermore, at Knossos the first damage an earthquake of such magnitude would have done would be to shake down the Domestic Quarters and particularly the Grand Staircase, where four floors at least were supported on wooden columns. A very mild earthquake in 1931 snapped and shifted the upper part of a reinforced concrete column no less than 6 cm. But the Grand Staircase remained complete and practically undamaged long enough for it to be silted up with debris and earth which preserved the landing on a level with the Central Court to within $1\frac{1}{2}$ metres of its original position. The marks of fire are most obvious on the Western or official wing.

Everything, indeed, points to a deliberate sacking on the part of enemies of the most powerful cities in Crete. We have seen the prosperity of the period and it is obvious that no mere Viking raid could have accomplished such destruction. It must have been a highly organized expedition with an avowed purpose. That this purpose was not to invade and colonize the island is clear from the way in which the Minoan culture continues, though in a very minor key, without any Mainland influence until the very end of L.M.III. The object of this thorough, relentless destruction must have been purely political.

There are two theories which will account for this. Both have much to be saip for them and, curiously enough, they are diametrically opposed. According to the first theory the Minoan domination over the Mainland has been grossly over-estimated. It has been pointed out that if we lacked all historical documents we should, if we used similar arguments, maintain that there was an Athenian domination of Etruria in later days. On this theory the Mainland and Crete were separate independent powers, the former merely adopting the outward trappings of a higher civilization. In L.M.II, however, the Mainland was strong enough to establish control over Crete. This would account for the extremely Mainland character of the Palace style. In that case the destruction of the Cretan cities was due to a nationalist revolt against the foreign 'harmosts'. Evidence for this is the fact that in the succeeding, L.M.III Period, the civilization of Crete has little connexion with that of the Mainland; it is indeed, as will be seen, rather markedly Minoan.

The other theory, to which the present writer adheres, would regard the Minoanization of the Mainland as too pronounced to be the result of mere influence. It is certainly far more complete than was the influence of Egypt in that country's highly organized empire. We would regard the archaeological results as supporting legend, the latter admittedly only referring to the Saronic Gulf, that Crete had by the end of L.M.I–II established a considerable domination over the rest of the Aegean. Her main dealings abroad were with Egypt and the Egyptian Empire in Syria. Egyptian objects and influence are so rare on the Mainland that it would seem as if that part of the Minoan Empire was barred from direct traffic with Egypt. The presence of Mainland vessels in Egypt is easily ex-plained by the fact that they were more suitable for travelling and that therefore the tribute of the Mainland to the Cretan overlord was sent direct to Egypt in payment of goods instead of being unloaded in Crete and reshipped thence.

We have seen that though superficially Minoanized, the Mainland still kept a good deal of its native culture and taste. The richest market in the world was barred and we may perhaps catch an echo of the attempt to find fresh markets in the story of Jason's voyage to the Black Sea. At all events it is not hard to imagine the rebellious feelings of the dominions, and we can well imagine things getting to the pitch of a concerted effort on their part to smash the capital state of the empire.

Now there is a name which is always associated, if not with the sack of Knossos, at least with the liberation of its subjects—Theseus. Names have a habit of being remembered when the deeds with which they are associated are forgotten or garbled. Who would recognize Alexander in Iskander of the two Horns, or Vergil in the necromancer of the Middle Ages? It has already been suggested that the seven youths and seven maidens may have been the Mainland quota for the bull-ring at Knossos. That is just the type of detail that would be remembered, the more so in that it may well have been the sentimental reason without which no purely commercial war can ever take place. No doubt the rape of Helen was a very good rallying cry when the Mycenaean Empire wished to break through to the Black Sea trade which Troy was keeping for itself.

And in the last decade of the fifteenth century on a spring day, when a strong South wind was blowing which carried the flames of the burning beams almost horizontally northwards, Knossos fell.

The final scene takes place in the most dramatic room ever excavated—the Throne Room. It was found in a state of complete confusion. A great oil jar lay overturned in one corner, ritual vessels were in the act of being used when the disaster came. It looks as if the king had been hurried here to undergo too late some last ceremony in the hopes of saving the people. Theseus and the Minotaur! Dare we believe that he wore the mask of a bull?

Such imaginings may not be suitable to archaeology but, with this possibility in mind, I defy anyone to enter the Throne Room without a strange thrill.

Crete had fallen and henceforward she was to be a mere satellite of the world centering round Greece, gradually drawing nearer until she was absorbed in the general Hellenic culture which she herself had done so much to found.

4. The Theory of Greek Supremacy*

1. The Settlement of Greece

Before the end of the Dark Age, the population of Greece had been made up for the rest of Antiquity. As finally constituted, the population consisted of four groups of peoples, viz. two groups of non-Greeks and two groups of Greeks. The order of arrival of these four groups is the first problem.

About one of them, viz. the Dorians, there is no question: they were the fourth and last to arrive. Their impact spread itself over many years, both before and after 1100 B.C., the approximate date usually given for convenience. With them came the Dark Age, and iron began to be used.

The major uncertainties are back in the Stone and Bronze Ages, long anterior to 1100 B.C. The three groups of peoples which have to be settled in Greece before (4) the Dorians are: (1) Neolithic peoples, (2) Anatolian peoples, (3) non-Dorian Greeks. No reliable explicit statement from Antiquity tells us when any of these peoples arrived, and it is still true that after the (metal-less) Neolithic period, no particular kind of archaeological remains—buildings, weapons, pottery, burials, or the like—comes to us positively associated with any of them. Indeed argument is needed to show that there *were* three groups of

peoples, and that no one group is identical with one of the others.

Archaeology does reveal, on many sites, though by no means on all sites, three distinct strata of general destruction; each destruction was followed, soon or late, by new kinds of pottery and other remains. Such interruptions of cultural continuity are usually and rightly taken to signalize the arrival of a new people. The Interruptions (if we may use the word as a specific term) are as follows: (A) end of Neolithic to beginning of Early Helladic; (B) end of Early Helladic to beginning of Middle Helladic and (C) end of Late Helladic, i.e.

NOTE. The pre-eminent book in the field is M. Ventris and J. Chadwick, *Documents in Mycenaean Greek* (1956), the contents of which are at least half historical. Yet of the thirty-one reviews that have been published (I have been at pains to read them all), only a very few contain any attempt at historical understanding. "Greeks in Knossos before 1400 are still something of an embarrassment," writes one of the most eminent of all students of Linear B: he expresses a lingering and compulsive mood, perhaps, not an accurate assessment of anyone's opinion. Actually for some time now it has been clear that *not* to find Greeks in full control of Knossos well before 1400 B.C. would be not merely embarrassing but astonishing. Linguistic studies must have priority where the understanding of documents is first of all a linguistic problem; but undoubtedly historic understanding of the Greeks in the Bronze Age despite some excellent studies, on the whole has lagged.

No one could be more aware than their author that the present pages do too little to fill the gap and that fuller treatments are needed. In particular, section III needs an article to itself, and might be somewhat better if there had been room for a projected historical treatment of Pylos. The text is written for non-specialists; except in some of the later sections, argumentation is reserved for the notes.

* Sterling Dow, "The Greeks in the Bronze Age," *Rapports II* (Stockholm: International Committee of Historical Sciences, XIth Congress of Historical Sciences, August 1960), pp. 2–26. Reprinted by permission of the author and of Almqvist & Wiksell Förlag.

end of the Bronze Age to beginning of Sub-Minoan, and then of Protogeometric, i.e. beginning of the Iron Age. This last Interruption (C) undoubtedly marks the arrival of (4) the Dorians. The two earlier Interruptions, (A) and (B), must mark the arrival of two out of the three earlier peoples.

The (2) Anatolians are known to have been in Greece from the fact that many place-names in Greece have certain specific suffixes, which have been virtually proved not to be Greek. These place-name suffixes are abundant, however, in Asia Minor. They are found also in Crete and in the Islands. The natural presumption is that people from Asia Minor spread over the Aegean, moving at about the same time into both Crete and Greece. The immigration introduced a degree of cultural unity sufficient to spread similar place names over Crete, over the Mainland, the Islands, and north into Macedonia. The question was put: When did such unity prevail over the whole area? The answer was: Clearly *not* in the Neolithic period; *nor* in Middle Helladic; *nor* in Late Helladic, because in Late Helladic a common culture developed only in the last phase, and a simultaneous Anatolian (or any other) invasion of Crete, the Islands, and the Mainland in that period is out of the question. Archaeology does, however, prove a common and unified culture in the Early Helladic period. This being so, the (2) Anatolians are conjectured to have arrived at the Interruption (A) between Neolithic and Early Helladic.

It has long been assumed that Mykenai in its great days was under Greek domination—back into the Middle Helladic period, sometime not long before ca. 1600 B.C. and down to Agamemnon, whose name is Greek. The development reflected in the graves at Mykenai appeared to be continuous, but there was a gap between the graves (ending at ca. 1300 B.C.) and Agamemnon (then dated ca. 1200).

Although it was all but certain that Greece was in Greek hands, still nothing clinched the argument. The evidence was primarily archaeological, but it amounted only to features of Mainland culture which were Northern, and which persisted in the face of strong Minoanization (the Minoans who inhabited Crete and spread their Minoan culture to the Mainland were certainly not Greeks). There was also linguistic evidence, but it was merely the interpretation, still disputed, of some names in Hittite documents to give recognizable Greek names. Add tradition, mostly Homeric—which after all is only myth for this period, including names such as Agamemnon—and the evidence available was exhausted.

Now there is much more. The decipherment of the Linear B script as Greek proves absolutely that there were Greeks in Pylos by ca. 1200 B.C., where they were well established, with a complicated bureaucracy certainly not created overnight. It proves also that Greeks were in control of Knossos (and Crete) by 1400 B.C., whereas earlier this had merely seemed to some scholars highly probable on archaeological grounds. If Greeks controlled Crete in 1400, they must have been based on the Mainland, i.e. presumably on Mykenai. In Mykenai (or wherever) they could not have just arrived, but the whole long development, uninterrupted and organic, back through the great Tholos Tomb Dynasty, and beyond that through the Shaft Grave Dynasty, must be Greek. And so the decipherment of Linear B has shown what no one is likely ever to doubt again, that Greeks were firmly in control of the country during all the five Late Helladic centuries, ca. 1600 to ca. 1100 B.C. Since, moreover, as has been stated in note 3 *supra*. there is no sharp archaeological break (i.e. no level of destruction) between Middle and Late Helladic, it is proper to assume that the Greeks were in Greece during the Middle Helladic period also, and hence that the first (i.e. non-Dorian) Greeks came to Greece at the beginning of the Middle Helladic period, ca. 2000 B.C. The signal of their arrival is the stratum of destruction, Interruption (B) at the end of Early Helladic III. To non-Dorian Greeks, therefore, belong the Middle and Late Helladic periods.

These findings are helpful. As we have seen, the arrival of the (4) Dorian Greeks at the end of Late Helladic, ca. 1100 B.C., i.e. at Interruption (C), is undisputed. The decipherment of Linear B as Greek provides assurance that the (3) non-Dorian Greeks came to Greece at the end of Early Helladic, ca. 2000 B.C., i.e. at Interruption (B). By elimination, Interruption (A), at the end of Neolithic, is confirmed as the time of arrival of the (2) Anatolians. This reinforces the conclusion already reached by Blegen in 1928 on the basis of archaeological evidence, as we have seen.

The resulting scheme is more solid than ever before:

	PEOPLE	
Number		Interruption
(1)	Neolithic	
(2)	Anatolians	(A)
(3)	Non-Dorian Greeks	(B)
(4)	Dorian Greeks	(C)

TIME OF ARRIVAL

(1) Some remote date, unknown.
(2) Beginning of Early Helladic, ca. 3000 B.C. (Also to Crete.)
(3) Beginning of Middle Helladic, ca. 2000 B.C. (None to Crete.)
(4) Beginning of Dark (Iron) Age, usual date ca. 1100 B.C. (Also to Crete.)

Greeks came to Greece by the start of MH I: that may be regarded now as certain.

II. BACKGROUND: EARLY PERIODS AND SITES

1. NEOLITHIC. The Neolithic peoples of the Mainland were quite different in culture from those of Crete; they did not settle even the Kyklades. Probably therefore they came by land. Culturally, they are said to have remained provincial throughout a period of tremendous duration, viz. "the Neolithic and to a large extent the Early Bronze Age." No one contribution of theirs to the later Greece of the Hellenes has been definitely specified, but something historical can perhaps be learned from the principal site of the second of the two main Neolithic periods.

Dimini. Whatever its absolute dates, Dimini in Thessaly is a fortified Neolithic town, of which there are few. Its neighbor and predecessor, Sesklo, preserves only one apparent stretch of city wall, but Dimini boasted a sextuple circumvallation, a thing unique in Greece at any period. The walls were curved to follow the contours of the hill, so that at times the walls are close together. There were no towers. The height of the walls is stated, on no obvious basis, to have been probably not over ca. 2.90 m; there was a low parapet behind. The design makes the purpose clear: the walls were breast-works. The purpose was not to put six successive obstacles in front of the enemy, but rather to give body protection to many rows of archers and slingers. Taken by itself, as a type, this is doubtless an early fortification, but in relative chronology its phase of Thessalian Neolithic (the second of two phases) may be so late in absolute time as to come after e.g. the fortification of Lerna (*infra*). This impairs the value of Dimini as a monument of the military art. Be this as it may, the innermost-topmost wall is the thickest, approaches most to a rectangular shape, and encloses a court on the long axis of which is a "megaron". No scheme could more strongly suggest monarchy, control literally central. Such as it is, this is the first major fact—or better, not "fact" but "observation"—in the political history of Europe.

2. EARLY HELLADIC. Since their place-names are found in the Islands, the Ana-

tolian peoples probably came by sea. Many more long centuries were drawn out before Greeks arrived, but in the Early Helladic periods as in the Neolithic, there were spectacular events and achievements of which some memory may have been transmitted until finally the Greeks heard it. On the whole, to be sure, the Anatolian peoples on the Greek Mainland, as in Crete, seem to have lived quietly, in towns numerous, small, unwalled, and self-contained. Commerce was minimal, war apparently unusual. But to all this there is one known startling exception.

Lerna. At Lerna there was that long continuity of occupation which is favorable to a high culture. There had been two Neolithic phases. In the second phase, levels could be counted, and the deposit from the first phase, where no such definite count could be made, but which is approximately as deep, suggests somewhat the same order of duration. At the beginning of Early Helladic occupation, a distinct break occurred. Early Helladic also is divided into two phases, the first of which had at least six architectural stages.

In this first EH phase, two different fortification walls were built at Lerna, an earlier wall and a later; the later, so far as it has been recovered, replaced the earlier. The earlier appears, though we cannot judge, to have been simple. Over it was built a massive new fortification, consisting of two thick walls joined at intervals by heavy cross-walls which strengthened the whole and formed chambers. Towers projected from the angles. Again, as at Dimini (but quite different in form), we encounter a developed design without known antecedents on the site (the earlier wall being so fragmentary that its form cannot be fully made out, but apparently it was a single wall without towers). A house ('BG') of equally massive construction—we may as well call it the then palace—and showing two or three building periods, stood within this impressive and (for EH times) uncommon fort.

A sensational sequence of events followed. Palace BG and the fortification walls were razed to the ground in order to build a new and perhaps even grander palace, 'The House of the Tiles.' Defences were evidently considered superfluous, but the sequel suggests that this was an error. Not at once but after some little time the House of the Tiles was destroyed in a great conflagration. Whether the House was first pillaged is not clear, but the catastrophe was evidently no mere accident, since the building was never replaced. Instead, the debris was reverently gathered into a low tumulus, perfectly circular in plan, ringed with stones, and evidently forbidden to be built upon. During the long remainder of EH, a series of three or four lesser building periods produced only small houses, and no fortification. The tumulus was not violated.

The House of the Tiles is the greatest known monument of the Anatolians in Greece. After its destruction, the culminating peak of the culture was past, so that when the Greeks arrived, they could learn only the humbler crafts, not strong monarchy symbolized by grand palaces. A few other Early Bronze sites had walls, and enough of them may have survived (not at Lerna but Aigina) to teach the Greeks their first lessons in military architecture, and perhaps to endow them with a small but pernicious heritage of inter-polis warfare.

3. MIDDLE HELLADIC. Like their predecessors the Anatolians, the Greeks came to most areas as violent conquerors, but to some areas peacefully enough so that their arrival was not disruptive nor marked by conflagrations. With this evidence of archaeology, the one known cultural borrowing agrees. Enough Anatolians survived throughout most of Greece, and their intercourse with the new settlers was peaceful and prolonged enough, to communicate the names of natural features, town-sites, and a few other words; the latter two

items suggest some continuity of occupation.

Beyond this all is guess-work. The Greeks may well have learned much in a minor way from the inhabitants—crafts and skills, local lore, legends of men and walled cities, tales of gods and heroes, and most important, sea-faring. It *might* even be true that just as the Greeks later (from 1600 B.C. on) received their higher education from the Minoans (who were kin to the Anatolian inhabitants of Greece), so earlier the Greeks received elementary education from the Neolithic peoples (if anything survived from them) and more importantly from the Anatolian inhabitants of Greece. Analogies could be given, however, to show how easily false inferences can be made about cultural borrowings by conquerors from the conquered: a new, superior people may adopt place-names and vegetables but little else. In the present instance, moreover, there is the fact of pottery: the invaders used, or came to use, pottery wares ('Minyan') superior to anything known earlier in Greece, and moreover the frequent imitation of metal shapes indicates that the newcomers disposed of enough metal so that not infrequently they could afford to make a vessel of it.

For history the most significant general fact is that some of the Middle Helladic sites were fortified: Aigina, Malthi, Mykenai, Tiryns are the ones known to have been. The fortifications are not impressive compared either to those of Dimini and of Lerna, or to later walls, and in some instances the MH walls may have been constructed primarily not against massive attacks—none of the MM cities is known to have been violently destroyed within the period—but merely against stray marauders.

Dorion-Malthi, however, in the middle of the Middle Helladic period, was made into a real fort. In the Neolithic and Early Helladic periods it had been an unfortified country town, and it never became a city and a power of consequence, even comparable for instance to Gla; but from its hilltop north-west of Mt. Ithome it dominated the route from the north into the plain of Messenia. The first distinction of Malthi is a rare one: it was possible to excavate the whole.

After residing there awhile, the Middle Helladic occupants, who had conquered and burned the old EH country town, decided to make the site a strong-point. Excavation showed that the plans went well beyond mere fortifications, to include other features of some interest. Among these, the palace itself is the least impressive, being not conspicuously larger than the other buildings, nor isolated, nor planted on a central axis. Nevertheless it is recognizable. Sharing with it the central, topmost terrace were a series of artisans' shops—smiths, millers, potters. This central, topmost area was surrounded by a wall of its own, which in places served also as a retaining wall. Less than a half of the heavy construction is preserved, but there were evidently five gates, some of them flanked by towers.

A fairly large area surrounded this central fort all the way round: there was space for some 320 houses in all, plus certain areas evidently left empty for markets, herds, or whatnot. But not all the buildings were houses. Along part of the west side, and using the city-wall itself for a back-wall, 15 commodious magazines were constructed. They were obviously built as part of the whole plan. The dominating feature is the city wall, which can be traced throughout most of its length. The gates are narrow. Outworks of some sort were noted at three points: they may have been towers. The wall follows the contours of the hill.

Whoever the people were who built this city ("Dorion IV"), and whatever the source of their inspiration, plainly the whole reflects strong central authority. But powerful monarchy was not evident at first. The first city built on the site by the Middle Helladic occupiers, "Dorion III," was apparently not thus planned, unified, and fortified. The conquest itself may have been led by an autocrat; if so, it took his successors some time to learn the architectural possibilities. But they were bold and imaginative. No Classical polis is quite so literally centralized and so schematically neat as Malthi.

A still more remarkable feature, but never commented upon, is the presence of artisans' shops near the palace, and the great row of capacious magazines along the outer wall. In a sense the city appears to be actually in large part if not wholly an extension of the palace. As elsewhere, far the larger number of the community would live outside. And so here at Malthi, as early as at distant Knossos, and far earlier than at nearby Pylos, we may recognize the characteristic Mykenaian combination of manufacturing, storage, and military facilities which supported, and were directed by, a palace bureaucracy.

III. The Minoan Thalassocracy

Knossos and Crete in Late Minoan I. For more than a millenium, Cretan culture had developed undisturbed, indeed essentially uninfluenced, from outside, passing through many phases. If the history of the palace is any indication, the power of the leading city, Knossos, at first had grown only slowly. But the consolidation of the Palace, in Middle Minoan II, i.e. in the first half of the Second Millenium B.C., may well have been preceded and supported by an extension of territory, income, and, in a mild form, of military strength. In Late Minoan I, the Palace attained its maximum size. Concomitantly, the power of its kings reached out landwards.

There is some evidence that not only the Palace itself at Knossos, but also some of the other sites in Crete, had had walls of a sort in the Middle Minoan period. In no case, apparently, were the fortifications powerful; when expansion started, Knossos was not impeded by them. Mallia, almost a neighbor, was her greatest rival, and there is some reason to think that Knossos destroyed Mallia at this very time.

The only other large power, Phaistos, was reduced to accepting peaceful coexistence. Knossos took as much of Crete as she wanted, which was doubtless as much as she thought she could control. An extensive road system was developed, with numerous stations which have been military guard-posts. In Late Minoan I Crete, Knossos occupied a commanding position.

There need be no doubt also that Cretan foreign relations were Knossian foreign relations. It was Knossos which brought the advanced arts to the Mainland of Europe and civilized the Greeks. With regard, moreover, to economic and political power, quite apart from the civilizing arts, it was natural that the city which had gained the hegemony of Crete should not stop at the water's edge, but should seek markets and spheres of influence overseas.

The Minoanization of the Mainland. The story told by the six famous shaft Graves of Mykenai is familiar and undisputed. The 19 burials, unviolated, of royal persons can plausibly be assigned to one dynasty. In the span of their rule, which reached from sometime in Middle Helladic III down into Late Minoan I, roundly from ca. 1600 B.C. to ca. 1500, Minoan cultural influence on Mainland Greece can be followed from an early stage to a mounting ascendancy. In content and in manner the culture of the Mainland became Minoan. Major arts and minor crafts were equally and completely affected; so much so that it is often impossible to say whether a given object, such as a dagger with multiple metal inlays, was made in Crete and exported, or was made on the Mainland by a Cretan craftsman who had gone abroad to make his fortune, or was made on the Mainland by a Mainland craftsman trained in Crete. The first really powerful Greeks failed to develop plastic arts of their own, but they learned with utter thoroughness from others.

The fact of Cretan influence on the Mainland ("Minoanization") has been familiar long enough so that we fail to consider that it was not inevitable that the civilizing arts should have been imported from Crete and from Crete alone. Asia Minor and Egypt had much to offer. Hence behind the tremendous Minoan cultural impetus, one expects to find extensive commerce, and behind the commerce very likely some political and military power.

The Empire: Founder, Date, Character. The first individual man named by Thucydides in his History (1.4) is put down as Minos, and the first specific organized power is stated to be Minos' Sea Empire. Of the person still nothing positive is known. "Minos" may have been merely a title. It may also have been a title which came from the proper name of an actual famous emperor; we shall see that the circumstances surrounding the myth are such as virtually to make him real.

The date of the Empire is not difficult to determine. In Middle Minoan III, Knossian power at home is still not consolidated, and Minoan cultural influence abroad has to establish itself. But if we come down as far as Late Minoan II, on the other hand, i.e. to the period from ca. 1450 to ca. 1400, Minoan Knossos was in no position to control anybody, as we shall see *infra*; and this condition may have begun as early as say 1480, though 1460 or even 1450 might be the correct date for the beginning of Knossian helplessness. In any case at least 100 years (1580–1480) are available, and they are *the* 100 years when Knossos has been seen to be at her peak, viz. in Late Minoan I. The Minoan Thalassocracy probably occupied most of this century.

The Minoans plainly loved sport more than war, but very dangerous sport. They had a military organization, with officers distinguished from privates—it was no mere rabble, but *may* have been a professional army—and they hired mercenaries from distant parts, doubtless because the manpower on which they could draw was limited. None of their cities being walled, they knew nothing of siege warfare.

Whether their navy included any ships specially constructed for combat may be doubted. Ships interested their artists, but the representations are all small, so that the comparatively large ships, which doubtless existed, could not be adequately depicted. Certainly they used sails as well as oars, but one fact alone proves that the ships were larger than mere sailing rowboats: they could (then or a very little later, *infra*) transport horses, which requires a larger ship. Timbers of any desired size were doubtless available, and carpentry was well advanced. Adhering, however, to minimum probabilities for this, the first thalassocracy, it is proper to imagine small fleets of one-masted merchant vessels which, aided by a store of arms, turned pirate when the occasion seemed favorable, and likewise descended upon seacoast towns.

But it would not take long to discover that devastating raids might well cut down future booty. The next step would be the exaction of tribute, presently fixed in amounts and payable on the occasion of regular visits. Unless the seacoast towns were large and armed, this was not difficult. If a town was too large to control, or was too well fortified, or was inaccessible, the fleets of Minos simply got what they could by trade.

The most promising area for exploitation was not Egypt or the strong states of Asia, but the Aegean—the islands and the coasts of the Mainland. Mykenai was altogether too strong, hence trade was indicated. But precisely as in the case of the Athenian Empire later (Thucydides was right in seeing a general resemblance), the islands and many coastal hamlets were helpless, and trade was replaced by seizure. So long as Knossos, like Athens later, had strong naval superiority, it was not difficult. The peculiarity of a sea empire is precisely that imperial command of the sea prevents subjects from uniting, and without being garrisoned they can be bilked separately for tribute.

Outposts and Organization. In time, no doubt, the advantages became apparent of permanent stations of some sort (trading posts, factories) with perhaps enough troops in each for protection and to make easier the collection of regular tribute. The name Minoa was given, or became attached, to several of these trading posts. All the known Minoas are on the coast: the trading-revenue fleet would put in for supplies and to help in collecting tribute. It may well be significant that none of them became a large or powerful city: they occupied fringe positions: they were only supply depots for the fleets, plus a modicum of trade. The (general) location and the name are all that is positively known.

But again, in time, the further advantages became apparent of actual Minoan cities, permanently rooted, perhaps inland, and supported not merely by trade and tribute but by agriculture and industry. And so Crete sent out the first European colonies. There may not have been many: only two have as yet been discovered, Phylakopi in Melos, and Ialysos in Rhodes; Miletos in Asia Minor is doubtful. In contrast with all the Minoas, these known colonies became important towns.

The Minoan Thalassocracy was far-flung but not grandiose. On a map it would be patches of tribute-paying areas—necessarily the coastal areas of Greece too weak to maintain independence—plus a few colonies; the rest would be trade. Knossos flooded the Mainland with works of the arts and the crafts; her fresco painters and other technicians travelled from city to city. Coinage being virtually non-existent, the form of payment can only be conjectured; one natural conjecture is precious metals.

The organization of this first European Empire need not be imagined as impressive. In other Cretan palaces, and doubtless also at Knossos, bureaucratic records were kept on clay tablets, but the tablets (Linear A) have a slovenly appearance. The Minoans never became great organizers; were never rigorous enough to develop fierce bureaucratic precision or to burn cities (unless Mallia?). The reason for their easy-going ways was not so much that they were at an early stage of imperialism, as that the gay Minoan temperament, developed in many centuries of insular security, would never have found the exacting tasks of governing a big empire congenial at any stage. Their enthusiasm for records and writings was indeed so weak that although they transmitted, and secured the full acceptance of, graphic images in abundance, hardly anyone outside Crete learned Linear A writing.

The Myth of the Minotaur. Minoan culture was loved, as it deserved to be, but Minoan tribute was hated. No doubt they were harsh masters. In revenge the Athenians concocted the myth of the Minotaur. Several of its features are palpably inventions. Theseus was inevitably made the hero, and the revenge motif required that he, like Aeneas, jilt the loving enemy princess after heroic conduct and a safe escape. The tribute too is personalized: for seven youths and seven maidens read *X* measures of wheat or barley, *vel sim.* Myth loves "human" touches. The Athenians did not love paying tribute, yet their myth presupposes tribute. Myth often puts a good face on things, sometimes concealing the truth almost completely, as the Romans for instance concealed in myth the fact of a century of hated Etruscan domination. The Athenians could not do likewise. It is notable, for instance, that Minos himself is left alive: Theseus is not made to kill the hated oppressor. That claim would have been absurd, so the myth adhered to fact. Again, if the Athenians were to conceal the tribute, the story would have no point. But they would never in the world invent so disgraceful a circumstance. The myth embodies a fact, the fact of tribute.

If it were all, it would still be telling evidence for the existence of a Minoan

Thalassocracy. But besides the "human elements" which were certainly invented, and the bitter facts which had to be kept, the myth has certain other elements, occurring uniquely in this one myth, chiefly the *Minotaur*, and the maze-like *labyrinth* in which he was kept. Recalling the place-name suffix -inth-, we see that *labyrinthos* should mean "place of the labrys"; and "labrys" means double-axe. The Palace at Knossos is eminently the place of double-axes; they are incised in its very piers. "Minotaur" is Greek for "minos-bull," and is patently a monstrous duplication of Minos himself. The Minoans were devoted to a peculiar and very hazardous bull-sport, in which girls as well as youths participated. Most recently there is evidence that the performances took place, not outside, but in the central courtyards of the palaces themselves. There is no need to add that the very plan of the Palace at Knossos is labyrinthine in its maze-like elaboration.

No myth whatever from all Antiquity preserves more truthfully such a constellation of facts otherwise unknowable later; the 27,000+ lines of Homer have nothing to compare with this. The Cretan local details of the myth can reasonably be held to be corroboration of the truth of the underlying facts. Minos was known far and wide; more place-names echoed his name than any other mortal's till Alexander the Great; and an immortal myth, telling of Athenian dislike, tells also perforce of Minos' Empire. Later, Herodotos, who had heard too many good stories to be easily convinced by any, passed it by without a thought; but Thucydides, intent on piercing through to the realities, saw reality in Minos' Thalassocracy. True, Thucydides could only fill out the picture by sketching in general details of the Athenian Empire of his own time; the area was the same, and the fundamental conditions were similar enough to make his account plausible.

Centralized freebooting rather than an empire, Minos nevertheless inspired respect and hate. It was doubtless just what might be expected of Cretans: wild, irregular, venturesome, colorful. It succeeded because there was no organized opposition. The Greeks had come as conquerors, but after two or three placid centuries not all were able to face Minos. Such was the first supra-national entity of European history.

IV. THE GREEKS IN CRETE

The Conquest. Beginning in the period Middle Minoan III, Cretan merchants and craftsmen had come to the Mainland. Presently, in return, Greeks from Mykenai and other cities, travelling as merchants, sailors, envoys, or mere tourists, doubtless visited the great metropolis of culture. But they did not all go to genuflect. Athens and the other places in the Empire hated the levies of tribute and resented subjugation. Mykenai herself doubtless became tired of learning, paying, admiring, and envying. It may not have taken the visitors long to observe that Knossos, unwalled, was defended by troops without body armor; and to observe that the Mainland, perhaps Mykenai alone with her immediate allies, was stronger than Knossos.

Two facts about the conquest are known. One is that command of the sea was a prerequisite. Under the eyes of the Cretans, Mykenai created a navy: it was probably easy, since already Mykenai had extensive commerce, and so far as is known, merchantmen were the only warships, i.e. there were no ships specialized solely for combat. Allied fleets were doubtless enlisted: if so, the coalition against Troy was not the first foreign expedition Mykenai had commanded.

On the whole peaceful, the Cretans were mainly a dagger people, or a dagger-and-rapier people, in contrast to the Mykenaian kings, who were buried with a small arsenal of slashing swords. The Cretans were only good enough at military affairs to maintain for a few generations their ramshackle, piratical "empire." There was of course no siege, no long exacerbating campaign such as would lead to furious carnage and destruction: archaeology records no destruction.

Like the Macedonians later, the Mykenaians struck against their civilizers (and it may well be that one battle, like Khaironeia, sufficed). What Athens earlier, under "Theseus," would have liked to do but could not, Mykenai did. Knossos, unconquered since the Bronze Age began, was defeated, and Greeks occupied the Labyrinth.

Permanent occupation with full control of a foreign city was perhaps itself a new thing in the Aegean world. Like Minos before, the new Thalassocracy could ill afford the men. But Mykenai now held Knossos itself, an incomparable treasure: the schoolmaster of Greece more fundamentally than Athens ever was to be, Knossos had also been, again as Athens was to be, a tyrannical denier of liberties. The Greeks stayed in Knossos, mainly no doubt for profit, secondarily to prevent revival of tyranny; but also, as it turned out, to go on learning.

To account for far-flung Knossian overseas power, it was necessary to assume that Knossos controlled other cities. The Linear B tablets now appear to tell us that Greek Knossos was master of many cities in Crete, perhaps of the whole island. The cities were defenseless, i.e. unwalled, and had had no experience in forming a union of their own, i.e. not under Knossos. Some few may have got themselves destroyed by rebelling later, when the Greeks were well established, but none is alleged to have been destroyed at the time of the conquest.

Date of the Greek Conquest. The kind of changes shown by archaeology in Late Minoan II at Knossos would have taken some time to develop. The script also, as we see it in the tablets, which were inscribed presumably in the last year or two before the destruction, is well standardized, fixed for 200 years. The Greeks would have taken years to settle in (it was a foreign country

they were trying to rule), to conquer as much as they wanted, to observe Linear A, to get the elaborate new Linear B signary developed, to teach it and to use it. Late Minoan II is usually dated from ca. 1450, i.e. the changes, except the script, become clearly marked about then. The conquest itself, for a guess, may have been as early as 1480 or as late as 1460. If the impression gained from Linear B is correct, by ca. 1410 an elaborate bureaucratic system has been built up. The earlier date, ca. 1480, seems preferable for the conquest itself.

Knossos under Greeks. The capture of Knossos was followed by military occupation. In addition to being, as before, a royal residence, a cult center, a place of (bull) sports, an administrative capitol with archives, and a battery of magazines (for the storage of payment in kind), the Palace now became an arsenal. A conspicuous new feature was the numerous chariots; large numbers of horses must have been stabled near the palace. For the first time troops were seen drilling in body armor. The number of arrows in the arsenal was high in the thousands, though not more than should be expected. But the Palace remained unprotected by any fortification: like their predecessors, the Mykenaians doubtless asked, Whom have we to fear?

In the building itself the Greeks made few changes. Most conspicuous was the creation of a Throne Room. It was not a very large chamber, and we do not know what went on in it: but definitely it is similar to the design of Mainland throne rooms. At the humble other extreme, Mainland pottery, the so-called Palace Style, was introduced; it was of course ultimately Minoan-derived, but certain shapes of vase and of decoration distinguished it.

The Creation of Linear B. In a sense, literacy had existed in Crete for some three centuries; but the Minoans had made little use of it. The surviving Linear A tablets, as we have seen, are so poor clerically as to suggest negligence if not actual incompetence. It is not strange that very little writing had crossed to the Mainland, which may be regarded as virtually illiterate until Knossos was captured. At Knossos, including the neighboring sites, only 16 Linear A inscriptions have survived; but on the analogy of Hagia Triada, we may imagine that the Greeks found accounts being kept there in Linear A. Such accounts were the more necessary because Knossos controlled a large part of Crete.

Upon capturing Knossos and its Cretan holdings, the Greeks were faced with administrative tasks never faced by them before. They pressed into their own service some at least of the Knossian administrative staff, and in no time at all (we may imagine) the Greeks learned from the scribes the advantages for administration of the ability to write and read. The language had to be Greek, but trial showed that Linear A, doubtless none too good for the Minoan language, was impossible for Greek. Accordingly orders were given to the (Minoan) scribes, and largely by them Linear B was created. The basis was of course Linear A; but the process of creation, so far as it is now understood, was by no means completely systematic. The result was what might be expected. A syllabary need not be, for Greek, grossly defective, and Linear B conceivably could be worse. On the other hand, and without being able to judge, except from external appearances, about Linear A, one can only say that an instrument was created barely adequate to the administrative records for which the Greeks wanted it.

The Wanax at Knossos. The Linear B tablets have revealed a fact of prime historical importance. The head of state at Knossos bore the title *Wanax* (ἄναξ), the Linear B word for King (actually attested only at Pylos on the Mainland). With him too there was a *Lawagetas*, a high official whose duties and relationship to the Wanax are unknown. Knossos, in short, was under rulers whose titles suggest an independent kingdom. For instance, in Mykenai Agamemnon was doubtless called Wanax, and

Nestor in Pylos. It might well seem therefore that Knossos was no part of an empire, but rather was as completely independent of Mykenai as was, e.g., Pylos. The objections to this view are strong but not conclusive. They are two. In the first place, some Mainland power had to organize and pay for a large-scale expedition: it is unlikely that that power would voluntarily forego the profits. On the contrary, wealth derived from Crete would be one likely source of funds to pay for the walls, the palace, and the tholoi (with their lost furnishings) at Mykenai. In the second place, Linear B was transmitted to the Mainland with such utter faithfulness as to suggest that close touch with Knossos was maintained. Possibly the Wanax of Knossos belonged, like Menelaos, to a cadet branch of the house of Mykenai, or may otherwise have been under Mykenaian control.

The Destruction in ca. 1400 B.C. One April day when there was a brisk wind blowing, the Palace at Knossos was burned throughout. The almost complete lack of valuable objects found by the excavators makes it appear that the Palace was looted first, and consequently that the fire was intentional. Stone vases were left where they were being made, and the Throne Room was in confusion.

At or about the same time, other places were destroyed or were abandoned without destruction: Tylissos, Nirou Khani, perhaps Plate. A couple of decades earlier, apparently, the same thing had happened to Phaistos itself (and Hagia Triada), to several places in the East, to Gournia and other small towns. It has sometimes been suggested, strangely, that these were acts of natives directed against their Greek masters. To burn a dozen cities of your own is no sure way to rid yourself of tyranny, but only to invite, as in World War II, savage reprisals at once and worse tyranny to follow. The way to get rid of an occupying force is to kill its troops, and there is every reason to believe that the Cretans were powerless against the arms stacked at

Knossos and their users. Neither is there any evidence or probability that any foreign, i.e. non-Greek, power invaded Crete and destroyed cities. No foreign power at this time is known to have launched great overseas expeditions. The perpetrators must be identified by more positive reasoning.

The first clue is that certain of the towns now deserted were not reoccupied for over a thousand years: Mokhlos, Pseira, Nirou Khani. The Palace itself at Knossos was apparently deserted for a time, then cleared and partly repaired.

The evidence can be extended. In J. D. S. Pendlebury, *Archaeology of Crete* (London 1939), all the known sites of Crete were mapped and also tabulated. For all three Late Minoan sub-periods together (LM I, LM II, LM III, plus sites assignable only to LM as a whole), the total is 192. The figure is large enough to encourage further exploration. LM II, being a local (Knossian) period, may be omitted, and of course the sites assignable only to LM as a whole. For LM I alone, 69 sites are known; for LM III, a longer period, 88.

This is not the place to discuss the various refinements and qualifications which caution may suggest: when they are taken into account and the necessary allowances are made the conclusions will not be impaired. The striking fact is that of the 69 LM I sites, only 22 sites, which constitute only 11 per cent of the total of 192 different sites for LM as a whole, are known to have been occupied in both LM I and LM III.

Evidently there was a major disruption before the beginning of LM III. The disruption extended beyond the 12 cities where there is definite evidence of destruction or sudden abandonment. The sites themselves, physically, were as good as before. One suspects that the explanation may be grim, viz. enslavement or the massacre of all who did not escape to the hills. Even little Trianda in Rhodes was abandoned suddenly; the people left cheap things (pots etc.) on the floor just where they happened to be. It is ominous that there was a Mykenaian town nearby.

In all this there is nothing to suggest a foreign invasion, nor is it the kind of disruption which a civil disturbance would suggest. The destruction was rather an act of hate. Further light on who did it is shed by the subsequent fate of Crete. During the entire next period, Late Minoan III, or more generally Late Bronze III (formerly called "Mycenaean" but that is no longer possible), Crete was reduced to being isolated and quiet. That is the evidence of archaeology. Except for what the Homeric epics, and most specifically the Catalogue of Ships, allege about participation in the Trojan Expedition, Crete has no part in the events of LB III. It seems that Mykenai, after the destruction, left Crete to itself for some time. The outside power had been there in full control: the Linear B tablets make that plain. It is natural, and I think correct, to assume that the power which had the control was the power which abandoned the island. Mykenai was supreme. It was Mykenai which committed the enslavements, massacres, and burnings. On some of the sites, where these awful events had taken place, including Knossos itself for a time, the Cretans no longer wished to live.

Why did Mykenai kill a goose that was laying golden eggs? An explanation is not hard to imagine. The Cretans have never been comfortable to govern. A dagger people from way back, gay and irresponsible ("all Cretans are liars," said a Cretan), they doubtless took their first conquest hard. The pride of an island free of invasion longer than even England has been, aware that recently they had ruled the seas and educated their future conquerors, was a pride which could turn to any and all forms of desperation. There may have been a long series of incidents, culminating in some such act as the assassination of a *wanax*.

It is a construction, but I think it fits. Mykenai presently had had enough. To hold the island in chains was out of the question. They lacked the manpower. They could find (and did find) more tranquil fields to dominate. And so, in utter exasperation, Mykenai pillaged, massacred, burned, and withdrew.

Later, in the long Late Bronze age, a Greek dynasty returned, somehow managed better, and sent the mighty King Idomeneus, with Meriones and 80 ships, a large contingent, to Troy.

Tradition. The decipherment of the Linear B tablets has had yet one further result, hitherto unnoticed. We know now that at some time there was massive Greek conquest not only of Knossos but also of the erstwhile dependencies of Knossos. Such an achievement makes the capture of poor little Troy VIIa seem petty. We know also that Knossos and many other places in Crete, and even Minoan colonies outside Crete, at some later time were pillaged and destroyed. Here were awful and mighty acts: why is there no epic about them? Theseus earlier was remembered in a story that proved to be unforgettable. Troy later was remembered in two epics that are immortal. Yet neither myth nor tradition in any other form remembered the events of ca. 1480 or of ca. 1400 B.C. The fact calls for understanding.

An explanation can, I think, be given, and it is fundamental to the nature of mythical tradition. The *Chanson de Roland*, by whomever composed (evidently the process of its development was not precisely the same as that of the *Iliad*), selected a petty rearguard action, that at Roncesvalles, and proceeded to make a hero and a villain and a moving story out of unlikely material. Plainly in the formation of epic there can operate what may be called a principle of whimsicality. In the second place, study of modern living epics in Jugoslavia has shown that a large number of epics normally co-exist. Each singer has several. The epics compete for favor, and those that achieve popularity persist because of the story, and because of the talent some unusual singers expend upon it. Quite likely there *were* epics about Knossos. They lacked intrinsic interest, and no singer, adopting their themes, made them live. We have the *Iliad*, the *Odyssey*, and parts of many other epics clustered about them: the inferiority of these others is evident even in the fragments, and they illustrate the process, essentially whimsical and in a sense accidental, which normally operates. History is the loser on a vast scale; but the singers are concerned, not with history in our sense, but with history as material which they can use to please and enthrall their hearers.

V. THE MYKENAIAN HEGEMONY

Mykenai in Greece. Apart from the usual farms, pastures, and groves, the resources of Mykenai are altogether unknown to us: how was procured the gold of the Shaft Graves and the wherewithal to build a fleet. Mykenai itself was well situated, but so were many other towns. With silver, marble, and clay, Classical Athens had at least modest non-agricultural resources for Empire; but for Mykenai no special local sources of wealth whatever can be specified.

It was the start which was difficult. In time, perhaps early in the 300–400 years of Greek occupation before Grave Circle A, territory was surely added. The minimum which ought to be imagined is shown best by Pylos in the Linear B tablets: however their detail is to be interpreted, unquestionably they show extensive territorial control. Something like this, as much or more, should be imagined for Mykenai.

A second stage, whenever attained, would be the close alliance, based on marriage perhaps rather than on conquest, with Lakedaimon, thus giving control all the way south to the Lakonian Gulf, also the Taygetan promontory, and in Messenia as far as, and including, Pedasos-Methone. Earlier perhaps than this Mainland expansion was a third phase, the conquest of Crete. In any case the problem of resources, difficult (for us) in the Sixteenth Century—so that the obtaining of the gold etc. for the 19 burials in Grave Circle A remains a problem—in the later Fifteenth and in the Fourteenth Century is no problem at all. Revenues sufficed for the walls, the palace, the tholoi; for all the furnishings, of which just enough remains to give a hint, of the palace; and of the tholoi, where virtually nothing remains.

The Form of the Hegemony. If we try to formulate some notion of the organization of the Aegean under Mykenai, we find a number of indications as guides:

1. In the Ancient tradition as a whole, Mykenai is not given a thalassocracy. Thucydides makes Minos, but not Agamemnon, anticipate the features of the Athenian Empire. Agamemnon has naval power and islands, but their character would seem to be that of an extension of the kingdom.

2. The Catalogue of Ships, however doubtful its division of the Argolid into two, may well echo historical truth in not making the *relation* (not of course, the absolute figures) of Agamemnon's naval power to the rest of Greece resemble that of Athens later. Agamemnon has available 160 ships, of which he loans the Arkadioi 60: the implicit suggestion that he could man only 100 is in the direction of realism. The next largest power, Pylos, has 90; then come Tiryns and Crete each with 80.

3. The Linear B tablets from Knossos, as we have seen, reveal there a chief of state (*Wanax*) with a high official at his side, just as in an independent kingdom. Mykenai may well have controlled the place and received much of the income, but in form Knossos was apparently independent.

4. In the *Iliad*, Agamemnon does not by any means occupy the position of Emperor in relation to the other Kings. He is a *primus inter pares*, though with the emphasis on the *primus*. The weaker he

appears personally, the more he must be conceded to owe to his acknowledged headship of Greece; close reading will show, I think, that this position is really conceded very fully by the poet, however much his plot forced him to make Agamemnon appear weak personally.

5. These considerations, varied in source and doubtless in value, accord best with the Hittite evidence as most recently interpreted. This interpretation leads not for the first time, but more imperatively than before to the identification of Rhodes as the great Greek power with which the Hittites dealt. Hittite documents of the Fourteenth and Thirteenth centuries refer some 20 times to Akhkhijawā, more easily transliterated Ahhijawa, which was evidently their (inaccurate) rendition of 'Αχαιϝία, that is, Achaea. If Ahhijawa cannot be Mykenai itself—the evidence is awkward both ways—then what we have is an independent state of considerable power in the eastern Aegean. Here again Mykenai appears as having no empire, or rather, Greek power is fragmented.

If the foregoing does not mislead, we can contrast the Minoan Thalassocracy with the Mykenaian Hegemony. Like Classical Corinth, perhaps, Mykenai was content with the profits of trade, and sought no empire. Colonies were sent out, but for the revenue of trade if for any; not for other power, and not for the extortion of tribute. As against the many Minoas, spread abroad, there is only the one Mykenai.

Tiryns, and a Theory of Walls. The Bronze Age is crowded with problems, of which one of the most intractable has been the walls of Tiryns. Tiryns is not much over six miles, or ten kilometres, from Mykenai, yet Tiryns managed to build walls (and subsequently enlarged them to double the free area protected) under the very eyes of Mykenai. Why did Mykenai permit it? So long as the question remains unanswered—a question inherent, not in fallible texts, but in solid visible facts—our knowledge of the very elements of the Bronze Age is incomplete. Yet no satisfactory answer has been given.

If a theory may be ventured, it will start from the size of the citadels in question. All are small. In two or three minutes a man could walk from one end to the other of the Athenian Akropolis. Mykenai was not larger, Tiryns was smaller. Dimini, Lerna (only a fraction is excavated, but there is no reason to believe that it had any unusual size), Malthi—the known forts of the past were no larger. Gla alone had any size, but that was because of terrain. This feature, smallness, has itself always been a difficulty, though usually not discussed. How could Troy stand a ten-year siege if it were so small that a swift runner, as D. L. Page points out, could cross it lengthwise in some 25 seconds?

The essential consideration is that fortifications can be defensive or offensive. Messene and the other Fourth-Century B.C. forts were offensive, i.e. built to encircle and contain Sparta. The classic walls of Messene enclosed a whole city, i.e. they sheltered an army which could sally forth to threaten any army passing by, or to ruin its communications. For this purpose size, speaking generally, is essential. Such walls are built to provide ample safe space.

Prehistoric walls were built around the palace. Their purpose was to protect the king's house and as much as was feasible of the cluster of offices, storerooms, workrooms, archives, etc., which excavation has discovered within them and which the Linear B tablets associate with the palace bureaucracy. Most of all, they were built to shelter the royal treasure. They were defensive. They would hold enough men to man the walls and, under the then conditions of siege warfare, to stand a siege. A small force could do it.

This being so, it seems likely enough that the Kings of Mykenai saw no reason to object to the building of walls at Tiryns. If the King of Tiryns wished to be safe, i.e. to build a fence around his valuables, that was unobjectionable. Even when enlarged, the fort would not hold enough men to block the access of Mykenai to the sea. Tiryns might harass Mykenaian traders going to and fro, but only at the price of a war which the two neighbors did not wish to contemplate; their lands were vulnerable even if their stored-up treasures were not. The walls were built as defences against more remote enemies.

Troy. If this view of Bronze Age fortifications is acceptable, the expedition against Troy can be explained in simple terms. The old notion that Troy obnoxiously controlled the Dardanelles, and thus Black Sea commerce, by levying toll on shipping, or on goods trans-shipped, is happily defunct. There was no such commerce, and the destruction of Troy VIIa did not open it up. Another explanation of the war is needed.

Like all such forts, Troy VIIa held royal treasure. It was not the rich place that Troy VI had been, but the prospective plunder was worth the effort. Epic poetry later altered the purpose to a romantic one, and glamorized the whole expedition, just as epic poetry would be expected to do.

A few facts appear to survive criticism. There *was* a Greek expedition against Troy VIIa; Mykenai under Agamemnon commanded it; numerous allies took part. The fort was packed with people, and proved hard to capture. The Greeks succeeded, after which they pillaged, burned, and departed. Epic exaggerated all the details, especially the size of the Greek force, and the time it took. Gross inaccuracies about the site crept in: they would not worry epic poets. So much seems clear. The real problems are in another sphere, viz. chronology.

The Relative Order of Events. Until closer absolute dates can be fixed from the pottery, the historian can only attempt a rational relative arrangement.

In Greece itself, all the great forts had already been built, probably in the Fourteenth Century. The danger envisaged at that time is totally unknown, but the fact that the walls were often repaired, improved, and sometimes extended shows that they were not built for mere display of strength; and they are much too strong to have been built against mere marauders. Danger did not materialize effectively until the end of the pottery period Myk III B. Close to the walls of Mykenai itself three fine houses, more likely to have been appurtenances of the Palace than mere private dwellings, were destroyed by fire at that time. The Kings of Pylos had presumably felt that their remote location and their wide domains were protection enough, and so they had built no walls. Also at the end of Myk III B, the attack on Pylos came by sea; moderate forces were dispatched to a series of possible landing-places, but it was a mistake (one can guess) thus to divide up the army—it is as if only raids were feared, whereas the actual attack was massive. The Palace was easily entered, savagely despoiled, and burned.

History records many acts of colossal folly, but it stretches credulity to put the Trojan expedition *after* such events—not to mention the violence such a dating would do to the tradition of a large fleet from Pylos, under the venerable and prominent Nestor. Moreover the likely dating of the pottery found in Troy VIIa is earlier. The traditional dating of the expedition to some year soon after 1200 B.C. is therefore coming to be generally regarded as improbable.

The great movement of peoples that attacked Egypt by land and sea ca. 1223 B.C. is the next earlier event. The age of unrest had already begun. There was another attack on Egypt, this time by a great fleet of sea raiders, in ca. 1190 B.C. The connection of these events somehow with the destructions at Mykenai and Pylos is surely mandatory. A Trojan expedition in the midst of all this may not be inconceivable, but would have been folly. Moreover the heroes on their returns would have encountered somewhere, sometime, the masses of migrants and raiders, but the tradition preserves no memory of it.

One further indication is the ending of the commerce of Mykenai. It had been extensive and voluminous, but at some date in the second half of the Thirteenth Century it is reduced to almost nothing. The cause, again, would be the movements of uprooted peoples, who must have been on the move for a score of years before they reached Egypt. The Trojan expedition *ought* not to have been launched when revenues from commerce were decimated, the world was unsettled abroad, and there was a threat to the home cities.

And yet it is impossible to recede very far in fixing a date for the Trojan expedition, because unlike its predecessor, Troy VIIa contains very little Mykenaian pottery: 80 sherds of Myk III B, none whatever of Myk III C. There are two choices. One is to suppose that the expedition was launched when conditions were already so upset that Mykenaian exports had dwindled. In that case it would have been a comparatively small but thoroughly desperate raid, wildly distorted by the poets later. And again there is the fact that forces were abroad sufficient to ruin very extensive commerce, yet of such forces the tradition preserves no memory. The alternative is to conceive that Troy itself, before world conditions were upset and commerce ruined, became too poor to import luxury wares from Greece, so that Myk III B wares, still being exported elsewhere in quantity, could rarely be afforded at Troy. This latter alternative would permit a date conformable to the conditions represented in the *Iliad* and *Odyssey*, i.e. a world not yet thrown into turmoil. The epics are surprisingly scrupulous, as if well informed generally, about, e.g., the Dorians; some knowledge of the peoples known to the Egyptians by name as their attackers might be expected if such peoples were then at large.

Of these two alternatives, neither of which is comfortable, the latter seems preferable. Troy fell, in that case, ca. 1240, but before Myk III B ceased to be exported.

The Destruction of the Palace Bureaucracies. Certain phenomena, when seen in relation, give an insight into the "mind" of Bronze Age Greece. (1) With their interest in astonishingly petty details, the tablets show a bookkeeping–shopkeeping mentality. (2) The economy in some sense is planned. The object of the plan, or at least *one* object, is to fill the palace magazines with agricultural produce (Knossos) and the shelves with thousands of vases (Pylos), the sale of which would increase the royal treasures (Mykenai, Grave Circle A). (3) In other royal economies, i.e. in states where the king's income is very large (taxes, tribute, booty), and his expenses (army/bodyguard, court, royal burials) are less, treasure can accumulate to enormous totals (cf. the Achaemenids and the Ptolemies). (4) The safety of the treasure naturally becomes a grave concern: hence walls are built if a menace exists. (5) The treasures cannot be kept secret, but become known, however inaccurately; hence wars such as the expedition against Troy, since people who are obsessed with their own treasures naturally want to add to them the treasures of others.

(6) Within each such state, and considering them from the point of view of the subjects, it seems clear that the authority of the monarch and his bureaucracy over a great many subjects was tremendous. People appear to have lived within an elaborate framework of *system*, features of which were specialization under central control, with writing used to communicate and preserve orders and records. To some extent intricate and complex, the different functions—commerce and agriculture and manufacture—depended on each other. If treasure and the safe-guarding of it were dominant concerns in the king's mind, subservience and care in fulfilling his duties in the system dominated the subject. the subject knew no other way of life.

All of this was highly "civilized" and one may conjecture that it was fragile. Destroy the palace, and the whole community was wrecked. This happened. Pylos, the last palace to be built, was perhaps the first to go, ca. 1200 B.C., the rest very soon, in the next decades, at latest not after 1150. The Dorian destroyers were savage enough to have ended less fragile organizations than the palace bureaucracies. As it was, the disruption of commerce brought down the whole of society. This fragility explains why, even without Dorians on the Akropolis, Attika also went under. The economy was geared to certain exports and imports; they ended, and the invaders were soon ravaging the Attic countryside. The Akropolis they could not take, but destruction was complete without that.

Linear B can teach us two large facts, still not wholly assimilated, about the destruction. One is about illiteracy. Hitherto it has been fairly clear that illiteracy was due to the failure of interest on the part of older people in teaching the younger to read and write; and in an equally complete failure of interest on the part of the younger to want to learn. Now we can understand much better the failure of interest. It was caused by the utter collapse of a system which had engrossed the lives of those who wrote and who read. When the system collapsed overnight, the incentive to literacy was not all that went with it, but people's very lives. There were no more careers for the palace bureaucrats, the craftsmen, the officers, even for the more highly trained slaves. Probably most of them had to go dig in the fields. There was a reversion to primitive economy.

The other large historical fact taught by Linear B is the abruptness of the governmental change. The Classical Greeks were inherently, persistently conservative, in that the greatest changes were regularly accompanied by retention of something old. As in Rome and in other states also, the King might be largely or almost completely supplanted; but there was still at Athens, throughout its history down to

Constantine or beyond, an officer entitled *Basileus*, not to mention, for centuries at least, four *Phylobasileis*. But when the destruction of the Twelfth Century took place, the chief of state, the *Wanax*, was evidently completely abolished. He was part of the bureaucracy, the supreme part, so integral that his title did not survive, even in some conservative nominal manner, any more than did the bureaucracy. The epic tradition too lost any accurate and conscious memory of the office.

The effect of the Dorian invasions was not just the destruction of property. It was profoundly a mental event. The state was almost literally decapitated. The whole organization and the whole mentality at the top—that of the palace bureaucracy— went. Small local officials, numerous in each state, whose title had been *Basileus* and was significantly kept, replaced the one Wanax. The state was broken up into smaller local units. Attika, for instance, had to be united all over again.

The Dorians and the three centuries *plus* of Dark Age which they initiated were the most fearful and (for civilization at the time) costly disaster in European history. But they were not an unmixed evil. Linear B literacy, had it lasted any length of time, would have been an incubus upon the Greek mind. That has been clear for some time. Can we not add to it a similar statement about the palace bureaucracies ? They had created Mykenai, Tiryns, Pylos, much else; but their work was done, they had no future, at least none easily imagined. Even in cities where there may have been opportunities, as in Athens, no one tried to recreate palace bureaucracies. They too would have become an incubus, a faulty syllabary of thought where a flexible alphabet was needed. Even though fine things were rubbed out by the Dorians, too many and unnecessarily, on the whole it was well for Europe that the slate was wiped clean. Hesiod knew enough to deplore the Iron Age, yet without it there would have been no Hesiod, and all that came down to his greater compeer Homer would never have had the qualities which oral testing produces.

5. A CHALLENGE TO ORTHODOXY*

This ["Biography of the Book"] may seem a strange title for an Introduction, but the fact is that this book claimed a will of its own, and eventually took a course and assumed a form contrary to the original plan and intentions of the author. Its life-history will serve simultaneously as apologia, summary, and guide through the labyrinth.

The book began with an invitation from the publishers to write an account for the general reader of the work on the Mycenaean Greek texts written in the Linear B script. This is the form of writing used by the Greeks of the Mycenaean age, whose decipherment by the late Michael Ventris marked a turning point in the study of the Late Bronze Age of the Aegean. I responded to this invitation all the more gladly because Linear B remains something of a mystery even to some professional classical scholars, with the consequence that ideas and results, reached tentatively in the infancy of this new branch of study, but later discarded, were beginning to find their way into general accounts of the Greek Bronze Age over the signature of authoritative names. Let it be freely confessed that at the beginning we all made mistakes in dealing with these bald counting-house dockets from the Mycenaean palaces, which give only the barest of hints at a form of Greek some five centuries earlier

* Leonard R. Palmer, *Mycenaeans and Minoans,* 2nd ed. (New York, Alfred A. Knopf, 1955), pp. 17–32. Copyright © 1961, 1965 by Leonard R. Palmer. Reprinted by permission of Alfred A. Knopf, Inc. and of the British publishers, Faber and Faber Limited, London.

than any dialect of that tongue we had hitherto encountered. It was necessary to work out the best scientific method of coaxing the truth from these reluctant witnesses. After trial and error it proved that the safest way was to abandon the Greek lexicon and to try the way of pure analysis. In other words we repeated the experience of decipherers in other fields: the 'etymological' method of guessing at Greek words, long since discredited, had to give way to the 'combinatory' method, which attempts first to arrive at the meaning of the syllabically written words by contextual analysis before going on to the second step of equating these words with later words listed in the Greek lexicon of Liddell and Scott.

Provided at an early stage by Ventris, with his exemplary generosity, with much unpublished material, I began a systematic attempt to analyse the Linear B archives along these lines. Handwriting, size and shape of tablet, signs of cutting and breaking, the grouping of scattered texts into ordered series as the successive 'pages' of a book, arithmetical analysis of the quantities —all the results gradually accumulated by the patient labours of an international team were applied, and little by little the Mycenaean world began to take on an appearance less strange than that conjured up by the earlier method. A motley band of women described as 'headband makers, musicians and sweepers' turned out to be simply named after the villages from which they came. 'Absent carpenters,' an entry of remarkable frequency, were petrified into a place-name of the pattern Newcastle-upon-Tyne. 'Female barley-reapers,' of curiously mixed parentage, were found to be women attached to a temple establishment. Beneath this bright microscopic lamp 'kings,' 'palaces,' and 'Councils of Elders' all faded into insubstantiality and were consigned to a limbo reigned over by that short-lived Linear B character, 'Aigeus the Cretan,' who turned out to be of greater importance when transformed into the

description of a tripod: 'with goat's head handles, of Cretan workmanship.'

By the beginning of 1960; this re-examination was finished, and a work *The Interpretation of Mycenaean Greek Texts* was sent to press.

The task of summarizing the results for presentation to non-specialists in the first draft of this book proved far from easy. The many differences between this account and others which have appeared rules out any simple categorical statement of my own results with the bland implication that the others are wrong and it is sufficient that I say so. Moreover, the message of these new documents concerns a wide circle beyond the limits of classical studies. The Bronze Age of Greece is one of the most formative periods of our civilization, and the results of investigation in this field have repercussions far outside the Aegean. The pre-history of much of Europe hinges on correct interpretation of excavations in Greek lands. Consequently the reader had to be admitted to full partnership. The problems had to be stated, the material presented, and the workings shown, despite their difficulty. So I have not shunned the quotation of actual texts or the elucidation of the methods of analysis involved.

On reflection it seemed best to base the exposition on the finds made at Pylos, the site near Navarino in southern Greece where Professor C. W. Blegen in 1939 uncovered what he believed, rightly in my opinion, to be the palace of the Homeric King Nestor. Here was found the best preserved and the most coherent archive of documents written on clay tablets in the Linear B script. Without them the decipherment would hardly have been possible; without them it would have been difficult to make sense of the more fragmentary texts discovered by Sir Arthur Evans at Knossos in Crete at the beginning of the century. We begin, therefore, with Pylos and an historical account of the long scholarly controversy concerned with this place. It began in antiquity when Greek exponents of Homer tried to locate the places which figure in the stories of the Iliad and the Odyssey, and in particular 'sandy Pylos,' where the aged King Nestor had his palace. This quarrel raged through the ages among Homeric philologues. In the late nineteenth century archaeologists brought their expertise to bear, only to make confusion worse confounded. For they split evenly, and the 'Greens' and 'Blues' of this ancient feud could each flourish an archaeological site to substantiate their claim. Our first chapter ends with an appeal by an archaeologist to the then undeciphered texts which held the decisive answer to the riddle.

Our second chapter is then perforce concerned with the dispute over the decipherment. The story of that remarkable achievement has already been told in moving terms by Michael Ventris's collaborator, Dr. J. Chadwick. But attacks still continue, sometimes in a disquieting form. Since the validity of the decipherment is basic to our whole enterprise, the question 'What constitutes a proof of any decipherment whatsoever?' has been considered in detail and the objections examined and assessed.

This essential preliminary completed, we return in the third chapter to the question which closed the first. The answer is unequivocal: the texts show that the place where Professor Blegen's palace is sited was called Pylos. To be more precise, we have a fairly clear and detailed picture of the geography of the territory controlled by this palace. Gratifyingly enough, its limits coincide almost exactly with the extent of Pylian territory such as we can piece together from the scattered references to this Mycenaean kingdom contained in the Homeric poems. We can see that administratively its territory was divided into two provinces, the Hither Province and the Further Province, the demarcation being the cape which marks the southern point of the Messenian peninsula, Cape Acritas. Pylos is the chief place of the Hither Province. Still more gratifying, renewed archaeological exploration of the region mapped out in our analysis as the Further Province has revealed important new Mycenaean sites.

Our geographical setting outlined, we turn in Chapter Four to the Bronze Age society which lived there, to encounter a surprise. The picture would have astonished Homer, on whose witness we had previously to rely for the reconstruction of the Greek Heroic Age, but not, I believe, Thucydides. The great historican, with his penetrating vision, remarked that there were many features about the way of life in early Greece which resembled the Orient of his own day. In fact, the picture of the Mycenaean polity which has gradually emerged from the combined labours of Linear B scholars recalls the temple states of the Orient. A king who shares his title 'Wanax' with a god is intimately linked with a goddess simply called 'The Lady' or 'The Mistress.' This close association shows itself in a variety of ways, in none more clearly or more fundamentally than the texts dealing with land-tenure. For the student of the structure of society there is no subject of greater importance; and we are fortunate indeed that virtually a complete land register, in two separate versions, has been preserved to us, relating to what I believe was the King's estate at the holy town of Pylos, where 'The Mistress' had her shrine. From these and other similar texts we gather some idea of the various classes of landholders, among whom, the 'servants (male and female) of the God' are especially numerous.

But this is no mere offshoot of the Orient. The God-King or the King-God is certainly paramount, but the *demos* also figures prominently as a land-holding entity, leasing its lands and upholding its rights *vis-à-vis* the palace in a case of disputed tenure.

The duality King-Mistress is particularly evident in the texts relating to bronze, for we have a great part of what must have been a census of the bronze-smiths of the Kingdom; it records those with allotted tasks, together with the amount of bronze issued, and also the bronze-smiths who are idle. It is here that we find the workers divided into those belonging to Potnia ('The Mistress') and the others, mentioned first, who presumably belonged to the royal establishment.

Yet another census concerns the cattle herds of both provinces of the kingdom. Here we find listed first the beasts of the king; then those belonging to a number of palace notabilities, whom we encounter elsewhere; and finally again the animals entered as belonging to Potnia. Gradually these dour archives reveal to us a complex administration with its queer titulature, practically nothing of which survived into later Greek, and many aspects of the economy. We need nothing to convince us of the importance of wheat, wine, oil and cattle in Mycenaean Greece. But one of the most welcome pieces of information gives some answer to a Bronze Age riddle: how did an intrinsically poor country like Greece manage to pay for its luxury imports? From the records of Pylos, Mycenae and Knossos we can now see the importance attached by all the palaces to the collection of aromatic substances for the manufacture of perfumed oil. The texts also give us interesting indications of the uses to which it was put. This dove-tails nicely with an archaeological fact of unique importance— the ubiquity of the stirrup-jar. Without undue distortion we may say that our picture of the extent of Mycenaean expansion and influence is little more than the distribution of this type of vessel on the archaeological map. The stirrup-jar is the *Leitfossil* of Mycenaean culture. We now know from the texts that they were used to contain perfumed oil.

Of no less interest is another set of facts of basic economic significance. It has proved possible to elucidate the grain ration scales, and it has become clear that a scheme of allocations according to social grade and function was in operation, a complex scheme common to both Pylos and Knossos. Again we are struck by the resemblance of the whole system to certain systems of the Orient which had been analysed by students of cuneiform texts. But this is not the only significant feature: the ratios of the corn-measures themselves are Mesopotamian in origin. They are dictated by the practical necessity of issuing a basic daily ration at monthly intervals. Moreover, the determination of these daily ration scales enables us to get some idea of the number of men and women the palace at Knossos was catering for; again by a lucky chance we have a number of texts recording the monthly allocation for certain dependent places, notably Phaestos in the south of Crete.

Finally the texts recording the things and substances offered to the gods, notably perfumed oil, enable us to give the precision of cult-titles, places, festivals and dates to the accounts of Mycenaean religion based hitherto on the dumb 'picture book' presented by the artefacts of Minoan and Mycenaean craftsmen. The result is gratifying to all concerned. It confirms in the main the deductions of the chief exponents in this delicate field of study. The Mycenaean religion shows itself profoundly under the influence of the Orient. For all the presence of Zeus, Hera, Artemis, Poseidon and Hermes, the views of Sir Arthur Evans and others that the Aegean, religiously speaking, was an offshoot of the Orient have been largely substantiated.

One simple physical fact about these clay tablets now focuses attention on a problem which has an undeniable fascination though authoritative cold water has diminished its historical pretensions. The records were originally inscribed on sun-dried clay which would soon have disintegrated. They present themselves to the scrutiny of twentieth century scholars only because they were unintentionally baked in the fire which finally destroyed the Palace of Nestor about 1200 B.C. They thus record the doings of the palace in the final months of Mycenaean civilization in those parts. Was it possible that the scribes and their masters were totally oblivious of their impending doom? This is the question to which we address ourselves in Chapter Five. We can answer it briefly: we see a society organizing itself with meticulous bureaucratic detail for its final ordeal. Women and children are gathered together into two main concentration areas, and arrangements are recorded for their supervision and provisioning. Bronze-smiths are allotted tasks, and it is recorded that officials are to yield up 'temple bronze' for armaments. Watchers are posted to guard an immense stretch of coast, a thinly spread line, with named officers and commanders. All this was clear by 1955–56. Further analysis has disclosed other facts of interest. The chain of watcher posts along the coast showed a great gap around the southern tip of the peninsula. We can now see, thanks to the analysis of what appeared to be a totally unrelated set of texts, that this gap is filled by the places where 'rowers' are recorded. Such complementarity shown by two different sets of texts can hardly be accidental, and I have ventured to conclude that these 'rower' texts reflect dimly the main concentration of the Pylian fleet in the area embracing the southern parts of the peninsula facing the Ionian Sea and the Gulf of Messenia, and that the complementary screen of coast watchers is the common-sense reaction of men faced with a sea-borne attack of unknown target area.

But this is not the only information which fits in here. Yet another set of texts is concerned with the allocation of craftsmen, especially bronze-smiths. Once again as minute analysis fitted the facts into place, it could be seen that these allocations affected the same area, and often the same places, as those recorded in the 'rower' texts. Here, too, a random coincidence seems excluded. We deduce that the craftsmen — chariot-wrights, 'sewers,' masons, bronze-smiths, etc. — are being posted to

the military headquarters. Pylian society was facing its emergency with the clear rationality we associate with the Greek mind. Strategic concentration and organization of local defence units, with civil defence measures to protect the women and children housed in villages scattered over the open countryside against possible marauders—an evacuation in reverse. The last mentioned pieces in this complex jigsaw puzzle we have been able to put in place thanks to the detailed ration lists which this movement of population necessitated. It was arithmetical analysis of these lists which revealed the basic rationing system which was also found to apply to Knossos.

At this point my original undertaking to write the new story of Mycenaean society under the title 'Nestor of Pylos' seemed virtually completed. All that remained was to compose a final synthesis, working these results into the accepted framework of prehistoric archaeology. It was at this point that the book took a new turn which necessitated the writing of a second part not envisaged in the original plan. It completely changed the character of the book. I had imagined that the final conspectus would not take much longer than a week, for once Ventris's decipherment had won acceptance, a clear picture of the Late Aegean Bronze age had achieved orthodoxy. But it gradually became clear that my results could not be fitted into this accepted framework.

This received opinion was given clear and cogent expression at the Eleventh International Congress of Historical Sciences held in Stockholm in August 1960. Among the reports submitted for discussion was one by Professor S. Dow of Harvard on 'The Greeks in the Bronze Age.' Its findings are that the Greeks entered Greece shortly after 2000 B.C. and introduced the Middle Helladic Culture. It was, however, not until Late Helladic times (beginning c. 1580 B.C.) that a concentration of power is to be observed centring around Mycenae. About 1480 B.C., according to Professor Dow, the Mycenaeans launched a successful invasion of Crete and ruled the island from the Palace of Knossos, where their period of dominance coincides with the Late Minoan II culture. The burning of this palace at the end of this period, c. 1400 B.C. is thought to mark the end of Minoan civilization. Professor Dow correctly summarizes archaeological opinion when he says that during the whole Late Minoan III period (c. 1400–1150) Crete was but a shadow of its former self, being isolated and quiet. In this, like all other Aegean specialists, he is following in the footsteps of Sir Arthur Evans, who called this the Period of Partial Reoccupation, when the denizens of the ruined palace were mere 'squatters.'

My own findings could hardly be a greater contrast. I have been forced to the conclusion that during this so-called 'squatter' period Knossos was in fact at the height of its power and that its Greek king controlled most of the island. Moreover, I now believe that many of the famous works of art, such as the Bull Relief Fresco, are also of this period, when the Greeks were in control. The steps which have led to this complete revolution in the accepted picture are set forth in Chapter Six. All that is necessary to say here is that interpretation of the texts had convinced me by February 1960 that Sir Arthur Evans's dating of the Linear B tablets to the end of the Late Minoan II period, c. 1400 B.C., must be wrong. In particular my suspicions were focused precisely on his key stratigraphical statements concerning a little room called The Room of the Stirrup Jar. These doubts prompted a series of enquiries which revealed the existence in the archives of the Ashmolean Museum, Oxford, of important primary sources for the Knossos excavations, which had remained unexploited. The first to emerge was the Day Book of the Knossos excavations meticulously kept by Sir Arthur Evans's assistant and official recorder, Duncan Mackenzie. This document showed that the alleged clear stratification of the Room of the Stirrup Jar, on which my doubts had been concentrated, had not been observed at the time when the said room was excavated and the objects removed, thus destroying the evidence once and for all. The find objects were not in fact arranged in their neat and convincing stratigraphical pattern until the end of the fourth season, in 1903. The next document I examined confirmed this: it was Sir Arthur Evans's own notebook for the said year. He, like Mackenzie, had drawn a plan of the area, and they both agreed in siting the objects on the same level with no hint of a vertical section which later was to figure so prominently in the published discussions.

Chapter Six, which sets forth these doubts, the progress of the search and its culmination, was already in the press in its present form when another document of the first importance came to light. On returning from vacation at the beginning of September 1960 I was informed that more of the papers left to the Ashmolean by the late Sir John Myres had been brought up from the basement. Among them was the document for which I had been looking from the start of my enquiries. This was Sir Arthur Evans's own Handlist of the Linear B tablets, complete with drawings and indications of the find-places. It is a paste-up of his original notebooks which he had cut up and rearranged. In his first excavation report of 1900 Evans wrote: 'I have copied over nine hundred of these tablets which I hope carefully to revise with the aid of the originals on my return to Crete. . . . No effort will be spared to publish the whole collected material at the earliest possible moment. The Oxford University Press (Clarendon Press) has undertaken the publication, and has already set in hand the preliminary work, including a Mycenaean Fount.' In fact over half a century was to elapse before the tablets were published. But from the snippets in the later paste-up it has proved possible to reconstruct Evans's notebook in what must have been its original form of 1900.

Study of this document brought complete confirmation of the doubts my researches had raised about Evans's chosen key to the stratigraphy of the tablets, to which he had lent emphasis by every device of typography. The heading of this important section of his monumental work reads thus: 'Hoard of Tablets referring to Painted Clay "Stirrup Vases" from Area above "Early Keep". Its Stratigraphical Relations.' The Handlist shows that there was only one such tablet and not a hoard; and that it was found 'Near Southwest Entrance' and not in the little Room of the Stirrup Jar lying to the west of the Northern Entrance Passage. I may add that a little later I found an unpublished commentary on the Knossos tablets by the late Sir John Myres, the literary executor of Sir Arthur Evans. He too places the said tablet 'near the southwest entrance.'

Throughout this investigation and discussion we have been at pains merely to record the documentary facts and to observe that the earlier and the later statements 'cannot be reconciled.' We stress again that the question of 'deliberate misrepresentation' is an irrelevance. Defenders of Evans, however, continue to insist publicly that the question of integrity is involved. If we are thus compelled to face it, then the problem will be most objectively considered as one aspect of the relationship between Volume Four of the *Palace of Minos* as a whole to the Handlist of 1900; for it was in this part of his work that Evans made his first extensive communication concerning the Linear B tablets to the world of scholarship thirty-five years after the discovery of the first tablets.

It may be said at once that throughout his exposition Evans makes intensive use of his Handlist, reproducing the drawings and quoting the texts by their HL number while discussing such minutiae as the variations in the shape of individual signs. Moreover he sometimes cut out the

drawings and sent them to the press for making blocks for the figures. There are many instances where the drawings have been re-pasted along with pulls from the blocks.

Among the texts drawn in this original notebook of 1900 is the famous stirrup-vase tablet. The corresponding figure is *PoM* iv, fig. 719, p. 734. It is an exact replica *of the same size*. A tracing made of the figure fits exactly over the drawing. Now the drawing on the page of the Handlist is singled out by the word. 'This, written alongside, while the drawing above is distinguished by the note 'not this.' The stirrup-vase tablet is also marked off by four crosses drawn in red ink and below in the same red ink are written the words 'same size'. There can be little doubt that these are instructions to the press for making figure 719. Above the drawing written in ink in Evans's own hand stands his original indication of the find place: W. Area: Nr SW entrance. Thus while Evans was preparing the copy and assembling the facts which were to offer to his fellow scholars 'decisive evidence for relative dating of "stirrup Vase Tablets"'; while he was preparing to announce to the world of scholarship that the tablets in question were separated by a deposit 'about 20 cm thick' from the Late Minoan III stirrup-jars on the floor above, he had before his eyes his own record that the tablet in question was found in an entirely different part of the Palace. Hence there is a conflict of testimony relating to all the alleged facts about the 'stratigraphic relation of this deposit.'

Even so my comment takes the limited and prudent form that we had best ignore the data relating to the Room of the Stirrup-Jar. I have found that no doubt attaches to other detailed statements relating to finds of Linear B tablets. It is fortunate that, as the records now show, only a few miserable scraps of tablet were in fact found in the said room and that there was after all only one 'stirrup-jar tablet,' the one we have just assigned to a different locality. It is surprising that Evans should so have singled out these scraps and this one stratigraphic statement. We must infer that this was the clearest case in his eyes. Yet only a few yards away is one of the most extensive and coherent of all tablet deposits, and unmistakably associated with, one may say entangled with, whole pots of clear late Reoccupation date. All the evidence, published and unpublished, harmonizes. No less clear and acknowledged by Evans himself are the facts relating to the four hundred and fifty tablets found within a space of ten metres in the East Wing of the Palace, the so-called Domestic Quarters, which Evans himself declared had remained in continuous occupation down to the end of Late Minoan III times, after the great catastrophe dated to 1400 B.C. The Little Palace, some hundreds of yards to the northwest of the main palace, offers evidence which Evans himself originally found cogent, for here there was no conflagration until the end of LM III. We are told in fact that the wooden columns of this building still retained their flutings which left their impression on the later plaster which set round them. But without conflagration these sun-dried tablets and sealings could not have survived. The facts in the important West Wing, where were situated the Throne Room, the shrines and the all-important magazines, are more confused. But fortunately the unity of all the archives can be demonstrated by internal cross-references.

To avoid friction due to misunderstanding we stress that throughout Chapter Six our method has been to let Evans tell his own story and to follow his own analyses. He discusses the various artefacts drawn on these tablets and we accept his analysis without question simply in order to observe where the echoes of resemblance lie. It will be seen that once his key statement is disregarded, all his arguments lead to the same conclusion, confirmed by the Day

Book, that the tablets are of LM III date. The same is true of his study of many of the works of art such as the Bull Relief Fresco. Furthermore, by a curious irony, our new dating restores to Evans the victory, awarded by almost universal consent since 1952 to his main opponent in an archaeological dispute which had for decades divided Aegean archaeologists into opposing camps. A. J. B. Wace was the chief spokesman for the 'mainlanders,' who argued that the Late Minoan II palace of Knossos had been the seat of Greek conquerors from the Mycenaean mainland. Once the language of these tablets was seen to be Greek, Wace's thesis, tentatively propounded by him, attracted a large following. But if the tablets are to be dated to c. 1150, then Evans's stubbornly held views are shown to be right after all.

There are other important consequences. The end of LM III Knossos is dated by archaeologists a half century or so later than the destruction of the Palace of Nestor at Pylos. This implies that the Knossos tablets, with their new dating, are somewhat later than those of Pylos. This purely archaeological conclusion is supported by observations of language and orthography. If the new date is right, then we must re-open the whole question of the history of the script. Serious doubt is cast on the idea that the Linear B script was evolved by Minoan scribes in Crete for their Greek masters in the fifteenth century or earlier. It would now seem more likely that the Greek invaders brought this form of script with them from the mainland. This would account better for a more important fact left unexplained by the previous theory: there is a totally different system of measurements of capacity from those of Linear A.

This brings us to the third important point where I would disagree with the accepted picture of the Greek Bronze Age. What evidence have we for associating the Greeks with the Middle Helladic invasion dated to c. 2000 B.C.? The Linear B texts are our first indubitable evidence for the presence of Greeks. If they are all to be dated to 1200 B.C. or later, then we are a long way from 2000 B.C. Now Professor Blegen has stressed that the whole history of the palace of Pylos was played out within the short period LH III B, i.e. 1300–1200 B.C. The rise of the palace at the beginning of this period marks, he believes, the arrival of a new dynasty, which legend suggests came from north of the isthmus of Corinth. Thus in the present state of knowledge we cannot safely go back further than 1300 B.C. for the use of Linear B at Pylos to write the Greek language. However, it would not be forcing the evidence overmuch if we say that the beginning of the Late Helladic period (*c.* 1580 B.C.) marks the arrival of the Greeks in Greece.

Who then brought the Middle Helladic culture to Greece? This is the subject of our ninth chapter. In the first place we follow the majority opinion among archaeologists about the affinities of this culture. They agree in the main in associating it with northwest Asia Minor; and more recent investigations show a distribution of its characteristic 'Grey Minyan' pottery as far south as the Maeander valley. If this is where the Middle Helladic folk came from, then they can hardly have been Greeks. There is not a shred of evidence for the use of the Greek language in those parts at that early date.

On the other hand, we have plenty of evidence for another Indo-European family of languages used throughout the second millennium in Asia Minor. These are the Anatolian languages, the best known of which is Hittite. But in the south and west, in the regions nearest to Crete, we find a closely related language, Luvian. Quite unexpectedly, while engaged in work in this field, I found some remarkable Luvian echoes in the Linear A texts. The possibility argued in Chapter Seven that the predecessors of the Greeks were Luvians from western Asia Minor should please both philologists and archaeologists. Before the decipherment the most important linguistic

evidence for the pre-Greek people was place-names. Among these none figures more prominently in scholarly discussion than those of the type *Parnassos*. Now such names are particularly common in Luvian territory. Furthermore, Parnassos turns out to be a perfectly transparent word: it means 'belonging to the *parna*'. In the Luvian tongue *parna* means 'house' and in particular 'house of god,' 'temple,' a spread of meaning such as we observe in the German *Dom* 'cathedral,' which is nothing more than the Latin word *domus*. Thus the Greek mountain name Parnassos not only has Asianic counterparts, as scholars had long observed; it also has an appropriate meaning in Luvian. While much remains to be done on the Linear A texts, which present the next important philological task in this area, as a working hypothesis I should propose to equate the archaeological 'Grey Minyan' folk with my philological 'Parnassos folk.' This would satisfactorily harmonize the results long reached through the study of pottery and place-names by two different disciplines. It would appear that Greece and Crete were twice invaded by Indo-European peoples during the second millennium B.C. in much the same way as our own island was first invaded by Celts and later by our Anglo-Saxon forebears. First came the Luvians, causing the Middle Helladic revolution; they were followed by the Greeks, who caused the less violent archaeological break at the beginning of Late Helladic. So far no archaeological evidence has come to light which suggests where they came from. That it was from the regions north of Greece seems, however, inescapable.

The book, in its drastically revised form, was already with the printers when the question of the credibility of the central witness was again raised in an acute form. It had been objected that if the Linear B tablets are all assigned to the late date, 1150 B.C., then there is a gap of some 400 years of apparent illiteracy in the history of the Knossian palace. This stimulated new enquiry, which is set forth in the inserted addendum. From this it emerges that once again, precisely at two key points of the evidence, we observe retrospective adjustments of the observed facts. In the starkest case 'good painted pottery of the Palace style' has been altered into 'characteristic vessels of the Third Middle Minoan class.' Once again we choose the most objective presentation of the course of events. We say that our results are more compatible with the statements contained in the primary sources than with the second thoughts of later years. All scholars justly claim the right to re-interpret their primary facts in the light of later information and experience. But once the archaeologist has removed a given set of objects from the ground, he cannot retrospectively endow them with forms, or rearrange them in positions, more convenient to a favoured hypothesis.

If, in the absence of any decisive association of Palace Style LM II pottery with an undisturbed deposit of Linear B tablets, we regard the LM II dating as a pure hypothesis, then the drastic readjustments of the primary facts required to save the hypothesis are a measure of its validity. We state the course of our own investigation likewise in terms of the fundamental steps of any scientific inquiry whatsoever. First comes observation and analysis of the facts, leading to the framing of a hypothesis as a tentative explanation. In our case what serves as the hypothesis is Ventris's decipherment. From the hypothesis a scientist draws deductions which lead to the expectation of making verificatory observations. To do this experimental situations are devised or a suitable natural situation is awaited, such as an eclipse of the sun. In our case the deductions from the 'hypothesis' of the decipherment are the philological workings we have outlined. These cast doubt on a certain set of statements made by Sir Arthur Evans. The setting up of the experiment corresponds to our search for the missing documents. Then

we make at the expected point the verificatory observations. It is necessary to stress once again that from this vast range of buildings and all the statements made about them in the excavation reports and Evans's huge work, we focused the experimental situation narrowly on the few pages devoted to this insignificant little room. It was precisely apropos of this that we found the statement which we had 'predicted.' No other statement relating to the Linear B tablets was challenged, and all are consistent both with the primary records and with our own findings.

Thus if we ignore these inadmissible retrospective adjustments in the physical positions of the objects found, if we keep to the statements of the primary sources—the Day Book, and the notebooks and Handlist of Evans himself—then the alleged gap between the two sorts of writing at Knossos disappears. Greeks using Linear B directly succeeded Luvians using Linear A. It is also satisfactory that we have been able to detect some evidence for the use of Linear B at a date earlier than the very end of the long period LM III, to which the archaeologists allocate no less than 250 years.

Such was the life history of this book with its modest original plan and scope. The new philological wine had burst the old archaeological bottle. Yet its results were virtually the same as the conclusions reached in the meantime by the distinguished archaeologist to whom philologists owe the tablets from Pylos. We have accepted them gratefully from his hand and gone our own way of truth. After seven years of research we find ourselves at the same goal. For in the meantime Professor Blegen, who had so firmly supported Professor Wace in contending that the LM II palace was under the control of Greeks from the mainland, had for various reasons come to believe that the Throne Room was after all an LM III reconstruction and that the Knossos tablets formed part of an archive contemporary with those of Pylos and Mycenae.

6. THE EXPLOSION ON SANTORINI (THERA) AND ITS PLACE IN THE AEGEAN BRONZE AGE*

Archaeological evidence usually consists of a very few, hard, unassailable facts. If the excavated and still visible floor of a building is of such and such a size and is made of gypsum, that can be considered a fact. But if, as often happens, an excavator has removed that floor to get at strata beneath it, the floor moves into a somewhat more shadowy realm—the "observed fact." We assume it to be true, but we can't test it. If the excavator then goes on to conclude that some pots which he found beneath the floor are earlier than the floor itself (because they were sealed in by it), we move into a still more insubstantial realm—the "primary inference." From there, like the soul in the neo-Platonic universe, we move rapidly outward toward a world that consists of inferences based on other inferences.

Now, what happens if scholars begin to question not the outer fringe of this circle of inferences but its very core? What happens if they challenge the "observed facts" and the "primary inferences" of the excavator. What can happen is that a grand archaeological edifice, perhaps already sanctified as a "chapter in human history," can collapse like a house of cards. Something of this sort is now threatening to take place in the archaeology of Bronze Age Greece.

Minoan archaeology began with, in fact was created by, Sir Arthur Evans, whose excavations at Knossos beginning in 1900 have, for better or worse, left an ineradicable stamp on the field. Evans had gone to Crete to look for examples of writing which

could be connected with the Mycenaean civilization first brought to light by Heinrich Schliemann some 25 years before. Evans did find writing, particularly some ancient Greek writing or Linear B tablets which were not deciphered during his long lifetime. But his principal discovery was a great palace unlike anything known on the Greek mainland. Its labyrinthine plan, its vibrant, rhythmic frescoes, its civilized, sophisticated appurtenances (including plumbing, which today seems to be one of the indispensable indices of civilization) stirred a visionary quality in Evans. At first *it* impressed itself on him; but as time passed, *he* began to impress himself on *it*. He gave it a name—Minoan—thus forever associating it with the later Greek legend of Minos, Theseus, and the Minotaur. He also gave it a kind of physical form by restoring many parts of the palace itself, by restoring vast fresco panels from tiny fragments, and by conjuring up—through vivid, graphic restorations and engaging prose—a picture of the religious life, amusements, and catastrophes that marked the life of the palace.

But most important for scholars today is that he gave the palace a chronology. Evans recognized in his excavations a pre-Palatial phase extending from the Stone Age to about 2000 B.C., an early Palatial phase extending from about 2000 to 1700 B.C., and a major Palatial phase—the great age of Minoan Crete, which lasted from about 1700 to 1400 B.C. Around 1400 B.C. a great disaster, probably caused by an earthquake in Evans's opinion, thoroughly destroyed the palace. For the next time sequence, from 1400 to 1100 B.C., Evans postulated his now controversial "squatter period" at Knossos, during which a few surviving Minoans lived out a ghostly existence amid the ruins of the great palace. At the end of this period, Bronze Age Crete merges into

---

* Jerome J. Pollitt, "Atlantis and Minoan Crete: An Archaeological Nexus," *Yale Alumni Magazine*, February 1970, pp. 20–29. Reprinted with permission from the February 1970 issue of the *Yale Alumni Magazine;* copyright by Yale Alumni Publications, Inc.

the Greek dark ages, and in its later history it follows the development of Greece as a whole.

Evans refined this general chronology by establishing a sequence of pottery types which fell into three phases—Early Minoan (EM), Middle Minoan (MM), and Late Minoan (LM). (Late Minoan extended from about 1050 B.C. to 1575 B.C. Middle Minoan lasted from 1575 B.C. to 2000 B.C.) There were also many subphases, such as EM II, LM Ia. The major Palatial phases occurred from MM III (about 1700 B.C.) to the end of LM II (about 1400 B.C.) To the long and supposedly dreary squatter period belonged the pottery called LM III.

The nature of the last phases of Minoan civilization—their dates, what happened during them, and to whom—has recently become very controversial. Evans's chronological system and his interpretation of the historical situation in which Minoan Crete is to be viewed have been seriously challenged. New pictures of the chronology of late Minoan civilization and new visions of a Minoan apocalypse have been offered. But before we can evaluate these new proposals, we must cross the southern Agean and look at what was happening on the Greek mainland.

Although the Bronze Age civilization of the Greek mainland had been known and studied since Schliemann's famous excavations at Mycenae in 1876, a coherent picture was largely the work of a Yale man, Carl W. Blegen, '08, '20 Ph.D., '27 M.A.H. In fact, the report of Blegen's excavations at Korakou, near Corinth, on which "Helladic chronology" is based, was a Yale doctoral dissertation submitted to the department of classics in 1920. In working out his chronological system Blegen followed Evans's model for Crete; he recognized an early, middle, and late phase for the Bronze Age of the mainland. The Early Helladic (EH) period, like the early Minoan, was seen to have occupied most of the third millenium B.C., a period during which cultural developments on

the Cycladic islands were of particular importance. Around 2000 B.C. a drastic change in pottery types, an increased use of bronze, new burial procedures, and new types of houses all seem to signal the advent of new peoples in Greece. This relatively simple Middle Helladic (MH) culture developed without any ostensible break into the Late Helladic (LH) phase, more generally referred to as "Mycenaean culture," around 1600 B.C. Since there was no break between Middle Helladic and Mycenaean, and since Mycenaean had such close connections in myth and legend with later Greece, Blegen and the distinguished British archaeologist Alan Wace, suggested, long before the decipherment of the Linear B tablets, that the Middle Helladic period marked the coming of Greek-speaking peoples to Greece.

The Mycenaean period covered nearly five centuries. Its first phases, LH I and II, from roughly 1600 to 1400 B.C., distinguished principally by the fabulous shaft graves found by Schliemann and later at Mycenae, were contemporary with the high point (and also supposed collapse) of Minoan Crete. Some objects in the shaft graves clearly seem to be Minoan, and others show a distinct Minoan influence. But the great days of Mycenaean Greece really seem to have come in the period between 1400 and 1200 B.C., LH III and its subdivisions. During this period the great palaces at Mycenae, Tiryns, Pylos and elsewhere, and most of the great tombs were built. It was also at this time that the foreign connections of Greece, traceable through finds of Mycenaean pottery, spread far and wide—to Italy and apparently to Spain in the west, to Egypt, and to the Near East. A Mycenaean trading empire seems to have developed.

What was the relationship between the Minoan and Mycenaean cultures? The answer has been disputed for a long time. Until the mid 1950's there were two main lines of thought. Sir Arthur Evans always maintained that down to 1400 B.C. the Mycenaean culture was simply a provincial, colonial offshoot of Minoan Crete. Hardy rustics of Hellenic stock served sophisticated Minoan overlords. The Mycenaean world did not strike out on its own until 1400 B.C., the end of LM II, when, in the view of Evans and his followers, a great earthquake or revolution led to the destruction of the great palaces of Minoan Crete. In Crete itself, it was held, no outside influence had any effect on the course of events. From the great days of LM I through the "squatter period," the people who inhabited Crete remained the same.

Those who worked mostly with Mycenaean material, however, particularly Wace, developed a different point of view. They felt that an unbiased examination of many objects from Knossos assigned by Evans to LM II, the period between 1450–1400 B.C., just before the destruction of the palace, seemed to point not to Minoan domination of the mainland but to exactly the reverse. Certain types of pottery characteristic of this period—the Ephyraean cups, alabastra, and the Palace style of painted pottery—were most common on the mainland and their presence at Knossos (and not, incidentally, at the other Cretan sites) seemed to mark an intrusion. It was also noted that the Minoan frescoes of this late phase appeared more similar to those of the mainland than to those at other Cretan sites, and that a well-known Mycenaean raw material, a green porphyry found only near Sparta, now appeared at Knossos for the first time. All of this suggested to Wace and others that during LM II Knossos had actually been seized and occupied by Mycenaean invaders, Greeks from the supposedly subservient mainland.

The choice between these alternatives was a matter of taste until 1952 when Michael Ventris deciphered the Linear B tablets. Clay tablets of this type had been found by Evans as early as 1900, but relatively few of them were published before

he died in 1941. It was assumed, of course, that the script of the tablets was used to write a lost "Minoan" language. But when Blegen, on the first day of his renowned excavation at Pylos in 1939, discovered a second archive of Linear B tablets, the problem of what these tablets were became more complex. What were tablets written in a supposedly Minoan language doing on the Greek mainland in a context dating them around 1200 B.C., well into the time of the Minoan squatter period? The problem became even more acute when further tablets were found at Mycenae in the early 1950's. (Recently, still others have appeared at Thebes.) It was still possible for those who took a pro-Minoan view of the relationship between Crete and the mainland to hold that somehow a Minoan aristocracy had survived in Greece and still had managed to dominate the mainland people at palaces like Pylos and Mycenae. But then, in 1952–53, Ventris brilliantly demonstrated that the Linear B tablets were written in an early form of the language which we now call Greek. Not only the tablets of Pylos and Mycenae, but those of Knossos too, were written in the language of the mainland. Wace's view of Crete and the mainland in the late Bronze Age seemed to be confirmed.

Almost as a symbol of victory, Wace was invited to write a historical introduction to Ventris and Chadwick's *Documents in Mycenaean Greek*. Reading it gives the impression that everything has finally fallen into place, that whatever details might have to be clarified, we know what happened in the Greek Bronze Age. The Minoan civilization reached its zenith between 1600–1450 B.C. During this time it exercised a strong cultural influence on the more backward but perhaps also more martial people of the mainland. Then, in about 1450 B.C., the Mycenaean Greeks seized control of Knossos and controlled it for about 50 years (LM II). This seizure may have come through a violent invasion, or possibly the Mycenaeans simply occupied

Years B.C.	Egypt		Greek Mainland	Crete		Cyclades
1000				Sub-Minoan		
1100	Decline		Proto-Geometric			Platon Notation
			LH IIIC			
1200	XX Dynasty					
		Meremptah	LH IIIB	LM IIIC		PP III
1300		Rameses II		LM IIIB		PP II
	XIX Dynasty					
		Akhenaton	LH IIIA			Post Pal I
1400		Amenhotep III		LM IIIA		Earthquakes
		Thutmosis IV		LM II Knossos	LM III	NP III	Thera Collapse
		Amenhotep II	LH II			
1500		Thutmosis III		LM IB		Thera Eruption
		Hatshepsut				
		Thutmosis I & II				
	New Kingdom	XVIII Dynasty · Amenhotep I	LH I	LM IA	New Palaces II	Earthquakes
1600		Ahmose I	Mycenaean			
		XV-XVI Dynasties Hyksos XVII		MM IIIB		
1700				MM IIIA	NP I	
1800	2nd Int. Period	XIII-XIV		MM IIB		
1900				Middle Minoan IIA		
		XII Dynasty			Old Palaces	Middle Cycladic
2000	Middle Kingdom	XI Dynasty		MM IB		
			Middle Helladic			
2100						EC III

A comparative dating chart, showing the chronology for Egypt, the Greek mainland, Crete, and the Cyclades for the period described in the article.

Crete after it had been devastated by one of its many earthquakes. Around 1400 B.C. or slightly later, this Mycenaean domination of Knossos was thrown off, perhaps by revolution. The palace of Knossos was destroyed once and for all. Destruction, either from violence or from natural causes, also swept the other Cretan sites. It was a *Götterdämmerung* of the Minoans, followed by the long innocuous squatter period. The Mycenaean Greeks lost interest in Crete, and while it languished, they proceeded to build their own civilization on the mainland to new heights.

This view lasted for less than a decade; it was then beset with the same revolutions and natural disasters that it postulated for Crete. The leader of this revolution has been an Oxford philologist, Leonard R. Palmer, who became interested in the general field of Minoan archaeology while working on the Linear B tablets. Palmer had been engaged by a publisher to write a semi-popular book on the world of Bronze Age Greece as revealed by the tablets. Not even he had any inkling at the beginning that this seemingly innocuous book would become the center of a major storm of scholarly controversy.

In working out a historical synthesis of what happened in Crete and Greece in the late Bronze Age, Palmer was puzzled by the fact that the Knossos tablets were thought to have been baked and preserved in a great conflagration about 1400 B.C. (the end of LM II or slightly later) while the Pylos tablets underwent the same fate nearly 200 years later, around 1200 B.C. Yet in language and form the tablets from the two places were astonishingly similar. The standard chronology would imply that the process of writing and recording underwent scarcely any alteration for two centuries. Before Palmer, Blegen had also raised this problem and had suggested that the findspots of the Knossos tablets should be reinvestigated to see if there was any evidence linking them with LM IIIB instead

of LM II, bringing their date more in line with the Pylos tablets.

Palmer felt driven to follow up Blegen's suggestion because, in addition to the discrepancy in the date of the tablets, there were other facts which bothered him about Evans's picture of Crete between 1400–1200 B.C. as a land of insignificant squatters.

First, there was the contradiction between the squatter theory and Homer's picture of Crete. As classical archaeologists have known since the time of Schliemann, Homer has much to tell us about Greece in the Bronze Age. And in the *Iliad* and the *Odyssey*, Crete, far from being a land of squatters, is the realm of wealthy cities and powerful kings. Idomeneus, who led the Cretan contingent to the Trojan War, is depicted as the peer of Agamemnon, Achilles, and the other Achaean warriors.

The megaron, a typical architectural form, known at Pylos, Mycenae, and Tiryns, is also found in Crete at Haghia Triada, Tylissos, and, scarcely known but extremely important, at Knossos, where it was built into part of the palace. All of this is peculiar if only ghostly Minoan squatters inhabited these sites between 1400–1200 B.C.

In addition, the Linear B tablets at Knossos refer to sites in western Crete, particularly Cydonia and Aptara, which according to the evidence provided by Minoan pottery, were not even founded until LM III, that is, *after* the time when Knossos was supposedly destroyed.

False-necked jars, commonly called "stirrup jars," are very rare in LM II, the period in which Knossos was destroyed. In LM III, on the other hand, they abound. Yet one of the Linear B tablets lists 1800 of them. (Stirrup jars, it should be noted, do exist before LM III; it is the quantity which is at issue.)

The tablets also indicate that Knossos and Phaistos, the great Minoan palace sites to the south, are closely related. Yet the Palace Style of pottery, distinctive of LM II and characteristic of the supposed era of destruction at Knossos, doesn't even exist at Phaistos.

Except in disturbed deposits, Palace Style sherds and Linear B tablets seem to be mutually exclusive.

In any case the date of the Palace Style itself seems shaky. At Alalakh in northern Syria, Sir Leonard Woolley found a type of pottery in an archaeological stratum datable to around 1250 B.C. that seemed to be strongly under the influence of the Palace Style, even though that style supposedly went out of existence 150 years earlier.

There is evidence that some of the Minoan pottery styles, hitherto considered stratified and mutually exclusive, were in use at the same time. A recent excavation at Gortyna, north of Phaistos, by distinguished Italian archaeologist Doro Levi, found that LM I and LM II pottery was apparently in simultaneous use.

The type of chariot illustrated on the Knossos tablets shows a close resemblance to the type illustrated on frescoes of LH III from Tiryns.

The ideogram for a horse on the tablets shows three tufts on the horse's mane. The same arrangement appears on LM III sealings and again in Mycenaean wall-paintings of LH II.

The ideogram for a corselet on the tablets from Knossos and Pylos shows that exactly the same type of armor was in use in both places.

The swords illustrated on the tablets are of LM III and LH III type.

Some of the stirrup jars described on the Pylos tablets are spoken of as being "of Cretan workmanship," a peculiar designation if Crete at this time was a land of degenerate squatters.

Inscribed stirrup jars from the mainland (Thebes, Eleusis, Tiryns, Mycenae) have Cretan place names written on them, apparently designating Crete as their place of origin.

Finally, the tablets indicate that there were similar supervisory and rationing systems at Pylos and Knossos.

With all this in mind, Palmer began to check the evidence available for the findspots of the Knossos tablets. He found that the information given in *Scripta Minoa* II, the second volume of the publication of the Knossos tablets, which appeared after Evans's death, was unreliable in some ways. He therefore asked permission of the Ashmolean Museum at Oxford to examine Evans's original records in storage there. He found some of Evans's notebooks and papers, but he also came upon a quite remarkable document for which he was totally unprepared: the Day-Book of the Knossos excavations kept by Duncan MacKenzie, Evans's chief assistant for many years. This day-book was a day-by-day record of what had been found at Knossos since 1900.

In Palmer's opinion this newly recovered evidence shows that the findspots of the Knossos tablets have in every case been misrepresented in Evans's publication. Palmer does not openly say whether this misinterpretation was deliberate or accidental, but he darkly hints that Evans's dispute with Wace might have been the motivating force behind it. It would be too complicated and time-consuming to examine all Palmer's arguments in detail, but let me give one key example which can stand for the whole. Evans claimed that the decisive key to the dating of the Knossos tablets was to be found in a small room just west of the north entrance passage to the palace, known as the "room of the stirrup jars." In the fourth volume of the *Palace of Minos*, we are told that three floor levels were found in this room. According to the report, some late stirrup jars were found on the uppermost level, about 80 cm. below the surface. Another 20 cm. below this, on a second floor, a hoard of Linear B tablets were said to have been found, and 60 cm. below this second floor still a third was found.

What Palmer claims to have learned about these rooms on the basis of the original records is so devastating that I will quote him: "The documents to which I have referred were to show, step by step, that this elaborate stratigraphical picture was a total fabrication: there were no such three floors in that room; the tablet was the sole one and it had been found near the southeast entrance [of the palace]. . . . The room of the stirrup-jars had only two floors and not three. The three floor levels were actually observed in the neighboring room of the saffron gatherer, and here all three levels had been occupied in the LM III period. This is how Evans achieved his 'decisive stratigraphy.'"

The publication of the first edition of Palmer's *Mycenaeans and Minoans* in 1961 set off a series of bitter exchanges with the defenders of Evans's ideas and honor. In order to give the public a chance to judge for itself, Oxford University Press arranged to publish a volume in which Palmer would state his arguments in detail and a spokesman for the traditional point of view, the able and distinguished archaeologist, John Boardman, would defend Evans and criticize the arguments in the first edition of Palmer's *Mycenaeans and Minoans.* Neither man was allowed, however, to read the other's portion of this composite book before its publication.

The unbiased reader who struggles through the Palmer-Boardman book will probably judge it a standoff. There are lucid arguments on both sides, and one is hard pressed to know what to think. But Palmer has had, at this point, the last word. Thanks to a generous publisher, he has been able to produce an expanded second edition of *Mycenaeans and Minoans* in which he not only restates his own case but also answers Boardman.

At the very least, it seems to me, Palmer has cast enough doubt on the reliability of Evans's chronology so that one need no longer feel obligated to do it honor. It is now perfectly reasonable to believe that during the high point of the Mycenaean Empire, from around 1400–1200 B.C., Crete was a thriving part of the Mycenaean

world, not a land of squatters, and that the final destruction of Bronze Age civilization in Crete has to be viewed as part of the same pattern which brought an end to Mycenae, Tiryns, Pylos, and the other great sites of the mainland in the period between 1200–1100 B.C.

This opportunity to rethink the whole question of how Bronze Age civilization in the Aegean came to an end brings us to what I call the "New Apocalypse" in Minoan archaeology—the theory that associates the destruction of Minoan Crete with the later Greek myth of the lost continent of Atlantis. The story of Atlantis is preserved in the two dialogues of Plato, the *Critias* and the *Timaeus.* Plato tells us the story was handed down from the Athenian philosopher-statesman Solon, who was said to have learned it from Egyptian priests. The *Timaeus* sets Atlantis in a remote age, some 9,000 years before Solon. The people of Atlantis, a race of divine descent that dwelt on a large island in the Atlantic Ocean, attacked and enslaved many of the countries around the Mediterranean. At length they were opposed by the ancient Athenians who defeated them after a long struggle. The Athenians set about to liberate the countries enslaved by Atlantis, but as they were doing so, a dreadful day of earthquakes and floods caused Atlantis to sink and the ancient Athenians, as well as the Atlanteans, to perish. In the *Critias*, Plato adds a strange physical description of the island of Atlantis: it was circular, about 11 miles in diameter, and consisted of a plain and a mountain in the center surrounded by alternating concentric rings of land and sea. On the central islet were palaces, religious sanctuaries sacred particularly to Poseidon, and springs of warm and cold water. The rings were linked by a great canal. The island was densely inhabited.

In the last few years a number of scholars writing in newspapers and popular magazines have proposed that there are real historical roots in the Atlantis story—not in the Atlantic Ocean, where occult literature has looked for centuries, but on the Cycladic island of Thera.

Thera and the smaller islets near it form a broken circle which resembles the crater-rim of a great volcano. In fact, within this broken circle there is a still-active volcanic center. It has been proposed that this broken circle once consisted mostly of rich, fertile, volcanic earth, penetrated by inlets, and that it was a flourishing, densely populated center of Minoan civilization. Minoan remains on the ·island were discovered as long ago as 1867. There are also many traces of ancient and recent volcanic activity on the island. Might there not have been a great volcanic eruption in the Minoan period, it has been asked, an eruption followed by the sinking of the center of the island into a caldera, a large crater formed by the collapse of the volcano's central part. Might not this event be the source of the myth of Atlantis?

The idea that Thera was Atlantis is not new, although it has lately gained a new popularity. It was suggested as early as 1885 by a Frenchman named Nicaise. The idea that the civilization on Atlantis might actually have been what we call Minoan civilization was clearly stated by British archaeologist J. K. Frost as early as 1909. By 1939 the theory had been thoroughly outlined by the Greek archaeologist, Spyridon Marinatos, who is now the Inspector General of the Antiquities Service in Greece. Marinatos's own discovery of pumice and what seemed to be evidence of a tidal wave at Amnisos in Crete suggested to him that the effects of the Thera eruption may have been responsible for the destruction not only of Thera itself but of Minoan civilization as a whole. He compared, as some geologists have done before him, the probable effects of the Thera explosion with the effects of the explosion of Krakatoa in the Dutch East Indies in 1883.

Since then, geologists and oceanographers have added scientific data and expertise to the theory. The most notable were the Columbia geologists, Heezen and Ninkovich, who have studied the seabottom cores from around Thera; the Greek seismologist, Angelos Galanopoulos, who has drawn elaborate analogies between Plato's description of Atlantis and the probable pre-eruption geology of Thera; and the oceanographer, James W. Mavor Jr., whose enthusiasm brought about a new series of excavations on Thera. (The new excavations, I might add, are under the direction of Marinatos; Mavor has been barred from the excavation for a variety of reasons which he endeavors to explain in his 1969 book, *Voyage to Atlantis*.)

At this point, let me summarize the picture that has been drawn of the geological history of Thera and the probable effects of its eruption. The sea-core tests of Heezen and Ninkovich show that Thera has had two great eruptions in recent geological history, one about 25,000 years ago the other within the last 5,000 years. [*Editors' note: A new calculation by Dr. William Ryan of Columbia University suggests that the first great eruption actually took place 80,000 years ago.*] The first perhaps formed a caldera, resembling Thera today. In time, this caldera filled up with a new volcanic matter, forming a fertile island that eventually became a center of Minoan culture. A second great eruption and collapse is thought to have taken place around 1400 B.C., with a force five times greater than Krakatoa. It is hypothesized that a black cloud caused by the eruption darkened the sky for days and affected the atmosphere for years afterwards. Poisonous vapors spread for miles. A huge wave, estimated by some to have been as high as 700 feet and to have traveled at 350 miles an hour, overwhelmed Crete. Whatever was left standing after the wave was destroyed by great earthquakes and shock waves in the air. The volcanic debris, which fell on Crete in particular, made the land infertile for decades, perhaps centuries. Thousands upon thousands of people perished. It was the end of Minoan civilization. In the turmoil of the subsequent age, the Greeks forgot the great catastrophe, but it was preserved in the records of Egyptian priests and in time came back to Greece in the form of Plato's myth of Atlantis.

Those who accept this grim picture and a date for the Thera disaster around 1400 B.C. suggest that a few cultured Minoans escaped the catastrophe and migrated to Greece, where they were responsible for the cultural efflorescence at sites like Pylos after 1400 B.C. They also see some of the "lamentation literature" of the Near East, familiar to us from the Old Testament and from Egyptian records, as reflecting the Thera disaster.

It should be emphasized, however, that this date of 1450–1400 B.C. for the eruption is not precise. Geologists took it from the traditional Minoan chronology. All the geologists can tell us is that the eruption probably occurred within the last 5,000 years. True, some wood samples from quarries on Thera have been dated by carbon [14] to somewhere between 1700 B.C. and 1400 B.C., but the trees from which these samples came could easily predate the major eruption by centuries. And since Thera has been subjected to repeated volcanic eruptions over the centuries, they could also postdate the major eruption and still be buried in volcanic ash.

We could, in other words, assign the new apocalypse to the new chronology and connect the eruption of Thera with Palmer's date of around 1200 B.C. for the destruction of Knossos. What implications follow? Obviously, it might suggest that not only the destruction of civilization in Crete but the destruction of Bronze Age civilization in Greece as a whole was caused by the Thera disaster. Crete and Mycenae went down on the same ship, so to speak. In fact, such an interpretation was implied recently by Leon Pomerance, one of the participants in the current

excavation of the Minoan palace at Kato Zakros in eastern Crete. It remains to be seen whether the Kato Zakros evidence will support Pomerance's theory and bring about a major revision of Minoan chronology. I might point out, however, that a carbon [14] sample from Kato Zakros yielded the date 1150, plus or minus 120 years. The director of the excavation, Nicholas Platon, is reluctant to accept the date provided by his own excavation because it does not fit the traditional chronology. But Palmerites will be perhaps less reluctant.

If the destruction of Greece's Bronze Age civilization did result from a great natural catastrophe, how precisely did it happen? Can a calamity even of the presumed dimensions of the Thera eruption really bring an entire civilization to an end? The human species has a way of pulling itself together in spite of the most incredible calamities, as the inhabitants of Hiroshima and the earthquake-torn belts of Turkey and Iran attest. Is it possible that the modern enthusiasm for the apocalypse of Atlantis is more a reflection of our own nuclear anxieties than it is a respect for historical truth?

In any case there are reasons for being cautious about the Atlantis theory. As I have said, the date of the Thera eruption cannot really be pinned down. It could have happened around 1400 B.C. or 1200 B.C., but it also could have happened in 2500 B.C. or even in 900 B.C. The fact that the Minoan remains on Thera are covered with ash is not conclusive. Thera has volcanic eruptions an average of every 50 years. There have been many eruptions since the Greek Bronze Age, some of major proportions. The position of the Minoan remains within the successive deposits of volcanic debris on the island, if it can be determined, has not been made clear by the excavation reports. Moreover, we do not know at what speed the caldera of Thera formed. The extent of the shock waves and the presumed infertility of the soil are only hypotheses.

And if we associate the presumed Thera disaster with the end of *both* Minoan and Mycenaean civilization, we must take into account the increasingly abundant evidence which demonstrates that the Mycenaean world did not collapse all at once. It is true that around 1200 B.C. there are signs of trouble in the Mycenaean world. Emergency fortifications and water supplies are built at Mycenae, Tiryns, and Athens (fortifications are built for protection from people, not volcanoes). Pylos, it is true, was destroyed by fire around 1200 B.C., but whatever the storm was, most Mycenaean centers seem to have weathered it. In Athens, civilization never came to an abrupt break. Mycenae and Tiryns seem to die of attrition around 1100 B.C., but in the century between 1200 B.C. and 1100 B.C. there is no single, great calamity. In fact, at times there are some signs of reviving prosperity.

This slow decline of Mycenaean civilization has recently led the distinguished American archaeologist, Rhys, Carpenter, to propose yet another natural calamity as the cause of the decline of Bronze Age civilization in Greece. In a brilliant little book entitled *Discontinuity in Greek Civilization*, Carpenter suggests that the cause was not a great explosion but rather a prolonged drought extending from about 1200 to 900 B.C. He conjectures that a world-wide climatic change at this time caused the cyclonic storms that normally bring rain to Greece throughout all seasons except summer to shift northward, so that instead of the three dry months which Greece now experiences there were eight such months. In the wake of this change came famine, disease, and depopulation. He suggests that the Dorians and Herakleidai, who in Greek literary tradition displaced the Mycenaeans, came not as conquerors but as nomads or as refugees returning to a nearly deserted land.

Carpenter's enthralling book, however, cannot really prove its case. Meteorologists who have commented on it note that the mechanics of climatic change are not as simple and predictable as he makes them out to be. Moreover, analyses of samples of ancient pollen from Greece, although scarce at the moment, do not substantiate Carpenter's hypothetical drought.

So, at this point in history our knowledge of what really happened at the end of the Greek Bronze Age is very much up in the air. I would like to compound the confusion by adding an observation of my own. To the archaeologist who looks beyond the confines of the Aegean toward other parts of the Mediterranean and Europe, it is clear that the period between 1250 B.C. and 1100 B.C. was an era of great turmoil and instability everywhere. In Asia Minor the once mighty Hittite Empire began to crumble, There are major destruction levels in Syria, Palestine, and on Cyprus. Egypt, during the reign of Ramses III in the early 12th Century, suffered attacks from foreign hordes known collectively as the "Peoples of the Sea. . . ."

Historians of the Greek Bronze Age more often look east rather than west, because it is from the east that the elements of so-called "higher" civilization emanated at this time. Yet Italy, at the end of the Bronze Age, has perhaps much to tell us about what happened in Greece. Around 1200 B.C. connections with the Aegean are shattered and here many sites are abandoned. In Sicily, the survivors of the Bronze Age Castelluccio and Thapsos cultures seem to flee up into the hills. On the Aeolian Islands, where a series of trading stations that seems to have passed on obsidian and metals to the Aegean has flourished for 2,000 years or more, civilization is all but annihilated.

In all these areas—Aegean, East, and West—there seems to be one consistent element that accompanies the turmoil and sets its stamp on it. This is the rite of cremation burial with certain types of swords, pins, and ornaments accompanying the cremation. . . . The aggregate of this rite and these implements, suddenly and in so many places at roughly the same time, must reflect more than just a coincidental change of custom. And the place where this combination of cremation, flange-hilted swords, and safety pins makes its earliest appearance is in the Urn-field cultures of the Balkans and Central Europe.

The idea that the Bronze Age civilization of Greece might have been destroyed by an invasion from the north has been out of fashion for some time because, in the form in which it was originally proposed, it was simplistic and did not fit the archaeological evidence. But perhaps it is due for a comeback in an altered form. The picture of piratical groups of footloose Urn-fielders from central Europe, in concert perhaps with other disaffected elements of the Mediterranean population, attacking Egypt, driving the inhabitants of Crete and south Italy into the hills, sacking Pylos (causing the building of emergency fortifications in other Mycenaen cities), and starting a general chain reaction of piracy, civil strife, and economic dislocation throughout the Mediterranean, is not beyond the evidence.

The process may have resembled the invasion of the Roman Empire by semi-barbarian northerners from the third to the fifth centuries A.D. This was also a gradual process. There is no single archaeological stratum to mark where "the invaders" replaced the "established culture." But in several centuries a great and long-standing civilization passed from the scene. If we did not know what really happened from ancient historians, what calamities and disasters would we not hypothesize for the fall of the Roman Empire? In the end, I wonder if the fall of Mycenaean Greece might not turn out to be the result not of strange and unexpected natural forces, but rather of strange and unexpected people.

SECTION V

The World of Homer

ONE OF THE OLDEST of scholarly debates is that which surrounds the poems of Homer. From ancient times men have asked who wrote the poems: Was there a single author for both, for each, or for neither? Since the discoveries of Schliemann new questions have been added to the old Homeric question. What is the relationship between the world described by Homer and the world inhabited by the Mycenaeans? Are the Homeric heroes Mycenaeans, or men of the Dark Ages, or a combination of these? Further questions have been raised by the apparent decipherment of the Linear B tablets at Cnossus and Pylos by Michael Ventris. If these are truly written in Greek does it mean that the story of Greek civilization is an unbroken tale beginning with the Mycenaeans? All these problems emphasize the importance of seeking the true character of the world of Homer. Since a complete investigation is impossible this chapter will emphasize the political aspects of Homeric society.

1. THE QUARREL OF ACHILLES AND AGAMEMNON*

Sing, goddess, the wrath of Achilles Peleus' son, the ruinous wrath that brought on the Achaians woes innumerable, and hurled down into Hades many strong souls of heroes, and gave their bodies to be a prey to dogs and all winged fowls; and so the counsel of Zeus wrought out its accomplishment from the day when first strife parted Atreides king of men and noble Achilles.

Who then among the gods set the twain at strife and variance? Even the son of Leto and of Zeus; for he in anger at the king sent a sore plague upon the host, that the folk began to perish, because Atreides had done dishonour to Chryses the priest. For he had come to the Achaians' fleet ships to win his daughter's freedom, and brought a ransom beyond telling; and bare in his hands the fillet of Apollo the Far-darter upon a golden staff; and made his prayer unto all the Achaians, and most of all to the two sons of Atreus, orderers of the host: "Ye sons of Atreus and all ye well-greaved Achaians, now may the gods that dwell in the mansions of Olympus grant you to lay waste the city of Priam, and to fare happily homeward; only set ye my dear child free, and accept the ransom in reverence to the son of Zeus, far-darting Apollo."

---

* The *Iliad*, translated by Andrew Lang, Walter Leaf, and Ernest Myers, rev. ed. (London: Macmillan & Co., Ltd., 1907), pp. 1–10. Used by permission.

Then all the other Achaians cried assent, to reverence the priest and accept his goodly ransom; yet the thing pleased not the heart of Agamemnon son of Atreus, but he roughly sent him away, and laid stern charge upon him, saying: "Let me not find thee, old man, amid the hollow ships, whether tarrying now or returning again hereafter, lest the staff and fillet of the god avail thee naught. And her will I not set free; nay, ere that shall old age come on her in our house, in Argos, far from her native land, where she shall ply the loom and serve my couch. But depart, provoke me not, that thou mayest the rather go in peace."

So said he, and the old man was afraid and obeyed his word, and fared silently along the shore of the loud-sounding sea. Then went that aged man apart and prayed aloud to king Apollo, whom Leto of the fair locks bare: "Hear me, god of the silver bow, that standest over Chryse and holy Killa, and rulest Tenedos with might, O Smintheus! If ever I built a temple gracious in thine eyes, or if ever I burnt to thee fat flesh of thighs of bulls or goats, fulfil thou this my desire; let the Danaans pay by thine arrows for my tears."

So spake he in prayer, and Phoebus Apollo heard him, and came down from the peaks of Olympus wroth at heart, bearing on his shoulders his bow and covered quiver. And the arrows clanged upon his shoulders in his wrath, as the god moved; and he descended like to night. Then he sate him aloof from the ships, and let an arrow fly; and there was heard a dread clanging of the silver bow. First did he assail the mules and fleet dogs, but afterward, aiming at the men his piercing dart, he smote; and the pyres of the dead burnt continually in multitude.

Now for nine days ranged the god's shafts through the host; but on the tenth Achilles summoned the folk to assembly, for in his mind did goddess Hera of the white arms put the thought, because she had pity on the Danaans when she beheld them perishing. Now when they had gathered and were met in assembly, then Achilles fleet of foot stood up and spake among them: "Son of Atreus, now deem I that we shall return wandering home again—if verily we might escape death—if war at once and pestilence must indeed ravage the Achaians. But come, let us now inquire of some soothsayer or priest, yea, or an interpreter of dreams—seeing that a dream too is of Zeus—who shall say wherefore Phoebus Apollo is so wroth, whether he blame us by reason of vow or hetacomb; if perchance he would accept the savour of lambs or unblemished goats, and so would take away the pestilence from us."

So spake he and sate him down; and there stood up before them Kalchas son of Thestor, most excellent far of augurs, who knew both things that were and that should be and that had been before, and guided the ships of the Achaians to Ilios by his soothsaying that Phoebus Apollo bestowed on him. He of good intent made harangue and spake amid them: "Achilles, dear to Zeus, thou biddest me tell the wrath of Apollo, the king that smiteth afar. Therefore will I speak; but do thou make convenant with me, and swear that verily with all thy heart thou wilt aid me both by word and deed. For of a truth I deem that I shall provoke one that ruleth all the Argives with might, and whom the Achaians obey. For a king is more of might when he is wroth with a meaner man; even though for the one day he swallow his anger, yet doth he still keep his displeasure thereafter in his breast till he accomplish it. Consider thou, then, if thou wilt hold me safe."

And Achilles fleet of foot made answer and spake to him: "Yea, be of good courage, speak whatever soothsaying thou knowest; for by Apollo dear to Zeus, him by whose worship thou, O Kalchas, declarest thy soothsaying to the Danaans, no man while I live and behold light on earth shall lay violent hands upon thee amid the hollow ships; no man of all the Danaans, not even if thou mean Agamemnon, that now avoweth him to be greatest far of the Achaians."

Then was the noble seer of good courage, and spake: "Neither by reason of a vow is he displeased, nor for any hecatomb, but for his priest's sake to whom Agamemnon did despite, and set not his daughter free and accepted not the ransom; therefore hath the Far-darter brought woes upon us, yea, and will bring. Nor will he ever remove the loathly pestilence from the Danaans till we have given the bright-eyed damsel to her father, unbought, unransomed, and carried a holy hecatomb to Chryse; then might we propitiate him to our prayer."

So said he and sate him down, and there stood up before them the hero son of Atreus, wide-ruling Agamemnon, sore displeased; and his dark heart within him was greatly filled with anger, and his eyes were like flashing fire. To Kalchas first spake he with look of ill: "Thou seer of evil, never yet hast thou told me the thing that is pleasant. Evil is ever the joy of thy heart to prophesy, but never yet didst thou tell any good matter nor bring it to pass. And now with soothsaying thou makest harangue among the Danaans, how that the Far-darter bringeth woes upon them because, forsooth, I would not take the goodly ransom of the damsel Chryseis, seeing I am the rather fain to keep her own self within mine house. Yea, I prefer her before Klytaimnestra my wedded wife; in no wise is she lacking beside her, neither in favour nor stature, nor wit nor skill. Yet for all this will I give her back, if that is better; rather would I see my folk whole than perishing. Only make ye me ready a prize of honour forthwith, lest I alone of all the Argives be disprized, which thing beseemeth not; for ye all behold how my prize is departing from me."

To him then made answer fleet-footed goodly Achilles: "Most noble son of Atreus, of all men most covetous, how shall the great-hearted Achaians give thee a meed of honour? We know naught of any wealth of common store, but what spoil soe'er we took from captured cities hath been apportioned, and it beseemeth not to beg all this back from the folk. Nay, yield thou the damsel to the god, and we Achaians will pay thee back threefold and fourfold, if ever Zeus grant us to sack some well-walled town of Troyland."

To him lord Agamemnon made answer and said: "Not in this wise, strong as thou art, O godlike Achilles, beguile thou me by craft; thou shalt not outwit me nor persuade me. Dost thou wish, that thou mayest keep thy meed of honour, for me to sit idle in bereavement, and biddest me give her back? Nay, if the great-hearted Achaians will give me a meed suited to my mind, that the recompense be equal—but if they give it not, then I myself will go and take a meed of honour, thine be it or Aias', or Odysseus' that I will take unto me; wroth shall he be to whomsoever I come. But for this we will take counsel hereafter; now let us launch a black ship on the great sea, and gather picked oarsmen, and set therein a hecatomb, and embark Chryseis of the fair cheeks herself, and let one of our counsellors be captain, Aias or Idomeneus or goodly Odysseus, or thou, Peleides, most redoubtable of men, to do sacrifice for us and propitiate the Far-darter."

Then Achilles fleet of foot looked at him scowling and said: "Ah me, thou clothed in shamelessness, thou of crafty mind, how shall any Achaian hearken to thy bidding with all his heart, be it to go a journey or to fight the foe amain? Not by reason of the Trojan spearmen came I hither to fight, for they have not wronged me; never did they harry mine oxen nor my horses, nor ever waste my harvest in deep-soiled Phthia, the nurse of men; seeing there lieth between us long space of shadowy mountains and sounding sea; but thee, thou shameless one, followed we hither to make thee glad, by earning recompense at the Trojans' hands for Menelaos and for thee, thou dog-face! All this thou reckonest not nor takest thought thereof; and now thou threatenest thyself to take my meed of honour, wherefor I travailed much, and the sons of the Achaians gave it me. Never win I meed like unto thine, when the Achaians sack any populous citadel of Trojan men; my hands bear the brunt of furious war, but when the apportioning cometh then is thy meed far ampler, and I betake me to the ships with some small thing, yet mine own, when I have fought to weariness. Now will I depart to Phthia, seeing it is far better to return home on my beaked ships; nor am I minded here in dishonour to draw thee thy fill of riches and wealth."

Then Agamemnon king of men made answer to him: "Yea, flee, if thy soul be set thereon. It is not I that beseech thee to tarry for my sake; I have others by my side that shall do me honour, and above all Zeus, lord of counsel. Most hateful art thou to me of all kings, fosterlings of Zeus; thou ever lovest strife and wars and fightings. Though thou be very strong, yet that I ween is a gift to thee of God. Go home with thy ships and company and lord it among thy Myrmidons; I reck not aught of thee nor care I for thine indignation; and this shall be my threat to thee: seeing Phoebus Apollo bereaveth me of Chryseis, her with my ship and my company will I send back; and mine own self will I go to thy hut and take Briseis of the fair cheeks, even that thy meed of honour, that thou mayest well know how far greater I am than thou, and so shall another hereafter abhor to match his words with mine and rival me to my face."

So said he, and grief came upon Peleus' son, and his heart within his shaggy breast was divided in counsel, whether to draw his keen blade from his thigh and set the company aside and so slay Atreides, or to assuage his anger and curb his soul. While yet he doubted thereof in heart and soul, and was drawing his great sword from his sheath, Athene came to him from heaven, sent forth of the white-armed goddess Hera, whose heart loved both alike and had care for them. She stood behind Peleus' son and caught him by his golden hair, to him only visible, and of the rest no man beheld her. Then Achilles marvelled, and turned him about, and straightway knew Pallas Athene; and terribly shone her eyes. He spake to her winged words, and said: "Why now art thou come hither, thou daughter of aegis-bearing Zeus? Is it to behold the insolence of Agamemnon son of Atreus? Yea, I will tell thee that I deem shall even be brought to pass: by his own haughtinesses shall he soon lose his life."

Then the bright-eyed goddess Athene spake to him again: "I came from heaven to stay thine anger, if perchance thou wilt hearken to me, being sent forth of the white-armed goddess Hera, that loveth you twain alike and careth for you. Go to now, cease from strife, and let not thine hand draw the sword; yet with words indeed revile him, even as it shall come to pass. For thus will I say to thee, and so it shall be fulfilled; hereafter shall goodly gifts come to thee, yea in threefold measure, by reason of this despite; hold thou thine hand, and hearken to us."

And Achilles fleet of foot made answer and said to her: "Goddess, needs must a man observe the saying of you twain, even though he be very wroth at heart; for so is the better way. Whosoever obeyeth the gods, to him they gladly hearken."

He said, and stayed his heavy hand on the silver hilt, and thrust the great sword back into the sheath, and was not disobedient to the saying of Athene; and she forthwith was departed to Olympus, to the other gods in the palace of aegis-bearing Zeus.

Then Peleus' son spake again with bitter words to Atreus' son, and in no wise ceased from anger: "Thou heavy with wine, thou with face of dog and heart of deer, never didst thou take courage to arm for battle among thy folk or to lay ambush with the princes of the Achaians; that to thee were even as death. Far better booteth it, forsooth, to seize for thyself the meed of honour of every man through the wide host of the Achaians that speaketh contrary to thee. Folk-devouring king! seeing thou rulest men of naught; else were this despite, thou son of Atreus, thy last. But I will speak my word to thee, and swear a mighty oath therewith: verily by this staff that shall no more put forth leaf or twig, seeing it hath for ever left its trunk among the hills, neither shall it grow green again, because the axe hath stripped it of leaves and bark; and now the sons of the Achaians that exercise judgment bear it in their hands, even they that by Zeus' command watch over the traditions—so shall this be a mighty oath in thine eyes—verily shall longing for Achilles come hereafter upon the sons of the Achaians one and all; and then wilt thou in no wise avail to save them, for all thy grief, when multitudes fall dying before manslaying Hector. Then shalt thou tear thy heart within thee for anger that thou didst in no wise honour the best of the Achaians."

So said Peleides and dashed to earth the staff studded with golden nails, and himself sat down; and over against him Atreides waxed furious. Then in their midst rose up Nestor, pleasant of speech, the clear-voiced orator of the Pylians, he from whose tongue flowed discourse sweeter than honey. Two generations of mortal men already had he seen perish, that had been of old time born and nurtured with him in goodly Pylos, and he was king among the third. He of good intent made harangue to them and said: "Alas, of a truth sore lamentation cometh upon the land of Achaia. Verily Priam would be glad and Priam's sons, and all the Trojans would have great joy of heart, were they to hear all this tale of strife between you twain that are chiefest of the Danaans in counsel and chiefest in battle. Nay, hearken to me; ye are younger both than I. Of old days held I converse with better men even than you, and never did they make light of me. Yea, I never beheld such warriors, nor shall behold, as were Peirithoos and Dryas shepherd of the host and Kaineous and Exadios and godlike Polyphemos [and Theseus son of Aigeus, like to the immortals]. Mightiest of growth were they of all men upon the earth; mightiest they were and with the mightiest fought they, even the wild tribes of the mountain caves, and destroyed them utterly. And with these held I converse, being come from Pylos, from a distant land afar; for of themselves they summoned me. So I played my part in fight; and with them could none of men that are now on earth do battle. And they laid to heart my counsels and hearkened to my voice. Even so hearken ye also, for better is it to hearken. Neither do thou, though thou art very great, seize from him his damsel, but leave her as she was given at the first by the sons of the Achaians to be a meed of honour; nor do thou, son of Peleus, think to strive with a king, might against might; seeing that no common honour pertaineth to a sceptred king to whom Zeus apportioneth glory. Though thou be strong, and a goddess mother bare thee, yet his is the greater place, for he is king over more. And thou, Atreides, abate thy fury; nay, it is even I that beseech thee to let go thine anger with Achilles, who is made unto all the Achaians a mighty bulwark of evil war."

Then lord Agamemnon answered and said: "Yea verily, old man, all this thou sayest is according unto right. But this fellow would be above all others, he would be lord of all and king among all and captain to all; wherein I deem none will hearken to him. Though the immortal gods made him a spearman, do they therefore put revilings in his mouth for him to utter?"

Then goodly Achilles brake in on him

and answered: "Yea, for I should be called coward and man of naught, if I yield to thee in every matter, howsoe'er thou bid. To others give now thine orders, not to me [play master; for thee I deem that I shall no more obey]. This, moreover, will I say to thee, and do thou lay it to thy heart. Know that not by violence will I strive for the damsel's sake, neither with thee not any other; ye gave and ye have taken away. But of all else that is mine beside my fleet black ship, thereof shalt thou not take anything or bear it away against my will. Yea, go to now, make trial, that all these may see; forthwith thy dark blood shall gush about my spear."

2. ODYSSEUS AND THERSITES*

In the Second Book of the *Iliad* Agamemnon is inspired to test the spirit of his troops by suggesting that they give up the siege of Troy and return home. But the stratagem fails; the men run to their ships. Then the goddess Athena intervenes and urges Odysseus to stop their flight.

So spake she [Penelope], and the bright-eyed goddess Athene disregarded not; but went darting down from the peaks of Olympus, and came with speed to the fleet ships of the Achaians. There found she Odysseus standing, peer of Zeus in counsel, neither laid he any hand upon his decked black ship, because grief had entered into his heart and soul. And bright-eyed Athene stood by him and said: "Heaven-sprung son of Laertes, Odysseus of many devices, will ye indeed fling yourselves upon your benched ships to flee homeward to your dear native land? But ye would leave to Priam and the Trojans their boast, even Helen of Argos, for whose sake many an Achaian hath perished in Troy, far from his dear native land. But go thou now amid the host of the Achaians, and tarry not; and with thy gentle words refrain every man, neither suffer them to draw their curved ships down to the salt sea."

So said she, and he knew the voice of the goddess speaking to him, and set him to run, and cast away his mantle, the which his herald gathered up, even Eurybates of Ithaca, that waited on him. And himself he went to meet Agamemnon son of Atreus, and at his hand received the sceptre of his sires, imperishable for ever, wherewith he took his way amid the ships of the mail-clad Achaians.

Whenever he found one that was a captain and a man of mark, he stood by his side, and refrained him with gentle words: "Good sir, it is not seemly to affright thee like a coward, but do thou sit thyself and make all thy folk sit down. For thou knowest not yet clearly what is the purpose of Atreus' son; now is he but making trial, and soon he will afflict the sons of the Achaians. And heard we not all of us what he spake in the council? Beware lest in his anger he evilly entreat the sons of the Achaians. For proud is the soul of heaven-fostered kings; because their honour is of Zeus, and the god of counsel loveth them."

But whatever man of the people he saw and found him shouting, him he drave with his sceptre and chode him with loud words: "Good sir, sit still and hearken to the words of others that are thy betters; but thou art no warrior, and a weakling, never reckoned whether in battle or in council. In no wise can we Achaians all be kings here. A multitude of masters is no good thing; let there be one master, one king, to whom the son of crooked-counselling Kronos hath granted it, [even the

---

* *Iliad*, translated by Lang, Leaf, and Myers, rev. ed. (London: Macmillan & Co., Ltd., 1907), pp. 24–30. Used by permission.

sceptre and judgments, that he may rule among you]."

So masterfully ranged he the host; and they hasted back to the assembly from ships and huts, with noise as when a wave of the loud-sounding sea roareth on the long beach and the main resoundeth.

Now all the rest sat down and kept their place upon the benches, only Thersites still chattered on, the uncontrolled of speech, whose mind was full of words many and disorderly, wherewith to strive against the chiefs idly and in no good order, but even as he deemed that he should make the Argives laugh. And he was ill-favoured beyond all men that came to Ilios. Bandy-legged was he, and lame of one foot, and his two shoulders rounded, arched down upon his chest; and over them his head was warped, and a scanty stubble sprouted on it. Hateful was he to Achilles above all and to Odysseus, for them he was wont to revile. But now with shrill shout he poured forth his upbraidings upon goodly Agamemnon. With him the Achaians were sore vexed and had indignation in their souls. But he with loud shout spake and reviled Agamemnon: "Atreides, for what art thou now ill content and lacking? Surely thy huts are full of bronze and many women are in thy huts, the chosen spoils that we Achaians give thee first of all, whene'er we take a town. Can it be that thou yet wantest gold as well, such as some one of the horse-taming Trojans may bring from Ilios to ransom his son, whom I perchance or some other Achaian have led captive; or else some young girl, to know in love, whom thou mayest keep apart to thyself? But it is not seemly for one that is their captain to bring the sons of the Achaians to ill. Soft fools, base things of shame, ye women of Achaia and men no more, let us depart home with our ships, and leave this fellow here in Troy-land to gorge him with meeds of honour, that he may see whether our aid avail him aught or no; even he that hath now done dishonour to Achilles, a

far better man than he; for he hath taken away his meed of honour and keepeth it by his own violent deed. Of a very surety is there no wrath at all in Achilles' mind, but he is slack; else this despite, thou son of Atreus, were thy last."

So spake Thersites, reviling Agamemnon shepherd of the host. But goodly Odysseus came straight to his side, and looking sternly at him with hard words rebuked him: "Thersites, reckless in words, shrill orator though thou art, refrain thyself, nor aim to strive simply against kings. For I deem that no mortal is baser than thou of all that with the sons of Atreus came before Ilios. Therefore were it well that thou shouldest not have kings in thy mouth as thou talkest, and utter revilings against them and be on the watch for departure. We know not yet clearly how these things shall be, whether we sons of the Achaians shall return for good or for ill. Therefore now dost thou revile continually Agamemnon son of Atreus, shepherd of the host, because the Danaan warriors give him many gifts, and so thou talkest tauntingly. But I will tell thee plain, and that I say shall even be brought to pass: if I find thee again raving as now thou art, then may Odysseus' head no longer abide upon his shoulders, nor may I any more be called father of Telemachos, if I take thee not and strip from thee thy garments, thy mantle and tunic that cover thy nakedness, and for thyself send thee weeping to the fleet ships, and beat thee out of the assembly with shameful blows."

So spake he, and with his staff smote his back and shoulders: and he bowed down and a big tear fell from him, and a bloody weal stood up from his back beneath the golden sceptre. Then he sat down and was amazed, and in pain with helpless look wiped away the tear. But the rest, though they were sorry, laughed lightly at him, and thus would one speak looking at another standing by: "Go to, of a truth Odysseus hath wrought good deeds without number ere now, standing foremost in wise counsels and setting battle in array, but now is this thing the best by far that he hath wrought among the Argives, to wit, that he hath stayed this prating railer from his harangues. Never again, forsooth, will his proud soul henceforth bid him revile the kings with slanderous words."

3. The Shield of Achilles*

In Book Eighteen of the *Iliad* a new shield is fashioned for Achilles on which several scenes of the life of Homeric society are depicted. The following passage describes an aspect of political life.

Also he fashioned therein two fair cities of mortal men. In the one were espousals and marriage feasts, and beneath the blaze of torches they were leading the brides from their chambers through the city, and loud arose the bridal song. And young men were whirling in the dance, and among them flutes and viols sounded high; and the women standing each at her door were marvelling. But the folk were gathered in the assembly place; for there a strife was arisen, two men striving about the blood-price of a man slain; the one claimed to pay full atonement, expounding to the people, but the other denied him and would take naught; and both were fain to receive arbitrament at the hand of a daysman. And the folk were cheering both, as they took part on either side. And heralds kept order among the folk, while the elders on polished stones were sitting in the sacred circle, and holding in their hands staves from the loud-voiced heralds. Then before the people they rose up and gave judgment each in turn. And in the midst lay two talents of gold, to be given unto him who should plead among them most righteously.

* *Iliad*, translated by Lang, Leaf, and Myers, rev. ed. (London: Macmillan & Co., Ltd., 1907), p. 351. Used by permission.

4. Kingship at Ithaca*

In the First Book of the *Odyssey* Telemachus calls an assembly to deal with the problems of Ithaca, and especially his family. The discussion reveals much about the nature of Homeric kingship.

Now the wooers clamoured throughout the shadowy halls, and each one uttered a prayer to be her bedfellow. And wise Telemachus first spake among them:

'Wooers of my mother, men despiteful out of measure, let us feast now and make merry and let there be no brawling; for, lo, it is a good thing to list to a minstrel such as him, like to the gods in voice. But in the morning let us all go to the assembly and sit us down, that I may declare my saying outright, to wit that ye leave these halls: and busy yourselves with other feasts, eating your own substance, going in turn from house to house. But if ye deem this a likelier and a better thing, that one man's goods should perish without atonement, then waste ye as ye will; and I will call upon the everlasting gods, if haply Zeus may grant that acts of recompense be made: so should ye hereafter perish within the halls without atonement.'

* The *Odyssey*, translated by S. H. Butcher and A. Lang (London: Macmillan & Co., Ltd., 1930), pp. 12–13.

So spake he, and all that heard him bit their lips and marvelled at Telemachus, in that he spake boldly.

Then Antinous, son of Eupeithes, answered him: 'Telemachus, in very truth the gods themselves instruct thee to be proud of speech and boldly to harangue. Never may Cronion make thee king in seagirt Ithaca, which thing is of inheritance thy right!'

Then wise Telemachus answered him, and said: 'Antinous, wilt thou indeed be wroth at the word that I shall say? Yea, at the hand of Zeus would I be fain to take even this thing upon me. Sayest thou that this is the worst hap that can befall a man? Nay, verily, it is no ill thing to be a king: the house of such an one quickly waxeth rich and himself is held in greater honour. Howsoever there are many other kings of the Achaeans in seagirt Ithaca, kings young and old; some one of them shall surely have this kingship since goodly Odysseus is dead. But as for me, I will be lord of our own house and thralls, that goodly Odysseus gat me with his spear.'

Then Eurymachus, son of Polybus, answered him, saying: 'Telemachus, on the knees of the gods it surely lies, what man is to be king over the Achaeans in seagirt Ithaca. But mayest thou keep thine own possessions and be lord in thine own house! Never may that man come, who shall wrest from thee thy substance violently in thine own despite, while Ithaca yet stands. But I would ask thee, friend, concerning the stranger—whence he is, and of what land he avows him to be? Where are his kin and his native fields? Doth he bear some tidings of thy father on his road, or cometh he thus to speed some matter of his own? In such wise did he start up, and lo, he was gone, nor tarried he that we should know him;— and yet he seemed no mean man to look upon.'

Then wise Telemachus answered him, and said: 'Eurymachus, surely the day of my father's returning hath gone by. Therefore no more do I put faith in tidings, whencesoever they may come, neither have I regard unto any divination, whereof my mother may inquire at the lips of a diviner, when she hath bidden him to the hall. But as for that man, he is a friend of my house from Taphos, and he avows him to be Mentes, son of wise Anchialus, and he hath lordship among the Taphians, lovers of the oar.'

So spake Telemachus, but in his heart he knew the deathless goddess. Now the wooers turned them to the dance and the delightsome song, and made merry, and waited till evening should come on. And as they made merry, dusk evening came upon them. They they went each one to his own house to lie down to rest.

5. THE EVIDENCE OF THE TABLETS: SOCIAL ORGANIZATION*

The following selection is a summary of the evidence of the Linear B Tablets provided by Ventris and Chadwick, the decipherers of the script.

The frequent qualification of people by occupational names makes it possible to draw some general deductions about the structure of society in a Mycenaean kingdom; further work will no doubt extend and correct the picture offered here. Most of the evidence comes from Pylos, but many of the important words recur at Knossos, and there is no indication that

* Michael Ventris and John Chadwick, *Documents in Mycenaean Greek* (Cambridge: Cambridge University Press, 1956), pp. 119–125.

the social structure was significantly different. The absence of any palace records from Mycenae excludes any deductions about that kingdom, though there seems no reason to assume that Pylos was exceptional. The apparent differences between the Mycenaean and Homeric patterns are explicable in terms of the Homeric question.

A monarchical system of government is proved for both Knossos and Pylos by references to the king (*wanax*); the absence of any further qualification shows that the state knew one king only. The suggestion of Palmer that he was a priest-king is likely enough on archaeological as well as comparative grounds; but that his power was temporal as well as spiritual is guaranteed by the elaborate records of his civil service. A number of tradesmen—a potter, a fuller and an armourer (?)—are referred to as 'royal' (*wanakteros*), and the same word in a doubtful context on a jar from Thebes seems at least to prove the existence of another kingdom there. The king is never referred to by name and title at once, though he may be mentioned by name alone: Ekhelawon at Pylos is clearly a man of supreme importance, and the precedence accorded him in 171=Un718* makes it almost certain that we have here the first contemporarily attested Mycenaean monarch.

The Pylos distribution of τεμένη ranks next to the king's the allocation of the *lāwāgetās*. His name is a known Greek compound, surviving in verse in the form λαγέτας, though apparently meaning only 'leader', 'prince', without the technical sense it must bear in Mycenaean. There is no direct clue in the tablets to his peculiar function, but both the etymology and the Teutonic parallels adduced by Palmer suggest that he was the military commander whose duty it was to lead the host in war. If the Germanic parallel were exact (cf. Tacitus, *Germania*, 7), we might expect

him to be elected only in time of war; and we may be sure from the military tablets that Pylos was at this time on a war footing. But he is also found at Knossos, where so far there is no indication of preparations against an attack. Compare §§ 1, 22–4 of the autobiography of the Hittite king Hattusilis III: 'But when my father Mursilis became a god, my brother Muwatallis seated himself on the throne of his father; and before the face of my brother I became *chief of the armed forces* (EN KI.KAL.BAD).' Occupational names are also qualified by the adjective *lāwāgesios*.

The *temenos* list enumerates next some officials called *te-re-ta*, τελεσταί, an official title which survived in Elis down to the classical period. They are assigned jointly the same amount of grain (land?) as the king, but it is divided among three holders, so that the individual holdings are the same as that of the *lāwāgetās*. Palmer equates the *telestai* with the Hittite LÚ *ILKI* 'fief-holders' owing a special duty to the king, and contrasts them with the 'artisans', whom he equates with the Homeric δημιοεργοί, a word not found yet in the tablets, though *dāmos* is very common. Some sort of feudal system of land tenure is certain; but Palmer's view is open to objection, especially because of the newly published Pylos text 171=Un718, where the *telestai* seem to be equated with the *dāmos*. Considerable numbers of *telestai* seem to be proved by the instance of 114=En02, where the district *Pa-ki-ja-* alone contains fourteen, and at Knossos by 47=Am826 where no less than forty-five *telestai* of Aptara are mentioned. It is likely that the verb *te-re-ja-e* (*teleiaen?*) expresses the function of the *telestās*, and since it is replaced in other cases by *wo-ze-e* (*worzeen*) which seems to be the function of the *ka-ma-e-u*, it probably indicates some kind of feudal service.

The *ka-ma-e-u* is plainly the holder of the land called *ka-ma*. The most natural explanation of this is that it is the obsolete noun *χαμά from which the locative

---

* References are to the documents.

χαμαί was formed, a conclusion supported by a Cretan gloss in Hesychius. Its meaning, however, is more specialized and it denotes a particular kind of feudal holding. The men distinguished by this title seem to be of humble status; they include a baker (?) and a 'slave of the god'.

A more important title is the *e-qe-ta*, *heq″etās*=ἐπέτης. It is a rare word in classical Greek and seems to mean no more than 'companion, follower'. But Palmer is probably right in seeing in this word the equivalent of the Homeric ἑταῖρος, and understanding it to mean 'companion of the king' like the late Latin *comes* and similar words in Celtic and Germanic. The proof of their position emerges from the military tablets, where they are regularly dignified by a patronymic, a rare distinction elsewhere. They seem to be attached to bodies of troops in the capacity of staff officers, possibly as liaison officers representing the central authority, the command being in the hands of the local lords. On the other hand they are occasionally mentioned in contexts relating to land tenure (e.g. PY 55= An724, and 142=Eb32 where one (or more) is coupled with the priestess, the key-bearers and a man called *We-te-re-u*). They may have slaves, and they have a distinctive kind of garment.

In addition to these we find also a number of officials who appear to be confined to outlying regions. We do not find them associated with Pylos or Knossos, but with subordinate towns. The title *pa₂-si-re-u* is clearly to be connected with the Homeric βασιλεύς, who is not a king, but a kind of feudal lord, master of his own territory but owning allegiance to the king. Carratelli disagrees with this view (also expressed by Furumark) and would see in these βασιλεῖς religious functionaries like the φυδοβασιλεῖς. But their association with the outlying towns is significant. They have a *pa₂-si-re-wi-ja*, probably 'retinue', less likely 'palace', and in KN 38= As1516 it is noteworthy that this term

follows the place-name *Se-to-i-ja* and another name (*Phaistos?*) lost in a lacuna, while the first section contains the heading *Knōsiā lāwāge⟨si⟩ā*, implying a parallel between the *lāwāgetās* at Knossos and the *basileus* elsewhere.

The *ke-ro-si-ja*, *geronsia*=γερουσία is perhaps the council of a *basileus* since on PY 40=An22 this word is associated with a man who is elsewhere called *pa₂-si-re-u*. It is less certain whether the erased *ke-ro-te* in KN B 800 is *gerontes*, and if so whether it should be connected as proposed by Carratelli.

Another title which seems likewise to be provincial is *mo-ro-pa₂*, probably to be interpreted *moroppās* (Palmer: μοιρόπᾱs) 'possessor of a portion, shareholder'. His importance is vouched for by the fact that Klumenos who is *moroppās* in PY 43= Sn01 is on 58=An654 commander of a regiment. Their regional location is to be inferred from a variety of indications: their presence in the tribute list 258=Kn01; the fact that *Ka-do-wo moroppas* of 43= Sn01 is elsewhere associated with the place-name *Ma-ro-*; the entry on the same tablet which shows that Klumenos was *ko-re-te* of the place *I-te-re-wa*.

Finally we hear of a local official called the *ko-re-te*, who seems to be a kind of mayor (Furumark: Dorfschulze). The word is an agent noun in -*tēr*, not yet satisfactorily interpreted, but his status emerges clearly enough from PY 257= Jn09, where we have sixteen places named and contributions of bronze from the *ko-re-te* and *po-ro-ko-re-te* of each. The prefix *pro-* must mean in this case 'vice-' or 'sub-', a sense not preserved in any classical compound. The heading to this tablet enumerates not only these two, but also a variety of other titles which are not mentioned again below. Is the explanation that the heading gives all the possible alternative titles which are equivalent to the two general terms *ko-re-te* and *po-ro-ko-re-te*? Against this it may be argued that the *klawiphoroi* are elsewhere feminine, though it is less likely that the same is true of *du-ma-te*. The *da-mo-ko-ro* who is mentioned a few times may perhaps be another title or another local official appointed by the king. There are occasional references to *ki-ti-ta* 'settlers' and *me-ta-ki-ti-ta* 'colonists (?)', but it would not seem safe to draw any conclusions from these words yet.

Of the humbler members of the population we can say less. The variety of trades followed shows a highly developed division of labour, but it is not clear how far the craftsmen were royal servants, or even slaves, or what other status they enjoyed. There is one very obvious omission from the list of trades, the absence of any word implying that the raising of crops was a specific occupation. On the contrary land tenure documents mention craftsmen such as fullers and agricultural workers such as shepherds. This suggests that everyone in addition to his special occupation also farmed a portion of land.

Among the occupational names there are many still not satisfactorily interpreted, and in some other cases the precise significance of the word is lost; etymology is often a poor guide to meaning. Thus the list of trades must be regarded as incomplete.

Among the public servants we hear of a messenger and a herald (*a-ke-ro*, *ka-ru-ke*); but the name of the scribe still eludes us. The agricultural workers named include shepherds (*po-me*), goat-herds (*ai-ki-pa-ta*), huntsmen (*ku-na-ke-ta-i*), and wood-cutters (*du-ru-to-mo*). The building trades are represented by masons (*to-ko-do-mo*) and carpenters (*te-ko-to*); ship construction is a separate trade (*na-u-do-mo*). Metal-workers include bronzesmiths (*ka-ke-u*) and cutlers (?, *pi-ri-je-te*), and other manufacturers are bow-makers (*to-ko-so-wo-ko*), chair(?)-makers (*to-ro-no-wo-ko*) and potters (*ke-ra-me-we*). The making of cloth was a women's occupation; we hear of carders, spinners and weavers (*pe-ki-ti-*

ra$_2$, *a-ra-ka-te-ja*, *i-te-ja-o*), and there are separate designations for flax-workers (*ri-ne-ja*), and perhaps for the makers of some of the other special kinds of garment (*a-pu-ko-wo-ko*, *e-ne-re-ja*, *o-nu-ke-ja*). The fulling of cloth was a man's trade (*ka-na-pe-u*) and the king had his own fuller. The making of garments was shared by men and women (*ra-pte*, *ra-pi-ti-ra$_2$*). Luxury trades are attested by unguent-ilers (*a-re-pa-zo-o*) and goldsmiths (*ku-ru-so-wo-ko*). We have one reference to a physician (*i-ja-te*). The grinding and measuring out of grain were done by women (*me-re-ti-ri-ja*, *si-to-ko-wo*), but the making of bread by men (*a-to-po-qo*); Blegen seems unjustified in his assumption that the Mycenaean figurine of a bread-maker is female. More menial occupations seem to be indicated by stokers (*pu-ka-wo*), ox-drivers (?, *ze-u-ke-u-si*) and, among the women, bath-attendants (*re-wo-to-ro-ko-wo*) and serving women (*a-pi-qo-ro*).

The existence of slavery in some form is certain. Some slaves (*do-e-ro*, *do-e-ra*) are plainly stated to be the property of individuals: e.g. the women of *Amphiq^u-hoitās*, or those belonging to the smiths and following their masters' trade. The slave of *We-da-ne-u* is even in the position of having to contribute to his master's revenue and is not distinguished in his treatment from the rest of the group who appear to be free men. The Pylos tablet 28 = An42 suggests that a single slave parent of either sex made the child a slave, contrary to the rule of classical Greece; but this deduction is not inevitable. The Pylos tablets of the classes *Aa* and *Ab* imply that the labour force was recruited by raids in which captive women and children were brought home and taught trades, and this conclusion seems to be confirmed by the word 'captives' (*ra-wi-ja-ja*) applied to some of these women: others are referred to by ethnic adjectives. The *Ad* series suggests that the children of slaves were an important element in the manpower available. On the other hand there is some evidence that women of this class also worked for wages (*e-ke-ro-qo-no*); but possibly these were not wage-earners on their own account, but were hired out to augment the palace revenues.

But by far the greater number of slaves named at Pylos are 'slaves of the god (or goddess)'. Two explanations of this phrase are possible: we may either suppose that a number of slaves became the property of a deity instead of a man, or that the title really conceals some quite different status from that of ordinary slaves. In the former case we need not think exclusively of the ἱερόδουλοι or temple-slaves of later times; dedication to a deity could be a method of holding public property, as we see to be the case with the lands of Dionysus and Athena recorded in the famous tables of Heraclea. The other alternative is made attractive by the fact that slaves of the god have leases of land and seem in fact to live on much the same terms as free men. The translation 'slave' is probably here leading us to a false conception of social status, and it might be preferable to adopt feudal terminology, such as 'serf' or 'villein'. The parallel of Near Eastern societies in which similar titles are actually honorific probably does not hold good for Mycenaean Greece; for there are a few isolated cases in which the slave of a man seems to enjoy the same status as a slave of the god; and the slaves of the priestess raise an awkward point in social precedence.

At Knossos we learn almost nothing of the military organization apart from the existence of the *lāwāgetās*; but at Pylos preparations were being made against an attack, and a series of tablets are concerned with naval and military matters. From these it appears that the command of the bodies of men detailed to watch the coast was in the hands of local lords, each of whom was assisted by a small group of officers; while each sector had allocated as well a *heqᵘetās*, who may have been a liaison officer representing the king. The details of the troops are obscure, since the words applied to them, *ke-ki-de* and *ku-re-we*, are not satisfactorily explained; Palmer suggests that the latter word means elsewhere 'men-at-arms', but insists that it is here a place-name. Other groups of men are merely referred to by ethnic adjectives. The total number of troops recorded on the surviving tablets of the military series is 740.

Rowers to man warships seem to have been drawn as necessary from the coastal towns; it is probable that they were conscripts rather than professionals, at least if our interpretation of 55=An724 is correct. Rowers are also mentioned as the fathers of the sons of some slave women at Pylos (15=Ad684). At Knossos rowers surprisingly figure in a list of local officials who are supplying or receiving cattle.

6. HOMER AND MYCENAE*

Many scholars have argued for the essential identity of the Homeric and Mycenaean worlds—none more forcefully than Martin Nilsson. The following discussion of political organization is typical of this view.

There is one side of life in which we may especially hope to discover through this method elements handed down from the Mycenaean age—the state organization, for though undeveloped this is closely bound up with the background of epics, and is therefore likely to be preserved

* Martin Nilsson, *Homer and Mycenae* (London: Methuen and Co., Ltd., 1933), pp. 214–235 (abridged).

through the epic technique, although not without alterations and misunderstandings. It may be expected to be so in Greek epics also, because it is the rule in other epics that the old social and political conditions are retained and form the background of the epics, in spite of later and profound changes in the life of the people. Other epics centre around a chief figure, a king or a prince, and this figure is often depicted as an overlord of vassals, and he is often treated not too reverently. The similarity was often noted between Charlemagne in the *chansons de geste*, Vladimir the Great in the *bylinas*, and Agamemnon in the Iliad. The former comparison was especially advanced by Andrew Lang. He describes the Homeric society justly as a loose feudalism of princes ruled by an overlord who ruled by undisputed divine right, but was often both weak and violent, being subject to gusts of arrogance as well as to abuse of his vassals. This similarity is due to the similarity of cultural conditions, the aristocratic and even feudalistic organization of the state and society which is peculiar to the Heroic Age, i.e. the age in which epics originate.

Analogies are useful but they may be misleading, especially if they are pressed too hard. The political conditions of the Middle Ages which Lang especially takes into account are not the best comparison, being much more sophisticated than the more primitive Homeric society. The chief value of analogies is to show what is possible and what may be reasonably expected; they do not prove anything in special or specified details. In trying to discern the Mycenaean elements in the Homeric descriptions of the state and the social organization, more reliable proofs are wanted, but the external criteria being absent we must rely upon internal criteria. Thus the task is extremely difficult and delicate. Our main method will be the same as that which in philosophy is called the criterion of reality, viz. the reasonable connection of phenomena with each other

agreeing with our other experience of reality. In applying this method a great measure of tact and sound common sense is required, and above all, one-sidedness and attempts to carry through preconceived opinions must be strictly avoided.

1. THE KINGSHIP

* * *

The command in war was essential to the old kingship. Only later, during that development which led to the weakening and final abolition of the kingship, was it taken from the king and entrusted to other officials. For example, it is related that the polemarchos was put at the side of the king in Athens earlier than any of the other archons. The institution of this official is attributed to mythical times. There is a trace of this development in the Odyssey in a fictitious narrative of Odysseus, who passes himself off for a Cretan and says that the Cretans asked him and Idomeneus to conduct their ships to Troy. This is a sign of a late date of this passage and does not apply to the old background of the epics.

The king appears in the Iliad as a leader in war, just as the Spartan and Macedonian kings were. He was no Pharaoh nor was he a king by right of divine standing like the Hellenistic kings and the late Roman emperors, a conception which was inherited by the European monarchs of later ages. But Zeus who gave him the kingship protected him, just as he gave their lots to men and protected their rights. He who was the protector of moral life and laws ought especially to protect the man whom he had made the ruler of men according to the laws. If the Greek kingship had once been founded upon the belief in the religious position and magic efficiency of the king, this idea had receded into the background, pressed back by the urgent needs of a war-leader in this stormy age.

Nor was the administering of justice any essential part of the king's power.

The king is never represented as a judge in Homer, except for the above-quoted passage, if the words εὐδικίας ἀνέχῃσι are to be referred to judicial functions. In certain cases the popular assembly administers justice in a somewhat rough and ready manner reminding us of lynch justice; this is due to the primitive and undeveloped conditions. In several places judges are mentioned and they are twice called by a special name δικασπόλοι. In a passage in the Nekyia they seem to be a class identified with the noblemen. This is, of course, a late development in which the nobility monopolized the courts, and to this later time belongs also a striking simile in the Iliad, which foretells the cry of Hesiod for justice against the crooked judgments of the gift-devouring noblemen. The most detailed reference to court and justice is a scene in the description of Achilles' shield. The judge who is surrounded by elders is here called ἵστωρ, "he who knows," i.e. knows the prescriptions of law. The administration of justice was undeveloped, and it seems that in their quarrels people applied to a man who was known for his knowledge of the traditional decrees of the law. Hence he is called ἵστωρ. This resembles not a little conditions in Scandinavia, where a certain man in every province was recognized for the same knowledge, the *lagmän*. He recited to the assembled people the decrees of the law which he kept in his memory, and administered justice in their meetings. Similar old conditions may be the reason why the judges in old Persia were independent of the king and could be deposed only for flagrant breach of their duty. On the other hand, the popular assembly had the right of administering justice, especially in cases where a man had acted against the public welfare. Such are the cases mentioned above. The judicial power of the Macedonian army assembly agrees with this principle. The little we know of it suggests that cases of high treason were referred to its judgment. In this judicial power of the popular assembly the starting-point is found of a far-reaching development.

Homer proves that the kingship was an old time-honoured institution protected by Zeus and by divine law. The sign of this power is the sceptre given by Zeus himself. With this in his hand Agamemnon appears in the assembly of the army, and the same idea is met with elsewhere. It is true that Agamemnon is sometimes treated with little respect and even contemptuously, but on the other hand other passages show that the reverence for the king was deep-rooted. The aged Nestor warns Achilles not to quarrel with the king who bears the sceptre, for he, to whom Zeus has given the glory, has received a far greater honour than others. Diomedes acknowledges that Zeus has given a far greater honour to Agamemnon than to other men because of the sceptre, but he adds that Zeus has not, however, given him strength and valour. Some verses farther on Nestor uses words which would become a real courtier: "Most noble son of Atreus, Agamemnon, king of men, with thee will I end and with thee begin, for thou art king of many peoples and upon thee Zeus has bestowed the sceptre and the privileges that thou shouldst take counsel for them. Therefore especially it behoves thee both to speak and to listen and to perform whatsoever some other may say whose heart hath prompted him well." And lastly there is the much-quoted verse: "A multitude of masters is an evil thing, let there be one master." There is no reason whatever to restrict these words to the position of commander-in-chief; they refer clearly to the king whose chief duty was the military leadership. All these passages show a kingship implying great and real power, and great and special honour.

We have noted that the kingship comprising the leadership in war as its chief duty was hereditary among the Teutons in Macedonia and in Sparta. Agamemnon's kingship is also hereditary, he had received it from his forefathers whose sceptre he bore. The hereditary principle was so deep-rooted that the throne when empty was given away with the hand of the queen-dowager. That is known from the myth of Oedipus and from the Odyssey, where the young noblemen woo Penelope in order to get the kingship. Then it is objected that there existed a son of Odysseus, who might claim the kingship by hereditary right. But the hereditary right was among the Greeks as well as among the old Teutons subject to a restriction, which was self-evident to a people who gave themselves a king in order that he should command them in war. He must be able to fulfil his kingly duties himself. They were never capable of the idea of a regency during a king's minority. If we take this into consideration, the state of things in Ithaca is wholly clear and consistent. The hereditary right of Telemachos is recognized, even by the foremost of the suitors, Antinoos himself, but because the young prince is not of such an age as to be able to exercise the functions of a king, it is necessary at once to procure another king, if Odysseus should be dead, and the way to the throne is laid open by the hand of the queen with which it is given away. Thus a nobleman will be able to possess himself of the kingship by marrying the queen. Hence the reply of Telemachos shows a certain amount of resignation. Although he does not cede his hereditary right, he himself takes the possibility into account that he may be put aside. The cause of the ambush laid by the suitors to Telemachos on his return is precisely this hereditary right and the fact that he soon will come of age. He is a youth, and will soon be a man capable of exercising the kingship. His resolution to go to Pylos, carried through in spite of obstacles, makes the suitors aware that this time is drawing near. There is really *periculum in mora*, if they wish to possess themselves of the throne. Hence their attempt to get rid of the heir by assassination.

2. THE ARMY ASSEMBLY

At the side of the king was the army assembly. What a prominent part it played in the camp before Troy is well known, especially from the first book of the Iliad. It is not to be understood as an occasional institution, an assembly of the allied troops before Troy, like certain instances from the Historical Age of Greece, in which we find army assemblies of a wholly occasional character, e.g. that which Lysander summoned after the battle of Aigospotamoi in order to condemn the Athenian captives, or that which was formed by the Ten Thousand during their march from Mesopotamia to the Black Sea. The assembly which the Athenian mariners instituted on Samos in 411 B.C. in order to check the conservative revolution at home, posed as the popular assembly of the Athenians. These late examples are, however, a recrudescence of a much older state of things in which the assembly of the armed men was the regular popular assembly. It is the oldest form of popular assembly, and we find it in Macedonia, in Sparta, although its true nature is a little veiled by later development of state institutions, and among the old Teutonic peoples. The army assembly in Homer is not, as it is in the above-mentioned examples, an occasional creation in order to draw up an organization of the allied troops and their leaders, but is founded on old customs.

This is proved by the king's relation to it. The king summons the army assembly in order to deliberate on important matters, e.g. his proposal to abandon the war and to go back home, the peace proposals of the Trojans, etc. The assembly gives voice to its opinions by cries, but the decision belongs to the king alone. He turns Chryses off in spite of the applause with which his request is greeted by the assembly. This power is acknowledged by old Nestor in the words already quoted. If the king shares the opinion of the assembly, he may refer to it, as he does when Idaios brings the offer of the Trojans to give back the treasures but to keep Helen. He says to the herald: "You hear the word of the Achaeans yourself, Idaios," but adds the kingly sanction: "to me also it is pleasing."

Except this we know next to nothing of the rights of the assembly. Only one thing is clear, freedom of speech was inherent in the nature of this institution. But what might happen to a commoner who ventured obloquy is well known from the famous episode of Thersites. This is only natural, for the chiefs were the representatives of their contingents and spoke in their name. Further, the mode of fighting gave prominence to the chiefs and the noblemen who possessed horses and chariots. In this respect conditions were similar to those of feudal Europe in the Middle Ages. The noblemen played the most prominent rôle both on the battle-field and in the assembly. They spoke and fought for the people. The people were accordingly little more than a chorus both in the assembly place and in battle. How old these conditions are we cannot say. They can only have come into existence after the horse had been introduced and brought about a revolution in the art of fighting. The horse was unknown in an earlier age, but known during the Mycenaean Age. It was probably introduced by the immigrating Greeks.

Two other points must be noted. Old age prevents a man from being prominent on the battle-field but not from giving his counsels in the assembly and the council of the chiefs. Here, on the contrary, his experience and eloquence may be held in high esteem. Here he has a chance of gaining fame and influence, as old Nestor did. This is nowise contrary to an undeveloped society; we may think of the high esteem in which eloquence is held by the American Indians.

Further, the assembly is summoned not only by the king but by others also, e.g. by Telemachos or by Achilles. The first example may be excused by the abnormal state of things on Ithaca, but not the second. We do not know whether this was so from the beginning; or if it is a sign of incipient decay of the king's power. It has been pertinently observed that the people may have daily assembled in the *agora*, as the Athenians did, and that the Greeks had a natural instinct to resort to the place of assembly even without special summons when something happened to the community; so an assembly might come about without being summoned formally.

3. VASSALS AND RETAINERS

If the king is the leader in war, he must possess the right and power to summon his subjects to follow him, and so it is in the Iliad. The plot of the story is founded on this right, for only a later age, which did not understand this right of the king, invented the story that Tyndareos took an oath of Helen's suitors to help the one who was chosen to avenge any wrong which might be done to him because of his wife. In the last book of the Odyssey it is stated that Odysseus was fetched by the Atreidae to the war, and according to the Cypria he tried to escape his duty by a ruse. The presumption is that he was bound to follow Agamemnon's call, being his vassal.

This duty to take the field is mentioned in some passages of the Iliad. It is told that Polyctor's sons cast lots which of them was to take the field, and that Echepolos from Sicyon bought himself free by giving to Agamemnon a costly horse. If anybody tried to escape his duty it might be enforced; it is said that the Achaeans compelled Euchenor from Corinth to follow by imposing a fine. It has hardly been noticed how remarkable this information is. If the war against Troy was waged by a league, a town might take part or not according to its own wish, and if it took part, it elected its contingent itself; the league had no right to pick out individuals in an allied town. In the quoted passages, we find on the contrary, a supreme authority compelling a man from Corinth and another from Sicyon, and we may reasonably add, from other towns also, to take the field. This authority is in one passage said to be that of the Achaeans, but it must be supposed that this is only a vague phrase. The authority was originally the king as is said in the passage concerning Echepolos who gave a costly horse to Agamemnon in order to be released from taking part in the war. I do not think that this is to be understood as bribery, but that the duty of personal service might be exchanged against some other tribute according to the king's discretion.

The king was surrounded by vassals and each of these commanded his own troops. That is the immediate impression given by a reading of the Iliad, but certain peculiar features appear on a closer inspection of certain passages. The vassals are sometimes called "kings" in the Iliad; in the Odyssey this name belongs to all members of the nobility. Agamemnon was, in fact, a King of Kings, a Great King, though he is never called by this name. In regard to the position of the vassals it is natural that they spoke on behalf of their troops in the army assembly, as was noted already, and that the king summoned them to deliberation and took their counsel in all matters of importance. Hence they are called γέροντες, seniors, but this word does not necessarily imply old age. The king was free to summon such vassals as he liked, but this liberty was, of course, rather strictly limited by the power of the individual vassals. If he neglected some, open or secret opposition followed.

* * *

It is decisive that "friends" and "servants" are identical. Patroclos, who very often is called the dearest friend of Achilles, says himself that Pelias called him his servant, and also another friend of Achilles, Automedon, is called his servant. Both words are at the same time used of the same person. In one passage it is told that two servants followed Achilles, Automedon and Alkimos, whom he honoured most among his friends after Patroclos' death. In another place it is said that Aias' servant Lycophron was killed, and a few lines farther on, speaking of the same man, that his faithful friend was killed. Patroclos exhorts the Myrmidons, who are said to be the friends of Achilles, calling them his servants. I am afraid that the translation of θεράπων by "servant" may be misleading for us who think of a class distinction between servants and friends according to later conditions, which, moreover, already begin to appear in the Odyssey. A "servant" attends to a hero, they take the weapons of Menelaos and they take care of his horses; Poseidon himself does the same service to his brother, the king of the gods. The "friends" do the like humble service, e.g. they skin the sacrificed animal and divide its flesh. It is characteristic of a certain cultural stage that the personal entourage of a chief perform such services, that they are his friends and his servants at the same time. What a so-called servant is in reality, is shown by a tale of Nestor. When Lycurgos grew old he gave his weapons which he had taken as plunder from the slain Areithoos and thereafter always worn, to his servant Eurythion. This man is mentioned also as the most prominent hero in the war of the Pylians with the Arcadians.

It appears that "friends" and "servants" denote the same men only from a different aspect. They are the personal attendants of a king, they eat at his table, they perform all kinds of services for him and they surround him in the battle. Most prominent among them is his chariot-driver. He was a most trusted man, on whose skill the life and luck of the hero in the battle depended. It is characteristic of the part played by servants in battle that when Idomeneus has slain Phaistos his servants strip the slain of his weapons. In this light, the stock expressions applied even to such heroes as Pelias and Neleus, "Ares' servants" or "servants of the great Zeus," will be better understood. These "friends" and "servants" being the personal entourage of the great and the petty kings, are in all respects to be compared with the *hird* of the kings of the Teutonic tribes in the age of the great migrations and of the Scandinavian kings in the Viking Age. In later Greece we find nothing similar except in backward Macedonia, where the old kingship and old conditions lingered on late into the Historical Age. Such an organization, if the word may be used, is characteristic of a stage of society but little developed, and is found especially in the Heroic Age of wandering peoples and in the Viking Age of Scandinavia, which was but the continuation of the migrations of the Teutonic tribes. We may confidently take it as belonging to the Viking Age of Greece too, the Mycenaean Age.

The power of the king was especially based on this retinue, and the more retainers his wealth permitted him to entertain, the greater was his power. A mighty vassal with a numerous and valiant retinue may have a strong position even against the king. And the power of the Great King also was ultimately based upon his personal retinue. As always happens under similar conditions the interests of the king and the vassals clashed, for the former strove to assert his power over the vassals and these to extend their independence. That is self-evident, even if we had not the illustrations in Homer of the self-assertion and obstinacy of the Achaean chiefs. The position of these vassals, their command of their retinues who were devoted to them personally made it possible for them to assert their independence, and their position was strengthened by the fact (which is always

implied in the myths), that their dominions were hereditary, as was the kingship. Thus it is not surprising that chiefs are sometimes called "kings" in the Iliad. There may have been among these chiefs, men who were princes by origin as well as others who had received dominions as their part of the plunder. They belonged perhaps to old families of petty kings, and the Great King may have been chosen from among them, as happened among the Teutonic tribes. The hereditary principle was the rule, and was applied even to vassals whose dominions were given them by the king.

Consequently the relation between the king and his vassals was not always amiable. Achilles goes far in showering abuse upon Agamemnon, and others also permit themselves to say harsh words to him. The Homeric image of the great king has irreverent features. This is so in other epics in which a Great King appears, in the *chansons de geste* and in the *bylinas*, and is to be explained from the similarity of conditions. The epic songs were chanted at the courts of the vassals who tried to assert themselves and their valour against their overlord, and in a certain sense were hostile to him. Hence the lack of respect for the overlord which colours epics both in Greece and elsewhere.

From the hints in Homer we are thus able to piece together a picture of the state organization during the Mycenaean Age, consistent with the conditions which for other reasons we may surmise obtained during this stormy age, and which we find among other peoples under similar circumstances. A hereditary king who was the chief leader in war ruled over a number of vassals whose position was also hereditary, and who had to go to war with their troops under his command. Both the king and the vassals were surrounded by retinues; the bond uniting the vassals to the king was loose, and the vassals strove continually to assert their independence.

7. The Documents from Pylos and Cnossos*

Nilsson wrote before the evidence of the Linear B tablets was available. In the view of Denys Page and many other scholars that evidence makes it impossible to equate the world of Homer with Agamemnon's Mycenae. The following selection describes the contents of the tablets and offers an interpretation of their meaning which sharply contradicts Nilsson's thesis.

Between the latest of the Linear B documents and the golden age of Homeric poetry three or four hundred years elapse. The time is long enough: but it is not the only or even the opaquest barrier. Near the beginning of this interval the Mycenaean civilization was overturned and buried: between the documents and the poems lie the Dark Ages of Greece. The world which the Homeric poets pretend to describe is one which had disappeared from the face of the earth hundreds of years before: yet there remained one thread unbroken, uniting the memory of past and present,—Homeric poetry itself, continuously composed and transmitted from the Mycenaean to the modern age. Surely some traces of the past may be found in it: though few perhaps and faint, for the Greek Epic was continually developing; it was reborn and to some extent reattired according to the fashion prevalent in each new generation. There are indeed certain formular phrases in which even today the ancient music dwells lingering: but the echoes become ever fainter, for the Iliad marches on continually, farther and farther from the past; and the final product, the poems in their present form, may well reflect much more of the recent than of that remoter world.

It is worth while to compare the two, poems and documents, and to notice resemblance and contrast. But as a rule we can do this only in broadest outlines. We are very seldom able to make valid comparisons in detail. For it is no good putting

poems and documents side by side and observing, this in the one is like that in the other. Where the poems agree with the documents on a point of detail, that detail may have come to the later poets from their own times or from comparatively recent times; it is very seldom possible to prove that it must have come down from the Mycenaean period and could not have been known at first hand in any later period.

I proceed to examine one aspect only of this many-sided Mycenaean world as revealed by the documents,—its relation to the world of the Iliad; and I shall do this in broadest outlines only. It soon becomes apparent that the differences between the two are many and great, the points of contact few and superficial. Here and there we may find that the language of the poem has preserved some relic of its Mycenaean past; and it is likely that the number of such relics identifiable is only a small proportion of the number actually existing. We must constantly remember how scanty and one-sided our information is; and how great the difference between a poem and a taxation-form. The Mycenaean clerk and the Mycenaean poet had different traditions, different purposes, and different audiences; as a rule they talk about quite different things. In general it becomes clear that the tale of Troy, which has a continuous history from the 12th to the 9th century B.C., in its latest phase reflects nothing of its Mycenaean past except misty outlines and a few dim-seen details: but the disparity must not be exaggerated. Much that we learn for the first time from the Tablets may be of a

* Denys Page, *History and the Homeric Iliad*, (Berkeley: University of California Press, 1959), pp. 178–187; 202.

type which was below the level, or alien to the purposes, of Mycenaean poetry.

Let us begin by scanning the outline of the Mycenaean world revealed by the Tablets; first noticing the astonishing fact that the sign-forms, spelling, dialect, phraseology, and tablet-shapes at Pylos on the mainland about 1200 B.C. are almost identical with those at Cnossos overseas 200 years earlier,—this almost incredible uniformity is perhaps the most persuasive of several proofs "that writing was the preserve of specialists trained in a rigidly conservative scribal school." The decipherment of the Tablets has fully confirmed what the intelligible ideograms had already suggested: that the Kingdoms of Pylos and Cnossos were bureaucratic monarchies of a type quite unexpected in Hellas but in many ways similar to some contemporary and earlier kingdoms in the eastern Mediterranean. This is the immediate and enduring impression made by the Tablets: that their world is essentially similar to the societies of Ugarit and Alalakh and Hattusas; it is very unlike anything that we associate with Greeks or anything that ever again existed in Hellas.

These palace archives are the records of a comprehensive and pervasive bureaucracy, administering for hundreds of years a most elaborately organized society. We did not, and could not, know that it ever existed: for suddenly the whole complex system disappeared from the earth, soon to be forgotten, never to be revived. The total extinction of a system so long-enduring, so elaborately constructed, and so rigidly administered, bears eloquent testimony to the depth and darkness of the flood which submerged Hellas when the Dorian peoples settled in the realms of Agamemnon and Menelaus and Nestor.

Observe now these bureaucrats, how wide their scope and how insatiable their thirst for information. They probe into the affairs of people in every gradation of society, from the highest officers of state down to the slave of a manual worker.

They have the power to demand, and the duty to record, infinite detail about men and women and children, industrial manufactures and materials, agricultural produce and livestock, all kinds of holdings of all kinds of land, the administration of religious ritual, movements of troops and the manning of ships. There is endless counting and classifying, measuring and weighing, assessing and collecting and distributing. It is as if everything done by everybody was open to official inquiry and subject to official orders. We possess a part only of the archives for a single year at Pylos: they record thousands of transactions in hundreds of places.

Here, for example, are eighteen places, each obliged to make contributions of six commodities, and relative assessments are fixed for each of the places and for each of the commodities with in the schedule. Here again is a distribution of bronze, enough to make half a million arrowheads or 2,300 swords, allocated to a large number of places, with a note to say how many smiths in each place are active, how many inactive, and what is the allocation to each. In Crete we count sheep up to 25,051; and again up to 19,000.

But more astonishing and significant is the omniscience, the insatiable thirst for intimate detail. Sheep may be counted up to a glittering total of twenty-five thousand: but there is still a purpose to be served by recording the fact that *one* animal was contributed by Komawens and another by *E-te-wa-no*. Restless officialdom notes the presence in *Pe-se-ro*'s house of one woman and two children; the employment of two nurses, one girl, and one boy, in a Cretan village; the fattening of an insignificant number of hogs in nine places; the existence somewhere of a single pair of brassbound chariot wheels labelled "useless,"—these things and hundreds more of the same type were duly recorded in the palaces of Pylos and Cnossos. A glance at these documents enables you at once to answer such questions as these: How many slaves has Korudallos, and what are they doing? How many sons did the weaving women from *Ti-nwa-to* bear to the rowing-men at *A-pu-ne-we*? Who is watching over the cattle of Thalamatas? What are the wheat and fig rations for thirty-seven female bath attendants and twenty-eight children at Pylos? What is the acreage of Alektruon's estate, and how much ought he to pay (1) in annual tax, (2) to Poseidon, (3) to Diwieus? How much linen is to be expected from Rhion; what deduction must be made by reason of the exemption of what class of craftsman? In a given room or other space, how many pans, cauldrons, lamps, hammers, brushes, and fire tongs are to be found? To whom, in what amounts, and for what purpose, did *A-ko-so-ta* issue coriander, cyperus, fruits, wine, honey, and what else? How much is due from Dunios to the palace?—Answer: 2,220 litres of barley, 526 of olives, 468 of wine; 15 rams, 8 yearlings, 1 ewe, 13 he-goats, 12 pigs, 1 fat hog, 1 cow, and 2 bulls. What are the personal names of two oxen belonging to *Ta-za-ro*?— Answer: *Glossy* and *Blackie*.

I do not say that these are questions which anyone was likely to ask: the point is that these—and hundreds if not thousand like them—can all be *answered* from the records. They serve to illustrate the omniscience of the bureaucracy. One would suppose that not a seed could be sown, not a gram of bronze worked, not a cloth woven, not a goat reared or a hog fattened, without the filling of a form in the Royal Palace; such is the impression made by only part of the files for a single year.

What was the purpose of this annual amassing of infinite detail about so many activities is so many places? Some of the Tablets are simply inventories,—descriptions of furniture and equipment of various kinds, presumably in use at the Palace or in store near by. But the great majority are records of assessments, deliveries, and distributions,—distributions

both of materials for production and of commodities so produced. And now we must ask, what is the political background necessarily implied by this wonderfully elaborate and centralized administrative system? One thing is surely manifest: that whoever controlled this secretariat must to some extent have authorized and controlled the transactions which it records. These archives were not compiled without the exercise of extensive powers, especially the power to extract information about all kinds of activities from all classes in the kingdom. And presumably the source of that power is the same as that which authorized the actions consequent upon the information thus collected,— the fixing of assessments, the exacting of dues, the allocation of rations. From the fact that the archives were found *in the palaces* we naturally infer that the supreme central authority was that of the king himself; though we do not know whether his power was absolute or limited (whether by a council of state or by some other body).

So much is clear in outline. When we proceed to inquire into the structure of this bureaucratic state, we find the detail fragmentary and obscure.

Two characteristics of Mycenaean civilization unfamiliar to the Greek Epic are clearly attested,—slavery, and the specialization of labour. Here are things of which the Homeric poems have no notion,— numerous male and female "slaves of the goddess (or god)"; slaves of a palace official, 32 female slaves of Amphiphoitas; slaves of one man after another, slave even of a bronzesmith. And division of labour is thoroughly systematic: the list of occupational names is a long one, including doctor, herald, goldsmith, potter, forester, baker, carpenter, shipbuilder, bowmaker, flaxworker, carder, spinner, weaver, fuller, stitcher, bath attendant, and unguent boiler.

These at least are hard facts: when we turn to the higher levels of society we enter the realm of theory, if not of dreams.

The Tablets mention (but seldom) a person called *wanax*, apparently "the sovereign," at Cnossos and Pylos and perhaps also at Thebes. There is nothing to contradict the opinion that in each place there was only *one* "sovereign"; but we know very little about him. He has (of course) a *temenos*, a slice of land; he appoints bureaucratic officials; he has "royal servants"—the king's potter, the king's fuller, the king's *e-te-do-mo*; there are textiles "belonging to the king"; his title is recorded in obscure connexions with the places *Pa-ki-ja-* and *Pi-ka-na*; and we are told how much seed he had for condiments at Cnossos. This is a small sum of knowledge; and the rest is guess-work. The comprehensive and centralized administrative system suggests an auto-cratic monarchic régime: we suppose that the *wanax* was head of the state and supreme in authority, for his palace officials seem to be all-powerful every-where. I notice in passing one most significant omission in the Tablets; there is not a word about the administration of *justice*, no reference whatsoever to *law*. It is natural to infer that the king, all-powerful controller of the all-seeing bureaucracy, possessed supreme authority also in the region of lawmaking and law enforcement: but it is not a very secure inference, since we know nothing whatever about the king's relation to other great men in his dominions.

Let us leave him, uneasy on doubtful throne, and look to see who comes next. Professor Palmer has reconstructed a feudal hierarchy of alleged Indo-European pattern, with King and Duke and Barons; but the Tablets themselves afford no evidence that such ranks, thus inter-related, ever existed in Mycenaean Hellas. The reconstruction is based on analogies from other societies in combination with the etymologies of certain titles in the Tablets. It is purely theoretical: it might be true, or it might be false,—and we now

believe that it is false, for it looks as though the so-called barons must be with-drawn from the system and assigned to religious duties, apparently not in the higher strata of society. In any case it must be admitted that there is nothing in the Tablets to suggest that Mycenaean society was constructed in any such way,—that the so-called duke performed the duties, and possessed the privileges, of a military leader; or that the so-called duke and barons stood in this particular relation to each other and to the so-called king. The whole system is an hypothesis, a pattern not revealed by the Tablets but impressed upon them from outside.

Let us briefly examine the doubtful credentials of the "duke." No. 152 records the *temenê*, slices of land, belonging to the king and to a person called *lawagetas*, in that order; then, after a gap, come the landholdings of certain officials, *telestai* and *worgiones*. It is a safe inference that the *lawagetas*, "leader of the people," was an important officer. The Epic knows nothing of him, and the Tablets tell us nothing about his functions. It is suggested that he was an *army* leader, a duke or Herzog: if it were so, it would be sur-prising that his title found—or retained—no place in poetry about war. The Epic assigns the military leadership to the king: and the Tablets neither confirm nor contradict it. But in truth the "army command" of the *lawagetas* remains a mere speculation, unsupported by the Tablets; and his claim to the second position in the state, too hastily inferred from his mention next the king in a single document, is vigorously contested by other Tablets.

For somewhere in this exalted sphere we must make room for another great personage, known by name but not by title,—*Echelawon*. In no. 171, a record of offerings to Poseidon, he has pride of place, and makes by far the greatest contribution; the *lawagetas* comes third, below even the *damos*, and his offerings are relatively contemptible. Ventris and Chadwick say that the precedence assigned to Echelawon in this record "makes it almost certain that we have here the first contemporarily attested Mycenaean monarch": but this claim is opposed by no. 54, where Echelawon's name occurs near the bottom of a long list of places and persons with numbers of oarsmen attached; and by no. 55, where he is included in a list of authorities responsible for a *deficit* of oarsmen, and again his name is not first in the order. Neither the contents of these lists nor the position of Echelawon in them is easily reconciled with the theory that he was the Great King of Pylos. Yet he is obviously of exalted standing: and we cannot possibly rank him *lower* than the *lawagetas*; for in nos. 55 and 171, when both are mentioned, Echelawon comes in front, and in 171 he makes the *lawagetas* look very small. The hard fact is that we do not know what functions these officers performed, or how they stood in relation to each other and to the king.

Moving downwards (or so we suppose) in the social hierarchy we are soon lost in a wilderness of titles, most of them new to us and all but a few obscure or incomprehensible. They seem to come from a variety of categories. There are titles such as "settler" and "immigrant"; there is the volatile term *damos*, a body empowered to lease certain kinds of land and obliged to make certain ritual offerings. There are titles for classes of landholders,—*mo-ro-pa₂*, ktoinoochoi, ktoinetai, kamaeus; there are names for provincial grandees,— *ko-re-te, po-ro-ko-re-te, du-ma, po-ro-du-ma, me-ri-du-ma*. There are titles for religious officers, "priest" and "priestess," "telestai," "keybearers," and a body called "worgiones." There are bureaucrats, both of the palace and provincial, some of the former known by name,—*A-ko-so-ta, We-da-ne-u, We-we-si-jo, A-ke-o, U-ta-jo*, Diwieus, and Amphimedes; others by title,—*e-sa-re-u* in high places, *o-pi-su-ko* and *o-pi-ka-pe-u* in the provinces. There are other obscure titles, such as *hequetas*: this officer is dignified by a patronymic adjective; he accompanies troops of soldiers; he may possess slaves; cloaks and even chariot wheels seem to be named after his title; but we know nothing whatsoever about his relation to other persons or parties in the state.

Among these titles we come at last to one already familiar from the Greek Epic, *basileus*. There are few mentions of him; and there are numerous documents in which his absence is conspicuous. There is one tablet which suggests that in Crete the *basileus* occupied a post in provincial towns comparable with that of the *lawagetas* in the capital: but at Pylos he seems to be one among numerous officials, *ko-re-te-re, mo-ro-pa₂*, and the like, who contribute gold or distribute bronze or receive rations of barley. At first sight he appears rather an insignificant person: a *basileus* may be named low on a list of officials of different types; and his retinue may be lumped together with bakers and leatherworkers and even the slaves of other men. But at least it looks as though he *has* a retinue, and so much cannot yet be said about anyone else in the state. There is a further possibility, at present unconfirmed: that he kept a Council of Elders, *geronsia*. It is prudent to admit that, despite some appearances, the *basileus* may have been a more important official than most: nevertheless it is clear that he and his retinue are subservient to the bureaucrats at Pylos.

Such in briefest outline are some of the most prominent aspects of the world of Mycenaean Greece: how much of all this was remembered in the Ionian Epic? The answer is surely not in doubt. . . . the Epic touches this real world at the surface here and there: but it has no conception of what lay beneath the surface. The Iliad and Odyssey have no notion of a society of this type, an autocratic bureaucratic government, pervasive and penetrating, assessing and collecting and distributing, measuring and counting and recording. They are not even aware that labour was so highly specialized, or that slavery was an integral institution in social and religious life. They have lost, if they ever possessed, almost all the titles of rank in all walks of life: they have forgotten the very commonest terms, *lawagetas* and *hequetas*, *ktoina* and *kama*, *o-pa* and *qe-te-a₂* and *dosmos* and the rest. In Mycenaean Greece the vocabulary was bound up with the system: the system disappeared from the earth,—and with it disappeared the technical terms, for there was no longer any meaning in them or use for them.

* * *

Looking back over the scene, we are satisfied that our first impression has been strongly confirmed by closer acquaintance. The world of the Tablets is one of which the Homeric poems retain only the faintest conception. The whole complex structure of society passed away, and the memory of it faded and perished: only a few points of contact, as a rule slight and superficial, have survived through the Dark Ages . . ..

8. A MORE RECENT ARGUMENT FOR IDENTITY*

T. B. L. Webster is an able advocate of the view that the evidence of the tablets does not contradict the assertion that the Homeric poems depict the Mycenaean world.

Michael Ventris' decipherment of Linear B in 1952 proved that Greek was spoken in the Mycenaean world. This fact had long been suspected by archaeologists and, to quote two outstanding examples, Nilsson had maintained that much of Greek mythology was Mycenaean in origin and Miss Lorimer claimed that Homer's knowledge of perishable Mycenaean objects came from a poetic tradition which went back to the time of the shaft-graves of Mycenae. On the linguistic side, Bowra had shown the probability that words common to the Homeric poems and Arcado-Cypriote came to both from Mycenaean Greek.

Ventris' discovery not only confirmed these views but provided a considerable mass of varied material in the tablets recovered from the Mycenaean palaces (even the houses in which the tablets were found at Mycenae were probably outhouses of the palace). In reviewing the great work, *Documents in Mycenaean Greek*, in which Ventris and Chadwick described the discovery, discussed the

picture of the Mycenaean world which the tablets give, and translated and commented on a large selection of tablets, I tried to point out the consequences which follow from reading these documents.

'Because they are written in Greek, they tell us a great deal about the Greek language half a millennium and more before Homer. Because they record Mycenaean civilization in Mycenaean terminology, while Homer was writing in Ionian Greek at the beginning of the *polis* civilization, they show, when joined with other evidence, how much in Homer is Mycenaean; and where we can say that these Mycenaean elements cannot have survived till Homer's time, they tell us something of the poetry which bridged the gap. Because many of the personal names are known from mythology, which was already supposed to go back to Mycenaean times, they pose the question of what Greek mythology was already existent. Because they give us the names of Greek gods then worshipped, they make a new assessment of the earliest Greek religion and its relation to Minoan religion desirable. Because they prove that Mycenaean civilization was a Greek-speaking civilization, they also show that Mycenaean art is Greek art; except for a comparatively small number of imports, objects of art on the mainland from the Shaft-Grave

---

* T. B. L. Webster, *From Mycenae to Homer* (London: Methuen and Co., 1958), pp. 1–3; 22–26.

period and in Knossos at least from the middle of the fifteenth century must have made sense to their Greek-speaking owners and must have been explicable in Greek terms. Because Linear B is derived from Linear A, communication between Greeks and Minoans is proved, and the Greek occupation of Knossos (and probably many other parts of Crete, as the tablets and Idomeneus' contingent suggest) is likely to have been followed by the borrowing not only of script but also of stories, and by the borrowing not only of art techniques and forms but also of the ideas conveyed by those forms, since here Greek and Minoan artists were working side by side and could communicate with each other. Because Asiatic words were found in the tablets, we can suppose that the Mycenaean out-stations in Ugarit and the port of Alalakh were to some extent bilingual (and the Hittite correspondence shows that verbal communication between the Greek world and the Hittite world was possible); we can therefore surmise that Eastern stories entered the Mycenaean repertoire, but there is no reason to suppose that Eastern works of art which found their way to Greece carried their interpretation with them, except on the possible occasions when the artist himself travelled; when Mycenaean artists on the mainland were inspired by imported works of art, their interpretation would be a new Greek interpretation, which need bear no relation to what the Eastern artist meant. Because the Mycenaean palaces used tablets and the tablets can now be read, Mycenaean civilization becomes comparable with other civilizations which used tablets at this time.'

The possibility of drawing a picture of Mycenaean civilization from its documents and not only from archaeology (which continues to provide more and more material), the linguistic evidence that Mycenaean Greeks were in contact with the East, and the determination of Mycenaean Greek as a stage which can be distinguished in the development of the Greek language have come at a time when knowledge of the contemporary Eastern world is both fuller and more accessible to the classical scholar than it has ever been before. This is partly due to recent

discoveries and partly to the number of reliable and convenient translations (often with text indices) which have been issued in the last few years. It is therefore now possible to see Mycenaean civilization against contemporary civilization and form some opinion of the contacts between the Greek world and the Near East. By seeing the Greeks against this background we can measure more clearly than ever before the achievement of the Greeks in leaping out of this context to become the founders of modern civilization.

* * *

Such a survey, based on a very large number of detailed and fragmentary documents, is necessarily unsatisfactory. But it may serve to show that the range of the records in Pylos, Knossos, and the Eastern sites is much the same, and that quite often particular documents or classes of document can be closely compared. Undoubtedly Ugarit and Alalakh were more concerned with manufactures than Knossos or Pylos, and silver by weight was already for them performing the function of money, whereas, as far as can be seen, in the Mycenaean centres no such standard existed. But against these differences must be set the similarities of a palace keeping minute records of every department of life in war and peace, of a divine or at least god-like King at its head surrounded by court officials, who were partly military leaders and partly administrative officials, of a wider circle of nobility owning large estates worked by their tenants, a nobility some of whom formed the chariotry, while some were the mayors of the towns and villages, and were responsible for the craftsmen and land-workers in their districts. All grades were held together by the services which they paid to the palace and by the gifts, which came from the palace particularly when promotions were made by the King; gifts and counter-gifts were also the cement of relations between kingdoms. Thus the records fully agree with the material remains in showing that the rich, elaborate, and highly centralized Mycenaean civilization was much more akin to contemporary Near Eastern kingdoms than to the city states of archaic and classical Greece.

In spite of the likenesses two differences are interesting. We do not even know the Mycenaean word for scribes, although elsewhere they advertise themselves proudly; they appear in the census and ration lists of Alalakh, and of the tablets from Ugarit used in this survey more than sixty are signed by scribes, some of whom give also the name of their father or teacher; in Mari 'the scribes have organized the daily labour for a canal' and 'clever scribes' are sent to the capital to carry out a census and a land-survey. Yet if Mycenaean writing was handed down from fifteenth-century Knossos to thirteenth-century Pylos and Mycenae with extraordinarily little change of form, it must have been a traditional craft, and the Mycenaeans showed no reticence about the names of crafts. It is possible that some other craft-name such as 'herald', which is found in Pylos, covered the activity of the scribes. It is tempting to argue that writing itself was not regarded so highly as in the East.

The other difference is the absence of literary texts, letters, and juridical texts from Mycenaean sites, although, as has been said, longer and more continuous texts are found as near as Cyprus. There are several possible reasons for this absence which must be considered. Two possibilities are so obvious that they prevent us from asserting confidently that the Mycenaeans did not possess such texts. They may have been written on clay and stored apart from the documents which have been found. We have noticed that in Ugarit the poetic texts were stored in the temple instead of the palace, and that the palace archives were divided according to subject. There is always the possibility that stores of other kinds of documents at Knossos or Pylos escaped the conflagration

which baked and preserved the tablets that have been discovered; what has survived is in fact not a selection of all sorts of material but a remarkably full collection of some sorts of material—very full on sheep and chariots at Knossos, a nearly complete account of the land tenure of one of the nine towns of Pylos, etc. The other possibility is that another material, such as papyrus or skin, was used for documents which the Mycenaeans themselves wished to preserve. There are two reasons for supposing this. One is that the forms of the letters, which survived so remarkably unchanged through the centuries, are much easier to make with a pen or a brush than with an incising tool, and it is difficult to believe that they would not have been simplified if they had only or primarily been used for inscriptions on clay. The other reason is Marinatos' observation that a clay sealing at Knossos shows very fine lines on the back which look as though it had been attached to a papyrus document. It has been noticed that, except for the monthly offerings in Knossos and possibly the *damokoros* tablet, if that in fact gives a date, the records are undated and therefore consolidated records may have been made on another material instead of on clay as in Babylon; against this must be set the fact that the big Pylos land tablets are consolidated records, compiled from brief tablets, many of which survive.

It is then possible that other kinds of texts existed and have perished. Poetry we shall have to consider later more fully; here a caution may be expressed; in the East poetic texts have been found in temples and writing schools. We have them partly because scribes practised writing them, partly because they were needed for recitation at religious festivals. We do not know whether either of these needs existed in the Mycenaean age; we might even go further and say that the absence of reference to scribes makes the existence of developed writing schools unlikely and that we have no evidence that Mycenaean festivals were accompanied by the kind of recitation or song which required a written text. But it is equally true that we have no evidence against the existence of recited poetry.

Linear B, as we have it, is only used for internal palace records, which would probably be read by the scribes who wrote them. A very little adaptation, notably the recording of all double consonants and final consonants, would make the script precise enough to be read without difficulty by scribes in other palaces.

For the moment we can only say that the Mycenaeans had an adequate script for recording poetry, if they needed it, and for written correspondence between the Mycenaean palaces and between the Mycenaean palaces and places outside the Mycenaean world. Two points suggest the existence of such a correspondence. If the King of the Hittites wrote to the King of Ahhiyawa, the King of Ahhiyawa must surely have been able to reply; moreover the letter from the King of the Hittites to the King of Ahhiyawa about troubles in Lycia and the Homeric letter from the King of Argos to the King of Lycia, recommending Bellerophon as an expendable brigand, sound extraordinarily like the Eastern and Western ends of the same story. The second point is the likeness of the script wherever Linear B is found; it may be argued that one reason for this similarity is the use of Linear B for correspondence between Mycenaean Kings, and some such medium of communication would clearly be convenient if there is any truth in Homer's picture of a Mycenaean world knit together by allegiance to Agamemnon and capable of undertaking an overseas expedition on a large scale.

The third general kind of text which we lack is the juridical text, whether individual contracts and rulings or collections of generalized rulings such as the Babylonian code, the Hittite code, or the edict of Harmhab of Egypt. Again the answer may be the chance of survival, whether such texts were written on clay and have been lost or were written on some more perishable material. Certainly the orders for coastal defence and instructions for sacrifices, the detailed description of chariots, the long summary of land tenure with its notes of default and disagreement, prove the possibility and even the likelihood that there were Mycenaean juridical texts. We can say at least that Homer preserves the picture of the King as appointed by Zeus to dispense justice, as he did in the East. The Homeric phrase 'preserve the rulings from (i.e. given by) Zeus' naturally reminds us of Hammurabi of Babylon, who is depicted receiving his laws from the god of justice. Rather similar is the picture on a ring from Mycenae, which shows a goddess instructing a King. In Homer Minos of Crete is described as 'the familiar friend of Zeus', and in the Underworld he gives *themistes* to those who ask him for rulings. *Themistes* are the rulings which the King preserves and from which he selects for the particular case. The same word is used once in Homer and at least twice on the Knossos tablets for a feudal due, which is a particular kind of royal ruling. The dues were recorded as we have seen. Perhaps the juridical rulings too were recorded in some form, so that the King and his household and his successors knew them. Such records were *themistes*, and the King chose one which applied. The word for choose is *krinein*, the word which comes to mean simply 'judge'. The development of meaning is clear if it originated in the choice of an applicable ruling from among the recorded rulings. This however is conjecture; Homer gives us evidence enough that like other rulers of the second millennium the Mycenaean King was also the dispenser of justice.

9. A MIDDLE WAY*

Before the decipherment of Linear B, which enabled us to read contemporary records of Bronze Age Greece, we were dependent for our knowledge of Mycenaean institutions and social life on the *Iliad* and *Odyssey*. These poems, written in the eighth and seventh centuries B.C. respectively, do not picture the contemporary world of the poets but describe a more or less remote past. But how remote? Ostensibly the background of the poems belongs to the Age of Heroes, to the world of Agamemnon and his associates, say the thirteenth century B.C. Palace bards must have begun to celebrate the exploits of the great Mycenaean kings and lords soon after the Sack of Troy, and an unbroken tradition of oral poetry linked Homer with those first unknown lays of the Heroic Age of Greece. Can we be sure that no distortion of the picture took place in those five or six centuries of bardic transmission which separated 'Homer' from the events he purports to describe? Certainly the spade of the archaeologist has verified the existence of the palaces where Homer's heroes lived, and Professor Martin Nilsson showed that the Mycenaean sites thus revealed correspond in importance to the main centres of Greek heroic legends and myths. However, in a recent, stimulating, and richly informative book Dr. M. I. Finley has challenged the long held view that the picture which emerges from Homer can be attributed to the late Bronze Age of Mycenae. We must distinguish, he argues, the Heroic Age depicted in the Greek epic from the Mycenaean Age of the archaeological finds. Claiming a 'historian's licence', he would pin down the world of Odysseus to the tenth and ninth centuries B.C. As for Homer, 'On the whole

he knew where the Mycenaean civilization flourished, and his heroes lived in great Bronze Age palaces unknown in Homer's day. And that is virtually all he knew about Mycenaean times. . . .'

The study of the texts reveals that the truth lies between this revolutionary notion and the traditional picture based on Homer. Certainly there is much in this complex, bureaucratically controlled society that recalls the temple economies of the contemporary Orient. Yet curiously enough it was the abundant new information on land tenure, a subject to which Dr. Finley has devoted much attention, that showed a social structure which in its main lines is reconcilable with that of Homer's Heroic Age and wholly different from the Orient.

1. THE SOCIAL STRUCTURE

That the society of the Heroic Age of Greece was feudal in form has often been asserted and as often denied. By feudal we mean, of course, that the bonds of society were 'baronial' in nature: in other words that land was held of an overlord in return for an obligation to render military service. The word *baron* in its original sense carries this implication. A baron, according to an attractive interpretation, is a 'man of the service', the underlying word being connected with the verb 'bear'. The 'burden' undertaken is that of 'service'. Homer provides a significant pointer to such obligations in the behaviour of Echepolus of Sicyon (west of Corinth on the Corinthian Gulf), who when called upon to join the expedition against Troy gave Agamemnon instead a fine mare named Aithe ('Blazing'), which Menelaus yoked to his chariot when competing in the funeral games of Patroclus. Sicyon was one of the cities ascribed to Agamemnon in the 'Catalogue', which lists the contributions,

* L. R. Palmer, *Mycenaeans and Minoans* (New York: Alfred A. Knopf, Inc., and London: Faber and Faber, 1962), pp. 90–99.

measured in terms of ships, made by the various Greek potentates to the expedition against Troy. Then there was the case of Euchenor of Corinth. His father was a seer and had foretold that his son would either die of disease if he stayed at home or be killed in battle if he went to Troy. So he joined the expedition, thus 'avoiding a grievous fine and loathesome disease'. His father's prophecy was fulfilled when he was struck by the spear of Paris 'beneath the jaws and the ears'. The mention of a technical word for a legal penalty (*thoē*) as an alternative to military service implies an obligation to an overlord, and Corinth like Sicyon is listed among the cities of Agamemnon.

The key to the feudal mode of organization is land tenure. Agriculture was the basis of ancient society and the structure of power should be reflected in the arrangements governing the ownership and the use of land. Sir William Ridgeway long ago made a close study of the references to land tenure scattered in the Greek epic and constructed a picture of Homeric land tenure. For instance, the elaborate description of the Shield which Hephaestus, the craftsman god, was commissioned to make for Achilles in preparation for his final duel with Hector includes vignettes of Greek society. One panel of the shield described by the poet depicts the large cattle grazing in the water meadows, while the sheep are on the upland pastures. The description of the shield suggests that the arable land of the typical 'heroic' community was divided between the large open field of the commune, on which many plough teams operate simultaneously, and the personal holding of the 'king' (*basileus*), who stands and supervises the gathering of the harvest.

Again, when the Trojans and Greeks are locked in close struggle over the wall enclosing the Greek ships drawn up on the Trojan shore, the poet compares the scene with a quarrel between 'two men who in a common field on each side of the boundary stones with measuring rods in their hands dispute about their share in a small plot'. Boundary stones are mentioned in another passage of the *Iliad* when Odysseus and Diomede set a trap for the Trojan Dolon ('*Trickster*'), who passes them as they lie in wait. They let him get as far ahead 'as the boundary marks of mules are wont to be, which surpass oxen in drawing the plough over the deep fallow'. These 'marks' imply a division of the fallow, and the distance between them must have been conventionally established, otherwise it could not be referred to as a standard of measurement.

From such occasional hints Ridgeway and others pieced together a picture of 'heroic' land tenure. Much land and indeed whole cities were dedicated to the gods and priests were men of great wealth. One of them provided Odysseus with seven talents of gold and also with the wonderful wine which was the undoing of the Cyclops. The king and the war captains received personal allocations of land called 'cuts' (*temenos*), a word which survived later only with a religious connotation. Yet all these deductions from the scanty and ambiguous Homeric evidence have been disputed, and it could be asserted that the Homeric picture may merely be that of Greece after the collapse of the Mycenaean world and the ensuing Age of Migrations.

By a great piece of good fortune we can now by-pass many of these interpretational difficulties and disputed points. We now have much more detailed information about the complex land tenure system of the last years of the Mycenaean Age than, for instance, about seventh-century Sparta. Perhaps the most important documents for the historian which were contained in the Archive Room at Pylos are those dealing with land holding. Much work was needed on these particularly difficult texts before they became reasonably clear. But the general picture which has emerged enables us to sit in judgement on the various accounts of 'heroic' land tenure based on the study of Homer. The palm must unquestionably be awarded to Sir William Ridgeway. His picture approximates most closely to that which we shall now describe.

The chief categories of land-holders at Pylos are set forth in a document which consists of two tablets. The first entry relates to the *Wanax*, the King. He is credited with a *temenos*, literally a 'cut', measured as thirty units of seed corn. A *temenos* is registered in the next line against the *Lawagetas*, literally the 'Leader of the War-Host', for the word *lawos* 'folk' in Homer has the narrower meaning 'the body of warriors'. The scribe now leaves a blank line after these two *temenos* entries to show that they are *sui generis*. The following entry relates to *telestai* a word about which there has been some dispute but which, I shall argue, means 'service men'. There are three of them and the seed corn entry is thirty units, so that they each have as much land in this place as the *Lawagetas* himself, whose allocation is ten units. Next we have an entry for the *damos*, the 'commune' and then an obscure reference to 'deserted' or 'uninhabited' land which may have been set aside for cult purposes.

The document is continued on the second tablet, which is in the same hand. It refers to one who seems to have been a great noble, *Echelawon* by name. Ventris and Chadwick identified him with the King. However, once it became clear, thanks to the work of Professor E. M. Bennett, that these two tablets formed a single document such identification was ruled out. The beginning of the tablet is slightly mutilated, but it seems reasonably clear that at the place in question Echelawon had two arable plots and two pieces of land planted with trees. The seed corn allocation is 94 measures. What is of importance is that his arable is referred to by the term *ki-ti-me-na* and not *temenos*.

This technical word recurs in the most complex document we possess relating to land holding. It concerns the holy place *Pa-ki-ja-nes*, which we have sited close to Pylos itself and where there was an important shrine of the goddess Potnia, 'The Lady, the Mistress'. Two versions survive of this register. The first consists mainly of a number of tablets of the elongated 'palm-leaf' type, each of which records the provisional 'proposals' for given individuals. In the later version these individual proposals are consolidated in a 'book' consisting of a series of tablets of the oblong 'page' type. It was naturally of importance to be able to establish the correct order of the 'pages' in the book. After careful examination of the tablets in Athens in the spring of 1959 it proved possible to deduce the original order, and this threw a flood of light on the nature and grouping of the entries in the register.

The document falls into two halves. The first is concerned with land called *ki-ti-me-na* and the second with holdings of *ke-ke-me-na* land. At first these two terms were regarded as synonymous, but it soon became clear that the first type of land was always held from a named individual of the *telestas* class whereas the *ke-ke-me-na* type is always held 'from the *damos*'. We have already seen that Echelawon's huge holding was also designated *ki-ti-me-na*. So far from being equivalent terms, the distinction between *ki-ti-me-na* and *ke-ke-me-na* represents a fundamental cleavage in Mycenaean society. As we shall see, the *telestai* are men in royal service and they presumably held their land of the King. The etymological analysis of *ki-ti-me-na* will occupy us below, but what delimits the meaning of the word is its opposition to *ke-ke-me-na* land, which being held of the *damos* I shall call 'common land'. The details of the register will be discussed later. What is of importance is that some entries suggest that the main estate of the King was at *Pa-ki-ja-nes*, where he is closely associated with the goddess Potnia. This has an interesting Homeric echo. It is characteristic of the casual nature of the

Homeric evidence that we learn of such an arrangement only incidentally in the course of Nausicaa's conversation with Odysseus. The girl modestly explains that it will excite unfavourable comment if she accompanies him in person and she proceeds to describe the way to the town of the Scherians. 'You will find a lovely poplar grove of Athena near the road. In it a spring flows and about it is a meadow. There is the *temenos* of my father and his fruitful orchard.' In this way we learn that Alcinous, Wanax of Scheria and father of Nausicaa, had his *temenos* closely conjoined with the precincts of Athena. The link of the royal *temenos* with his religious functions appears clearly even in post-Homeric times. Herodotus records that when the constitution of Cyrene was reformed on the advice of Delphi, king Battus was allowed to keep his '*temenea* and his priesthoods'.

A *temenos* of the 'War-leader' also appears clearly in a number of Homeric passages. Thus Meleager ('He who cares for the chase') was offered a *temenos* to persuade him to take part in the fighting against the Curetes. The military aspect of the War-leader's *temenos* is explicitly stressed by Sarpedon, the Lycian, in addressing his comrade-in-arms Glaucus. 'Why do the Lycians honour us and why do we enjoy a large *temenos* beside the banks of the Xanthus river? . . . For that reason we must take our stand in the front ranks of the Lycians. . . .'

Now there is another smaller register in the Pylian archives and a number of its entries strongly suggest that it is concerned with the estate of the Lawagetas. Notable among the tenants is one who is described as 'the Charioteer of the Lawagetas' and a number of others are dubbed *lawagesioi*, that is 'belonging to the Lawagetas'. Two separate lines of enquiry indicate that the land recorded in this set of texts was at a place called *Ti-no*. On the back of one of the tablets the scribe has tallied the amount of seed corn. It is some 130 measures as against 170 or so measures recorded for the estate at *Pa-ki-ja-nes*. On the front of the tablet showing the tallying there is a puzzling entry which indicates that one of the most prominent tenants had a holding in respect of 'a horse'. The holding is large, and at first it was supposed that the man in question held this land by way of upkeep for a war-horse. But this was not very convincing. New light was thrown on this problem when a text came to hand which recorded the issue of quantities of cyperus to *I-qo* ('Horse'). Cyperus is an aromatic plant used in the making of perfumes and in offerings to divinities. It could no longer be supposed that this was any ordinary horse. The recipient *I-qo* was evidently the name of a god. Below we shall discuss the evidence bearing on the god Hippos. At all events such a god is congenial company for a Mycenaean War-leader, on whose land we find the Charioteer of the War-leader. It may well be that the noble horse depicted on the seal from the Little Palace at Knossos represents this god of the Mycenaean warriors and is more than a mere indication of cargo as Evans suggested. Here then are the facts relating to the Wanax and the Lawagetas which our study has elicited from the Pylian texts:

Wanax: *temenos*: estate at *Pa-ki-ja-nes*: *wa-na-ka-te-ro* holders: 170 units: goddess Potnia.

Lawagetas: *temenos*: estate at *Ti-no*: *ra-wa-ke-si-jo* holders: 130 units: god Hippos.

We now return to the great land register of *Pa-ki-ja-nes* with its division into two parts contrasting *ki-ti-me-na* land with *ke-ke-me-na*. *ki-ti-me-na* land, as we have said, is leased from *telestai*. This word means literally 'men of the *telos*', and *telos* is a noun connected with the root meaning 'lift'. Its basic meaning is 'what is lifted, burden', but it has the derived meanings 'charge, due, obligation' and the like. Suggestions have been made that these men were 'initiation priests', but this will not bear examination. In the first place the *telestai* include a fuller, a potter, and a shepherd. Moreover, when the pages of the register were put in their proper order, it could be seen that the document grouped the holders according to function. The *telestai* were not grouped with the cult functionaries. This was confirmed by yet another observation. Another set of tablets summarizes the entries of the register and gives the total amount of seed corn involved. The groupings here are the same as those of the register. Again the *telestai* do not appear along with the cult personnel.

No less cogent was an observation made apropos of the other sort of land. After listing the *ki-ti-me-na* land of the *telestai*, 'service men', the register goes on to record in its second part the *ke-ke-me-na* land held from the *damos*. The first entries of this second part relate to personalities some of whom we know as *telestai*. What is important is that now they are no longer given this description but receive a new appellation—'*ktoina* holders' (*ktoina* is a word which survived later in the dialect of Rhodes and signified a division of land with predominantly religious connexions). From this it was clear that the *telestai* were designated as such only in respect of their holdings of *ki-ti-me-na* land. In other words *telestas* is a tenure-bound status word. A *telestas* owed *telos* to the Wanax (the king) presumably in return for his holding of *ki-ti-me-na* land.

We have said that this class of *telestai* includes men designated shepherd, fuller and potter. However, the size of their holdings suggests that these terms are not to be taken in their literal sense any more than words like 'Steward', 'Constable', etc. in our own medieval terminology. The 'shepherd' will have been the Master of the Royal herds, the 'potter' the Master of the Royal Potteries and the 'fuller' perhaps the Master of the Cloth.

That the Mycenaean polity was no absolute despotism of the Oriental type is clear from the character of the *damos* or 'commune'. The *damos*, from which so much of the land here recorded was held, was no subservient and downtrodden body. This emerges clearly from a pair of texts recording a case of disputed tenure. The earlier version runs 'The priestess declares that the god has an *e-to-ni-jo* (this being the term for a large religious holding), but the *ktoina*-holder says that she has leases of *ke-ke-me-na* plots.' We have said that the term '*ktoina*-holder' designates a person of *telestas* status in respect of his holding of *damos* land. What is significant is that in the later consolidated document the protest by the *ktoina*-holder is taken up by the *damos*. The version now reads '. . . but the *damos* says that she has leases of *ke-ke-me-na* plots'. Here the *damos* acts as a collective, as it also does when making certain deliveries for religious purposes. A protest in the name of the *damos* implies an organ to deliberate and speak on its behalf, as indeed the leases 'from the damos' also do. What is of interest is that the protest is duly recorded in the palace register. In this entry, then, we see enshrined an acknowledgement of the vested rights of the commune. This is not the *damos* of the *Iliad*, where Odysseus beats a man of the *damos* for venturing to raise his voice in the assembly. But doubt-less in the field the commoner would be well advised not to run foul of the princely warriors. There are some indications that the bulk of the land was held by the *damos* and that their holdings are only reflected in the palace archives in so far as palace folk had some concern in them.

It remains to review briefly the other classes of tenants on the *damos* land. After the '*ktoina*-holders' we find entries relating to a type of holding designated *ka-ma*. With such land we find constantly references to three kinds of obligation. The words have been difficult to identify but I have argued that the three obligations are to occupy, to render services, or to pay. After the *ka-ma* holding the register goes on to record the most numerous holdings: these are by persons designated 'slave of the god', both men and women. Then follow the entries relating to the slaves of the prominent cult personages and finally the priestess, the priest and other officiants. We summarize the main classes of holders and the type of land which they hold and lease to others.

Wanax:	*temenos*
Lawagetas:	*temenos*
Echelawon:	*ko-to-na ki-ti-me-na*
telestai:	*ko-to-na ki-ti-me-na*
damos:	*ko-to-na ke-ke-me-na*

The distinction between the two technical terms for the two sorts of land is clear in that they refer to *telestas* and *damos* land respectively. There is no difficulty about the etymological identification of *ki-ti-me-na*: it is the participle *ktimena* from a verb whose range of meaning centres about 'win from the waste, set in order, settle'. A rough English equivalent would be 'assart land'. *ke-ke-me-na* has proved more difficult, although it clearly means 'common land'. I have brought the verb into connexion with the Greek word *koinos* 'common' and analysed the Mycenaean word as the participle of a verb *kei* with the original meaning 'split, share'. Thus *ke-ke-me-na* means literally 'share-land'. It is of interest that we find terms for the common land having precisely this significance in other languages. In Old English we have *gedalland* and in Welsh *rhandir*. Hittite has a closely resemblant term in *takšannaš*, literally 'joint land', this also being apparently the word for the 'village land' as opposed to land held from the palace.

These purely philological analyses harmonize with the results reached by students of early land tenure systems in Western Europe. Geographers had independently commented on the importance of the institution of the 'share-land' in early European society. It lies beyond the scope of this book to consider whether this resemblance is due to independent evolution in the societies concerned or whether there is a historical connexion between them. But in view of statements to the contrary it must be insisted that the picture of Mycenaean society sketched above has emerged entirely from analysis of the texts. It was not based on an 'Indo-European hypothesis', and imposed from without on the texts.

SECTION VI

The Spartan Revolution

THE SPARTAN STATE, its constitution and the mode of life of its citizens, have exercised a fascination on the ancient Greeks as well as on modern students of the Greek world. Ancient tradition assigned Sparta's peculiar constitution to a single lawgiver, Lycurgus, who is said to have reformed the state and set forth a new way of life at a single stroke as early as the eighth or even the ninth century B.C. Many modern scholars reject the idea of a single reform by a single lawgiver and some even deny that "Lycurgus" ever existed. Most scholars, in any case, agree on a more gradual change but one so fundamental as to deserve the name "revolution." They do not agree on the date of the change or, more important, its causes. The following selections include most of the important ancient evidence as well as two modern discussions of the problems.

1. PLUTARCH'S LIFE OF LYCURGUS*

There is so much uncertainty in the accounts which historians have left us of Lycurgus, the lawgiver of Sparta, that scarcely anything is asserted by one of them which is not called into question or contradicted by the rest. Their sentiments are quite different as to the family he came of, the voyages he undertook, the place and manner of his death, but most of all when they speak of the laws he made and the commonwealth which he founded. They cannot, by any means, be brought to an agreement as to the very age in which he lived; for some of them say that he flourished in the time of Iphitus, and that they

two jointly contrived the ordinance for the cessation of arms during the solemnity of the Olympic games. Of this opinion was Aristotle; and for confirmation of it, he alleges an inscription upon one of the copper quoits used in those sports, upon which the name of Lycurgus continued uneffaced to his time. But Eratosthenes and Apollodorus and other chronologers, computing the time by the successions of the Spartan kings, pretend to demonstrate that he was much more ancient than the institution of the Olympic games. Timæus conjectures that there were two of this name, and in diverse times, but that the one of them being much more famous than the other, men gave to him the glory of the exploits of both; the elder of the two,

---

* Plutarch, *Lycurgus* (abridged), translated by John Dryden.

180

according to him, was not long after Homer; and some are so particular as to say that he had seen him. But that he was of great antiquity may be gathered from a passage in Xenophon, where he makes him contemporary with the Heraclidæ. By descent, indeed, the very last kings of Sparta were Heraclidæ too; but he seems in that place to speak of the first and more immediate successors of Hercules. But notwithstanding this confusion and obscurity, we shall endeavour to compose the history of his life, adhering to those statements which are least contradicted, and depending upon those authors who are most worthy of credit.

* * *

Lycurgus was much missed at Sparta, and often sent for, "for kings indeed we have," they said, "who wear the marks and assume the titles of royalty, but as for the qualities of their minds, they have nothing by which they are to be distinguished from their subjects;" adding, that in him alone was the true foundation of sovereignty to be seen, a nature made to rule, and a genius to gain obedience. Nor were the kings themselves averse to see him back, for they looked upon his presence as a bulwark against the insolence of the people.

Things being in this posture at his return, he applied himself, without loss of time, to a thorough reformation, and resolved to change the whole face of the commonwealth; for what could a few particular laws and a partial alteration avail? He must act as wise physicians do, in the case of one who labours under a complication of diseases, by force of medicines reduce and exhaust him, change his whole temperament, and then set him upon a totally new regimen of diet. Having thus, projected things, away he goes to Delphi to consult Apollo there; which having done, and offered his sacrifice, he returned with that renowned oracle, in which he is called beloved of God, and rather God than man; that his prayers

were heard, that his laws should be the best, and the commonwealth which observed them the most famous in the world. Encouraged by these things he set himself to bring over to his side the leading men of Sparta, exhorting them to give him a helping hand in his great undertaking; he broke it first to his particular friends, and then by degrees, gained others, and animated them all to put his design in execution. When things were ripe for action, he gave orders to thirty of the principal men of Sparta to be ready armed at the market-place by break of day, to the end that he might strike a terror into the opposite party. Hermippus hath set down the names of twenty of the most eminent of them; but the name of him whom Lycurgus most confided in, and who was of most use to him, both in making his laws and putting them in execution was Arthmiadas. Things growing to a tumult, King Charilaus, apprehending that it was a conspiracy against his person, took sanctuary in the temple of Minerva of the Brazen House; but, being soon after undeceived, and having taken an oath of them that they had no designs against him, he quitted his refuge, and himself also entered into the confederacy with them; of so gentle and flexible a disposition he was, to which Archelaus, his brother-king, alluded, when, hearing him extolled for his goodness, he said, "Who can say he is anything but good? he is so even to the bad."

Amongst the many changes and alterations which Lycurgus made, the first and of greatest importance was the establishment of the senate, which having a power equal to the king's in matters of great consequence, and, as Plato expresses it, allaying and qualifying the fiery genius of the royal office, gave steadiness and safety to the commonwealth. For the state, which before had no firm basis to stand upon, but learned one while towards an absolute monarchy, when the kings had the upper hand, and another while towards a pure democracy, when the people had the better, found in this establishment of the senate a central weight, like ballast in a ship, which always kept things in a just equilibrium; the twenty-eight always adhering to the kings so far as to resist democracy, and on the other hand, supporting the people against the establishment of absolute monarchy. As for the determinate number of twenty-eight Aristotle states, that it so fell out because two of the original associates, for want of courage, fell off from the enterprise; but Sphærus assures us that there were but twenty-eight of the confederates at first; perhaps there is some mystery in the number, which consists of seven multiplied by four, and is the first of perfect numbers after six, being, as that is, equal to all its parts. For my part, I believe Lycurgus fixed upon the number of twenty-eight, that, the two kings being reckoned amongst them, they might be thirty in all. So eagerly set was he upon this establishment, that he took the trouble to obtain an oracle about it from Delphi, the Rhetra, which runs thus: "After that you have built a temple to Jupiter Helianius, and to Minerva Hellania, and after that you have *phyle'd* the people into *phyles*, and *obe'd* them into *obes*, you shall establish a council of thirty elders, the leaders included, and shall, from time to time, *apellazein* the people betwixt Babyca and Cnacion, there propound and put to the vote. The commons have the final voice and decision." By *phyles* and *obes* are meant the divisions of the people; by the *leaders*, the two kings; *apellazein*, referring to the Pythian Apollo, signifies to assemble; Babyca and Cnacion they now call Œnus; Aristotle says Cnacion is a river, and Babyca a bridge. Betwixt this Babyca and Cnacion, their assemblies were held, for they had no council-house or building to meet in. Lycurgus was of opinion that ornaments were so far from advantaging them in their counsels, that they were rather an hindrance, by diverting their attention from the business before them to statues and pictures, and roofs curiously

fretted, the usual embellishments of such places amongst the other Greeks. The people then being thus assembled in the open air, it was not allowed to any one of their order to give his advice, but only either to ratify or reject what should be propounded to them by the king or senate. But because it fell out afterwards that the people, by adding or omitting words, distorted and perverted the sense of propositions, Kings Polydorus and Theopompus inserted into the Rhetra, or grand covenant, the following clause: "That if the people decided crookedly it should be lawful for the elders and leaders to dissolve;" that is to say, refuse ratification, and dismiss the people as depravers and perverters of their counsel. It passed among the people, by their management, as being equally authentic with the rest of the Rhetra, as appears by these verses of Tyrætus,—

"These oracles they from Apollo heard,
And brought from Pytho home the perfect
    word:
The heaven-appointed kings, who love the
    land,
Shall foremost in the nation's council stand;
The elders next to them: the commons last;
Let a straight *Rhetra* among all be passed."

Although Lycurgus had, in this manner, used all the qualifications possible in the constitution of his commonwealth, yet those who succeeded him found the oligarchical element still too strong and dominant, and to check its high temper and its violence, put, as Plato says, a bit in its mouth, which was the power of the ephori, established an hundred and thirty years after the death of Lycurgus. Elatus and his colleagues were the first who had this dignity conferred upon them in the reign of King Theopompus, who, when his queen upbraided him one day that he would leave the regal power to his children less than he had received it from his ancestors, said in answer, "No, greater; for it will last longer." For, indeed, their prerogative being thus reduced within reasonable bounds, the Spartan kings were at once freed from all further jealousies and consequent danger, and never experienced the calamities of their neighbours at Messene and Argos, who, by maintaining their prerogative too strictly, for want of yielding a little to the populace, lost it all.

Indeed, whosoever shall look at the sedition and misgovernment which befell these bordering nations to whom they were as near related in blood as situation, will find in them the best reason to admire the wisdom and foresight of Lycurgus. For these three states, in their first rise, were equal, or, if there were any odds, they lay on the side of the Messenians and Argives, who, in the first allotment, were thought to have been luckier than the Spartans; yet was their happiness of but small continuance, partly the tyrannical temper of their kings and partly the ungovernableness of the people quickly bringing upon them such disorders, and so complete an overthrow of all existing institutions, as clearly to show how truly divine a blessing the Spartans had had in that wise lawgiver who gave their government its happy balance and temper. But of this I shall say more in its due place.

After the creation of the thirty senators, his next task, and, indeed, the most hazardous he ever undertook, was the making a new division of their lands. For there was an extreme inequality amongst them, and their state was overloaded with a multitude of indigent and necessitous persons, while its whole wealth had centred upon a very few. To the end, therefore, that he might expel from the state arrogance and envy, luxury and crime, and those yet more inveterate diseases of want and superfluity, he obtained of them to renounce their properties, and to consent to a new division of the land, and that they should live all together on an equal footing; merit to be their only road to eminence, and the disgrace of evil, and credit of worthy acts, their one measure of difference between man and man.

Upon their consent to these proposals, proceeding at once to put them into execution, he divided the country of Laconia in general into thirty thousand equal shares, and the part attached to the city of Sparta into nine thousand; these he distributed among the Spartans, as he did the others to the country citizens. Some authors say that he made but six thousand lots for the citizens of Sparta, and that King Polydorus added three thousand more. Others say that Polydorus doubled the number Lycurgus had made, which, according to them, was but four thousand five hundred. A lot was so much as to yield, one year with another, about seventy bushels of grain for the master of the family, and twelve for his wife, with a suitable proportion of oil and wine. And this he thought sufficient to keep their bodies in good health and strength; superfluities they were better without. It is reported, that, as he returned from a journey shortly after the division of the lands, in harvest time, the ground being newly reaped, seeing the stacks all standing equal and alike, he smiled, and said to those about him, "Methinks all Laconia looks like one family estate just divided among a number of brothers."

Not contented with this, he resolved to make a division of their moveables too, that there might be no odious distinction or inequality left amongst them; but finding that it would be very dangerous to go about it openly, he took another course, and defeated their avarice by the following stratagem: he commanded that all gold and silver coin should be called in, and that only a sort of money made of iron should be current, a great weight and quantity of which was very little worth; so that to lay up twenty or thirty pounds there was required a pretty large closet, and, to remove it, nothing less than a yoke of oxen. With the diffusion of this money, at once a number of vices were banished from Lacedæmon; for who would rob another of such a coin? Who would unjustly detain or take by force, or accept as a bribe, a thing which it was not easy to hide, nor a credit to have, nor indeed of any use to cut in pieces? For when it was just red hot, they quenched it in vinegar, and by that means spoilt it, and made it almost incapable of being worked.

In the next place, he declared an outlawry of all needless and superfluous arts; but here he might almost have spared his proclamation; for they of themselves would have gone after the gold and silver, the money which remained being not so proper payment for curious work; for, being of iron, it was scarcely portable, neither, if they should take the means to export it, would it pass amongst the other Greeks, who ridiculed it. So there was now no more means of purchasing foreign goods and small wares; merchants sent no shiploads into Laconian ports; no rhetoric-master, no itinerate fortune-teller, no harlot-monger, or gold or silver-smith, engraver, or jeweller, set foot in a country which had no money; so that luxury, deprived little by little of that which fed and fomented it, wasted to nothing and died away of itself. For the rich had no advantage here over the poor, as their wealth and abundance had no road to come abroad by but were shut up at home doing nothing. And in this way they became excellent artists in common, necessary things; bedsteads, chairs, and tables, and such like staple utensils in a family, were admirably well made there; their cup, particularly, was very much in fashion, and eagerly bought up by soldiers, as Critias reports; for its colour was such as to prevent water, drunk upon necessity and disagreeable to look at, from being noticed and the shape of it was such that the mud stuck to the sides, so that only the purer part came to the drinker's mouth. For this, also, they had to thank their lawgiver, who, by relieving the artisans of the trouble of making useless things, set them to show their skill in giving beauty to those of daily and indispensable use.

The third and most masterly stroke of this great lawgiver, by which he struck a yet more effectual blow against luxury and the desire of riches, was the ordinance he made, that they should all eat in common, of the same bread and same meat, and of kinds that were specified, and should not spend their lives at home, laid on costly couches at splendid tables, delivering themselves up into the hands of their tradesmen and cooks, to fatten them in corners, like greedy brutes, and to ruin not their minds only but their very bodies which, enfeebled by indulgence and excess, would stand in need of long sleep, warm bathing, freedom from work, and, in a word, of as much care and attendance as if they were continually sick. It was certainly an extraordinary thing to have brought about such a result as this, but a greater yet to have taken away from wealth, as Theophrastus observes, not merely the property of being coveted, but its very nature of being wealth. For the rich, being obliged to go to the same table with the poor, could not make use of or enjoy their abundance, nor so much as please their vanity by looking at or displaying it. So that the common proverb, that Plutus, the god of riches, is blind, was nowhere in all the world literally verified but in Sparta. There, indeed, he was not only blind, but like a picture, without either life or motion. Nor were they allowed to take food at home first, and then attend the public tables, for every one had an eye upon those who did not eat and drink like the rest, and reproached them with being dainty and effeminate.

* * *

Lycurgus would never reduce his laws into writing; nay there is a Rhetra expressly to forbid it. For he thought that the most material points, and such as most directly tendered to the public welfare, being imprinted on the hearts of their youth by a good discipline, would be sure to remain, and would find a stronger security, than any compulsion would be, in the principles of action formed in them by their best lawgiver, education. And as for things of lesser importance, as pecuniary contracts, and such like, the forms of which have to be changed as occasion requires, he thought it the best way to prescribe no positive rule or inviolable usage in such cases, willing that their manner and form should be altered according to the circumstances of time, and determinations of men of sound judgment. Every end and object of law and enactment it was his design education should effect.

One, then, of the Rhetras was, that their laws should not be written; another is particularly levelled against luxury and expensiveness, for by it was ordained that the ceilings of their houses should only be wrought by the axe, and their gates and doors smoothed only by the saw. Epaminondas's famous dictum about his own table, that "Treason and a dinner like this do not keep company together," may be said to have been anticipated by Lycurgus. Luxury and a house of this kind could not well be companions. For a man might have a less than ordinary share of sense that would furnish such plain and common rooms with silver-footed couches and purple coverlets and gold and silver plate. Doubtless he had good reason to think that they would proportion their beds to their houses, and their coverlets to their beds, and the rest of their goods and furniture to these. It is reported that king Leotychides, the first of that name, was so little used to the sight of any other kind of work, that, being entertained at Corinth in a stately room, he was much surprised to see the timber and ceiling so finely carved and panelled, and asked his host whether the trees grew so in his country.

A third ordinance of Rhetra was, that they should not make war often, or long, with the same enemy, lest that they should train and instruct them in war, by habituating them to defend themselves. And this is what Agesilaus was much blamed for, a long time after; it being thought, that, by his continual incursions into Bœotia, he made the Thebans a match for the Lacedæmonians; and therefore Antalcidas, seeing him wounded one day, said to him, that he was very well paid for taking such pains to make the Thebans good soldiers, whether they would or no. These laws were called the Rhetras, to intimate that they were divine sanctions and revelations.

In order to the good education of their youth (which, as I said before, he thought the most important and noblest work of a lawgiver), he went so far back as to take into consideration their very conception and birth, by regulating their marriages. For Aristotle is wrong in saying, that, after he had tried all ways to reduce the women to more modesty and sobriety, he was at last forced to leave them as they were, because that in the absence of their husbands, who spent the best part of their lives in the wars, their wives, whom they were obliged to leave absolute mistresses at home, took great liberties and assumed the superiority; and were treated with overmuch respect and called by the title of lady or queen. The truth is, he took in their case, also, all the care that was possible; he ordered the maidens to exercise themselves with wrestling, running, throwing the quoit, and casting the dart, to the end that the fruit they conceived might, in strong and healthy bodies, take firmer root and find better growth, and withal that they, with this greater vigour, might be the more able to undergo the pains of child-bearing. And to the end he might take away their overgreat tenderness and fear of exposure to the air, and all acquired womanishness, he ordered that the young women should go naked in the processions, as well as the young men, and dance, too, in that condition, at certain solemn feasts, singing certain songs, whilst the young men stood around, seeing and hearing them. On these occasions they now and then made, by jests, a befitting reflection upon those who had misbehaved themselves in the wars; and again sang encomiums upon those who had done any gallant action, and by these means inspired the younger sort with an emulation of their glory. Those that were thus commended went away proud, elated, and gratified with their honour among the maidens; and those who were rallied were as sensibly touched with it as if they had been formally reprimanded; and so much the more, because the kings and the elders, as well as the rest of the city, saw and heard all that passed. Nor was there anything shameful in this nakedness of the young women; modesty attended them, and all wantonness was excluded. It taught them simplicity and a care for good health, and gave them some taste of higher feelings, admitted as they thus were to the field of noble action and glory. Hence it was natural for them to think and speak as Gorgo, for example, the wife of Leonidas, is said to have done, when some foreign lady, as it would seem, told her that the women of Lacedæmon were the only women in the world who could rule men; "With good reason," she said, "for we are the only women who bring forth men."

These public processions of the maidens, and their appearing naked in their exercises and dancings, were incitements to marriage, operating upon the young with the rigour and certainty, as Plato says, of love, if not of mathematics. But besides all this, to promote it yet more effectually, those who continued bachelors were in a degree disfranchised by law; for they were excluded from the sight of those public processions in which the young men and maidens danced naked, and, in winter-time, the officers compelled them to march naked themselves round the market-place, singing as they went a certain song to their own disgrace, that they justly suffered this punishment for disobeying the laws. More-over, they were denied that respect and observance which the younger men paid their elders; and no man, for example, found fault with what was said to Dercylli-das, though so eminent a commander;

upon whose approach one day, a young man, instead of rising, retained his seat, remarking, "No child of yours will make room for me."

In their marriages, the husband carried off his bride by a sort of force; nor were their brides ever small and of tender years, but in their full bloom and ripeness. After this, she who superintended the wedding comes and clips the hair of the bride close round her head, dresses her up in man's clothes, and leaves her upon a mattress in the dark; afterwards comes the bride-groom, in his everyday clothes, sober and composed, as having supped at the common table, and, entering privately into the room where the bride lies, unties her virgin zone, and takes her to himself; and, after staying some time together, he returns composedly to his own apartment, to sleep as usual with the other young men. And so he continues to do, spending his days, and, indeed, his nights, with them, visiting his bride in fear and shame, and with circumspection, when he thought he should not be observed; she, also, on her part, using her wit to help and find favourable opportunities for their meeting, when company was out of the way. In this manner they lived a long time, insomuch that they sometimes had children by their wives before ever they saw their faces by daylight. Their interviews, being thus difficult and rare, served not only for continual exercise of their self-control, but brought them together with their bodies healthy and vigorous, and their affections fresh and lively, unsated and undulled by easy access and long continuance with each other; while their partings were always early enough to leave behind unextinguished in each of them some remaining fire of longing and mutual delight. After guarding mar-riage with this modesty and reserve, he was equally careful to banish empty and womanish jealousy. For this object, exclud-ing all licentious disorders, he made it, nevertheless, honourable for men to give the use of their wives to those whom they should think fit, that so they might have children by them; ridiculing those in whose opinion such favours are so unfit for participation as to fight and shed blood and go to war about it. Lycurgus allowed a man who was advanced in years and had a young wife to recommend some virtuous and approved young man, that she might have a child by him, who might inherit the good qualities of the father, and be a son to himself. On the other side, an honest man who had love for a married woman upon account of her modesty and the well-favouredness of her children, might, without formality, beg her company of her husband, that he might raise, as it were, from this plot of good ground, worthy and well-allied children for himself. And indeed, Lycurgus was of a persuasion that children were not so much the property of their parents as of the whole commonwealth, and, therefore, would not have his citizens begot by the first-comers, but by the best men that could be found; the laws of other nations seemed to him very absurd and inconsistent, where people would be so solicitous for their dogs and horses as to exert interest and to pay money to procure fine breeding, and yet kept their wives shut up, to be made mothers only by themselves, who might be foolish, infirm, or diseased; as if it were not apparent that children of a bad breed would prove their bad qualities first upon those who kept and were rearing them, and well-born children, in like manner, their good qualities. These regulations, founded on natural and social grounds, were certainly so far from that scandalous liberty which was afterwards charged upon their women, that they knew not what adultery meant. It is told, for instance, of Geradas, a very ancient Spartan, that, being asked by a stranger what punishment their law had appointed for adulterers, he answered, "There are no adulterers in our country." "But" replied the stranger, "suppose there were?" "Then," answered he, "the offender would have to give the plaintiff a bull with a neck so long as that he might drink from the top of Taygetus of the Eurotas river below it." The man, surprised at this, said, "Why, 'tis impossible to find such a bull." Geradas smilingly replied, "'Tis as possible as to find an adulterer in Sparta." So much I had to say of their marriages.

Nor was it in the power of the father to dispose of the child as he thought fit; he was obliged to carry it before certain triers at a place called Lesche; these were some of the elders of the tribe to which the child belonged; their business it was carefully to view the infant, and, if they found it stout and well made, they gave order for its rearing, and allotted to it one of the nine thousand shares of land above mentioned for its maintenance, but, if they found it puny and ill-shaped, ordered it to be taken to what was called the Apothetæ, a sort of chasm under Taygetus; as thinking it neither for the good of the child itself, nor for the public interest, that it should be brought up, if it did not, from the very outset, appear made to be healthy and vigorous. Upon the same account, the women did not bathe the new-born children with water, as is the custom in all other countries, but with wine, to prove the temper and complexion of their bodies; from a notion they had that epileptic and weakly children faint and waste away upon their being thus bathed, while, on the contrary, those of a strong and vigorous habit acquire firmness and get a temper by it, like steel. There was much care and art, too, used by the nurses; they had no swaddling bands; the children grew up free and unconstrained in limb and form, and not dainty and fanciful about their food; not afraid in the dark, or of being left alone; and without peevishness, or ill-humour, or crying. Upon this account Spartan nurses were often bought up, or hired by people of other countries; and it is recorded that she who suckled Alcibiades was a Spartan; who, however, if fortunate in his nurse, was not so in his preceptor; his guardian, Pericles, as Plato tells us, chose a servant for that office called Zopyrus, no better than any common slave.

Lycurgus was of another mind; he would not have masters bought out of the market for his young Spartans, nor such as should sell their pains; nor was it lawful, indeed, for the father himself to breed up the children after his own fancy; but as soon as they were seven years old they were to be enrolled in certain companies and classes, where they all lived under the same order and discipline, doing their exercises and taking their play together. Of these, he who showed the most conduct and courage was made captain; they had their eyes always upon him, obeyed his orders, and underwent patiently whatsoever punishment he inflicted; so that the whole course of their education was one continued exercise of a ready and perfect obedience. The old men, too, were spectators of their performances, and often raised quarrels and disputes among them, to have a good opportunity of finding out their different characters, and of seeing which would be valiant, which a coward, when they should come to more dangerous encounters. Reading and writing they gave them, just enough to serve their turn: their chief care was to make them good subjects, and to teach them to endure pain and conquer in battle. To this end, as they grew in years, their discipline was proportionately increased; their heads were close-clipped, they were accustomed to go barefoot, and for the most part to play naked.

After they were twelve years old, they were no longer allowed to wear any undergarments, they had one coat to serve them a year; their bodies were hard and dry, with but little acquaintance of baths and unguents; these human indulgences they were allowed only on some few particular days in the year. They lodged together in little bands upon beds made of the rushes which grew by the banks of the river Eurotas, which they were to break off with their hands without a knife; if it were

winter, they mingled some thistledown with their rushes, which it was thought had the property of giving warmth. By the time they were come to this age there was not any of the more hopeful boys who had not a lover to bear him company. The old men, too, had an eye upon them, coming often to the grounds to hear and see them contend either in wit or strength with one another, and this as seriously and with as much concern as if they were their fathers, their tutors, or their magistrates; so that there scarcely was any time or place without some one present to put them in mind of their duty, and punish them if they had neglected it.

Besides all this, there was always one of the best and honestest men in the city appointed to undertake the charge and governance of them; he again arranged them into their several bands, and set over each of them for their captain the most temperate and boldest of those they called Irens, who were usually twenty years old, two years out of the boys; and the oldest of the boys, again, were Mell-Irens, as much as to say, who would shortly be men. This young man, therefore, was their captain when they fought and their master at home, using them for the offices of his house; sending the eldest of them to fetch wood, and the weaker and less able to gather salads and herbs, and these they must either go without or steal; which they did by creeping into the gardens, or conveying themselves cunningly and closely into the eating-houses; if they were taken in the fact, they were whipped without mercy, for thieving so ill and awkwardly. They stole, too, all other meat they could lay their hands on, looking out and watching all opportunities, when people were asleep or more careless than usual. If they were caught, they were not only punished with whipping, but hunger, too, being reduced to their ordinary allowance, which was but very slender, and so contrived on purpose, that they might set about to help themselves, and be forced to exercise their energy and address. This was the principal design of their hard fare; there was another not inconsiderable, that they might grow taller; for the vital spirits, not being overburdened and oppressed by too great a quantity of nourishment, which necessarily discharges itself into thickness and breadth, do, by their natural lightness, rise, and the body, giving and yielding because it is pliant, grows in height. The same thing seems, also, to conduce to beauty of shape; a dry and lean habit is a better subject for nature's configuration, which the gross and over-fed are too heavy to submit to properly. Just as we find that women who take physic whilst they are with child, bear leaner and smaller but better-shaped and prettier children; the material they come of having been more pliable and easily moulded. The reason, however, I leave others to determine.

To return from whence we have digressed. So seriously did the Lacedæmonian children go about their stealing, that a youth, having stolen a young fox and hid it under his coat, suffered it to tear out his very bowels with its teeth and claws and died upon the place, rather than let it be seen. What is practised to this very day in Lacedæmon is enough to gain credit to this story, for I myself have seen several of the youths endure whipping to death at the foot of the altar of Diana surnamed Orthia.

* * *

To return to the Lacedæmonians. Their discipline continued still after they were full-grown men. No one was allowed to live after his own fancy; but the city was a sort of camp, in which every man had his share of provisions and business set out, and looked upon himself not so much born to serve his own ends as the interest of his country. Therefore if they were commanded nothing else, they went to see the boys perform their exercises, to teach them something useful or to learn it them-

selves of those who knew better. And indeed one of the greatest and highest blessings Lycurgus procured his people was the abundance of leisure which proceeded from his forbidding to them the exercise of any mean and mechanical trade. Of the money-making that depends on troublesome going about and seeing people and doing business, they had no need at all in a state where wealth obtained no honour or respect. The Helots tilled their ground for them, and paid them yearly in kind the appointed quantity, without any trouble of theirs. To this purpose there goes a story of a Lacedæmonian who, happening to be at Athens when the courts were sitting, was told of a citizen that had been fined for living an idle life, and was being escorted home in much distress of mind by his condoling friends; the Lacedæmonian was much surprised at it and desired his friend to show him the man who was condemned for living like a freeman. So much beneath them did they esteem the frivolous devotion of time and attention to the mechanical arts and to money-making.

It need not be said that upon the prohibition of gold and silver, all lawsuits immediately ceased, for there was now neither avarice nor poverty amongst them, but equality, where every one's wants were supplied, and independence, because those wants were so small. All their time, except when they were in the field, was taken up by the choral dancers and the festivals, in hunting, and in attendance on the exercise-grounds and the places of public conversation. Those who were under thirty years of age were not allowed to go into the market-place, but had the necessaries of their family supplied by the care of their relations and lovers; nor was it for the credit of elderly men to be seen too often in the market-place; it was esteemed more suitable for them to frequent the exercise-grounds and places of conversation, where they spent their leisure rationally in conversation, not on money-making and market-prices, but for the most part in passing judgment on some action worth considering; extolling the good, and censuring those who were otherwise, and that in a light and sportive manner, conveying, without too much gravity, lessons of advice and improvement. Nor was Lycurgus himself unduly austere; it was he who dedicated, says Sosibius, the little statue of Laughter. Mirth, introduced seasonably at their suppers and places of common entertainment, was to serve as a sort of sweetmeat to accompany their strict and hard life. To conclude, he bred up his citizens in such a way that they neither would nor could live by themselves; they were to make themselves one with the public good, and, clustering like bees around their commander, be by their zeal and public spirit carried all but out of themselves, and devoted wholly to their country. What their sentiments were will better appear by a few of their sayings. Pædaretus, not being admitted into the list of the three hundred, returned home with a joyful face, well pleased to find that there were in Sparta three hundred better men than himself. And Polycratidas, being sent with some others ambassador to the lieutenants of the king of Persia, being asked by them whether they came in a private or in a public character, answered, 'In a public, if we succeed; if not, in a private character." Argileonis, asking some who came from Amphipolis if her son Brasidas died courageously and as became a Spartan, on their beginning to praise him to a high degree, and saying there was not such another left in Sparta, answered, "Do not say so; Brasidas was a good and brave man, but there are in Sparta many better than he."

The senate, as I said before, consisted of those who were Lycurgus's chief aiders and assistants in his plans. The vacancies he ordered to be supplied out of the best and most deserving men past sixty years old, and we need not wonder if there was much striving for it; for what more glorious competition could there be amongst men,

than one in which it was not contested who was swiftest among the swift or strongest of the strong, but who of many wise and good was wisest and best, and fittest to be intrusted for ever after, as the reward of his merits, with the supreme authority of the commonwealth, and with power over the lives, franchises, and highest interests of all his countrymen? The manner of their election was as follows: The people being called together, some selected persons were locked up in a room near the place of election, so contrived that they could neither see nor be seen, but could only hear the noise of the assembly without; for they decided this, as most other affairs of moment, by the shouts of the people. This done, the competitors were not brought in and presented all together, but one after another by lot, and passed in order through the assembly without speaking a word. Those who were locked up had writing-tables with them, in which they recorded and marked each shout by its loudness, without knowing in favour of which candidate each of them was made, but merely that they came first, second, third, and so forth. He who was found to have the most and loudest acclamations was declared senator duly elected. Upon this he had a garland set upon his head, and went in procession to all the temples to give thanks to the gods; a great number of young men followed him with applauses, and women, also, singing verses in his honour, and extolling the virtue and happiness of his life. As he went round the city in this manner, each of his relations and friends set a table before him, saying "The city honours you with this banquet;" but he, instead of accepting, passed round to the common table where he formerly used to eat, and was served as before, excepting that now he had a second allowance, which he took and put by. By the time supper was ended, the women who were of kin to him had come about the door; and he, beckoning to her whom he most esteemed, presented to her the portion he had saved, saying, that it had been a mark of esteem to him, and was so now to her; upon which she was triumphantly waited upon home by the women.

Touching burials, Lycurgus made very wise regulations; for, first of all, to cut off all superstition, he allowed them to bury their dead within the city, and even round about their temples, to the end that their youth might be accustomed to such spectacles, and not be afraid to see a dead body, or imagine that to touch a corpse or to tread upon a grave would defile a man. In the next place, he commanded them to put nothing into the ground with them, except, if they pleased, a few olive leaves, and the scarlet cloth that they were wrapped in. He would not suffer the names to be inscribed, except only of men who fell in the wars, of women who died in a sacred office. The time, too, appointed for mourning, was very short, eleven days; on the twelfth, they were to do sacrifice to Ceres, and leave it off; so that we may see, that as he cut off all superfluity, so in things necessary there was nothing so small and trivial which did not express some homage of virtue or scorn of vice. He filled Lacedæmon all through with proofs and examples of good conduct; with the constant sight of which from their youth up the people would hardly fail to be gradually formed and advanced in virtue.

And this was the reason why he forbade them to travel abroad, and go about acquainting themselves with foreign rules of morality, the habits of ill-educated people, and different views of government. Withal he banished from Lacedæmon all strangers who would not give a very good reason for their coming thither; not because he was afraid lest they should inform themthemselves of and imitate his manner of government (as Thucydides says), or learn anything to their good; but rather lest they should introduce something contrary to good manners. With strange people, strange words must be admitted; these novelties produce novelties in thought; and on these

follow views and feelings whose discordant character destroys the harmony of the state. He was as careful to save his city from the infection of foreign bad habits, as men usually are to prevent the introduction of a pestilence.

Hitherto I, for my part, see no sign of injustice or want of equity in the laws of Lycurgus, though some who admit them to be well contrived to make good soldiers, pronounce them defective in point of justice. The Cryptia, perhaps (if it were one of Lycurgus's ordinances, as Aristotle says it was), gave both him and Plato, too, this opinion alike of the lawgiver and his government. By this ordinance, the magistrates despatched privately some of the ablest of the young men into the country, from time to time, armed only with their daggers, and taking a little necessary provision with them; in the daytime, they hid themselves in out-of-the-way places, and there lay close, but in the night issued out into the highways, and killed all the Helots they could light upon; sometimes they set upon them by day, as they were at work in the fields, and murdered them. As, also, Thucydides, in his history of the Peloponnesian war, tells us, that a good number of them, after being singled out for their bravery by the Spartans, garlanded, as enfranchised persons, and led about to all the temples in token of honours, shortly after disappeared all of a sudden, being about the number of two thousand; and no man either then or since could give an account how they came by their deaths. And Aristotle, in particular, adds, that the ephori, so soon as they were entered into their office, used to declare war against them, that they might be massacred without a breach of religion. It is confessed, on all hands, that the Spartans dealt with them very hardly; for it was a common thing to force them to drink to excess, and to lead them in that condition into their public halls, that the children might see what a sight a drunken man is; they made them to dance low dances, and sing ridiculous songs, forbidding them expressly to meddle with any of a better kind. And accordingly, when the Thebans made their invasion into Laconia, and took a great number of the Helots, they could by no means persuade them to sing the verses of Terpander, Alcman, or Spendon, "For," said they, "the masters do not like it." So that it was truly observed by one, that in Sparta he who was free was most so, and he that was a slave there, the greatest slave in the world. For my part, I am of opinion that these outrages and cruelties began to be exercised in Sparta at a later time, especially after the great earthquake, when the Helots made a general insurrection, and, joining with the Messenians, laid the country waste, and brought the greatest danger upon the city. For I cannot persuade myself to ascribe to Lycurgus so wicked and barbarous a course, judging of him from the gentleness of his disposition and justice upon all other occasions; to which the oracle also testified.

When he perceived that his more important institutions had taken root in the minds of his countrymen, that custom had rendered them familiar and easy, that his commonwealth was now grown up and able to go alone, then, as Plato somewhere tells us, the Maker of the world, when first he saw it existing and beginning its motion, felt joy, even so Lycurgus, viewing with joy and satisfaction the greatness and beauty of his political structure, now fairly at work and in motion, conceived the thought to make it immortal too, and, as far as human forecast could reach, to deliver it down unchangeable to posterity. He called an extraordinary assembly of all the people, and told them that he now thought everything reasonably well established, both for the happiness and the virtue of the state; but that there was one thing still behind, of the greatest importance, which he thought not fit to impart until he had consulted the oracle; in the meantime, his desire was that they would observe the laws without

any the least alteration until his return, and then he would do as the god should direct him. They all consented readily, and bade him hasten his journey; but, before he departed, he administered an oath to the two kings, the senate, and the whole commons, to abide by and maintain the established form of polity until Lycurgus should be come back. This done, he set out for Delphi, and, having sacrificed to Apollo, asked him whether the laws he had established were good, and sufficient for a people's happiness and virtue. The oracle answered that the laws were excellent, and that the people, while it observed them, should live in the height of renown. Lycurgus took the oracle in writing, and sent it over to Sparta; and, having sacrificed the second time to Apollo, and taken leave of his friends and his son, he resolved that the Spartans should not be released from the oath they had taken, and that he would, of his own act, close his life where he was. He was now about that age in which life was still tolerable, and yet might be quitted without regret. Everything, moreover, about him was in a sufficiently prosperous condition. He therefore made an end of himself by a total abstinence from food, thinking it a statesman's duty to make his very death, if possible, an act of service to the state, and even in the end of his life to give some example of virtue and effect some useful purpose. He would, on the one hand, crown and consummate his own happiness by a death suitable to so honourable a life, and on the other hand, would secure to his countrymen the enjoyment of the advantages he had spent his life in obtaining for them, since they had solemnly sworn the maintenance of his institutions until his return. Nor was he deceived in his expectations, for the city of Lacedæmon continued the chief city of all Greece for the space of five hundred years, in strict observance of Lycurgus's laws; in all which time there was no manner of alteration made, during the reign of fourteen kings down to the time of Agis, the son of Archidamus. For the new creation of the ephori, though thought to be in favour of the people, was so far from diminishing, that it very much heightened, the aristocratical character of the government.

2. XENOPHON'S *CONSTITUTION OF THE SPARTANS*[*]

Xenophon (*ca.* 430–354 B.C.) was an Athenian who was exiled and lived much of his life in the Peloponnesus. He fought in the Spartan army under King Agesilaus whose friend and admirer he was.

1. I recall the astonishment with which I first noted the unique position of Sparta among the states of Hellas, the relatively sparse population, and at the same time the extraordinary power and prestige of the community. I was puzzled to account for the fact. It was only when I came to consider the peculiar institutions of the Spartans that my wonderment ceased. Or rather, it is transferred to the legislator who gave them those laws, obedience to which has been the secret of their prosperity. This legislator, Lycurgus, I admire, and hold him to have been one of the wisest of mankind. Certainly he was no servile imitator of other states. It was by a stroke of invention rather, and on a pattern much in opposition to the commonly-accepted one, that he brought his fatherland to this pinnacle of prosperity.

Take for example—and it is well to begin at the beginning—the whole topic of the begetting and rearing of children. Throughout the rest of the world the young girl, who will one day become a mother (and I speak of those who may be held to be well brought up), is nurtured on the plainest food attainable, with the scantiest addition of meat or other condiments; while as to wine they train them either to total abstinence or to take it highly diluted with water. And in imitation, as it were, of the handicraft type, since the majority of artificers are sedentary, we, the rest of the Hellenes, are content that our girls should sit quietly and work wools. That is all we

demand of them. But how are we to expect that women nurtured in this fashion should produce a splendid offspring?

Lycurgus pursued a different path. Clothes were things, he held, the furnishing of which might well enough be left to female slaves. And, believing that the highest function of a free woman was the bearing of children, in the first place he insisted on the training of the body as incumbent no less on the female than the male; and in pursuit of the same idea instituted rival contests in running and feats of strength for women as for men. His belief was that where both parents were strong their progency would be found to be more vigorous.

And so again after marriage. In view of the fact that immoderate intercourse is elsewhere permitted during the earlier period of matrimony, he adopted a principle directly opposite. He laid it down as an ordinance that a man should be ashamed to be seen visiting the chamber of his wife, whether going in or coming out. When they did meet under such restraint the mutual longing of these lovers could not but be increased, and the fruit which might spring from such intercourse would tend to be more robust than theirs whose affections are cloyed by satiety. By a farther step in the same direction he refused to allow marriages to be contracted at any period of life according to the fancy of the parties concerned. Marriage, as he ordained it, must only take place in the prime of bodily vigour, this too being, as he believed, a condition conducive to the production of

[*] Translated by Henry Dakyns.

healthy offspring. Or again, to meet the case which might occur of an old man wedded to a young wife. Considering the jealous watch which such husbands are apt to keep over their wives, he introduced a directly opposite custom; that is to say, he made it incumbent on the aged husband to introduce some one whose qualities, physical and moral, he admired, to beget him children. Or again, in the case of a man who might not desire to live with a wife permanently, but yet might still be anxious to have children of his own worthy the name, the lawgiver laid down a law in his behalf. Such an one might select some woman, the wife of some man, well born herself and blest with fair offspring, and, the sanction and consent of her husband first obtained, raise up children for himself through her.

These and many other adaptations of a like sort the lawgiver sanctioned. As, for instance, at Sparta a wife will not object to bear the burden of a double establishment, or a husband to adopt sons as foster-brothers of his own children, with a full share in his family and position, but possessing no claim to his wealth and property.

So opposed to those of the rest of the world are the principles which Lycurgus devised in reference to the production of children. Whether they enabled him to provide Sparta with a race of men superior to all in size and strength I leave to the judgment of whomsoever it may concern.

2. With this exposition of the customs in connection with the birth of children, I wish now to explain the systems of education in fashion here and elsewhere. Throughout the rest of Hellas the custom on the part of those who claim to educate their sons in the best way is as follows. As soon as the children are of an age to understand what is said to them they are immediately placed under the charge of Paidagogoi (or tutors), who are also attendants, and sent off to the school of some teacher to be taught grammar, music,

and the concerns of the palaestra. Besides this they are given shoes to wear which tend to make their feet tender, and their bodies are enervated by various changes of clothing. And as for food, the only measure recognised is that which is fixed by appetite.

But when we turn to Lycurgus, instead of leaving it to each member of the state privately to appoint a slave to be his son's tutor, he set over the young Spartans a public guardian, the Paidonomos, to give him his proper title, with complete authority over them. This guardian was selected from those who filled the highest magistracies. He had authority to hold musters of the boys, and as their overseer, in case of any misbehaviour, to chastise severely. The legislator further provided the pastor with a body of youths in the prime of life, and bearing whips, to inflict punishment when necessary, with this happy result that in Sparta modesty and obedience ever go hand in hand, nor is there lack of either.

Instead of softening their feet with shoe or sandal, his rule was to make them hardy through going barefoot. This habit, if practised, would, as he believed, enable them to scale heights more easily and clamber down precipices with less danger. In fact, with his feet so trained the young Spartan would leap and spring and run faster unshod than another shod in the ordinary way.

Instead of making them effeminate with a variety of clothes, his rule was to habituate them to a single garment the whole year through, thinking that so they would be better prepared to withstand the variations of heat and cold.

Again, as regards food, according to his regulation the prefect, or head of the flock, must see that his messmates gathered to the club meal, with such moderate food as to avoid that heaviness which is engendered by repletion, and yet not to remain altogether unacquainted with the pains of penurious living. His belief was that by such training in boyhood they would be better able when occasion demanded to continue toiling on an empty stomach. They would be all the fitter, if the word of command were given, to remain on the stretch for a long time without extra dieting. The craving for luxuries would be less, the readiness to take any victual set before them greater, and, in general, the regime would be found more healthy. Under it he thought the lads would increase in stature and shape into finer men, since, as he maintained, a dietary which gave suppleness to the limbs must be more conducive to both ends than one which added thickness to the bodily parts by feeding.

On the other hand, in order to guard against a too great pinch of starvation, though he did not actually allow the boys to help themselves without further trouble to what they needed more, he did give them permission to steal this thing or that in the effort to alleviate their hunger. It was not of course from any real difficulty how else to supply them with nutriment that he left it to them to provide themselves by this crafty method. Nor can I conceive that any one will so misinterpret the custom. Clearly its explanation lies in the fact that he who would live the life of a robber must forgo sleep by night, and in the daytime he must employ shifts and lie in ambuscade; he must prepare and make ready his scouts, and so forth, if he is to succeed in capturing the quarry.

It is obvious, I say, that the whole of this education was intended, to make the boys craftier and more inventive in getting in supplies, while at the same time it cultivated their warlike instincts. An objector may retort, "But if he thought it so fine a feat to steal, why did he inflict all those blows on the unfortunate who was caught?" My answer is: for the self-same reason which induces people, in other matters which are taught, to punish the mal-performance of a service. So they, the Lacedaemonians, visit penalties on the boy who is detected thieving as being but a sorry bungler in the art. So to steal as many cheeses as

possible [off the shrine of Orhia][1] 'twas a feat to be encouraged; but, at the same moment, others were enjoined to scourge the thief, which would point a moral not obscurely, that by pain endured for a brief season a man may earn the joyous reward of lasting glory. Herein, too, it is plainly shown that where speed is requisite the sluggard will win for himself much trouble and scant good.

Furthermore, and in order that the boys should not want a ruler, even in case the guardian himself were absent, he gave to any citizen who chanced to be present authority to lay upon them injunctions for their good, and to chastise them for any trespass committed. By so doing he created in the boys of Sparta a most rare modesty and reverence. And indeed there is nothing which, whether as boys or men, they respect more highly than the ruler. Lastly, and with the same intention, that the boys must never be reft of a ruler, even if by chance there were no grown man present, he laid down the rule that in such a case the most active of the Leaders or Prefects was to become ruler each of his own division. The conclusion being that under no circumstances whatever are the boys of Sparta destitute of one to rule them.

I ought, as it seems to me, not to omit some remark on the subject of homosexuality, it being a topic in close connection with that of boyhood and the training of boys.

We know that the rest of the Hellenes deal with this relationship in different ways, either after the manner of the Boeotians, where man and boy are intimately united by a bond like that of wedlock, or after the manner of the Eleians, where the enjoyment of beauty is gained by favours; while there are others who would absolutely debar the lover from all conversation and discourse with the beloved.

---

[1] Artemis of the Steep, a title connecting the goddess with Mount Orthion or Orthosion. The words are out of their right place.

Lycurgus adopted a system opposed to all of these alike. Given that some one, himself being all that a man ought to be, should in admiration of a boy's soul endeavour to discover in him a true friend without reproach, and to consort with him —this was a relationship which Lycurgus commended, and indeed regarded as the noblest type of bringing up. But if, as was evident, it was not an attachment to the soul, but a yearning merely towards the body, he stamped this thing as foul and horrible; and with this result, to the credit of Lycurgus be it said, that in Lacedaemon the relationship of lover and beloved is like that of parent and child or brother and brother where carnal appetite is in abeyance.

That this, however, which is the fact, should be scarcely credited in some quarters does not surprise me, seeing that in many states the laws do not oppose the desires in question.

I have now described the two chief methods of education in vogue; that is to say, the Lacedaemonian as contrasted with that of the rest of Hellas, and I leave it to the judgment of him whom it may concern, which of the two has produced the finer type of men. And by finer I mean the better disciplined, the more modest and reverential, and, in matters where self-restraint is a virtue, the more continent.

3. Coming to the critical period at which a boy ceases to be a boy and becomes a youth, we find that it is just then that the rest of the world proceed to emancipate their children from the private tutor and the schoolmaster, and, without substituting any further ruler, are content to launch them into absolute independence.

Here, again, Lycurgus took an entirely opposite view of the matter. This, if observation might be trusted, was the season when the tide of animal spirits flows fast, and the froth of insolence rises to the surface; when, too, the most violent appetites for pleasures invade the mind. This, then, was the right moment at which to impose constant labours upon the growing youth, and to devise for him a subtle system of absorbing occupation. And by a crowning enactment, which said that he who shrank from the duties imposed on him would forfeit henceforth all claim to the glorious honours of the state, he caused, not only the public authorities, but those personally interested in the youths to take serious pains so that no single individual of them should by an act of cowardice find himself utterly despised within the body politic.

Furthermore, in his desire firmly to implant modesty in them he imposed a special rule. In the streets they were to keep their hands within the folds of the cloak; they were to walk in silence and without turning their heads to gaze, but rather to keep their eyes fixed upon the ground before them. And hereby it would seem to be proved conclusively that, even in the matter of quiet bearing and sobriety, the masculine type may claim greater strength than that which we attribute to the nature of women. At any rate, you might sooner expect a stone image to find voice than one of those Spartan youths; to divert the eyes of some bronze statue were less difficult. And as to quiet bearing, no bride ever stepped in bridal bower with more natural modesty. Note them when they have reached the public table. The plainest answer to the question asked, that is all you need expect to hear from their lips.

4. But if he was thus careful in the education of the stripling, the Spartan lawgiver showed a still greater anxiety in dealing with those who had reached the prime of opening manhood; considering their immense importance to the city in the scale of good, if only they proved themselves the men they should be. He had only to look around to see that wherever the spirit of emulation is most deeply seated, there, too, their choruses and gymnastic contests will present alike a far higher charm to eye and ear. And on the same principle he

persuaded himself that he needed only to confront his youthful warriors in the strife of valour, and with like result. They also, in their degree, might be expected to attain to some unknown height of manly virtue.

What method he adopted to engage these combatants I will now explain. Their ephors select three men out of the whole body of the citizens in the prime of life. These three are named masters of the horse. Each of these selects 100 others, being bound to explain for what reason he prefers in honour these and disapproves of those. The result is that those who fail to obtain the distinction are now at open war, not only with those who rejected them, but with those who were chosen in their stead; and they keep ever a jealous eye on one another to detect some slip of conduct contrary to the high code of honour there held customary. And so is set on foot that strife, in truest sense acceptable to heaven, and for the purposes of state most politic. It is a strife in which not only is the pattern of a brave man's conduct fully set forth, but where, too, each against other and in separate camps, the rival parties train for victory. One day the superiority shall be theirs; or, in the day of need, one and all to the last man, they will be ready to aid the fatherland with all their strength.

Necessity, moreover, is laid upon them to study a good habit of the body, coming as they do to blows with their fists for very strife's sake wherever they meet. However, any one present has a right to separate the combatants, and, if obedience is not shown to the peacemaker, the Guardian of youth hales the delinquent before the ephors, and the ephors inflict heavy damages, since they will have it plainly understood that rage must never override obedience to law.

With regard to those who have already passed the vigour of early manhood, and on whom the highest magistracies henceforth devolve, there is a like contrast. In Hellas generally we find that at this age the need of further attention to physical strength is removed, although the imposition of military service continues. But Lycurgus made it customary for that section of his citizens to regard hunting as the highest honour suited to their age; but not to the exclusion of any public duty. And his aim was that they might be equally able to undergo the fatigues of war with those in the prime of early manhood.

5. The above is a fairly exhaustive statement of the institutions traceable to the legislation of Lycurgus in connection with the successive stages of a citizen's life. It remains that I should endeavour to describe the style of living which he established for the whole body, irrespective of age. It will be understood that, when Lycurgus first came to deal with the question, the Spartans, like the rest of the Hellenes, used to mess privately at home. Tracing more than half the current misdemeanours to this custom, he was determined to drag his people out into the daylight, and so he invented the public mess-rooms. Whereby he expected at any rate to minimise the transgression of orders.

As to food, his ordinance allowed them so much as, while not inducing repletion, should guard them from actual want. And, in fact, there are many exceptional dishes in the shape of game supplied from the hunting field. Or, as a substitute for these, rich men will occasionally garnish the feast with wheaten loaves. So that from beginning to end, till the mess breaks up, the common board is never stinted for viands, nor yet extravagantly furnished.

So also in the matter of drink. While putting a stop to all unnecessary potations, detrimental alike to a firm brain and a steady gait, he left them free to quench thirst when nature dictated; a method which would at once add to the pleasure while it diminished the danger of drinking. And indeed one may fairly ask how, on such a system of common meals, it would be possible for any one to ruin either himself or his family through either gluttony or wine-bibbing.

This too must be borne in mind, that in other states equals in age, for the most part, associate together, and such an atmosphere is little conducive to modesty. Whereas in Sparta Lycurgus was careful so to blend the ages that the younger men must benefit largely by the experience of the elder—an education in itself, and the more so since by custom of the country conversation at the common meal has reference to the honourable acts which this man or that man may have performed in relation to the state. The scene, in fact, but little lends itself to the intrusion of violence or drunken riot; ugly speech and ugly deeds alike are out of place. Among other good results obtained through this out-door system of meals may be mentioned these: There is the necessity of walking home when the meal is over, and a consequent anxiety not to be caught tripping under the influence of wine, since they all know of course that the supper-table must be presently abandoned, and that they must move as freely in the dark as in the day, even the help of a torch to guide the steps being forbidden to all on active service.

In connection with this matter, Lycurgus had not failed to observe the effect of equal amounts of food on different persons. The hardworking man has a good complexion, his muscles are well fed, he is robust and strong. The man who abstains from work, on the other hand, may be detected by his miserable appearance; he is blotched and puffy, and devoid of strength. This observation, I say, was not wasted on him. On the contrary, turning it over in his mind that any one who chooses, as a matter of private judgment, to devote himself to toil may hope to present a very creditable appearance physically, he enjoined upon the eldest for the time being in every gymnasium to see to it that the labours of the class were proportional to the meats. and to my mind he was not out of his reckoning in this matter more than elsewhere. At any rate, it would be hard to discover a healthier or more completely

developed human being, physically speaking, than the Spartan. Their gymnastic training, in fact, makes demands alike on the legs, arms and neck equally.

6. There are other points in which this legislator's views run counter to those commonly accepted. Thus: in other states the individual citizen is master over his own children, servants and belongings generally; but Lycurgus, whose aim was to secure to all the citizens a considerable share in one another's goods without mutual injury, enacted that each one should have an equal power over his neighbour's children as over his own. The principle is this. When a man knows that this, that, and the other person are fathers of children subject to his own authority, he must perforce deal by them even as he desires his own children to be dealt by. And, if a boy chance to have received a whipping, not from his own father but some other, and goes and complains to his own father, it would be thought wrong on the part of that father if he did not inflict a second whipping on his son. A striking proof, in its way, how completely they trust each other not to impose dishonourable commands upon their children.

In the same way he empowered them to use their neighbour's servants in case of need. This communism he applied also to dogs used for the chase; in so far that a party in need of dogs will invite the owner to the chase, and if he is not at leisure to attend himself, at any rate he is happy to let his dogs go. The same applies to the use of horses. Some one has fallen sick perhaps, or is in want of a carriage, or is anxious to reach some point or other quickly—in any case he has a right, if he sees a horse anywhere, to take and use it, and restores it safe and sound when he has done with it.

And here is another institution attributed to Lycurgus which scarcely coincides with the customs elsewhere in vogue. A hunting party returns from the chase, belated. They want provisions—they have nothing prepared themselves. To meet this contingency he made it a rule that owners are to leave behind the food that has been dressed; and the party in need will open the seals, take out what they want, seal up the remainder, and leave it. Accordingly, by his system of give-and-take even those with next to nothing have a share in all that the country can supply, if ever they stand in need of anything.

7. There are yet other customs in Sparta which Lycurgus instituted in opposition to those of the rest of Hellas, and the following among them. We all know that in the generality of states every one devotes his full energy to the business of making money: one man as a tiller of the soil, another as a mariner, a third as a merchant, whilst others depend on various arts to earn a living. But at Sparta Lycurgus forbade his freeborn citizens to have anything whatsoever to do with the concerns of money-making. As freemen, he enjoined upon them to regard as their concern exclusively those activities upon which the foundations of civic liberty are based.

And indeed, one may well ask, for what reason should wealth be regarded as a matter for serious pursuit in a community where, partly by a system of equal contributions to the necessaries of life, and partly by the maintenance of a common standard of living, the lawgiver placed so effectual a check upon the desire for riches for the sake of luxury? What inducement, for instance, would there be to make money, even for the sake of wearing apparel, in a state where personal adornment is held to lie not in the costliness of the clothes they wear, but in the healthy condition of the body to be clothed? Nor again could there be much inducement to amass wealth, in order to be able to expend it on the members of a common mess, where the legislator had made it seem far more glorious that a man should help his fellows by the labour of his body than by costly outlay. The latter being, as he finely phrased it, the function of wealth, the former an activity of the soul.

He went a step farther, and set up a strong barrier (even in a society such as I have described) against the pursuance of money-making by wrongful means. In the first place, he established a coinage of so extraordinary a sort, that even a single sum of ten minas could not come into a house without attracting the notice, either of the master himself, or of some member of his household. In fact, it would occupy a considerable space, and need a waggon to carry it. Gold and silver themselves, moreover, are liable to search, and in case of detection, the possessor subjected to a penalty. In fact, to repeat the question asked above, for what reason should money-making become an earnest pursuit in a community where the possession of wealth entails more pain than its employment brings satisfaction?

8. But to proceed. We are all aware that there is no state in the world in which greater obedience is shown to magistrates, and to the laws themselves, than Sparta. But, for my part, I am disposed to think that Lycurgus could never have attempted to establish this healthy condition, until he had first secured the unanimity of the most powerful members of the state. I infer this for the following reasons. In other states the leaders in rank and influence do not even desire to be thought to fear the magistrates. Such a thing they would regard as in itself a symbol of servility. In Sparta, on the contrary, the stronger a man is the more readily does he bow before constituted authority. And indeed, they pride themselves on their humility, and on a prompt obedience, running, or at any rate not crawling with laggard step, at the word of command. Such an example of eager discipline, they are persuaded, set by themselves, will not fail to be followed by the rest. And this is precisely what has taken place. It is reasonable to suppose that it was these same noblest members of the state who combined to lay the foundation of the ephorate, after they had come to the conclusion themselves that of all the blessings

which a state, or an army, or a household can enjoy, obedience is the greatest. Since, as they could not but reason, the greater the power with which men fence about authority, the greater the fascination it will exercise upon the mind of the citizen, to the enforcement of obedience.

Accordingly the ephors are competent to punish whomsoever they choose; they have power to exact fines on the spur of the moment; they have power to depose magistrates in mid career, nay, actually to imprison and bring them to trial on the capital charge. Entrusted with these vast powers, they do not, as do the rest of states, allow the magistrates elected to exercise authority as they like, right through the year of office; but, in the style rather of despotic monarchs, or presidents of the games, at the first symptom of an offence against the law they inflict chastisement without warning and without hesitation.

But of all the many beautiful contrivances invented by Lycurgus to kindle a willing obedience to the laws in the hearts of the citizens, none, to my mind, was happier or more excellent than his unwillingness to deliver his code to the people at large, until, attended by the most powerful members of the state, he had betaken himself to Delphi, and there made inquiry of the god whether it were better for Sparta, and conducive to her interests, to obey the laws which he had framed. And not until the divine answer came, "Better will it be in every way," did he deliver them, laying it down as a last ordinance that to refuse obedience to a code which had the sanction of the Pythian god himself was a thing not illegal only, but impious.

9. The following too may well excite our admiration for Lycurgus. I speak of the consummate skill with which he induced the whole state of Sparta to regard an honourable death as preferable to an ignoble life. And indeed if any one will investigate the matter, he will find that by comparison with those who make it a principle to retreat in face of danger, actually fewer of

these Spartans die in battle, since, to speak truth, salvation, it would seem, attends on virtue far more frequently than on cowardice—virtue, which is at once easier and sweeter, richer in resource and stronger of arm, than her opposite. And that virtue has another familiar attendant—to wit, glory—needs no showing, since all wish to ally themselves somehow with the good.

Yet the actual means by which he gave currency to these principles is a point which it were well not to overlook. It is clear that the lawgiver set himself deliberately to provide all the blessings of heaven for the good man, and a sorry and ill-starred existence for the coward.

In other states the man who shows himself base and cowardly wins to himself an evil reputation and the nickname of a coward, but that is all. For the rest he buys and sells in the same market-place with the good man; he sits beside him at the play; he exercises with him in the same. gymnasium, and all as suits his humour. But at Lacedaemon there is not one man who would not feel ashamed to welcome the coward at the common mess-table, or to try conclusions with such an antagonist in a wrestling bout. Consider the day's round of his existence. The sides are being picked for a game of ball, but he is left out as the odd man: there is no place for him. During the choric dance he is driven away into ignominious quarters. Nay, in the very streets it is he who must step aside for others to pass, or, being seated, he must rise and make room, even for a younger man. At home he will have his maiden relatives to support in their isolation (and they will hold him to blame for their unwedded lives). A hearth with no wife to bless it—that is a condition he must face, and yet he will have to pay damages for incurring it. Let him not roam abroad with a smiling countenance; let him not imitate men whose fame is irreproachable, or he shall feel on his back the blows of his superiors. Such being the weight of infamy which is laid upon all cowards, I, for my part, am not surprised if in Sparta they deem death preferable to a life so steeped in dishonour and reproach.

10. That too was a happy enactment, in my opinion, by which Lycurgus provided for the continual cultivation of virtue, even to old age. By fixing the election to the council of elders as a last ordeal at the goal of life, he made it impossible for a high standard of virtuous living to be disregarded even in old age. (So, too, it is worthy of admiration in him that he lent his helping hand to virtuous old age. Thus, by making the elders sole arbiters in the trial for life, he contrived to charge old age with a greater weight of honour than that which is accorded to the strength of mature manhood.) And assuredly such a contest as this must appeal to the zeal of mortal man beyond all others in a supreme degree. Fair, doubtless, are contests of gymnastic skill, yet are they but trials of bodily excellence, but this contest for the seniory is of a higher sort—it is an ordeal of the soul itself. In proportion, therefore, as the soul is worthier than the body, so must these contests of the soul appeal to a stronger enthusiasm than their bodily antitypes.

And yet another point may well excite our admiration for Lycurgus largely. It had not escaped his observation that communities exist where those who are willing to make virtue their study and delight fail somehow in ability to add to the glory of their fatherland. That lesson the legislator laid to heart, and in Sparta he enforced, as a matter of public duty, the practice of every virtue by every citizen. And so it is that, just as man differs from man in some excellence, according as he cultivates or neglects to cultivate it, this city of Sparta, with good reason, outshines all other states in virtue; since she, and she alone, has made the attainment of a high standard of noble living a public duty.

And was not this a noble enactment, that whereas other states are content to inflict punishment only in cases where a man does wrong against his neighbour, Lycurgus imposed penalties no less severe on him who openly neglected to make himself as good as possible? For this, it seems, was his principle: in the one case, where a man is robbed, or defrauded, or kidnapped, and made a slave of, the injury of the misdeed, whatever it be, is personal to the individual so maltreated; but in the other case whole communities suffer foul treason at the hands of the base man and the coward. So that it was only reasonable, in my opinion, that he should visit the heaviest penalty upon these latter.

Moreover, he laid upon them, like some irresistible necessity, the obligation to cultivate the whole virtue of a citizen. Provided they duly performed the injunctions of the law, the city belonged to them, each and all, in absolute possession and on an equal footing. Weakness of limb or want of wealth was no drawback in his eyes. But as for him who, out of the cowardice of his heart, shrank from the performance of the law's injunction, the legislator pointed him out as disqualified to be regarded longer as a member of the brotherhood of peers.

It may be added that there is no doubt as to the great antiquity of this code of laws. The point is clear so far, that Lycurgus himself is said to have lived in the days of the Heracleidae. But being of so long standing, these laws, even at this day, still are stamped in the eyes of other men with all the novelty of youth. And the most marvellous thing of all is that, while everybody is agreed to praise these remarkable institutions, there is not a single state which cares to imitate them.

11. The above form a common stock of blessings, open to every Spartan to enjoy, alike in peace and in war. But if any one desires to be informed in what way the legislator improved upon the ordinary machinery of warfare and in reference to an army in the field, it is easy to satisfy his curiosity.

In the first instance, the ephors announce by proclamation the limit of age to which the service applies for cavalry and heavy infantry; and in the next place, for the various handicraftsmen. So that, even on active service, the Lacedaemonians are well supplied with all the conveniences enjoyed by people living as citizens at home. All implements and instruments whatsoever, which an army may need in common, are ordered to be in readiness, some on waggons and others on baggage animals. In this way anything omitted can hardly escape detection.

For the actual encounter under arms, the following inventions are attributed to him. The soldier has a crimson-coloured uniform and a heavy shield of bronze; his theory being that such an equipment has no sort of feminine association, and is altogether most warrior-like. It is most quickly burnished; it is least readily tarnished.

He further permitted those who were above the age of early manhood to wear their hair long. For so, he conceived, they would appear of larger stature, more free and indomitable, and of a more terrible aspect.

So furnished and accoutred, he divided his citinze soldiers into six *morae* (regimental divisions) of cavalry and heavy infantry. Each of these citizen regiments has one polemarch (colonel), four captains of companies, eight lieutenants, each in command of a half company, and sixteen commanders of sections. At the word of command any such regimental division can be formed readily either into single file or into three files abreast, or into six files abreast.

As to the idea, commonly entertained, that the tactical arrangement of the Laconian heavy infantry is highly complicated, no conception could be more opposed to fact. For in the Laconian order the front rank men are all leaders, so that each file has everything necessary to play its part efficiently. In fact, this disposition is so easy to understand that no one who can distinguish one human being from another could fail to follow it. One set have the privilege of leaders, the other the duty of followers. The evolutional orders, by which greater depth or shallowness is given to the battle line, are given by word of mouth by the commander of the section, who plays the part of the herald, and they cannot be mistaken. None of these manoeuvres presents any difficulty whatsoever to the understanding.

But when it comes to their ability to do battle equally well in spite of some confusion which has been set up, and whatever the chapter of accidents may confront them with, I admit that the tactics here are not so easy to understand, except for people trained under the laws of Lycurgus. Even movements which an instructor in heavy-armed warfare might look upon as difficult are performed by the Lacedaemonians with the utmost ease. Thus, the troops, we will suppose, are marching in column; one section of a company is of course stepping up behind another from the rear. Now, if at such a moment a hostile force appears in front in battle order, the word is passed down to the commander of each section, "Deploy into line to the left." And so throughout the whole length of the column, until the line is formed facing the enemy. Or supposing while in this position an enemy appears in the rear. Each file performs a countermarch with the effect of bringing the best men face to face with the enemy all along the line. As to the point that the leader previously on the right finds himself now on the left, they do not consider that they are necessarily losers thereby, but, as it may turn out, even gainers. If, for instance, the enemy attempted to turn their flank, he would find himself wrapping round, not their exposed, but their shielded flank. Or if, for any reason, it be thought advisable for the general to keep the right wing, they turn the corps about, and counter-march by ranks, until the leader is on the right, and the rear rank on the left. Or again, supposing a division of the enemy appears on the right while they are marching in column, they have nothing further to do but to wheel each company to the right, like a trireme, prow forwards, to meet the enemy, and thus the rear company again finds itself on the right. If, however, the enemy should attack on the left, either they will not allow of that and push him aside, or else they wheel their companies to the left to face the antagonist, and thus the rear company once more falls into position on the left.

12. I will now speak of the mode of encampment sanctioned by the regulation of Lycurgus. To avoid the waste incidental to the angles of a square, the encampment, according to him, should be circular, except where there was the security of a hill, or fortification, or where they had a river in their rear. He had sentinels posted during the day along the place of arms and facing inwards; since they are appointed not so much for the sake of the enemy as to keep an eye on friends. The enemy is sufficiently watched by mounted troopers perched on various points commanding the widest prospect.

To guard against hostile approach by night, sentinel duty according to the ordinance was performed by the Sciritae outside the main body. At the present time the rule is so far modified that the duty is entrusted to foreigners, if there be a foreign contingent present, with a leaven of Spartans themselves to keep them company.

The custom of always taking their spears with them when they go their rounds must certainly be attributed to the same cause which makes them exclude their slaves from the place of arms. Nor need we be surprised if, when retiring for necessary purposes, they only withdraw just far enough from one another, or from the place of arms itself, not to create annoyance. The need of precaution is the whole explanation.

The frequency with which they change their encampments is another point. It is done quite as much for the sake of benefiting their friends as of annoying their enemies.

Further, the law enjoins upon all Lacedaemonians, during the whole period of an expedition, the constant practice of gymnastic exercises, whereby their pride in themselves is increased, and they appear freer and of a more liberal aspect than the rest of the world. The walk and the running ground must not exceed in length the space covered by a regimental division, so that no one may find himself far from his own stand of arms. After the gymnastic exercises the senior polemarch gives the order by herald to be seated. This serves all the purposes of an inspection. After this the order is given to get breakfast, and for the outposts to be relieved. After this, again, come pastimes and relaxations before the evening exercises, after which the herald's cry is heard to take the evening meal. When they have sung a hymn to the gods to whom the offerings of happy omen have been performed, the final order, "Retire to rest at the place of arms," is given.

If the story is a little long the reader must not be surprised, since it would be difficult to find any point in military matters omitted by the Lacedaemonians which seems to demand attention.

13. I will now give a detailed account of the power and privilege assigned by Lycurgus to the king during a campaign. To begin with, so long as he is on active service, the state maintains the king and those with him. The polemarchs mess with him and share his quarters, so that by constant intercourse they may be all the better able to consult in common in case of need. Besides the polemarch three other members of the peers share the royal quarters. The duty of these is to attend to all matters of commissariat, in order that the king and the rest may have unbroken leisure to attend to affairs of actual warfare.

But I will resume at a somewhat higher point and describe the manner in which the king sets out on an expedition. As a preliminary step, before leaving home he offers sacrifice in company with his staff to Zeus the Leader, and if the victims prove favourable then and there the priest, who bears the sacred fire, takes thereof from off the altar and leads the way to the boundaries of the land. Here for the second time the king does sacrifice to Zeus and Athena; and as soon as the offerings are accepted by those two divinities he steps across the boundaries of the land. And all the while the fire from those sacrifices leads the way, and is never suffered to go out. Behind follow beasts for sacrifice of every sort.

Invariably when he offers sacrifice the king begins the work before the day has broken, being minded to anticipate the goodwill of the god. And round about the place of sacrifice are present the polemarchs and captains, the lieutenants and sub-lieutenants, with the commandants of the baggage train, and any general of the states who may care to assist. There, too, are to be seen two of the ephors, who never interfere, save only at the summons of the king, yet have they their eyes fixed on the proceedings of each one there and keep all in order, as may well be guessed. When the sacrifices are accomplished the king summons all and issues his orders as to what has to be done. And all with such method that, to witness the proceedings, you might fairly suppose the rest of the world to be but bungling experimenters, and the Lacedaemonians alone true handicrafts-men in the art of soldiering.

Then the king puts himself at the head of the troops, and if no enemy appears he heads the line of march, no one preceding him except the Sciritae, and the mounted troopers exploring in front. If, however, there is any reason to anticipate a battle, the king takes the leading column of the first army corps and wheels to the right until he has got into position with two army corps and two generals of division on either flank. The disposition of the supports is assigned to the eldest of the royal council acting as brigadier, the staff consisting of all peers who share the royal mess and quarters, with the soothsayers, surgeons, and flute-players, whose place is in the front of the troops, with, finally, any vol-unteers who happen to be present. So that

there is no check or hesitation in anything to be done; every contingency is provided for.

The following details also seem to me of high utility among the inventions of Ly-curgus with a view to the actual battle. Whenever, the enemy being now close enough to watch the proceedings, the goat is sacrificed; then, says the law, let all the flute-players, in their places, play upon the flutes, and let every Lacedaemonian don a wreath. Then, too, so runs the order, let the shields be brightly polished. The privilege is accorded to the young man to enter battle with his long locks combed. To be of a cheery countenance—that, too, is of good repute. Onwards they pass the word of command to the subaltern in command of his section, since it is impossible to hear along the whole of each section from the particular subaltern posted on the outside. It devolves, finally, on the polemarch to see that all goes well.

When the right moment for encamping has come, the king is responsible for that, and has to point out the proper place. The despatch of embassies, however, whether to friends or to foes, is not the king's affair. Petitioners in general wishing to transact anything treat, in the first instance, with the king. If the case concerns some point of justice, the king despatches the petitioner to the Hellanodicae (who form the court-martial); if of money, to the paymasters. If the petitioner brings booty, he is sent off to the sellers of spoil. This being the mode of procedure, no other duty is left to the king, while he is on active service, except to play the part of priest in matters concerning the gods and of commander-in-chief in his relationship to men.

14. Now, if the question be put to me whether the laws of Lycurgus remain still to this day unchanged, that indeed is an assertion which I should no longer venture to maintain; knowing, as I do, that in former times the Lacedaemonians preferred to live at home on moderate means, content to associate exclusively with themselves

rather than to play the part of governor-general in foreign states and to be corrupted by flattery; knowing further, as I do, that formerly they dreaded to be detected in the possession of gold, whereas nowadays there are not a few who make it their glory and their boast to be possessed of it. I am very well aware that in former days alien acts were put in force for this very object. To live abroad was not allowed. And why? Simply in order that the citizens of Sparta might not take the infection of dishonesty and light-living from foreigners; whereas now I am very well aware that those who are reputed to be leading citizens have but one ambition, and that is to live to the end of their days as governors-general on a foreign soil. The days were when their sole anxiety was to fit themselves to lead the rest of Hellas. But nowadays they concern themselves much more to wield command than to be fit themselves to rule. And so it has come to pass that whereas in old days the states of Hellas flocked to Lacedaemon seeking her leadership against the supposed wrongdoer, now numbers are inviting one another to prevent the Lacedaemonians again recovering their empire. Yet, if they have incurred all these reproaches, we need not wonder, seeing that they are so plainly disobedient to the god himself and to the laws of their own lawgiver Lycurgus.

15. I wish to explain with sufficient detail the nature of the covenant between king and state as instituted by Lycurgus; for this, I take it, is the sole type of rule which still preserves the original form in which it was first established; whereas other constitutions will be found either to have been already modified or else to be still undergoing modifications at this moment.

Lycurgus laid it down as law that the king shall offer in behalf of the state all public sacrifices, as being himself of divine descent, and whithersoever the state shall despatch her armies the king shall take the lead. He granted him to receive honorary gifts of the things offered in sacrifice, and he appointed him choice land in many of the provincial cities, enough to satisfy moderate needs without excess of wealth. and in order that the kings also might camp and mess in public he appointed them public quarters; and he honoured them with a double portion each at the evening meal, not in order that they might actually eat twice as much as others, but that the king might have wherewithal to honour whomsoever he desired. He also granted as a gift to each of the two kings to choose two mess-fellows, which same are called Pythii. He also granted them to receive out of every litter of swine one pig, so that the king might never be at a loss for victims if he wished to consult the gods.

Close by the palace a lake affords an unrestricted supply of water; and how useful that is for various purposes they best can tell who lack the luxury. Moreover, all rise from their seats to give place to the king, save only that the ephors rise not from their thrones of office. Monthly they exchange oaths, the ephors in behalf of the state, the king himself in his own behalf. And this is the oath on the king's part, "I will exercise my kingship in accordance with the established laws of the state." And on the part of the State the oath runs, "so long as he (who exercises kingship) shall abide by his oath we will not suffer his kingdom to be shaken."

These then are the honours bestowed upon the king during his lifetime at home, honours by no means much exceeding those of private citizens, since the lawgiver was minded neither to suggest to the kings the pride of the despotic monarch, nor, on the other hand, to engender in the heart of the citizen envy of their power. As to those other honours which are given to the king at his death, the laws of Lycurgus would seem plainly to signify hereby that these kings of Lacedaemon are not mere mortals but heroic beings, and that is why they are preferred in honour.

3. TYRTAEUS*

Tyrtaeus was an elegiac poet contemporary with the Second Messenian War in the seventh century B.C. The fragments of his poems which survive are a major source of our knowledge of the early history of Sparta.

Pausanias *Description of Greece* [the Second Messenian War]: The man who brought the war to an end was this Theopompus, as is testified by the Elegiac lines of Tyrtaeus, which say 'to our King' etc. (ll. 1–2).

Scholiast on Plato: On Tyrtaeus' arrival in Lacedaemon he became inspired, and urged the Spartans to end the war against the Messenians by every means in his power, among others by the famous line 'Messenè is good,' etc.

Strabo *Geography*: Messenè was taken after a war of nineteen years; compare Tyrtaeus: (ll. 4–8).

... to our king, the friend of the Gods, Theopompus, through whom we took spacious Messenè, Messenè so good to plough and so good to plant, for which there fought ever unceasingly nineteen years, keeping an unfaltering heart, the spearmen fathers of our fathers, and in the twentieth year the foeman left his rich lands and fled from the great uplands of Ithomè.

Pausanias *Description of Greece*: The vengeance the Spartans took on the Messenians is referred to in these lines of Tyrtaeus:

galled with great burdens like asses, bringing to their lords under grievous necessity a half of all the fruit of the soil.

And that they were obliged to join in their lamentations he shows in the following couplet:

making lamentation for their lords both themselves and their wives, whenever one was overtaken with the dolorous fate of Death.

Strabo *Geography*: They fought more than

once because of rebellion on the part of the Messenians. The first conquest, according to the poems of Tyrtaeus, took place two generations before his time, and the second, when they rebelled in alliance with the Argives, Arcadians, and Pisatans, the Arcadians making Aristocrates king of Orchomenus their general and the Pisatans Pantaleon son of Omphalion; in the latter war he declares that he led the Lacedaemonians himself.

* * *

Lycurgus *Against Leocrates* [to the Athenians about their ancestors]: So great was the energy, both public and private, of the men who then inhabited Athens, that the bravest people of Greece, in their war of long ago against the Messenians, received an oracle which bade them if they would defeat their enemies to take a leader from us. Now if the God preferred a general of Athens above the two Heracleid kings who rule at Sparta, that general must have been a man of extraordinary valour. Everyone in Greece knows that the general they took from our city was Tyrtaeus, by whose aid, with a wisdom that looked far beyond the dangers of that day, they both defeated their enemies and established their system of education. Tyrtaeus left behind him Elegiac Poems which are used to teach them courage, and a people whose practice is to take no account of poets, have made so much of Tyrtaeus as to pass a law that whenever they take the field under arms they shall all be summoned to the king's tent to hear his poems, in the belief that this will make them most willing to die for their country. And it would be well for you to hear the Elegiac verses, so that you may know what it was that made men famous among them:

For 'tis a fair thing for a good man to fall and die fighting in the van for his native land, whereas to leave his city and his rich fields and go a-begging is of all things the most miserable, wandering with mother

* Reprinted by permission of the publishers and the Loeb Classical Library, From *Greek Elegy and Iambus*, Vol. I, fragments 5–8, 10–12, translated by J. M. Edmonds (Cambridge, Mass.: Harvard University Press, 1931).

dear and aged father, with little children and wedded wife. For hateful shall such an one be among all those to whom he shall come in bondage to Want and loathsome Penury, and doth shame his lineage and belie his noble beauty, followed by all evil and dishonour. Now if so little thought be taken of a wanderer, and so little honour, respect, or pity, let us fight with a will for this land, and die for our children and never spare our lives.

Abide then, O young men, shoulder to shoulder and fight; begin not foul flight nor yet be afraid, but make the heart in your breasts both great and stout, and never shrink when you fight the foe. And the elder sort, whose knees are no longer nimble, fly not ye to leave them fallen to earth. For 'tis a foul thing, in sooth, for an elder to fall in the van and lie before the younger, his head white and his beard hoary, breathing forth his stout soul in the dust, with his privities all bloody in his hands, a sight so foul to see and fraught with such ill to the seer, and his flesh also all naked; yet to a young man all is seemly enough, so long as he have the noble bloom of lovely youth, aye a marvel he for men to behold, and desirable unto women, so long as ever he be alive, and fair in like manner when he be fallen in the vanguard. So let each man bite his lip with his teeth and abide firm-set astride upon the ground.

Stobaeus *Anthology* [on war]: Tyrtaeus:

Ye are of the lineage of the invincible Heracles; so be ye of good cheer; not yet is the head of Zeus turned away. Fear ye not a multitude of men, nor flinch, but let every man hold his shield straight towards the van, making Life his enemy and the black Spirits of Death dear as the rays of the sun. For ye know the destroying deeds of lamentable Ares, and well have learnt the disposition of woeful War; ye have tasted both of the fleeing and the pursuing, lads, and had more than your fill of either. Those who abiding shoulder to shoulder go with a will into the mellay and the van, of

these are fewer slain, these save the people afterward; as for them that turn to fear, all their valour is lost—no man could tell in words each and all the ills that befall a man if he once come to dishonour. For pleasant it is in dreadful warfare to pierce the midriff of a flying man, and disgraced is the dead that lieth in the dust with a spear-point in his back. So let each man bite his lip and abide firm-set astride upon the ground, covering with the belly of his broad buckler thighs and legs below and breast and shoulders above; let him brandish the massy spear in his right hand, let him wave the dire crest upon his head; let him learn how to fight by doing doughty deeds, and not stand shield in hand beyond the missiles. Nay, let each man close the foe, and with his own long spear, or else with his sword, wound and take an enemy, and setting foot beside foot, resting shield against shield, crest beside crest, helm beside helm, fight his man breast to breast with sword or long spear in hand. And ye also, ye lightarmed, crouch ye on either hand beneath the shield and fling your great hurlstones and throw against them your smooth javelins, in your place beside the men of heavier armament.

Stobaeus *Anthology* [praise of valour]: Tyrtaeus:

I would neither call a man to mind nor put him in my tale for prowess in the race or the wrestling, not even had he the stature and strength of a Cyclops and surpassed in swiftness the Thracian North-wind, nor were he a comelier man than Tithonus and a richer than Midas or Cinyras, nor though he were a greater king than Pelops son of Tantalus, and had Adrastus' suasiveness of tongue, nor yet though all fame were his save of warlike strength; for a man is not good in war if he have not endured the sight of bloody slaughter and stood nigh and reached forth to strike the foe. This is prowess, this is the noblest prize and the fairest for a lad to win in the world; a common good this both for the city and all her people, when a man standeth firm in the forefront without ceasing, and making heart and soul to abide, forgetteth foul flight altogether and hearteneth by his words him that he standeth by. Such a man is good in war; he quickly turneth the savage hosts of the enemy, and stemmeth the wave of battle with a will; moreover he that falleth in the van and loseth dear life to the glory of his city and his countrymen and his father, with many a frontwise wound through breast and breastplate and through bossy shield, he is bewailed alike by young and old, and lamented with sore regret by all the city. His grave and his children are conspicuous among men, and his children's children and his line after them; nor ever doth his name and good fame perish, but though he be underground he liveth evermore, seeing that he was doing nobly and abiding in the fight for country's and children's sake when fierce Ares brought him low. But and if he escape the doom of outstretched Death and by victory make good the splendid boast of battle, he hath honour of all, alike young as old, and cometh to his death after happiness; as he groweth old he standeth out among his people, and there's none that will do him hurt either in honour or in right; all yield him place on the benches, alike the young and his peers and his elders. This is the prowess each man should this day aspire to, never relaxing from war.

4. ARISTOTLE ON THE SPARTAN CONSTITUTION*

Aristotle lived in the fourth century B.C. and his criticisms of Sparta's constitution are influenced by the events of his time. Yet it is the institutions themselves rather than their corruption which are judged and so the criticisms remain significant for the entirety of the Spartan experience.

In the governments of Lacedaemon and Crete, and indeed in all governments, two points have to be considered: first, whether any particular law is good or bad, when compared with the perfect state; secondly, whether it is or is not consistent with the idea and character which the lawgiver has set before his citizens. That in a well-ordered state the citizens should have leisure and not have to provide for their daily wants is generally acknowledged, but there is a difficulty in seeing how this leisure is to be attained. The Thessalian Penestae have often risen against their masters, and the Helots in like manner against the Lacedaemonians, for whose misfortunes they are always lying in wait. Nothing, however, of this kind has as yet happened to the Cretans; the reason probably is that the neighbouring cities, even when at war with one another, never form an alliance with rebellious serfs, rebellions not being for their interest, since they themselves have a dependent population. Whereas all the neighbours of the Lacedaemonians, whether Argives, Messenians, or Arcadians, were their enemies. In Thessaly, again, the original revolt of the slaves occurred because the Thessalians were still at war with the neighbouring Achaeans, Perrhaebians and Magnesians. Besides, if there were no other difficulty, the treatment or management of slaves is a troublesome affair; for, if not kept in hand, they are insolent, and think that they are as good as their masters, and, if harshly treated, they hate and conspire against them. Now it is clear that when these are the results the citizens of a state have not found out the secret of managing their subject population.

* Aristotle, *Politics*, 1269a–1271b, translated by Benjamin Jowett.

Again, the licence of the Lacedaemonian women defeats the intention of the Spartan constitution, and is adverse to the happiness of the state. For, a husband and a wife being each a part of every family, the state may be considered as about equally divided into men and women; and, therefore, in those states in which the condition of the women is bad, half the city may be regarded as having no laws. And this is what has actually happened at Sparta; the legislator wanted to make the whole state hardy and temperate, and he has carried out his intention in the case of the men, but he has neglected the women, who live in every sort of intemperance and luxury. The consequence is that in such a state wealth is too highly valued, especially if the citizens fall under the dominion of their wives, after the manner of most warlike races, except the Celts and a few others who openly approve of male loves. The old mythologer would seem to have been right in uniting Ares and Aphrodite, for all warlike races are prone to the love either of men or of women. This was exemplified among the Spartans in the days of their greatness; many things were managed by their women. But what difference does it make whether women rule, or the rulers are ruled by women? The result is the same. Even in regard to courage, which is of no use in daily life, and is needed only in war, the influence of the Lacedaemonian women has been most mischievous. The evil showed itself in the Theban invasion, when, unlike the women in other cities, they were utterly useless and caused more confusion than the enemy. This licence of the Lacedaemonian women existed from the earliest times, and was only what might be expected. For, during the wars of the Lacedaemonians, first against the Argives, and afterwards against the Arcadians and Messenians, the men were long away from home, and, on the return of peace, they gave themselves into the legislator's hand, already prepared by the discipline of a soldier's life (in which there are many

elements of virtue), to receive his enactments. But, when Lycurgus, as tradition says, wanted to bring the women under his laws, they resisted, and he gave up the attempt. These then are the causes of what then happened, and this defect in the constitution is clearly to be attributed to them. We are not, however, considering what is or is not to be excused, but what is right or wrong, and the disorder of the women, as I have already said, not only gives an air of indecorum to the constitution considered in itself, but tends in a measure to foster avarice.

The mention of avarice naturally suggests a criticism on the inequality of property. While some of the Spartan citizens have quite small properties, others have very large ones; hence the land has passed into the hands of a few. And this is due also to faulty laws; for, although the legislator rightly holds up to shame the sale or purchase of an inheritance, he allows anybody who likes to give or bequeath it. Yet both practices lead to the same result. And nearly two-fifths of the whole country are held by women; this is owing to the number of heiresses and to the large dowries which are customary. It would surely have been better to have given no dowries at all, or, if any, but small or moderate ones. As the law now stands, a man may bestow his heiress on any one whom he pleases, and, if he die intestate, the privilege of giving her away descends to his heir. Hence, although the country is able to maintain 1500 cavalry and 30,000 hoplites, the whole number of Spartan citizens fell below 1000. The result proves the faulty nature of their laws respecting property; for the city sank under a single defeat; the want of men was their ruin. There is a tradition that, in the days of their ancient kings, they were in the habit of giving the rights of citizenship to strangers, and therefore, in spite of their long wars, no lack of population was experienced by them; indeed, at one time Sparta is said to have numbered not less than 10,000 citizens. Whether this statement is true or not, it would certainly have been better to have maintained their numbers by the equalization of property. Again, the law which relates to the procreation of children is adverse to the correction of this inequality. For the legislator, wanting to have as many Spartans as he could, encouraged the citizens to have large families; and there is a law at Sparta that the father of three sons shall be exempt from military service, and he who has four from all the burdens of the state. Yet it is obvious that, if there were many children, the land being distributed as it is, many of them must necessarily fall into poverty.

The Lacedaemonian constitution is defective in another point; I mean the Ephoralty. This magistracy has authority in the highest matters, but the Ephors are chosen from the whole people, and so the office is apt to fall into the hands of very poor men, who, being badly off, are open to bribes. There have been many examples at Sparta of this evil in former times; and quite recently, in the matter of the Andrians, certain of the Ephors who were bribed did their best to ruin the state. And so great and tyrannical is their power, that even the kings have been compelled to court them, so that, in this way as well, together with the royal office the whole constitution has deteriorated, and from being an aristocracy has turned into a democracy. The Ephoralty certainly does keep the state together; for the people are contented when they have a share in the highest office, and the result, whether due to the legislator or to chance, has been advantageous. For if a constitution is to be permanent, all the parts of the state must wish that it should exist and the same arrangements be maintained. This is the case at Sparta, where the kings desire its permanence because they have due honour in their own persons; the nobles because they are represented in the council of elders (for the office of elder is a reward of virtue); and the people, because all are eligible to the Ephoralty. The election of

Ephors out of the whole people is perfectly right, but ought not to be carried on in the present fashion, which is too childish. Again, they have the decision of great causes, although they are quite ordinary men, and therefore they should not determine them merely on their own judgement, but according to written rules, and to the laws. Their way of life, too, is not in accordance with the spirit of the constitution—they have a deal too much licence; whereas, in the case of the other citizens, the excess of strictness is so intolerable that they run away from the law into the secret indulgence of sensual pleasures.

Again, the council of elders is not free from defects. It may be said that the elders are good men and well trained in manly virtue; and that, therefore, there is an advantage to the state in having them. But that judges of important causes should hold office for life is a disputable thing, for the mind grows old as well as the body. And when men have been educated in such a manner that even the legislator himself cannot trust them, there is real danger. Many of the elders are well known to have taken bribes and to have been guilty of partiality in public affairs. And therefore they ought not to be irresponsible; yet at Sparta they are so. But (it may be replied), 'All magistracies are accountable to the Ephors.' Yes, but this prerogative is too great for them, and we maintain that the control should be exercised in some other manner. Further, the mode in which the Spartans elect their elders is childish; and it is improper that the person to be elected should canvass for the office; the worthiest should be appointed, whether he chooses or not. And there the legislator clearly indicates the same intention which appears in other parts of his constitution; he would have his citizens ambitious, and he has reckoned upon this quality in the election of the elders; for no one would ask to be elected if he were not. Yet ambition and avarice, almost more than any other passions, are the motives of crime.

Whether kings are or are not an advantage to states, I will consider at another time, they should at any rate be chosen, not as they are now, but with regard to their personal life and conduct. The legislator himself obviously did not suppose that he could make them really good men; at least he shows a great distrust of their virtue. For this reason the Spartans used to join enemies with them in the same embassy, and the quarrels between the kings were held to be conservative of the state.

Neither did the first introducer of the common meals, called 'phiditia', regulate them well. The entertainment ought to have been provided at the public cost, as in Crete, but among the Lacedaemonians every one is expected to contribute, and some of them are too poor to afford the expense; thus the intention of the legislator is frustrated. The common meals were meant to be a popular institution, but the existing manner of regulating them is the reverse of popular. For the very poor can scarcely take part in them; and, according to ancient custom, those who cannot contribute are not allowed to retain their rights of citizenship.

The law about the Spartan admirals has often been censured, and with justice; it is a source of dissension, for the kings are perpetual generals, and this office of admiral is but the setting up of another king.

The charge which Plato brings, in the *Laws*, against the intention of the legislator, is likewise justified; the whole constitution has regard to one part of virtue only—the virtue of the soldier, which gives victory in war. So long as they were at war, therefore, their power was preserved, but when they had attained empire they fell, for of the arts of peace they knew nothing, and had never engaged in any employment higher than war. There is another error, equally great, into which they have fallen. Although they truly think that the goods for which men contend are to be acquired by virtue rather than by vice, they err in supposing that these goods are to be preferred to the virtue which gains them.

Once more: the revenues of the state are ill-managed; there is no money in the treasury, although they are obliged to carry on great wars, and they are unwilling to pay taxes. The greater part of the land being in the hands of the Spartans, they do not look closely into one another's contributions. The result which the legislator has produced is the reverse of beneficial; for he has made his city poor, and his citizens greedy.

Enough respecting the Spartan constitution, of which these are the principal defects.

5. REVOLUTION IN SPARTA*

Forrest sees the revolution in Sparta as part of a general upheaval in Archaic Greece. He offers a possible explanation of the creation of the unique aspects of Spartan society based on his interpretation of ancient traditions about early Sparta.

THE DATE

In one way the example of Korinth does help to provide positive information on the

* George W. Forrest, *The Emergence of Greek Democracy* (London: Weidenfeld and Nicholson, 1966), pp. 123–140. Reprinted by permission of the McGraw-Hill Book Company, New York, and of the British publishers, Weidenfeld and Nicholson, London. Copyright © 1966 by McGraw-Hill, Inc.

revolution. It gives one fixed point between the first signs of economic awakening in the early eighth century and the comparatively well-documented story of political development which begins with Athens in the late seventh. By 657 B.C. in a state which had been among the leaders of the economic revolution, the resulting upheaval had produced a sufficient amount of confusion among the aristocracy to bring a different section of that class to power; it had given them and a large enough number of lesser men sufficient independence to conceive of and welcome the possibility of change; and it had given the lesser men the weapons with which to effect the change.

Pheidon, the tyrants of Sikyon, Megara or Miletos, though roughly or even exactly datable, are much too shadowy to provide any such fixed point except on the assumption, which I should certainly make, that their background was much the same, but it is an assumption, and they throw no fresh light on the nature of the development; on the other hand Sparta, the one state which does tell us something about the desires of ordinary men, presents, at the same time, one of the most tricky chronological problems in Greek history.

At some early date Sparta acquired a constitution, the work, it was said, of a great law-giver, Lykourgos. But at first glance the ancient evidence shows little agreement about this early genius—so little that many modern historians, in even deeper despair than one Greek historian who finally decided to postulate two *Lykourgoi*, have simply dismissed the man himself as a fiction and relied on their intuition to fix the date of 'his' work. For us the identity of the law-giver is unimportant—someone devised a Spartan constitution and we may as well call him Lykourgos—but the date does matter and fortunately the problem, though perhaps insoluble, is not nearly so complicated as has been supposed. Most of the divergent dates in the authorities are the result either of the use of different chronological systems (chronology was another fifth-century invention) or of the propaganda battle that was later fought over Sparta's oligarchic stability and it is clear that in fact the bulk of the ancient evidence either dated or was consistent with the dating of Lykourgos to the reign of King Charillos, which must have covered, roughly, the years 775–750 and the dissentients, with one doubtful exception, place him even earlier.

The issue, then, is this. Can we accept law-making in Sparta in the early eighth century? Some modern scholars can, the majority find it impossible before the seventh, but even with them there is no agreement on the precise context. To some the second half of the seventh century seems preferable; to others, including myself, the years around 675. I cannot discuss the evidence here; it must suffice to set out the general considerations which make the traditional early date impossible and to consider, very briefly, how the different later dates should affect the interpretation of the changes as a whole.

Our chief evidence for the nature of the reform is a document preserved by Plutarch in his life of Lykourgos, a document which he calls a *Rhetra* or 'law' but which he rather confusedly describes as an oracle delivered to the Spartans by Delphi (the language certainly has some oracular elements in it). The text embodies some of the main provisions of the new constitution:

(i) When a sanctuary has been set up to Zeus Sullanios and Athena Sullania, when the people has been drawn up in tribes and in *obai* and a *Gerousia* [or Senate] established with thirty members including the kings; (ii) meetings of the assembly shall be held from time to time on Apollo's feast-day between Babyka and Knakion; (iii) here questions shall be introduced and the *Gerousia* shall stand aside; (iv) the assembly of the people shall have the final say.

There follows what Plutarch regards as a later amendment:

(v) But if the people should speak with a crooked voice, the Elders (sc. the *Gerousia*) and the Leaders (sc. the Kings) shall dismiss them. (*Lykourgos*, 6)

At one point, in clause iv, the text is corrupt; where it is certain the meaning is often obscure (the word I have translated 'stand aside' has been variously rendered 'dismiss,' 'refuse to introduce proposals,' 'reach a final decision'); even where the meaning of the words is clear, the significance of them often escapes us (what exactly is a "crooked" voice?) but the general drift is firm enough and is confirmed by some verses of the mid-seventh-century Spartan poet, Tyrtaios, who seems to have summed up the new constitution in one poem, the bulk of which is unfortunately lost:

They listened to Apollo and brought home from Delphi the oracle of the God, his sure words. . . . 'The kings who are honoured by the gods shall show the way in counsel, they and the Elders, wise in years, whose care is lovely Sparta. After them the men of the people answering with straight decisions . . .' (Fragment 4).

Now it is just possible to conceive of a defined constitution such as this existing in an unlettered world, waiting to be written down when Greeks recovered the art of writing about 750 B.C. but it is far more likely that the document should be contemporary with the institution of the system which it describes, and 750 therefore becomes a *terminus post quem* for the revolution. Tyrtaios, on the other hand, cannot have written much outside the years 680–620 B.C. Hence the limits 750–620.

Again Tyrtaios ascribes the oracle to Delphi and although we cannot be certain that Tyrtaios is talking of the whole document or that he is telling the truth (in later centuries Delphi attracted much activity to which it had no real claim), the text itself is probably oracular in origin and Delphi, which had been Sparta's friend from its earliest days, is the obvious source. But we now know that Delphi did not exist as an oracular centre before the mid-eighth century. So the upper limit is confirmed.

Finally and decisively, the new constitution recognised a citizen body of some 9,000 'Equals' (this from other sources) who were to form the assembly. This can only be the Spartan hoplite army. But 9,000 Spartan hoplites did not exist before, at the outside, 725 and cannot have become a coherent political force before,

again at the outside, 700. So the limits are narrowed. Whatever the origin of the tradition associating Lykourgos with King Charillos, however firmly held by the Greeks themselves, it must be abandoned.

Had Sparta been, in every respect, a normal Greek state we should have had no difficulty in moving on to a more precise date, between 660 and 620. It would be almost unthinkable that a lesser city than Korinth should have outstripped her by much in political development. Indeed the nearer we could get to 620 and the later we could make Tyrtaios, the happier we should feel. But Sparta was abnormal in two important ways.

Like Korinth, she was a Dorian city but unlike Korinth (as far as we can tell) she had retained some of her primitive Dorian tribal customs (common messes for her citizens; an elaborate tribal—rather than family—education for her young), this perhaps explained by the fact that, unlike Korinth, she was surrounded by a number of surviving non-Dorian communities which she gradually incorporated or reduced to something approaching servile status, so providing herself with a valuable, but potentially dangerous, subject population, the so-called Helots, which she could exploit but which she had to guard herself against. From an early date Spartans were surrounded by a large body of men from whom they felt distinct and such a feeling of distinction easily leads to a feeling of community and consequently to a blurring of distinctions inside the privileged group. So it is readily understandable that Spartans could develop a greater sense of 'belonging' earlier than Korinthians and that they might therefore demand recognition of this belonging sooner than their other Dorian or non-Dorian fellows.

Secondly, like Korinth, she went through an economic revolution in the eighth century. But although, as far as we can tell, she had been open to all the same influences and pressures which provoked change elsewhere she had not reacted to them in the same way. Instead of solving her problems by colonisation, trade and manufacture she indulged in a war of conquest against the neighbouring territory of Messenia, the SW. Pelopponnese, and by 715, having already conquered much of the SE., i.e. the later Lakonia, doubled her agricultural land by its annexation. From then on Sparta could prosper without the aid of commerce; she had committed herself to an almost exclusively agricultural future. The results were twofold. For one thing, although it is unlikely that a conflict of economic interest played any direct and significant part in the Korinthian crisis the mere existence of two interests, agricultural and commercial, however intertwined, must necessarily exacerbate any other tensions that there may be and it is undoubtedly true that the political trouble in Korinth was ultimately the result of the introduction of the new commercial element. It was not introduced into Sparta and could not therefore cause or exacerbate these tensions there. All Spartans were farmers and remained farmers. To that extent they had less to quarrel about than Korinthians and we should expect their quarrels to be milder if they ever arose.

At the same time Korinthian prosperity came gradually, starting with a tentative probing towards the west after 800, growing steadily through the days of colonisation and more quickly thereafter with the increase of trade and manufacture which followed it. Sparta's wealth was won on the day she completed the conquest of Messenia's fertile plain and was spread among the whole Spartan population, unequally no doubt, as soon as that plain was divided up.

The suddenness of Spartan expansion and the peculiarity of Spartan society could, then, explain why the revolution there came early—as early as, say, 675; the homogeneity of this same society and of its economy could explain why the revolution was achieved without much bloodshed, without the destruction of the aristocracy,

without the installation of a tyrant. The reader must judge for himself from the books mentioned in the bibliography whether the detailed evidence supports this *a priori* justification of a date early in the seventh century. The discussion which follows is based on the belief that it does; if it does not, some detail will have to be altered and Spartans will lose some, though by no means all, of the credit which I am about to give them—they will learn by others' mistakes rather than set an example which others failed to follow. But in either case the basic nature of the revolution is the same and in either case the revolution belongs to the same wider context—that of the seventh-century growth of hoplite self-confidence.

THE CHANGES

The Sparta which conquered Messenia was ruled by two kings from different families, the Agiadai and the Eurypontidai, a strange institution which the Spartans traced back to the twin sons of an early leader but is more probably to be explained by some earlier compromise between and coalition of rival Dorian groups. Beneath them an aristocratic council, the *gerousia*, then the free Spartan farmers and finally a largely non-Dorian labour-force, the helots. In later history this series was further complicated by the existence of a number of *perioikoi* ('dwellers round-about'), the inhabitants of other cities in Lakonia which, although technically self-governing, were in fact completely subject to Sparta. But at this date it is unlikely that Sparta was either strong enough or well-organised enough to have absorbed these men into her own system; no doubt their cities already acknowledged Spartan superiority but their status was probably nearer that of the satellite than the subject; they would impinge only rarely on Spartan affairs and we may ignore them. As political animals we may also ignore the helots—so long as we take care to remember that their existence posed a constant threat to Spartan security, a constant encouragement to internal unity and a constant supply of Spartan wealth.

The body of the citizens, to use a word that is still anachronistic, was organised on the common aristocratic pattern, in tribes (the three Dorian tribes) composed of phratries, whose leaders, no doubt, manned the *gerousia*. Each phratry maintained by the contribution of its members one (some historians would say more than one) public mess (*sussition*) for its adult males, in effect the barracks for its own fighting unit; each phratry handled the education of its children through a series of age-groups up till the time when they graduated to membership of the mess. How far these primitive customs had fallen into disuse by, say, 700 we do not know; nor do we know whether there had grown up substantial distinctions within the body of Spartans, whether, that is, some phratries had become depressed at the expense of others or whether within each phratry some members had grown too poor to maintain their position, now tolerated as hangers-on, or perhaps not tolerated and expelled, or even whether there had been some recent influx to community which had not been admitted to full membership. But we do know that one of the chief elements in the change was the reaffirmation if not a tightening up of the system as a whole and the declaration that all Spartans should now begin again as equal members of equal groups with sufficient resources (an allotment of land provided by the state with helots to work it) to maintain themselves in that position. If they failed, it was their fault—they were expelled, they ceased to be what it is now almost right to call full citizens—but at least they started with a fair chance. The fact was advertised—the Spartans were now known as *Homoioi*—'Equals'. Measures like this surely imply considerable disorder and considerable inequality before.

But although the old system was maintained, even rejuvenated, it was no longer based on the same tribal background. A Spartan remained a member of his tribe but he now became as well the member of a new unit called an *oba*, a unit based not on (a mythical) common ancestry but on residence, for the *obai* were the wards of the city of Sparta and those parts of the surrounding countryside where Spartans lived. Somehow or other an integrated system of local *obai* and ancestral tribes was built up out of the basic units, the messes. How this was achieved is completely uncertain. The number of the *obai*, their relationship with the tribes, how the messes were fitted in to either, whether messes themselves remained either in practice unchanged—all this is dark. And as a result we have no way of knowing how the new system affected either the composition of the Spartan governing class or of what became under the new régime the Spartan citizen body. But that it did affect both can hardly be doubted.

THE NEW RULING CLASS

Tyrtaios appears to say (some vital words are missing) that the Oracle which proclaimed the broad lines of the new constitution was brought from Delphi by the Kings Theopompos (*c*. 720–perhaps *c*. 670) and Polydoros (*c*. 700–*c*. 665). Both kings later had a reputation as reformers, Theopompos as a rather unwilling supporter of change, Polydoros as a radical popular hero (he was even said to have been assassinated by a disgruntled aristocrat). These are some of the details that have to be abandoned with a later dating, but, if true, they suggest very strongly that these kings, like Pheidon in Argos, were making use of popular discontent to confirm their royal authority over the aristocrats. A view made more plausible by the fact that, at some date, probably in the reign of these same kings, a new magistracy was created, the Ephorate which must in origin have been designed as an aristocratic check on royal authority and indeed always retained some of its original flavour. Moreover the Oracle itself gives great prominence to the constitution of the *gerousia* under the new system while later authorities (among them Aristotle) emphasise again and again 'Lykourgos'' interest in its composition and its powers. From now on its numbers were fixed at thirty (including the two kings) and its members were elected, though choice was for life and was limited to candidates over sixty years of age from a defined group of aristocratic houses. It would be strange if the imposition of these rules alone did not produce some new aristocratic faces in the *gerousia* of 674 and even stranger if this result was not intended.

In other words, in Sparta, as in Korinth, the struggle for power was being conducted at the highest level in society; the picture is complicated by the existence of the kings and, perhaps, of a rather more coherent and vocal *demos*; it is obscured by an almost complete lack of reliable detailed evidence (did Lykourgos, as Plutarch says, choose the first *gerousia* himself? genuine tradition or historian's guess?), but its subject is clear—a ruling class which had so lost its internal stability in the face of unaccustomed problems and pressures that one section was prepared to look outside for help in holding or winning domination over another.

THE NEW 'DEMOS'

The ruling class is easy enough to define both before and after the reforms—roughly the royal houses and those other families which provided or could aspire to provide members of the *gerousia*. The *demos*, on the other hand, was in a very real sense created by the reforms, and it is almost impossible to describe the elements of which it was made up, or the distinctions which were removed to create the 'Equals,' impossible not only because the evidence is lacking but because we do not even know the kind of language to use in describing them. Was the desired equality simply the status of

being a hoplite? Did Lykourgos, that is, create new hoplites by a redistribution of land? Or was it equality among existing hoplites? If the second, was the inequality simply one of wealth, poor hoplites against rich hoplites, or of status? If of status, was it between phratry-member and outsider or was it between or even inside the phratries? The only certainty is that to be a full Spartan after 675 meant more than simply not to be a helot, that a line was drawn around some 9,000 men who from now on were to have similar rights and similar duties. It is likely enough that some non-helots were still left outside; certain that provision was made for demoting failures from the 9,000 without robbing them of their freedom and possibly for promoting promising outsiders. But the exceptions are irrelevant. What matters is that the question, what is a citizen, had now become meaningful. The answer, a man who shared these rights and duties, who belonged to the society not just because he had a sense of belonging but because he could produce a list of his privileges and his commitments.

The latter were simple if not light. As a boy the Spartan had to endure the various unpleasant exercises prescribed in the training programme, until, if he passed successfully, he was admitted to the *sussition*; from then on he had to provide from his allotment of land the appropriate contribution in kind to maintain his membership and, as a member, he devoted himself entirely to further exercise when not actually showing in the field the military excellence the exercise was designed to produce. His life was that of a soldier in barracks. But in return he had his land, a number of helots to work it and to serve him. And, more important for us if not for him, he was a member of a community which did more than guarantee his physical survival.

Of his legal rights nothing is known (nor indeed of the Spartan legal system as a whole); Sparta was not given to advertising the details of her administration abroad, and much of it was conducted by precedent rather than according to any written code. But Spartans believed that Lykourgos had first established the precedents and, although he was certainly lauded as the originator of much in later Sparta which would have surprised him greatly, his reputation as the creator of her legal code cannot be entirely baseless. Details hardly matter; at least it is certain that he laid down some laws, that after 675 the Spartan knew what was expected of him and, more important, precisely what would happen to him if he failed to do it, knew too that the same was expected of everyone else and that the same penalties would be exacted. Even without evidence it is a safe assumption that he had not known this before.

Like the Korinthian the Spartan had his city 'set to rights' and it is a curious and comforting coincidence that the very words used by our sources, good and bad, to describe Bakchiad wickedness and Kypselos' virtue, reappears in the sources, good and bad again, for Sparta. The Bakchiads were men 'who used force,' who 'exceeded the rule' and Kypselos won support against them by his generosity in administering the law; Polydoros, the reforming king, according to Pausanias, 'neither used violence nor exceeded the rule in word or deed but maintained strict justice tempered with kindness in conducting cases in the courts.' Pausanias, a guide-book writer of the second century A.D., is never better than his source and in this case the quality of his source is unknown; but a poet who visited Sparta in 675, Terpander of Lesbos, has left two lines describing the Sparta of his day, I would say the new Sparta which Lykourgos had created:

Spear-points of young men blossom there:
Clear-voiced the Muse's songs arise:
Justice is done in open air
The help of gallant enterprise.
(Tr. Sir Maurice Bowra)

'Justice' again has overtones which the Greek '*dike*' (the noun behind *dikaios*) probably lacked in the seventh century; the emphasis again is on the existence of laws rather than on their quality and the same idea is reflected in another word used by contemporary Spartans (by Tyrtaios for example) to describe their new condition—*eunomia*, 'good order'. Law where there had been no law; order in place of disorder, and in this case we can be fairly sure that the ordinary Spartan actually wanted both.

The use of *eunomia* in the propaganda strongly suggests that they did—Tyrtaios was not writing only for the aristocrats; the ostentatious introduction of 'Equality' almost proves it, for this equality can hardly have been simply economic—all Spartans received an allotment of land, perhaps an equal allotment, but it is hard to believe that the rich lost everything they already held above the new minimum. It can only mean equality of status, not in all respects because just as there were rich and poor in later Sparta so there were aristocrats and commoners, but at least in some respects that mattered to ordinary men. Of these equality before the law is an obvious, almost necessary example.

It is still impossible to see how the seventh-century Spartan would formulate his demands for justice; quite impossible to know whether he also made demands for some political recognition, although this too he did receive. The text of the *Rhetra* enjoins the reorganisation of the citizen body by tribes and *obai*; also the new constitution of the *gerousia*; but it then goes on to appoint and regulate procedure for fixed meetings of a citizen assembly and, although the text at this point is corrupt, appears to affirm that this assembly should be sovereign; the final clause, probably as Plutarch says a later amendment, then seems to impose some restriction on this sovereignty.

Basically the form of constitution which is laid down here is typical of the developed constitutions of almost all later Greek states, oligarchic or democratic, where a comparatively small council conducted the day-to-day administration, prepared business for and presided over the deliberations of a sovereign assembly. There were vast differences between states in the membership and competence of both Council and Assembly but the pattern was constant and it first appears in Sparta. Not unnaturally some historians have been led to confuse form with content and have gone on to write as if Sparta too achieved together with the system some form of democracy in embryo and consequently to argue that if they achieved it they also wanted it. To some extent both steps are justified but I am not sure that it is to any significant extent.

To put the case against in an extreme form: neither democracy nor a constitutional oligarchy exists without democratic or constitutionally oligarchic spirit and it is at least as true that form encourages the growth of spirit as that spirit creates the form. In Sparta even within the circle of the 'Equals' there is very little sign that the assembly ever became conscious of its apparent theoretical power, that it ever acquired much spirit. If the final clause of the *Rhetra* is a later restriction on the power of the assembly, then the assembly was prepared to accept it. And when the assembly was consulted what form did the consultation take? 'Questions shall be introduced and [on my hesitantly offered translation] the *gerousia* shall stand aside; the assembly . . . shall have the final say.' What process does this imply? On two later occasions where we have a comparatively full account of procedure at an assembly, one in the fifth century (Diodoros, xi, 50), one in the third (Plutarch, *Agis*, ix–xi), neither of them wholly unambiguous or reliable, it would seem that the *gerousia* puts forward a question for discussion but not for decision and then holds a separate meeting ('stands aside'?) at which it formulates a proposal under the influence of the 'sense' of the assembly's reaction—under the influence of but not necessarily

in accordance with the assembly's will. In fact in both cases, for special reasons, it seems to go against the assembly's will, and in both cases its decision seems to emerge in the end as established policy. All this is very much more like the activity of a Homeric assembly than of anything we know or imagine of later Greek democratic practice. Indeed throughout Spartan history there is no occasion on which the assembly is said to have taken any positive part in the direction of Spartan policy (as distinct from influencing that policy by its attitude).

It is just conceivable that an early sense of independence was gradually crushed by a consistently encroaching executive but it is far more likely that this independence never existed; that Spartans, unlike Athenians, simply failed to be trained by their constitutional forms into an awareness of what could be done with them, that in 675 they were delighted to meet and shout their approval or disapproval of this or that proposal put before them, as they did for centuries after, without ever realising that their shouts could or should be decisive, likely that they were, in fact, far nearer to the spirit of Homer's Ionian assembly than to anything we should find elsewhere in fifth-century Greece. If this is true another argument follows. There had no doubt been Homeric-type assemblies in Sparta before the time of Lykourgos; the only difference now was that they met by law, not at the whim of the kings of *gerousia*, hardly a major constitutional advance.

This, as I said, is an extreme form of the case. To prescribe assemblies *is* to do more than to convene them casually, much more; to affirm the sovereignty of the *demos* as the *Rhetra* does means something even if that sovereignty is never respected in any real sense and it is likely that both prescription and affirmation were welcomed even demanded by the average Spartan. But, as I see it, the answer lies in moving as little as possible from this extreme rather than as near as we can to the idea of full democratic responsibility, or vocal democratic agitation.

CONCLUSION

In the case of Korinth I offered a guess to illustrate the kind of political crisis which might have brought Kypselos to power. Perhaps I may be allowed to do the same for Sparta. Lykourgos and the kings I would imagine were concerned to alter the composition of the aristocracy. To do this they enlisted the support of the Spartan hoplite army with promises of land, justice and that way of life which the Spartans called *eunomia*. They kept their promises. They achieved their ends without destroying the existing aristocrats and the result at the start would have been a new governing class divided against itself; it would be too much to ask that the old should give way without a struggle to the new. In such a situation the continued support of the hoplites might seem vital and this could be assured by providing a regular means of demonstrating the support to any opposition—the assembly (it is always easy to encourage popular feeling when it is in your favour). But once the initial question of status inside the aristocracy was settled common agricultural interests, a common fear of helots, possibly even the beginnings of a common suspicion of the hoplites might well bring a quick merging of the old and new; quite soon the *gerousia* could have seen that it was politic to present a solid front, to settle its disagreements without appeal to popular opinion. Meanwhile

a happy accident may have helped to crush any hoplite independence that there was. In 669 B.C. Polydoros led out the new army in an attack on Argos and the new army was decisively beaten by the Argives under Pheidon at the Battle of Hysiai. Just as the Athenian disaster in Sicily in 413 brought temporary disgrace on the democracy that had voted for the expedition, so it is easy to see how defeat might break the confidence of the Spartan hoplite, particularly as that defeat was immediately followed by a long and desperate struggle against a Messenian revolt, a struggle which could not but unite all Spartans.

So, perhaps, the Spartan aristocracy survived the crisis which broke so many of the other aristocracies of Greece; the economic and social demands of the hoplites had been satisfied, the political demands were not and because of Sparta's peculiar position never became so pressing that another revolution could be built around them alone; the concessions made in 675 did not materially alter the distribution of power inside the state—they could be absorbed, perhaps in part ignored, perhaps even withdrawn (by the final clause of the *Rhetra*) without trouble. When King Polydoros was assassinated by an aristocrat, his murderer was honoured with a tomb in Sparta and Pausanias, who reports it, was surprised—'either the assassin had been a good man before or possibly his relatives buried him secretly' (iii, 3). Rather, I should think, the Spartans had forgotten what they owed and did not realise what might have been owed to their king.

6. SPARTAN SOCIETY*

Professor Finley takes a sceptical view of most ancient tales of the early history of Sparta and believes that the major changes in its way of life came in the sixth century.

* M. I. Finley, "Sparta," *Problèmes de la Guerre en Grèce Ancienne*, ed. Jean-Pierre Vernant (The Hague: Mouton & Co., 1968). Reprinted by permission of Edicom, N.V., Laren, Holland.

I

The Sparta I shall consider falls within a rather restricted period, from about the middle of the sixth century to the battle of Leuctra in 371 B.C. I exclude the earlier history—apart from a few certain events and general trends—because I believe that our information is almost wholly fictitious (especially anything referring to Lycurgus); that all attempts to reconstruct that early history in detail, with names and exact dates, rest on totally unsound methodological principles; and that the excessive concentration on assumed distant origins in a mythical *Wanderungszeit* is almost equally unsound in method. I stop at Leuctra because I accept the virtually unanimous Greek tradition that a qualitative change set in early in the fourth century. Thereafter, despite certain continuities, Sparta was being transformed into a different kind of society again.

What this means is that I accept that the decisive turning-point in Spartan history came in or about the reign of Leon and Agasicles (Herod. 1.65–66), soon after 600 B.C., as the culmination of a crisis perhaps a century old, a crisis in which the so-called Second Messenian War was the main catalytic occurrence, and which produced persistently revolutionary potentialities and threats. Much about that war is obscure, not to say legendary, but the poetry of Tyrtaeus is contemporary and illuminating. It demonstrates that the Spartan army was in a disorder and turmoil unlike anything known from the classical period, the community in a state of *stasis*; and that the Lycurgus myth was not yet current. Once the war was finally won, a number of profound changes were introduced: political, economic and ideological. I do not know how rapidly they were brought about (a question to which I shall return), or by whom, but in the end we have the Sparta which was a unique structure in the Greek world, which the Sparta of Alcman was not. I stress the word *structure* in order to divert attention from the customary overconcentration on certain elements in the system, and on what regularly goes with them in the modern literature, namely, a mystique about Dorians and Dorianism in general and a few largely irrelevant Cretan parallels in particular, the latter, in my judgment, essentially misleading constructs of fourth-century theories or propaganda (in which Carthage also figured, at least for Aristotle, let it be noted).

If the excavations of the shrine of Artemis Orthia were as revealing of the transformation in Sparta as it is sometimes said, we could date the break rather near the year 600 (or several decades later in Boardman's new chronology). However, apart from the rather problematical disappearance of ivory from the deposits, I do not see that Artemis Orthia provides evidence from which to prove anything. The "evidence," which it had been rather more fashionable to stress ten or twenty years ago than it is now, turns out to consist of little more than highly subjective judgments about the quality of Laconian pottery in various periods, on which the experts do not agree. Besides, we do not know whether the Spartans ever made this pottery themselves or whether much (or even all) of it was already in the hands of the *perioeci* well before 600, in which case the decline is irrelevant anyway, even if it really could be placed in the middle of the sixth century. On the other hand, if those who believe the ephor Chilon to have been the great reforming "lawgiver" could be shown to be right, then we should have a firm date about 550, although I cannot imagine how we should then fill out the very long interval between the end of the Second Messenian War and 550. Since all this is largely irrelevant to my subject, I propose to by-pass the chronological puzzles and speak, as a kind of shorthand, of the "sixth-century revolution."

Let me elaborate a bit on this "revolution." Schematically (and rather inexactly) one may divide the classical Spartan structure into three broad strands:

1. the infra-structure of land allotments, helots and *perioeci*, with everything that

includes with respect to labour, production and circulation;

2. the governmental system (including the military);

3. the ritual system: *rites de passage*, the *agoge*, the age-classes, *syssitia*, etc.

These strands had different origins and a different history; they did not develop and shift *en bloc*; and they did not have the same unchanged functions at all times. The "sixth-century revolution" was therefore a complex process of some innovation and much modification and re-institutionalization of the elements which appear to have survived "unchanged." I use the word "revolution" even more loosely than is perhaps customary, but I do not use it capriciously. It is loose because I do not for a moment suggest, or believe, that the classical Spartan system was created at one stroke, or even in one reign. After all, the introduction of the hoplite army was one of its necessary conditions, and that must go back early in the seventh century, at least before the Second Messenian War. Helotage in some form was even older. And we must not rule out the possibility that other elements were effectively introduced (or raised to new prominence) as late as the fifth century (as we know certain changes in the army organization to have been). On the other hand, it was not a system that somehow just evolved. Some innovations and modifications *had* to be introduced at a single stroke (whether one at a time or in combination). The Great Rhetra, for example, reflects something very fundamental of this kind. In a negative way, the prohibition of the use of silver coinage by Spartiates was another obviously sharp decision made by somebody at some moment (and one, incidentally, which more than most can be almost exactly dated to the time of Leon and Agasicles).

By speaking of the "sixth-century revolution," in sum, I am trying to underscore the necessity for looking at the structure, and not at isolated elements and their antiquity or persistence. I include the whole of the ritual system in this argument, particularly in what I have called rather awkwardly "re-institutionalization," because even if it were the case that the ritual externals were all very old and unaltered (a most unlikely possibility), their function within the new structure was necessarily a new one in significant respects, in effect if not always by deliberate intent. No one will pretend that the whipping ceremony at Artemis Orthia in Roman times, when a great theatre was built for the convenience of the spectators, bore any meaningful connection with the superficially similar rite of Xenophon's day. *A priori* we must assume the same discontinuity in function between the fifth century and, say, the eighth, and sometimes we have evidence to confirm the assumption, as in the case of the *krypteia*.

Classical Sparta may have had an archaic, and even a pre-archaic look about it, but the function of the "survivals" is what chiefly matters, not the mere fact of survival. Before the reign of Leon and Agasicles, writes Herodotus, the Spartans were the *kakonomotatoi* of all the Greeks; then they switched to *eunomia*. Both *eunomia* and *kakonomos* characterize a whole way of life, and not only (or perhaps not at all) a form of constitution. That transformation was the "sixth-century revolution."

II

At this stage I want to consider the structure as an ideal type. In what follows, furthermore, I am not much concerned with the accuracy of any individual text. Unless one believes that the picture the Greeks have left us is altogether a fiction, few of the details are of themselves crucial for an apprehension of the ideal type.

I go immediately to the *homoioi*, who are our subject. We must, at the start, take the word in its full connotation-Equals. (The fact that it first appears as a "technical term" in Xenophon, whereas Herodotus (7.234) uses the word in its ordinary Greek connotation, and that Xenophon alone speaks of *hypomeiones*, Inferiors, does not impress me as having any significance; the Spartan "technical" social terminology is filled with comparable words, e.g. *tresantes*, *agathoergoi*, *neodamodeis*.) At birth, if they were permitted to remain alive, all Spartan males were strictly "equal" with two exceptions: 1) two of them were potential heirs to the kingship; 2) some were richer than others; the *anthropoi olbioi* of Herodotus (6.61; cf. 7.134); the *plousioi* of Xenophon (*Lac. Pol.* 5.3), who provided wheaten-bread for the *syssitia*; or the winners of Olympic chariot-races, of whom there are eleven within my time-limits in Moretti's catalogue, one a king and another the daughter of a king. Being equal meant sharing a common, well-defined life-cycle, including:

An important part of the buttressing was negative, so to speak, the reduction to the barest minimum of the disruptive, centrifugal effects of property and the family. We may permit ourselves to be more "sociological" and less moralistic than Xenophon, for example, in analyzing the functions of the Spartan regime of property and family.

1. *Property*—extensive comment is unnecessary at this point, though I shall have to return in the next seciton to the inequality in wealth. The total withdrawal from economic (and not merely banausic) activity, the austerity, the sharing were meant to be cohesive factors, and they were.

2. *Family*—a mere enumeration of certain rites and institutions is sufficient to reveal the scale of the effort to transfer allegiance away from the family or kinship group to various male groups, Xenophon's *teknopoiia* (with which he opens his *Lac. Pol.*), the right of any father or indeed of any adult Spartiate to exercise authority over any child, the singularly joyless marriage ceremony with its rare transvestite ritual, the barrack life. The family, in sum, was minimized as a unit of either affection

or authority, and replaced by overlapping male groupings—the age-classes, the homosexual pairings between younger and older men (whether "Platonic" or not), the élite corps such as the *hippeis*, the *syssitia*. Two details are perhaps worth mentioning here, though I shall have to return to them at the end.

1. The age-group system was unusually ramified, extending considerably beyond the simple division between *neoi* and *gerontes*. I have no precise idea of what its effects were, but at least the ramified system greatly increased the occasions for ritual reinforcement.

2. On entry into adulthood, the Spartiate was at least partly divorced from his age-group by the practice of individual co-optation into a *syssition*. Any device which cuts across a "natural" grouping, whether family or age-group, can be seen as one more way of strengthening the structure as a whole against its individual parts.

So much buttressing was necessary, in part at least, because the Equals turned out, in the end, to be meshed in a complex of inequalities. There were leaders, élites, at all levels, and the primary principles of selection were appointment and cooptation, and never, it should be stressed, selection by lot, the standard Greek device for imposing equality. All *homoioi* were eligible in principle and that fact differentiated the Spartan army from those, like the Prussian, which had an officer corps drawn solely from a pre-existing and exclusive élite. The end-result, however, was the same in one respect: there was a chain of command in which the authority-obedience syndrome moved in one direction only, from the top down. To be sure, there were two exceptions in the method of selection: the *gerousia* and the ephors were elected in open competition. It is a pity that we know virtually nothing about this procedure or about the men elected. Just who lie concealed behind Aristotle's *kaloi kagathoi* (*Pol.* 1270b24)? Were they usually the same men who had already come out on top through cooptation? That is what I should expect in this society, and I shall come back to the question shortly.

In so far as the success of the system is to be measured by its military successes, the verdict must, of course, be favourable. The Spartan army *was* better than any other, with more stamina and greater manœuvrability, thanks to superior physical condition, better training and discipline, more obedience. Thought seems to have been given to military organization; at least the not infrequent changes in organization suggest that. On the other hand, there is no evidence of interest in tactics or weaponry beyond the maintenance of both at the best traditional level.

The production and distribution of weapons remain something of a puzzle. I think we can take it that the procurement of metals and the manufacture of arms were the responsibility (and also the privilege) of the *perioeci*. But how did the individual Spartiate obtain his arms and armour? The traditional Greek conception of *hoi hopla parechomenoi*, of the hoplite as by definition the citizen (or metic) rich enough to equip himself, does not apply. All Spartiates were "rich" enough, but none had the proper market mechanism. The choice lies between (*a*) individual procurement from *perioeci* by payment in *naturalia* (or, conceivably, iron spits), and (*b*) procurement and distribution by the state. I know of no ancient text which gives the answer. Nor does archaeology help in the absence of systematic excavation of any perioecic community. One can argue either way from the shields, all of which were required to have a Lambda inscribed on them, but many (if not all) of which also had a personal blazon. My own preference is for the public supply system, because the other seems insufficiently reliable and because we do have textual evidence (Xen., *Lac. Pol.* 11.2; 13.11; cf. *Ages.* 1.26) that once the army had marched off, the state took responsibility for repair and replacement (as it must have done for the initial

procurement even at home when helots were enrolled as hoplites, e.g. Thuc. 4.80.5).

III

So much for the ideal type. In actual practice the system was filled with tensions and anomie.

1. To begin with, the Spartan army was not always big enough for its needs—needs which were more cause of the system than consequence. *Perioeci* were an integral part of the hoplite army, and, at least on major occasions such as the Peloponnesian War, substantial numbers of helots and ex-helots (*neodamodeis*) were also enlisted. I have no answer to the very important question of how helots were selected and trained for hoplite fighting (or to any possible connection with the mysterious *mothakes*). Spartans were regularly accompanied by helot orderlies or batmen and there is no particular problem in using such people as light-armed auxiliaries. Hoplite training, however, could not be achieved casually; the essence was movement in formation, and it was for their unique skills at this in particular that the Spartans were commended by ancient writers. That helot and ex-helot hoplites were a serious flaw in the system is self-evidence, psychologically as well as in its overt functioning.

2. For Aristotle the greatest vice was financial corruption. Perhaps he was thinking primarily of the changed Sparta of the later fourth century, but bribery is already a major theme in Herodotus (3.148, 5.51, 6.50, 6.72, 6.82, 8.5). Even before the law of Epitadeus, the infrastructure was flawed. The regime of property and inheritance, like the political system, was a compromise. Heavy as the pressures of austerity and withdrawal from all economic activity may have been, they were insufficient to overcome completely the counter-pressures of inequalities in wealth, or the fears of impoverishment whether through large

families or otherwise. The prohibition of business activity (*chrematismos* is Xenophon's carefully chosen word) does not eliminate a desire for—and an ability to employ—wealth, not even if the prohibition can be perfectly enforced. Xenophon's statement (*Lac. Pol.* 7.6) that the possession of gold and silver was prohibited must be understood, in my opinion, to refer only to coin (as his context implies). But gold and silver have other functions, revealed by Herodotus, perhaps unconsciously, when he employs the good old Homeric word *keimelion* (treasure) in his story (6.62) of how King Ariston acquired his third wife, the mother of Damaratus. Coined money is not essential for exchange, and there were exchanges in Sparta. Even if one were for some reason unwilling to accept the accuracy of Thucydides' inclusion of buying and selling among the activities forbidden to a Spartiate when he suffered *atimia* (5.34.2), there is no getting away from Damonon and his son Enymakritidas, who made a dedication to Athena Chalkioikos, probably in the middle of the fifth century, recording twenty or more victories. The text stresses that they won with their own horses and their own chariots, and the latter had to be acquired by the exchange of wealth in some form.

Presumably a sufficient equilibrium could be maintained despite the pressures so long as the Spartans remained safely cocooned within their own world. But not when they were drawn abroad.

3. There was structural tension within and about the leadership. I am not concerned with disagreements over policy which are inevitable whenever there is shared leadership—examples are abundant, e.g. with respect to the situation in Athens after the overthrow of the Peisistratids, or whether to go to war with Athens in 431—but with the tensions inherent in the positions themselves, in the efforts to attain and then to maintain and enhance positions of leadership. We must not allow ourselves to be bemused by the Greek obsession with

the "lawgiver": the sixth-century revolution had to strike some sort of balance among the social elements that were then in existence, and this balance meant failure to institute a unified leadership principle. Hence there were hereditary kings, elected elders and ephors, and appointed leaders at other levels. Again we must not be bemused by a Greek obsession, this time with "mixed constitution." Instead of an equilibrium there was permanent conflict, which could not be cushioned by the self-confidence and stability which are generrated, for exemple, by an exclusive leadership caste. Even the kings, in Aristotle's words, were compelled to court (*demagogein*) the ephors (*Pol.* 1270b14).

The leitmotif, I think, was not so much a conflict between kings and ephors, as such, as between men of energy and ambition—the men imbued with excessive *philonikia*, The Lysanders as well as the Cleomenes, actual and potential—and the rest. One source of *stasis*, Aristotle noted (*Pol.* 1306b31–33), was the dishonourable treatment of men of *arete* by others whose *arete* was no greater but who had more honour, and the specific example he gave was the treatment of Lysander by the kings. That the kings were a persistently disruptive force of a special kind and magnitude in classical Spartan history needs no demonstration. What deserves notice, however, is that they were potentially disruptive by definition, so to speak, that their very existence was a contradiction of the ideal type of Spartan equality. Cleomenes I, wrote Herodotus (5.39), reigned not because of his own *andragathia* but by heredity. That sums it up. Given the psychological underpinning of being born to high office and the various charismatic practices and institutions attached to Spartan kingship—Herodotus knew what he was saying when he called the royal funeral rites "barbarian" it depended solely on the personality of the individual king whether he was a force for *eunomia* or for *anomia*, or no force at all.

The hereditary principle also injected the family into the picture, again in violation of the Spartan ideal. The various recorded manœuvres on behalf of younger sons and other kin of kings, including the classic employment of allegations of illegitimacy, belong to the courts of tyrants and barbarian monarchs, not to a Greek *polis*. It then becomes necessary to consider whether kinship did not also play some part in the leadership struggles outside the kingship. I have already said that it is my guess that the men chosen for the *gerousia*, the ephorate and the magistracies were those who had earlier come out on top through the appointment procedures. All *homoioi* were, in a formal sense, equally eligible. But were they in practice? Who, then, were the men whom Herodotus called "among the first by birth" (7.134); and what did Aristotle mean when he said that election to the *gerousia* was "oligarchical" (*dynasteutikos*, which implies manipulation as well), whereas everyone was eligible for the *ephorate* (*Pol.* 1306a18, 1294b29–31)? It is true that such texts are very rare: the more common reference is to individuals being or wishing to be "first" or "among the most powerful," which need mean nothing more than to achieve leadership by their own efforts. But the few texts remain, and they say what we should have guessed without them, namely, that there were families who were able to influence the appointment procedures in favour of their own members, beginning at the first opportunity, among the children. That means, in effect, that there developed an element of hereditary aristocracy within the system, far from closed, but not without considerable influence nevertheless. And I have no doubt that wealth played its part here (as Herodotus 7.134 implies). There were others, in sum, besides Cleomenes who achieved positions, lower or higher in the ranking, by birth rather than by *andragathia*.

Inevitably when there is struggle for leadership, disagreements over policy reflect calculations of personal advantage in the struggle alongside, and confused with, calculations about the desirability of a proposed policy as such. Sometimes these differences were brought before the *damos* in assembly, and that raises one further question respecting equals and unequals. The time has long passed when any serious historian or political scientist thinks in 19th-century liberal terms about voting behaviour, with its image of the "reasonable man" weighing the issues "rationally" and free from all prejudices, pressures and emotions. It is nevertheless legitimate to ask whether there was something in the Spartan structure which makes the "reasonable man" approach even less applicable, even more of a caricature, than, say, for the Athenian assembly. I will put the question very bluntly. Can we imagine that the obedient, disciplined Spartan soldier dropped his normal habits on those occasions when he was assembled not as a soldier but as a citizen, while he listened to debates among those from whom he otherwise was taught to take orders without questioning or hesitation? I do not think we have any evidence from which to answer concretely, but my guess is that the Spartan assembly in function and psychology was much closer to the Homeric than to the Athenian. Archidamus and Sthenelaidas harangued each other before the assembled *damos* as Agamemnon and Achilles did. That is not open discussion. But neither is it mere puppetry: when the leadership divided over policy, someone had to make the decision, and that was the *damos*.

4. There was too much social mobility in both directions, too much, that is, for a society which in principle was completely closed and rigid, and which therefore lacked the mechanism (and the psychology) necessary to adjust the mobile elements properly in their new statuses.

a) There were Spartiates who lost status, yet somehow remained within the community in a curiously inferior position (as distinct from exiles). These were not always economic failures (men who could not maintain their *syssition* quotas); a depreciation in status could also follow from failure at some stage in the *agoge*, failure in battle (the *tresantes*), *atimia*, or the like.

b) There were helots who rose in status, many even achieving membership in the *damos* (for that is what *neodamodeis* has to mean, whatever inferiority in shading it may imply).

I am frankly unable to visualize these people, how they lived or even, in many cases, where they lived. Brasidas's helots, Thucydides says (5.34.1), were first given permission to reside where they wished, but then they were settled with the *neodamodeis* at Lepreon on the Elean border to help serve as buffers against the hostile Eleans. Neither Thucydides nor anyone else explains what it meant in practice to be "settled" or to reside where they wished, or where and how the degraded Spartiates lived. That all these groups were an undigested lump within the system is self-evident, and the released prisoners from Sphacteria were treated as such by the regime, too, simply because they could anticipate *atimia* (Thuc. 5.34.2). Interestingly enough, this particular group came from the first families (Thuc. 5.15.1, however one prefers to heal the corrupt text). Yet it must be recorded that neither separately nor together were the misplaced elements able to destroy the system directly. We are told of only one actual attempt, and that a failure, the abortive revolt led by Cinadon in 397 B.C. Several aspects of that revolt are neatly symbolic. Cinadon himself had been employed by the ephors on secret missions. Aristotle (*Pol.* 1306b34) described him as "manly" (*androdes*), and it would be nice to know whether Aristotle had any more information than we have on which to base that perhaps suprising adjective. When asked why he had conspired, Cinadon's reply was, "in order to be inferior to no one in Lacedaemon" (Xen., *Hell.* 3.3.11). Appropriately, the chief

agents in suppressing the revolt before it started were drawn from the super-élite corps, the *hippeis*.

5. For the sake of completeness, I record without discussion two further sources of tension: (*a*) the women, if Plato and Aristotle are to be believed; and (*b*) experience abroad.

IV

I have said very little so far about war or "la fonction guerrière." The paradox is that militarism in Sparta was in a low key. Among the more than 100,000 lead figurines found in the ruins of Artemis Orthia, neither soldiers nor arms are particularly prominent (though they exist). There were no war games, no warrior-graves. The latter disappeared abruptly throughout the Greek world, barring strikingly few exceptions on the fringes, more or less at the same time as the appearance of the hoplite, that is, with the extension of the military role from the "heroic" aristocrat to a broader sector of the population. Sparta was no exception. Sparta seems not even to have included removal from the army among the punishments for military disgrace. At least that is the implication in Herodotus' story (7.229–31 + 9.71) about Aristodamos, the survivor of Themopylae who was permitted to die a glorious death (though officially not recognized as such) at Plataea. And the men who surrendered at Sphacteria, temporarily declared *atimoi* though they were, soon found their rights restored. There is also no trace of the "war habit" characteristic, for example, of the Assyrians, the tendency to go out and fight simply because that is what warriors are for. After the Second Messenian War and the sixth-century revolution, Sparta was, if anything, less willing to join battle than many other Greek states. The Corinthians were not wrong when, in Thucydides' account in his first book, they made a special point of that.

If we look on the whole of Laconia and

Messenia as a unit, then of course there was a pyramidal social structure with the Spartiates as a military élite at the top. However, it was not a military élite in the sense of the Junkers or even the Theban Sacred Band. Instead we must think of a (conceptually) closed system as a whole, which had a military function but not a wholly militaristic stamp. I am using these words as they are distinguished by Alfred Vagts in his excellent *History of Militarism*. "The military way," he writes, "is marked by a primary concentration of men and materials on winning specific objectives of power with the utmost efficiency... Militarism, on the other hand, presents a vast array of customs, interests, prestige, actions and thought associated with armies and wars and yet transcending true military purposes." In a sense both are of course visible in Sparta, but a further quotation from Vagts's book will show why I said "not a wholly militaristic stamp." Vagts continues: "An army so built that it serves military men, not war, is militaristic; so is everything in an army which is not preparation for fighting, but merely exists for diversion or to satisfy peace-time whims like the long anachronistic cavalry today ... enterprises for sheer glory or the reputation of leaders, which reduce the fighting strength of armies and wreck them from within, come under that head."

That may conceivably describe a Cleomenes I, for example, but he was rejected. It is not until the fourth century that the refrain becomes insistent in Greek writers that the Spartan *politeia* was like an army camp (Isoc. 6.81; Plato, *Laws* 666E); that the sole aim of the lawgiver was war; that in consequence Spartans were too underdeveloped in all other human aspects (or, contrariwise, that they were praised for precisely those narrow qualities which Plato and Aristotle condemned); that, in sum, they were not only efficiently military but also excessively militaristic. All this is well known and requires no elaboration. But it is not unnecessary or out of place to

say that this was not the whole picture even in fourth-century writers. Why did Plato, who criticized Sparta so brutally in the eighth book of the *Republic* (547 D–549 A), not simply dismiss her? Why did he instead select Cleinias to be one of the trio who were to set up the new state of the *Laws*?

The answer, of course, is that for Plato Sparta had much to offer despite her one-sidedness, not in her laws or institutions narrowly conceived (which are hardly reflected in Plato's book) but in her fundamental conception of a total community, in her *eunomia* or *peitharchia* as a way of life, one which he wished to strip of its militaristic side (but not of its military function). Sparta had long been a bulwark against tyranny, after all, both at home and abroad; that may not be very true, especially not about Sparta's activities abroad, but it was firmly believed to be true by many Greeks, and it was repeated *ad nauseam*. Pindar believed it. There are not many references to Sparta in Pindar's surviving poems, but they are more significant than their rarity might imply precisely because they are all gratuitous. Pindar wrote no odes for Spartan victors and he did not have to drag Sparta in at all. In the *First Pythian*, celebrating a victory by Hiero I of Syracuse, the poet comments in these words on Hiero's new foundation at Etna (lines 61–70):

the city in liberty built
of gods, and ordinances of Hyllos' rule, and the
          descendants of Pamphylos,
those, too, of Heracles' seed,
who dwell beside Taygetos' slopes, are minded
    to abide forever in the decrees of Aigimios,
Dorians ...
By your (Zeus's) aid, this leader of men,
enjoining it upon his son also, might glorify his
    people and turn them to peace and harmony.

Some quite remarkable nonsense has been, and is still being, written about those lines. The absurd suggestion is offered that Hiero, following a brutal expulsion of population of the type so familiar in

Sicilian history, actually planned to introduce the Spartan constitution and *agoge* at Etna under the kingship of his son Deinomenes. If it is not obvious that all Pindar had in mind was a traditional royal and aristocratic set-up, in which the *damos* would find its freedom in discipline, piety and honourable rule by their betters, then Edouard Will has settled the point by drawing attention to the remarkably parallel lines in a fragment (n° 1 Schroeder) about Aegina. If there was anything political, in the narrow sense, in Pindar's mind, then it was to whisper a reminder of Sparta's anti-tyrant tradition. There is never anything more in Pindar, never a suggestion that Sparta was somehow peculiar or unique; in particular, not that Sparta was militaristic in a way that set it apart from the states and the aristocracies of the old school in which the values he accepted were to be found.

There they surpass in counsels of elders,
And in the spears of young men,
And in choirs, and the Muse, and Glory.

That was sung about Sparta in another fragment (189 Bowra); it could as well have been used for Thebes, Thessaly, Aegina or Cyrene, or even for the kind of Athens that Miltiades and Cimon stood for in his eyes.

Nor is the picture in Herodotus very different on the essential question. Given his subject-matter, Herodotus was bound to stress the military skill of the Spartans and their unfailing obedience to the *nomos* never to retreat in battle. Being Herodotus, he was also bound to dwell on certain oddities, such as the honours and rituals surrounding the kings or the penalties meted out to the *tresantes*. Herodotus was alert to, and often very subtle about, nuances differentiating Greek states from each other. But that was still some way from the altogether odd Sparta of the fourth-century mirage. For him the Greek world was divided into two kinds of communities, those ruled by tyrants, which were a bad thing, and those ruled by them-

selves. The latter in turn were either fully democratic or they were not, and Sparta was the most important, the most powerful and the most interesting of those which were not.

I have gone on at some length about the way in which Sparta was classed with a whole category of Greek *poleis* because it is essential to be clear on what was really different and unique about Sparta. At the beginning I made the point that we must not think of the various strands in the Spartan structure as monolithic in their history and movement. If we look at these elements again, this time from the point of view of their uniqueness or familiarity, we find the following (details apart):

1. Helotage was not altogether rare; it was found in Thessaly, in Crete, in Sicily, and probably throughout the Danubian and Black Sea areas of Greek settlement.

2. The Spartan governmental machinery had its peculiarities to be sure, but not a single feature of significance other than the kings that can legitimately be called unique among the Greeks.

3. Every Greek community had its *rites de passage*—at birth, on entering adulthood, at marriage, at death. The variations were endless, and, looked at in isolation, the only things that stand out about the Spartan rites were their perhaps greater frequency and their apparently greater stress on physical punishment and brutality.

4. There is absolutely nothing to my knowledge in Spartan cults or cult practices deserving of notice in our context.

5. Not even the *syssitia* or the age-groups were of themselves unique.

This last point requires elaboration. Some form of table fellowship can be found in all human societies. The association of *syssitia* with age-classes is specifically attested in several Greek communities, and there is every reason to suspect that our information is fragmentary and incomplete. Age-classes, in turn, are common under a great diversity of circumstances. Armies regularly employ them whenever there is conscription, both for the initial training and for call-up when their services are required. On the other hand, Jeanmaire himself noted the proliferation of societies of *neoi* in Hellenistic and Roman times, precisely the period when they had lost all military function and turned instead to the gymnasium and the palaestra. *Philonikia* in the *agon* could take a sporting form just as well as a military—as Pindar bears witness.

What was unique about Sparta was the way all these elements were combined into a coherent structure, and the pivotal organizing mechanism, the *agoge*. I must insist that there is nothing inherent in age-classes which has to end in the Spartan *agoge*, or even in its ethos of obedience and self-effacement before the interests of the state. There is no self-evident reason why the division into, and the conflict between, *neoi* and *gerontes*, which Jeanmaire worked out so brilliantly, should evolve into the complexity of the Spartan age-class system. It is the complexity and the function that are unique in Sparta, not the division into confraternities of the old and the young. Nor is there any inherent reason why helotage should have led to the Spartan system; and so on through each of the elements. But when the system finally emerged, each element was re-institutionalized in a process that never quite came to an end. And the *agoge* was invented. That last is a pure speculation, of course, but of all the elements in Sparta the *agoge* is the one of which it is most impossible to find traces in our earliest Greek record or traditions, the one which alone "makes" the Spartan system, so to speak, and therefore I am driven to the inference that, as a pattern of life for the young and as an attempt to fix the individual Spartan's behaviour and ideology for a lifetime, the *agoge* was a late invention, however old some of the initiation rites and similar external aspects of it may have been. It was

the *agoge*, finally, and the *eunomia* it was held responsible for, which in the end caught the Greek fancy and lay at the heart of the Spartan mirage. "One of the finest of your laws," said Plato's Athenian (*Laws* 634D), "is the one absolutely prohibiting any of the *neoi* from inquiring whether any of the laws is good or not."

I have come nearly to the end of my discussion without having yet mentioned Jeanmaire's thesis of the Spartan *damos* as their heir of the Homeric *laos*. My silence, I regret to say, is the measure of my disagreement. This is not the place for an extended discussion, but I will just note that I have elsewhere discussed my inability to accept the feudal conception of the Homeric *compagnonnage*, which is absolutely basic to Jeanmaire's analysis, and I find nothing to justify his identification of the *kleros* with a fief, and much against it. After all, the appearance of the hoplite marks the transfer of the military function from the *laos* to the *demos* everywhere in the archaic Greek world. That is not what is special about Sparta, but the way that new function of the *demos* was finally meshed into a unique structure, one which shows no trace of the alleged feudal origin. Jeanmaire is not unaware of that difficulty, and the way he gets round the later sense of *kleros* in Sparta or the form the *syssitia* took, which they really should not have on his theory, exposes the weakness of the whole argument, in my view.

The one reason I wish I could follow Jeanmaire is that it offers an explanation for the survival of kinship (though not of two kings, for which no plausible explanation has ever been offered). I have no alternative to put forward, but I will suggest that "survival" may not be the precisely correct word. What do we know about Spartan kings or kinship between Menelaus and Leon (or Cleomenes I for that matter)? Genealogies and stories told by Plutarch add up to very little history. Prerogatives in sacrifice and the like were commonplace in Greece whenever anyone exercised the priestly function, whatever his title; guards of honour are so obvious that they can, and have been, thought up time and again in history; double rations in the *syssitia* are really not the same as the Homeric prerogatives, no matter how often they are said to be; and, above all, the funeral rites —which Herodotus found to be the most striking thing of all about the Spartan kings—cannot be survivals in any sense, since we know of no precedent in the Greek tradition, nor did Herodotus, who called them "barbarian." It is at least a defensible hypothesis that the Spartan kingship in the institutional form that we know was as much, or more, a product of the sixth-century revolution, stimulated by the failures of the Second Messenian War, as of inertia, which we have the habit of calling, in the absence of an explanation, "survival."

There remains, finally, to look at one other unusual feature of Sparta. No other Greek state was a territorial state like her, in which *polis* and territory were not synonymous, so to speak (as they were between Athens and Attica); in which the *polis*, at least ideally, consisted of a single class of Equals ruling over a relatively vast subject population. The Second Messenian War was decisive in this respect, too.

Thereafter the *fonction guerrière* became a police function rather than a proper military function. It was aimed against an enemy within rather than at enemies real or potential without. To preserve the difficult position of a ruling class in those special circumstances, the whole society was structured to fulfill the police function. Even the efforts expended to found and maintain the Peloponnesian League, though they required repeated warfare, may be accurately described as part of the police function. Sparta's tragedy thereafter stemmed from a familiar cause: she did not live in a vacuum. The Persian invasions foreshadowed what was to come in the Peloponnesian War. Against her will almost, Sparta was drawn into extensive military activity, genuinely military. That entailed severe pressure on manpower and a dangerously extensive incorporation of non-equals into the army if not into the ruling class, unprecedented opportunities for ambitious individuals, extensive travel abroad and a breach in the traditional *xenelasia*, the impossibility of holding the line against the seductions of wealth. The system could not and did not long survive. And so the final paradox is that her greatest military success destroyed the model military state.

SECTION VII

The Origin of Greek Tyranny

THE PASSING of the Greek dark ages produced a period of rapid change in the eighth and seventh centuries. The isolation of the several districts of the Greek world gave way to a period of easy and frequent commercial intercourse. The growth of population produced a great wave of colonization which carried the Greeks and their way of life as far west as Spain and as far east as the Caucasus Mountains. Industry grew and with it the importance of technology. At the same time slavery became more significant and the lower classes were pushed into an ever more precarious economic position. In the military realm the hoplite phalanx became the backbone of Greek armies.

All of these developments had political consequences, and in many states combinations of them caused the overthrow of the traditional aristocratic republics and the establishment of tyrannies. The problem set by this chapter is to determine the factors which produced tyranny and in this way to gain an insight into its true nature and significance.

First are presented three examples of major tyrannies.

1. TYRANNY AT CORINTH*

The following selection presents the reply of the Corinthian Sosicles to a Spartan request for help in restoring the tyrant Hippias to the throne in Athens.

Such was the address of the Spartans. The greater number of the allies listened without being persuaded. None however broke silence, but Sosicles the Corinthian, who exclaimed:

"Surely the heaven will soon be below, and the earth above, and men will henceforth live in the sea, and fish take their place upon the dry land, since you, Lacedaemonians, propose to put down free governments in the cities of Greece, and to set up tyrannies in their stead. There is nothing in the whole world so unjust, nothing so bloody, as a tyranny. If, however, it seems to you a desirable thing to have the cities under despotic rule, begin by putting a tyrant over yourselves, and then establish despots in the other states. While you continue

* Herodotus, 5. 92, translated by George Rawlinson.

231

yourselves, as you have always been, unacquainted with tyranny, and take such excellent care that Sparta may not suffer from it, to act as you are now doing is to treat your allies unworthily. If you knew what tyranny was as well as ourselves, you would be better advised than you now are in regard to it. The government at Corinth was once an oligarchy—a single race, called Bacchiadae, who intermarried only among themselves, held the management of affairs. Now it happened that Amphion, one of these, had a daughter, named Labda, who was lame, and whom therefore none of the Bacchiadae would consent to marry; so she was taken to wife by Aetion, son of Echecrates, a man of the township of Petra, who was, however, by descent of the race of the Lapithae, and of the house of Caeneus. Aetion, as he had no child either by this wife, or by any other, went to Delphi to consult the oracle concerning the matter. Scarcely had he entered the temple when the priestess saluted him in these words:

No one honours thee now, Aetion, worthy of honour;
Labda shall soon be a mother—her offspring a rock, that will one day
Fall on the kingly race, and right the city of Corinth.

By some chance this address of the oracle to Aetion came to the ears of the Bacchiadae, who till then had been unable to perceive the meaning of another earlier prophecy which likewise bore upon Corinth, and pointed to the same event as Aetion's prediction. It was the following:

When mid the rocks an eagle shall bear a carnivorous lion,
Mighty and fierce, he shall loosen the limbs of many beneath them—
Brood ye well upon this, all ye Corinthian people,
Ye who dwell by fair Peirene, and beetling Corinth.

The Bacchiadae had possessed this oracle for some time, but they were quite at a loss to know what it meant until they heard the response given to Aetion; then however they at once perceived its meaning, since the two agreed so well together. Nevertheless, though the bearing of the first prophecy was now clear to them, they remained quiet, intending to put to death the child which Aetion was expecting. As soon, therefore, as his wife was delivered, they sent ten of their number to the township where Aetion lived, with orders to make away with the baby. So the men came to Petra, and went into Aetion's house, and there asked if they might see the child; and Labda, who knew nothing of their purpose, but thought their inquiries arose from a kindly feeling towards her husband, brought the child, and laid him in the arms of one of them. Now they had agreed by the way that whoever first got hold of the child should dash it against the ground. It happened, however, by a providential chance, that the babe, just as Labda put him into the man's arms, smiled in his face. The man saw the smile, and was touched with pity, so that he could not kill it; he therefore passed it on to his next neighbour, who gave it to a third; and so it went through all the ten without any one choosing to be the murderer. The mother received her child back, and the men went out of the house, and stood near the door, and there blamed and reproached one another; chiefly however accusing the man who had first had the child in his arms, because he had not done as had been agreed upon. At last, after much time had been thus spent, they resolved to go into the house again and all take part in the murder. But it was fated that evil should come upon Corinth from the progeny of Aetion, and so it chanced that Labda, as she stood near the door, heard all that the men said to one another, and fearful of their changing their mind, and returning to destroy her baby, she carried him off and hid him in what seemed to her the most unlikely place to be suspected, a cypsel or corn-bin.

She knew that if they came back to look for the child, they would search all her house; and so indeed they did, but not finding the child after looking everywhere, they thought it best to go away, and declare to those by whom they had been sent that they had done their bidding. And thus they reported on their return home. Aetion's son grew up, and, in remembrance of the danger from which he had escaped, was named Cypselus, after the corn-bin. When he reached to man's estate, he went to Delphi, and on consulting the oracle, received a response which was two-sided. It was the following:

See there comes to my dwelling a man much favour'd of fortune,
Cypselus, son of Aetion, and king of the glorious Corinth,—
He and his children too, but not his children's children.

Such was the oracle; and Cypselus put so much faith in it that he forthwith made his attempt, and thereby became master of Corinth. Having thus got the tyranny, he showed himself a harsh ruler—many of the Corinthians he drove into banishment, many he deprived of their fortunes, and a still greater number of their lives. His reign lasted thirty years, and was prosperous to its close; insomuch that he left the government to Periander, his son. This prince at the beginning of his reign was of a milder temper than his father; but after he corresponded by means of messengers with Thrasybulus, tyrant of Miletus, he became even more sanguinary. On one occasion he sent a herald to ask Thrasybulus what mode of government it was safest to set up in order to rule with honour. Thrasybulus led the messenger without the city, and took him into a field of corn, through which he began to walk, while he asked him again and again concerning his coming from Corinth, ever as he went breaking off and throwing away all such ears of corn as over-topped the rest. In this way he went through the whole

field, and destroyed all the best and richest part of the crop; then, without a word, he sent the messenger back. On the return of the man to Corinth, Periander was eager to know what Thrasybulus had counselled, but the messenger reported that he had said nothing; and he wondered that Periander had sent him to so strange a man, who seemed to have lost his senses, since he did nothing but destroy his own property. And upon this he told how Thrasybulus had behaved at the interview. Periander, perceiving what the action meant, and knowing that Thrasybulus advised the destruction of all the leading citizens, treated his subjects from this time forward with the very greatest cruelty. Where Cypselus had spared many, and had neither put them to death nor banished them, Periander completed what his father had left unfinished. One day he stripped all the women of Corinth stark naked, for the sake of his own wife Melissa. He had sent messengers into Thesprotia to consult the oracle of the dead upon the Acheron concerning a pledge which had been given into his charge by a stranger, and Melissa appeared, but refused to speak or tell where the pledge was. 'She was chill,' she said, 'having no clothes; the garments buried with her were of no manner of use, since they had not been burnt. And this should be her token to Periander, that what she said was true—the oven was cold when he baked his loaves in it.' When this message was brought him, Periander knew the token for he had had intercourse with the dead body of Melissa; wherefore he straightway made proclamation, that all the wives of the Corinthians should go forth to the temple of Hera. So the women apparelled themselves in their bravest, and went forth, as if to a festival. Then, with the help of his guards, whom he had placed for the purpose, he stripped them one and all, making no difference between the free women and the slaves; and, taking their clothes to a pit, he called on the name of

Melissa, and burnt the whole heap. This done, he sent a second time to the oracle, and Melissa's ghost told him where he would find the stranger's pledge. Such, Lacedaemonians, is tyranny, and such are the deeds which spring from it. We Corinthians marvelled greatly when we first knew of your having sent for Hippias, and now it surprises us still more to hear you speak as you do. We adjure you, by the common gods of Greece, plant not despots in her cities. If however you are determined, if you persist, against all justice, in seeking to restore Hippias, know, at least, that the Corinthians will not approve your conduct."

2. TYRANNY AT SICYON*

Herodotus here has described the tribal reforms of Cleisthenes of Athens. In the following passage he offers a possible reason for his action.

My belief is that in acting thus he did but imitate his maternal grandfather, Cleisthenes, king of Sicyon. This king, when he was at war with Argos, put an end to the contest of the rhapsodists at Sicyon, because in the Homeric poems Argos and the Argives were so constantly the theme of song. He likewise conceived the wish to drive Adrastus, the son of Talaus, out of his country, seeing that he was an Argive hero. For Adrastus had a shrine at Sicyon, which yet stands in the market-place of the town. Cleisthenes therefore went to Delphi, and asked the oracle if he might expel Adrastus. To this the priestess is reported to have answered, "Adrastus is the Sicyonians' king, but you are only a robber." So when the god would not grant his request, he went home and began to think how he might contrive to make Adrastus withdraw of his own accord. After a while he hit upon a plan which he thought would succeed. He sent envoys to Thebes in Boeotia, and informed the Thebans that he wished to bring Melanippus the son of Astacus to Sicyon. The Thebans consenting, Cleisthenes carried Melanippus back with him, assigned him a precinct within the town-hall, and built him a shrine there in the safest and strongest part. The reason for his so doing (which I must not forbear to mention) was, because Melanippus was Adrastus' great enemy, having slain both his brother Mecistes and his son-in-law Tydeus. Cleisthenes, after assigning the precinct to Melanippus, took away from Adrastus the sacrifices and festivals wherewith he had till then been honoured, and transferred them to his adversary. Hitherto the Sicyonians had paid extraordinary honours to Adrastus, because the country had belonged to Polybus, and Adrastus was Polybus' daughter's son, whence it came to pass that Polybus, dying childless, left Adrastus his kingdom. Besides other ceremonies, it had been their custom to honour Adrastus with tragic choruses, which they assigned to him rather than Dionysus, on account of his calamities. Cleisthenes now gave the choruses to Dionysus, transferring to Melanippus the rest of the sacred rites.

Such were his doings in the matter of Adrastus. With respect to the Dorian tribes, not choosing the Sicyonians to have the same tribes as the Argives, he changed all the old names for new ones; and here he took special occasion to mock the Sicyonians, for he drew his new names from the words pig, and ass, adding thereto the usual tribe endings; only in the case of his own tribe he did nothing of the sort, but gave them a name drawn from his own kingly office. For

* Herodotus, 5. 67–68; 6. 126–130. Translated by *Rawlinson*.

he called his own tribe the Archelai, or Rulers, while the others he named Hyatae, or Pig-folk, Oneatae, or Ass-folk, and Choereatae, or Swine-folk. The Sicyonians kept these names, not only during the reign of Cleisthenes, but even after his death, for sixty years: then, however, they took counsel together, and changed to the well-known names of Hyllaeans, Pamphylians, and Dymanatae, taking at the same time, as a fourth name, the title of Aegialeans, from Aegialeus the son of Adrastus.

* * *

Afterwards, in the generation which followed, Cleisthenes, king of Sicyon, raised the family to still greater eminence among the Greeks than even that to which it had attained before. For this Cleisthenes, who was the son of Aristonymus, the grandson of Myron, and the great-grandson of Andreas, had a daughter, called Agarista, whom he wished to marry to the best husband that he could find in the whole of Greece. At the Olympic games, therefore, having gained the prize in the chariot-race, he caused public proclamation to be made to the following effect, "Whoever among the Greeks deems himself worthy to become the son-in-law of Cleisthenes, let him come, sixty days hence, or, if he will, sooner, to Sicyon; for within a year's time, counting from the end of the sixty days, Cleisthenes will decide on the man to whom he shall contract his daughter." So all the Greeks who were proud of their own merit or of their country flocked to Sicyon as suitors; and Cleisthenes had a foot-course and a wrestling-ground made ready, to try their powers.

From Italy there came Smindyrides, the son of Hippocrates, a native of Sybaris—which city about that time was at the very height of its prosperity. He was a man who in luxuriousness of living exceeded all other persons. Likewise there came Damasus, the son of Amyris, surnamed the Wise, a native of Siris. These

two were the only suitors from Italy. From the Ionian Gulf appeared Amphimnestus, the son of Epistrophus, an Epidamnian; from Aetolia Males, the brother of that Titormus who excelled all the Greeks in strength, and who, wishing to avoid his fellow-men, withdrew himself into the remotest parts of the Aetolian territory. From the Peloponnese came several—Leocedes, son of that Pheidon, king of the Argives, who established weights and measures throughout the Peloponnese, and was the most insolent of all the Grecians—the same who drove out the Elean directors of the games, and himself presided over the contests at Olympia—Leocedes, I say, appeared, this Pheidon's son; and likewise Amiantus, son of Lycurgus, an Arcadian of the city of Trapezus; Laphanes, an Azenian of Paeus, whose father, Euphorion, as the story goes in Arcadia, entertained the Dioscuri at his residence, and thenceforth kept open house for all comers; and lastly, Onomastus, son of Agaeus, a native of Elis. These four came from the Peloponnese. From Athens there arrived Megacles, the son of that Alcmaeon who visited Croesus, and Tisander's son, Hippocleides, the wealthiest and handsomest of the Athenians. There was likewise one Euboean, Lysanias, who came from Eretria, then a flourishing city. From Thessaly came Diactorides, a Cranonian, of the race of the Scopadae; and Akcon arrived from the Molossians. This was the list of the suitors.

Now when they were all come, and the day appointed had arrived, Cleisthenes first of all inquired of each concerning his country and his family; after which he kept them with him a year, and made trial of their manly bearing, their temper, their accomplishments, and their disposition, sometimes drawing them apart for converse, sometimes bringing them all together. Such as were still youths he took with him from time to time to the gymnasia; but the greatest trial of all was at the banquet-table. During the whole period of their stay he lived with them as I have said, and, further, from first to last he entertained them sumptuously. Somehow or other the suitors who came from Athens pleased him the best of all; and of these Hippocleides, Tisander's son, was specially in favour, partly on account of his manly bearing, and partly also because his ancestors were of kin to the Corinthian Cypselids.

When at length the day arrived which had been fixed for the espousals, and Cleisthenes had to speak out and declare his choice, he first of all made a sacrifice of 100 oxen, and held a banquet whereat he entertained all the suitors, and the whole people of Sicyon. After the feast was ended, the suitors vied with each other in music and in speaking on a given subject. Presently, as the drinking advanced, Hippocleides, who quite dumbfounded the rest, called aloud to the flute-player, and bade him strike up a dance; which the man did, and Hippocleides danced to it. And he fancied that he was dancing excellently well; but Cleisthenes, who was observing him, began to misdoubt the whole business. Then Hippocleides, after a pause, told an attendant to bring in a table; and when it was brought he mounted upon it and danced first of all some Laconian figures, then some Attic ones; after which he stood on his head upon the table, and began to toss his

legs about. Cleisthenes, notwithstanding that he now loathed Hippocleides for a son-in-law, by reason of his dancing and his shamelessness, still, as he wished to avoid an outbreak, had restrained himself during the first and likewise during the second dance; when, however, he saw him tossing his legs in the air, he could no longer contain himself, but cried out, "Son of Tisander, you have danced your wife away!" "What does Hippocleides care?" was the other's answer. And hence the proverb arose.

Then Cleisthenes commanded silence, and spake thus before the assembled company:

"Suitors of my daughter, well pleased am I with you all, and right willingly, if it were possible, would I content you all, and not by making choice of one appear to put a slight upon the rest. But as it is out of my power, seeing that I have but one daughter, to grant to all their wishes, I will present to each of you whom I must needs dismiss a talent of silver, for the honour that you have done me in seeking to ally yourselves with my house, and for your long absence from your homes. But my daughter, Agarista, I betroth to Megacles, the son of Alcmaeon, to be his wife, according to the usage and wont of Athens."

Then Megacles expressed his readiness, and Cleisthenes had the marriage solemnized.

3. TYRANNY AT ATHENS*

The *Athenian Constitution* is one of the 158 constitutions compiled by Aristotle and his students and used as the basis for the *Politics*. It is usually attributed to Aristotle himself, although it may have been written by one of his students.

Accordingly Solon made his journey abroad for these reasons. And when he

* Reprinted by permission of the publishers from *Loeb Classical Library*, Aristotle, *The Athenian Constitution*, 13–19, translated by H. Rackham (Cambridge, Mass.: Harvard University Press, 1935).

had gone abroad, though the city was still disturbed, for four years they kept at peace; but in the fifth year after Solon's archonship because of party strife they did not appoint an archon, and again in the fifth year after that they enacted a suspension of the archonship for the same cause. After this at the same interval of time Damasias was elected Archon, and held the post for two years and two months, until he was driven out of the office by force. Then because of the civil strife they decided to elect ten Archons, five from the nobles, three from the farmers and two from the artisans, and these held office for the year after Damasias. This shows that the Archon had very great power; for we find that they were always engaging in party strife about this office. And they continued in a state of general internal disorder, some having as their incentive and excuse the cancellation of debts (for it had resulted in their having become poor), others discontented with the constitution because a great change had taken place, and some because of their mutual rivalry. The factions were three: one was the party of the Men of the Coast, whose head was Megacles the son of Alcmaeon, and they were thought chiefly to aim at the middle form of constitution; another was the party of the Men of the Plain, who desired the oligarchy, and their leader was Lycurgus; third was the party of the Hillmen, which had appointed Peisistratus over it, as he was thought to be an extreme advocate of the people. And on the side of this party were also arrayed, from the motive of poverty, those who had been deprived of the debts due to them, and, from the motive of fear, those who were not of pure descent; and this is proved by the fact that after the deposition of the tyrants the Athenians enacted a revision of the roll, because many people shared the citizenship who had no right to it. The different parties derived their names from the places where their farms were situated.

Peisistratus, being thought to be an extreme advocate of the people, and having won great fame in the war against Megara, inflicted a wound on himself with his own hand and then gave out that it had been done by the members of the opposite factions, and so persuaded the people to give him a bodyguard, the resolution being proposed by Aristophon. He was given the retainers called Club-bearers, and with their aid he rose against the people and seized the Acropolis, in the thirty-second year after the enactment of his laws, in the archonship of Comeas. It is said that when Peisistratus asked for the guard Solon opposed the request, and said that he was wiser than some men and braver than others—he was wiser than those who did not know that Peisistratus was aiming at tyranny, and braver than those who knew it but held their tongues. But as he failed to carry them with him by saying this, he brought his armour out in front of his door and said that for his part he had come to his country's aid as far as he could (for he was now a very old man), and that he called on the others also to do the same. Solon's exhortations on this occasion had no effect and Peisistratus having seized the government proceeded to carry on the public business in a manner more constitutional than tyrannical. But before his government had taken root the partisans of Megacles and Lycurgus made common cause and expelled him, in the sixth year after his first establishment, in the archonship of Hegesias. In the twelfth year after this Megacles, being harried by party faction, made overtures again to Peisistratus, and on terms of receiving his daughter in marriage brought him back, in an old-fashioned and extremely simple manner. Having first spread a rumour that Athena was bringing Peisistratus back, he found a tall and beautiful woman, according to Herodotus a member of the Paeanian deme, but according to some accounts a Thracian flower-girl from Collytus named Phyē, dressed her up to look like the goddess, and brought her to the city with him, and Peisistratus drove in a chariot with the woman standing at his side, while the people in the city marvelled and received them with acts of reverence.

In this way his first return took place.

Afterwards, as he was expelled a second time in about the seventh year after his return—for he did not maintain his hold for long, but came to be afraid of both the factions owing to his unwillingness to live with Megacles' daughter as his wife, and secretly withdrew—; and first he collected a settlement at a place near the Gulf of Thermae called Rhaecelus, but from there he went on to the neighbourhood of Pangaeus, from where he got money and hired soldiers, and in the eleventh year went again to Eretria, and now for the first time set about an attempt to recover his power by force, being supported in this by a number of people, especially the Thebans and Lygdamis of Naxos, and also the knights who controlled the government of Eretria. Winning the battle of Pallenis, he seized the goverᴄment and disarmed the people; and now he held the tyranny firmly, and he took Naxos and appointed Lygdamis ruler. The way in which he disarmed the people was this: he held an armed muster at the Temple of Theseus, and began to hold an Assembly, but he lowered his voice a little, and when they said they could not hear him, he told them to come up to the forecourt of the Acropolis, in order that his voice might carry better; and while he used up time in making a speech, the men told off for this purpose gathered up the arms, locked them up in the neighbouring buildings of the Temple of Theseus, and came and informed Peisistratus. He, when he had finished the rest of his speech, told his audience not to be surprised at what had happened about their arms, and not to be dismayed, but to go away and occupy themselves with their private affairs, while he would attend to all public business.

This was the way, therefore, in which the tyranny of Peisistratus was originally set up, and this is a list of the changes that it underwent. Peisistratus's administration of the state was, as has been said, moderate, and more constitutional than tyrannic; he was kindly and mild in everything, and

in particular he was merciful to offenders, and moreover he advanced loans of money to the poor for their industries, so that they might support themselves by farming. In doing this he had two objects, to prevent their stopping in the city and make them stay scattered about the country, and to cause them to have a moderate competence and be engaged in their private affairs, so as not to desire nor to have time to attend to public business. And also the land's being thoroughly cultivated resulted in increasing his revenues; for he levied a tithe from the produce. And for this reason he organized the Local Justices, and often went to the country on circuit in person, inspecting and settling disputes, in order that men might not neglect their agriculture by coming into the city. For it was when Peisistratus was making an expedition of this kind that the affair of the man on Hymettus cultivating the farm afterwards called Tax-free Farm is said to have occurred. He saw a man at farm-work, digging mere rocks, and because of his surprise ordered his servant to ask what crop the farm grew; and the man said, "All the aches and pains that there are, and of these aches and pains Peisistratus has to get the tithe." The man did not know who it was when he answered, but Peisistratus was pleased by his free speech and by his industry, and made him free from all taxes. And in all other matters too he gave the multitude no trouble during his rule, but always worked for peace and safeguarded tranquillity; so that men were often to be heard saying that the tyranny of Peisistratus was the Golden Age of Cronos; for it came about later when his sons had succeeded him that the government became much harsher. And the greatest of all the things said of him was that he was popular and kindly in temper. For he was willing to administer everything according to the laws in all matters, never giving himself any advantage; and once in particular when he was summoned to the Areopagus to be tried on a charge of murder, he appeared in person to make his defence, and the issuer of the summons was frightened and left. Owing to this he remained in his office for a long period, and every time that he was thrown out of it he easily got it back again. For both the notables and the men of the people were most of them willing for him to govern, since he won over the former by his hospitality and the latter by his assistance in their private affairs, and was good-natured to both. And also the laws of Athens concerning tyrants were mild at those periods, among the rest particularly the one that referred to the establishment of tyranny. For they had the following law: 'These are the ordinances and ancestral principles of Athens: if any persons rise in insurrection in order to govern tyrannically, or if any person assists in establishing the tyranny, he himself and his family shall be disfranchised.'

Peisistratus, therefore, grew old in office, and died of disease in the archonship of Philoneos, having lived thirty-three years since he first established himself as tyrant, but the time that he remained in office was nineteen years, as he was in exile for the remainder. Therefore the story that Peisistratus was a lover of Solon and that he commanded in the war against Megara for the recovery of Salamis is clearly nonsense, for it is made impossible by their ages, if one reckons up the life of each and the archonship in which he died. When Peisistratus was dead, his sons held the government, carrying on affairs in the same way. He had two sons by his wedded wife, Hippias and Hipparchus, and two by his Argive consort, Iophon and Hegesistratus surnamed Thettalus. For Peisistratus married a consort from Argos, Timonassa, the daughter of a man of Argos named Gorgilus, who had previously been the wife of Archinus, a man of Ambracia of the Cypselid family. This was the cause of Peisistratus's friendship with Argos, and a thousand Argives brought by Hegesistratus fought for him in the battle of Pallenis. Some people date his marriage with the Argive lady during his first banishment, others in a period of office.

Affairs were now under the authority of Hipparchus and Hippias, owing to their station and their ages, but the government was controlled by Hippias, who was the elder and was statesmanlike and wise by nature; whereas Hipparchus was fond of amusement and love-making, and had literary tastes: it was he who brought to Athens poets such as Anacreon and Simonides, and the others. Thettalus was much younger, and bold and insolent in his mode of life, which proved to be the source of all their misfortunes. For he fell in love with Harmodius, and when his advances were continually unsuccessful he could not restrain his anger, but displayed it bitterly in various ways, and finally when Harmodius's sister was going to be a Basket-carrier in the procession at the Panathenaic Festival he prevented her by uttering some insult against Harmodius as being effeminate; and the consequent wrath of Harmodius led him and Aristogeiton to enter on their plot with a number of accomplices. At the Panathenaic Festival on the Acropolis they were already keeping a watch on Hippias (who happened to be receiving the procession, while Hipparchus was directing its start), when they saw one of their partners in the plot conversing in a friendly way with Hippias. They thought that he was giving information, and wishing to do something before their arrest they went down and took the initiative without waiting for their confederates, killing Hipparchus as he was arranging the procession by the Leocoreum. This played havoc with the whole plot. Of the two of them Harmodius was at once dispatched by the spearmen, and Aristogeiton died later, having been taken into custody and tortured for a long time. Under the strain of the tortures he gave the names of a number of men that belonged by birth to families of distinction, and were friends of the tyrants, as confederates. For they were not able immediately to find any trace of the plot, but the current story that Hippias made the people in the procession fall out away from their arms and searched for those that retained their daggers is not true, for in those days they did not walk in the procession armed, but this custom was instituted later by the democracy. According to the account of people of popular sympathies, Aristogeiton accused the tyrants' friends for the purpose of making his captors commit an impiety and weaken themselves at the same time by making away with men who were innocent and their own friends, but others say that his accusations were not fictitious but that he disclosed his actual accomplices. Finally, as do what he would he was unable to die, he offered to give information against many more, and induced Hippias to give him his right hand as a pledge of good faith, and when he grasped it he taunted him with giving his hand to his brother's murderer, and so enraged Hippias that in his anger he could not control himself but drew his dagger and made away with him.

After this it began to come about that the tyranny was much harsher; for Hippias's numerous executions and sentences of exile in revenge for his brother led to his being suspicious of everybody and embittered. About four years after Hipparchus's death the state of affairs in the city was so bad that he set about fortifying Munychia, with the intention of moving his establishment there. While engaged in this he was driven out by the king of Sparta, Cleomenes, as oracles were constantly being given to the Spartans to put down the tyranny, for the following reason. The exiles headed by the Alcmeonidae were not able to effect their return by their own unaided efforts, but were always meeting reverses; for besides the other plans that were complete failures,

they built the fort of Leipsydrion in the country, on the slopes of Parnes, where some of their friends in the city came out and joined them, but they were besieged and dislodged by the tyrants, owing to which afterwards they used to refer to this disaster in singing their catches:

Faithless Dry Fountain! Lackaday,
What good men's lives you threw away!
True patriots and fighters game,
They showed the stock from which they came!

So as they were failing in everything else, they contracted to build the temple at Delphi, and so acquired a supply of money for the assistance of the Spartans. And the Pythian priestess constantly uttered a command to the Spartans, when they consulted the oracle, to liberate Athens, until she brought the Spartiates to the point, although the Peisistratidae were strangers to them; and an equally great amount of incitement was contributed to the Spartans by the friendship that subsisted between the Argives and the Peisistratidae. As a first step, therefore, they dispatched Anchimolus with a force by sea; but he was defeated and lost his life, because the Thessalian Cineas came to the defence with a thousand cavalry. Enraged at this occurrence, they dispatched their king Cleomenes by land with a larger array; he won a victory over the Thessalian cavalry who tried to prevent his reaching Attica, and so shut up Hippias in the fortress called the Pelargicum and began to lay siege to it with the aid of the Athenians. While he was sitting down against it, it occurred that the sons of the Peisistratidae were caught when trying secretly to get away; and these being taken they came to terms on the condition of the boys' safety, and conveyed away their belongings in five days, surrendering the Acropolis to the Athenians; this was in the archonship of Harpactides, and Peisistratus's sons had retained the tyranny for about seventeen years after their father's death, making when added to the period of their father's power a total of forty-nine years.

4. Aristotle on the Origin of Tyranny*

It remains to speak of monarchy, the causes that destroy it and the natural means of its preservation. And the things that happen about royal governments and tyrannies are almost similar to those that have been narrated about constitutional governments. For royal government corresponds with aristocracy, while tyranny is a combination of the last form of oligarchy and of democracy; and for that very reason it is most harmful to its subjects, inasmuch as it is a combination of two bad things, and is liable to the deviations and errors that spring from both forms of constitution. And these two different sorts of monarchy have their origins from directly opposite sources; royalty has come into existence for the assistance of the distinguished against the people, and a king is appointed from those distinguished by superiority in virtue or the actions that spring from virtue, or by superiority in coming from a family of that character, while a tyrant is set up from among the people and the multitude to oppose the notables, in order that the people may suffer no injustice from them. And this is manifest from the facts of history. For almost the greatest number of tyrants have risen, it may be said, from being demagogues, having won the people's confidence by slandering the notables. For some tyrannies were set up in this manner when the states had already grown great, but others that came before them arose from kings departing from the ancestral customs and aiming at a more despotic rule, and others from the men elected to fill the supreme magistracies (for in old times the peoples used to appoint the popular officials and the sacred embassies for long terms of office), and others from

oligarchies electing some one supreme official for the greatest magistracies. For in all these methods they had it in their power to effect their purpose easily, if only they wished, because they already possessed the power of royal rule in the one set of cases and of their honourable office in the other, for example Phidon in Argos and others became tyrants when they possessed royal power already, while the Ionian tyrants and Phalaris rose from offices of honour, and Panaetius at Leontini and Cypselus at Corinth and Pisistratus at Athens and Dionysius at Syracuse and others in the same manner from the position of demagogue. Therefore, as we said, royalty is ranged in correspondence with aristocracy, for it goes by merit, either by private virtue or by family or by services or by a combination of these things and ability. For in every instance this honour fell to men after they had conferred benefit or because they had the ability to confer benefit on their cities or their nations, some having prevented their enslavement in war, for instance Codrus, others having set them free, for instance Cyrus, or having settled or acquired territory, for instance the kings of Sparta and Macedon and the Molossians. And a king wishes to be a guardian, to protect the owners of estates from suffering injustice and the people from suffering insult, but tyranny, as has repeatedly been said, pays regard to no common interest unless for the sake of its private benefit; and the aim of tyranny is what is pleasant, that of royalty what is noble. Hence even in their requisitions money is the aim of tyrants but rather marks of honour that of kings; and a king's bodyguard consists of citizens, a tyrant's of foreign mercenaries. And it is manifest that tyranny has the evils of both democracy and oligarchy; it copies oligarchy in making wealth its object (for inevitably that is the only way in which

* Reprinted by permission of the publishers from *Loeb Classical Library*, Aristotle, *Politics*, 1310a–1311a, translated by H. Rackham (Cambridge, Mass.: Harvard University Press, 1959).

the tyrant's bodyguard and his luxury can be kept up) and in putting no trust in the multitude (which is why they resort to the measure of stripping the people of arms, and why ill-treatment of the mob and its expulsion from the city and settlement in scattered places is common to both forms of government, both oligarchy and tyranny), while it copies democracy in making war on the notables and destroying

them secretly and openly and banishing them as plotting against it and obstructive to its rule. For it is from them that counter-movements actually spring, some of them wishing themselves to rule, and others not to be slaves. Hence comes the advice of Periander to Thrasybulus, his docking of the prominent corn-stalks, meaning that the prominent citizens must always be made away with.

5. THE MEANING OF TYRANNY*

The word tyranny in Greek history does not denote one simple, unchanging institution, nor should it be assumed that it means a form of government essentially similar in all the cases to which it is applied. I shall discuss here only the earliest tyrannies in the Greek world—the tyrannies of the seventh and sixth centuries B.C., which arose under quite different conditions and were, for that reason, different in character and purpose from the later dictatorships of various times and places in the Greek world. Tyranny or dictatorship was, of course, in Greece as elsewhere a recurring phenomenon. In the late sixth and early fifth centuries it was a device used by Persia to govern the Greek cities of Asia Minor within the Persian Empire. The famous western tyrants of Sicily and South Italy appeared in the sixth and especially the fifth and fourth centuries; and there occurred elsewhere shorter or longer periods of tyranny. These belong to a time when in Greece itself conditions had changed; the early tyrannies had been overthrown, and a reaction against tyranny had set in owing to the combined influence of Sparta, who was proud of the fact that she had been always without tyrants (αἰεὶ ἀτυράννευτος Thuc. I. 18. 1) and

had helped in the expulsion of some of the tyrants, and of Athens where, after the tyranny, the triumphant progress of democracy and imperialism exercised great influence on political thought.

These later tyrannies conform to the modern meaning of the term; indeed, the term acquired its technical meaning from their character and from discussions of different types of government by historians and philosophers, who had them in mind when they described tyranny as a form of demagogy, a perversion of monarchy, oligarchy, or democracy. The earliest tyrants were not demagogues for the simple reason that there was as yet no *demos* upon whose shoulders they could rise. They belong to an earlier stage of political development and can more accurately be described as the successful champions of a growing middle class, who overthrew the restrictive aristocracies of birth and so freed their cities for a development which under favourable circumstances could and sometimes did lead to democracy.

The early tyrannies are thus *sui generis* and must be studied in the context of their times to be understood. It is even doubtful whether the term τύραννος was commonly and generally applied to them in their own day. The word was still rare at that time and had a variety of meanings; certainly it had no restricted and technical meaning until the end of the fifth century. Its

* Mary White, "Greek Tyranny," *Phoenix*, 9 (1955), pp. 1–8. Copyright, 1955, by The Classical Association of Canada (Toronto: University of Toronto Press, 1955).

origins are obscure, it is not a Greek nor Indo-European term. Whatmough's opinion, which has won wide acceptance, is that it is Lydian and is related to a group of Lydian names: Τύρσα, Turnus, Τυρσανοί and its alternative form Τυρρηνοί (the Greek term for the Etruscans), Tuscus and the older Tursco, and Turan, the Etruscan name for Venus. The probability of Lydian origin derives some support from the fact that the earliest use of any form of the word in Greek is by Archilochos referring to his contemporary, Gyges of Lydia (ca. 687–652 B.C.):

I care not for the wealth of golden Gyges, nor ever have envied him; I am not jealous of the works of Gods, and I have no desire for lofty despotism (μεγάλης δ' οὐκ ἐρέω τυραννίδος); for such things are far beyond my ken.

Here τυραννίς denotes the sovereign power of a wealthy monarch, and is probably simply a synonym for absolute or royal power. Such continues to be one of its common meanings in both poetry and prose. But as early as Alkaios, Theognis, and Solon it has the derogatory sense of despotic power based on fraud or violence. There may be some suggestion of this meaning even in the first use by Archilochos of Gyges, a resourceful usurper who in a palace intrigue killed his predecessor, married his queen, and by a vigorous and devious policy established the Mermnad dynasty as the ruling power in Anatolia (Hdt. 1. 8–12).

Alkaios (Frs. 48 and 87) is the first to use the word of a Greek leader. He applies it to Pittakos, the *aesymnetes* or dictator elected as mediator between the aristocrats, among whom Alkaios and his brothers were prominent, and the party of Melanchros and Myrsilos. Aristotle (*Politics* 1285 a30-b4) describes *aesymnetes* as an elective form of tyranny, resembling tyranny in being despotic, but resembling kingship in being elective and constitutional. Alkaios has all the aristocratic contempt for an upstart, and objects to

Pittakos because he is low-born, κακοπατρίδας. When he says that all praised Pittakos and set him up as tyrant (ἐστάσαντο τύραννον), he uses τύραννος as a term of personal abuse and not as the proper word to use of the constitutional nature of his position. Pittakos was scarcely more a tyrant in the later accepted sense of the term than was Solon in Athens, who held similar power for the year of his archonship (Aristotle, *Ath. Pol.* 5.2. εἵλοντο κοινῇ διαλλακτὴν καὶ ἄρχοντα Σόλωνα). Theognis uses various forms of the term in three passages (823–824; 1181–1182; 1204), Solon three times (Fr. 23, lines 6, 9, 19; *cf.* Fr. 10, 3–4 where the word is not used but the idea is present), both poets in the sense of despotic rule but neither referring to a particular individual.

In the fifth century, when the tyrants had been driven out and, in Athens especially, democracy had won its glorious victories over the Persian, in whose train had been the ex-tyrant Hippias and the other Peisistratidai, all forms of one-man rule were execrated, Persian monarchy and Greek tyranny alike. This can be seen in the honours paid to Harmodios and Aristogeiton who murdered Hipparchos. They became the tyrannicides, their statues were set up in the Agora, and in the scolion or drinking song celebrating their deed the refrain reads:

ὅτε τὸν τύραννον κανέτην
ἰσονόμους τ' Ἀθήνας ἐποιησάτην

When they slew the tyrant and gave equal laws to Athens

Here tyranny is specifically contrasted with *isonomia*, an earlier term for democracy.

The Athenian dramatists have a similar attitude towards absolute power. They use the word *tyrannos* frequently, both of the power of the gods—Zeus, Apollo, and Eros—and of human princes; almost always it contains the suggestion of a newly acquired or dangerously arbitrary power which is likely to be irresponsibly misused. Sometimes this is explicit, as in Sophocles' *Oedipus Tyrannus* 873:

ὕβρις φυτεύει τύραννον

Pride breeds tyranny.

In other passages there can be seen an effective *double entendre* between the conventional meaning of king and the derogatory meaning of despot.

Although the Attic use of the word was becoming increasingly coloured with this derogatory meaning, the Ionic continued to have both senses. The two fifth-century historians, the Ionian Herodotos and the Athenian Thucydides illustrate this. Herodotos applies it constantly to oriental kings and their power, occasionally even to governors or satraps, and regularly to the various Greek tyrants, in fact to one-man rule of any kind with no implication about the character of the rule. But in other places, and these are the more emphatic, it is despotic power as opposed to freedom (ἐλευθερίη 1. 62.2), or to oligarchic government (ἰσοκρατία 5. 92. a2); and in the famous Persian debate on the virtues of democracy, oligarchy, and monarchy (3. 80–82) it is significant that Otanes, who recommends democracy, uses both μούναρχος and τύραννος interchangeably of one-man rule while Dareios, who recommends the retention of the monarchy, uses μούναρχος only. Thucydides, on the other hand, restricts the term to the well known tyrants of Greece and the West or to tyranny as an illegal and despotic form of government. The two most striking passages in the latter sense describe the Athenian Empire: Perikles' remark in the second book (2. 63. 2: ὡς τυραννίδα γὰρ ἤδη ἔχετε αὐτήν, ἣν λαβεῖν μὲν ἄδικον δοκεῖ εἶναι, ἀφεῖναι δὲ ἐπικίνδυνον.) "For what you hold is, to speak somewhat plainly, a tyranny; to take it perhaps was wrong, but to let it go is unsafe," is echoed by Kleon later, in his speech about the punishment of Mitylene (3. 37. 2: ὅτι τυραννίδα ἔχετε τὴν ἀρχήν).

Even this brief account of the history of the term indicates that there is no certainty that the tyrants of the seventh and sixth centuries were so called by their contemporaries. If they were, it denoted their absolute power, or was a term of censure and abuse; it was not a technical description of a type of government. In the fifth century it *is* applied to them, but has two other distinct uses: as a synonym for royal or absolute power, and as a synonym for ill gotten or despotically exercised power. Only by the end of the century is the latter restricted and technical meaning established.

When it was the fashion to regard Ionia as the pioneer in all things Greek, it was thought that Greek tyranny was modelled on Gyges of Lydia, and the probable Lydian origins of the word and its first application to him were cited as corroborative evidence. On this theory the idea of tyranny first took root in the Greek cities of Asia Minor, perhaps in Ephesos where we hear of Melas the son-in-law of Gyges, or in Miletos where Thrasyboulos was a famous tyrant; thence it spread to mainland Greece. But Melas is nothing but a name, and Thrasyboulos was a contemporary of Periander, who belonged to the second generation of tyranny in Corinth. What evidence we have points in the opposite direction, to the conclusion that the earliest tyrants were in Greece itself, the group at the Isthmus, the Kypselids in Corinth, the Orthagorids in Sikyon, and Theagenes in Megara. Whether the career and methods of Gyges provided a pattern for the Isthmian tyrants can be only a conjecture from the fact that during and after Gyges' reign Greek-Lydian relations first became frequent and close. On the other hand it is certain that the conditions which gave rise to these tyrannies were peculiarly Greek, and bear little relation to anything we know, or can guess, of the circumstances attending the palace revolution and change of dynasty in Lydia.

In the Isthmian cities Dorian aristocracies had succeeded the kingships established at the time of the Dorian invasions, kingships which still persisted at Argos and Sparta. We know more of the Corinthian aristocracy than of the others; they were the Bacchiads, a group of Heraklid land-owning families who intermarried among themselves and jealously monopolized all political power in Corinth. They were an able and vigorous group who in the early days of the colonial movement to the West planted two of the most famous and successful colonies, Corcyra and Syracuse in 733 B.C. They seem to have been the first to see the commercial possibilities opened up by this Greek expansion to the West, and instead of remaining merely a land-owning aristocracy, solving the problems of growth by continuing to export population in colonies, they encouraged Corinth to supplement her limited agricultural resources by crafts and trade. Strabo (8. 6. 20, C378) says of them: τὸ ἐμπόριον ἀδεῶς ἐκαρπώσαντο, "they fearlessly reaped the fruits of commerce." It is significant that Corinth sent out only the two early colonies; thereafter it is her pottery, Proto-Corinthian, one of the loveliest of the 'Orientalizing' wares, which appears in ever increasing quantities not merely in the West but throughout the Greek markets. Corinth became famous for her innovations in naval architecture and *ca.* 704 (Thuc. 1. 13. 3) lent one of her shipwrights to Samos to build four ships of the new style. This was probably the penteconter, a type of ship which, with its fifty rowers as well as sails, was much less dependent on winds and currents and could make faster and safer journeys than the older ships.

The very success of the Bacchiads in availing themselves of and adapting themselves to the expanding opportunities of the early seventh century was their undoing. The twin claims of land and birth upon which an aristocracy relies for its exclusive political control were challenged by the appearance of a growing middle class. This middle class was not an exclusively mercantile group in contrast to a land-owning aristocracy; there seems to have been no such clear distinction. Both groups had both agricultural and mercantile interests, and land was still the principal form of security. Inevitably, as some families outside the aristocratic group grew wealthy and prominent, intermarriages took place. Alkaios and Theognis, themselves die-hard aristocrats, complain bitterly of such marriages, which corrupt noble blood with base-born stock.

The new prosperity was reflected in a change of military equipment and tactics. Hoplite tactics replaced the older long-range type of fighting in which the aristocratic cavalry had borne the burden and heat of the day, supported by a lightly armed and poorly trained militia. Although less expensive than cavalry equipment, hoplite armour was much heavier and more expensive than that formerly used by the fighters in the ranks, and hoplite tactics involved long training and drilling by a compact body of fighters whose success depended upon their discipline and effective cooperation. The middle classes contributed the hoplite phalanx, and this gave added force to their resentment against the aristocratic monopoly of political power and exclusive right to interpret justice. Hesiod of Boeotia, the earliest poet of mainland Greece, voices the gathering storm of protest against princes who twist justice to their own ends.

The answer of the Bacchiads to both criticism and demands was the frequent answer of a privileged class, greater harshness and repression. When, in addition, Corinth was unsuccessful in wars with her neighbours Argos and Megara and her colony Corcyra, the situation was ripe for a revolution. Kypselos brought the discontent to a head for his own personal advantage and seized power with the support of the middle classes. The stories of Kypselos' parentage, of his rise to power, and of his policy thereafter all stress that hatred of the oppression of the Bacchiads was the sentiment that rallied support for him. Claims to rule based on the prestige of birth are notoriously hard to break, and a strong personality, able, resourceful, and ruthless, is needed to initiate a successful revolution. Kypselos was a man of these qualities. Nicolaus of Damascus says that Kypselos became polemarch, in which office the mildness of his judicial decisions contrasting with the harsh decisions of the Bacchiads made him popular so that he was able to make himself tyrant without the usual bodyguard. We may be sceptical of some of the details of the story, but there is little reason to doubt that Kypselos had the loyal support of the middle-class hoplite soldiers. The first thing he did was to kill or drive out the Bacchiads, some of whom fled to Corcyra, Sparta, and the West. Periander, Kypselos' son and successor, displayed the same implacable hatred of the Bacchiads. They were expelled from their refuge in Corcyra, and a son of Periander installed as regent. It seems clear, therefore, that the Corinthian tyranny arose in protest against the Bacchiad monopoly of power, and that the studied policy of the Kypselids was to break that power for ever.

In Sikyon the pattern was similar. The Orthagorid tyrants were animated by hostility to the aristocratic Dorian families, and themselves belonged to the fourth and non-Dorian tribe. The renaming of the tribes (Hdt. 5. 68), to us a childishly spiteful gesture, was Kleisthenes' telling attack upon the prestige of the Dorian aristocracy. Orthagoras, the founder of the tyranny, is described as the son of a cook or a butcher (μάγειρος). As a young man he distinguished himself in his military service with the περιπόλοι, frontier guards, became their commander, and eventually polemarch. Then with the help of the hoplites he seized the tyranny.

For Megara there is less evidence about the establishment of Theagenes, but the little there is is significant. Aristotle says in the *Politics* (1305a) that Theagenes secured power after slaughtering the flocks and herds of the wealthy. In the *Rhetoric* (1357b) he says that, urged by the poor who hated the wealthy, he obtained a bodyguard and so became tyrant. It should be remembered that Megara in the seventh century had founded a group of colonies at and around the Bosporus, the two most famous being Chalkedon, an agricultural colony in a quiet bay on the southern shore, and seventeen years later Byzantion on the northern shore at the gates of the Euxine in a position to control the trade in and out of the Black Sea. Megara had an aristocracy which, like the Bacchiads, had exploited the possibilities of colonization; their flocks and herds and the wool trade, as Ure suggests, were an important part of their wealth. Aristotle's evidence indicates that in Megara too the tyranny was a movement to overthrow aristocracy.

These Isthmian tyrannies are the earliest Greek tyrannies, so far as can be inferred from the evidence we have. They begin in the second half of the seventh century; Kypselos is usually dated *ca.* 655, Orthagoras about the same time, and Theagenes in the 630's.

It seems to me that, if it is correct to say that tyranny in these places was a movement against the aristocracies of birth led and supported by a rising middle class, its geographic position is significant. The Isthmus, lying between the Corinthian and Saronic gulfs, stands at the centre of the principal trade routes: the route to the West which had been opened up by the early colonial movement, and the routes to the East, to Asia Minor, Syria, and Egypt, and to the Black Sea. Here the impact of new developments was most quickly and most acutely felt, and brought in its wake political change. The idea spread eastward, and many cities in Asia Minor seem to have had tyrannies in the early sixth century. What we know of Thrasyboulos of Miletos and the struggles in Mitylene in which the poet Alkaios participated suggests that in these places also it was a reaction against aristocracy. In Samos, where I have attempted to show that the tyranny began as early as the 560's with the piratical activities of Aiakes, it was the overthrow of the landowners, the γεωμόροι, which gave Aiakes the opportunity to seize personal power. In Athens, tyranny appeared with Peisistratos in 561/60 under special circumstances which I shall discuss later. Although the first

tyrannies in the newer cities of the West arose in the early part of the sixth century, it was not until the end of the century and the beginning of the fifth century that most of the cities had tyrants. By this time tyranny had become simply a designation for personal power or dictatorship and had lost its former significance as a symptom of social and political development. Similarly the later tyrannies in Asia Minor supported by Lydia or Persia were an artificial prolongation of the earlier institution and cease to have any real interest for us.

6. THE TYRANT AS CAPITALIST*

The seventh and sixth centuries B.C. constitute from many points of view one of the most momentous periods in the whole of the world's history. No doubt the greatest final achievements of the Greek race belong to the two centuries that followed. But practically all that is meant by the Greek spirit and the Greek genius had its birth in the earlier period. Literature and art, philosophy and science are at this present day largely following the lines that were then laid down for them, and this is equally the case with commerce. It was at the opening of this epoch that the Greeks or their half hellenized neighbours the Lydians brought about perhaps the most epoch-making revolution in the whole history of commerce by the invention of a metal coinage like those that are still in circulation throughout the civilized world.

It was no accident that the invention was made precisely at this time. Industry and commerce were simultaneously making enormous strides. About the beginning of the seventh century the new Lydian dynasty of the Mermnadae made Sardis one of the most important trading centres

that have arisen in the world's history. The Lydian merchants became middlemen between Greece and the Far East. Egypt recovered its prosperity and began rapidly to develop commercial and other relations with its neighbours, including the Greeks. Greek traders were pushing their goods by sea in all directions from Spain to the Crimea. Concrete evidence of this activity is still to be seen in the Corinthian and Milesian pottery of the period that has been so abundantly unearthed as far afield as Northern Italy and Southern Russia. It was a time of extraordinary intellectual alertness. Thales and the numerous other philosophers of the Ionian School were in close touch with the merchants and manufacturers of their age. They were in fact men of science rather than philosophers in the narrow modern sense of the latter word, and most of them were ready to apply their science to practical and commercial ends, as for example Thales, who is said to have made a fortune by buying up all the oil presses in advance when his agricultural observations had led him to expect a particularly plentiful harvest. A corner in oil sounds very modern, and in fact the whole of the evidence shows that in many ways this ancient epoch curiously anticipated the present age.

* P. N. Ure, *The Origin of Tyranny* (Cambridge: Cambridge University Press, 1922), pp. 1–3, 290–295, 296–297, 300–301, 306.

Politically these two centuries are generally known as the age of tyrants. The view that the prevalence of tyranny was in some way connected with the invention of coinage has been occasionally expressed. Radet has even gone so far as to suggest that the first tyrant was also the first coiner. He does not however go further than to suggest that the tyrant started a mint and coinage when already on the throne.

The evidence appears to me to point to conclusions of a more wide-reaching character. Briefly stated they are these: that the seventh and sixth century Greek tyrants were the first men in their various cities to realize the political possibilities of the new conditions created by the introduction of the new coinage, and that to a large extent they owed their position as tyrants to a financial or commercial supremacy which they had already established before they attained to supreme political power in their several states.

In other words their position as I understand it has considerable resemblances to that built up in the fourteenth and fifteenth centuries A.D. by the rich bankers and merchants who made themselves despots in so many of the city states of Italy. The most famous of these are the Medici, the family who gave a new power to the currency by their development of the banking business, and mainly as a result of this became tyrants of Florence. Santo Bentivoglio of Bologna passed from a wool factory to the throne. Another despot of Bologna was the rich usurer Roméo Pepoli. At Pisa the supreme power was grasped by the Gambacorti with an old merchant named Pietro at their head. At Lodi it was seized by the millionaire Giovanni Vignate. The above instances are taken from Symonds' sixth class of despots of whom he says that "in most cases great wealth was the original source of despotic ascendancy."

* * *

The age of the first known metal coins is also the age of the first rulers to be called tyrants. Ancient evidence and modern analogy both suggest that the new form of government was based on the new form of capital. The modern analogy is to be found in the financial revolution which has largely replaced metal coins by paper (thereby rendering capital very much more mobile, just as was done by the financial revolution of the age of the tyrants) and has led many people to fear a new tyranny of wealth. The ancient evidence is to be found in the scanty extant writings of the sixth century B.C. (Solon and Theognis), in scattered notices about early tyrants or tyranny in fifth century writers (Thucydides, Herodotus, Pindar), in certain statements of Aristotle, in references to industrial conditions both during and after the age of the tyrants, in the history of the states where there was never a tyranny, and in the steps taken to prevent a recurrence of tyranny.

If the commercial origin of the early tyranny is not explicitly formulated by any ancient writer it should be remembered how meagre are contemporary documents and how little Greek writers say about economic causes. It is true also that my view is at variance with statements of Plato, Aristotle, and subsequent writers: but their picture of the rise of tyranny clashes with known facts about the seventh and sixth centuries and is due to false generalizations from the conditions of their own days and particularly from the career of Dionysius of Syracuse.

Peisistratus made himself tyrant by organizing the Attic "hill men" (Diakrioi, Epakrioi) against the two previously existing rival factions of the "plain" and the "coast." The accepted explanations of these "hill men" are improbable. They cannot have been farmers or shepherds, who were always very conservative, are not recorded as having subsequently supported Peisistratus, and must have lived principally in the plain and very little in the forest-clad mountains where modern theories generally locate them. Nor were the "hill men" confined to the mountainous district of North Attica, the mistaken identification of which with the "hill country" is due to mistaken views as to the triple division of Attica into "hill," "coast," and "plain," which wrongly assigns all South Attica to the "coast" and limits the "coast" to South Attica. These views on the triple division of Attica in the days of Peisistratus are based on the weakest of evidence and are made improbable by the subsequent topographical arrangements of Cleisthenes (502 B.C.), and by the later uses of the terms Diakria and Epakria. The Epakria contained a village named Semachidai which, as shown by a recently found inscription, lay in the hilly mining district of South Attica. Furthermore the Attic "akron" *par excellence* was Cape Sunium, the Southern apex of the Attic mining district and of the whole Attic peninsula. In view of these facts it becomes probable that the Sunium and Laurium mining district was the "hill country" *par excellence*. The mines were almost certainly in full work at this period, and the miners, unlike those of later ages, free men, good material for a political faction.

That Peisistratus based his power on silver mines is made very likely by what is known of his subsequent career. He finally "rooted his power" on money derived partly from home, partly from the Thracian mining district; he went to the Thracian mining district to prepare for his second restoration; his first restoration is attributed to the dressing up as Athena of a Thracian woman named Phye, who is very possibly to be explained away as the Athena who begins about this time to appear on Attic coins: for this interpretation of the Phye story compare the names "girl," "virgin," "Pallas" colloquially given to the Attic coins, and the jest about Agesilaus being driven out of Asia by the Great King's archers, a colloquial name for Persian gold coins.

The tyranny fell at Athens when the tyrants lost control of the Thracian mining district. Shortly afterwards the ambitious Histiaeus, the Greek friend of the Persian king into whose power the mines had passed, incurred the suspicions of the Persian sovereign through attempting to build up a political power on these very mines and miners.

The history of the Alcmaeonid opposition to the house of Peisistratus likewise suggests that the government of Athens at this period depended first and foremost on the power of the purse.

Polycrates is perhaps best known for his piracies, but it seems not unlikely that these piracies were in fact an elaborate commercial blockade of Persia that proved almost as unpopular among Greek neutrals as among the subjects of the Great King against whom it was mainly directed. As tyrant Polycrates is found controlling the commercial and industrial activities of his state, building ships, harbour works, and waterworks, and very possibly a great bazaar, and probably employing much free labour on these works. Before he became tyrant he already had an interest in the chief Samian industries, the working of metal and the manufacture of woollen goods. Aiakes the father of Polycrates is probably the Aiakes whom a recently discovered Samian inscription appears to connect with the sea-borne trade of the island. The tyrant is said to have owed his fall to an attempt to get money enough to rule all Greece, a statement of particular value considering the tendency to administer poetic justice that is so frequently displayed by Herodotus, who is our authority for this statement.

The great developments of trade and industry that just preceded the age of tyranny in Greece had their parallel if not their origin in Egypt. At the height of this development in Egypt a new and powerful dynasty arises which bases its power on commerce and on the commercial and industrial classes. Already towards the end of the eighth century we find King Boc-choris (somewhat after the manner of the Argive Pheidon) devoting special attention to commercial legislation. His successor Sethon is said by Herodotus to have based his power on "hucksters and artizans and tradespeople." During these reigns the country was always being occupied or threatened by foreign invaders from Ethiopia or Assyria. The first Egyptian king of this period to rule all Egypt in normal conditions of peace and quietness was Psammetichus I, who rose to power about the same time as Cypselus in Corinth and Orthagoras in Sicyon. Psam-metichus according to Diodorus converted his position from that of a petty Delta chieftain (one of twelve who shared the rule of the part of the country not in foreign occupation) into that of supreme ruler of the whole country as a result of the wealth and influence that he won by trad-ing with Phoenicians and Greeks.

This last statement if true establishes Psammetichus as a commercial tyrant. It occurs only in Diodorus, and receives no direct confirmation in earlier writers, but it is in entire harmony with all that is known about events and conditions in Egypt at this period, and more particularly with the notices just quoted as to Bocchoris and Sethon, with the history of Amasis and the other later Saites as recorded in Hero-dotus, and with the conclusions to be drawn from the excavation of Naukratis and the other Greek settlements that played so important a part in Saite Egypt.

From the middle of the eighth century B.C. till the early part of the fifth Lydia appears to have been a power in which the ruler based his position on wealth and struggles for the throne were fought with the weapons of trade and finance. This according to the accounts is the case with Spermos and Ardys in the eighth century and with Croesus in the sixth: the story of Gyges and his magic ring may also be explained in the same sense. A similar state of things is indicated in the advice which Croesus is made by Herodotus to give to Cyrus, in the story of the revolt of Pactyes, and in that of Xerxes and the rich Pythes.

At about the time to which we can trace back this state of things in Lydia, two events were taking place that are both attributed to Lydia, namely the striking of the first metal coins and the appearance of the first tyrant. In neither case are the dates very precise. The first coins are more probably to be placed late in the eighth century than early in the seventh, and though Gyges is stated to have been the first tyrant, there are reasons for suspecting that he may have been merely the first ruler of his kind to attract the attention of the Greeks. The magic ring too by which he secured his tyranny is sometimes attri-buted not to Gyges but to some (not very remote) ancestor of his or to the eighth century plutocrat Midas king of the neigh-bouring Phrygia. But on any showing the ring falls within the limits of time and place to which may be ascribed the earliest coins and the earliest tyrant. Rings are one common form of early currency and it is not impossible that it was to the ring in this sense that the first tyrant owed his tyranny. This view, which implies that the earliest coins were private issues and that the coinage was only nationalized when the principal coiner became chief of the state, is supported alike by evidence and analogies.

Pheidon, who was probably the first ruler to be called tyrant in European Greece, is described by Herodotus as "the man who created for the Pelopon-nesians their measures," a description that at once suggests that it was this commercial step that differentiated Pheidon the tyrant from the kings who preceded him. Later writers, of whom the earliest is Ephorus, go further and state that silver was first coined by Pheidon in Aegina. The state-ment has been called in question, but it is confirmed by the chapters of Herodotus (v. 82 f.) which describe the early relations between Argos, Aegina, and Athens. In the light of recent archaeological enquiries it becomes highly probable that Argos became predominant in Aegina as described in these chapters of Herodotus (which are unfortunately most vague in their chronology) just about the time when Pheidon most probably reigned; and this probability is increased by the tradition that Pheidon recovered the lot of Temenos, the domain of the kings of Argos in early Dorian times, which included the island of Aegina. The occupation of Aegina by Argos which we have seen reason to associate with Pheidon gave rise according to Herodotus to a change in the "measures" (which probably included the weights system) in use on the island, the new measures being half as great again as those previously in use. The Aeginetan standard on which the Aeginetan coins were struck is roughly half as great again as the other and probably earlier standard used in ancient Greece. The statement of Ephorus that silver was first coined by Pheidon in Aegina is thus strikingly confirmed, which means that the first ruler to strike coins in European Greece was also the first to be called tyrant.

The tyranny at Corinth coincides with the great industrial and commercial developments of the city described by Thucydides (I. 13) in words that are a paraphrase of his description of the state of things that led to the rise of tyrannies in Greece generally. Scholars agree that the tyrants had a direct interest in some of these developments, notably shipping, colonizing and coinage. The main industry of Corinth at this period seems to have been pottery, with which she supplied much of the Greek world. Of the early career of the first tyrant, Cypselus, very little is known beyond the story in Herodotus which professes to explain how the infant Cypselus got his curious name. We have examined in some detail the meaning of the words cypselus and cypsele, and found that they probably mean potter and

pot, so that the man who established the tyranny at Corinth seems to have borne a name that associates him with the main industry of his city.

* * *

In Chapter IX we surveyed the evidence for the origin of the early tyrannies at Sicyon, Megara, Miletus, Ephesus, Leontini, Agrigentum, and Cumae. The material is scanty and it is enough here to recall that as far as it goes it supports the theory of a commercial origin. At Sicyon the tyranny is founded by a tradesman the son of a tradesman. At Megara Theagenes rises to power as the result of what looks very like the creation of a corner in the staple product of his city. At Miletus and Leontini we find tyrants arising as the result of something like class war between rich and poor, while a later tyrant of Miletus tries to establish a great political position by getting control of the mines and miners of Thrace. At Ephesus and Cumae the tyrants' power is said to be based on the money that they distributed among the poorer classes, while at Agrigentum the tyrant is definitely stated to have secured the tyranny through his position as a great employer.

In the times of Aristotle there are several cases in the Pergamene district of rich bankers and the like making attempts, of which one at least was successful, to secure supreme political power in their cities by means of their wealth. The close personal relationship in which Aristotle stood to some of them partly explains why they are not classed by him as tyrants.

Not long afterwards the far more important power of the rulers of Pergamum owed its origin entirely to the enormous wealth of the founder of the dynasty.

Later still at Olbia chance has preserved an inscription which records how a very rich Olbiopolitan named Protogenes became "financial director" of his city.

Though there is no evidence that Proto-genes ever became a tyrant the inscription shows that the sort of position which we have imagined to have been normally built up by the would-be tyrant of the seventh or sixth century was actually secured some three or four centuries later by a wealthy individual in this remote and backward Greek city on the Black Sea.

* * *

If once the commercial origin of the tyrants' power is admitted, the various facts recorded about individual tyrants certainly gain in meaning and coherence. The mercenaries, the monetary reforms and innovations, the public works, the labour legislation, the colonial policy and the commercial alliances with foreign states, which have been repeatedly found associated with the early tyrants and which give the preserved accounts of them such a distinct stamp, become far more significant if it is granted that the tyrant's power was based on his control of the labour and trade of his city. As has been already observed, the fact that a theory explains the connexions between an obviously connected group of phenomena is no proof of its truth: but on the other hand a theory which fails to explain satis-factorily such a connexion is at an obvious disadvantage as compared with one which does. That is one further reason why the typical tyrant is not to be explained as a successful soldier or demagogue whose riches came to him suddenly at the same moment as his throne. The adventurer of either of these types might indeed further the commercial developments of the city that he had seized. It would be of course to his interest to do so. But as a general rule the man who has secured a fortune at a single stroke does not care to improve it by years of patient and organized effort. If all or any considerable number of the tyrants reviewed above had owed their positions to their sword or their tongue,

there would inevitably have been some cases of commercial retrogression under the tyrannies, whereas in fact there are none.

This is a fundamental fact. The tyrants were one and all first-class business men. If they did not deliberately use their wealth to secure their position, there is only one other possible explanation of their history; their financial abilities must have led their fellow-countrymen to put them in the way of seizing the throne, and that is roughly the account of them that is to be found in some modern histories, where they are vaguely pictured as the more or less passive products of blind economic forces. This view seems to me untenable. It cannot be reconciled with the impression made by the early tyrants on writers like Aristotle. More fatal still, we have a series of "lawgivers" like Solon, who was a business man who gained his position precisely in the way just indicated. Some of Solon's friends reproached him with his folly in not making himself tyrant. But the fact remains that no "lawgiver" of the period did so, and that the titles of νομοθέτης and αἰσυμνήτης that were given these legally appointed dictators were never applied either by friends or enemies to any of the tyrants at any period of their careers.

* * *

The age of the tyrants lasted for little more than five generations, and never so long as that in any one city. This fact may have some consolation for those who fear a modern tyranny of wealth, and offers perhaps an analogy for the observations of H. G. Wells on the transitory character of the modern financial boss. The determina-tion not to be permanently governed by mere wealth is as strong to-day as it was twenty-five centuries ago. "The loathing of capital with which our labouring classes to-day are growing more and more infected" is explained by William James as "largely composed of this sound sentiment of antipathy for lives based on mere having." He contrasts the "military and aristocratic" ideal of the "well-born man without possessions."

It is of course particularly hard to test the scorn of possessions of a class that can always help itself to them at a crisis, and, as William James himself admits, the ideal has always been "hideously corrupted." Certainly at the present day the antipathies between aristocracy and militarism and capitalism are, to say the least of it, not particularly marked. It is the democracy that loathes capitalism. But this may be merely a phase. The anti-capitalist movement may end by labour becoming fatally materialised or fatally impoverished, and in any country where that happens the way will be open for a new Peisistratus.

7. THE TYRANT AS SOCIAL REFORMER*

My subject is the age of the early Greek tyrants, viz. the seventh and sixth centuries B.C. It is not the dawn of Greek history but the morning before it reaches its glorious apogee after the great struggle with Persia. I know historians who value this age much higher than the full-grown classical age of the fifth and fourth centuries B.C. I know connoisseurs of art to whom the great classical art of the age of Pheidias is dull and monotonous as compared with the art of the age of the Peisistratidae. I can understand it. For the charm of the half-enclosed rose bud is lovelier and more tender, more promising than the spell of the fully blossoming flower. The age of which I speak to-night is an age of great and promising and very varied beginnings, an age of great, almost unlimited possibilities, and in this respect richer than the following classical age. For mastership is only attained by concentrating and limiting the efforts in one or a few directions. The old saying is true: "In der Begrenzung zeigt sich der Meister." The glorious harmony of classical art and life is won only by throwing away certain beginnings which in themselves may have been valuable and promising and by developing those which were selected and kept fully and harmoniously.

I permit myself to illustrate this point by a few instances. To begin with religion, Orphism was created and became important in these centuries. In many respects it was an original creation of some religious genius and dissimilar to Greek religious standards. It came as near as possible to a revealed religion having sacred books and certain doctrines, it had a touch of intolerance and developed perhaps something not unlike our congregations, it was a religion of the elect. It addressed itself to the poor and humble, to those who had a contrite heart and longed for justice. It taught the composite nature of man being a mixture of good and evil and his duty to conquer his Titanic nature by asceticism and righteousness. It demanded justice and the punishment of wrong-doing, if not in this world, at any rate in another, it transformed the lower world into a place of punishment by the adaptation of the demand for retribution to the old idea that the hereafter is a repetition of the present, it believed in the happier lot of the purified and initiated. The most original ideas of the Orphics are that they scorned this life and attributed a higher value to the other life, comparing the body with a tomb in which the higher part of man, his soul, is enclosed, and that they made the individual in his relationship to guilt and retribution the centre of their teaching. The background of these religious ideas is the need and distress of the age of which we shall speak later, for it

---

* Martin Nilsson, *The Age of the Early Greek Tyrants* (Belfast: The Queen's University, 1936), pp. 4–24.

directed the minds of men from this poor and disastrous life to seek consolation in religious and spiritual values. But the Orphics covered their deep ideas with a thick and grotesque garb of myths. Social conditions became better, the victory over the Persians caused a great national exaltation in which the Greeks returned to their innate propensities of clarity and plastic beauty. The mists and figures of clouds were dissipated, but when the Greek mind had worn itself out and was scorched by the winds from the Orient, Orphism put up its head again and became an important part of the syncretism of late antiquity.

Let us turn our eyes to another aspect of human life which is considered to be the most materialistic of all, craftsmanship and engineering. That technical skill made progress can be seen from the rapid development of sculpture, for which the ability to cut and chisel stone and marble is a premise. We have at least some information, however scanty, in regard to inventions. I do not discuss the question whether these inventions were made for the first time or borrowed, perhaps they were, but that they are recorded proves the interest which the age took in technical matters. In the sixth century Rhoikos and Theodoros from Samos are said to have invented the method of casting bronze *à cire perdue* and Glaukos from Chios the art of welding iron. To some extent we may appreciate the skill of the engineers from aqueducts built at this time and still extant at Megara, at Athens, and on Samos. These aqueducts were underground pipe-lines and it required not a little skill in measuring and levelling to find out where the channel could be cut and the pipes laid down with the least cost and labour. A real masterpiece of engineering work is the aqueduct built on Samos by Eupalinos from Megara. A tunnel was cut through a mountain, about 750 feet high, its length was two-thirds of a mile. The work was begun on both sides of the mountain and met in the middle. It was a great achievement that the errors in the side direction was but 15 feet and in the vertical direction something between six and nine feet. The Corinthians built the first triremes, ships with three rows of oars on each side, a revolutionizing improvement of the men of war; and the trireme remained the standard type down to the Hellenistic age.

Moreover the engineers were proud of their work. This appears from the inscription of the large stand of a mixing vessel made by Glaukos and dedicated by King Alyattes at Delphi, an inscription which evidently Herodotus read. Glaukos says that he alone of all men invented the welding of iron. Mandrokles from Samos, who built the bridge across the Bosporos over which the army of King Darius marched to the war against the Scythians, commemorated his achievement by having a picture painted of the event and by exposing it in the temple of Hera on Samos with an epigram which testifies to his self-esteem; the epigram says that he made a wreath of honour for himself and glory for his compatriots.

In the hey-day of Athens it was otherwise. An architect got the same wages as a stone-cutter, a drachma a day, only twice the wage of an unskilled labourer. It is true that the technique in building temples, *e.g.* the Parthenon, was admirable, but it had come to a standstill, there was no progress before the Hellenistic age, and even then technical skill was not highly valued except for military engineering. The only period of antiquity which is similar to our times in its esteem of technical skill and progress was the age of the tyrants.

It is not accidental that the nature philosophers arose in Ionia at the same time. There is a connecting link between the construction of the universe by the philosophers and the constructions of the engineers. But I shall not allow myself to be lost in wild speculations, but only to remind you that to-day in a time of great engineering constructions seemingly wild speculations on the construction of the expanding universe do appear. I wish only to call attention to the enlarging of the geographical horizon, due to the adventurous sea expeditions and still more to the busy work of recording and coordinating these discoveries and making them scientifically and practically useful by maps and sailing directions. Astronomical knowledge was borrowed from Babylonia and converted to the use of the sailors.

Some people may object that the last mentioned achievements belong to Ionia, but let me state that in this age there was no barrier between Ionia and the mother country. Eupalinos was summoned from Megara to build the aqueduct on Samos, Ameinokles from Corinth to Samos to build triremes, and Bathykyles from Magnesia on Maeander to construct the throne of Apollo at Amyklai, to mention only a few instances which are near at hand.

It is a fascinating age. Its very obscurity is for many a part of its spell. It provides them with a grand guessing game in which even the most daring hypothesis has a sporting chance of proving right. For it is only in art that our materials are rich, richer than in any other age; original sculptures in abundance have been discovered in great excavations. But of our historical information the reverse is true. It is more or less fragmentary, it has been worked over by later authors who continually confused it and it has been overgrown by the luxuriant growth of legend. Just as the archaeologists not only pull down the overgrowth and remove later accretions, but, not allowing the mutilated fragments to remain in their nakedness, try to reconstruct the venerable old buildings, so it is the duty of the historical scholar not only to criticize the sources and to remove the legends but to try and reconstruct the history of the age. Or he

would do a flagrant injustice to an age so rich and interesting as this is. It is certainly an arduous task and in order to grasp and elucidate the underlying problems it may be useful to pay attention to some other matters than those which belong to the daily routine of historical research.

I shall not enter on the time-honoured controversial points, the date of the reign of the Cypselidae, the tyrant family of Corinth, the date of the revolutionary attempt of Kylon at Athens, the question whether Peisistratos was driven out and came back three times or not, except for the fact that some archaeological evidence mentioned below agrees with the traditional dating of the rule of the Cypselidae. I cannot summon any enthusiasm for these doctrinaire questions; my aim is to get at a better understanding of the economic and social conditions which underlie this rich and varied, but also turbulent age.

I may begin with a remark which is found in most handbooks. Tyrants appear only in some geographically limited areas of Greece in which the most progressive cities of the age were situated. Of Asia Minor, especially Ionia, very little is known except for Miletos, the spiritual and commercial capital of the Greek people before the Persian Conquest of Asia Minor. On the mainland tyrants appear in certain cities around the Isthmus, Corinth, Sicyon, Epidauros, Megara, Athens. The rest of the mainland remained in the old backward conditions—Corinth and Megara were great industrial, commercial, and colonizing centres.

Another such town was Chalkis on Euboea, the importance of which is proved by its many colonies; its commerce and industry must also have been considerable. It is an exception to the rule; no tyrants existed there. But Chalkis was involved in a lengthy war with the neighbouring town of Eretria at the end of the eighth century; it was victorious but evidently its progress was checked and it succumbed to Athens before the end of our period. The hey-day of Chalkis was so early that it escaped tyranny. In the ensuing wars the knightly nobility kept the upper hand.

Another exception is Aegina, the most famous and richest commercial city of the mainland in the sixth century. Many of the odes of Pindar are composed in the honour of young Aeginetan noblemen. Its importance is proved by the fact that its standards of coins and measurements were widely accepted. The remarkable fact is that Aegina has not founded a single colony, nor had it tyrants. Aeginetan industry is unknown, there is very little of Aeginetan ceramics. These facts seem to prove that Aegina was a purely commercial town without any important industry of its own, it was a transit harbour busy with transit commerce. This agrees with the fact that it kept its aristocratic constitution and social conditions. We shall see that the assembling in a town of a numerous poor population with homogeneous occupations and interests is the ground from which tyranny sprang and on which it throve. In a purely commercial town the population is much more differentiated in occupations, interests, and habits of life. The merchants, whose business demands a psychological understanding of man, know how to handle men, how to humour the lower classes by well considered concessions and at the same time to keep the essential parts of government to themselves. And even the lower classes, if occupied with trade, enter into a closer understanding of the conditions of economic life than the workers of industry. Commercial republics have therefore often shown a great stability of political life, e.g., in antiquity Carthage and Rhodes and in later times Venice.

If we start from the social and political conditions in the beginning of the archaic age during which the nobles kept the political power, there are some hints in the Odyssey proving that there was a numerous free population earning a beg-garly pittance and employed especially for seasonal work in agriculture. Evidently there was a surplus population which the country was not able to feed. Hesiod shows what the conditions of the small peasants were, famine was near at hand, and in Attica we know that many, not being able to pay their debts, became slaves or tenants of the wealthy.

There are other methods than emigration to relieve the pressure of over-population and to dispose of the surplus population which the country cannot feed. It is superfluous to speak of the colonization from which sometimes two centuries of Greek history are named. I remark only that the cities which are called founders and mother cities of colonies were in reality emigration harbours. Megara and Chalkis had not such a stock of population as to be able to provide the colonists for all the colonies which are ascribed to them. The poor Boeotians of Hesiod may certainly have been prone to emigrate and to try their luck in a foreign country. For this they had to turn to the nearest town where ships were to be found. These were precisely merchant cities such as Chalkis and Megara. The poor peasants from the northern Peloponnese went to Corinth. The city which lent the ships organized of course the expedition and the new colony, consequently it figured as the mother city. In reality the colonists came from various places and there is evidence to prove how mixed the population of a colony was.

The other means of relieving the pressure of overpopulation is to find new work for them, i.e., to create an industry the products of which can be exported and exchanged against the food stuffs which are needed but which the country itself cannot produce. That this was the case to a great extent in the age of the tyrants has not been properly realized because of the common opinion that slaves were employed in Greek industry. It was lightly assumed that they were employed in the age of the tyrants too, although

Periander is said to have prohibited the acquiring of slaves. Against this common opinion Professor Ure delivered a vigorous attack in a stimulating and well-known book. To him the tyrants were big business men, who founded their power on the great mass of free labourers who were dependent on them. I shall not enter upon details on which opinions may vary, but Ure seems to have proved thus much with certainty; namely that the labourers in the age of the tyrants were free men, although of a low standing and very poor.

It is in fact but natural that the surplus population sought relief not only in emigration but also in other work than agriculture, if they were able to find it. And we know that they could, for the age of colonization is also the age in which Greek industry and commerce grew up and developed increasingly. Colonization and commerce went hand in hand, the colonies became markets and starting points for commerce and the voyages of the merchants prepared the way for colonization.

The common opinion that slave labour dominated in the age of the tyrants, as in fact it did in the fifth century and later, is influenced by the known aversion of the Greeks against *banausia*, manual labour. There were many *banausoi*, labourers, in fifth century Athens, certainly the majority of the citizens, but they draped themselves in the rags of the aristocratic ideal that earning one's livelihood by manual labour is not worthy of a free man.

There are signs that in the age of the tyrants quite another opinion asserted itself, one which affirmed instead of denying the dignity of manual labour. The salient point in many anecdotes of Periander is that he did not permit people to lounge idle in the market place; the most explicit information states that he "forbade the citizens to acquire slaves and live in idleness, and continually found them some employment." Of Peisistratos it is told that he incited the country folk to strenuous

work and rewarded those who did such. Solon who was a merchant shared this view. He enjoined that only the man who had taught his children a profession had the right to be supported by them in old age. A new valuation of manual labour corresponding to the conditions of the new age, free labour, was making its way but was soon repressed. When slave labour became dominant in the fifth century the people shared the aristocrats' prejudice against manual labour.

It can be readily understood that the destitute population of the country-side flocked into the city when a prospect appeared of earning a livelihood, which of course was poor but a little better because not so much dependent on seasonal labour. There is information to this effect which was overlooked. Periander is said not to have allowed anybody and everybody to live in the city, just as the Ptolemies prohibited the rural population from dwelling in Alexandra. When the poet Theognis cries out against the people who until recently lived outside the town clad in goat skins but now were masters, his invective gains point if it was directed against the rural population which had flowed into the city and ousted the noblemen from their predominance.

There are facts which show that the increase of the city population in this age was exceptionally large. This is the reason why Theagenes at Megara and Peisistratos at Athens built aqueducts with costs and labour which are astounding in comparison with the standards of the age. The old wells did not suffice for the growing population. In the fifth and fourth centuries we do not hear of such works of public utility. The American excavators discovered recently parts of the city walls of old Corinth which allow to trace the circuit. The result is so astonishing that in a personal interview I asked Mr. Broneer if it was right, and he stated that he had himself traced the walls. The circuit enclosed an area whose diameter is about three miles in the east-west and a mile and a half in the north-south direction. Even if we leave a liberal part for unoccupied ground the extent of the city area surpasses all that we expected and thought probable. Corinth was a big town in the age of the tyrants. It can only have become so through immigration from the countryside and the immigration cannot have taken place if people did not trust that they would find sustenance in the city.

Its greatness cannot have come save through industry and trade. Our information concerning industry and trade is lamentably meagre; the wares have vanished with one important exception, ceramics. We must remember that earthenware vessels played a much greater part at that time than later, not to speak of our own days. Not only common and fine vases were made of clay but clay vessels served also for storing certain wares and as receptacles of fluids. In certain ceramic styles certain forms of vessels predominate, sometimes almost to the exclusion of other forms, e.g., of the proto-Corinthian ware the small, graceful, slender lecythi and of the Corinthian ware, the round, squat aryballi, which are found in thousands and thousands. This is explained by the fact that they served as receptacles for unguents and perfumes, and this fact allows us certain inferences in regard to the industry of the city from which they came. Not only the vessels but probably also their contents were produced there.

Except for Mycenaean vases and sherds proto-Corinthian vases are the first Greek export found in Italy in considerable number. They were made at Corinth. This has been doubted but is proved by the finds of the Americans. Corinthian vases too were exported to Italy in great quantities.

Of course vases were not Corinth's only export nor Italy their only destination. The finds at Calydon prove that architectural terracottas were exported ready-made with marks and numbers so that they could be fitted together on the place. The large and interesting finds of the English excavators at Perachora are a new proof of the great activity and the brisk trade of Corinth, for this harbour place belonged to Corinth. Still more the recent finds at Corinth itself testify to its flourishing and important ceramic industry. A mile west of the ancient market place near a ravine potters' workshops were found at a place where clay of the finest quality is available and there is a supply of water. Enormous masses of pottery were found, among them lumps of clay, crude or worked, unfired bowls, mis-shapen vases, apprentice- and trial-pieces, factory rejects. Scattered fragments and three deposits of proto-Corinthian ware prove that this kind of pottery was made at Corinth. There are many figurines and moulds for them. The majority of the finds belong to the Orientalizing Corinthian style but they go down to the fifth and fourth centuries and testify to a gradual decline of Corinthian ceramics in the fifth and following centuries, as they testify to its activity and prosperity in the seventh and early sixth centuries.

In recent years there has been a dispute whether we are entitled to speak of an industry at all in ancient times. Some scholars have said we must not. They point to the smallness of the factories even in the great days of Athens, the small number of workers employed in them and the absence of machines. We ought, they say, not speak of industry but of handicraft. This is true in regard to the methods of production. There were no machines, only the common tools of the craftsman and simple machines driven by the hand of man, e.g. the potter's wheel. The factories were workshops and fifty slave labourers in a workshop were a great number in the first part of the fourth century. It is not, however, the technical aspect that is decisive but the economic. Many small workshops may together bring forth a large output, at least as compared with the markets of the age. The real criterion is, whether the production is made on order and for the home market, or for export and for a foreign market which may be calculated but is always largely uncertain. The latter was the case in the great cities of the age of the tyrants. Goods were produced not simply to the order of some local customers, but in large quantities ready for such market as should turn up. Thus I think that we may speak of an industry and of industrial cities in this age, if only the word is understood rightly.

Some archaeological facts may perhaps be utilised in order to illustrate these conditions. I have already mentioned the well-known fact that in certain ceramic styles certain forms of vessels are predominant, e.g. small lecythi in the proto-Corinthian and aryballi in a certain phase of the Corinthian ware. This has been explained by the fact that these small vases served as receptacles of unguents and perfumes and were manufactured for this purpose. But there is still another fact which may be taken into account in this connexion, viz. the abrupt appearance of certain ceramic styles which are characteristic of this mass production.

The proto-Corinthian style springs from the Geometric and is quite geometric in its first phase. Still it has a peculiar character of its own, a soberness and exactness which make it easily distinguishable from ordinary Geometric ware. The Corinthian style proper is different from it *toto caelo* not only by its orientalizing elements but also by its very spirit, its turgid design which is very prone to carelessness. It cannot be derived from the proto-Corinthian style, but is created by a thoroughly dissimilar mind, although there was some cross influence, apparent in proto-Corinthian ware of the type of the Berlin lecythos; they show how Corinthian looks translated into proto-Corinthian. There is a kind of pottery, a variety of the Orientalizing Corinthian animal style, which is found in most museums but generally overlooked because of its base quality; it is called Attico-Corinthian. It seems to belong chiefly to western Attica, the animal style of Attica is another represented by the Vourva vases, the greatest quantities of it are in the museum at Eleusis. At one time I guessed, rather hastily, that it represents the missing Megarian pottery, or it may be Eleusinian. Eleusis was independent of Athens at the time in which it was made. Although the design is a base variety of Corinthian, the ware is very characteristic and easily recognizable.

Vase painting was very low in Attica at the end of the seventh century. There are vases which are really hideous and childish in design. The more admirable is the severe and exact though not dry style which appears with Sophilos and Klitias and Ergotimos, the makers of the François vase, in the very years in which Peisistratos seized the power. The style of the Chalcidian vases is very characteristic, but there is no preceding and no succeeding stage. Quite recently it was maintained that they were made in Etruria.

My purpose in referring to these instances was to call attention to the abrupt appearance of very definite and standardized styles of ceramics which were characteristic of mass production. The common evolutionist explanation, the gradual development of one style from another, does not suffice to explain the break by which such a style with an almost personal note comes into existence nor the tenacity with which it is kept and applied to thousands and thousands of vessels. It seems to me that the only sufficient explanation is to recognize the decisive will of a single person who put his imprint on the design and made the many painters paint the many vessels in precisely the same manner.

The reason is easily understood. Not only was the manufacture of these vases a mass production which always tends to mechanize design but the style of decoration served the same aims as trade marks of wares and styles of packages in our days. If some one, say in Italy, bought a proto-Corinthian lecythos with perfume he recognized its origin and knew what he was buying. A great manufacturer invented the style and applied it to his wares in order that they might be easily recognized in the market. It was a piece of early commercial advertisement. For the same reason styles which had won popularity in the market were imitated by others, just as trade marks and packings are counterfeited nowadays. *E.g.*, Corinthian ware was imitated in Boeotia to a great extent.

If I am right in these inferences it follows that there were big industrial and commercial men whose influence was decisive in regard to the ornamentation of the mass production of ceramics. It remains to ask if they were big industrialists in our sense of the word who employed numerous labourers. Such men Professor Ure thinks the tyrants were. I am not quite sure of that. It is pretty certain that the workshops of the potters were not such big establishments as ours are. According to our notions they were mere workshops, but there were many of them, so many that they have given their name to a large part of the town of Athens, Kerameikos. It is possible that these big industrial and commercial men were investors who furnished the owners of small workshops with capital, perhaps with the raw material and tools they needed, collected their products, brought them on the market, and exported them. That is just the way in which industrial activity often begins. It was so in my country and at one time also in England. These advancers of capital had a great economic power over the craftsmen who were wholly dependent on them. They were able to dictate to them the manner in which the vessels were to be made and painted. For they knew the brand in which the purchasers had confidence.

Whether it was such men as these who appropriated the political power to themselves and became tyrants is a question upon which I do not enter. For it seems impossible to give any answer. But it is evident that the investors of capital took as much as possible of the profit for themselves—or they would not have been Greeks—allowing to the labourers and craftsmen only so much as was necessary for a bare sustenance. Thus in a big industrial city like Corinth there was a numerous population of a homogeneous character in occupations and interests, men on a low standard of life, toiling hard and incessantly for small pay. They had no prospect of rising from this low level; they had no political rights, for the nobles ruled the city, but they were free men and they knew it. Their burning wish was a bettering of their miserable conditions, but they were not able to wrest the power from the nobles nor did they know how to organize state life in their own interest. But they were willing to follow whosoever gave a prospect of helping them.

The growth of the city population explains the origin, the glory, and the fall of tyranny. Social needs and distress arose, but the ruling class of the nobles which adhered to the old ways was unwilling to relieve them. The labouring people who had common wants and interests but no organization to support their wishes, who had no political rights but were free men, wanted only a head and they would take the lead by the sheer force of their number. No wonder that a man appeared who saw the opportunity and seized it, perhaps for love of power, perhaps because he understood that the present state was untenable and that something must be done in order to relieve the pressing needs of the small people.

It must be acknowledged that the tyrants did their best to care for the labouring people to whom they owed their power. They brought water into the towns, they built magnificent temples, of which the seven upright columns in old Corinth and the pediment sculptures of the Peisistratos temple on the Acropolis at Athens still are left. They humoured the people by instituting splendid festivals and games, *e.g.* the Panathenaean games and the great Dionysia, the origin of the drama, brought into Athens from the newly conquered village of Eleutherai. Above all they favoured commerce and industry on which the sustenance of the people depended.

An industrial and commercial power is always prone to use political means, and if necessary, weapons and men of war in order to secure and dominate trade routes and markets. An imperialistic foreign policy is but the consequence. The Cypselidae of Corinth led such a policy with much energy and success especially in order to secure their most important trade route towards the West. In their time Corinth was an exception to the Greek rule that a colony was independent of its mother city and connected with it by bonds of piety only. Kypselos forced Kerkyra to submit and made it a vice-royalty for the Heir Apparent of his house. His son Gorgos took possession of Leukas and dug a channel through the low shelf by which it was united with the mainland, and he founded the colony of Ambrakia. Periander's son Euagoras founded Potidaia on the Chalkidike which still in the year 433 B.C. had its highest official, the *damiourgos*, sent from Corinth.

Peisistratos imitated the tyrants of Corinth. In order to control the trade route to the Black Sea he took possession of Sigeion near Troy, and we cannot believe that Miltiades the elder established himself as prince of the Chersonnese on the other side of the straits without his will and consent. It is said that Miltiades went into exile because he loathed the tyrant, but his family (the Philaidae) had its reasons to veil their connexions with the tyrant when they became leaders of the Athenian republic. Peisistratos was the first to purify the holy territory of Delos, a

sign that he held sway over the old commercial and religious centre of the Aegean, and his relations to the tyrants of the islands are well known. It is a common saying that he laid the foundations of the empire of Athens which was developed under other auspices. But it ought also to be recognized that the fall of his sons was not due to their own faults principally but to the fact that the imperialistic policy of the family broke down because of the advance of the Persians. They took their key-points, Sigeion and the Chersonnese, and the gold mines of Pangaion and ousted their ships from the Aegean.

A comparison between the two foremost tyrant cities, Athens and Corinth, is very instructive. Their periods of success are not contemporary, tyranny arose at Athens about two decades after its fall at Corinth.

Corinth dominated the Italian market in the later part of the seventh and the earlier part of the sixth century. This period coincides well with the traditional dating of the rule of the Cypselidae, 657—585 B.C. The import of vessels from Athens began before the middle of the sixth century and in the later part of the century it completely ousted the Corinthian ware. The period of Athens' predominance in the Italian market coincides also with the rule of its tyrants, though it continued after their fall. They were the last of the early tyrants. The great industrial development at Corinth as well as at Athens was contemporary with the rule of the tyrants, a valuable confirmation of my views.

It appears that Athens remained much longer than Corinth in the old agrarian conditions; this we may infer from what we know of Solon too. This will also explain why Athens did not found any colonies, the age of colonization was past when Athens began to emerge. But when she began her industrial and commercial competition, then she went forward with fresh vigour and full force. Corinth was weakened when the tyrants were overthrown, it returned to a modified and milder aristocratic *régime* which was not able to keep up its colonial empire. The colonies in the West which had been subject to the tyrants became independent. We do not know if the aristocrats cared less for industry than the tyrants, perhaps they did, for before long Corinthian ceramics were ousted from their market in Italy. Corinth remained always an important trading and industrial city; during the rule of the tyrants it had occupied the first place, after their fall it had to be content to come second to the rising Athens.

I have tried to describe the ground on which tyranny grew, a fertile soil for dictatorship, a numerous, homogeneous, distressed, and discontented population which only needed a leader to make revolt against the ruling class. He came, he needed only a small guard to overthrow the few aristocrats.

There is no doubt that social conditions went on improving and the tyrants did much for that improvement. Social progress clamours for more and it was not possible for anybody to fulfil all the wishes, reasonable or not. The people knew that they were free men, but they knew also that the tyrants had the power of not allowing them to use their freedom as they liked. As time went on the compulsion exercised by the tyrant was resented more and more and the harshness, iniquity, and selfishness shown by the once ruling nobles was gradually forgotten. The enemies of the tyrant joined and overthrew him. The results were various, at Corinth a modified aristocracy, at Athens an outspoken democracy.

This is a schematic picture, true as far as it is founded on common human nature, but too simple to cover the complicated course of history. In Athens things turned out otherwise but we know the growing discontent and Hippias would have been overthrown even if the Spartan army had not driven him out. But afterwards people spoke of the golden days of Peisistratos, not unjustly. The tyrants were no angels, nor were they the blackguards of later Greek historians. They seized their opportunity as men do who have a will to power. They have filled their mission well, but their rule was an interlude conditioned by passing circumstances. The Moor had done his service, the Moor might go.

SECTION VIII

Greek Strategy in the Persian War

IN THE SUMMER of 480 B.C., Xerxes, Great King of Persia, took an enormous invading army into Greece. During the previous year those Greeks who meant to resist met to plan a defence. After abandoning an attempt to make a stand at Tempe in Thessaly they fell back to central Greece, at Thermopylae on land and Artemisium at sea. Herodotus is our main source and his account of the Greek strategy is not clear. How did the Greeks hope to check the Persians? Did they hope to stop them for good at Thermopylae, or was the idea to force a sea battle at Artemisium? Were both the army and the fleet intended only to fight holding actions until the Athenians fled to Salamis and the Peloponnesus? Scholars have long argued these questions which have been sharpened by the discovery of the "Themistocles Decree," an inscription from the third century B.C. which purports to be an Athenian decree passed in 480 before the Battle of Artemisium. The authenticity of the decree is still in question, but if it reflects a reliable tradition it must influence our view in important ways.

1. THE ACCOUNT OF HERODOTUS*

Some time in 481 the Greeks received word of Xerxes' approach. Herodotus describes the Greek response.[1]

138. To return, however, to my main subject, the expedition of the Persian king, though it was in name directed against Athens, threatened really the whole of Greece. And of this the Greeks were aware some time before, but they did not all view the matter in the same light. Some of them had given the Persian earth and water, and were bold on this account, deeming themselves thereby secured against suffering hurt from the barbarian army; while others, who had refused compliance, were thrown into extreme alarm. For whereas they considered all the ships in Greece too few to engage the enemy, it was plain that the greater number of states would take no part in the war, but warmly favoured the Medes.

139. And here I feel constrained to deliver an opinion, which most men, I

* Selections are from Herodotus, *Histories*, translated by George Rawlinson.
[1] 7.138–145.

263

know, will dislike, but which, as it seems to me to be true; I am determined not to withhold. Had the Athenians, from fear of the approaching danger, quitted their country, or had they without quitting it submitted to the power of Xerxes, there would certainly have been no attempt to resist the Persians by sea; in which case, the course of events by land would have been the following. Though the Peloponnesians might have carried ever so many breastworks across the Isthmus, yet their allies would have fallen off from the Lacedaemonians, not by voluntary desertion, but because town after town must have been taken by the fleet of the barbarians; and so the Lacedaemonians would at last have stood alone, and, standing alone, would have displayed prodigies of valour, and died nobly. Either they would have done thus, or else, before it came to that extremity, seeing one Greek state after another embrace the cause of the Medes, they would have come to terms with King Xerxes; and thus, either way Greece would have been brought under Persia. For I cannot understand of what possible use the walls across the Isthmus could have been, if the King had had the mastery of the sea. If then a man should now say that the Athenians were the saviours of Greece, he would not exceed the truth. For they truly held the scales, and whichever side they espoused must have carried the day. They too it was who, when they had determined to maintain the freedom of Greece, roused up that portion of the Greek nation which had not gone over to the Medes, and so, next to the gods, they repulsed the invader. Even the terrible oracles which reached them from Delphi, and struck fear into their hearts, failed to persuade them to fly from Greece. They had the courage to remain faithful to their land, and await the coming of the foe.

140. When the Athenians, anxious to consult the oracle, sent their messengers to Delphi, hardly had the envoys completed the customary rites about the sacred precinct, and taken their seats inside the sanctuary of the god, when the priestess, Aristonice by name, thus prophesied:

Wretches, why sit ye here? Fly, fly to the ends of creation,
Quitting your homes, and the crags which your city crowns with her circlet.
Neither the head, nor the body is firm in its place, nor at bottom
Firm the feet, nor the hands, nor resteth the middle uninjur'd.
　All—all ruined and lost. Since fire, and impetuous Ares,
Speeding along in a Syrian chariot, hastes to destroy her.
Not alone shalt thou suffer; full many the towers he will level,
Many the shrines of the gods he will give to a fiery destruction.
Even now they stand with dark sweat horribly dripping,
Trembling and quaking for fear, and lo! from the high roofs trickleth
Black blood, sign prophetic of hard distresses impending.
Get ye away from the temple, and brood on the ills that await ye!

141. When the Athenian messengers heard this reply, they were filled with the deepest affliction: whereupon Timon, the son of Androbulus, one of the men of most mark among the Delphians, seeing how utterly cast down they were at the gloomy prophecy, advised them to take an olive-branch, and entering the sanctuary again, consult the oracle as suppliants. The Athenians followed this advice, and going in once more, said, "O King, we pray thee reverence these boughs of supplication which we bear in our hands, and deliver to us something more comforting concerning our country. Else we will not leave thy sanctuary, but will stay here till we die." Upon this the priestess gave them a second answer, which was the following:

Pallas has not been able to soften the lord of Olympus,
Though she has often prayed him, and urged him with excellent counsel.

Yet once more I address thee in words than
  adamant firmer.
When the foe shall have taken whatever the
  limit of Cecrops
Holds within it, and all which divine Cithaeron
  shelters,
Then far-seeing Zeus grants this to the prayers
  of Athena;
Safe shall the wooden wall continue for thee
  and thy children.
Wait not the tramp of the horse, nor the foot-
  men mightily moving
Over the land, but turn your back to the foe,
  and retire ye.
Yet shall a day arrive when ye shall meet him
  in battle.
Holy Salamis, thou shalt destroy the offspring
  of women,
When men scatter the seed, or when they
  gather the harvest.

142. This answer seemed, as indeed it
was, gentler than the former one; so the
envoys wrote it down, and went back with
it to Athens. When, however, upon their
arrival, they produced it before the people,
and inquiry began to be made into its true
meaning, many and various were the interpretations which men put on it; two, more
especially, seemed to be directly opposed
to one another. Certain of the old men
were of opinion that the god meant to
tell them the citadel would escape; for this
was anciently defended by a palisade; and
they supposed that barrier to be the
wooden wall of the oracle. Others maintained that the fleet was what the god
pointed at; and their advice was that
nothing should be thought of except the
ships, which had best be at once got ready.
Still such as said the wooden wall meant
the fleet, were perplexed by the last two
lines of the oracle:

Holy Salamis, thou shalt destroy the offspring
  of women,
When men scatter the seed, or when they
  gather the harvest.

These words caused great disturbance
among those who took the wooden wall to

be the ships; since the interpreters understood them to mean, that, if they made
preparations for a sea-fight, they would
suffer a defeat off Salamis.

143. Now there was at Athens a man
who had lately made his way into the first
rank of citizens; his true name was Themistocles, but he was known more generally
as the son of Neocles. This man came forward and said, that the interpreters had
not explained the oracle altogether aright,
"For if," he argued, "the clause in question
had really respected the Athenians, it
would not have been expressed so mildly;
the phrase used would have been Luckless
Salamis, rather than Holy Salamis, had
those to whom the island belonged been
about to perish in its neighbourhood.
Rightly taken, the response of the god
threatened the enemy, much more than the
Athenians." He therefore counselled his
countrymen to make ready to fight on
board their ships, since they were the
wooden wall in which the god told them to
trust. When Themistocles had thus cleared
the matter, the Athenians embraced his
view, preferring it to that of the interpreters.
The advice of these last had been against
engaging in a sea-fight. "All the Athenians
could do," they said, "was, without lifting
a hand in their defence, to quit Attica, and
make a settlement in some other country."

144. Themistocles had before this given
a counsel which prevailed very seasonably.
The Athenians, having a large sum of
money in their treasury, the produce of the
mines at Laureium, were about to share it
among the full-grown citizens, who would
have received ten drachmas apiece, when
Themistocles persuaded them to forbear
the distribution, and build with the money
200 ships, to help them in their war
against the Aeginetans. It was the breaking
out of the Aeginetan war which was at this
time the saving of Greece, for hereby
were the Athenians forced to become a
maritime power. The new ships were not
used for the purpose for which they had
been built, but became a help to Greece in

her hour of need. And the Athenians had not only these vessels ready before the war, but they likewise set to work to build more; while they determined, in a council which was held after the debate upon the oracle, that, according to the advice of the god, they would embark their whole force aboard their ships, and with such Greeks as chose to join them, give battle to the barbarian invader. Such, then, were the oracles which had been received by the Athenians.

145. The Greeks who were well affected to the Grecian cause, having assembled in one place, and there consulted together, and interchanged pledges with each other, agreed that, before any other step was taken, the feuds and enmities which existed between the different nations should first of all be appeased. Many such there were; but one was of more importance than the rest, namely, the war which was still going on between the Athenians and the Aeginetans. When this business was concluded, understanding that Xerxes had reached Sardis with his army, they resolved to despatch spies into Asia to take note of the king's affairs. At the same time they determined to send ambassadors to the Argives, and conclude a league with them against the Persians; while they likewise despatched messengers to Gelo, the son of Deinomenes, in Sicily, to the people of Corcyra, and to those of Crete, exhorting them to send help to Greece. Their wish was to unite, if possible, the entire Greek name in one, and so to bring all to join in the same plan of defence, inasmuch as the approaching dangers threatened all alike. Now the power of Gelo was said to be very great, far greater than that of any single Grecian people.

After unsuccessful missions to secure aid from Argos, Syracuse, Corcyra, and Crete and a quickly abandoned expedition to Tempe the Greeks met again at the Isthmus of Corinth.[2]

175. The Greeks, on their return to the Isthmus, took counsel together . . . and considered where they should fix the war, and what places they should occupy. The opinion which prevailed was, that they should guard the pass of Thermopylae; since it was narrower than the Thessalian defile, and at the same time nearer to them. Of the pathway, by which the Greeks who fell at Thermopylae were intercepted, they had no knowledge, until, on their arrival at Thermopylae, it was discovered to them by the Trachinians. This pass then it was determined that they should guard, in order to prevent the barbarians from penetrating into Greece through it; and at the same time it was resolved that the fleet should proceed to Artemisium, in the region of Histiaeotis; for as those places are near to one another, it would be easy for the fleet and army to hold communication.

* * *

The Persian fleet coming south encountered and captured three look-out ships.[3]

182. Thus did the Persians succeed in taking two of the vessels. The third, a trireme commanded by Phormus of Athens, took to flight and ran aground at the mouth of the river Peneus. The barbarians got possession of the bark, but not of the men. For the Athenians had no sooner run their vessel aground than they leaped out, and made their way through Thessaly back to Athens.

---

[2] 7.175.
[3] 7.182–184.1.

When the Greeks stationed at Artemisium learned what had happened by fire-signals from Sciathus, so terrified were they, that, quitting their anchorage-ground at Artemisium, and leaving scouts to watch the foe on the high lands of Euboea, they removed to Chalcis, intending to guard the Euripus.

183. Meantime three of the ten vessels sent forward by the barbarians advanced as far as the sunken rock between Sciathus and Magnesia, which is called the Ant, and there set up a stone pillar which they had brought with them for that purpose. After

this, their course being now clear, the barbarians set sail with all their ships from Therma, eleven days from the time that the king quitted the town. The rock, which lay directly in their course, had been made known to them by Pammon of Scyros. A day's voyage without a stop brought them to Sepias in Magnesia, and to the strip of coast which lies between the town of Casthanaea and the promontory of Sepias.

184. As far as this point then, and on land, as far as Thermopylae, the armament of Xerxes had been free from mischance....

At this point Herodotus gives very large figures for the size of the Persian army and navy. A fierce storm, however, destroyed a vast number of the ships and encouraged the Greeks who waited at Artemisium opposite the Persian fleet. At the same time Xerxes marched his army to Thermopylae where he faced the Greeks under the Spartan King Leonidas.[4]

...He had now come to Thermopylae, accompanied by the 300 men which the law assigned him, whom he had himself chosen from among the citizens, and who were all of them fathers with sons living. On his way he had taken the troops from Thebes, whose number I have already mentioned, and who were under the command of Leontiades the son of Eurymachus. The reason why he made a point of taking troops from Thebes and Thebes only was, that the Thebans were strongly suspected of being well inclined to the Medes. Leonidas therefore called on them to come with him to the war, wishing to see whether they would comply with his demand, or openly refuse, and disclaim the Greek alliance. They, however, though their wishes leant the other way, nevertheless sent the men.

206. The force with Leonidas was sent forward by the Spartans in advance of their main body, that the sight of them might encourage the allies to fight, and hinder them from going over to the Medes, as it was likely they might have done had they seen Sparta backward. They intended

presently, when they had celebrated the Carneian festival, which was what now kept them at home, to leave a garrison in Sparta, and hasten in full force to join the army. The rest of the allies also intended to act similarly; for it happened that the Olympic festival fell exactly at this same period. None of them looked to see the contest at Thermopylae decided so speedily; wherefore they were content to send forward a mere advanced guard. Such accordingly were the intentions of the allies.

207. The Greek forces at Thermopylae, when the Persian army drew near to the entrance of the pass, were seized with fear, and a council was held to consider about a retreat. It was the wish of the Peloponnesians generally that the army should fall back upon the Peloponnese, and there guard the Isthmus. But Leonidas, who saw with what indignation the Phocians and Locrians heard of this plan, gave his voice for remaining where they were, while they sent envoys to the several cities to ask for help, since they were too few to make a stand against an army like that of the Medes.

4 7.205–207.

* * *

After a delay of some days the Persians attacked, but the Greeks withstood their assaults, inflicting heavy casualties and holding the pass for several days.[5]

213. Now, as the king was at a loss, and knew not how he should deal with the emergency, Ephialtes, the son of Eurydemus, a man of Malis, came to him and was admitted to a conference. Stirred by the hope of receiving a rich reward at the king's hands, he had come to tell him of the pathway which led across the mountain to Thermopylae; by which disclosure he brought destruction on the band of Greeks who had there withstood the barbarians. . . .

217. The Persians took this path, and crossing the Asopus, continued their march through the whole of the night, having the mountains of Oeta on their right hand, and on their left those of Trachis. At dawn of day they found themselves close to the summit. Now the hill was guarded, as I have already said, by 1,000 Phocian men-at-arms, who were placed there to defend the pathway, and at the same time to secure their own country. They had been given the guard of the mountain path, while the other Greeks defended the pass below, because they had volunteered for the service, and had pledged themselves to Leonidas to maintain the post.

218. The ascent of the Persians became known to the Phocians in the following manner: During all the time that they were making their way up, the Greeks remained unconscious of it, inasmuch as the whole mountain was covered with groves of oak; but it happened that the air was very still, and the leaves which the Persians stirred with their feet made, as it was likely they would, a loud rustling, whereupon the Phocians jumped up and flew to seize their arms. In a moment the barbarians came in sight, and perceiving men arming themselves, were greatly amazed; for they had fallen in with an enemy when they expected no opposition. Hydarnes, alarmed at the sight, and fearing lest the Phocians might be Lacedaemonians, inquired to Ephialtes to what nation these troops belonged. Ephialtes told him the exact truth, whereupon he arrayed his Persians for battle. The Phocians, galled by the showers of arrows to which they were exposed, and imagining themselves the special object of the Persian attack, fled hastily to the crest of the mountain, and there made ready to meet death; but while their mistake continued, the Persians, with Ephialtes and Hydarnes, not thinking it worth their while to delay on account of Phocians, passed on and descended the mountain with all possible speed.

219. The Greeks at Thermopylae received the first warning of the destruction which the dawn would bring on them from the seer Megistias, who read their fate in the victims as he was sacrificing. After this deserters came in, and brought the news that the Persians were marching round by the hills: it was still night when these men arrived. Last of all, the scouts came running down from the heights, and brought in the same accounts, when the day was just beginning to break. Then the Greeks 'held a council to consider what they should do, and here opinions were divided: some were strong against quitting their post, while others contended to the contrary. So when the council had broken up, part of the troops departed and went their ways homeward to their several states; part however resolved to remain, and to stand by Leonidas to the last.

220. It is said that Leonidas himself sent away the troops who departed, because he tendered their safety, but thought it unseemly that either he or his Spartans should quit the post which they had been especially sent to guard. For my own part, I incline to think that Leonidas gave the

order, because he perceived the allies to be out of heart and unwilling to encounter the danger to which his own mind was made up. He therefore commanded them to retreat, but said that he himself could not draw back with honour; knowing that, if he stayed, glory awaited him, and that Sparta in that case would not lose her prosperity. For when the Spartans, at the very beginning of the war, sent to consult the oracle concerning it, the answer which they received from the priestess was that either Sparta must be overthrown by the barbarians, or one of her kings must perish. The prophecy was delivered in hexameter verse, and ran thus:

Oh! ye men who dwell in the streets of broad Lacedaemon,
Either your glorious town shall be sacked by the children of Perseus,
Or, in exchange, must all through the whole Laconian country
Mourn for the loss of a king, descendant of great Heracles.
HE cannot be withstood by the courage of bulls or of lions,
Strive as they may; he is mighty as Zeus; there is nought that shall stay him,
Till he have got for his prey your king, or your glorious city.

The remembrance of this answer, I think, and the wish to secure the whole glory for the Spartans, caused Leonidas to send the allies away. This is more likely than that they quarrelled with him, and took their departure in such unruly fashion.

* * *

222. So the allies, when Leonidas ordered them to retire, obeyed him and forthwith departed. Only the Thespians and the Thebans remained with the Spartans; and of these the Thebans were kept back by Leonidas as hostages, very much against their will. The Thespians, on the contrary, stayed entirely of their own accord, refusing to retreat, and declaring that they would not forsake Leonidas and

his followers. So they abode with the Spartans, and died with them. Their leader was Demophilus, the son of Diadromes.

223. At sunrise Xerxes made libations, after which he waited until the time when the market-place is wont to fill, and then began his advance. Ephialtes had instructed him thus, as the descent of the mountain is much quicker, and the distance much shorter, than the way round the hills, and the ascent. So the barbarians under Xerxes began to draw nigh; and the Greeks under Leonidas, as they now went forth determined to die, advanced much further than on previous days, until they reached the more open portion of the pass. Hitherto they had held their station within the wall, and from this had gone forth to fight at the point where the pass was the narrowest. Now they joined battle beyond the defile, and carried slaughter among the barbarians, who fell in neaps. Behind them the captains of the squadrons, armed with whips, urged their men forward with continual blows. Many were thrust into the sea, and there perished; a still greater number were trampled to death by their own soldiers; no one heeded the dying. For the Greeks, reckless of their own safety and desperate, since they knew that, as the mountain had been crossed, their destruction was nigh at hand, exerted themselves with the most furious valour against the barbarians.

224. By this time the spears of the greater number were all shivered, and with their swords they hewed down the ranks of the Persians; and here, as they strove, Leonidas fell fighting bravely, together with many other famous Spartans, whose names I have taken care to learn on account of their great worthiness, as indeed I have those of all the 300. There fell too at the same time very many famous Persians: among them, two sons of Darius, Abrocomes and Hyperanthes, his children by Phratagune, the daughter of Artanes. Artanes was brother of King Darius, being a son of Hystaspes, the son of Arsames;

and when he gave his daughter to the king, he made him heir likewise of all his substance; for she was his only child.

225. Thus two brothers of Xerxes here fought and fell. And now there arose a fierce struggle between the Persians and the Lacedaemonians over the body of Leonidas, in which the Greeks four times drove back the enemy, and at last by their great bravery succeeded in bearing off the body. This combat was scarcely ended when the Persians with Ephialtes approached; and the Greeks, informed that they drew nigh, made a change in the manner of their fighting. Drawing back into the narrowest part of the pass, and retreating even behind the cross wall, they posted themselves upon a hillock, where they stood all drawn up together in one close body, except only the Thebans. The hillock whereof I speak is at the entrance of the straits, where the stone lion stands which was set up in honour of Leonidas. Here they defended themselves to the last, such as still had swords using them, and the others resisting with their hands and teeth; till the barbarians, who in part had pulled down the wall and attacked them in front, in part had gone round and now encircled them upon every side, overwhelmed and buried the remnant left beneath showers of missile weapons.

* * *

228. The slain were buried where they fell; and in their honour, nor less in honour of those who died before Leonidas sent the allies away, an incription was set up, which said:

Here did four thousand men from Pelops' land
Against three hundred myriads bravely stand.

This was in honour of all. Another was for the Spartans alone:

Go, stranger, and to Lacedaemon tell
That here, obeying her behests, we fell.

This was for the Lacedaemonians. The seer had the following:

The great Megistias' tomb you here may view,
Whom slew the Medes, fresh from Spercheius'
    fords.
Well the wise seer the coming death foreknew,
Yet scorned he to forsake his Spartan lords.

These inscriptions, and the pillars likewise, were all set up by the Amphictyons, except that in honour of Megistias, which was inscribed to him (on account of their sworn friendship) by Simonides, the son of Leoprepes.

THE EIGHTH BOOK, ENTITLED URANIA

1. The Greeks engaged in the sea-service were the following. The Athenians furnished 127 vessels to the fleet, which were manned in part by the Plataeans, who, though unskilled in such matters, were led by their active and daring spirit to undertake this duty; the Corinthians furnished a contingent of forty vessels; the Megarians sent twenty; the Chalcideans also manned twenty, which had been furnished to them by the Athenians; the Aeginetans came with eighteen; the Sicyonians with twelve; the Lacedaemonians with ten; the Epidaurians with eight; the Eretrians with seven; the Troezenians with five; the Styreans with two; and the Ceans with two triremes and two fifty-oared galleys. Last of all, the Locrians of Opus came in aid with a squadron of seven fifty-oared galleys.

2. Such were the nations which furnished vessels to the fleet now at Artemisium; and in mentioning them I have given the number of ships furnished by each. The total number of the ships thus brought together, without counting the fifty-oared galleys, was 271; and the captain, who had the chief command over the whole fleet, was Eurybiades the son of Eurycleides. He was furnished by Sparta, since the allies had said, "If a Lacedaemonian did not take the command, they

would break up the fleet, for never would they serve under the Athenians."

* * *

4. At the present time the Greeks, on their arrival at Artemisium, when they saw the number of the ships which lay at anchor near Aphetae, and the abundance of troops everywhere, feeling disappointed that matters had gone with the barbarians so far otherwise than they had expected, and full of alarm at what they saw, began to speak of drawing back from Artemisium towards the inner parts of their country. So when the Euboeans heard what was in debate, they went to Eurybiades, and besought him to wait a few days, while they removed their children and their slaves to a place of safety. But as they found that they prevailed nothing, they left him and went to Themistocles, the Athenian commander, to whom they gave a bribe of thirty talents, on his promise that the fleet should remain and risk a battle in defence of Euboea.

5. And Themistocles succeeded in detaining the fleet in the way which I will now relate. He made over to Eurybiades five talents out of the thirty paid him, which he gave as if they came from himself; and having in this way gained over the admiral, he addressed himself to Adeimantus, the son of Ocytus, the Corinthian leader, who was the only remonstrant now, and who still threatened to sail away from Artemisium and not wait for the other captains. Addressing himself to this man, Themistocles said with an oath, "You forsake us? By no means! I will pay you better for remaining than the Mede would for leaving your friends"—and straightway he sent on board the ship of Adeimantus a present of three talents of silver. So these two captains were won by gifts, and came over to the views of Themistocles, who was thereby enabled to gratify the wishes of the Euboeans. He likewise made his own gain on the occasion; for he kept the rest of the money, and no one knew of it. The com-

manders who took the gifts thought that the sums were furnished by Athens, and had been sent to be used in this way.

6. Thus it came to pass that the Greeks stayed at Euboea and there gave battle to the enemy. Now the battle was on this wise. The barbarians reached Aphetae early in the afternoon, and then saw (as they had previously heard reported) that a fleet of Greek ships, weak in number, lay at Artemisium. At once they were eager to engage, fearing that the Greeks would fly, and hoping to capture them before they should get away. They did not however think it wise to make straight for the Greek station, lest the enemy should see them as they bore down, and betake themselves to flight immediately; in which case night might close in before they came up with the fugitives, and so they might get clean off and make their escape from them; whereas the Persians were minded not to let even a torch-bearer slip through their hands.

7. They therefore contrived a plan, which was the following: They detached 200 of their ships from the rest, and—to prevent the enemy from seeing them start —sent them round outside the island of Sciathos, to make the circuit of Euboea by Caphareus and Geraestus, and so to reach the Euripus. By this plan they thought to enclose the Greeks on every side; for the ships detached would block up the only way by which they could retreat, while the others would press upon them in front. With these designs therefore they dispatched the two hundred ships, while they themselves waited, since they did not mean to attack the Greeks upon that day, or until they knew, by signal, of the arrival of the detachment which had been ordered to sail round Euboea. Meanwhile they made a muster of the other ships at Aphetae.

8. Now the Persians had with them a man named Scyllias, a native of Scione, who was the most expert diver of this day. At the time of the shipwreck off Mount Pelion he had recovered for the Persians a

great part of what they lost, and at the same time he had taken care to obtain for himself a good share of the treasure. He had for some time been wishing to go over to the Greeks; but no good opportunity had offered till now, when the Persians were making the muster of their ships. In what way he contrived to reach the Greeks I am not able to say for certain: I marvel much if the tale that is commonly told be true. It is said he dived into the sea at Aphetae, and did not once come to the surface till he reached Artemisium, a distance of nearly ten miles. Now many things are related of this man which are plainly false, but some of the stories seem to be true. My own opinion is that on this occasion he made the passage to Artemisium in a boat.

However this might be, Scyllias no sooner reached Artemisium than he gave the Greek captains a full account of the damage done by the storm, and likewise told them of the ships sent to make the circuit of Euboea.

9. So the Greeks on receiving these tidings held a council, whereat, after much debate, it was resolved that they should stay quiet for the present where they were, and remain at their moorings, but that after midnight they should put out to sea, and encounter the ships which were on their way round the island. Later in the day, when they found that no one meddled with them, they formed a new plan, which was to wait till near evening, and then sail out against the main body of the barbarians, for the purpose of trying their mode of fighting and skill in manoeuvring.

10. When the Persian commanders and crews saw the Greeks thus boldly sailing towards them with their few ships, they thought them possessed with madness, and went out to meet them, expecting (as indeed seemed likely enough) that they would take all their vessels with the greatest ease. The Greek ships were so few, and their own so far outnumbered them, and sailed so much better, that they resolved, seeing their advantage, to encompass their foe on every side. And now such of the Ionians as wished well to the Grecian cause and served in the Persian fleet unwillingly, seeing their countrymen surrounded, were sorely distressed; for they felt sure that not one of them would ever make his escape, so poor an opinion had they of the strength of the Greeks. On the other hand, such as saw with pleasure the attack on Greece, now vied eagerly with each other which should be the first to make prize of an Athenian ship, and thereby to secure himself a rich reward from the king. For through both the hosts none were so much talked of as the Athenians.

11. The Greeks, at a signal, brought the sterns of their ships together into a small compass, and turned their prows on every side towards the barbarians; after which, at a second signal, although inclosed within a narrow space, and closely pressed upon by the foe, yet they fell bravely to work, and captured thirty ships of the barbarians, at the same time taking prisoner Philaon, the son of Chersis, and brother of Gorgus, king of Salamis, a man of much repute in the fleet. The first who made prize of a ship of the enemy was Lycomedes the son of Aeschreas, an Athenian, who afterwards received the prize for valour. Victory however was still doubtful when night came on, and put a stop to the combat. The Greeks sailed back to Artemisium and the barbarians to Aphetae, much surprised at the result, which was far other than they had looked for. In this battle only one of the Greeks who fought on the side of the king deserted and joined his countrymen. This was Antidorus of Lemnos, whom the Athenians rewarded for his desertion by the present of a piece of land in Salamis.

12. Evening had barely closed in when a heavy rain, it was about midsummer, began to fall, which continued the whole night, with terrible thunderings and lightnings from Mount Pelion: the bodies of the slain and the broken pieces of the damaged ships were drifted in the direction of Aphetae, and floated about the prows of the vessels

there, disturbing the action of the oars. The barbarians, hearing the storm, were greatly dismayed, expecting certainly to perish, as they had fallen into such a multitude of misfortunes. For before they were well recovered from the tempest and the wreck of their vessels off Mount Pelion, they had been surprised by a sea-fight which had taxed all their strength, and now the sea-fight was scarcely over when they were exposed to floods of rain, and the rush of swollen streams into the sea, and violent thunderings.

13. If, however, they who lay at Aphetae passed a comfortless night, far worse were the sufferings of those who had been sent to make the circuit of Euboea; in as much as the storm fell on them out at sea, whereby the issue was indeed calamitous. They were sailing along near the Hollows of Euboea, when the wind began to rise and the rain to pour: overpowered by the force of the gale, and driven they knew not whither, at the last they fell upon rocks, Heaven so contriving, in order that the Persian fleet might not greatly exceed the Greek, but be brought nearly to its level. This squadron, therefore, was entirely lost about the Hollows of Euboea.

14. The barbarians at Aphetae were glad when day dawned, and remained in quiet at their station, content if they might enjoy a little peace after so many sufferings. Meanwhile there came to the aid of the Greeks a reinforcement of fifty-three ships from Attica. Their arrival, and the news which reached Artemisium about the same time of the complete destruction by the storm of the ships sent to sail round Euboea, greatly cheered the spirits of the Greek sailors. So they waited again till the same hour as the day before, and, once more putting out to sea, attacked the enemy. This time they fell in with some Cilician vessels, which they sank; when night came on, and they withdrew to Artemisium.

15. The third day was now come, and the captains of the barbarians, ashamed that so small a number of ships should harass their fleet, and afraid of the anger of Xerxes, instead of waiting for the others to begin the battle, weighed anchor themselves, and advanced against the Greeks about the hour of noon, with shouts encouraging one another. Now it happened that these sea-fights took place on the very same days with the combats at Thermopylae; and as the aim of the struggle was in the one case to maintain the pass, so in the other it was to defend the Euripus. While the Greeks, therefore, exhorted one another not to let the barbarians burst in upon Greece, these latter shouted to their fellows to destroy the Grecian fleet, and get possession of the channel.

16. And now the fleet of Xerxes advanced in good order to the attack, while the Greeks on their side remained quite motionless at Artemisium. The Persians therefore spread themselves, and came forward in a half moon, seeking to encircle the Greeks on all sides, and thereby prevent them from escaping. When they saw this, the Greeks sailed out to meet their assailants; and the battle forthwith began. In this engagement the two fleets contended with no clear advantage to either, for the armament of Xerxes injured itself by its own greatness, the vessels falling into disorder, and often running foul of one another; yet still they did not give way, but made a stout fight, since the crews felt it would indeed be a disgrace to turn and fly from a fleet so inferior in number. The Greeks therefore suffered much, both in ships and men; but the barbarians experienced a far larger loss of each. So the fleets separated after such a combat as I have described.

* * *

18. The two fleets, on separating, hastened very gladly to their anchorage-grounds. The Greeks, indeed, when the battle was over, became masters of the bodies of the slain and the wrecks of the vessels; but they had been so roughly handled, especially the Athenians, one-half of whose vessels had

suffered damage, that they determined to break up from their station, and withdraw to the inner parts of their country.

* * *

21. While the Greeks were employed in the way described above, the scout who had been on the watch at Trachis arrived at Artemisium. For the Greeks had employed two watchers: Polyas, a native of Anticyra, had been stationed off Artemisium, with a row-boat at his command ready to sail at any moment, his orders being that, if an engagement took place by sea, he should convey the news at once to the Greeks at Thermopylae; and in like manner Abronychus, the son of Lysicles, an Athenian, had been stationed with a thirty-oared ship near Leonidas, to be ready, in case of disaster befalling the land force, to carry tidings of it to Artemisium. It was this Abronychus who now arrived with news of what had befallen Leonidas and those who were with him. When the Greeks heard the tidings they no longer delayed to retreat, but withdrew in the order wherein they had been stationed, the Corinthians leading, and the Athenians sailing last of all.

The Persians next marched south toward Attica.[6]

40. Meanwhile, the Grecian fleet, which had left Artemisium, proceeded to Salamis, at the request of the Athenians, and there cast anchor. The Athenians had begged them to take up this position, in order that they might convey their women and children out of Attica, and further might deliberate upon the course which it now behoved them to follow. Disappointed in the hopes which they had previously entertained, they were about to hold a council concerning the present posture of their affairs. For they had looked to see the Peloponnesians drawn up in full force to resist the enemy in Boeotia, but found nothing of what they had expected; nay, they learnt that the Greeks of those parts, only concerning themselves about their own safety, were building a wall across the Isthmus, and intended to guard the Peloponnese, and let the rest of Greece take its chance. These tidings caused them to make the request whereof I spoke, that the combined fleet should anchor at Salamis.

41. So while the rest of the fleet lay to off this island, the Athenians cast anchor along their own coast. Immediately upon their arrival, proclamation was made, that every Athenian should save his children and household as he best could; whereupon some sent their families to Aegina, some to Salamis, but the greater number to Troezen. This removal was made with all possible haste, partly from a desire to obey the advice of the oracle, but still more for another reason. The Athenians say that they have in their acropolis a huge serpent which lives in the temple, and is the guardian of the whole place. Nor do they only say this, but, as if the serpent really dwelt there, every month they lay out its food, which consists of a honey-cake. Up to this time the honey-cake had always been consumed; but now it remained untouched. So the priestess told the people what had happened; whereupon they left Athens the more readily, since they believed that the goddess had already abandoned the citadel. As soon as all was removed, the Athenians sailed back to their station.

42. And now, the remainder of the Grecian sea-force, hearing that the fleet which had been at Artemisium, was come to Salamis, joined it at that island from Troezen—orders having been issued previously that the ships should muster at Pogon, the port of the Troezenians. The vessels collected were many more in number than those which had fought at Artemisium, and were furnished by more

cities. The admiral was the same who had commanded before, Eurybiades, the son of Eurycleides, who was a Spartan, but not of the family of the kings: the city, however, which sent by far the greatest number of ships, and the best sailers, was Athens.

* * *

After giving a catalogue of the Greeks at Salamis, Herodotus describes the decision to fight.[7]

49. When the captains from these various nations were come together at Salamis, a council of war was summoned; and Eurybiades proposed that any one who liked to advise, should say which place seemed to him the fittest, amongst those still in the possession of the Greeks, to be the scene of a naval combat. Attica, he said, was not to be thought of now; but he desired their counsel as to the remainder. The speakers mostly advised, that the fleet should sail away to the Isthmus, and there give battle in defence of the Peloponnese; and they urged as a reason for this, that if they were worsted in a sea-fight at Salamis, they would be shut up in an island, where they could get no help; but if they were beaten near the Isthmus, they could escape to their homes.

50. As the captains from the Peloponnese were thus advising, there came an Athenian to the camp, who brought word that the barbarians had entered Attica, and were ravaging and burning everything. For the division of the army under Xerxes was just arrived at Athens from its march through Boeotia, where it had burnt Thespiae and Plartea—both which cities were forsaken by their inhabitants, who had fled to the Peloponnese—and now it was laying waste all the possessions of the Athenians. Thespiae and Plataea had been burnt by the Persians, because they knew from the Thebans that neither of those cities had espoused their side.

51. Since the passage of the Hellespont and the commencement of the march upon Greece, a space of four months had gone by; one while the army made the crossing, and delayed about the region of the Hellespont; and three while they proceeded thence to Attica, which they entered in the archonship of Calliades. They found the city forsaken; a few people only remained in the temple, either keepers of the treasures, or men of the poorer sort. These persons having fortified the acropolis with planks and boards, held out against the enemy. It was in some measure their poverty which had prevented them from seeking shelter in Salamis; but there was likewise another reason which in part induced them to remain. They imagined themselves to have discovered the true meaning of the oracle uttered by the priestess, which promised "The wooden wall should never be taken." The wooden wall, they thought, did not mean the ships, but the place where they had taken refuge.

52. The Persians encamped upon the hill over against the citadel, which is called Ares' hill by the Athenians, and began the siege of the place, attacking the Greeks with arrows whereto pieces of lighted tow were attached, which they shot at the barricade. And now those who were within the citadel found themselves in a most woeful case, for their wooden rampart betrayed them; still, however, they continued to resist. It was in vain that the Pisistratidae came to them and offered terms of surrender—they stoutly refused all parley, and among their other modes of defence, rolled down huge masses of stone upon the barbarians as they were mounting up to the gates: so that Xerxes was for a long time very greatly perplexed, and could not contrive any way to take them.

53. At last, however, in the midst of these many difficulties, the barbarians made

---

7 8.49–53; 56–63.

discovery of an access. For verily the oracle had spoken truth; and it was fated that the whole mainland of Attica should fall beneath the sway of the Persians. Right in front of the Acropolis, but behind the gates and the common ascent—where no watch was kept, and no one would have thought it possible that any foot of man could climb—a few soldiers mounted from the sanctuary of Aglaurus, Cecrops' daughter, notwithstanding the steepness of the precipice. As soon as the Athenians saw them upon the summit, some threw themselves headlong from the wall, and so perished; while others fled for refuge to the inner part of the temple. The Persians rushed to the gates and opened them, after which they massacred the suppliants. When all were slain, they plundered the temple, and fired every part of the Acropolis.

* * *

56. Meanwhile, at Salamis, the Greeks no sooner heard what had befallen the Athenian citadel, than they fell into such alarm that some of the captains did not even wait for the council to come to a vote, but embarked hastily on board their vessels, and hoisted sail as though they would take to flight immediately. The rest, who stayed at the council board, came to a vote that the fleet should give battle at the Isthmus. Night now drew on, and the captains, dispersing from the meeting, proceeded on board their respective ships.

57. Themistocles, as he entered his own vessel, was met by Mnesiphilus, an Athenian, who asked him what the council had resolved to do. On learning that the resolve was to stand away for the Isthmus, and there give battle on behalf of the Peloponnese, Mnesiphilus exclaimed, "If these men shall sail away from Salamis, you will have no fight at all for the one fatherland; for they will all scatter themselves to their own homes; and neither Eurybiades nor any one else will be able to hinder them, or to stop the breaking up

of the armanent. Thus will Greece be brought to ruin through evil counsels. But hurry now; and, if there be any possible way, seek to unsettle these resolves—perhaps you might persuade Eurybiades to change his mind, and continue here."

58. The suggestion greatly pleased Themistocles; and without answering a word, he went straight to the vessel of Eurybiades. Arrived there, he let him know that he wanted to speak with him on a matter touching the public service. So Eurybiades bade him come on board, and say whatever he wished. Then Themistocles, seating himself at his side, went over all the arguments which he had heard from Mnesiphilus, pretending as if they were his own, and added to them many new ones besides; until at last he persuaded Eurybiades, by his importunity, to quit his ship and again collect the captains to council.

59. As soon as they were come, and before Eurybiades had opened to them his purpose in assembling them together, Themistocles, as men do when they are very anxious, spoke much to them; whereupon the Corinthian captain, Adeimantus, the son of Ocytus, observed, "Themistocles, at the games they who start too soon are scourged." "True," rejoined the other in his excuse, "but they who wait too late are not crowned."

60. Thus he gave the Corinthian at this time a mild answer; and towards Eurybiades himself he did not now use any of those arguments which he had urged before, or say aught of the allies betaking themselves to flight if once they broke up from Salamis; it would have been ungraceful for him, when the confederates were present, to make accusation against any; but he had recourse to quite a new sort of reasoning, and addressed him as follows:

"With you it rests, Eurybiades, to save Greece, if you will only listen to me, and give the enemy battle here, rather than yield to the advice of those among us, who would have the fleet withdrawn to the Isthmus. Hear now, I beseech you, and judge between the two courses. At the Isthmus you will fight in an open sea, which is greatly to our disadvantage, since our ships are heavier and fewer in number than the enemy's; and further, you will in any case lose Salamis, Megara, and Aegina, even if all the rest goes well with us. The land and sea force of the Persians will advance together; and your retreat will but draw them towards the Peloponnese, and so bring all Greece into peril. If, on the other hand, you do as I advise, these are the advantages which you will secure: in the first place, as we shall fight in a narrow sea with few ships against many, if the war follows the common course, we shall gain a great victory: for to fight in a narrow space is favourable to us—in an open sea, to them. Again, Salamis will in this case be preserved, where we have placed our wives and children. Nay, that very point by which you set most store, is secured as much by this course as by the other; for whether we fight here or at the Isthmus, we shall equally give battle in defence of the Peloponnese. Assuredly you will not do wisely to draw the Persians upon that region. For if things turn out as I anticipate, and we beat them by sea, then we shall have kept your Isthmus free from the barbarians, and they will have advanced no further than Attica, but from thence have fled back in disorder; and we shall, moreover, have saved Megara, Aegina, and Salamis itself, where an oracle has said that we are to overcome our enemies. When men counsel reasonably, reasonable success ensues; but when in their counsels they reject reason, God does not choose to follow the wanderings of human fancies."

61. When Themistocles had thus spoken,

Adeimantus the Corinthian again attacked him, and bade him be silent, since he was a man without a city; at the same time, he called on Eurybiades not to put the question at the instance of one who had no country, and urged that Themistocles should show of what state he was envoy, before he gave his voice with the rest. This reproach he made, because the city of Athens had been taken, and was in the hands of the barbarians. Hereupon Themistocles spake many bitter things against Adeimantus and the Corinthians generally; and for proof that he had a country, reminded the captains, that with 200 ships at his command all fully manned for battle, he had both city and territory as good as theirs; since there was no Grecian state which could resist his men if they were to make a descent.

62. After this declaration, he turned to Eurybiades, and addressing him with greater warmth and earnestness, "If you stay here," he said, "and behave like a brave man, all will be well—if not, you will bring Greece to ruin. For the whole fortune of the war depends on our ships. Be persuaded by my words. If not, we will take our families on board, and go, just as we are, to Siris in Italy, which is ours from of old, and which the prophecies declare we are to colonise some day or other. You then, when you have lost allies like us, will hereafter call to mind what I have now said."

63. At these words of Themistocles, Eurybiades changed his determination; principally, as I believe, because he feared that if he withdrew the fleet to the Isthmus, the Athenians would sail away, and knew that without the Athenians, the rest of their ships could be no match for the fleet of the enemy. He therefore decided to remain, and give battle at Salamis.

2. THE ACCOUNT OF PLUTARCH*

When the king of Persia sent messengers into Greece, with an interpreter, to demand earth and water, as an acknowledgment of subjection, Themistocles, by the consent of the people, seized upon the interpreter, and put him to death, for presuming to publish the barbarian orders and decrees in the Greek language; this is one of the actions he is commended for, as also for what he did to Arthmius of Zelea, who brought gold from the king of Persia to corrupt the Greeks, and was, by an order from Themistocles, degraded and disfranchised, he and his children and his posterity; but that which most of all redounded to his credit was, that he put an end to all the civil wars of Greece, composed their differences, and persuaded them to lay aside all enmity during the war with the Persians; and in this great work, Chileus the Arcadian was, it is said, of great assistance to him.

Having taken upon himself the command of the Athenian forces, he immediately endeavoured to persuade the citizens to leave the city, and to embark upon their galleys, and meet with the Persians at a great distance from Greece; but many being against this, he led a large force, together with the Lacedæmonians, into Tempe, that in this pass they might maintain the safety of Thessaly, which had not as yet declared for the king; but when they returned without performing anything, and it was known that not only the Thessalians, but all as far as Bœotia, was going over to Xerxes, then the Athenians more willingly hearkened to the advice of Themistocles to fight by sea, and sent him with a fleet to guard the straits of Artemisium.

When the contingents met here, the Greeks would have the Lacedæmonians to command, and Eurybiades to be their admiral; but the Athenians, who surpassed all the rest together in number of vessels, would not submit to come after any other, till Themistocles, perceiving the danger of the contest, yielded his own command to Eurybiades, and got thr Athenians to submit, extenuating the loss by persuading them, that if in this war they behaved themselves like men, he would answer for it after that, that the Greeks, of their own will, would submit to their command. And by this moderation of his, it is evident that he was the chief means of the deliverance of Greece, and gained the Athenians the glory of alike surpassing their enemies in valour, and their confederates in wisdom.

As soon as the Persian armada arrived at Aphetæ, Eurybiades was astonished to see such a vast number of vessels before him, and being informed that two hundred more were sailing around behind the island of Sciathus, he immediately determined to retire farther into Greece, and to sail back into some part of Peloponnesus, where their land army and their fleet might join, for he looked upon the Persian forces to be altogether unassailable by sea. But the Eubœans, fearing that the Greeks would forsake them, and leave them to the mercy of the enemy, sent Pelagon to confer privately with Themistocles, taking with him a good sum of money, which, as Herodotus reports, he accepted and gave to Eurybiades. In this affair none of his own countrymen opposed him so much as Architeles, captain of the sacred galley, who, having no money to supply his seamen, was eager to go home; but Themistocles so incensed the Athenians against them, that they set upon him and left him not so much as his supper, at which Architeles was much surprised, and took it very ill; but Themistocles immediately sent him in a chest a service of provisions, and at the bottom of it a talent of silver, desiring him to sup tonight, and to-

* Plutarch, *Themistocles*, 6–15. Translated by John Dryden.

morrow provide for his seamen; if not, he would report it among the Athenians that he had received money from the enemy. So Phanias the Lesbian tells the story.

Though the fights between the Greeks and Persians in the straits of Eubœa were not so important as to make any final decision of the war, yet the experience which the Greeks obtained in them was of great advantage; for thus, by actual trial and in real danger, they found out that neither number of ships, nor riches and ornaments, nor boasting shouts, nor barbarous songs of victory, were any way terrible to men that knew how to fight, and were resolved to come hand to hand with their enemies; these things they were to despise, and to come up close and grapple with their foes. This Pindar appears to have seen, and says justly enough of the fight at Artemisium, that—

"There the sons of Athens set
The stone that freedom stands on yet."

For the first step towards victory undoubtedly is to gain courage, Artemisium is in Eubœa, beyond the city of Histiæa, a sea-beach open to the north; most nearly opposite to it stands Olizon, in the country which formally was under Philoctetes; there is a small temple there, dedicated to Diana, surnamed of the Dawn, and trees about it, around which again stand pillars of white marble; and if you rub them with your hand, they send forth both the smell and colour of saffron. On one of these pillars these verses are engraved:

"With numerous tribes from Asia's region brought
The sons of Athens on these waters fought;
Erecting, after they had quelled the Mede,
To Artemis this record of the deed."

There is a place still to be seen upon this shore, where, in the middle of a great heap of sand, they take out from the bottom a dark powder like ashes, or something that has passed the fire; and here, it is supposed, the shipwrecks and bodies of the dead were burnt.

But when news came from Thermopylæ to Artemisium informing them that king Leonidas was slain, and that Xerxes had made himself master of all the passages by land, they returned back to the interior of Greece, the Athenians having the command of the rear, the place of honour and danger, and much elated by what had been done.

As Themistocles sailed along the coasts, he took notice of the harbours and fit places for the enemy's ships to come to land at, and engraved large letters in such stones as he found there by chance, as also in others which he set up on purpose near to the landing-places, or where they were to water; in which inscriptions he called upon the Ionians to forsake the Medes, if it were possible, and to come over to the Greeks, who were their proper founders and fathers, and were now hazarding all for their liberties; but, if this could not be done, at any rate to impede and disturb the Persians in all engagements. He hoped that these writings would prevail with the Ionians to revolt, or raise some trouble by making their fidelity doubtful to the Persians.

Now, though Xerxes has already passed through Doris and invaded the country of Phocis, and was burning and destroying the cities of the Phocians, yet the Greeks sent them no relief; and, though the Athenians earnestly desired them to meet the Persians in Bœotia, before they could come into Attica, as they themselves had come forward by sea at Artemisium, they gave no ear to their requests, being wholly intent upon Peloponnesus, and resolved to gather all their forces together within the Isthmus, and to build a wall from sea to sea in that narrow neck of land; so that the Athenians were enraged to see themselves betrayed, and at the same time afflicted and dejected at their own destitution. For to fight alone against such a numerous army was to no purpose, and the only expedient now left them was to leave their city and cling to their ships; which the people were very unwilling to submit to, imagining that it would signify little now to gain a victory, and not understanding how there could be deliverance any longer after they had once forsaken the temples of their gods and exposed the tombs and monuments of their ancestors to the fury of their enemies.

Themistocles, being at a loss, and not able to draw the people over to his opinion by any human reason, set his machines to work, as in a theatre, and employed prodigies and oracles. The serpent of Minerva, kept in the inner part of her temple, disappeared; the priest gave it out to the people that the offerings which were set for it were found untouched, and declared, by the suggestion of Themistocles, that the goddess had left the city, and taken her flight before them towards the sea. And he often urged them with the oracle which bade them trust to walls of wood, showing them that walls of wood could signify nothing else but ships; and that the island of Salamis was termed in it, not miserable or unhappy, but had the epithet of divine, for that it should one day be associated with a great good fortune of the Greeks. At length his opinion prevailed, and he obtained a decree that the city should be committed to the protection of Minerva, "Queen of Athens"; that they who were of age to bear arms should embark, and that each should see to sending away his children, women, and slaves where he could. This decree being confirmed, most of the Athenians removed their parents, wives, and children to Trœzen, where they were received with eager good-will by the Trœzenians, who passed a vote that they should be maintained at the public charge, by a daily payment of two obols to every one, and leave be given to the children to gather fruit where they pleased, and schoolmasters paid to instruct them. This vote was proposed by Nicagoras.

There was no public treasure at that time in Athens; but the council of Areo-pagus, as Aristotle says, distributed to every one that served eight drachmas, which was a great help to the manning of the fleet; but Clidemus ascribes this also to the art of Themistocles. When the Athenians were on their way down to the haven of Piræus, the shield with the head of Medusa was missing; and he, under the pretext of searching for it, ransacked all places, and found among their goods considerable sums of money concealed, which he applied to the public use; and with this the soldiers and seamen were well provided for their voyage.

When the whole city of Athens were going on board, it afforded a spectacle worthy alike of pity and admiration, to see them thus send away their fathers and children before them, and, unmoved with their cries and tears, passed over into the island. But that which stirred compassion most of all was, that many old men, by reason of their great age, were left behind; and even the tame domestic animals could not be seen without some pity, running about the town and howling, as desirous to be carried along with their masters that had kept them; among which it is reported that Xanthippus, the father of Pericles, had a dog that would not endure to stay behind, but leaped into the sea, and swam along by the galley's side till he came to the island of Salamis, where he fainted away and died, and that spot in the island, which is still called the Dog's Grave, is said to be his.

Among the great actions of Themistocles at this crisis, the recall of Aristides was not the least, for, before the war, he had been ostracised by the party which Themistocles headed, and was in banishment; but now, perceiving that the people regretted his absence, and were fearful that he might go over to the Persians to revenge himself, and thereby ruin the affairs of Greece, Themistocles proposed a decree that those who were banished for a time might return again, to give assistance by word and deed to the cause of Greece with the rest of their fellow-citizens.

Eurybiades, by reason of the greatness of Sparta, was admiral of the Greek fleet, but yet was faint-hearted in time of danger, and willing to weigh anchor and set sail for the isthmus of Corinth, near which the land army lay encamped; which Themistocles resisted; and this was the occasion of the well-known words, when Eurybiades, to check his impatience, told him that at the Olympic games they that start up before the rest are lashed; "And they," replied Themistocles, "that are left behind are not crowned." Again, Eurybiades lifting up his staff as if he were going to strike, Themistocles said, "Strike if you will, but hear;" Eurybiades, wondering much at his moderation, desired him to speak, and Themistocles now brought him to a better understanding. And when one who stood by him told him that it did not become those who had either city nor house to lose, to persuade others to relinquish their habitations and forsake their countries, Themistocles gave this reply: "We have indeed left our houses and our walls, base fellow, not thinking it fit to become slaves for the sake of things that have no life nor soul; and yet our city is the greatest of all Greece, consisting of two hundred galleys, which are here to defend you, if you please; but if you run away and betray us, as you did once before, the Greeks shall soon hear news of the Athenians possessing as fair a country, and as large and free a city, as that they have lost." These expressions of Themistocles made Eurybiades suspect that if he retreated the Athenians would fall off from him. When one of Eretria began to oppose him, he said, "Have you anything to say of war, that are like an inkfish? you have a sword, but no heart." Some say that while Themistocles was thus speaking upon the deck, an owl was seen flying to the right hand of the fleet, which came and sate upon the top of the mast; and this happy omen so far disposed the Greeks to follow his advice, that they presently prepared to fight. Yet, when the enemy's fleet was arrived at the haven of Phalerum, upon the coast of Attica, and with the number of their ships concealed all the shore, and when they saw the king himself in person come down with his land army to the seaside, with all his forces united, then the good counsel of Themistocles was soon forgotten, and the Peloponnesians cast their eyes again towards the isthmus, and took it very ill if any one spoke against their returning home; and, resolving to depart that night, the pilots had orders what course to steer.

Themistocles, in great distress that the Greeks should retire, and lose the advantage of the narrow seas and strait passage, and slip home every one to his own city, considered with himself, and contrived that stratagem that was carried out by Sicinnus. This Sicinnus was a Persian captive, but a great lover of Themistocles, and the attendant of his children. Upon this occasion, he sent him privately to Xerxes, commanding him to tell the king that Themistocles, the admiral of the Athenians, having espoused his interest, wished to be the first to inform him that the Greeks were ready to make their escape, and that he counselled him to hinder their flight, to set upon them while they were in this confusion and at a distance from their land army, and hereby destroy all their forces by sea. Xerxes was very joyful at this message, and received it as from one who wished him all that was good, and immediately issued instructions to the commanders of his ships, that they should instantly set out with two hundred galleys to encompass all the islands, and enclose all the straits and passages, that none of the Greeks might escape, and that they should afterwards follow with the rest of their fleet at leisure. This being done, Aristides, the son of Lysimachus, was the first man that perceived it, and went to the tent of Themistocles, not out of any friendship, for he had been formerly banished by his means, as has been related, but to inform him how they were encompassed by their enemies. Themistocles, knowing the generosity of Aristides, and much struck by his visit at that time, imparted to him all that he had transacted by Sicinnus, and entreated him that, as he would be more readily believed among the Greeks, he would make use of his credit to help to induce them to stay and fight their enemies in the narrow seas. Aristides applauded Themistocles, and went to the other commanders and captains of the galleys, and encouraged them to engage; yet they did not perfectly assent to him, till a galley of Tenos, which deserted from the Persians, of which Panætius was commander, came in, while they were still doubting, and confirmed the news that all the straits and passages were beset; and then their rage and fury, as well as their necessity, provoked them all to fight.

As soon as it was day, Xerxes placed himself high up, to view his fleet, and how it was set in order. Phanodemus says, he sat upon a promontory above the temple of Hercules, where the coast of Attica is separated from the island by a narrow channel; but Acestodorus writes, that it was in the confines of Megara, upon those hills which are called the Horns, where he sat in a chair of gold, with many secretaries about him to write down all that was done in the fight.

When Themistocles was about to sacrifice, close to the admiral's galley, there were three prisoners brought to him, fine looking men, and richly dressed in ornamented clothing and gold, said to be the children of Artayctes and Sandauce, sister to Xerxes. As soon as the prophet Euphrantides saw them, and observed that at the same time the fire blazed out from the offerings with a more than ordinary flame, and a man sneezed on the right, which was an intimation of a fortunate event, he took Themistocles by the hand, and bade him concentrate the three young men for sacrifice, and offer them up with prayers for vitory to Bacchus the Devourer; so should the Greeks not only save themselves, but

also obtain victory. Themistocles was much disturbed at this strange and terrible prophecy, but the common people, who in any difficult crisis and great exigency ever look for relief rather to strange and extravagant than to reasonable means, calling upon Bacchus with one voice, led the captives to the altar, and compelled the execution of the sacrifice as the prophet had commanded. This is reported by Phanias the Lesbian, a philosopher well read in history.

The number of the enemy's ships the poet Æschylus gives in his tragedy called *The Persians*, as on his certain knowledge, in the following words:

"Xerxes, I know, did into battle lead
One thousand ships; of more than usual
  speed
Seven and two hundred. So it is agreed."

The Athenians had a hundred and eighty; in every ship eighteen men fought upon the deck, four of whom were archers and the rest men at arms.

As Themistocles had fixed upon the most advantageous place, so, with no less sagacity, he chose the best time of fighting; for he would not run the prows of his galleys against the Persians, nor begin the fight till the time of day was come, when there regularly blows in a fresh breeze from the open sea, and brings in with it a strong swell into the channel; which was no inconvenience to the Greek ships, which were low-built, and little above the water, but did much to hurt the Persians, which had high sterns and lofty decks, and were heavy and cumbrous in their movements, as it presented them broadside to the quick charges of the Greeks, who kept their eyes upon the motions of Themistocles, as their best example, and more particularly because, opposed to his ship, Ariamenes, admiral to Xerxes, a brave man and by far the best and worthiest of the king's brothers, was seen throwing darts and shooting arrows from his huge galley, as from the walls of a castle. Aminias the

Decelean and Sosicles the Pedian, who sailed in the same vessel, upon the ships meeting stem to stem, and transfixing each the other with their brazen prows, so that they were fastened together, when Ariamenes attempted to board theirs, ran at him with their pikes, and thrust him into the sea; his body, as it floated amongst other shipwrecks, was known to Artemisia, and carried to Xerxes.

It is reported that, in the middle of the fight, a great flame rose into the air above the city of Eleusis, and that sounds and voices were heard through all the Thriasian plain, as far as the sea, sounding like a number of men accompanying and escorting the mystic Iacchus, and that a mist seemed to form and rise from the place from whence the sounds came, and, passing forward, fell upon the galleys. Others believed that they saw apparitions, in the shape of armed men, reaching out their hands from the island of Ægina before the Grecian galleys; and supposed they were the Æacidæ, whom they had invoked to their aid before the battle. The first man that took a ship was Lycomedes the Athenian, captain of the galley, who cut down its ensign, and dedicated it to Apollo the Laurel-crowned. And as the Persians fought in a narrow arm of the sea, and could bring but part of their fleet to fight, and fell foul of one another, the Greeks thus equalled them in strength, and fought with them till the evening forced them back, and obtained, as says Simonides, that noble and famous victory, than which neither amongst the Greeks nor barbarians was ever known more glorious exploit on the seas; by the joint valour, indeed, and zeal of all who fought, but by the wisdom and sagacity of Themistocles.

3. THE THEMISTOCLES DECREE AND THE EVACUATION OF ATTICA*

Few periods in all ancient history are more familiar than the months from May to September of 480 B.C., when the enormous army and navy of Xerxes, King of the Persians, crossed from Asia to Europe and bore down upon the heart of Greece. Few battles are more famous than Salamis, where Xerxes, after carrying all before him, crushing Leonidas at Thermopylai and forcing the Greek fleet to withdraw from Artemision, sacking and burning Athens saw his navy defeated by a far smaller force and the tide of Persian might begin to ebb. How did the Greeks prepare to face the Persian threat, the greatest they had ever met, and what planning achieved this remarkable result?

Most of our information comes from Herodotos, writing some fifty years later and basing his account on the versions that were current among the Greeks states in his own time. He gives major credit to the Athenians for having given up a public distribution of revenue from their silvermines in order to build a fleet of two qundred ships. This judgement has, as he himself expected, brought the charge of Athenian bias, but no one has suggested that he shows favour towards Themistokles, the author of the policy, about whom he tells a number of scandalous stories. Later writers add little that goes back to contemporary evidence. There is the account of the fourth-century historian Ephoros, from Kyme in Asia Minor, condensed in Diodorus Siculus, and some of the biographies of Nepos and Plutarch, of Roman date. What little we have had in the way of early documents takes the form of

* Michael H. Jameson, "Waiting for the Barbarian," *Greece and Rome*, second series, 8 (Oxford, 1961), pp. 5–18. Reprinted by permission of The Clarendon Press, Oxford.

memorials after the event: the grave epigram for Leonidas and his comrades, for instance, which tells us that they died at Thermopylai 'obedient to the words' of the Lacedaemonians, but does not say what those words were. Were they really told not to retreat even when the pass had been lost? And Aeschylus, undoubtedly an eye-witness, has a magnificent description of the battle of Salamis in his tragedy, *The Persians*, produced at Athens eight years later, but the only clue he gives to the Greek preparations is the remark of the Chorus (line 238), 'They [the Athenians] have a font of silver, a treasury in the earth', which reminds us of how the fleet was built. Plutarch, however, knew and even seemed to quote a few words from an Athenians decree, moved by Themistokles after the loss of Thermopylai and Arte-mision, for the evacuation from the city of the women and children to safety in Troizen (across the Saronic Gulf, in the Peloponnese) and the embarkation of all men on board ship. Even this tantalizing scrap of information had been called into question by Bury, who pointed out that there would be no room for all men if the fleet had already been manned to stop the enemy at Artemision. So the account of Herodotos has remained the most reliable and the most complete, as well as the earliest.

In 1932 or 1933 Anargyros Titires, a farmer of the village of Damala, near the site of ancient Troizen, found the grave of a child while digging a pit for a lemon-tree; on one side of the grave was a marble slab. It was the upper part of an inscribed stele, about 2 feet high, 15 inches wide, and 3 inches thick. Titres' land is near the ruins of the old church of Saint Soteira, which may continue the title of Artemis Soteira whose shrine bordered the ancient agora of Troizen, according to Pausanias. The farmer used the stele as a step in his house for some years, and later left it out in the farmyard. In these years, if not earlier, the left side of the inscribed surface was badly damaged. In April of 1959, Christos Phourniades, the French master of the *gymnasion* in the town of Poros, near by, persuaded the farmer to contribute his stone to a collection of in-scriptions and minor antiquities being gathered together in a local coffee-house, a good example of a worthy and unsung enterprise whereby schoolmasters through-out Greece help to preserve her antiquities. In July of the same year my wife and I came to Troizen on our way to the village of Hermione, over the mountains, whose history and archaeology had been a special interest since our student days in Athens. We were curious to see if the villagers here, as in Hermione, had come upon inscriptions in recent years which might throw light on the relations of the two neighbouring city-states in antiquity. We took notes on the stones housed in the *kapheneion* as well as on others in the village. Titires's stele and a two-word gravestone were the only new texts we saw. A few weeks later, when I had finished my work in Hermione, I returned to make a full transcription.

It soon became clear that the inscription was important—an Athenian, not Troi-zenian, decree with talk of Salamis, Arte-mision, and 'the Barbarian'. It could only have to do with Troizen's hospitality to the Athenian refugees of 480 B.C. But it was not until I was back at the University of Pennsylvania and had an opportunity to study the text more carefully that I realized that, although the inscription might date from the fourth century, its contents did not. Since the inscription was engraved *stoichedon* (with the same amount of space for each letter) it was possible to determine exactly how many letters there had been in each line even where the surface of the stone was most battered. A growing suspicion made me decide to plot the words of Plutarch's quotation from Themistokles' decree on the graph paper on which I had written the mutilated be-ginning of this decree. There could be no mistaking the results: the first nine words

agreed exactly—τὴν μὲν πόλιν παρακατα-
θέσθαι τῇ ᾽Αθηνᾷ τῇ ᾽Αθηναίων μεδεούσῃ.
Then the 'Themistokles, son of Neokles, of
the deme Phrearrhoi,' who in the line before was listed as having made the motion,
was not the fourth-century Athenian of that
name and that township, as I had first
thought—it must be his ancestor, the great
Themistokles himself.

I have described this process of identification in full (at the risk of seeming
incredibly slow to realize the truth) in
order to share with others something of the
excitement of a discovery no student of
Greek history could ever have hoped to
make by his own deliberate efforts. The
forty-seven lines of the Greek text, probably the greater part of the decree, as
restored by me and the generous fraternity
of scholars that has advised me, have been
published with a detailed commentary in
the second issue for 1960 of *Hesperia*, the
journal of the American School of Classical
Studies at Athens (vol. xxix, pp. 198–223);
[a revised version of the text of the inscription resulting from the comments of
other scholars and a visit to Greece in 1961
has been published in the same journal
(vol. xxxi, 1962, pp. 310–15). From the
revised text] I give a translation of the
decree without indicating which words
have been restored on damaged parts of
the stone, except to note that the initial
invocation, 'The Gods,' no longer legible
on the stone, seems demanded by the
solemnity and the piety of the decree. I
insert a few explanatory notes in brackets.

The Gods

Resolved by the Council and the People

Themistokles, son of Neokles, of Phrearroi,
made the motion:

To entrust the city to Athena the Mistress of
Athens and to all the other Gods to guard and
defend from the Barbarian for the sake of the
land. The Athenians themselves and the
foreigners who live in Athens are to send their
children and women to safety in Troizen, their
protector being Pittheus, the founding hero of
the land. They are to send the old men and

their movable possessions to safety on Salamis.
The treasurers and priestesses are to remain on
the acropolis guarding the property of the gods.

All the other Athenians and foreigners of
military age are to embark on the 200 ships
that are ready and defend against the Barbarian
for the sake of their own freedom and that of
the rest of the Greeks along with the Lakedaim-
onians, the Korinthians, the Aiginetans, and
all others who wish to share the danger.

The generals are to appoint, starting tomorrow, 200 trierarchs, one to a ship, from among
those who have land and house in Athens and
legitimate children and who are not older than
fifty; to these men the ships are to be assigned
by lot. They are to enlist marines, 10 to each
ship, from men between the ages of twenty and
thirty, and four archers. They are to distribute
the servicemen [the marines and archers] by
lot at the same time as they assign the trierarchs
to the ships by lot. The generals are to write
up the rest ship by ship on white boards,
(taking) the Athenians from the lexiarchic
registers, the foreigners from those registered
with the polemarch. They are to write them up
assigning them by divisions, 200 of about one
hundred (men) each, and to write above each
division the name of the trireme and of the
trierarch and the servicemen, so that they may
know on which trireme each division is to
embark. When all the divisions have been composed and allotted to the triremes, the Council
and the generals are to man all the 200 ships,
after sacrificing a placatory offering to Zeus the
Almighty and Athena and Nike and Poseidon
the Securer.

When the ships have been manned, with 100
of them they are to meet the enemy at Artemision in Euboia, and with the other 100 they
are to lie off Salamis and the coast of Attica
and keep guard over the land. In order that all
Athenians may be united in their defense
against the Barbarian those who have been
sent into exile for ten years are to go to Salamis
and to stay there until the People come to some
decision about them, while those who have
been deprived of citizen rights are to have
their rights restored . . .

What is the historical significance of this
text? First of all there is the date of the
decree, that is, the date on which the
Athenians resolved to abandon their homes
and lands, send their families away, and

risk everything at sea. The naval engagements off Artemision in Euboea had still to be fought (in August) while the near-by 'gates' of Thermopylai were being defended by Leonidas. But all thought of defending, with the participation of Athenian hoplites, the passage of Tempe below Mt. Olympos in the far north of Greece had clearly been abandoned. The time then is after Themistokles' return from the congress of Greek states at the Isthmus of Corinth, following the abandonment of Tempe, probably early in June while Xerxes was still in Thrace. Now it has been customary to suppose that the Athenians only decided to leave their city when Thermopylai had been lost, the fleet had withdrawn from Artemision, and the Persians were pouring through central Greece. Certainly it is at this moment that Plutarch cites the decree. Not so Herodotos, who has heard a phrase, at least, from the decree (vii. 144. 3, '. . . along with those of the Greeks who wish') but does not date it; that is because he mentions the Athenian decision to take to the sea in his *introductory* discussion of the Greek preparations, when he singles out the Athenians for special praise. The evacuation of the civilians he mentions only when his narrative brings the Greek navy, followed by the Persians, to Attica, at which point he mentions a proclamation to clear the land. Plutarch and most modern historians have identified the proclamation and the decree. The error is understandable—there is no reason to think that Plutarch, or any later historian, knew more than the first two patriotic paragraphs of the text printed above, and so he did not have the vital reference to Artemision. His view has been reinforced by Herodotos' report, echoed by Athenians writers, that the Athenians had expected a Peloponnesian force in Boeotia to stop the Persians; they felt they had been betrayed and so were forced to the desperate measure of abandoning their city. It may well have been that in the summer of 480 B.C. many Athenians still expected, or hoped, that the

Persians would be stopped short of Attica, and it is even more likely that in the forties and thirties of the fifth century, when Herodotos was gathering his information, the Athenians were more inclined to blame the Spartans than the Persians for their hardships. But reflection will show that before Athens had her long walls, linking the city to the sea and isolating her from the land, a decision to put all her manpower on shipboard could only mean abandoning the city; the decree confirms that the two decisions go together, and, incidentally, Bury's objection is removed. The truth in fact seems more complimentary to both Spartans and Athenians. The Spartans did not betray the Athenians in order to hide behind a wall across the Isthmus of Corinth. The Athenians did not act out of panic but deliberately chose the bold policy of Themistokles while Xerxes was still far from his own borders. They had not been blinded by their brief moment of hoplite glory at Marathon in 490 B.C., but had already entered upon Themistokles' shipbuilding programme. If the foresight and leadership of Themistokles emerge all the more brilliant from a fog of anecdote and scandal, the courage of the Athenian people, who chose to follow him, is equally remarkable.

A second point follows closely upon the date of the decree: the Athenians planned to send only half of their 200 ships to Artemision. Whatever the final figures of their contingent, this decision reveals their intentions toward Artemision. It was not to be an all-out effort, and, indeed, it proved indecisive. There has never been any question but that only a fraction of the Greek land forces were engaged in the simultaneous action at Thermopylai (only 3,100 Peloponnesian hoplites compared to 23,800 at Plataia), and many explanations have been offered, in ancient and modern times—that Sparta's safety demanded the predicted death of a king, that the main force was delayed by the Karneian and Olympian festivals, that a token force was sent to secure Athenian support, that only a small force was needed to hold the pass while the fleet forced a decisive engagement. The decree shows that this last view (which never had ancient support) must now be abandoned, and that the Athenians, evacuating Attica, did not expect a full-scale resistance on land north of the Isthmus. Instead, the plan was to hold off the Persians as long as possible while Athens was evacuated, a larger fleet was mustered at Pogon, the harbour of Troizen (ships were expected from the West), and the defences of the Isthmus were strengthened. All but the Spartans, Thespiaians, and Thebans were detached and withdrew from Thermopylai in time. Leonidas is said to have known that a detachment of Persians had taken a mountain path and would come out in his rear. Perhaps he delayed his own withdrawal too long. When caught front and rear the Thebans surrendered, and it is only to be wondered that they fought so long; without an Isthmus to protect their city or a fleet to evacuate their families, they had sent only a small contingent to match the Spartans, and with the loss of Thermopylai their resistance was at an end. Leonidas and the rest fought to the last man. Their valour is no less commendable if we suppose it was not planned as a useless sacrifice.

If Artemision and Thermopylai were not intended to be the main defence line, Salamis and the Isthmus gain in importance; and it is worth remembering that the Persians never landed on Salamis nor breached the Isthmus defences. The straits of Salamis had distinct advantages over those between Euboea and Thessaly. The entrances at their narrowest were only one sea mile wide (compared to the two miles west of Artemision) and the widest stretch was only two sea miles, as against the five miles over which most of the fighting at Artemision actually took place. These were important considerations for a smaller, slower fleet. At Salamis the Athenians were supported by their own home guard of men over fifty and (probably) under twenty, and finally there was the incalculable effect on their morale of having their country before them and their families at their back. 'O sons of the Greeks, come now, free your fatherland, free your children and your wives, the seats of your ancestral gods, the graves of your forefathers. Now the fight is for everything.' Perhaps, then, it needed less prophetic foresight than insight into the plans of Themistokles for the Delphic priestess to tell the Athenians, 'divine Salamis will destroy many sons of women when Dementer is scattered or when she is gathered in [at the autumn ploughing and sowing, or the early summer harvest],' while recommending a 'wooden wall' but saying not a word of Artemision.

One detail of the Athenian plans has always puzzled historians: Themistokles had convinced the Athenians that when Apollo's priestess recommended the 'wooden wall' she meant the 200 ships, but others argued that she meant a wooden barricade on the acropolis. When the Persians sacked the city they found on the acropolis (and put to death) a few Athenians, treasurers of the sanctuary and poor men who had stayed, trusting in their interpretation of the oracle or out of poverty (the meaning of the latter, I would guess, is that in the absence of any public commissariat some of those without resources of their own thought themselves as well off at Athens with the Persians as with their countrymen on Salamis). From the decree we now see that treasurers (probably) and priestesses (certainly) were *required* to stay on the acropolis. I would take this to be a concession to the most conservative and religious element in Athens that *wanted* to stay on the acropolis. At the time there may still have been hope that the Persians would respect the gods if the city itself were abandoned, and that the gods would not, in the end, permit the destruction of their shrines. Later the Athenians were willing enough to dwell on the barbarities of the Persians, but preferred to pass over their own instructions that doomed the keepers of the acropolis. It is only in the Roman Nepos' *Life of Themistokles* (2. 8) that we come close to the intent of the decree.

The decree gives us a vivid picture of the young Athenian democracy at work in the moment of its greatest danger. There is no distinction drawn between classes; knights, hoplites, thetes are all to row; marines are selected by age alone. The trierarchs are chosen for qualities of command: they must be of regular military age and have a heavy stake in the future of Athens—landed property and legitimate children, the latter being the same qualification as Leonidas demanded of the men who came with him to Thermopylai. Later the trierarchy came to be little more than a burdensome tax on the rich. The ten elected generals appoint the trierarchs and supervise the distribution of men to the ships. The polemarch who, as late as Marathon ten years earlier, had been the commander-in-chief, is now only the magistrates who keeps the rolls of foreigners resident in Athens (metics, distinguished here from the citizens only in that they are not eligible for the trierarchy). Citizens are enrolled in registers kept in their demes, the ληξιαρχικὰ γραμματεῖα; since the names of *all* citizens are to be found in them there is no support for the view that they were essentially property-owners' rolls, and it seems more likely that the λῆξις at the source of the word had originally to do with the assignment of citizens to the Council by lot. The Council that joins with the ten generals in the final outfitting of the ships is the annual council of 500 (50 from each tribe) established by Kleisthenes. There is no word of the Areopagus, the old council of ex-archons, to which later conservative sources had given major credit for the success of the complex operation.

The decree also confirms the prompt reconciliation with political enemies. The opponents of Themistokles who had been exiled for ten years by ostracism, notably Aristeides and Xanthippos, Perikles' father, are to come to Salamis where the assembly (of those citizens not on shipboard) are to decide the terms of their recall. It is a generous but at the same time a careful move. What followed the last words preserved on the stone was probably the formula of a general amnesty.

How, in fact, were the provisions of the decree carried out? Let us begin with the gods: 'The gods keep safe the city of divine Pallas'—so Aeschylus' Persian messenger (line 347) on the results of the battle of Salamis; and when Xerxes' fleet sailed away, Themistokles said, 'Not we, but the gods and heroes, have brought this to pass. . . .' The women and children, when the time came, seem to have gone to Salamis and Aigina, nearer to home and their men, as well as to Troizen. As we have seen, there was probably a strong feeling among many that they would not really have to leave. It had to be argued that even Athena had left, since her sacred snake on the acropolis had not touched his monthly honey cake. At Troizen the refugees were welcomed generously, and Plutarch cites a Troizenian decree moved by a certain Nikagoras to provide two obols per person per day for maintenance, to give the children permission to pick whatever fruit they wanted, and to pay the wages of their teachers.

The Athenians, in the end, may have sent more than a hundred ships to Artemision. There is reason to think that their total fleet numbered at least 240 triremes and that besides the 200 representing the emergency reserve there was a regular force on active duty at the time of the expedition to Tempe. Had some of these stayed on patrol at Artemision when the army was withdrawn from Tempe they might account, in part, for Herodotos' total of 127 or 180. But in any case it is only on the hypothesis of a large reserve lying off Attica that the Athenians could have made good their losses at Artemision and still have had 180 ships at Salamis. The choice of Salamis for a decision was amply justified in the event, though it took still more of Themistokles' skill to bring it off; but that is another story.

What was the history of the decree itself, and how is it that we find it preserved only in a late-fourth-century inscription from Troizen? No doubt the Council and the board of generals (specifically, their chairman, who at this time could only have been Themistokles) had copies as authority for their actions in the coming months. By the time of the Persians' final withdrawal from Greece in 479 B.C. after Plataia, any publication of the decree by engraving it on stone would have been for memorial rather than practical reasons, and its history would have been tied to the fluctuating fortunes of Themistokles, its author. After the war Themistokles built a shrine to Artemis of Good Counsel (*Aristoboule*) near his own house, an obvious reference to his services to Athens, thus causing much resentment; a text of the most famous sample of his good counsel would have stood appropriately beside his own likeness in the shrine (but that statue, to be sure, may have been dedicated later). Within ten years he was an exile in disgrace, and when he died a Persian governor in Magnesia on the Maeander his bones could not be returned openly to Attica for burial since he had been condemned as a traitor. It seems unlikely that any public memorials to his glory could have survived in Athens. But eventually his family was restored to citizen rights and made dedications in his honour. In the mid-fourth century a Themistokles of Phrearrhoi may have been the archon of 347/6 B.C.; the family survived to Plutarch's own day in the person of a Themistokles who was a fellow student at the Academy. It is probably to the family pride of Themistokles' descendants that we should attribute the survival of a text of the decree in one form or another into the fourth century.

Herodotos, who had little interest in public documents, seems to have heard at least a phrase from the decree. Although by reporting the Athenian feeling that the Peloponnesians should have met the Persians in Boeotia he gives the impression, no doubt common in the anti-Spartan atmosphere of Athens in the forties and thirties, that the decree was passed at the last minute, none of his *facts* is inconsistent with the decree. Thucydides, of course, deals only incidentally with this period; his own words permit an early date and a deliberate decision, but the Athenian arguments before the council of Sparta's Peloponnesian League in 432 B.C. claim 'we embarked on our ships and prepared to face the danger without resentment against you for not having come to our aid earlier,' an attitude that is most clearly expressed in the *Panegyric* of Isokrates, who either did not know or ignored the latter part of the decree. A few words of Lysias are reminiscent but could as well come from a memory of the facts as of the decree.

The first direct reference to the decree after Herodotos is a report in Demosthenes that his arch-enemy Aischines, in his anti-Macedonian phase, had read out in public the decrees of Miltiades vefore Marathon (to march out and face the enemy) and Themistokles before Salamis, and the Oath of Ephebes taken on the completion of their training. This marks a revival of interest in the patriotic documents of the past sharpened by awareness of the Macedonian threat, which reaches its climax in the years of Lykourgos' leadership in the thirties and twenties of the fourth century. Lykourgos himself had read out the Ephebic Oath and the Oath of the Greeks before Plataia, the latter being also known to Herodotos but deprived, like the decree, of chronological moorings. Both oaths have been found on a fourth-century inscription from the deme of Acharnai. This was also a time of local Attic historiography: Kleidemos wrote favourably of Themistokles' part in the evacuation of Athens, and we may be sure the great man's namesake was willing enough to furnish the historian with documents; Phanodemos also wrote of Themistokles, and was a close associate of Lykourgos. Consequently circumstances were favourable for the publications of the decree, and for publication in full, since there was no longer any need to blacken Sparta's name. Now the Troizenian text, as the orthography shows, is derived immediately either from a fourth-century Attic inscription or manuscript; there was, of course, no reason why the old Attic spelling in the old Attic alphabet should have been preserved. In the current style Themistokles' father's name and deme were included. We must look, therefore, for an occasion in the late fourth century when the Troizenians would have wanted to renew their old friendship with Athens and to remember the heroic days of Salamis and the welcome they gave the families of the Athenians.

The conditions are best met in the years 324 and 323 B.C., or perhaps shortly before, when a group of pro-Athenian Troizenians who had opposed the Macedonians, been exiled, and found refuge in Athens, where they were honoured with Athenian citizenship precisely because of their city's hospitality towards the Athenians in 480, finally returned home. In 323 their city welcomed the exiled Demosthenes and joined Athens in the short-lived 'Lamian War' against the Macedonians. By 322 all resistance had been crushed. The character of the letters on the stone permit such a date, and the atmosphere of patriotic enthusiasm, when the Macedonians were being likened to the Persian 'Barbarians,' is appropriate for recalling Troizen's short-lived glory. We may speculate that the stone also carried the recent Athenian decree granting citizenship to the Troizenian exiles, or possibly the Troizenian decree of Nikagoras welcoming the Athenians in 480 B.C. The location of the stone may have been the sanctuary of Apollo Thearios (mentioned in a number of inscriptions as the place where they were to be set up), or the stoa dedicated by Athenian refugees of 480 and containing statues of the women and children, both in the area of the ancient agora.

In later antiquity the decree was well known, but only the first lines, the first two patriotic paragraphs of our translation. The attic historians did not long survive in their original form, and were excerpted and condensed. These lines were eminently suitable for school books: Nepos, Quintilian, Plutarch, and Aristeides quote or paraphrase them; this last, a rhetorician of the second century A.D., has, surprisingly, the most complete version, a fact I would rather attribute to the presence of the beginning of the decree in the rhetorical handbooks than to his scholarship. In his usual overblown style he describes it as 'the fairest, most brilliant, and most perfect witness for virtue under the sun. . . . Some one of the gods spoke with the tongue of Themistokles.' Perhaps he was not altogether wrong, though we may prefer Thucydides' more sober remarks on Themistokles himself, that 'he was the best judge of the immediate situation after the briefest reflection, and most competent in his estimate of a very wide range of future events'—'a very wide range,' as an ancient commentator points out; not everything, for 'only god knows everything', and in the end Themistokles misjudged the men on whom his own greatness depended.

4. THE VALUE OF THE THEMISTOCLES DECREE*

The first wave of scholarship after the publication of the decree focused on the question of its authenticity. The following essay deals with that question in a penetrating way that leaves aside its more technical aspects.

Although most students of the question seem to have concluded that the Themistocles Decree is a forgery,[1] this consensus does not imply that the question of authenticity has been decisively answered. The difficulties involved in proving an ancient document spurious are easily imagined, and so it should not be surprising that no item in the decree, except the prescript, is demonstrably anachronistic or false. The arguments against authenticity have, necessarily, been as inferential and perhaps only as plausible as the counterarguments excogitated to meet them.[2] What has determined the prevailing negative attitude, therefore, is neither the intrinsics of the decree taken by themselves, though some seem suspicious, nor even its putatively fourth-century language.[3] All this can be got around.[4] The basic objection is that an important provision of the new version is contradicted by Herodotus, our major authority for the Persian Wars.[5] For

Herodotus explains the evacuation of Athens and the naval battle at Salamis as the unplanned consequence of the perfidy of the Spartans and their allies sometime after the Battle of Artemisium.[6] The Spartans, according to him, had engaged themselves to meet Xerxes somewhere in Boeotia, but turned instead to fortifying the Isthmus of Corinth and thereby necessitated the evacuation of Attica. The Themistocles Decree, on the other hand, provides for the evacuation of Athens and, probably, for a naval battle at Salamis before the issue of the Battles of Artemisium and Thermopylae could have been known.[7] These particulars are indeed mutually exclusive. But does it follow naturally and inevitably that the inscription therefore offers incorrect information?

The problem, I submit, is more complicated than would at first appear, and it involves a larger question even than the authenticity of the decree. It concerns our treatment of the ancient evidence and the degree to which we are willing to re-examine old assumptions in the light of freshly acquired information. For in rejecting the Themistocles Decree we seem to forget that we are asserting the superiority not of Herodotus' history but of our past interpretation of his history and that this interpretation has involved the rejection of some of his material because it has seemed improbable to us. Since, however, the decree has been rejected for containing these very same improbabilities, it is obvious that in quoting Herodotus against

* Charles W. Fornara, "The Value of the Themistocles Decree," *American Historical Review*, LXXII (1967), pp. 425–433.
[1] This was clear almost simultaneously with its discovery (cf. Sterling Dow, "Bibliography of the Purported Themistokles Inscription from Troizen," *Classical World*, LV [Jan. 1962], 105 B).
[2] Cf. Christian Habicht, "Falsche Urkunden zur Geschichte Athens im Zeitalter der Perserkriege," *Hermes*, LXXXIX (Jan. 1961), 1–35, and Helmut Berve, "Zur Themistokles-Inschrift von Troizen," *Bayerische Akademie der Wissenschaften, Philosophisch-Historische Klasse, Sitzungsberichte* (No. 3, 1961).
[3] See, above all, Mortimer Chambers, "The Authenticity of the Themistocles Decree," *American Historical Review*, LXVII (Jan. 1962), 306–16.
[4] See B. D. Meritt, "Greek Historical Studies," in *Lectures in Memory of Louise Taft Semple* (Cincinnati, Ohio, 1962), 21–34.
[5] So, e.g., Luigi Moretti, "Nota al Decreto di Temistocle trovato a Trezene," *Rivista di Filologia e di Istruzione Classica*, New Ser., XXXVIII (1960), 390–402; C. Hignett, *Xerxes' Invasion of Greece* (Oxford, Eng., 1963), 464; W. K. Pritchett, "Hero-

dotos and the Themistokles Decree," *American Journal of Archeology*, LXVI (Jan. 1962), 43–44; Chambers, "Authenticity of the Themistocles Decree," 309–10.
[6] Herodotus 8.40.2.
[7] Lines 6–9 with 40–44.

the decree as we have done, we argue in a circular manner. It is, in short, only a half-truth to say that Herodotus contradicts the Themistocles Decree; he also supports it. For there are passages in Herodotus, as will appear, that unambiguously imply an early decision to fight at Salamis and to evacuate the city. These passages have long been harshly treated. They have been interpreted out of all recognition, they have been rejected, or they have merely been ignored. The reason, of course, is that they strike us as improbable. We have decided what the proper sequence of events *must* have been. It is possible that we are right. I suggest, however, that it is now a question whether our correction of the ancient tradition may not have been pushed to an arbitrary extreme. There may be more reason to reject Herodotus' account of Spartan treachery as inconsistent with his own narrative than there is to use this possible inconsistency to reject the authenticity of the Themistocles Decree.

Before I begin, however, it would be well for me to state the premises crucial to my argument. They are, indeed, generally accepted.[8] They deserve repetition, nevertheless, for their relevance to the present question has perhaps been inadequately appreciated. I assume, what few would deny, that Herodotus' source, primarily oral, were diverse. There was not, that is to say, an Ur-Herodot, some coherent account of the Persian Wars which he simply repeated. It was Herodotus' contribution to seek out informants and to dovetail their remembrances in such a way as to create a connected and logically consequent narrative. Thus the coherence of the narrative, the interdependence of fact on fact, was largely his own creation. The facts themselves, on the other hand, derive from individuals who passed on to him their recollections of specific events or episodes. As to the accuracy of their recollection, we hardly needed Thucydides' celebrated criticism[9] of the uncertain memory of even contemporaries to be aware that Herodotus' informants guaranteed the existence of a tradition but not necessarily the truth of it. The corollary is important: inconsistencies in Herodotus' narrative attest his reliance upon divergent memories. We cannot, therefore, speak of "the tradition" as if it were ultimately uniform; nor ought we to proceed on the assumption that all of Herodotus' informants, *if only we properly interpret them*, had the same story to tell. It is methodologically improper to smooth away internal contradictions, for in doing so we obscure the vestiges of contemporary traditions in the presumption that one of them must be correct and that the others must be harmonious with it. Now if this is true, it bears significantly upon the question of the Themistocles Decree. Certain details in Herodotus presuppose a tradition very like that recorded in the recently discovered inscription.[10]

Herodotus tells the story (7.140–44) of the two oracles delivered at Delphi to the Athenians. The first advised the Athenians to flee to the ends of the earth; the second warned them against attempting any land battle with the barbarians, stating that though Attica would be ravaged wooden walls would save the citizenry and then added, disjunctively, that Salamis would be a scene of destruction. These oracles Herodotus dates unambiguously to the time before the Battles of Artemisium

---

[8] See Felix Jacoby, "Herodotos," in August von Pauly and Georg Wissowa, *Realencyclopädie*, Suppl. 2 (Stuttgart, 1913), cols. 392 ff.

[9] Thucydides 1.22.3.

[10] I should like to emphasize the word "tradition." Proponents of the authenticity of the decree, when they deal with the evidence in Herodotus that supports their position, are apt to assume that these passages prove the authenticity of the inscription. Actually, as I argue, they can provide confirmation only of the existence in the fifth century of an oral tradition transmitted to Herodotus that is similar to that embodied in the new document.

and Thermopylae.[11] The second oracle therefore implies—unless we attribute the power of true prophecy to Apollo's oracle—that Salamis was being at least considered as the location for a naval battle even before the failure at Artemisium. R. W. Macan, the shrewdest of Herodotus' commentators, observed that Herodotus' date is "out of the question, from a historical and psychological point of view." According to him, "the second oracle was obviously obtained with especial reference to the impending battle of Salamis." And this, he believed, presupposed that the Battle of Artemisium already had been fought. Macan's conclusions have generally been followed, and reasonably so. Herodotus' dating of an oracle, which implies that Salamis had been determined upon before the Battle of Artemisium was fought, is, as we know, contradicted by his later assertion that the selection of Salamis was the extemporaneous consequence of the failure of the Peloponnesian army to appear in Boeotia. There seemed little choice but to reject Herodotus' dating of the oracles and to set it down to some inexplicable confusion on his part. Surely the matter stands differently now. I do not see how we can avoid the conclusion that here he followed the tradition also preserved in the Themistocles Decree or, rather, that he related an episode embedded in that tradition. Of course, we may still choose to reject the date Herodotus assigns to the oracle. If we do so, however, we are in danger of proceeding in an arbitrary manner. We begin by rejecting the decree because Herodotus contradicts it, and we end by rejecting a relevant passage of Herodotus because it contradicts us.

Not merely the dating assigned by Herodotus to the oracles sustains the inference that the Themistocles Decree preserves genuine fifth-century tradition. Consider the implications of Herodotus'

discussion of that famous second oracle, that of the "wooden walls." The oracle is a double alternative. The first part states that all Athens will be destroyed except for the wooden walls and that the Athenians must run away. The second part begins with the line: "But you divine Salamis will destroy the sons of women." From the form of the oracle, therefore, we may infer that Delphi responded to a double question. And from the answer delivered we can reasonably infer what the questions were and, not improbably, what answers the questioners hoped for.

The first part of the oracle implies something like the following question: "Will Athens be destroyed and, if so, ought we not to emigrate in our ships to some remote corner of Hellas?" The second question put to the oracle seems to have been: "Would it not be better to stake everything upon a naval battle at Salamis?" Delphi, it appears, was asked to pronounce upon the crucial issue dividing the Athenians and seems to have done the best it could. It gave an answer acceptable to the advocates of emigration (the wooden walls are unquestionably ships), and, although negative about the prospects at Salamis, nevertheless Delphi was ambiguous enough to ensure that if a naval battle were attempted the oracle would be correct whatever the issue.

This reconstruction may appear hazardous. It is, however, fully supported by Herodotus, who informs us in considerable detail of the state of mind at Athens upon the receipt of the oracle. Athens, he says, was divided. One group wished to emigrate; another wished to fight. *Chresmologoi*, the expounders of oracles, men who would have known, if any could have, what Delphi intended by its oracle, understood the oracle to support the first alternative.[12]

11 This should not be disputed. (See Hignett, *Xerxes' Invasion*, 441.)

12 Herodotus 7.143.3. It should be unnecessary to enter here into a discussion characterized by the wildest flights of fancy. That part of the oracle which invokes Salamis is (at least) ambiguous. It cannot therefore be a mandate to Themistocles to

In Herodotus' words, these experts "were against preparing for a naval battle and the whole burden of what they said was that they should not even raise their hands in defense but should instead leave the land of Attica and settle in a new one." According to Herodotus, however, Themistocles gave his interpretation of the oracle, and the matter came to a vote. Themistocles won, and a decree was passed—dated by Herodotus to a time before the Battle of Artemisium—stipulating that the Athenians would engage the barbarian by sea with all their forces. The implication, obviously, is that the Athenians, in making this decision, renounced any hope of stopping the intruders by land. If so, they renounced Attica, precisely what we should have expected in view of what the oracle had predicted. They therefore had no choice but to evacuate or to plan for evacuation while they awaited the issue of naval combat. Is this not the Themistocles Decree? Herodotus, to be sure, does not mention Salamis when he alludes to the decree, and some scholars have maintained that he must have named it if Salamis were in fact then under consideration. Is it not enough that Herodotus

claims that the decree was passed as a consequence of the oracle and that the oracle mentions Salamis? It is plain enough, surely, that the Themistocles Decree has impeccable claims to being based on what is at least an authentic tradition. Whoever told Herodotus of the oracles and dated them as Herodotus indicated, and whoever added the account of political conflict at Athens, evidently reported a version of the bygone events that tallies remarkably with that third-century document (and incidentally permits a reasonable explanation of why the matter came to a vote in the first place). This tradition, then, is demonstrably not the idle speculation or tendentious combination of some forger of the *fourth* century. That Herodotus later gives another explanation for the evacuation of Athens merely proves that Herodotus speaks with many voices.

It will be alleged, perhaps, that Herodotus misdated the oracle and its consequences and that too much is being made of an error. Or, again, the discrepancy can be explained away. Thus one doubter of authenticity[13] admits, indeed, that Delphi was consulted. He denies, however, that the responses were those recorded by Herodotus. He proceeds to tell us what the oracles really said and how they really should be dated. Does he have private information? Only those passages of Herodotus which support his opinions, apparently, are truly authoritative. Surely this is an arbitrary way to treat the evidence and involves, as I have tried to show, a basic misunderstanding of the nature of oral tradition and the methods of Herodotus. If Herodotus' authority means anything, we are at least obligated to assume that he reported accurately what was told him. Ultimately, to be sure, we must reject or accept Herodotean traditions as true or untrue—or as likely or unlikely. Before we

---

fight at Salamis. What the Delphic priests intended by their oracle cannot perhaps be known, though if the Athenian *chresmologoi* (on which, see J. H. Oliver, *The Athenian Expounders of the Sacred and Ancestral Law* [Baltimore, 1950], 1 ff.) understood it as Herodotus reports, we must assume, as they were well versed in their profession, that their interpretation was right: that these men of the early fifth century, the sophisticated expounders of oracles, could accurately estimate the intended effect of an oracle propounded by Delphi. (I am assuming, of course, that the oracle was rational and intended some directive, and also that it is genuine. Our one criterion for determining what oracles are genuine and what oracles are fabrications after the event is their ambiguity or lack of it. This oracle, therefore, because it is ambiguous, must be presumed genuine, and so it has been judged by, among others, H. W. Parke and D. E. W. Wormell, *The Delphic Oracle* [Oxford, Eng., 1961] 170. I do not understand the logic of those scholars who allege that the oracle is a prediction after the event. The words of the oracle do not predict the vitory at Salamis; nor were they so interpreted, except by Themistocles, who wished to fight there. They are at best only reconcilable with it.)

---

13 Pierre Amandry, "Thémistocle: Un décret et un portrait," *Bulletin de la Faculté des Lettres de Strasbourg* (May–June 1961), 424–25.

come to that, however, we must try to isolate as objectively as possible what the traditions may have been. General considerations aside, however, the likelihood that Herodotus has committed an error is reduced considerably by the discovery of the Themistocles Decree. The coincidence, if accidental, is astonishing. One other item in Herodotus' history, in any case, will show conclusively, I think, that he actually is repeating a tradition (whether it be true or not) and not merely muddling his own history.

Herodotus relates (8.44.1) that the Plataeans proceeded *immediately upon their withdrawal* from Artemisium to evacuate their households. Herodotus is quite specific: "as the Greeks departed from Artemisium, the Plataeans, when they reached Chalcis, disembarked at the part of Boeotia over against Chalcis and turned to the removal of their households." There is no choice but to assume, therefore, as Macan long ago conceded, that the Plataeans (and the Athenians) had reached the decision to evacuate while at Artemisium. How can this be reconciled with the belief that the Athenians (and presumably the Plataeans) were forced to evacuate because of the subsequent lapse of the Peloponnesians? There seems to be only one way: to assume that it was the failure at Artemisium that crystallized the decision to evacuate, and it should be noted that many of the scholars who have quoted Herodotus against the Themistocles Decree have assumed precisely this. To use a phrase well worn in this controversy, their assumption is irreconcilable with Herodotus. It not only is not supported by Herodotus; it contradicts him. It stultifies the motivation Herodotus specifically supplies: the Spartans' failure to appear in Boeotia. It is ironic, perhaps, that the Themistocles Decree has been rejected because it is inconsistent with the Herodotean motivation of the evacuation of Athens and the Battle of Salamis and yet that this too is in effect rejected because it

fails to operate satisfactorily in our own reconstruction of the events. We have taken insufficient care, apparently, in separating Herodotus from our inferences from Herodotus. We ought to use the former as the yardstick to measure off the possible validity of the new evidence.

The burden is clear. Herodotus has merged at least two variant traditions into his general account or, perhaps more accurately, has inserted the tradition of Spartan betrayal into a narrative with which it is at odds. Probably Herodotus did not notice the contradictory implications of what he related. However that may be, the fact that some of the details he records presuppose the early decision to evacuate Athens and to engage the Persians at Salamis permits the conclusion that the tradition embodied in the Themistocles Decree is at least as old as that other tradition so censoriously quoted against it. If both traditions, consequently, may reasonably be traced to Herodotus and so to the fifth century, it follows that neither one is automatically preferable to the other. The major objection to the new version—that it was propounded in the fourth century—is removed,[14] and we must, therefore, choose between the two versions on other grounds. Which of the two, then, is more likely to be true?

Decision is by no means easy, and certainty is impossible. It is quite true that the resolve to evacuate, if made at some time after Artemisium, seems intrinsically more probable than the alternative. It is easy to imagine the Athenians suddenly turning to Delphi in desperation and being undecided after a naval defeat and the betrayal by the Spartans. Yet the alternative is not inconceivable and is supported—

14 See, e.g., Hignett, *Xerxes' Invasion*, 464–65: "there can be no compromise on this point between the Herodotean and the later (presumably Ephorean) account; one or other of them must be wrong, and Herodotus' informants, aristocrats [!] and contemporaries [!], were surely in a better position to know the facts."

positively by Herodotus' dating of the oracles, negatively by the difficulty of reconciling some other dating with Herodotus' narrative. For the one obvious place, where most scholars, in fact, would like to date them, is excluded by Herodotus' very words, which again we would be forced to correct. Herodotus (8.40) says:

The Greek expedition put its ships into Salamis at the request of the Athenians. The Athenians requested that they anchor at Salamis for the following reasons, namely, that they might remove their women and children from Attica and, *in addition*, that they might consider what was to be done by them.

Herodotus then alludes to the Spartan betrayal and the evacuation. Now if we assume that it was at this time that the Athenians consulted Delphi and decided, after contention, to stay and fight, we must recognize that Herodotus has reported the events in the wrong order. The request for assistance in the evacuation of Athenian women and children to Aegina, Salamis, and Troizen, which he places first, necessarily presupposes a prior decision to leave Athens but to remain in Greece to continue the struggle.[15] On the other hand, Herodotus clearly believed that the evacuation of Athens and the Battle of Salamis were unpremeditated. One should not, however, overestimate the importance of this, for it only proves that the motif of Spartan betrayal was a solid part of the tradition of the Persian Wars in Athens of the 440's. It does not prove, though this has been alleged, that a tradition substantially the same, if not exactly the same, as the Themistocles Decree was not known

to Herodotus or to his informants. That would be an oversimplification. Nothing stands in the way of assuming, and the assumption is supported by contradictions already mentioned, that the decree of Themistocles and the tradition of Spartan betrayal were not felt to be mutually exclusive. Modern historians may see the contradiction, but we know too much about the methods of Herodotus and about the ease with which erroneous notions arise to argue, or assume, that the prevalence of one tradition necessarily implies that the other was nonexistent. The proper question to ask is, therefore: would *fifth*-century Athenian oral tradition have been more likely to invent a tradition of Spartan betrayal or a Themistocles Decree? I think the answer is clear enough. The invention of a Themistocles Decree would have served little purpose. It might have enhanced Themistocles' reputation for sagacity, but he probably was already in Persia and beyond the need of it. Again, invention of the decree might have given the Athenians cause for self-congratulation on the grounds that the desertion of their city proceeded from themselves alone. It is possible, but it does not seem very likely. I cannot imagine the Athenians of the middle of the fifth century so desirous of yet another garland that they would be willing to sacrifice for it the gratifying story of a Sparta that failed to keep its promises. For the motif of Spartan treachery is tendentious. It had the undoubted virtue of heaping discredit upon Sparta at a time when the two states had become enemies. And how easy it would have been to impute blame to the Spartans for something that did *not* happen. How hard it would be to confute the allegation. Can we not imagine the Athenians—an orator, for example (surely they were not perjurious only in the fourth century)—asking why the Battle of Plataea had not been fought a year earlier so that Athens might then have been spared? The Peloponnesians tried to block the way to their cities at the very time the

---

[15] The Athenians would hardly have moved their women and children into the very path of the Persians unless they intended to fight in that quarter. If Herodotus is right, therefore, the plan to fight at Salamis and to evacuate was formulated prior to the deliberations that Herodotus vaguely hints at and scholars have identified as those leading to these very decisions.

Athenians were forced to leave their own, and yet, a year later, a decisive battle by land in Boeotia ended the threat of the Persians. Whatever the commitment undertaken by the Spartans, the bare sequence of events would have sufficed to engender in the Athenians, now wise in retrospect, the suspicion that the sacrifice of their city had been needless. It could have been avoided if the Greek land army, that is, the Peloponnesians, had confronted the enemy resolutely in the same place just one year earlier. By easy progression, in the light of suspicion and hostility, the responsibility for the delay could eventually have been ascribed to Spartan indifference and even malevolence. And would not the charge of Spartan treachery have been readily believed two or three decades after the event? Would someone have pointed to the Themistocles Decree and argued that the two versions were logically irreconcilable? I regard the idea of a Spartan army—a *Spartan* army—reneging on its commitment to allies without whom it could hope for nothing but defeat as unlikely as the corollary that the Athenians, so treated, would have come hat in hand to these

friends for help in evacuating the city.[16] Others will perhaps judge differently.[17] In any case, it is easier to explain the genesis of the tradition of Spartan treachery in a century when Athens and Sparta were at war with each other than it is to condemn the historical implications of the Themistocles Decree as a *fifth*-century fabrication. Whether, therefore, the decree is a (copy of a) fourth-century reconstruction or an authentic copy of a fifth-century decree is a comparatively trivial question. What is valuable is that the historical tradition it preserves is consistent with the main burden of Herodotus' narrative and therefore may very possibly be true. If we choose to reject this version, therefore, we must do so purely on grounds of probability and not by treating the ancient evidence as Procrustes did his victims.

16 It is not as if the Athenians had no choice: they could still remove themselves to Italy.

17 Arguments from silence have their limitations, no doubt, but it is surely strange that Thucydides, when he chronicles the genesis of Athenian and Spartan enmity (1.89 ff.), makes no allusion to an action that could not but have contributed to it. Again, so damning a testimony to Spartan irresolution would have been a splendid *topos* for Thucydidean speeches condemning it.

5. THE GREEK STRATEGY*

Many scholars now accept the authenticity of the tradition represented by the Themistocles Decree and, incorporating its evidence, have returned to the older question of the Greek strategy leading to the battle of Salamis. The following article offers one interpretation.

I

The general strategy of the Greek forces at Thermopylae and Artemisium has never been very clear, and the publication of the "Themistocles decree" from Troezen and the numerous studies which followed on its heels have reopened a number of questions.

* J. A. S. Evans, "Notes on Thermopylae and Artemisium," *Historia*, XVIII (1969), pp. 389–406. Reprinted by permission.

The trouble with the Thermopylae-Artemisium campaign is that whatever strategy the Greeks may have intended to use, it did not work out. Worse, at least for the historian: it developed a legend of its own. Leonidas and his little force of Lacedaemonians were surrounded at Thermopylae and died, unsupported by the reinforcements which he had urgently requested. Since Herodotus informs us explicitly elsewhere that the Spartans had never imagined that the action at Thermopylae would be over so soon, the fact that no reinforcements arrived tells us nothing of what Spartan intentions were. But, on the face of it, Thermopylae looks like a half-hearted effort which somehow became an act of heroism, and Leonidas appears the victim either of foul play or his countrymen's reluctance to act with dispatch.

The traditions about the naval battle have suffered a stranger fate. For the indecisive engagement at Artemisium was followed by the crucial victory at Salamis, which did turn the tide, and made the victorious campaign of 479 possible. Salamis was the vindication of Themistocles' naval policy. It proved the worth of the Greek fleet, and so there has been a tendency among historians to argue backwards, and assume that the Greeks put their confidence in the navy from the beginning. How and Wells put it well: "That the role of the land force (at Thermopylae) is defensive and subordinate is indicated by the small number of men who fought under Leonidas (cf. 7. 202n.) compared with the full muster of ships at Artemisium (8. 1); its sole object to hold the pass long enough to enable the fleet to cripple Xerxes' navy." The catastrophe at Thermopylae spoiled these plans, but at Salamis, the navy did what the Greek strategists had planned it to do at Artemisium.

Whatever the merit of this view, on *a priori* grounds alone it is difficult to imagine that the *probouloi* who dispatched the Greek forces to Thermopylae and Artemisium could conceive of tactics of this sort. The Greeks had put together a large fleet, though it was not yet fully mustered, but all told, it was still inferior in numbers to the Persian navy, and the Greeks had no way of knowing in advance that the two storms reported by Herodotus would help towards evening the odds. Second, the Greek fleet was untried and in part, untrained; the Persian navy, on the other hand, had just completed a modernization program and was apparently formidable. The new Athenian triremes

must have been manned only with difficulty, for among the sailors were Plataeans, eager enough but ἄπειροι τῆς ναυτικῆς and 20 ships had Chalcidian crews. The last time that Greek and Persian navies had clashed in a major battle had been Lade in 494 B.C. and its outcome can hardly have given the Greeks much confidence. Leonidas' little force may seem modest beside the muster of ships at Artemisium, but this may have been because the Greeks had more confidence in its ability to carry out its assignment. For when the Greeks at the Isthmus planned the defense of Thermopylae, they had no knowledge of the Anopaea path by which the Greek position was turned, and it must be admitted that had no such path existed, Leonidas could probably have held Thermopylae with no great difficulty. It should be noted in any case that a Spartan king commanded the land forces, while the navy was under the command of only a Spartiate, and this is a clear indication of what, in Spartan eyes at least, was the important sector of the Thermopylae-Artemisium operation.

However, the great argument against the theory that it was the Greek fleet which was to seek a decisive victory at Artemisium is simply that it does not act like a squadron whose orders are to seek out the enemy and destroy it. Its manoeuvres as described by Herodotus, accurately in their essentials as I hope to show, are the tentative movements of a force with little self-confidence but with two objectives: first to try out the Persian fleet with minimum risk to itself, and second, to cover Leonidas' position. When the admirals heard of the catastrophe at Thermopylae, they retired. The obvious reason is that once Thermopylae had fallen, there was no point in the fleet remaining at Artemisium for the Persian army could now advance freely. But there was no strategic necessity which forced the Greeks to retire *at once* any more than strategic necessity forced them to retire from behind Salamis immediately, once Attica was in Persian hands, and if they had been at Artemisium to win a decisive engagement, why would they have retreated immediately? But that was not their purpose. They were supporting Leonidas' position, who was also supporting theirs, and once Thermopylae fell, they retired without delay.

The publication of the Troezen decree has given rise to another view, that neither Thermopylae nor Artemisium were any more than delaying operations, designed to give the Athenians time to evacuate and the navy to muster, and quite apart from the question of whether or not the decree is genuine, this view deserves examination. We have every reason to believe that Thermopylae and Artemisium were part of a well-planned strategy. The Persian army had to pass through Thermopylae, and the Greeks were well aware of the strength of this position, as well as the superiority of the hoplite soldier in the sort of fighting which would take place there. If the Persian fleet was to support the army, it would have to pass between Euboea and the mainland, and whether it did this by pushing into the strait north of Euboea, thereby operating in restricted waters, or detached a squadron to circumnavigate the island, thus dividing the fleet, the result would be to the advantage of the Greeks. In addition, by taking a position at Artemisium, the Greeks could force the Persian navy to anchor in a relatively exposed position, and from mid-July to mid-September is the period when the *meltem* blows up sudden storms in the north Aegean. Sheltered behind Euboea, the Greek fleet could ride out a summer squall, but the Persians might be less fortunate. Storms, of course, could not be foreseen, and they could not bulk large in the Greek plans, but not for nothing did the Athenians pray to Boreas!

Yet the fleet was the weaker link in this Thermopylae-Artemisium line of defense. The geography of the area gave the Greek ships some advantage, but not enough to make up for their inferior numbers and

their inexperience. Yet if they were defeated and forced to retire, Leonidas' position at Thermopylae would be more than untenable; it would become a trap, for the Persians could land forces on his line of retreat with their ships, and he would have great difficulty extricating his men. The impressive muster of ships at Artemisium is a recognition of the navy's weakness, and not evidence that the Greeks expected it to win a decision.

In contrast to what looks like carefully-planned strategy at Thermopylae and Artemisium, the tactics of Salamis appear to have been put together in haste to meet the exigencies of the occasion. We may dismiss Herodotus' account of the quarrels in the Greek camp before Salamis as no evidence or as bias against Corinth, as Plutarch does, but it does show that if any long-range plans had been made to fight at Salamis after a delaying action at Artemisium, the Peloponnesians must never have been partial to them. Moreover, it takes two sides to make a battle, and although the Greeks may have planned a fight at Salamis long in advance, how could they be certain that the Persians would cooperate and push into the narrow waters between the island and the mainland where the advantage of their superior mobility would be thrown away? *Pace* Hignett, the Persian army and navy had the choice of pushing on to the Isthmus, by-passing the fleet behind Salamis, for, as Alexander the Great was to show later, it was quite possible for an army to advance along a coast without having command of the seas adjacent. Had the Greek ships been equipped with big guns like a modern fleet, this might have been a hazardous manoeuvre. But an ancient fleet could not bombard a land force effectively, and if the Persian fleet declined to fight at Salamis in a position which the Greeks chose, the only way in which the Greeks could force battle would be to close with the Persians and fight them in a position not of their own choice. Grundy was right to underline the enormous risk in the strategy of Salamis.

There was, of course, one factor which made it likely that the Persians would be impatient to destroy the Greek sea power and might even take risks to do it. If we put Salamis on or about September 23rd, Xerxes had at best four weeks before the campaigning season for 480 was over. November and December are the months of greatest rainfall in most of Greece and by then, the Persian army should be in winter camp, and the fleet would have to find some safe anchorage. For the general safety of the invading forces, it would be better if the Persians fleet had secure command of the sea before the campaigning season was out, and Xerxes was anxious to get it at Salamis and push on. Therefore, out of impatience, he attacked.

That was what happened. But can the Greek *probouloi* planning their strategy at the Isthmus have known that it would happen? Knowing that retreat in the face of a well-armed foe entailed great risks both on land and sea, and that there was no real certainty that the Persian fleet would attack at Salamis if given the opportunity, could the *probouloi* have conceived of the Thermopylae-Artemisium front as a delaying operation, designed only to give the Athenians time to evacuate, and the navy to muster for battle at Salamis? It is unlikely. One scholar has proposed the attractive alternative that the Athenians did in fact plan evacuation before the fleet was sent to Artemisium, as the Troezen decree states, but at the same time, Thermopylae and Artemisium were all-out efforts. This would give us the best of both worlds. But it appears to me that if we are to understand the Thermopylae-Artemisium operation properly we must explain two problems connected with it: first, why was Leonidas sent with so few men, and second, what sense can we make of the fleet's manoeuvres, assuming, for the sake of argument, that Herodotus has described them correctly.

II

It will not do to say that the force under Leonidas' command at Thermopylae was so small because Sparta was not interested in fighting north of the Isthmus of Corinth. For she had already sent a force to Tempe, and although it had withdrawn, it was for sound military reasons rather than tepid leadership. In the view of the Peloponnesians (Sparta was leader of the Peloponnesian League before she was leader of the so-called Hellenic League against Persia) the Isthmus was the last feasible line of defense, and Sparta could not adopt a strategy which would denude the Isthmus of troops, and still maintain the confidence of her Peloponnesian allies. But the force Sparta did send to Thermopylae was commanded by a king, which should, under ordinary circumstances, mean that the Spartans thought it was an important expedition. After the Persian invasion was over, Athenian tradition sought—quite successfully—to give special credit to Athens for winning the war and to stigmatize Sparta as dilatory, if not treacherous; and in 479, when the Spartans wait until the harvest is over in the Peloponnesus before marching out to Plataea, they give some grounds for their discredit. But not in 480, when the peril was general and was recognized as such. If the Spartans regarded the Isthmus of Corinth as the last line of defense if all else failed, and acted accordingly, there was the best possible reason for it. They were right.

The alternative, then, is to believe that Leonidas did have an adequate force at his command to carry out his objective.

Leonidas had no more than 7,000 troops at his disposal which compares unfavourably with the 10,000 sent to Tempe. The discrepancy is probably to be explained in two ways. First, the absence of any Athenian hoplites, who were at Tempe. This can probably be explained by the fact that the Athenians were using all available manpower on their fleet, although the rowers would be mostly *thetes*, and as Hignett points out, it *is* odd that the Athenians could spare no hoplites at all for Leonidas. The best reason for their absence is perhaps that no one thought they were needed. The second reason why Leonidas had fewer men than Euainetos at Tempe is that he may have expected more support from the states in north and central Greece. If we can believe Plutarch, Thebes sent 500 men to Tempe, but only 400 to Thermopylae, who were, as Diodorus says, ἀπὸ τῆς ἑτέρας μερίδος, and almost certainly not hostages. Conceivably, Leonidas even expected a degree of help from Thessaly; at least he sent a messenger there, presumably one of the messengers he sent out ἐς τὰς πόλιας to ask for help when he reached Thermopylae. But by this time, all Thessaly had medized.

When the Persians approached, Leonidas' army took fright and the Peloponnesians advised retreat to the Isthmus. The cause of the fright was no doubt the discovery of the Anopaea path, which the Trachinians revealed to Leonidas, and the realization that medism in central and northern Greece had gone further than the allies had expected, in spite of the king's brave proclamation that he was only the vanguard of a large army. But Leonidas knew that retreat was out of the question even without the urgings of the Phocians and Locrians. He probably sent for reinforcements; whether they could have arrived in time or not is an open question.

The fact is that Leonidas did hold the pass with his force until his position was turned. Had it not been for the Anopaea path, the Persians could not have forced their way past the Greek army provided, of course, that its casualties were made good by reinforcements, and therefore it follows that the *probouloi*, who acted in ignorance of this path's existence, did provide Leonidas with an adequate force to the best of their knowledge. The fact that there were fewer soldiers at Thermopylae than at Tempe may not have been intentional, but

it remains that it was the Anopaea path which destroyed Leonidas, not the small number of his soldiers.

However, Leonidas' force may have been adequate for the moment, but it could not hold its position indefinitely without some relieving forces, and one may wonder why some of the reinforcements which were to come to Thermopylae later could not have been included in the original force. The reason given by Herodotus is the Carneia at Sparta and the Olympic games. Dascalakis remarks, "It was in the character and traditions of Sparta to offer some pretext related to religious notions each time it dragged its feet on a distant military expedition." [*Translated by D. K.*] There was, however, a military reason.

If the navy failed to hold back the Persians at Artemisium Leonidas' position could rapidly become untenable, and he would have to attempt a withdrawal under cover of night, as Darius did on his Scythian expedition and Pausanias at Plataea. The hoplite was formidable when he faced the enemy in battle-line, each man protecting his neighbour as well as himself with his shield, and if we can judge from Plataea, neither the Persian infantry nor cavalry could stand up to a hoplite charge. But it was a different matter to retreat. Hoplite armour gave inadequate protection from the rear, and a Greek army in retreat was vulnerable, especially to mounted archers.

The Greek navy was untried. Themistocles might be an enthusiast, but the ordinary Peloponnesian, particularly a Spartan, must have had small confidence in it. Odds had been closer to even at Lade, where the Ionians had had a naval tradition which the Greeks of the Hellenic League, except Corinth and Aegina, had never had. But at Lade, the Greeks had lost. Until it could be seen how the Greek fleet would perform against the Persians, it was unwise to commit any great number of men to Thermopylae. There was no intention or hope of winning a decisive victory there, but Leonidas could maintain the line of defense.

III

Herodotus gives a clear order of the events at sea. The fleet waited 11 days after Xerxes' departure from Therma before it too left. Already (the day before?) ten Persian ships had captured three Greek vessels (although the Athenian crew got away), and the news of this signalled from Sciathos induced the Greek fleet at Artemisium to retire to Chalcis leaving scouts on the heights of Euboea to report enemy movements. The Persian fleet took a full day to reach Cape Sepias from Therma: a voyage of 90 to 100 miles directly across the open sea but longer if the fleet clung to the coast. Next morning, the *meltem* blew up a gale which lasted three days stopping on the fourth. On the second day of the storm, the ἡμεροσκόποι on the hills came down to tell the Greeks of the Persian shipwreck, and the Greek fleet returned from Chalcis to its former anchorage. We should not object here that the Greeks could not make the 70-mile voyage back to Artemisium in the time available, since the Persians were able to cover the 100 miles or so between Therma and Cape Sepias in full day's sailing. When the storm stopped, the fleet was back at Artemisium.

From Cape Sepias, the Persians proceeded to Aphetae. This is apparently still the day on which the gale ceased; presumably the wind dropped in the morning. On seeing that, the storm notwithstanding, there was still a formidable Persian fleet, the Greeks planned to retire ἔσω ἐς τὴν Ἑλλάδα but were prevented by Themistocles' judicious use of bribes. The Persians for their part detached a squadron of 200 ships and sent it around Euboea to cut off the Greek retreat south-east, Myres quite rightly points out that the text does not say that they were dispatched *from* Aphetae, but it is clear on when they were sent. News of this squadron was brought to

the Greek admirals at Artemisium by the diver Scyllias, and the Greeks planned to retire during the night to meet this threat in their rear. But, as evening approached, they joined battle with the Persians, which was interrupted by nightfall.

This first skirmish can be explained as an action to cover the Greek withdrawal. However, that night, a second storm blew up which destroyed the circumnavigating squadron and must also be the reason for the failure of the Greek fleet to withdraw as planned. The next day, 53 Attic ships arrived, and at the same time, a message that the circumnavigating squadron was destroyed. This day also, there was a skirmish with the enemy. The third day, the Persians attacked, and there was a major engagement in which the Greeks suffered heavily, particularly the Athenians. That night, as the Greeks plan withdrawal again ἔσω ἐς τὴν Ἑλλάδα, news arrives of the catastrophe at Thermopylae, and without further delay, the Greek fleet retires.

The chief difficulty with this description of events is to make sense of the three withdrawals or planned withdrawals from Artemisium, which Herodotus attributes simply to fright. The latest attempt to do so has been by J. F. Lazenby, who accepts the first withdrawal to Chalcis, suggesting that Leonidas may not yet have been in position at Thermopylae. The second decision to withdraw described in Herodotus 8. 8–9 was a planned manoeuvre to move back to a point where the Greeks might hope to catch the squadron circumnavigating Euboea isolated, but where they could still cover Leonidas. It would follow that the third projected withdrawal ἔσω ἐς τὴν Ἑλλάδα was likewise a strategic retreat to a less exposed situation, but one from which Leonidas could still be covered.

This hypothesis has the virtue of trying to make sense of Herodotus' account rather than simply rejecting those parts of it which do not fit into the preconceived schemes of modern scholars, but it is not entirely satisfactory. Leonidas may not have been in position when the Greek fleet withdrew to Chalcis (although according to my calculations, he was) but even if he were not, this is at best a negative reason. We cannot show that a move took place by proving that no harm would come of it if it did! The storm could be alleged as a reason; it is probable that Eurybiades would have had to pull back to some extent to escape its fury, but according to our sources, the withdrawal took place before the storm arose. It was a strategic withdrawal, not a panicstricken flight, as is apparent from the fact that ἡμεροσκόποι were posted, and the admirals took care to keep in touch with Persian movements. What was the reason for it?

The solution of despair would be that in the absence of any logical motive for this withdrawal to Chalcis, it never took place, but this requires us to believe that Herodotus or his informants have included a gratuitous fiction into their account for no apparent reason or that they have somehow converted a move into the harbour of Histiaea or somewhere in the vicinity, into a voyage as far as Chalcis. If this will not do, we are left with one solution. Eurybiades withdrew to Chalcis because he hoped to lure the Persian fleet after him.

It is argued that such a movement would uncover Leonidas' flank at Thermopylae. Not entirely. It would be possible for the Persian admirals to land men in the rear of Leonidas' position only if they detached a squadron to hold off the Greeks triremes, which were stationed within easy striking distance, for ships engaged in landing operations are particularly vulnerable to attack unless they are guarded. The Greek navy would hardly have passed through the narrows at Chalcis, but would be stationed in the open water north-west of the city waiting for an opportunity. If the Persians divided their navy, and assigned one part of it to fend off the enemy while the other attempted to cooperate with Xerxes' army by landing men in the rear of Leonidas, Eurybiades would have had his chance to atack one secction of their fleet at a time, in relatively restricted waters where the more mobile Persian ships would have less advantage.

Such tactics entailed great risks, but they are sufficiently similar to those at Salamis to allow us to see the brain of Themistocles behind them. However, it is doubtful if the Greek commanders were hoping for a decisive victory. Like Leonidas at Thermopylae, Eurybiades was trying to checkmate the Persian fleet, by putting it in a position where it could not cooperate with the land army unless it fought him in a position of his choice. If, as Herodotus indicates later, there was a plan to send a large Peloponnesian army into Boeotia, any Persian force which the fleet might land in the rear of Leonidas would have had only a remote chance of operating effectively. It would be easy for the Peloponnesian army to isolate it and destroy it. Like Leonidas at Thermopylae, Eurybiades was trying to maintain a line of defense.

News came of the first storm; the ἡμεροσκόποι need only have informed the Greek admirals where the Persian fleet was anchored and that the "Hellespontias" was raging, and they would guess the rest. Altering his plans to meet the opportunity, and hoping that the storm would damage the enemy more than it actually did, Eurybiades returned to Artemisium.

The second retreat which the Greeks planned but did not execute was, as Lazenby recognized, a strategic withdrawal to meet the threat of the squadron circumnavigating Euboea; it was also an attempt to draw the Persians into constricted waters. It was prevented by the second storm, which also destroyed the circumnavigating squadron. The next day, 53 Athenian ships arrived as reinforcements, bringing the number of Athenian triremes at Artemisium to an even 200, although twenty are manned by Chalcidians. It is hard to believe that these 53 ships had been detached to guard the Euripus against the Persian squadron sailing round Euboea, and were now returning with news of its destruction; if this were so, they must have been in a position where they could have witnessed the destruction of this squadron during the second storm (or been in touch with scouts who witnessed it) and yet be able to appear at Artemisium in good time the next day. In any case, Herodotus does not indicate that these 53 ships brought the news of the Persian squadron's destruction, but rather that the ships and the news arrived at the same time.

I prefer to regard these 53 ships as the Athenian reserve fleet, which had been guarding the coast of Attica; they also had heard of the storm (the first one, not the second) and realized that Boreas had answered Athenian prayers, and had evened the odds a little by wiping out a part of the Persian fleet. Therefore they hurried to join Eurybiades so that he might have a stronger force with which to join battle with the weakened navy of the enemy.

But it was still a formidable navy, and Eurybiades was not disposed to take chances. The tactics of the second day's fighting repeat the first's. But on the third day, the Persians force the attack, and inflict losses on the Greeks heavy enough to make them realize that they must pull back to more constricted waters if they are to hold back the Persians much longer. Then news comes of the catastrophe at Thermopylae, and the fleet retires during the night.

The whole battle at Artemisium, like Thermopylae, was designed as a holding operation. The first plan of the Greeks was to draw the Persian fleet between Euboea and the mainland, where it was hoped that it would place itself at a strategic disadvantage as it attempted to cooperate with Xerxes' army. With the first storm, the Greeks moved back to Artemisium, thinking the time was opportune for a naval engagement while the Persian fleet was in disarray, and the Athenian reserve fleet,

which had also heard of the storm and realized the opportunity, hurried to join them. But the Persians were still formidable and Eurybiades abandoned his plans for a naval battle; for the remaining two days, he fell back on his original plan of simply maintaining a line of defense. Eurybiades, therefore, was not attempting to seek out and destroy the enemy fleet at Artemisium. He was simply engaged in a holding action.

IV

It may be argued that there is something unsatisfactory about regarding the battle of Thermopylae and Artemisium as holding actions, thereby transforming the whole operation into a kind of simplified Maginot Line. Would not the Greeks have sought some more decisive action which did more than put off the inevitable? In fact, it did more than that. The events at Thermopylae coincided with the Olympic games of 480, which in turn coincided with the full moon of August 20th; hence the pass fell on or just after August 20th. The enormous difficulties of providing Xerxes' army with supplies, particularly water, during the summer in Greece have already been dealt with in detail; because of its very size, the army could not stay out of contact with the navy for long, for with it were corn transports with which to supplement what the army got by foraging, or carried in its own baggage train. Neither could the army stay in one position very long for fear of running out of water and pasture. Moreover the end of the campaigning season was approaching. The Persians could not afford to be delayed long at Thermopylae; if they were, they would have to abandon the objectives of their campaign for 480, and satisfy themselves with Thessaly and Macedonia.

The Greeks established the defense line at Thermopylae and Artemisium to delay the Persians, not as a feint to give time to evacuate Athens and build a wall across the

Isthmus, but to checkmate Xerxes at Thermopylae as the campaigning season ran out and his supplies ran short. For an army the size of the Persian one could not remain in one position for any length of time before it used up the available water supply and ran out of pasture for the pack animals. The geographical features made it relatively easy—or so it seemed—to hold back the Persian land forces. On sea, it was more difficult to block the Persian navy, but it had to be attempted, for without naval support, the pass of Thermopylae could not be held. But any sober realist must have realized that these tactics had somewhat less chance of success than a military operation usually has, and he must have known that Attica was more likely to suffer than the Peloponnesus if the Thermopylae-Artemisium defence-line gave way. For if Xerxes were delayed only a short time, it might still be too late in the season for him to invade the Peloponnesus in 480, but nothing could save Athens, for the Cithaeron range was not defensible. Ten years before, when Datis and Artaphernes had landed at Marathon, the Athenians had marched out to fight them, but there is no comparison between the Persian expeditionary force of 490 and Xerxes' army. There was no question of 10,000 hoplites chasing it away. Therefore we should expect Athens to map out a course of action in case the Thermopylae-Artemisium line failed.

V

There remain two problems. One is implicit in the "Themistocles decree" from Troezen. Here is not the place to enter into the question of whether or not this decree is genuine, although we can note that those scholars who have objected to it on linguistic grounds are widely at variance in deciding what terminology a genuine decree of 480 B.C. should have used. I wish to concern myself with only two points: the apparent division of the Athenian navy into equal active and reserve squadrons, and the prior evacuation of Attica. The second problem is closely related, although it has not been recognized as such: what forces, if any, did the Spartans intend to send to Thermopylae to reinforce Leonidas?

The provisions in the Troezen decree for manning the Athenian fleet (11. 18–40) have already been defended in detail, and here I can only add that if these provisions do not reflect genuine tradition, we would have to imagine something like them. For since the fleet was new, and the men who manned it for the most part untrained, the choosing of captains and crews could not be left to free enterprise; it had to be state-supervised. The provisions for evacuation are more surprising. They need not, of course, indicate either that the Athenians were certain of defeat at Artemisium, or that they regarded the whole operation as a delaying action desiged to allow time to prepare for a battle at Salamis but they do mean that the Athenians thought the navy commanded by Eurybiades had at best a 50% chance of success.

As for the reserve fleet, the best proof of its existence is that the Athenians had a grand total of 200 ships at Artemisium, including the triremes manned by the Chalcidians and the 53 late arrivals, while at Salamis, in spite of heavy losses at Artemisium the Athenian ships still total 200. I have already argued that the 53 Athenian ships which arrived on the second day of the battle belonged to this reserve fleet—probably as many as the Athenians could man adequately—which rushed to Artemisium on learning of the first storm, hoping that here was an opportunity to strike a victorious blow. The numbers in Herodotus do not correspond to those of the "Themistocles decree" and on the principle that round numbers are more suspect than odd ones, we should prefer the 127-ship battle fleet in Herodotus to the 100 ships of the decree. In practice, the size of the contingents at Artemisium was no doubt decided by the Greek commanders, not by the Athenian assembly, and so the discrepancy between the numbers in Herodotus and the decree is no argument against the decree's authenticity.

The argument over whether or not Sparta intended to reinforce Leonidas has been summarized by Hignett. If Thermopylae was a holding operation, as I have suggested, Leonidas would have to be reinforced at some time, but until it was clear how the navy would fare at Artemisium, the Spartans were unwilling to commit a large force to the pass. So an adequate army, as it was thought, and a good leader were sent; if they were wiped out or severely handled in a retreat necessitated by defeat at sea, their loss would not cripple the defense of the Peloponnesus. There is here the same realism as in the "Themistocles decree" when it provides for prior evacuation.

The Spartans did intend to send more hoplites, and they did not intend to abandon Leonidas and his men. But whereas the Athenian reinforcements did arrive in time at Artemisium, though they did not change the course of events, the Peloponnesian reinforcements which might have changed history, did not reach Thermopylae.

Significantly, both Herodotus who may or may not have known of the "Themistocles decree" and Plutarch who read at least part of it, represent the evacuation of Attica as a kind of *sauve qui peut* after Thermopylae has fallen. Cautiously realistic as the Greeks may have been about their chances of holding the Thermopylae-Artemisium line, they did not expect the action to be over so quickly, for if prior evacuation was planned, it was certainly not carried out. Since the Greeks do not seem to have contemplated catastrophe at Thermopylae, they must have expected the fleet to hold at Artemisium for a period, even if, in the end, it might have to retreat. And conceivably there were some who

thought the fleet might win an engagement, but not, I think, among the Spartans who led the Hellenic League.

This discussion is not intended as an argument for the authenticity of the "Themistocles decree," though if it can be shown that it fits into a reasonable concept of strategy, this would be added reason for accepting it. It is rather the contention of this paper that the Greeks regarded the actions at Thermopylae and Artemisium neither as an attempt to win a decisive victory nor as a feint designed to give time to muster forces for Salamis. Instead, they conceived of the operation as a forward line of defense, which could be reinforced as needed by reserves in the rear, and the aim of these tactics was to hold up Xerxes' advance until weather and lack of supplies forced him to abandon his campaign for that year, and perhaps indefinitely.

The operation was planned in the full realization that it could fail. The weak link was not the land force at Thermopylae, for the *probouloi* at the Isthmus did not know of the Anopaea path which upset their careful strategy. Rather it was the untried navy at Artemisium. Yet the Greeks had no choice but to use their navy, and conceivably there were some Greeks such as Themistocles himself who were reasonably sanguine about its chances. We can see that this view of the strategic concepts underlying the Greek campaign does not conflict essentially with the so-called "Thermistocles decree."

Things turned out otherwise. Thermopylae fell; Leonidas became a hero and the Spartan reinforcements did not arrive in time. Later, when Greece was divided into two hostile camps, Athens preferred to look on this failure as a betrayal, and Athenian tradition has coloured subsequent accounts. On sea, the Greeks were more fortunate than their *probouloi* who had gathered at the Isthmus earlier in 480 could have expected. Two storms helped to even the odds between the fleets, and a month after Eurybiades retired undefeated from

Artemisium, the fleet won a decisive victory at Salamis. Athenian tradition, followed by most subsequent historians, has been careful to give Eurybiades no credit personally for all this, but he can hardly have been a nonentity.

Looking back at it later, after Athens had been a great naval power with a superbly trained fleet, and Salamis had passed into the magnificent poetry of Aeschylus, ordinary Athenians must have found it incredible that their fathers could have had such little confidence in their navy in 480 B.C. Modern historians have by and large found it equally incredible; Athens must have been trying for a decisive battle at sea whether at Artemisium or at Salamis for surely there was in the back of Themistocles' mind a plan for Athens as a great naval power, and victory at Salamis was part of it. It does not detract from Themistocles' brilliance to say that he was no clairvoyant. When he urged his naval program, he had in mind more probably the example of the Phocaeans in 546 than Periclean Athens and the Athenian tribute lists. When Athens scraped together her available manpower to mobilize her new fleet in 480, it must have seemed to the Athenians quite as much as to the Spartans almost more than could be reasonably expected if the Greeks held back Xerxes at the Thermopylae-Artemisium front. Hence a small but adequate force went to Thermopylae, and Eurybiades led a comparatively large battle-fleet to Artemisium to try his fortune, while behind the Thermopylae-Artemisium line, the Greeks prepared for some alternative action in case Xerxes broke through.

SECTION IX

Periclean Athens—Was It Democratic?

THE ATHENIAN STATE in the Age of Pericles is usually taken to be the paradigm of direct and all but total democracy. It had universal suffrage for adult, male citizens, direct elections of magistrates and public officials for short terms, and careful supervision of their acts during and after their tenure of office. The assembly of all the citizens appeared to be fully sovereign and the popular courts had almost total jurisdiction. In spite of all this Thucydides, a contemporary witness, called it "a democracy in name but the rule of the first citizen in fact." The following selections will reveal the diversity of opinion among the ancient authors.

1. THE GREATNESS OF ATHENS:

PERICLES' FUNERAL ORATION*

In the winter following the first campaigns of the Peloponnesian War, Pericles was chosen to pronounce the customary eulogy over the fallen warriors. He turned it instead into an occasion to praise the Athenian state, its constitution and its way of life. Thucydides, who was almost surely present, reports it in full.

'Most of my predecessors in this place have commended him who made this speech part of the law, telling us that it is well that it should be delivered at the burial of those who fall in battle. For myself, I should have thought that the worth which had displayed itself in deeds, would be sufficiently rewarded by honours also shown by deeds; such as you now see in this funeral prepared at the people's cost.

And I could have wished that the reputations of many brave men were not to be imperilled in the mouth of a single individual, to stand or fall according as he spoke well or ill. For it is hard to speak properly upon a subject where it is even difficult to convince your hearers that you are speaking the truth. On the one hand, the friend who is familiar with every fact of the story, may think that some point has not been set forth with that fulness which he wishes and knows it to deserve; on the other, he who is a stranger to the matter

* Thucydides, 2. 35–46, translated by Richard Crawley.

308

may be led by envy to suspect exaggeration if he hears anything above his own nature. For men can endure to hear others praised only so long as they can severally persuade themselves of their own ability to equal the actions recounted: when this point is passed, envy comes in and with it incredulity. However, since our ancestors have stamped this custom with their approval, it becomes my duty to obey the law and to try to satisfy your several wishes and opinions as best I may.

'I shall begin with our ancestors: it is both just and proper that they should have the honour of the first mention on an occasion like the present. They dwelt in the country without break in the succession from generation to generation, and handed it down free to the present time by their valour. And if our more remote ancestors deserve praise, much more do our own fathers, who added to their inheritance the empire which we now possess, and spared no pains to be able to leave their acquisitions to us of the present generation. Lastly, there are few parts of our dominions that have not been augmented by those of us here, who are still more or less in the vigour of life; while the mother country has been furnished by us with everything that can enable her to depend on her own resources whether for war or for peace. That part of our history which tells of the military achievements which gave us our several possessions, or of the ready valour with which either we or our fathers stemmed the tide of Hellenic or foreign aggression, is a theme too familiar to my hearers for me to dilate on, and I shall therefore pass it by. But what was the road by which we reached our position, what the form of government under which our greatness grew, what the national habits out of which it sprang; these are questions which I may try to solve before I proceed to my panegyric upon these men; since I think this to be a subject upon which on the present occasion a speaker may properly dwell, and to which the whole assemblage, whether

citizens or foreigners, may listen with advantage.

'Our constitution does not copy the laws of neighbouring states; we are rather a pattern to others than imitators ourselves. Its administration favours the many instead of the few; this is why it is called a democracy. If we look to the laws, they afford equal justice to all in their private differences; if to social standing, advancement in public life falls to reputation for capacity, class considerations not being allowed to interfere with merit; nor again does poverty bar the way, if a man is able to serve the state, he is not hindered by the obscurity of his condition. The freedom which we enjoy in our government extends also to our ordinary life. There, far from exercising a jealous surveillance over each other, we do not feel called upon to be angry with our neighbour for doing what he likes, or even to indulge in those injurious looks which cannot fail to be offensive, although they inflict no positive penalty. But all this ease in our private relations does not make us lawless as citizens. Against this fear is our chief safeguard, teaching us to obey the magistrates and the laws, particularly such as regard the protection of the injured, whether they are actually on the statute book, or belong to that code which, although unwritten, yet cannot be broken without acknowledged disgrace.

'Further, we provide plenty of means for the mind to refresh itself from business. We celebrate games and sacrifices all the year round, and the elegance of our private establishments forms a daily source of pleasure and helps to banish the spleen; while the magnitude of our city draws the produce of the world into our harbour, so that to the Athenian the fruits of other countries are as familiar a luxury as those of his own.

'If we turn to our military policy, there also we differ from our antagonists. We throw open our city to the world, and never by alien acts exclude foreigners from any opportunity of learning or observing, although the eyes of an enemy may occasionally profit by our liberality; trusting less in system and policy than to the native spirit of our citizens; while in education, where our rivals from their very cradles by a painful discipliñe seek after manliness, at Athens we live exactly as we please, and yet are just as ready to encounter every legitimate danger. In proof of this it may be noticed that the Lacedæmonians do not invade our country alone, but bring with them all their confederates; while we Athenians advance unsupported into the territory of a neighbour, and fighting upon a foreign soil usually vanquish with ease men who are defending their homes. Our united force was never yet encountered by any enemy, because we have at once to attend to our marine and to despatch our citizens by land upon a hundred different services; so that, wherever they engage with some such fraction of our strength, a success against a detachment is magnified into a victory over the nation, and a defeat into a reverse suffered at the hands of our entire people. And yet if with habits not of labour but of ease, and courage not of art but of nature, we are still willing to encounter danger, we have the double advantage of escaping the experience of hardships in anticipation and of facing them in the hour of need as fearlessly as those who are never free from them.

'Nor are these the only points in which our city is worthy of admiration. We cultivate refinement without extravagance and knowledge without effeminacy; wealth we employ more for use than for show, and place the real disgrace of poverty not in owning to the fact but in declining the struggle against it. Our public men have, besides politics, their private affairs to attend to, and our ordinary citizens, though occupied with the pursuits of industry, are still fair judges of public matters; for, unlike any other nation, regarding him who takes no part in these duties not as unambitious but as useless, we

Athenians are able to judge at all events if we cannot originate, and instead of looking on discussion as a stumbling-block in the way of action, we think it an indispensable preliminary to any wise action at all. Again, in our enterprises we present the singular spectacle of daring and deliberation, each carried to its highest point, and both united in the same persons; although usually decision is the fruit of ignorance, hesitation of reflexion. But the palm of courage will surely be adjudged most justly to those, who best know the difference between hardship and pleasure and yet are never tempted to shrink from danger. In generosity we are equally singular, acquiring our friends by conferring not by receiving favours. Yet, of course, the doer of the favour is the firmer friend of the two, in order by continued kindness to keep the recipient in his debt; while the debtor feels less keenly from the very consciousness that the return he makes will be a payment, not a free gift. And it is only the Athenians who, fearless of consequences, confer their benefits not from calculations of expediency, but in the confidence of liberality.

'In short, I say that as a city we are the school of Hellas; while I doubt if the world can produce a man, who where he has only himself to depend upon, is equal to so many emergencies, and graced by so happy a versatility as the Athenian. And that this is no mere boast thrown out for the occasion, but plain matter of fact, the power of the state acquired by these habits proves. For Athens alone of her contemporaries is found when tested to be greater than her reputation, and alone gives no occasion to her assailants to blush at the antagonist by whom they have been worsted, or to her subjects to question her title by merit to rule. Rather, the admiration of the present and succeeding ages will be ours, since we have not left our power without witness, but have shown it by mighty proofs; and far from needing a Homer for our panegyrist, or other of his craft whose verses might charm for the moment only for the impression which they gave to melt at the touch of fact, we have forced every sea and land to be the highway of our daring, and everywhere, whether for evil or for good, have left imperishable monuments behind us. Such is the Athens for which these men, in ,the assertion of their resolve not to lose her, nobly fought and died; and well may every one of their survivors be ready to suffer in her cause.

'Indeed if I have dwelt at some length upon the character of our country, it has been to show that our stake in the struggle is not the same as theirs who have no such blessings to lose, and also that the panegyric of the men over whom I am now speaking might be by definite proofs established. That panegyric is now in a great measure complete; for the Athens that I have celebrated is only what the heroism of these and their like have made her, men whose fame, unlike that of most Hellenes, will be found to be only commensurate with their deserts. And if a test of worth be wanted, it is to be found in their closing scene, and this not only in the cases in which it set the final seal upon their merit, but also in those in which it gave the first intimation of their having any. For there is justice in the claim that steadfastness in his country's battles should be as a cloak to cover a man's other imperfections; since the good action has blotted out the bad, and his merit as a citizen more than outweighed his demerits as an individual. But none of these allowed either wealth with its prospect of future enjoyment to unnerve his spirit, or poverty with its hope of a day of freedom and riches to tempt him to shrink from danger. No, holding that vengeance upon their enemies was more to be desired than any personal blessings, and reckoning this to be the most glorious of hazards, they joyfully determined to accept the risk, to make sure of their vengeance and to let their wishes wait; and while committing to hope the uncertainty of final success, in the business before them they

thought fit to act boldly and trust in themselves. Thus choosing to die resisting, rather than to live submitting, they fled only from dishonour, but met danger face to face, and after one brief moment, while at the summit of their fortune, escaped, not from their fear, but from their glory.

'So died these men as became Athenians. You, their survivors, must determine to have as unaltering a resolution in the field, though you may pray that it may have a happier issue. And not contented with ideas derived only from words of the advantages which are bound up with the defence of your country, though these would furnish a valuable text to a speaker even before an audience so alive to them as the present, you must yourselves realise the power of Athens, and feed your eyes upon her from day to day, till love of her fills your hearts; and then when all her greatness shall break upon you, you must reflect that it was by courage, sense of duty, and a keen feeling of honour in action that men were enabled to win all this, and that no personal failure in an enterprise could make them consent to deprive their country of their valour, but they laid it at her feet as the most glorious contribution that they could offer. For this offering of their lives made in common by them all they each of them individually received that renown which never grows old, and for a sepulchre, not so much that in which their bones have been deposited, but that noblest of shrines wherein their glory is laid up to be eternally remembered upon every occasion on which deed or story shall fall for its commemoration. For heroes have the whole earth for their tomb; and in lands far from their own, where the column with its epitaph declares it, there is enshrined in every breast a record unwritten with no tablet to preserve it, except that of the heart. These take as your model, and judging happiness to be the fruit of freedom and freedom of valour, never decline the dangers of war. For it is not the miserable that would most justly be unsparing of their lives; these have nothing to hope for: it is rather they to whom continued life may bring reverses as yet unknown, and to whom a fall, if it came, would be most tremendous in its consequences. And surely, to a man of spirit, the degradation of cowardice must be immeasurably more grievous than the unfelt death which strikes him in the midst of his strength and patriotism!

'Comfort, therefore, not condolence, is what I have to offer to the parents of the dead who may be here. Numberless are the chances to which, as they know, the life of man is subject; but fortunate indeed are they who draw for their lot a death so glorious as that which has caused your mourning, and to whom life has been so exactly measured as to terminate in the happiness in which it has been passed. Still I know that this is a hard saying, especially when those are in question of whom you will constantly be reminded by seeing in the homes of others blessings of which once you also boasted: for grief is felt not so much for the want of what we have never known, as for the loss of that to which we have been long accustomed. Yet you who are still of an age to beget children must bear up in the hope of having others in their stead; not only will they help you to forget those whom you have lost, but will be to the state at once a reinforcement and a security; for never can a fair or just policy be expected of the citizen who does not, like his fellows, bring to the decision the interests and apprehensions of a father. While those of you who have passed your prime must congratulate yourselves with the thought that the best part of your life was fortunate, and that the brief span that

remains will be cheered by the fame of the departed. For it is only the love of honour that never grows old; and honour it is, not gain, as some would have it, that rejoices the heart of age and helplessness.

'Turning to the sons or brothers of the dead, I see an arduous struggle before you. When a man is gone, all are wont to praise him, and should your merit be ever so transcendent, you will still find it difficult not merely to overtake, but even to approach their renown. The living have envy to contend with, while those who are no longer in our path are honoured with a goodwill into which rivalry does not enter. On the other hand, if I must say anything on the subject of female excellence to those of you who will now be in widowhood, it will be all comprised in this brief exhortation. Great will be your glory in not falling short of your natural character; and greatest will be hers who is least talked of among the men whether for good or for bad.

'My task is now finished. I have performed it to the best of my ability, and in words, at least, the requirements of the law are now satisfied. If deeds be in question, those who are here interred have received part of their honours already, and for the rest, their children will be brought up till manhood at the public expense: the state thus offers a valuable prize, as the garland of victory in this race of valour, for the reward both of those who have fallen and their survivors. And where the rewards for merit are greatest, there are found the best citizens.

'And now that you have brought to a close your lamentations for your relatives, you may depart.'

2. ARISTOTLE ON PERICLEAN ATHENS*

The following selection is from the *Constitution of the Athenians*, probably written by Aristotle, although some scholars attribute it to one of his students. There is no doubt, however, that it was written about a century after the death of Pericles and represents the thinking of Aristotle and his school.

After this revolution the administration of the state became more and more lax, in consequence of the eager rivalry of candidates for popular favour. During this period the moderate party, as it happened, had no real chief, their leader being Cimon son of Miltiades, who was a comparatively young man, and had been late in entering public life; and at the same time the general populace suffered great losses by war. The soldiers for active service were selected at that time from the roll of citizens, and as the generals were men of no military experience, who owed their position solely to their family standing, it continually happened that some two or three thousand of the troops perished on an expedition; and in this way the best men alike of the lower and the upper classes were exhausted. Consequently in most matters of administration less heed was paid to the laws than had formerly been the case. No alteration, however, was made in the method of election of the nine Archons, except that five years after the death of Ephialtes it was decided that the candidates to be submitted to the lot for that office might be selected from the Zeugitae as well as from the higher classes. The first Archon from that class was Mnesitheides. Up to this time all the Archons had been taken from the Penta-cosiomedimni and Knights, while the Zeugitae were confined to the ordinary magistracies, save where an evasion of the law was overlooked. Four years later, in the archonship of Lysicrates, the thirty 'local justices', as they were called, were

re-established; and two years afterwards, in the archonship of Antidotus, in consequence of the great increase in the number of citizens, it was resolved, on the motion of Pericles, that no one should be admitted to the franchise who was not of citizen birth by both parents.

After this Pericles came forward as popular leader, having first distinguished himself while still a young man by prosecuting Cimon on the audit of his official accounts as general. Under his auspices the constitution became still more democratic. He took away some of the privileges of the Areopagus, and, above all, he turned the policy of the state in the direction of sea power, which caused the masses to acquire confidence in themselves and consequently to take the conduct of affairs more and more into their own hands. Moreover, forty-eight years after the battle of Salamis, in the archonship of Pythodorus, the Peloponnesian war broke out, during which the populace was shut up in the city and became accustomed to gain its livelihood by military service, and so, partly voluntarily and partly involuntarily, determined to assume the administration of the state itself. Pericles was also the first to institute pay for service in the law-courts, as a bid for popular favour to counterbalance the wealth of Cimon. The latter, having private possessions on a regal scale, not only performed the regular public services magnificently, but also maintained a large number of his fellow-demesmen. Any member of the deme of Laciadae could go every day to Cimon's house and there receive a reasonable provision; while his estate was guarded by no fences, so that any one who liked might help himself to

---

* Aristotle, *Constitution of the Athenians*, 26–28. Translated by F. G. Kenyon (London: G. Bell and Sons, 1891).

the fruit from it. Pericles' private property was quite unequal to this magnificence and accordingly he took the advice of Damonides of Oia (who was commonly supposed to be the person who prompted Pericles in most of his measures, and was therefore subsequently ostracised), which was that, as he was beaten in the matter of private possessions, he should make gifts to the people from their own property; and accordingly he instituted pay for the members of the juries. Some critics accuse him of thereby causing a deterioration in the character of the juries, since it was always the common people who put themselves forward for selection as jurors, rather than the men of better ·position. Moreover, bribery came into existence after this, the first person to introduce it being Anytus, after his command at Pylos. He was prosecuted by certain individuals on account of his loss of Pylos, but escaped by bribing the jury.

So long, however, as Pericles was leader of the people, things went tolerably well with the state; but when he was dead there was a great change for the worse. Then for the first time did the people choose a leader who was of no reputation among men of good standing, whereas up to this time such men had always been found as leaders of the democracy.

3. THUCYDIDES ON PERICLEAN DEMOCRACY*

The historian of the Peloponnesian War experienced Athenian democracy in its glory under Pericles and at its nadir at the end of the war. His account deserves the most respectful attention, for he was an eyewitness of acute and discerning judgment. The following selection follows an account of the response of the Athenians to the hardships of war; only the persuasiveness of Pericles had prevented them from seeking terms after a short period of fighting.

They not only gave up all idea of sending to Lacedæmon, but applied themselves with increased energy to the war; still as private individuals they could not help smarting under their sufferings, the common people having been deprived of the little that they ever possessed, while the higher orders had lost fine properties with costly establishments and buildings in the country, and, worst of all, had war instead of peace. In fact, the public feeling against him [Pericles] did not subside until he had been fined. Not long afterwards, however, according to the way of the multitude, they again elected him general and committed all their affairs to his hands, having now become less sensitive to their private and domestic afflictions, and understanding that he was the best man of all for

the public necessities. For as long as he was at the head of the state during the peace, he pursued a moderate and conservative policy; and in his time its greatness was at its height. When the war broke out, here also he seems to have rightly gauged the power of his country. He outlived its commencement two years and six months, and the correctness of his previsions respecting it became better known by his death. He told them to wait quietly, to pay attention to their marine, to attempt no new conquests, and to expose the city to no hazards during the war, and doing this, promised them a favourable result. What they did was the very contrary, allowing private ambitions and private interests, in matters apparently quite foreign to the war, to lead them into projects unjust both to themselves and to their allies—projects whose success would only conduce to the honour and advantage of private persons,

---

* Thucydides, 2. 65. Translated by Richard Crawley.

and whose failure entailed certain disaster on the country in the war. The causes of this are not far to seek. Pericles indeed, by his rank, ability, and known integrity, was enabled to exercise an independent control over the multitude—in short, to lead them instead of being led by them; for as he never sought power by improper means, he was never compelled to flatter them, but, on the contrary, enjoyed so high an estimation that he could afford to anger them by contradiction. Whenever he saw them unseasonably and insolently elated, he would with a word reduce them to alarm; on the other hand, if they fell victims to a panic, he could at once restore them to confidence. In short, what was nominally a democracy became in his hands government by the first citizen. With his successors it was different. More on a level with one another, and each grasping at supremacy, they ended by committing even the conduct of state affairs to the whims of the multitude. This, as might have been expected in a great and sovereign state, produced a host of blunders, and amongst them the Sicilian expedition; though this failed not so much through a miscalculation of the power of those against whom it was sent, as through a fault in the senders in not taking the best measures afterwards to assist those who had gone out, but choosing rather to occupy themselves with private cabals for the leadership of the commons, by which they not only paralysed operations in the field, but also first introduced civil discord at home. Yet after losing most of their fleet besides other forces in Sicily, and with faction already dominant in the city, they could still for three years make head against their original adversaries, joined not only by the Sicilians, but also by their own allies nearly all in revolt, and at last by the king's son, Cyrus, who furnished the funds for the Peloponnesian navy. Nor did they finally succumb till they fell the victims of their own intestine disorders. So superfluously abundant were the resources from which the genius of Pericles foresaw an easy triumph in the war over the unaided forces of the Peloponnesians.

4. THE "OLD OLIGARCH" ON PERICLEAN DEMOCRACY*

The following selections are from a pamphlet on the Athenian constitution which has come down to us among the works of Xenophon. In the long debate concerning its authorship the only fact generally agreed upon is that it could not have been written by Xenophon. Various authors have been proposed, among them Thucydides, the son of Melesias, a political opponent of Pericles. None of these attributions has won wide acceptance, and the anonymous author is usually called the "Old Oligarch." Internal evidence places the date of the treatise towards the beginning of the Peloponnesian War. Thus, the author, like Thucydides, is a contemporary of Pericles. His views, though contradictory to those of the historian, are not be dismissed.

Now, as for the constitution of the Athenians, and the type or manner of constitution which they have chosen, I praise it not, in so far as the very choice involves the welfare of the baser folk as opposed to that of the better class. I repeat, I withhold my praise so far; but, given the fact that this is the type agreed upon, I propose to show that they set about its preservation in the right way; and that those other transactions in connection with it, which are looked upon as blunders by the rest of the Hellenic world, are the reverse.

In the first place, I maintain, it is only just that the poorer classes and the common

* Pseudo-Xenophon, *Constitution of the Athenians*, 1, 3, translated by H. G. Dakyns.

people of Athens should be better off than the men of birth and wealth, seeing that it is the people who man the fleet, and have brought the city her power. The steersman, the boatswain, the lieutenant, the look-out-man at the prow, the shipwright—these are the people who supply the city with power far rather than her heavy infantry and men of birth and quality. This being the case, it seems only just that offices of state should be thrown open to every one both in the ballot and the show of hands, and that the right of speech should belong to any one who likes, without restriction. For, observe, there are many of these offices which, according as they are in good or in bad hands, are a source of safety or of danger to the People, and in these the People prudently abstains from sharing; as, for instance, it does not think it incumbent on itself to share in the functions of the general or of the commander of cavalry. The commons recognises the fact that in for-going the personal exercise of these offices, and leaving them to the control of the more powerful citizens, it secures the balance of advantage to itself. It is only those depart-ments of government which bring pay and assist the private estate that the People cares to keep in its own hands.

In the next place, in regard to what some people are puzzled to explain—the fact that everywhere greater consideration is shown to the base, to poor people and to common folk, than to persons of good quality,—so far from being a matter of surprise, this, as can be shown, is the key-stone of the preservation of the democracy. It is these poor people, this common folk, this worse element, whose prosperity, com-bined with the growth of their numbers, enhances the democracy. Whereas, a shifting of fortune to the advantage of the wealthy and the better classes implies the establishment on the part of the commons of a strong power in opposition to itself. In fact, all the world over, the cream of society is in opposition to the democracy. Naturally, since the smallest amount of

intemperance and injustice, together with the highest scrupulousness in the pursuit of excellence, is to be found in the ranks of the better class, while within the ranks of the People will be found the greatest amount of ignorance, disorderliness, rascal-ity,—poverty acting as a stronger incentive to base conduct, not to speak of lack of education and ignorance, traceable to the lack of means which afflicts the average of mankind.

The objection may be raised that it was a mistake to allow the universal right of speech and a seat in council. These should have been reserved for the cleverest, the flower of the community. But here, again, it will be found that they are acting with wise deliberation in granting to even the baser sort the right of speech, for supposing only the better people might speak, or sit in council, blessings would fall to the lot of those like themselves, but to the commons the reverse of blessings. Whereas now, any one who likes, any base fellow, may get up and discover something to the advantage of himself and his equals. It may be retorted, "And what sort of advantage either for himself or for the People can such a fellow be expected to hit upon?" The answer to which is, that in their judgment the ignorance and the baseness of this fellow, together with his goodwill, are worth a great deal more to them than your superior person's virtue and wisdom, coupled with animosity. What it comes to, therefore, is that a state founded upon such institutions will not be the best state; but, given a democracy, these are the right means to secure its preservation. The People, it must be borne in mind, does not demand that the city should be well governed and itself a slave. It desires to be free and to be master. As to bad legislation it does not concern itself about that. In fact, what you believe to be bad legislation is the very source of the People's strength and freedom. But if you seek for good legislation, in the first place you will see the cleverest members of the community laying down the laws for the rest. And in the next place, the better class will curb and chastise the lower orders; the better class will deliberate in behalf of the state, and not suffer crack-brained fellows to sit in council, or to speak or vote in the assemblies. No doubt; but under the weight of such blessings the People will in a very short time be reduced to slavery.

Another point is the extraordinary amount of license granted to slaves and resident aliens at Athens, where a blow is illegal, and a slave will not step aside to let you pass him in the street. I will explain the reason of this peculiar custom. Supposing it were legal for a slave to be beaten by a free citizen, or for a resident alien or freedman to be beaten by a citizen, it would frequently happen that an Athenian might be mistaken for a slave or an alien and receive a beating; since the Athenian People is not better clothed than the slave or alien, nor in personal appearance is there any superiority. Or if the fact itself that slaves in Athens are allowed to indulge in luxury, and indeed in some cases to live magnificently, be found astonishing, this too, it can be shown, is done of set purpose. Where you have a naval power dependent upon wealth we must perforce be slaves to our slaves, in order that we may get in our slave-rents, and let the real slave go free. Where you have wealthy slaves it ceases to be advantageous that my slave should stand in awe of you. In Lacedaemon my slave stands in awe of you. But if your slave is in awe of me there will be a risk of his giving away his own moneys to avoid running a risk in his own person. It is for this reason then that we have established an equality between our slaves and free men; and again between our resident aliens and full citizens, because the city stands in need of her resident aliens to meet the requirements of such a multiplicity of arts and for the purposes of her navy. That is, I repeat, the justification of the equality conferred upon our resident aliens.

The common people put a stop to citizens devoting their time to athletics and to the cultivation of music, disbelieving in the beauty of such training, and recognising the fact that these are things the cultivation of which is beyond its power. On the same principle, in the case of the choregia, the management of athletics, and the command of ships, the fact is recognised that it is the rich man who trains the chorus, and the People for whom the chorus is trained; it is the rich man who is naval commander or superintendent of athletics, and the People that profits by their labours. In fact, what the People looks upon as its right is to pocket the money. To sing and run and dance and man the vessels is well enough, but only in order that the People may be the gainer, while the rich are made poorer. And so in the courts of justice, justice is not more an object of concern to the jurymen than what touches personal advantage.

To speak next of the allies, and in reference to the point that emissaries from Athens come out, and, according to common opinion, calumniate and vent their hatred upon the better sort of people, this is done on the principle that the ruler cannot help being hated by those whom he rules; but that if wealth and respectability are to wield power in the subject cities the empire of the Athenian People has but a short lease of existence. This explains why the better people are punished with infamy, robbed of their money, driven from their homes, and put to death, while the baser sort are promoted to honour. On the other hand, the better Athenians protect the better class in the allied cities. And why? Because they recognise that it is to the interest of their own class at all times to protect the best element in the cities. It may be urged that if it comes to strength and power the real strength of Athens lies in the capacity of her allies to contribute their money quota. But to the democratic mind it appears a higher advantage still for the individual Athenian to get hold of the wealth of the allies, leaving them only enough to live upon and to cultivate their estates, but powerless to harbour treacherous designs.

Again, it is looked upon as a mistaken policy on the part of the Athenian democracy to compel her allies to voyage to Athens in order to have their cases tried. On the other hand, it is easy to reckon up what a number of advantages the Athenian People derives from the practice impugned. In the first place, there is the steady receipt of salaries throughout the year derived from the court fees. Next, it enables them to manage the affairs of the allied states while seated at home without the expense of naval expeditions. Thirdly, they thus preserve the partisans of the democracy, and ruin her opponents in the law courts. Whereas, supposing the several allied states tried their cases at home, being inspired by hostility to Athens, they would destroy those of their own citizens whose friendship to the Athenian People was most marked. But besides all this the democracy derives the following advantages from hearing the cases of her allies in Athens. In the first place, the one per cent levied in Piraeus is increased to the profit of the state; again, the owner of a lodging-house does better, and so, too, the owner of a pair of beasts, or of slaves to be let out on hire; again, heralds and criers are a class of people who fare better owing to the sojourn of foreigners at Athens. Further still, supposing the allies had not to resort to Athens for the hearing of cases, only the official representative of the imperial state would be held in honour, such as the general, or trierarch, or ambassador. Whereas now every single individual among the allies is forced to pay flattery to the People of Athens because he knows that he must betake himself to Athens and win or lose his case at the bar, not of any stray set of judges, but of the sovereign People itself, such being the law and custom at Athens. He is compelled to behave as a suppliant in the courts of justice, and when some juryman comes into court, to grasp his hand. For this reason, therefore, the allies find themselves more and more in the position of slaves to the people of Athens.

Furthermore, owing to the possession of property beyond the limits of Attica, and the exercise of magistracies which take them into regions beyond the frontier, they and their attendants have insensibly acquired the art of navigation. A man who is perpetually voyaging is forced to handle the oar, he and his domestic alike, and to learn the terms familiar in seamanship. Hence a stock of skilful mariners is produced, bred upon a wide experience of voyaging and practice. They have learned their business, some in piloting a small craft, others a merchant vessel, while others have been drafted off from these for service on a ship-of-war. So that the majority of them are able to row the moment they set foot on board a vessel, having been in a state of preliminary practice all their lives.

* * *

I repeat that my position concerning the constitution of the Athenians is this: the type of constitution is not to my taste, but given that a democratic form of government has been agreed upon, they do seem to me to go the right way to preserve the democracy by the adoption of the particular type which I have set forth.

5. Plato on Periclean Democracy*

In the *Gorgias* dialogue Plato makes his view of Pericles' contribution to the Athenian constitution perfectly clear. Plato was little more than a generation removed from the time of Pericles and undoubtedly had good second-hand evidence of its character. It is possible, however, that his opinion is influenced by his own experience of the Athenian democracy of the fourth century, which he cordially disliked.

Soc. And now, my friend, as you are already beginning to be a public character, and are admonishing and reproaching me for not being one, suppose that we ask a few questions of one another. Tell me, then, Callicles, how about making any of the citizens better? Was there ever a man who was once vicious, or unjust, or intemperate, or foolish, and became by the help of Callicles good and noble? Was there ever such a man, whether citizen or stranger, slave or freeman? Tell me, Callicles, if a person were to ask these questions of you, what would you answer? Whom would you say that you had improved by your conversation? There may have been good deeds of this sort which were done by you as a private person, before you came forward in public. Why will you not answer?

Cal. You are contentious, Socrates.

Soc. Nay, I ask you, not from a love of contention, but because I really want to know in what way you think that affairs should be administered among us—whether, whey you come to the administration of them, you have any other aim but the improvement of the citizens? Have we not already admitted many times over that such is the duty of a public man? Nay, we have surely said so; for if you will not answer for yourself I must answer for you. But if this is what the good man ought to effect for the benefit of his own state, allow me to recall to you the names of those whom you were just now mentioning, Pericles, and Cimon, and Miltiades, and

Themistocles, and ask whether you still think that they were good citizens.

Cal. I do.

Soc. But if they were good, then clearly each of them must have made the citizens better instead of worse?

Cal. Yes.

Soc. And, therefore, when Pericles first began to speak in the assembly, the Athenians were not so good as when he spoke last?

Cal. Very likely.

Soc. Nay, my friend, 'likely' is not the word; for if he was a good citizen, the inference is certain.

Cal. And what difference does that make?

Soc. None; only I should like further to know whether the Athenians are supposed to have been made better by Pericles, or, on the contrary, to have been corrupted by him; for I hear that he was the first who gave the people pay, and made them idle and cowardly, and encouraged them in the love of talk and of money.

Cal. You heard that, Socrates, from the laconising set who bruise their ears.

Soc. But what I am going to tell you now is not mere hearsay, but well known both to you and me: that at first, Pericles was glorious and his character unimpeached by any verdict of the Athenians—this was during the time when they were not so good—yet afterwards, when they had been made good and gentle by him, at the very end of his life they convicted him of theft, and almost put him to death, clearly under the notion that he was a malefactor.

Cal. Well, but how does that prove Pericles' badness?

* Plato, *Gorgias*, 515–517. Translated by Benjamin Jowett.

Soc. Why, surely you would say that he was a bad manager of asses or horses or oxen, who had received them originally neither kicking nor butting nor biting him, and implanted in them all these savage tricks? Would he not be a bad manager of any animals who received them gentle, and made them fiercer than they were when he received them? What do you say?

Cal. I will do you the favour of saying 'yes.'

Soc. And will you also do me the favour of saying whether man is an animal?

Cal. Certainly he is.

Soc. And was not Pericles a shepherd of men?

Cal. Yes.

Soc. And if he was a good political shepherd, ought not the animals who were his subjects, as we were just now acknowledging, to have become more just, and not more unjust?

Cal. Quite true.

Soc. And are not just men gentle, as Homer says?—or are you of another mind?

Cal. I agree.

Soc. And yet he really did make them more savage than he received them, and their savageness was shown towards himself; which he must have been very far from desiring.

Cal. Do you want me to agree with you?

Soc. Yes, if I seem to you to speak the truth.

Cal. Granted that.

Soc. And if they were more savage, must they not have been more unjust and inferior?

Cal. Granted again.

Soc. Then upon this view, Pericles was not a good statesman?

Cal. That is, upon your view.

Soc. Nay, the view is yours, after what you have admitted. Take the case of Cimon again. Did not the very persons whom he was serving ostracize him, in order that they might not hear his voice for ten years? and they did just the same to Themistocles, adding the penalty of exile; and they voted that Miltiades, the hero of Marathon, should be thrown into the pit of death, and he was only saved by the Prytanis. And yet, if they had been really good men, as you say, these things would never have happened to them. For the good charioteers are not those who at first keep their place, and then, when they have broken-in their horses, and themselves become better charioteers, are thrown out —that is not the way either in charioteering or in any profession.—What do you think?

Cal. I should think not.

Soc. Well, but if so, the truth is as I have said already, that in the Athenian State no one has every shown himself to be a good statesman—you admitted that this was true of our present statesmen, but not true of former ones, and you preferred them to the others; yet they have turned out to be no better than our present ones; and therefore, if they were rhetoricians, they did not use the true art of rhetoric or of flattery, or they would not have fallen out of favour.

Cal. But surely, Socrates, no living man ever came near any one of them in his performances.

Soc. O, my dear friend, I say nothing against them regarded as the serving-men of the State; and I do think that they were certainly more serviceable than those who are living now, and better able to gratify the wishes of the State; but as to transforming those desires and not allowing them to have their way, and using the powers which they had, whether of persuasion or of force, in the improvement of their fellow-citizens, which is the prime object of the truly good citizen, I do not see that in these respects they were a whit superior to our present statesmen, although I do admit that they were more clever at providing ships and walls and docks, and all that.

6. PLUTARCH ON PERICLEAN DEMOCRACY*

Plutarch of Chaeronea was a Greek who lived in the second century of our era, the author of many works. Certainly the best known of these is his collection of biographies of illustrious Greeks and Romans. He is not an historian but a biographer and he lacks the intellectual power of Thucydides, yet his *Lives* are peculiarly valuable. He used all the sources available to him almost indiscriminately. Many of these ancient sources are known to us only or chiefly through his citation of them, so that his work often throws important light on the events he describes. Thus, his *Life of Pericles* uses Thucydides but compares his views with those of other historians who may have employed reliable information not used by Thucydides. The first selection describes Pericles' rise to power and his early career.

Since Thucydides describes the rule of Pericles as an aristocratical government, that went by the name of a democracy, but was, indeed, the supremacy of a single great man, while many others say, on the contrary, that by him the common people were first encouraged and led on to such evils as appropriations of subject territory, allowances for attending theatres, payments for performing public duties, and by these bad habits were, under the influence of his public measures, changed from a sober, thrifty people, that maintained themselves by their own labours, to lovers of expense, intemperance, and licence, let us examine the cause of this change by the actual matters of fact.

At the first, as has been said, when he set himself against Cimon's great authority, he did caress the people. Finding himself come short of his competitor in wealth and money, by which advantages the other was enabled to take care of the poor, inviting every day some one or other of the citizens that was in want to supper, and bestowing clothes on the aged people, and breaking down the hedges and enclosures of his grounds, that all that would might freely gather what fruit they pleased, Pericles, thus outdone in popular arts, by the advice of one Damonides of Œa, as Aristotle states, turned to the distribution of the

public moneys; and in a short time having bought the people over, what with moneys allowed for shows and for service on juries, and what with other forms of pay and largess, he made use of them against the council of Areopagus of which he himself was no member, as having never been appointed by lot either chief archon, or lawgiver, or king, or captain. For from of old these offices were conferred on persons by lot, and they who had acquitted themselves duly in the discharge of them were advanced to the court of Areopagus. And so Pericles, having secured his power in interest with the populace, directed the exertions of his party against this council with such success, that most of these causes and matters which had been used to be tried there were, by the agency of Ephialtes, removed from its cognisance; Cimon, also, was banished by ostracism as a favourer of the Lacedæmonians and a hater of the people, though in wealth and noble birth he was among the first, and had won several most glorious victories over the barbarians, and had filled the city with money and spoils of war; as is recorded in the history of his life. So vast an authority had Pericles obtained among the people.

*   *   *

Cimon, while he was admiral, ended his days in the Isle of Cyprus. And the aristocratical party, seeing that Pericles was already before this grown to be the greatest

---

* Plutarch, *Pericles* (abridged). Translated by John Dryden.

and foremost man of all the city, but nevertheless wishing there should be somebody set up against him, to blunt and turn the edge of his power, that it might not altogether prove a monarchy, put forward Thucydides of Alopece, a discreet person, and a near kinsman of Cimon's, to conduct the opposition against him; who, indeed, though less skilled in warlike affairs than Cimon was, yet was better versed in speaking and political business and keeping close guard in the city, and, engaging with Pericles on the hustings, in a short time brought the government to an equality of parties. For he would not suffer those who were called the honest and good (persons of worth and distinction) to be scattered up and down and mix themselves and be lost among the populace, as formerly, diminishing and obscuring their superiority amongst the masses; but taking them apart by themselves and uniting them in one body, by their combined weight he was able, as it were upon the balance, to make a counterpoise to the other party.

For, indeed, there was from the beginning a sort of concealed split, or seam, as it might be in a piece of iron, marking the different popular and aristocratical tendencies; but the open rivalry and contention of these two opponents made the gash deep, and severed the city into the two parties of the people and the few. And so Pericles, at that time, more than at any other, let loose the reins to the people, and made his policy subservient to their pleasure, contriving continually to have some great public show or solemnity, some banquet, or some procession or other in the town to please them, coaxing his countrymen like children with such delights and pleasures as were not, however, unedifying. Besides that every year he sent out threescore galleys, on board of which there were numbers of the citizens, who were in pay eight months, learning at the same time and practising the art of seamanship.

He sent, moreover, a thousand of them into the Chersonese as planters, to share the land among them by lot, and five hundred more into the isle of Naxos, and half that number to Andros, a thousand into Thrace to dwell among the Bisaltæ.. and others into Italy, when the city Sybaris, which now was called Thurii, was to be repeopled. And this he did to ease and discharge the city of an idle, and, by reason of their idleness, a busy meddling crowd of people; and at the same time to meet the necessities and restore the fortunes of the poor townsmen, and to intimidate, also, and check their allies from attempting any change, by posting such garrisons, as it were, in the midst of them.

That which gave most pleasure and ornament to the city of Athens, and the greatest admiration and even astonishment to all strangers, and that which now is Greece's only evidence that the power she boasts of and her ancient wealth are no romance or idle story, was his construction of the public and sacred buildings. Yet this was that of all his actions in the government which his enemies most looked askance upon and cavilled at in the popular assemblies, crying out how that the commonwealth of Athens had lost its reputation and was ill-spoken of abroad for removing the common treasure of the Greeks from the isle of Delos into their own custody; and how that their fairest excuse for so doing, namely, that they took it away for fear the barbarians should seize it, and on purpose to secure it in a safe place, this Pericles had made unavailable, and how that "Greece cannot but resent it as an insufferable affront, and consider herself to be tyrannised over openly, when she sees the treasure, which was contributed by her upon a necessity for the war, wantonly lavished out by us upon our city, to gild her all over, and to adorn and set her forth, as it were some vain woman, hung round with precious stones and figures and temples, which cost a world of money."

Pericles, on the other hand, informed the people, that they were in no way obliged to give any account of those moneys to their allies, so long as they maintained their defence, and kept off the barbarians from attacking them; while in the meantime they did not so much as supply one horse or man or ship, but only found money for the service; "which money," said he, "is not theirs that give it, but theirs that receive it, if so be they perform the conditions upon which they receive it." And that it was good reason, that, now the city was sufficiently provided and stored with all things necessary for the war, they should convert the overplus of its wealth to such undertakings as would hereafter, when completed, give them eternal honour, and, for the present, while in process, freely supply all the inhabitants with plenty. With their variety of workmanship and of occasions for service, which summon all arts and trades and require all hands to be employed about them, they do actually put the whole city, in a manner, into state-pay; while at the same time she is both beautiful and maintained by herself. For as those who are of age and strength for war are provided for and maintained in the armaments abroad by their pay out of the public stock, so, it being his desire and design that the undisciplined mechanic multitude that stayed at home should not go without their share of public salaries, and yet should not have them given them for sitting still and doing nothing, to that end he thought fit to bring in among them, with the approbation of the people, these vast projects of buildings and designs of work, that would be of some continuance before they were finished, and would give employment to numerous arts, so that the part of the people that stayed at home might, no less than those that were at sea or in garrisons or on expeditions, have a fair and just occasion of receiving the benefit and having their share of the public moneys.

* * *

When the orators, who sided with Thucydides and his party, were at one time crying out, as their custom was, against Pericles, as one who squandered away the public money, and made havoc of the state revenues, he rose in the open assembly and put the question to the people, whether they thought that he had laid out much; and they saying, "Too much, a great deal," "Then," said he, "since it is so, let the cost not go to your account, but to mine; and let the inscription upon the buildings stand in my name." When they heard him say thus, whether it were out of a surprise to see the greatness of his spirit or out of emulation of the glory of the works, they cried aloud, bidding him to spend on, and lay out what he thought fit from the public purse, and to spare no cost, till all were finished.

At length, coming to a final contest with Thucydides which of the two should ostracise the other out of the country, and having gone through this peril, he threw his antagonist out, and broke up the confederacy that had been organised against him. So that now all schism and division being at an end, and the city brought to evenness and unity, he got all Athens and all affairs that pertained to the Athenians into his own hands, their tributes, their armies, and their galleys, the islands, the sea, and their wide-extended power, partly over other Greeks and partly over barbarians, and all that empire, which they possessed, founded and fortified upon subject nations and royal friendships and alliances.

After this he was no longer the same man he had been before, nor as tame and gentle and familiar as formerly with the populace, so as readily to yield to their pleasures and to comply with the desires of the multitude, as a steersman shifts with the winds. Quitting that loose, remiss, and, in some cases, licentious court of the popular will, he turned those soft and flowery modulations to the austerity of aristocratical and regal rule; and employing this uprightly and undeviatingly for the country's best interests, he was able generally to lead the people along, with their own wills and consents, by persuading and showing them what was to be done; and sometimes, too, urging and pressing them forward extremely against their will, he made them, whether they would or no, yield submission to what was for their advantage. In which, to say the truth, he did but like a skilful physician, who, in a complicated and chronic disease, as he sees occasion, at one while allows his patient the moderate use of such things as please him, at another while gives him keen pains and drug to work the cure. For there arising and growing up, as was natural, all manner of distempered feelings among a people which had so vast a command and dominion, he alone, as a great master, knowing how to handle and deal fitly with each one of them, and, in an especial manner, making that use of hopes and fears, as his two chief rudders, with the one to check the career of their confidence at any time, with the other to raise them up and cheer them when under any discouragement, plainly showed by this, that rhetoric, or the art of speaking, is, in Plato's language, the government of the souls of men, and that her chief business is to address the affections and passions, which are as it were the strings and keys to the soul, and require a skilful and careful touch to be played on as they should be. The source of this predominance was not barely his power of language, but, as Thucydides assures us, the reputation of his life, and the confidence felt in his character; his manifest freedom from every kind of corruption, and superiority to all considerations of money. Notwithstanding he had made the city of Athens, which was great of itself, as great and rich as can be imagined, and though he were himself in power and interest more than equal to many kings and absolute rulers, who some of them also bequeathed by will their power to their children, he, for his part, did not make the patrimony his father left him greater than it was by one drachma.

Thucydides, indeed, gives a plain statement of the greatness of his power; and the comic poets, in their spiteful manner, more than hint at it, styling his companions and friends the new Pisistratidæ, and calling on him to abjure any intention of usurpation, as one whose eminence was too great to be any longer proportionable to and compatible with a democracy or popular government. And Teleclides says the Athenians had surrendered up to him—

"The tribute of the cities, and with them, the cities too, to do with them as he pleases, and undo;
To build up, if he likes, stone walls around a town; and again, if so he likes, to pull them down;
Their treaties and alliances, power, empire, peace, and war, their wealth and their success forever more."

Nor was all this the luck of some happy occasion; nor was it the mere bloom and grace of a policy that flourished for a season; but having for forty years together maintained the first place among statesmen such as Ephialtes and Leocrates and Myronides and Cimon and Tolmides and Thucydides were, after the defeat and banishment of Thucydides, for no less than fifteen years longer, in the exercise of one continuous unintermitted command in the office, to which he was annually re-elected, of General, he preserved his integrity unspotted. . . .

[During the years just prior to the Peloponnesian War Pericles' political control was threatened by attacks on his friends and collaborators, among them the sculptor Phidias.]

Phidias then was carried away to prison, and there died of a disease; but, as some say, of poison, administered by the enemies of Pericles, to raise a slander, or a suspicion at least, as though he had procured it. The informer Menon, upon Glycon's proposal, the people made free from payment of taxes and customs, and ordered the generals to take care that nobody should do him any hurt. About the same time, Aspasia was indicted of impiety, upon the complaint of Hermippus the comedian, who also laid further to her charge that she received into her house freeborn women for the uses of Pericles. And Diopithes proposed a decree, that public accusations should be laid against persons who neglected religion, or taught new doctrines about things above, directing suspicion, by means of Anaxagoras, against Pericles himself. The people receiving and admitting these accusations and complaints, at length, by this means, they came to enact a decree, at the motion of Dracontides, that Pericles should bring in the accounts of the moneys he had expended, and lodge them with the Prytanes; and that the judges, carrying their suffrage from the altar in the Acropolis, should examine and determine the business in the city. This last clause Hagnon took out of the decree, and moved that the causes should be tried before fifteen hundred jurors, whether they should be styled prosecutions for robbery, or bribery, or any kind of malversation. Aspasia, Pericles begged off, shedding, as Æschines says, many tears at the trial, and personally entreating the jurors. But fearing how it might go with Anaxagoras, he sent him out of the city. And finding that in Phidias's case he had miscarried with the people, being afraid of impeachment, he kindled the war, which hitherto had lingered and smothered, and blew it up into a flame; hoping, by that means, to disperse and scatter these complaints and charges, and to allay their jealousy; the city usually throwing herself upon him alone, and trusting to his sole conduct, upon the urgency of great affairs and public dangers, by reason of his authority and the sway he bore.

These are given out to have been the reasons which induced Pericles not to suffer the people of Athens to yield to the proposals of the Lacedæmonians; but their truth is uncertain.

The Lacedæmonians, for their part, feeling sure that if they could once remove him, they might be at what terms they pleased with the Athenians, sent them word that they should expel the "Pollution" with which Pericles on the mother's side was tainted, as Thucydides tells us. But the issue proved quite contrary to what those who sent the message expected; instead of bringing Pericles under suspicion and reproach, they raised him into yet greater credit and esteem with the citizens, as a man whom their enemies most hated and feared. In the same way, also, before Archidamus, who was at the head of the Peloponnesians, made his invasion into Attica, he told the Athenians beforehand, that if Archidamus, while he laid waste the rest of the country, should forbear and spare his estate, either on the ground of friendship or right of hospitality that was betwixt them, or on purpose to give his enemies an occasion of traducing him; that then he did freely bestow upon the state all his land and the buildings upon it for the public use. The Lacedæmonians, therefore, and their allies, with a great army, invaded the Athenian territories, under the conduct of King Archidamus, and laying waste the country, marched on as far as Acharnæ, and there pitched their camp, presuming that the Athenians would never endure that, but would come out and fight them for their country's and their honour's sake. But Pericles looked upon it as dangerous to engage in battle, to the risk of the city itself, against sixty thousand men-at-arms of Peloponnesians and Bœotians; for so many they were in number that made the inroad at first; and he endeavoured to appease those who were desirous to fight, and were grieved and discontented to see how things went, and gave them good words, saying, that "trees, when they are lopped and cut, grow up again in a short time, but men, being once lost, cannot easily be recovered." He did not convene the people into an assembly, for fear lest they should force him to act against his judgment; but, like a skilful steersman or pilot of a ship, who, when a sudden squall comes on, out at sea, makes all his arrangements, sees that all is tight and fast, and then follows the dictates of his skill, and minds the business of the ship, taking no notice of the tears and entreaties of the sea-sick and fearful passengers, so he, having shut up the city gates, and placed guards at all posts for security, followed his own reason and judgment, little regarding those that cried out against him and were angry at his management, although there were a great many of his friends that urged him with requests, and many of his enemies threatened and accused him for doing as he did, and many made songs and lampoons upon him, which were sung about the town to his disgrace, reproaching him with the cowardly exercise of his office of general, and the tame abandonment of everything to the enemy's hands.

Cleon, also, already was among his assailants, making use of the feeling against him as a step to the leadership of the people, as appears in the anapæstic verses of Hermippus—

"Satyr-king, instead of swords,
Will you always handle words?
Very brave indeed we find them,
But a Teles lurks behind them.

"Yet to gnash your teeth you're seen,
When the little dagger keen,
Whetted every day anew,
Of sharp Cleon touches you."

Pericles, however, was not at all moved by any attacks, but took all patiently, and submitted in silence to the disgrace they threw upon him and the ill-will they bore him; and, sending out a fleet of a hundred galleys to Peloponnesus, he did not go along with it in person, but stayed behind, that he might watch at home and keep the city under his own control, till the Peloponnesians broke up their camp and were gone. Yet to soothe the common people, jaded and distressed with the war, he relieved them with distributions of public moneys, and ordained new divisions of subject land. For having turned out all the people of Ægina, he parted the island among the Athenians according to lot. Some comfort, also, and ease in their miseries, they might receive from what their enemies endured. For the fleet, sailing round the Peloponnese, ravaged a great deal of the country, and pillaged and plundered the towns and smaller cities; and by land he himself entered with an army the Megarian country, and made havoc of it all. Whence it is clear that the Peloponnesians, though they did the Athenians much mischief by land, yet suffering as much themselves from them by sea, would not have protracted the war to such a length, but would quickly have given it over, as Pericles at first foretold they would, had not some divine power crossed human purposes.

In the first place, the pestilential disease, or plague, seized upon the city, and ate up all the flower and prime of their youth and strength. Upon occasion of which, the people, distempered and afflicted in their souls, as well as in their bodies, were utterly enraged like madmen against Pericles, and, like patients grown delirious, sought to lay violent hands on their physician, or, as it were, their father. They had been possessed, by his enemies, with the belief that the occasion of the plague was the crowding of the country people together into the town, forced as they were now, in the heat of the summer-weather, to dwell many of them together even as they could, in small tenements and stifling hovels, and to be tied to a lazy course of life within doors, whereas before they lived in a pure, open, and free air. The cause and author of all this, said they, is he who on account of the war has poured a multitude of people in upon us within the walls, and uses all these men that he has here upon no employ or service, but keeps them pent up like cattle, to be overrun with infection from one another, affording them neither shift of quarters nor any refreshment.

With the design to remedy these evils, and do the enemy some inconvenience, Pericles got a hundred and fifty galleys ready, and having embarked many tried soldiers, both foot and horse, was about to sail out, giving great hope to his citizens, and no less alarm to his enemies, upon the sight of so great a force. And now the vessels having their complement of men, and Pericles being gone aboard his own galley, it happened that the sun was eclipsed, and it grew dark on a sudden, to the affright of all, for this was looked upon as extremely ominous. Pericles, therefore, perceiving the steersman seized with fear and at a loss what to do, took his cloak and held it up before the man's face, and screening him with it so that he could not see, asked him whether he imagined there was any great hurt, or the sign of any great hurt in this, and he answering No, "Why," said he, "and what does that differ from this, only that what has caused that darkness there, is something greater than a cloak?" This is a story which philosophers tell their scholars. Pericles, however, after putting out to sea, seems not to have done any other exploit befitting such preparations, and when he had laid siege to the holy city Epidaurus, which gave him some hope of surrender, miscarried in his design by reason of the sickness. For it not only seized upon the Athenians, but upon all others, too, that held any sort of communication with the army. Finding after

this the Athenians ill-affected and highly displeased with him, he tried and endeavoured what he could to appease and re-encourage them. But he could not pacify or allay their anger, nor persuade or prevail with them any way, till they freely passed their votes upon him, resumed their power, took away his command from him, and fined him in a sum of money; which by their account that say least, was fifteen talents, while they who reckon most, name fifty. The name prefixed to the accusation was Cleon, as Idomeneus tells us; Simmias, according to Theophrastus; and Heraclides Ponticus gives it as Lacratidas.

* * *

The city having made trial of other generals for the conduct of war, and orators for business of state, when they found there was no one who was of weight enough for such a charge, or of authority sufficient to be trusted with so great a command, regretted the loss of him, and invited him again to address and advise them, and to reassume the office of general. He, however, lay at home in dejection and mourning; but was persuaded by Alcibiades and others of his friends to come abroad and show himself to the people; who having, upon his appearance, made their acknowledgments, and apologised for their untowardly treatment of him, he undertook the public affairs once more. . . .

7. PERICLEAN ATHENS: DEMOCRACY OR DICTATORSHIP?*

In the following selection Malcolm McGregor critically examines and rejects the Thucydidean assertion that Athens was a democracy in name only during the Periclean Age. What is more, he goes on to explain why Thucydides made such a claim. The problem is posed by the fact that although Thucydides tells us that the oligarchic government installed by the Four Hundred in 411 was the best in his time, he also has high praise for the Athens of Pericles.

What we seek, ideally, is reconciliation of those comments by Thucydides on government that seem to conflict. Our investigation commences with Perikles. From the ostracism of Kimon in 461 to his own death in 429 he was not out of office for more than a year or two; for the last fifteen years consecutively he was elected *strategos*, often, probably, *strategos autokrator*. Long tenure of office, as we know, becomes in itself a ground for criticism and Perikles did not escape. The Olympian figure in Aristophanes surely reflects a phase of contemporary gossip. Today students are often told that Athens was not really a democracy at all; rather, it was a dictatorship. In more fashionable circles, we read of the principate of Perikles, a term which immediately summons Augustus Caesar from the shades. It must be granted that for this view there is weighty authority, Thucydides himself: "What was in theory democracy," he writes, "became in fact rule by the first citizen." The sentence has since been adopted by many as a fundamental text.

Perhaps the most quoted of Thucydides' opinions, it withstands analysis least; a cynic might remark that it is seldom subjected to analysis. Throughout Perikles' tenure of office the *ekklesia* met at least forty times a year. Each spring it elected the generals for the following year. Each year their fellow-citizens examined the

qualifications of the generals before they took office. Ten times during the year the *ekklesia* heard reports from the generals. As they left office each year a jury of their fellow-citizens audited their records. One may employ other terms: during Perikles' political life the constitution functioned without interruption and Perikles had to retain the confidence of the sovereign and sensitive *demos* in order to remain in office. Not only was it possible for him to fail of re-election, as indeed he did in 444 B.C.; he might be removed from office, as indeed he was in 430 B.C. In the autumn of that year a disgruntled citizenry deposed and fined Perikles; more than that, they actually despatched a peace-mission to Sparta, *while he remained in office*, in direct contravention of his established policy. Now if democracy means and is government by the citizens, if the *ekklesia* decided policy by vote, if free elections persisted at their constitutional intervals, if Perikles was at all times responsible to the sovereign *demos*, and if an unoppressed political opposition survived, as it surely did,—if all this is so, then Athens was as democratic, not only in theory but in day-to-day practice, as government can conceivably be. How such a system can be related to a dictatorship or to a principate is beyond my comprehension. The term principate is particularly unfortunate; for how does Augustus, the prototype, fit the conditions set out in this paragraph, which are not in dispute?

The principle of responsibility was paramount in the Athenian conception of democracy. The mere length of a responsible

---

* Malcolm McGregor, "The Politics of the Historian Thucydides," *Phoenix*, 10 (1956), pp. 97-98, 100-102. Published by the Classical Association of Canada (Toronto: University of Toronto Press, 1956).

magistrate's tenure of office should not, by rational judges, be adopted at any time as a criterion of dictatorship. Within our own memories, however, a prolonged term has evoked the same indefensible protest in democratic countries, which should help us to understand, from our own experience, Perikles' position amidst his critics (and admirers) at the beginning of the Peloponnesian War. And nowhere in the modern world is the citizen's control over his representatives more direct and more constant than was the Athenian's. The truth is that Perikles had so won the confidence of his fellow-citizens that they elected him year after year and (wisely, I should say) allowed him, as their elder statesman, to guide them and shape their policies. But that they never surrendered, or diminished, their control of their own destinies is proved no more convincingly by Perikles' failure at the polls in 444 and his deposition in 430 than by his rapid re-election by a repentant *demos* a few months later. Athens remained a full and direct democracy.

* * *

We may find it simpler to understand Thucydides if we recognise that the democratic party at Athens itself developed two wings, one radical and one conservative. Perikles ended his life as a member of the latter. He had had his fling with the radical, aggressively imperialistic type of popular leadership and, by 446/5 B.C., had failed. His failure was remarkable in that he confessed it; he at once abandoned the aggressive policy by land and turned to the consolidation of the naval empire. He was thus able to guide Athens—and so most of the Aegean states—through what was probably the longest period of continuous prosperity and peace that Hellenes could remember. His thorough-going reversal I deem the surest evidence of his superior statecraft. This was the man who commanded the allegiance of Thucydides.

With the death of Perikles the restraining voice was gone and the way cleared for the imperialistic radicals, who offered to an avid *demos* a policy that was to prove as disastrous as Perikles had predicted. This transition allows Thucydides to give vent to his natural antipathy to democracy. His indictment of popular government, implied before the death of Perikles, is explicit in his treatment of Kleon, reaches a climax in the shameful words of the Athenian in the Melian Dialogue, and passes inexorably to the final collapse, which Thucydides, who lived to see it, attributes to the folly of the democracy. The state under Perikles, which we, unlike Thucydides, call democracy, Thucydides could endorse with enthusiasm; but Kleon and his kind, in a state in which the machinery and the system had undergone not the slightest change, the oligarchic Thucydides could not stomach. To him Kleon was democracy; we know that Perikles was too. Worse was to come. Alkibiades, that brilliant renegade, borrowed the foreign policies of Kleon; having greater ability and less sense of responsibility, he wrought greater harm.

Yet there were those upon whom the mantle of Perikles fell. Of these Nikias was most prominent. Sometimes considered an oligarch, he was in truth, with his loyalty to Periklean tradition and policy, a conservative, or Periklean, democrat. Of him Thucydides, not surprisingly, writes with a nice appreciation, and in the increasingly grim pages one can detect a real sympathy for Nikias, so honest, so loyal, and, at the last, so ineffective.

The situation after Perikles has been neatly described by John Finley: "Pericles . . . had four characteristics: he could see and expound what was necessary, he was patriotic and above money. Athens' misfortune and the essential cause of her ruin was that none of his successors combined all these traits. Nicias, who was honest but inactive, had the last two; Alcibiades, who was able but utterly self-interested, had the first two . . . ."

This was Athens' tragedy, that she produced no successor who combined all the qualities of Perikles. I have heard it argued that Perikles was culpable for not having left a political heir, that is, that he did not brook rivalry. This, to be sure, is the charge that is commonly levelled at the great man. Apart from the fact that this assumes a principate that never existed and that Nikias *was* his heir, though not his intellectual peer, it is a formidable undertaking to show how one man could suppress others of comparable talent within his own party in a system in which an office-holder was ever subject to discipline and in which a popular assembly provided the ideal arena for the potential statesman to acquire education, training, and reputation. When we bewail the quality of those who received the reins from Perikles, we perhaps fail sufficiently to emphasise the surpassing genius of one who so excelled his contemporaries. "Perikles," Thucydides points out, "influential because of his reputation and intelligence and obvious integrity, was able freely to restrain the people; he led them rather than was led by them . . . . His successors were more evenly matched with one another, striving, each one of them, to be first."

Perikles commanded the respect and the loyalty of men of various political persuasions. Thucydides was one of those to whom the man was more significant than their own partly inherited political convictions. It is a truism that the inspired leader draws support from the state as a whole, irrespective of party-lines. To Thucydides the events that followed the death of Perikles must have come as a bitter, if not entirely unexpected, disappointment; not unexpected, because he had no real faith in democracy and the death of Perikles removed the source of his self-deception. Steadily, as he saw it, the Periklean state was being destroyed. When Theramenes' moderate oligarchy of Five Thousand, with its unrestricted citizenship but restricted privilege, emerged from the revolution of 411/0, Thucydides, reverting easily to his tradition, could follow the dictates of his intellect and pronounce this the best government enjoyed by the Athenians in his time. It is his only categorical judgement on government; it is the key to his political convictions.

One might draw a parallel between Thucydides and the Old Oligarch. The Old Oligarch, it will be recalled, is so named from the nature of his anti-democratic essay written about 425 B.C. He writes, in effect, "I do not approve of democracy, but, if you *must* have it, I admit that the Athenians make a fine job of it." Thucydides, the oligarch born, might have said, "I do not approve of democracy, I see no strength or wisdom in the rabble; but I do admire and will support the Periklean state, which of course is not democracy at all."

We are ready to summarise. Thucydides was reared in the conservative anti-democratic tradition. His orderly and impartial mind was impressed by the genius of Perikles, and so he became a Periklean, though not a democrat; nor could he admit that by so doing he was, in essence, approving of democracy. Later, the oligarchic tradition of his family, that had never been abandoned, reasserted itself, as he saw Periklean ideals forgotten, Periklean warnings ignored. He witnessed, with a brutally piercing eye, what seemed to him the evils of a democracy run to seed, its moral fibre weakening. He ended his life as he had begun it, a confirmed oligarch who had never renounced the creed of his fathers.

8. WAS ATHENS IN THE AGE OF PERICLES ARISTOCRATIC?*

The majority of the numerous books which deal with Athenian political and social life in the latter part of the fifth century B.C. convey to student and to reader the general, but emphatic, impression that the *polis* Athens, while theoretically a democracy, was, generally speaking, an aristocracy. It is hardly an exaggeration to say that the composite picture of Athens under Pericles, as represented in the traditional view of the handbooks, reveals a society brilliant in its achievements, but quite selfishly constituted, and gravely defective, save from the viewpoint of the favored few. Profound social distinctions, even among the citizens themselves, are insisted upon. The conception still is widely prevalent that the *élite* of Athenian society, few but fit, led a life of glorious but intensely selfish leisure, which was their lordly prerogative as the result of the ruthless exploitation of all professional men, artists, producers, traders, artisans, workers, resident aliens, and slaves. Almost everywhere we find the time-honored assertion that in Athens all work was despised, labor was contemned, the workers were disdained, and, in fact, that *any* service for which financial remuneration was received was in disrepute and branded the doer with a humiliating social stigma. The free man is supposed to have done little or no work, for surely the aristocratic citizen must have a completely independent and carefree existence for his manifold political, social, and religious duties.

Let me now present some typical quotations from some recent books on Athens which give this false, or exaggerated, as I think, impression of the nature of Athenian society in the second half of the fifth century B.C., in that they assert that it was essentially aristocratic. In the ninth edition (1915) of that very popular, widely influential, and, in many respects, admirable little book, *The Greek View of Life* by Mr. Lowes Dickinson, we read (italics are mine in every case): "In the Greek conception the citizen was an aristocrat. His excellence was thought to consist in public activity; and to the performance of public duties he ought therefore to be able to devote *the greater part of his time and energy*. But the existence of such a privileged class involved the existence of a class of producers to support them; and *the producers, by the nature of their calling*, be they slave or free, *were excluded from the life of the perfect citizen*. They had not the necessary leisure to devote to public business; neither had they the opportunity to acquire the mental and physical qualities which would enable them to transact it worthily. They were therefore regarded by the Greeks as an inferior class. . . . In Athens the most democratic of all the Greek communities, though they were admitted to the citizenship and enjoyed considerable political influence, *they never appear to have lost the stigma of social inferiority*. And the distinction which was more or less definitely drawn in practice *between the citizens proper* and *the productive class* was even more emphatically affirmed in theory" (pp. 74–75). "The obverse of the Greek *citizen*, who realized in the state the highest life, was *an inferior class of producers who realized only the means to subsistence*" (p. 75). "The *inferiority* of the artisan and the trader was further emphasized by the fact that *they were excluded by their calling* from the cultivation of the higher personal qualities; from the training of the body by gymnastics and of the mind by philosophy; *from habitual conversance with public affairs*; from that perfect balance, in a word, of the physical, intellectual, and moral powers,

---

* By LaRue Van Hook, "Was Athens in the Age of Pericles Aristocratic?" *The Classical Journal*, 14 (1918–19).

which was only to be attained by a process of *self-culture, incompatible with the pursuance of a trade for bread*" (p. 82). "The existence of the Greek citizen depended upon that of an inferior class who were regarded, not as ends in themselves, but as means to his perfection." "The aim of modern societies is not to separate off a privileged class of citizens, set free by the labour of others to live the perfect life, but rather to distribute impartially to all the burdens and advantages of the state, so that every one shall be at once a labourer for himself and a citizen of the state. But this idea is clearly incompatible with the Greek conception of the citizen" (p. 130). "It is because labour with the hands or at the desk distorts or impairs the body, and the petty cares of a calling pursued for bread pervert the soul, that so *strong a contempt was felt by the Greeks for manual labour and trade.*" "If then the artisan ... in Athens never altogether threw off *the stigma of inferiority attaching to his trade*, the reason was that the life he was compelled to lead was incompatible with the Greek conception of excellence" (p. 134). "The Greeks, on the whole, were quite content to sacrifice the majority to the minority. Their position was fundamentally aristocratic; they exaggerated rather than minimized the distinctions between men, the freeman and the slave, the gentleman and the artisan, regarding them as natural and fundamental, not as the casual product of circumstances. The 'equality' which they sought was proportional, not arithmetical, not of equal rights to all." "In a modern state it is different though class distinctions are clearly enough marked, yet the point of view from which they are regarded is fundamentally different. They are attributed rather to accidents of fortune than to varieties of nature. The artisan, for example, ranks no doubt lower than the professional man; but no one maintains that he is a different kind of being incapable by nature, as Aristotle asserts, of the characteristic excellence of man" (p. 79).

In *Greek Ideals*, by Mr. C. Delisle Burns, a study of Athenian social life of the period under consideration, the Greek aristocratic conception of individual liberty is likewise, I believe, overemphasized. Thus we find the statements: "It seemed essential that liberty and equality should only be the right of *a few* males. . . . Slaves and *workingmen had no time and no developed capacity for the 'good life'* " (p. 76). "Society was conceived only in terms . . . of *a small social caste*" (p. 109). "The Athenian citizen might object to doing manual labour" (p. 112).

Similar assertions are common. Thus Mr. Edwards in Whibley's *Companion to Greek Studies*: "The prejudice against trades and handicrafts was most pronounced in Sparta: elsewhere, though the political disabilities might be reduced or removed, the *social stigma was scarcely diminished*—indeed, even the fullest development of democracy at Athens did but stereotype the conventional horror of hard work, and proclaimed leisure, and not labour, to be the citizen's privilege. . . . The marvel is that, *amid all this depreciation*, mechanical skill and artistic taste should have attained so high a standard" (p. 437).

Gardner and Jevons, *Manual of Greek Antiquities* (p. 379), quote Aristotle and Plato to show the extreme *popular* prejudice against handiwork and the disesteem in which it was *universally* held—"only those too poor to buy slaves had to work themselves."

Gulick, in his excellent *Life of the Ancient Athenians*, says: "The class of artisans comprised callings which among us are regarded as the most dignified professions. Wherever one of these vocations *was in disrepute*, the cause is found in the fact that the person concerned *took money for his services*, and was to that extent not independent of others. Even the great artists, painters, and sculptors fell under *public contempt* simply because they earned money. A few artists, like Phidias, are said to have enjoyed the friendship of eminent men of aristocratic birth; but most of these stories of intimacy are later exaggerations which have not taken into account the conditions of ancient industrial life. Schoolmasters, teachers of music and gymnastics, sophists and even physicians were not highly regarded" (p. 233). "To the *emporos* attached some of *the stigma of personal labor.*" "Ancient communities (e.g., Athens) whose *citizens despised trade and manual labor*" (p. 65). "Art, letters, and politics, claimed the interest of the ordinary citizen far more than they do today, because it was the policy of Pericles *to render the democracy of Athens a leisure class, supported by their slaves and the revenues of the Empire*" (p. 118).

But enough of such representative quotations, they might be multiplied indefinitely. It is the aim of this paper to endeavor to correct, or, at least, to assist in the modification of this all too general conception of an essentially aristocratic Athenian society, a conception which is certainly false in some of its aspects and exaggerated or overemphasized in others.

Before a consideration of the subject proper it may well be asked, why is it that this view of Athenian society as aristocratic, if erroneous, is generally held? The reasons are, I believe, as follows: (1) Athens, like other Greek states, at an early period in its history, in fact, until after Solon and Cleisthenes, was, in large measure, oligarchic and aristocratic both politically and socially. Modern writers mistakenly assume that these early conditions, particularly in social life, continued. (2) Certain Greek states, e.g., Sparta, Thebes, and Crete never suffered democratization. The strictly aristocratic conditions which were permanently characteristic of these states are sometimes thought of as necessarily existing also in Athens. (3) Modern writers have the tendency implicitly to follow Plato and Aristotle as authorities and imagine that actual fifth century Athenian conditions are accurately re-

flected in the pages of these philosophers even when the latter are discussing theoretical polities and imaginary and ideal societies. Caution must always be observed surely in the case of these "Laconizing" theorizers who, furthermore, were intense aristocrats and distrusted democracy. (4) It is true that Athens was conservative in the granting of full and technically legal citizenship to foreigners and slaves. (5) Slavery was, of course, a recognized institution from time immemorial throughout the ancient world and Athens as well. (6) Physical *drudgery* was not relished by the Athenians. The ground is now cleared for our discussion.

1. POLITICAL CONDITIONS

Was Athens in the Age of Pericles really a political democracy? We are fortunate in having no less an authority than Pericles himself to testify for us; Pericles, the aristocrat, as reported by Thucydides, the aristocrat. "Our government is *not copied* from those of our neighbors; we are an example to them rather than they to us. Our constitution is named a *democracy*, because it is in the hands not of the few but of *the many*. Our laws secure *equal* justice for *all* in their private disputes, and our *public opinion* welcomes and honors talent in *every branch of achievement*, not for any sectional reason, but on grounds of excellence alone. And as we give free play to *all* in our public life, so we carry the same spirit into our daily relations with one another. We are obedient to whomsoever is set in authority, and to the laws, more especially to those which offer protection to the oppressed and those unwritten ordinances whose transgressions brings admitted shame. Wealth to us is not mere material for vainglory but an opportunity for achievement; and *poverty* we think is *no disgrace* to acknowledge but a real degradation to make no effort to overcome. *Our citizens attend both to public and private duties, and do not allow absorption in their own various affairs to interfere with their knowledge of the city's.* We differ from other states in regarding the man who *holds aloof from public life* not as quiet but as useless. In a word I claim that our city as a whole is an education to Greece, and that her members yield to none, man by man, for independence of spirit, many-sidedness of attainment, and complete self-reliance in limbs and brain."

In Athens, then, if not in Sparta and Plato's *Republic*, the state existed for the individual and not the individual for the state. It is unnecessary to do more than briefly to cite the facts which reveal Athens as a political democracy. *All* citizens over eighteen years of age were members of the Assembly; *all* citizens over thirty were eligible to membership in the Council of Five Hundred, the members of which were elected annually *by lot*; *all* citizens over thirty were eligible to election *by lot* to serve as jurymen in the Heliastic law courts. As Warde Fowler says: "Every citizen had the right to hold all offices, with the doubtful exception in 450, of the archonship; to serve on the Council; to take part in the Assembly; to sit as judge. There was no privileged class, no skilled politicians, no bureaucracy. The whole Athenian people were identified with, actually were the state. All shared equally in the government, education, and pleasures." For this complete political equality we may let Mr. Dickinson himself eloquently testify. Although he tells us (p. 83) that the artisan and the trader were excluded by their calling from habitual conversance with public affairs, later he says (p. 112): "Among the free citizens, who included persons of every rank, no political distinction at all was drawn. All of them from the lowest to the highest had the right to speak and vote in the great assembly of the people which was the ultimate authority; all were eligible to every administrative post; all sat in turn as jurors in the law courts. The disabilities of poverty were minimized by payment for attendance in

the assembly and courts. And what is more extraordinary, even distinctions of ability were levelled by the practice of filling all offices, except the highest, by lot. The citizenship was extended to every rank and calling; the poor man jostled the rich, the shopman the aristocrat, in the Assembly; cobblers, carpenters, smiths, farmers, merchants and retail dealers met together with the ancient landed gentry." "Politically the Athenian trader, and the Athenian artisan, was the equal of the aristocrat of purest blood" (p. 115).

We know that the power of the early Athenian aristocracy had been seriously curtailed by the legislation of Solon and Cleisthenes. After the Persian Wars its influence as an organized party became extremely small because of the democratic reforms of Ephialtes and Pericles through the blows dealt to the prestige of the Areopagus, the exile of Cimon, and the complete ascendency of Pericles. There was, then, in Athens in the Age of Pericles complete political equality among the citizens; poverty, wealth, station, family, occupation, and prestige all were of no consequence.

II. Social Conditions

1. *Social status of citizens in general.*— Let us now turn to an examination of the social conditions of Athenian life and scrutinize it for evidences of caste, class, snobbery, inequality, or injustice. In the city the house of the rich man and that of the poor man differed little in appearance. Private unostentation as contrasted with public magnificence was the rule. In fact, it was considered a breach of good taste to build and occupy a house of conspicuous cost or size. In the next place, simplicity in dress was general. Only the young (and, in particular, the Knights) dared to provoke possible derision or to invite popular prejudice by foppery of attire or appearance. Young Mantitheus apologizes to the Senate for his long hair and Strepsiades is

disgusted with his son's "dandyism." Wearing the hair long might arouse suspicion of Spartan or aristocratic sympathies. An ancient witness testifies that "the Athenian people are not better clothed than the slave or alien, nor in personal appearance is there any superiority." Of course the nature of the employment might influence the quality and nature of the costume.

In all forms of social activity all the citizens participated on a parity. All could attend the theater; all joined in the public festivals and in religious sacrifices and observances. In fact, if any element in Athens was favored it was the poor and lowly. Listen to the testimony of that unregenerate old Aristocrat (just quoted) who is bitterly opposed to Democracy as an institution but admits that it really exists in Athens. He says that if you *must* have Democracy Athens is a perfect example of it, "I do not praise the Polity of the Athenians, because the very choice involves the welfare of the *baser* folk as opposed to that of the *better* class. The poorer classes and the people of Athens should have the advantage over the men of birth and wealth because it is the people who row the vessels, and put around the city her girdle of power. Everywhere greater consideration is shown to the base, to poor people, and to common folk, than to persons of good quality—this should not surprise us, this is the keystone of the preservation of the democracy. It is these poor people, this common folk, this riff-raff, whose prosperity, combined with the growth of their numbers, enhance the democracy. All the world over the cream of society is in opposition to the democracy. The objection may be raised that it was a mistake to allow universal right of speech and a seat in the council; privileges which should have been reserved for the cleverest, the flower of the community. But if only the better people sat in council blessings would fall only to that class and the baser folk would get nothing. Whereas it is the other way round. The people desire to be free and to be masters and their bad legislation is the very source of the people's strength and freedom." The happy lot of the common people in ancient Athens is further described by this contemporary witness: "The rich man trains the chorus; it is the people for whom the chorus is trained. The rich man is trierarch or gymnasiarch and the people profit by their labors. The whole state sacrifices at public cost a large number of victims; the Attic Democracy keeps holiday. They build at public cost a number of palaestras, dressing-rooms, bathing establishments; the mob gets the benefit of the majority of these luxuries rather than the select few or the well-to-do. In the theater the people do not like to be caricatured in comedy; it is the wealthy or well-born or influential man who is lampooned."

Enough has been said to show that the door of opportunity was open to all in Athens at this time. Worth, ability, character, not accident of birth or position counted. The rich did not grow richer while the poor grew poorer. Surplus wealth was not at the disposal of the few. It was expended for the good of all upon religious observances, the drama, gymnasia, the navy, public buildings and their adornment, and the state support of orphans and those physically incapacitated for earning a living. The wealthier classes were expected, and, in fact, were compelled, to contribute according to their means to the common welfare through the various liturgies and taxes.

2. *The social status of the producer, artisan, etc.*—We come next to a study of the social and economic position of the workers of various kinds. As we have seen, the handbooks in general tell us that all work was regarded as degrading, every activity for which one was paid was condemned, and producers, artisans, and all workers were branded by a humiliating social stigma. No adequate proof of such a condition of affairs is forthcoming; indeed, the actual situation seems to have been

otherwise in democratic Athens of the time of Pericles. Why then is there this general mistaken notion? It is largely because of certain pronouncements in Plato and Aristotle. In the *Laws* and the *Republic* Plato insists on the gulf that should separate the citizen from the mechanic or trader. His ideal state rests upon agriculture and all the citizens are landed gentry forbidden to engage in trade. In this ideal *polis* trade and commerce are to be insignificant and the productive class is actually debarred from all political rights. A caste system is presupposed; governors and governed are sharply differentiated and each class is trained for its predestined position in the state. Aristotle, too, in his ideal state divides the population, on the one hand, into a ruling class of soldiers and judges and, on the other, into a subject class consisting of artisans and producers. As a mechanical trade renders the body and soul and intellect of free persons unfit for the exercise and practice of virtue Aristotle denies to the artisan the proper excellence of man on the ground that his occupation and status are unnatural. In an extreme Democracy the mechanic and hired laborer must needs be citizens; this is impossible in an Aristocracy in which virtue and desert constitute the sole claim to the honors of state. Other radical statements of Aristotle are that the producer only differs from a slave in being subject to all instead of to one man and that the sedentary and within-door nature of the crafts unfitted the man who exercised them for war and the chase, the most dignified employments. Physical labor is condemned by him in that it is cheapening to work for another for pay or material profit as this reduces one to the rank of a slave. This would seem to be the chief source for the curious statement everywhere repeated that all Athenians who did anything for pay were condemned. That Aristotle did not represent Athenian opinion is conclusively shown by his condemnation of agriculture as preventing leisure which is at the basis of virtue. But no one doubts that agriculture was generally and highly esteemed by the Athenians. In Xenophon in a passage which is represented as spoken by Socrates those base mechanic arts are condemned which ruin the bodies of all those engaged in them, as those who are forced to remain in sitting postures and hug the gloom or crouch whole days confronting a furnace. This results in physical enervation and enfeebling of the soul and the victims have no leisure to devote to the claims of friendship and the state. Such will be sorry friends and ill-defenders of the fatherland.

It is absolutely wrong to accept these passages as conclusively proving that the Athenians regarded work as degrading and workers as social outcasts. (1) These writers do not claim to be describing actual Athenian conditions. (2) They are postulating an "ideal" society. (3) They are ever admirers of Spartan, and not their own Athenian polity. (4) They were intense aristocrats in sympathy and mistrusted democracy. (5) They despised the body and its needs. (6) They had particularly in mind soul-destroying drudgery, not reasonable labor and skilled work; corrupt and petty business, not necessary and honest trade and affairs. Frequently they were contrasting the philosopher-statesmen set apart for ruling with the defective yokel. We can, indeed, if we wish, invoke the above-quoted writers in defense of work and the dignity of producing. Plato says in the *Laws*: "Retail trade in a city is not by nature intended to do any harm, but quite the contrary; for is not he a benefactor who reduces the inequalities and incommensurabilities of goods to equality and common measure? And this is what the power of money accomplishes, and the merchant may be said to be appointed for this purpose." Plato goes on to observe that many occupations have suffered ill-repute because of the inordinate love of gain and consequent corrupt practices on the part of the unscrupulous. He concludes: "If...we were to compel the best men everywhere to keep taverns for a time, or carry on retail trade, or do anything of that sort; or if, in consequence of some fate or necessity, the best women were compelled to follow similar callings, then we should know how agreeable and pleasant all these things are; and if all such occupations were managed on incorrupt principles, they would be honored as we honor a mother or nurse." Aristotle in the *Politics* condemns agriculture as we have seen, yet elsewhere he declares: "We honor the generous and brave and just. Such we conceive to be those who do not live upon others; and *such are they who live by labor* .... chiefly agriculturalists, and chief among the agriculturalists, the small farmers." Now these small farmers tilled their own fields; in the remote districts of Attica slavery had scarcely penetrated. Xenophon tells the story of Eutherus, an old friend of Socrates who, in poverty, as his property had been lost in the war, was gaining a livelihood by bodily toil. Socrates warns him that such employment in his case can be only temporary because of lack of necessary physical strength and urges him to secure a position as assistant to a large proprietor as manager of an estate. Eutherus fears the work may be servile. Socrates replies that heads of departments in a state who manage property are regarded not as performing undignified work but as having attained a higher dignity of freedom. Eutherus still demurs on the ground that he does not like to be accountable to anyone. Socrates replies that it is difficult to find work that is devoid of liability to account. It is difficult to avoid mistakes or unfriendly criticism. "Avoid captious critics," he says, "attach yourself to the considerate. Whatever you can do, do it heart and soul and make it your finest work." Another interesting and significant opinion of Socrates on this subject is reported by Xenophon which was expressed in a conversation between the philosopher and Aristarchus. The time was during the régime of the Thirty when economic and political conditions were

very bad. Aristarchus' house was full of his indigent female relatives, fourteen in all. As these ladies are all expert needlewomen, skilled in the making of garments, Socrates advises his friend to put them to work; Ceramon, for example, with a few slaves, is very prosperous. Aristarchus objects to this proposal; the situations are not comparable; the members of his large household are not barbarian slaves but are kinswomen and free-born. Socrates replies: "Then, on the ground that they are free-born and relatives you think they ought to do nothing but eat and sleep? Or is it your opinion that free-born people who live in this way lead happier lives and are more to be congratulated than those who devote themselves to such useful arts of life as they are skilled in? Are work and study of no value? Did your relatives learn what they know merely for useless information or as a future asset? Is the well-tempered life and a juster one attained rather through idleness or the practice of the useful? If they were called upon to do some shameful work, let them choose death rather than that; but it is otherwise. It is suitable work for women. The things which we know are those we can best perform; it is a joy to do them, and the result is fair."

Plenty of evidence is available to show that work was esteemed, not only in the times portrayed by Homer in the *Iliad* and *Odyssey* and Hesiod in his *Works and Days*, but in Athens of the fifth century, B.C. In Athens there was actually a law directed against idleness. That it was long in force is shown by the fact that Lysias wrote a speech in connection with a prosecution for ἀργία for which the penalty on conviction was a fine of one hundred drachmas and ἀτιμία if the accused were thrice convicted. Plutarch tells us that a son who had not been taught a trade by his father was thereby released from the obligation to support his parent in old age. We have already quoted Pericles to the effect that not poverty but indolence is degrading.

Now the old-fashioned assumption that

the Athenians found abundant leisure and opportunity for the *real life* (i.e., art, literature, politics, and philosophy) only because hirelings, slaves, and women did everything for them and the state treasury liberally supported them in *dolce far niente* is ridiculous. One thing is certain from all we know of the Athenians; they were not indolent; they were energetic in mind and body. Certainly in any state the wealthy are but a minority of the total population and even upon these rests the duty to manage their property and care for investments. Participation in public life and fulfilment of the demands and duties of good citizenship did not exact from the average Athenian anything like the major part of his waking hours. The Assembly met four times in each prytany (or tenth of a year period), i.e., less than once a week. As the attendance was voluntary only a fraction of all who were entitled to attend were ever present, as convenience or interest dictated. The Council was limited to five hundred citizens and no one might serve more than twice; furthermore, fifty only of the Council (οἱ πρυτάνεις, the standing committee) were continuously on duty so that the majority thus were free to attend to their private affairs. The Heliaea, or Courts of Justice, drew their dicasts or judges for jury service from a list of six thousand citizens. These were usually men of advanced years who had volunteered for such service. Universal military service at this time was not obligatory. Festivals and contests were generally attended but they occurred probably not oftener than once a week on the average. It has been estimated that a total of from two to three years of every citizen's life were required for deliberative and administrative duties. Many writers have emphasized the huge numbers of citizens who were supposedly pensioners luxuriously supported, apparently permanently and completely, by largess from the Periclean treasury. We have seen that public duties were not constant. As for the compensation it must be remembered that the daily living wage for the workman was from one drachma (about 18 cents), to one and a half. Now at the time under consideration Assemblymen received no compensation; jurymen received two obols (about six cents) daily for service; members of the Council of Five Hundred, elected annually by lot, were paid five obols (about fifteen cents). In the light of these facts how can it be claimed that Pericles *corrupted* the citizens generally by gifts of money, making them idle, cowardly, and greedy or to assume that these citizens were all dependent on public pay and could entirely support their households on these meager stipends. Mr. Grundy declares: "A condition of things in which a large proportion of a community is either practically or wholly dependent on the community for subsistence is unhealthy from both a social and political viewpoint." But only a minority of the fifty to sixty thousand adult male citizens received any state pay. The remuneration given was not a living wage; it was merely a contribution to support by which Pericles provided that *all*, and not merely the well-to-do, might participate, in turn, in civic affairs and obtain that benefit and culture from active personal public service to which he eloquently refers in the Funeral Oration. Nor was the remuneration intended as a sop to placate the discontented and starving proletariat. As Ferguson says: "Pericles did not intend to create a class of salaried officials; nor yet to make an advance toward communism. His ideal was political, not economic, equality—to enable all, irrespective of wealth or station, to use the opportunities and face the obligations which democracy brought in its train. Like all the great democratic leaders who preceded him, he was a nobleman by birth and breeding, and, like them, he did not doubt for a moment that the culture that enabled the life of his class would dignify and uplift that of the masses also. His aim was to unite the whole people in a community of high ideas and emotions. It was to make them a nation of noblemen." If this were not the case, Pericles' noble speech, which stands in history by the side of Lincoln's Gettysburg address, is the most hypocritical document preserved to us from the past.

Since the number of wealthy citizens was small how did the ordinary citizen gain his livelihood? It was by means of agriculture, handicrafts, trades, wholesale and retail business, and daily labor. No occupation was more respected and admired than agriculture. Farms were small, tenancy almost unknown. The small farmer tilled his fields with his own hands. In the arts and crafts and in labor no one needed to be idle for the state policies of Pericles and the great building operations not only gave employment to all the residents of Athens, whether free men or slaves, but attracted workers from far and near. Thousands of citizens, perhaps a third of the whole, gained a livelihood by labor. While commerce was largely in the hands of the resident-aliens, and the heaviest drudgery was performed by slaves, the mass of the skilled workers were free citizens. Stonecutters, masons, and sculptors had their shops or yards where they worked privately with their apprentices, or they might be engaged in public work, as the building operations on the Acropolis, working side by side with other citizens, with metics, and with slaves.

Modest means, even poverty (certainly *paupertas*), was the rule in Athens and was no bar to achievement and distinction. Life and its needs was simple, and money in itself as an accumulation was not desired. A uniform wage was paid practically to all skilled workmen alike. Everyone who had skill or art was an artist, a term applied to sculptors, painters, physicians, and cobblers. Our handbooks generally assert that every occupation or profession which brought any financial return was despised and its practitioner was socially held in contempt. Slight reflection should show

the absurdity of this thesis; there is no actual evidence to prove it. Plato, to be sure, who was wealthy and an aristocrat, sneers at those sophists and teachers who were compelled to take money for teaching. Of course there were some charlatans in this profession, but we may be certain that such sophists as Gorgias, Protagoras, Isocrates, and Alcidamas (all professors who accepted tuition from countless students who were only too glad to pay it) were held in high esteem in Athens. So were lawyers and speech-writers for pay, such as Antiphon, Lysias, and Isaeus. Literary men who accepted pay, poets who received purses for prizes, and actors who profited financially by their labors stood in the highest social esteem. The prestige of physicians depended on their skill and personality. The ignoramus and the charlatan were contemned; the skilled and public-spirited surgeon might be richly rewarded and given a honorary crown and public thanks. The elementary-school teacher, the music and gymnastic instructor, were not highly regarded, not because they received money for their services, but because most of them were ignorant men and often of inferior breeding. As for the great artists, sculptors, and painters it is simply impossible to believe such a statement as this: "Even the great artists, painters, and sculptors fell under public contempt simply because they earned money." Could this be true of a Phidias, a Polygnotus, an Ictinus, or a Mnesicles? But we know that Phidias was a warm and extremely intimate personal friend of Pericles. In fact, the statesman admired the sculptor so highly that the latter was entrusted with the greatest powers in superintending the ornamentation of the great temples. As for Polygnotus, a native of Thasos, he was the personal friend of Cimon, and was actually honored by the Athenians with citizenship. Expert potters and vase-painters were very numerous. While some of these were resident aliens (e.g. Amasis and Brygos), very many were citizens. Thus we find such names of prominent vase-makers as Klitias, Ergotimos, Nikosthenes, Epiktetes, Pamphaios, Euphronios, Hieron, and Megakles. A typical vase-making establishment would engage the services of some twelve persons who might be citizens, metics, and slaves all working side by side in equality. Citizen artists and artisans proclaim with pride, and do not conceal in shame, their occupations. Vase-painters and makers signed their wares. A scene (The Workshop of a Greek Vase-Painter) on a vase shows two Victories and Athena herself crowning the workmen, as Pottier says: "a poetic symbol to glorify the fame of Athenian industry." Indeed, artisans regarded themselves as under the special protection of Hephaestus, the smith, and of Athena, mistress of the arts and crafts, and were proud to claim descent from these deities. The potter, Euphronios, when making an offering to Athena calls himself in his dedication, κεραμεύς, and the same procedure is followed by the fuller Simon, the tanner Smikros, and the potters, Mnesiades and Nearchus. On a funeral bas-relief a cobbler was represented in a heroic attitude holding the insignia of his trade. In the neighborhood of the Agora shops were especially numerous. These places served as centers of gossip and of news for Athenians generally, as we are told in a graphic passage in an informative speech of Lysias.[1] It was among these craftsmen that Socrates, who had himself started in life as a stonecutter, spent much time in conversation. When he was, on an occasion, in search of a gentle-

man, he did not hesitate to go the round of various good carpenters, bronzeworkers, painters, and sculptors.

The comedies of Aristophanes are sometimes taken as proof of great social distinctions and inequalities existing among the citizens of Athens. Thus Mr. Dickinson, in an endeavor to maintain his thesis that Athens was politically democratic but socially intensely aristocratic, quotes at length the passage from the comedy of the *Knights* where the sausage-seller is assured that his crass ignorance, boorish vulgarity, and dense stupidity are the strongest possible recommendations and assets for the highest political distinction. We are apparently to infer that Aristophanes was himself a deep-dyed aristocrat who despised the people and their rule and that he was the spokesman for a large aristocratic section of Athenian society who were extremely hostile to democratic government. These views are unwarranted and, indeed, have been wholly discredited. Aristophanes was not a partisan; he was a conservative. He was not an opponent of democracy nor yet an aristocrat. It is true that he was a well-educated man of keen discernment, a friend of the Knights, and was doubtless on good terms with members of the aristocratic element in Athens. But he was friendly to the cause of democracy and sincerely wished to do it a favor by fearlessly revealing those defects to which a democratic form of government is especially liable and to give warning of possible dangers. This he constantly does in his plays with that exaggeration. and caricature which are characteristic of the Old Comedy. In the opinion of the poet grave danger to the democracy might arise from unscrupulous demagogy as represented by such knaves as Cleon. In the case of Cleon, who is lampooned in the play of the *Knights*, Aristophanes is actuated by intense animus as a result of previous personal encounters. Thus Cleon is excoriated as a vulgar, coarse, and despicable individual, and the dramatist tries to discredit his influence

---

[1] *On the Cripple* (No. 24), 19–20: "My accuser says that many unprincipled men gather at my shop. But you (the large jury) all know that this accusation is not directed at me more than other artisans, nor at those who frequent my place more than those who go to other shops. Each of you is accustomed to visit the establishment of the perfumer, or the barber, or the leatherworker, etc. If any of you shall condemn my visitors then he must condemn the frequenters of other places; and if these, then *all the Athenians*. Certainly *all* of you are accustomed to frequent these shops and spend time somewhere or other."

and popularity. It is a great mistake to take Aristophanes' savage attacks on vulgar demagogues and criticisms of weaknesses in democratic government as proof that Aristophanes was an aristocrat who condemned and arraigned the people as a whole for vulgarity and incompetency. That he did not despair of the democracy and that he sympathized and fraternized with the "lower classes' is shown by those plays in which the chief personages, although of low degree, are "sympathetic characters," e.g., Dicaeopolis, the charcoal-burner of the *Acharnians* and Strepsiades, the rough countryman of the *Clouds*.

In the opinion of Croiset, "the best Athenian society was the most open-hearted, most variously constituted, and most liberal society that has ever existed. The Athens that Plato shows us is a sort of talking place, where everybody is supposed to know everybody else, and where each person has a perfect right to make acquaintance with those he meets." As typical illustrations of this social democracy he refers to two social gatherings of which we have admirable accounts. In Xenophon's *Symposium* we have a description of a banquet held in 421 B.C., in the house of the wealthy Callias, son of Hipponicus, of a great and rich Athenian family. The guests include all sorts of people, rich, poor, philosophers and ignoramuses, and all converse familiarly on terms of equality and intimacy. In the same way, Plato, in his *Symposium*, an account of a dinner held at the house of Agathon in 416 B.C., reveals the same intermixture of classes and professions.

3. *The status of the metics.*—We have now completed our discussion of the essentially democratic political and social status of Athenian citizens. It remains to consider briefly the other two classes of the inhabitants of Attica who are commonly regarded, along with the poorer citizens, as the exploited victims of the Athenian aristocracy. These elements are the metics (resident aliens) and the slaves.

The rapid commercial growth and naval expansion of Athens early caused a shortage of workers and helpers of all kinds. The citizen population was numerically inadequate to assume these new duties in addition to the performance of their regular occupations and the prosecution of agriculture. This demand was met by extending a welcome to foreigners and this policy was continued and encouraged by Pericles. Their exact number in the year 431 B.C. is unknown. Meyer's estimate is adult male metics 14,000 to about 55,000 adult male citizens; Clerc estimates them at 24,000, followed by Zimmern, Ferguson gives the number of adult male citizens as 50,000, and a total population of Attica of 300,000 of which one-sixth was foreign and one-third servile. There may have been, then, one adult male metic for every two citizens.

What was the lot of the metics? It has been asserted that their social position was humiliating and that they were disliked and even despised by the ordinary citizen. But contemporary evidence does not indicate this. Pericles says: "We open our city to all and never drive out foreigners." The scene of Plato's dialogue, *The Republic*, is the house of Cephalus, a prominent and influential man, but a metic who had been invited to Attica by Pericles himself. Another contemporary speaks of "the equality between the metics and the full citizens, because the city stands in need of her resident aliens to meet the requirements of such a multiplicity of arts and for the purposes of her navy." Thucydides has Nicias say to metic sailors that they and not any friends or allies outside were the "only free partners with the Athenians in the Empire." The metics participated fully in the social and religious life of the city. Neither in dress nor appearance could they be distinguished from the citizens. They attended the theater, they had a prominent place and dress in the Panathenaïc procession, they were demesmen and worshipped the same deities as the citizens. Like the citizens they defrayed the expenses of the liturgies and served in the army and the navy. When any list of Athenian inhabitants is given the metics are always named as an essential element of the population. They worked in large numbers side by side and for equal pay with the citizens in all kinds of work as, for example, the construction of the Erechtheum. They are found engaged in all the occupations, as workers and artisans of all kinds, as merchants at Peiraeus and at Athens, as bankers and capitalists, as painters, sculptors, and artists, as architects, and as philosophers and orators. Many of the famous pupils of Isocrates were metics, and no less than three of the celebrated Canon of the Ten Orators were resident aliens, namely, Isaeus of Chalcis, Lysias of Syracuse, and Deinarchus of Corinth.

The fee of twelve drachmas (about $2.16) required of metics was a petty matter, a legal formality of registration and license and not an onerous tax burden, as it is often regarded. The liability to taxes beyond those required of citizens was not great. Perhaps the most serious limitation imposed upon aliens was the inability legally to own real property. But metics might be placed on equal terms as to taxation and the owning of property with the citizens thereby becoming ἰσοτελεῖς, and full citizenship might be conferred by vote of the Assembly. For example, an inscription is preserved which records the grant of full citizenship on those metics who participated in the return of the democrats from Phyle (in 404–3) and helped in the restoration. In the list occur some strangely sounding foreign names, e.g. Βενδιφάνης and Ψαμμίς, and their occupations as given are decidedly humble, such as cook, gardener, carpenter, fuller, etc.

The Athenians have been harshly criticized for not freely and generally granting citizenship to the metics. At first thought the criticism may seem valid and Athens illiberal. But the citizenship to the Athenian was not merely a political

privilege; it was a sacred and usually an *inherited* possession. Loss of citizenship was to be feared more than death itself. Athens was a small and homogeneous community and the Athenians regarded themselves as autochthonous, like their favorite and symbolic cicada, sprung from the very soil of Attica itself. There is danger to a state in a too rapid influx of aliens who are given the powers of citizenship before real political and social assimilation has taken place. Even free America requires a term of years of probation before naturalization, and one of our greatest problems surely is this very one of the assimilation of the large number of our resident aliens. As Aristotle says: "Another cause for revolution is difference of races which do not acquire a common spirit; for the state is not the growth of a day, neither is it a multitude brought together by accident. Hence the reception of strangers in colonies has generally produced revolution." It is true that the metics of Athens were not on full terms of political equality with the citizens but it has been shown that the yawning social and economic gulf postulated by modern writers between citizen and resident foreigner did not really exist.

4. *The status of the slaves.*—The institution of slavery existed throughout the ancient world from the earliest times. The Athenians, with but few exceptions, regarded slavery as natural and justifiable. It is again Aristotle, the fourth-century theorist and philosopher, who is made the starting-point for most modern discussions of slavery among the Greeks and the iniquity of the institution as maintained even by the cultured Athenians of the time of Pericles. In his treatment of this subject Aristotle characterizes in a cold-blooded legal fashion the slave as being merely "a breathing machine or tool, a piece of animated property" (ἔμψυχον ὄργανον, κτῆμά τι ἔμψυχον) and asserts that some men are so inferior that they may be regarded as slaves by nature. It is interesting to note,

however, that Aristotle in another passage admits that there were some who protested against such a view. He says: "Others regard slave owning as doing violence to nature on the ground that the distinction of slave and free man is wholly conventional and has no place in nature, and therefore is void of justice, as resting on mere force." Plato, too, regards slavery as natural and justifiable but would forbid the enslavement of Greeks, he admits, however, that "a slave is an embarrassing possession, the distinction between man and slave being a difficult one and slaves should be well-treated and not abused or insulted." Aristotle, also, advises good treatment for the slave.

Recent writers have been very severe in their strictures on the Athenians for tolerating slavery. Professor Mahaffy writes: "Our real superiority lies in our moral ideas, in our philanthropy, our care of the poor and the sick. I do not know whether the existence and justification of slavery as a natural institution are not the main cause of this difference. Xenophon tells us of the callous and brutal attitude to slaves and prisoners. If it was true then it must have been true ten times more in the colder, harsher, and more selfish society of the preceding generation. The milk of human kindness seems to have run dry among them. . . . . The association of the good with the beautiful and the true seems incomplete. The latter two are attained in no ordinary degree. The former, which is to us the most divine of the three, was but poorly represented." Mr. Dickinson goes so far as to say that Athenian slaves had *no political and social rights at all.* It is true that a minority of the slaves in Attica must have had an unenviable existence. These were the men who, in large numbers, slaved in the silver mines at Laurium. But what was the lot of the majority of the slaves in Attica? A contemporary testifies: "An extra-ordinary amount of license is granted to slaves . . . . where a blow is illegal, and a slave will not step aside to let

you pass him on the street. . . . . The Athenian people is not better clothed than the slave or alien, nor in personal appearance is there any superiority. . . . . Slaves in Athens are allowed to indulge in luxury, and indeed in some cases to live magnificently. . . . . We have established an equality between our slaves and free men." Newly acquired slaves were received into the household with showers ($\kappa\alpha\tau\alpha\chi\acute{\nu}\sigma\mu\alpha\tau\alpha$) of confections. They participated as members of the family in religious rites and sacrifices. They might attend the theater. They worked side by side with their masters in the workshop or might even be permitted to work on their own account exercising an independent profession ($\chi\omega\rho\grave{\iota}s$ $o\mathit{i}\kappa o\hat{\nu}\nu\tau\epsilon s$) either paying a commission to their masters or actually purchasing their freedom and gaining thereby the status of metics. The law protected a slave from being the victim of $\mathring{\nu}\beta\rho\iota s$ and the aggressor was subject to fine. The slave might not be put to death; a free man who had killed a slave was subject to prosecution for manslaughter. Refuge from a cruel master was afforded by flight to a temple as sanctuary, namely, to the Theseum, the Sanctuary of the Erinyes, and the altar of Athena Polias. Freedom might be granted outright by the master, while the state at times enfranchised slaves who had fought for Athens. In case of illness a slave might be affectionately cared for and at death mourned as a relative.

It is certainly a false assertion to claim that Athenian society *rested on slavery* and that slavery was the *dominant* factor in Athenian economic life. The slaves were in the minority in the total population at this period and the prosperity and greatness of the state was due to the industry, the initiative, and the efficiency of citizen and metic. Mr. Grundy says that "the ultimate controlling fact in Greek politics of the fifth and fourth centuries B.C. is the evil economic condition of the lower classes due to the competition of slave labour as competition with slave labour was impossible for the free proletariat." But this was not the case in the fifth century. There was no unemployment in Athens in the Age of Pericles. As we have seen, the demand for labor was so great that extensive immigration was encouraged and there was a living wage for all. It is undoubtedly true, however, that in the fourth century and later the competition of slave with free labor gave rise to economic distress at a time when the citizens had decreased in number but the slaves had enormously increased. Mr. Grundy further declares that all hand-labor became associated with slavery and hence became incompatible with the dignity of the free man. The absolute falsity of this conception has already been established.

CONCLUSION

As a result of this study the following conclusions may be made:

1. Perhaps the greatest error and most unscientific procedure of many writers is to disregard or underestimate local conditions and, in particular, the chronological factor. Far too often authors indulge in generalizations regarding "the ancient Greek." It is no more possible to make general sweeping statements correctly characterizing the institutions of "the ancient Greek" than it would be accurately to estimate the civilization of "the modern European." Sparta and Athens were as far apart politically and socially in numerous respects as Germany and America, while Athens of the second half of the fifth century B.C. in its political, social, and economic conditions was by no means the Athens of the sixth or fourth centuries.

2. The ideal, aristocratic conceptions of Plato and Aristotle must not, and cannot be taken literally to reflect actual Athenian conditions. Certainly Aristotle should not be taken as having "an average Greek mind" in his attitude toward society nor is he, or Plato, representative of fifth-century popular belief.

3. The time-honored tradition that Athenians despised all work and looked down upon all workers is false and our handbooks need revision in their treatment of this topic. It is true that in Athens, as with us, some occupations were thought less desirable and less dignified than others. In no land and at no time is the day laborer esteemed as highly as the statesman. Drudgery and menial employment the Athenians disliked and avoided; so do we. But the citizen who earned his living in some honest way and accepted money for his services was the rule and not the exception, nor was he as a result a social outcast but was a member, in good political and social standing, of the commonwealth.

4. The disabilities of the metics are generally exaggerated. Their position in Athenian society was not humiliating. While the resident aliens did not have full participation in political duties and privileges they did share, in a remarkable measure, the life of the citizens.

5. Slavery was, of course, an Athenian institution, and the right of owning slaves was, in general, not questioned. It is clear, however, that as a rule they were treated by their masters with humaneness and consideration, with the exception of the lowest class of public slaves who were employed in the mines.

6. It would be absurd to claim perfection for the Athenian democracy of the Age of Pericles, or to pretend that the Athenians had completely and happily solved the innumerable and complicated social, political, and economic problems which still vex the world and which still await solution even today. Athens was not, of course, at any time a perfect democracy. But that it was far more democratic and far less aristocratic in the time of Pericles than is generally assumed and asserted is certain.

SECTION X

The Causes of the Peloponnesian War

THE PELOPONNESIAN WAR was the turning point in the history of the Greek city-states. Until its outbreak they prospered and grew; agriculture, trade, and industry flourished. External threats had been repulsed and a golden age had descended upon the Hellenic world. The war was to end all that. It destroyed the economic prosperity of Greece, produced bitter class strife within the cities, opened the door to Persian control of Hellenic affairs, and set neighbor against neighbor in a long and bloody struggle. The causes of the war have been the subject of discussion since antiquity and agreement has by no means been reached by modern scholars. Should one seek impersonal causes or villains? Was any one state to blame or did several share it? Were internal politics responsible? What was the role of economic factors or of power politics? Was the war inevitable or could it have been avoided? All these are questions which have been asked and which remain vital.

1. THUCYDIDES ON THE CAUSES OF THE WAR:

THE CLASH OF EMPIRES*

In the first book of his *History* Thucydides describes the early history of Greece, concluding with an account of the growth of Spartan and Athenian power and the reasons for their clash.

But at last a time came when the tyrants of Athens and the far older tyrannies of the rest of Hellas were, with the exception of those in Sicily, once and for all put down by Lacedæmon; for this city, though after the settlement of the Dorians, its present inhabitants, it suffered from factions for an unparalleled length of time, still at a very early period obtained good laws, and enjoyed a freedom from tyrants which was unbroken; it has possessed the same form of government for more than four hundred years, reckoning to the end of the late war, and has thus been in a position to arrange the affairs of the other states. Not many years after the deposition of the tyrants, the battle of Marathon was fought between the Medes and the Athenians. Ten years afterwards the

* Thucydides, 1. 18–19, 23, translated by Richard Crawley.

barbarian returned with the armada for the subjugation of Hellas. In the face of this great danger the command of the confederate Hellenes was assumed by the Lacedæmonians in virtue of their superior power; and the Athenians having made up their minds to abandon their city, broke up their homes, threw themselves into their ships, and became a naval people. This coalition, after repulsing the barbarian, soon afterwards split into two sections, which included the Hellenes who had revolted from the king, as well as those who had aided him in the war. At the head of the one stood Athens, at the head of the other Lacedæmon, one the first naval, the other the first military power in Hellas. For a short time the league held together, till the Lacedæmonians and Athenians quarrelled, and made war upon each other with their allies, a duel into which all the Hellenes sooner or later were drawn, though some might at first remain neutral. So that the whole period from the Median war to this, with some peaceful intervals, was spent by each power in war, either with its rival, or with its own revolted allies, and consequently afforded them constant practice in military matters, and that experience which is learnt in the school of danger.

The policy of Lacedæmon was not to exact tribute from her allies, but merely to secure their subservience to her interests by establishing oligarchies among them; Athens, on the contrary, had by degrees deprived hers of their ships, and imposed instead contributions in money on all except Chios and Lesbos. Both found their resources for this war separately to exceed the sum of their strength when the alliance flourished intact.

* * *

The Median war, the greatest achievement of past times, yet found a speedy decision in two actions by sea and two by land. The Peloponnesian war was prolonged to an immense length, and long as it was it was short without parallel for the misfortunes that it brought upon Hellas. Never had so many cities been taken and laid desolate, here by the barbarians, here by the parties contending (the old inhabitants being sometimes removed to make room for others); never was there so much banishing and blood-shedding, now on the field of battle, now in the strife of action. Old stories of occurrences handed down by tradition, but scantily confirmed by experience, suddenly ceased to be incredible; there were earthquakes of unparalleled extent and violence; eclipses of the sun occurred with a frequency unrecorded in previous history; there were great droughts in sundry places and consequent famines, and that most calamitous and awfully fatal visitation, the plague. All this came upon them with the late war, which was begun by the Athenians and Peloponnesians by the dissolution of the thirty years' truce made after the conquest of Eubœa. To the question why they broke the treaty, I answer by placing first an account of their grounds of complaint and points of difference, that no one may ever have to ask the immediate cause which plunged the Hellenes into a war of such magnitude. The real cause I consider to be the one which was formally most kept out of sight. The growth of the power of Athens, and the alarm which this inspired in Lacedæmon, made war inevitable. Still it is well to give the grounds alleged by either side, which led to the dissolution of the treaty and the breaking out of the war.

2. THE CORCYRAEAN ALLIANCE*

One of the crucial turning points on the road to war was the Athenian decision to ally itself with Corcyra. Thucydides describes the arguments offered by both the Corcyraeans and the Corinthians to the Athenian assembly. In this way he dramatizes the issues confronting Athens; he then goes on to explain what considerations led to their decision. In 435 the Corcyraeans had defeated Corinth in a sea-battle. The debate in Athens took place two years later.

Corinth, exasperated by the war with the Corcyraeans, spent the whole of the year after the engagement and that succeeding it in building ships, and in straining every nerve to form an efficient fleet; rowers being drawn from Peloponnese and the rest of Hellas by the inducement of large bounties. The Corcyraeans, alarmed at the news of their preparations, being without a single ally in Hellas (for they had not enrolled themselves either in the Athenian or in the Lacedæmonian confederacy), decided to repair to Athens in order to enter into alliance, and to endeavour to procure support from her. Corinth also, hearing of their intentions, sent an embassy to Athens to prevent the Corcyræan navy being joined by the Athenian, and her prospect of ordering the war according to her wishes being thus impeded. An assembly was convoked, and the rival advocates appeared: the Corcyræans spoke as follows:

'Athenians! when a people that have not rendered any important service or support to their neighbours in times past, for which they might claim to be repaid, appear before them as we now appear before you to solicit their assistance, they may fairly be required to satisfy certain preliminary conditions. They should show, first, that it is expedient or at least safe to grant their request; next, that they will retain a lasting sense of the kindness. But if they cannot clearly establish any of these points, they must not be annoyed if they meet with a

rebuff. Now the Corcyræans believe that with their petition for assistance they can also give you a satisfactory answer on these points, and they have therefore despatched us hither. It has so happened that our policy as regards you, with respect to this request, turns out to be inconsistent, and as regards our interests, to be at the present crisis inexpedient. We say inconsistent, because a power which has never in the whole of her past history been willing to ally herself with any of her neighbours, is now found asking them to ally themselves with her. And we say inexpedient, because in our present war with Corinth it has left us in a position of entire isolation, and what once seemed the wise precaution of refusing to involve ourselves in alliances with other powers, lest we should also involve ourselves in risks of their choosing, has now proved to be folly and weakness. It is true that in the late naval engagement we drove back the Corinthians from our shores single-handed. But they have now got together a still larger armament from Peloponnese and the rest of Hellas; and we, seeing our utter inability to cope with them without foreign aid, and the magnitude of the danger which subjection to them implies, find it necessary to ask help from you and from every other power. And we hope to be excused if we forswear our old principle of complete political isolation, a principle which was not adopted with any sinister intention, but was rather the consequence of an error in judgment.

Now there are many reasons why in the event of your compliance you will

* Thucydides, 1. 31–44, translated by Richard Crawley.

congratulate yourselves on this request having been made to you. First, because your assistance will be rendered to a power which, herself inoffensive, is a victim to the injustice of others. Secondly, because all that we most value is at stake in the present contest, and your welcome of us under these circumstances will be a proof of good will which will ever keep alive the gratitude you will lay up in our hearts. Thirdly, yourselves expected, we are the greatest naval power in Hellas. Moreover, can you conceive a stroke of good fortune more rare in itself, or more disheartening to your enemies, than that the power whose adhesion you would have valued above much material and moral strength, should present herself self-invited, should deliver herself into your hands without danger and without expense, and should lastly put you in the way of gaining a high character in the eyes of the world, the gratitude of those whom you shall assist, and a great accession of strength for yourselves? You may search all history without finding many instances of a people gaining all these advantages at once, or many instances of a power that comes in quest of assistance being in a position to give to the people whose alliance she solicits as much safety and honour as she will receive. But it will be urged that it is only in the case of a war that we shall be found useful. To this we answer that if any of you imagine that that war is far off, he is grievously mistaken, and is blind to the fact that Lacedæmon regards you with jealousy and desires war, and that Corinth is powerful there,—the same, remember, that is your enemy, and is even now trying to subdue us as a preliminary to attacking you. And this she does to prevent our becoming united by a common enmity, and her having us both on her hands, and also to insure getting the start of you in one of two ways, either by crippling our power or by making its strength her own. Now it is our policy to be beforehand with her—that is, for Corcyra to make an offer of alliance

and for you to accept it; in fact, we ought to form plans against her instead of waiting to defeat the plans she forms against us.

'If she asserts that for you to receive a colony of hers into alliance is not right, let her know that every colony that is well treated honours its parent state, but becomes estranged from it by injustice. For colonists are not sent forth on the understanding that they are to be the slaves of those that remain behind, but that they are to be their equals. And that Corinth was injuring us is clear. Invited to refer the dispute about Epidamnus to arbitration, they chose to prosecute their complaints by war rather than by a fair trial. And let their conduct towards us who are their kindred be a warning to you not to be misled by their deceit, nor to yield to their direct requests; concessions to adversaries only end in self reproach, and the more strictly they are avoided the greater will be the chance of security.

'If it be urged that your reception of us will be a breach of the treaty existing between you and Lacedæmon, the answer is that we are a neutral state, and that one of the express provisions of that treaty is that if it shall be competent for any Hellenic state that is neutral to join whichever side it pleases. And it is intolerable for Corinth to be allowed to obtain men for her navy not only from her allies, but also from the rest of Hellas, no small number being furnished by your own subjects; while we are to be excluded both from the alliance left open to us by treaty, and from any assistance that we might get from other quarters, and you are to be accused of political immorality if you comply with our request. On the other hand, we shall have much greater cause to complain of you, if you do not comply with it; if we, who are in peril, and are no enemies of yours, meet with a repulse at your hands, while Corinth, who is the aggressor and your enemy, not only meets with no hindrance from you, but is even allowed to draw material for war from your dependencies. This ought not to be, but you should either forbid her enlisting men in your dominions, or you should lend us too what help you may think advisable.

'But your real policy is to afford us avowed countenance and support. The advantages of this course, as we premised in the beginning of our speech, are many. We mention one that is perhaps the chief. Could there be a clearer guarantee of our good faith than is offered by the fact that the power which is at enmity with you, is also at enmity with us, and that that power is fully able to punish defection. And there is a wide difference between declining the alliance of an inland and of a maritime power. For your first endeavour should be to prevent, if possible, the existence of any naval power except your own; failing this, to secure the friendship of the strongest that does exist. And if any of you believe that what we urge is expedient, but fear to act upon this belief, lest it should lead to a breach of the treaty, you must remember that on the one hand, whatever your fears, your strength will be formidable to your antagonists; on the other, whatever the confidence you derive from refusing to receive us, your weakness will have no terrors for a strong enemy. You must also remember that your decision is for Athens no less than for Corcyra, and that you are not making the best provision for her interests, if at a time when you are anxiously scanning the horizon that you may be in readiness for the breaking out of the war which is all but upon you, you hesitate to attach to your side a place whose adhesion or estrangement is alike pregnant with the most vital consequences. For it lies conveniently for the coast-navigation in the direction of Italy and Sicily, being able to bar the passage of naval reinforcements from thence to Peloponnese, and from Peloponnese thither; and it is in other respects a most desirable station. To sum up as shortly as possible, embracing both general and particular considerations, let

this show you the folly of sacrificing us. Remember that there are but three considerable naval powers in Hellas, Athens, Corcyra, and Corinth, and that if you allow two of these three to become one, and Corinth to secure us for herself, you will have to hold the sea against the united fleets of Corcyra and Peloponnese. But if you receive us, you will have our ships to reinforce you in the struggle.'

Such were the words of the Corcyraeans. After they had finished, the Corinthians spoke as follows:

'These Corcyraeans in the speech we have just heard do not confine themselves to the question of their reception into your alliance. They also talk of our being guilty of injustice, and their being the victims of an unjustifiable war. It becomes necessary for us to touch upon both these points before we proceed to the rest of what we have to say, that you may have a more correct idea of the grounds of our claim, and have good cause to reject their petition. According to them, their old policy of refusing all offers of alliance was a policy of moderation. It was in fact adopted for bad ends, not for good; indeed their conduct is such as to make them by no means desirous of having allies present to witness it, or of having the shame of asking their concurrence. Besides, their geographical situation makes them independent of others, and consequently the decision in cases where they injure any lies not with judges appointed by mutual agreement, but with themselves, because while they seldom make voyages to their neighbours, they are constantly being visited by foreign vessels which are compelled to put in to Corcyra. In short, the object that they propose to themselves in their specious policy of complete isolation, is not to avoid sharing in the crimes of others, but to secure a monopoly of crime to themselves,— the license of outrage wherever they can compel, of fraud wherever they can elude, and the enjoyment of their gains without shame. And yet if they were the honest men they pretend to be, the less hold that others had upon them, the stronger would be the light in which they might have put their honesty by giving and taking what was just.

'But such has not been their conduct either towards others or towards us. The attitude of our colony towards us has always been one of estrangement, and is now one of hostility; for, say they, "We were not sent out to be ill-treated." We rejoin that we did not found the colony to be insulted by them, but to be their head, and to be regarded with a proper respect. At any rate, our other colonies honour us, and we are very much beloved by our colonists; and clearly, if the majority are satisfied with us, these can have no good reason for a dissatisfaction in which they stand alone, and we are not acting improperly in making war against them, nor are we making war against them without having received signal provocation. Besides, if we were in the wrong, it would be honourable in them to give way to our wishes, and disgraceful for us to trample on their moderation; but in the pride and license of wealth they have sinned again and again against us, and never more deeply than when Epidamnus, our dependency, which they took no steps to claim in its distress, upon our coming to relieve it, was by them seized, and is now held by force of arms.

'As to their allegation that they wished the question to be first submitted to arbitration, it is obvious that a challenge coming from the party who is safe in a commanding position, cannot gain the credit due only to him who, before appealing to arms, in deeds as well as words, places himself on a level with his adversity. In their case, it was not before they laid siege to the place, but after they at length understood that we should not tamely suffer it, that they thought of the specious word arbitration. And not satisfied with their own misconduct there, they appear here now requiring you to join with

them not in alliance, but in crime, and to receive them in spite of their being at enmity with us. But it was when they stood firmly, that they should have made overtures to you, and not at a time when we have been wronged, and they are in peril; nor yet at a time when you will be admitting to a share in your protection those who never admitted you to a share in their power, and will be incurring an equal amount of blame from us with those in whose offences you had no hand. No, they should have shared their power with you before they asked you to share your fortunes with them.

'So then the reality of the grievances we come to complain of and the violence and rapacity of our opponents have both been proved. But that you cannot equitably receive them, this you have still to learn. It may be true that one of the provisions of the treaty is that it shall be competent for any state, whose name was not down on the list, to join whichever side it pleases. But this agreement is not meant for those whose object in joining is the injury of other powers, but for those whose need of support does not arise from the fact of defection, and whose adhesion will not bring to the power that is mad enough to receive them war instead of peace; which will be the case with you, if you refuse to listen to us. For you cannot become their auxiliary and remain our friend; if you join in their attack, you must share the punishment which the defenders inflict on them. And yet you have the best possible right to be neutral, or failing this, you should on the contrary join us against them. Corinth is at least in treaty with you; with Corcyra you were never even in truce. But do not lay down the principle that defection is to be patronised. Did we on the defection of the Samians record our vote against you, when the rest of the Peloponnesian powers were equally divided on the question whether they should assist them? No, we told them to their face that every power has a right to punish its own allies. Why, if you make it your policy to receive and assist all offenders, you will find that just as many of your dependencies will come over to us, and the principle that you establish will press less heavily on us than on yourselves.

'This then is what Hellenic law entitles us to demand as a right. But we have also advice to offer and claims on your gratitude, which, since there is no danger of our injuring you, as we are not enemies, and since our friendship does not amount to very frequent intercourse, we say ought to be liquidated at the present juncture. When you were in want of ships of war for the war against the Æginetans, before the Persian invasion, Corinth supplied you with twenty vessels. That good turn, and the line we took on the Samian question, when we were the cause of the Peloponnesians refusing to assist them, enabled you to conquer Ægina, and to punish Samos. And we acted thus at crises when, if ever, men are wont in their efforts against their enemies to forget everything for the sake of victory, regarding him who assists them then as a friend, even if thus far he has been a foe, and him who opposes them then as a foe, even if he has thus far been a friend; indeed they allow their real interests to suffer from their absorbing preoccupation in the struggle.

'Weigh well these considerations, and let your youth learn what they are from their elders, and let them determine to do unto us as we have done unto you. And let them not acknowledge the justice of what we say, but dispute its wisdom in the contingency of war. Not only is the straightest path generally speaking the wisest; but the coming of the war which the Corcyræans have used as a bugbear to persuade you to do wrong, is still uncertain, and it is not worth while to be carried away by it into gaining the instant and declared enmity of Corinth. It were, rather, wise to try and counteract the unfavourable impression which your conduct to Megara has created. For kindness opportunely

shown has a greater power of removing old grievances than the facts of the case may warrant. And do not be seduced by the prospect of a great naval alliance. Abstinence from all injustice to other first-rate powers is a greater tower of strength than anything that can be gained by the sacrifice of permanent tranquility for an apparent temporary advantage. It is now our turn to benefit by the principle that we laid down at Lacedæmon, that every power has a right to punish her own allies. We now claim to receive the same from you, and protest against your rewarding us for benefiting you by our vote by injuring us by yours. On the contrary, return us like for like, remembering that this is that very crisis in which he who lends aid is most a friend, and he who opposes is most a foe. And for these Corcyræans—neither receive them into alliance in our despite, nor be their abettors in crime. So do, and you will act as we have a right to expect of you, and at the same time best consult your own interests.'

Such were the words of the Corinthians.

When the Athenians had heard both out, two assemblies were held. In the first there was a manifest disposition to listen to the representations of Corinth; in the second, public feeling had changed, and an alliance with Corcyra was decided on, with certain reservations. It was to be a defensive, not an offensive alliance. It did not involve a breach of the treaty with Peloponnese: Athens could not be required to join Corcyra in any attack upon Corinth. But each of the contracting parties had a right to the other's assistance against invasion, whether of his own territory, or that of an ally. For it began now to be felt that the coming of the Peloponnesian war was only a question of time, and no one was willing to see a naval power of such magnitude as Corcyra sacrificed to Corinth; though if they could let them weaken each other by mutual conflict, it would be no bad preparation for the struggle which Athens might one day have to wage with Corinth and the other naval powers. At the same time the island seemed to lie conveniently on the coasting passage to Italy and Sicily. With these views, Athens received Corcyra into alliance, and on the departure of the Corinthians not long afterwards, sent ten ships to their assistance. They were commanded by Lacedæmonius, the son of Cimon, Diotimus, the son of Strombichus,

and Porteas, the son of Epicles. Their instructions were to avoid collision with the Corinthian fleet except under certain circumstances. If it sailed to Corcyra and threatened a landing on her coast, or in any of her possessions, they were to do their utmost to prevent it. These instructions were prompted by an anxiety to avoid a breach of the treaty.

3. THE CONGRESS AT SPARTA*

The Athenian alliance with Corcyra soon led to open combat between Athens and Corinth at the battle of Sybota. In the Spring of 432 Potidea, an ally of Athens but at the same time a colony of Corinth, revolted from Athens. The town was besieged by the Athenians and defended by a Corinthian army. Doubly enraged, the Corinthians called for a meeting of the Peloponnesian League.

[Thucydides reports speeches by the Corinthians and the Athenians who happened to be present. Then there is a debate among the Spartans: King Archidamus argues for a cautious policy, but he is answered by the Ephor, Sthenelaidas.]

... Last came forward Sthenelaidas, one of the Ephors for that year, and spoke to the Lacedæmonians as follows:

'The long speech of the Athenians I do not pretend to understand. They said a good deal in praise of themselves, but nowhere denied that they are injuring our allies and Peloponnese. And yet if they behaved well against the Mede then, but ill towards us now, they deserve double punishment for having ceased to be good and for having become bad. We meanwhile are the same then and now, and shall not, if we are wise, disregard the wrongs of our allies, or put off till to-morrow the duty of assisting those who must suffer to-day. Others have much money and ships and horses, but we have good allies whom we must not give up to the Athenians, nor by lawsuits and words decide the matter, as it

is anything but in word that we are harmed, but render instant and powerful help. And let us not be told that it is fitting for us to deliberate under injustice, long deliberation is rather fitting for those who have injustice in contemplation. Vote therefore, Lacedæmonians, for war, as the honour of Sparta demands, and neither allow the further aggrandisement of Athens, nor betray our allies to ruin, but with the gods let us advance against the aggressors.'

With these words he, as Ephor, himself put the question to the assembly of the Lacedæmonians. He said that he could not determine which was the loudest acclamation (their mode of decision is by acclamation not by voting); the fact being that he wished to make them declare their opinion openly and thus to increase their ardour for war. Accordingly he said, 'All Lacedæmonians who are of opinion that the treaty has been broken, and that Athens is guilty, leave your seats and go there,' pointing out a certain place; 'all who are of the opposite opinion, there.' They accordingly stood up and divided; and those who held that the treaty had been broken were in a decided majority. Summoning

* Thucydides, 1. 66–67; 85–88. Translated by Richard Crawley.

the allies, they told them that their opinion was that Athens had been guilty of injustice, but that they wished to convoke all the allies and put it to the vote; in order that they might make war, if they decided to do so, on a common resolution. Having thus gained their point, the delegates returned home at once; the Athenian envoys a little later, when they had despatched the objects of their mission. This decision of the assembly judging that the treaty had been broken, was made in the fourteenth year of the thirty years' truce, which was entered into after the affair of Euboea.

The Lacedæmonians voted that the treaty had been broken, and that war must be declared, not so much because they were persuaded by the arguments of the allies, as because they feared the growth of the power of the Athenians, seeing most of Hellas already subject to them.

4. Plutarch on the Causes of the War*

Plutarch used a variety of sources besides Thucydides. It is clearly from these other sources that he derives his account of the origins of the war. After telling of the Athenian suppression of the revolt of Samos in 440, he goes on to speak of the Peloponnesian War.

After this was over, the Peloponnesian war beginning to break out in full tide, he [Pericles] advised the people to send help to the Corcyræans, who were attacked by the Corinthians, and to secure to themselves an island possessed of great naval resources, since the Peloponnesians were already all but in actual hostilities against them. The people readily consenting to the motion, and voting an aid and succour for them, he despatched Lacedæmonius, Cimon's son, having only ten ships with him, as it were out of a design to affront him; for there was a great kindness and friendship betwixt Cimon's family and the Lacedæmonians; so, in order that Lacedæmonius might lie the more open to a charge, or suspicion at least, of favouring the Lacedæmonians and playing false, if he performed no considerable exploit in this service, he allowed him a small number of ships, and sent him out against his will; and indeed he made it somewhat his business to hinder Cimon's sons from rising in the state, professing that by their very names they were not to be looked upon as native and true Athenians, but foreigners and strangers, one being called Lacedæmonius, another Thessalus, and the third Eleus; and they were all three of them, it was thought, born of an Arcadian woman. Being, however, ill spoken of on account of these ten galleys, as having afforded but a small supply to the people that were in need, and yet given a great advantage to those who might complain of the act of intervention, Pericles sent out a larger force afterwards to Corcyra, which arrived after the fight was over. And when now the Corinthians angry and indignant with the Athenians, accused them publicly at Lacedæmon, the Megarians joined with them, complaining that they were, contrary to common right and the articles of peace sworn to among the Greeks, kept out and driven away from every market and from all ports under the control of the Athenians. The Æginetans, also, professing to be illused and treated with violence, made supplications in private to the Lacedæmonians for redress, though not daring openly to call the Athenians in question. In the meantime, also, the city Potidæa, under the dominion of the Athenians, but a colony formerly of the Corinthians, had revolted, and was beset with a formal siege, and was a further occasion of precipitating the war.

* Plutarch, *Pericles*, 29–33, translated by John Dryden.

Yet notwithstanding all this, there being embassies sent to Athens, and Archidamus, the King of the Lacedæmonians, endeavouring to bring the greater part of the complaints and matters in dispute to a fair determination, and to pacify and allay the heats of the allies, it is very likely that the war would not upon any other grounds of quarrel have fallen upon the Athenians, could they have been prevailed with to repeal the ordinance against the Megarians, and to be reconciled to them. Upon which account, since Pericles was the man who mainly opposed it, and stirred up the people's passions to persist in their contention with the Megarians, he was regarded as the sole cause of the war.

They say, moreover, that ambassadors went, by order, from Lacedæmon to Athens about this very business, and that when Pericles was urging a certain law which made it illegal to take down or withdraw the tablet of the decree, one of the ambassadors, Polyalces by name, said, "Well, do not take it down then, but *turn* it; there is no law, I suppose, which forbids that;" which, though prettily said, did not move Pericles from his resolution. There may have been, in all likelihood, something of a secret grudge and private animosity which he had against the Megarians. Yet, upon a public and open charge against them, that they had appropriated part of the sacred land on the frontier, he proposed a decree that a herald should be sent to them, and the same also to the Lacedæmonians, with an accusation of the Megarians; an order which certainly shows equitable and friendly proceeding enough. And after that the herald who was sent, by name Anthemocritus, died, and it was believed that the Megarians had contrived his death, then Charinus proposed a decree against them, that there should be an irreconcilable and implacable enmity thenceforward betwixt the two commonwealths; and that if any one of the Megarians should but set his foot in Attica, he should be put to death; and that the commanders, when they take the usual oath, should, over and above that, swear that they will twice every year make an inroad into the Megarian country; and that Anthemocritus should be buried near the Thracian Gates, which are now called the Dipylon, or Double Gate.

On the other hand, the Megarians, utterly denying and disowning the murder of Anthemocritus, throw the whole matter upon Aspasia and Pericles, availing themselves of the famous verses in the Acharnians—

"To Megara some of our madcaps ran,
    And stole Simætha thence, their courtesan.
Which exploit the Megarians to outdo,
    Came to Aspasia's house, and took off two."

The true occasion of the quarrel is not so easy to find out. But of inducing the refusal to annul the decree, all alike charge Pericles. Some say he met the request with a positive refusal, out of high spirit and a view of the state's best interest, accounting that the demand made in those embassies was designed for a trial of their compliance, and that a concession would be taken for a confession of weakness as if they durst not do otherwise; while other some there are who say that it was rather out of arrogance and a wilful spirit of contention, to show his own strength, that he took occasion to slight the Lacedæmonians. The worst motive of all, which is confirmed by most witnesses, is to the following effect: Phidias the Moulder had, as has before been said, undertaken to make the statue of Minerva. Now he, being admitted to friendship with Pericles, and a great favourite of his, had many enemies upon this account, who envied and maligned him; who also, to make trial in a case of his, what kind of judges the commons would prove, should there be occasion to bring Pericles himself before them, having tampered with Menon, one who had been a workman with Phidias, stationed him in the market-place, with a petition desiring public security upon his discovery and impeachment of Phidias. The people admitting the man to tell his story, and the prosecution proceeding in the assembly, there was nothing of theft or cheat proved against him; for Phidias, from the very first beginning, by the advice of Pericles, had so wrought and wrapt the gold that was used in the work about the statue, that they might take it all off, and make out the just weight of it, which Pericles at that time bade the accuser do. But the reputation of his works was what brought envy upon Phidias, especially that where he represents the fight of the Amazons upon the goddess's shield, he had introduced a likeness of himself as a bald old man holding up a great stone with both hands, and had put in a very fine representation of Pericles fighting with an Amazon. And the position of the hand which holds out the spear in front of the face, was ingeniously contrived to conceal in some degree the likeness, which meantime showed itself on either side.

Phidias then was carried away to prison, and there died of a disease; but, as some say, of poison, administered by the enemies of Pericles, to raise a slander, or a suspicion at least, as though he had procured it. The informer Menon, upon Glycon's proposal, the people made free from payment of taxes and customs, and ordered the generals to take care that nobody should do him any hurt. About the same time, Aspasia was indicted of impiety, upon the complaint of Hermippus the comedian, who also laid further to her charge that she received into her house freeborn women for the uses of Pericles. And Diopithes proposed a decree, that public accusations should be laid against persons who neglected religion, or taught new doctrines about things above, directing suspicion, by means of Anaxagoras, against Pericles himself. The people receiving and admitting these accusations and complaints, at length, by this means, they came to enact a decree, at the motion of Dracon-

tides, that Pericles should bring in the accounts of the moneys he had expended, and lodge them with the Prytanes; and that the judges, carrying their suffrage from the altar in the Acropolis, should examine and determine the business in the city. This last clause Hagnon took out of the decree, and moved that the causes should be tried before fifteen hundred jurors, whether they should be styled prosecutions for robbery, or bribery, or any kind of malversation. Aspasia, Pericles begged off, shedding, as Æschines says, many tears at the trial, and personally entreating the jurors. But fearing how it might go with Anaxagoras, he sent him out of the city. And finding that in Phidias's case he had miscarried with the people, being afraid of impeachment, he kindled the war, which hitherto had lingered and smothered, and blew it up into a flame; hoping, by that means, to disperse and scatter these complaints and charges, and to allay their jealousy; the city usually throwing herself upon him alone, and trusting to his sole conduct, upon the urgency of great affairs and public dangers, by reason of his authority and the sway he bore.

These are given out to have been the reasons which induced Pericles not to suffer the people of Athens to yield to the proposals of the Lacedæmonians; but their truth is uncertain.

The Lacedæmonians, for their part, feeling sure that if they could once remove him, they might be at what terms they pleased with the Athenians, sent them word that they should expel the "Pollution" with which Pericles on the mother's side was tainted, as Thucydides tells us. But the issue proved quite contrary to what those who sent the message expected; instead of bringing Pericles under suspicion and reproach, they raised him into yet greater credit and esteem with the citizens, as a man whom their enemies most hated and feared. . . .

5. DIODORUS SICULUS ON THE CAUSES OF THE WAR*

Diodorus was a Sicilian Greek who lived in the time of Caesar and Augustus. Between 60 and 30 B.C. he wrote a world history in forty volumes from the earliest times to Caesar's Gallic War (54 B.C.). His work is based on that of earlier writers and rarely on primary evidence. His chronology is often confused and his general reliability is debated. His greatest value is in preserving the works of historians now lost to us. In this passage he is probably following Ephorus of Cyme, a writer of the fourth century B.C., as well as the comic poets.

When Euthydemus was archon in Athens, the Romans elected in place of consuls three military tribunes, Manius Aemilianus Mamercus, Gaius Julius, and Lucius Quinctius. In this year there began the Peloponnesian War, as it has been called, between the Athenians and the Peloponnesians, the longest of all the wars which history records; and it is necessary and appropriate to the plan of our history to set forth at the outset the causes of the war.

While the Athenians were still striving for the mastery of the sea, the funds which had been collected as a common undertaking and placed at Delos, amounting to some eight thousand talents, they had transferred to Athens and given over to Pericles to guard. This man stood far above his fellow citizens in birth, renown, and ability as an orator. But after some time he had spent a very considerable amount of this money for his own purposes, and when he was called upon for an accounting he fell ill, since he was unable to render the statement of the monies with which he had been entrusted. While he was worried over the matter, Alcibiades, his nephew, who was an orphan and was being reared at the home of Pericles, though still a lad showed him a way out of making an explanation of the use of the money. Seeing how his uncle was troubled he asked him the cause of his worry. And

when Pericles said, "I am asked for the explanation of the use of the money and I am seeking some means whereby I may be able to render an accounting of it to the citizens," Alcibiades replied, "You should be seeking some means not how to render but how not to render an accounting." Consequently Pericles, accepting the reply of the boy, kept pondering in what way he could embroil the Athenians in a great war; for that would be the best way, he thought, because of the disturbance and distractions and fears which would beset the city, for him to escape giving an exact accounting of the money. Bearing upon this expedient an incident happened to him by mere chance for the following causes.

The statue of Athena was a work of Pheidias, and Pericles, the son of Xanthippus, had been appointed overseer of the undertaking. But some of the assistants of Pheidias, who had been prevailed upon by Pericles' enemies, took seats as suppliants at the altars of the gods; and when they were called upon to explain their surprising action, they claimed that they would show that Pheidias had possession of a large amount of the sacred funds, with the connivance and assistance of Pericles the overseer. Consequently, when the Assembly convened to consider the affair, the enemies of Pericles persuaded the people to arrest Pheidias and lodged a charge against Pericles himself of stealing sacred property. Furthermore, they falsely accused the sophist Anaxagoras, who was Pericles' teacher, of impiety against the gods; and they involved Pericles in their

* Reprinted by permission of the publishers from *Loeb Classical Library*, Diodorus Siculus, 12. 38–40, translated by C. H. Oldfather (Cambridge Mass.: Harvard University Press, 1933).

accusations and malicious charges, since jealousy made them eager to discredit the eminence as well as the fame of the man.

But Pericles, knowing that during the operations of war the populace has respect for noble men because of their urgent need of them, whereas in times of peace they keep bringing false accusations against the very same men because they have nothing to do and are envious, came to the conclusion that it would be to his own advantage to embroil the state in a great war, in order that the city, in its need of the ability and skill in generalship of Pericles, should pay no attention to the accusations being lodged against him and would have neither leisure nor time to scrutinize carefully the accounting he would render of the funds.

Now when the Athenians voted to exclude the Megarians from both their market and harbours, the Megarians turned to the Spartans for aid. And the Lacedaemonians, being won over by the Megarians, in the most open manner dispatched embassadors in accordance with the decision of the Council of the League, ordering the Athenians to rescind the action against the Megarians and theatening, if they did not accede, to wage war upon them together with the forces of their allies. When the Assembly convened to consider the matter, Pericles, who far excelled all his fellow citizens in skill of oratory, persuaded the Athenians not to rescind the action, saying that for them to accede to the demands of the Lacedaemonians, contrary to their own interests, would be the first step toward slavery. Accordingly he advised that they bring their possessions from the countryside into the city and fight it out with the Spartans by means of their command of the sea.

Speaking of the war, Pericles, after defending his course in well-considered words, enumerated first the multitude of allies Athens possessed and the superiority of its naval strength, and then the large

sum of money which had been removed from Delos to Athens and which had in fact been gathered from the tribute into one fund for the common use of the cities; from the ten thousand talents in the common fund four thousand had been expended on the building of the Propylaea and the siege of Potidaea; and each year there was an income from the tribute paid by the allies of four hundred and sixty talents. Beside this he declared that the vessels employed in solemn processions and the booty taken from the Medes were worth five hundred talents, and he pointed to the multitude of votive offerings in the various sanctuaries and to the fact that the fifty talents of gold on the statue of Athena for its embellishment was so constructed as to be removable; and he showed that all these, if dire need befell them, they could borrow from the gods and return to them again when peace came, and that also by reason of the long peace the manner of life of the citizens had made great strides toward prosperity.

In addition to these financial resources Pericles pointed out that, omitting the allies and garrisons, the city had available twelve thousand hoplites, the garrisons and metics amounted to more than seventeen thousand, and the triremes available to three hundred. He also pointed out that the Lacedaemonians were both lacking in money and far behind the Athenians in naval armaments. After he had recounted these facts and incited the citizens to war, he persuaded the people to pay no attention to the Lacedaemonians. This he accomplished readily by reason of his great ability as an orator, which is the reason he has been called "The Olympian." Mention has been made of this even·by Aristophanes, the poet of the Old Comedy, who lived in the period of Pericles, in the following tetrameters:

O ye farmers, wretched creatures,
　listen now and understand,
If you fain would learn the reason
　why it was Peace left the land.

Pheidias began the mischief,
  having come to grief and shame,
Pericles was next in order,
  fearing he might share the blame,
By his Megara-enactment
  lighting first a little flame,
Such a bitter smoke ascended
  while the flames of war he blew,
That from every eye in Hellas
  everywhere the tears it drew.

And again in another place:

The Olympian Pericles
Thundered and lightened
and confounded Hellas

And Eupolis the poet wrote:

One might say Persuasion rested
  On his lips; such charm he'd bring,
And alone of all the speakers
  In his list'ners left his sting.

6. PERICLES AS THE CAUSE OF THE WAR*

It was as leader of the demos, the great mass of the unpropertied, that Pericles had come to power. To this party he owed his victory over Cimon and Thucydides and with it his unexampled position of power at the head of Athens. But for Pericles demagogy was only a means to an end. As soon as he was free of rivals in the state, when nothing further was lacking to his monarchical power, he by no means wanted to push the bounds of extreme democracy any further. His regime would be no rule of a class, and least of all would it lead to the suppression of that social class from which the ruler himself had come. It was the continuing endeavor of Pericles to reconcile the educated and wealthy circles of the citizenry with the new order of things, to show that the un-limited rule of the masses, as he had established it in common with Ephialtes, was in no way identical with anarchy, that in spite of the popular courts and the ex-ended competence of the assembly, life and property would still be protected by the same guarantees as before. To be sure, he owed most of his success to the brilliant financial position which the long peace implied and which gave Pericles the possibility of satisfying the great mob in its material demands upon the state treasury, yet without needing to take away the goods of the rich for that purpose. But even if his own part in the settlement of the old struggle of interests between the propertied and the propertyless was smaller than it appeared outwardly, nevertheless, it was Pericles, in the public view, who had laid to rest the specter of social revolution, who, with a strong hand, had put the agitation which had begun after the Persian Wars back within bounds. How could the sympathy of the great majority of the propertied fail to fall to him? The old enmity was forgotten and men from the best families in the state such as Hagnon of Steiria, Nicias of Cydantidae, and Sophocles of Colonus placed their services at the disposal of the new ruler of the state.

But even now Pericles was not able to win over the totality of the upper classes. Thus, many of them could never forgive him for the fact that it was he who had raised the demos to an authoritative factor in the state, who had accustomed it to live and amuse itself at public expense, so that finally, from all of the democratic freedom not much more than the name was left. But in the disorganized state in which the supporters of this view had been since the ostracism of Thucydides, their opposition did not have much significance. It was much more important that Pericles had lost a large part of his popularity with the masses since he had stopped serving their interests exclusively and had become, instead of the leader of the demos, the leader of a new party devoted to him

* Taken from K. J. Beloch, *Die Attische Politik seit Perikles* (Leipzig, 1884), pp. 19–22, translated by Donald Kagan. By permission of B. G. Teubner, Verlagsgesellschaft, Stuttgart.

personally. Here too the belief grew that in the struggle for the extension of popular rights the goal of that struggle had itself gradually perished. Did one really live in a republic if one man, year in and year out, as president of the Strategia, as leading member of extraordinary commissions, had the military might of the state as well as its financial resources at his unlimited command, and conducted foreign affairs and relations with the allies at his discretion?

Thus the submerged opposition came to the surface. It was all the more dangerous since the means by which Pericles had established his influence over the masses was exhausted. The popular courts, jurymen's pay, gifts of grain, land distributions had now become organic institutions of the state. Whoever came to the helm at any time could not dare to jog it.

The first attack was naturally directed at the outer-works of the enemy position. Personal enemies of the ruler such as Cimon's son Lacedaemonius and Dracontides were elected to the generalship for 433/2. His confidants Phidias, Damon, and Anaxagoras were dragged before a court and condemned, his beloved Aspasia was acquitted only with great difficulty. For the present, Pericles' position at the head of state remained untouched; yet he felt that the earth under him was shaky, that every day his party was losing ground. Unless extraordinary events prevented the progress of affairs Pericles saw his own fall certain before his eyes.

Then came the war. Of course it is unfair to make Pericles responsible for the conflict between the two great Hellenic powers, between slavery and freedom, between unpropertied and propertied. Sooner or later, in one form or another the struggle was unavoidable. But it is, on the other hand, undeniable that Pericles did everything in his power to make the conflict break out precisely then, to make Athens show herself unwilling to grant even the slightest concessions to the Spartan demands. And yet there is hardly any doubt that as the parties stood in respect to one another in Sparta, even through a completely unimportant tractability in insignificant matters, even at this point, after the Corcyraean alliance and the battle of Sybota, the outbreak of the great war could have been put off. Thirteen years earlier Athens had bought peace with altogether different concessions and still not forfeited its position as a great power. It was a slogan that now the Megarian decree could not be lifted without a renunciation of national honor. And it is just as impossible to deny that the outbreak of the war at that moment was thoroughly in the interests of Pericles. Does history require any further evidence that public opinion in all of Hellas was right when it saw in Pericles the immediate author of the Peloponnesian War? Pericles had behaved like so many despots when their internal position totters; he sought to divert the dissatisfaction of the people with a great external action. He had as few scruples in the choice of means as do all tyrants. As he had once kindled class warfare in Athens, he now kindled a civil war among the Greeks.

7. THE ARGUMENT AGAINST INEVITABILITY*

The following account takes up the story after the affair at Potidaea.

Pericles was ready for war but also for peace, if peace could be kept without sacrifice. But what was needed was first a reply to Corinth which might daunt her friends. On the news that Aristeus had started, the Athenian Assembly passed the famous decree which excluded the Megarians from the markets of Attica and the harbours of the Athenian Empire. Pericles declared that this decree was not a violation of the Thirty Years Peace, and we may accept his testimony against that of the aggrieved Megarians. The Athenians had recent causes of complaint against Megara, and, besides, they had yet to revenge themselves for the massacre of their garrison fourteen years before. But, though anger may have chosen the victim, it was policy that directed the blow. The war which now seemed inevitable was to be a test of morale and Pericles chose this way of demonstrating from the very outset how formidable a power the enemies of Athens were daring to challenge. The decree was not what vulgar tradition came to see in it, a cause of war, it was an operation of war, the first blow at the courage and will of Athens' adversaries. The state which could, by a single decree, close a hundred harbours despite all the hoplites of the Peloponnese, was not an enemy to be lightly challenged, least of all by Corinth.

This shrewd stroke displays, alike in its force and adroitness, the intellectual clarity of Pericles, who believed that the issue whether Sparta would move must be made plain and that at once. Pericles forced the issue, not because his personal position was shaken, but because, if war

came, it must come before he was too old to guide Athens to victory. He was now sixty and it was no easy task to control for ever the sanguine fickle adventurous Athenian demos, and he foresaw how lightly they might squander the strength which he had built up.

The Athenians were thus ready to bring matters to a head but their zeal was cold beside that of the Corinthians. Even before the news came of the Athenian victory before Potidaea they had stirred up all the allies of Sparta who had grievances against Athens, and before the month of September ended they gathered at Sparta to persuade the Lacedaemonians that the Thirty Years Peace was at an end. The Megarians had their new grievance which they declared meant the breaking of the Peace, and envoys came secretly from Aegina complaining that Athens did not leave them autonomous as the Thirty Years Peace had provided. Their precise grievance is not revealed to us, but Aegina had once been a member of the Peloponnesian League and in the Thirty Years Peace there may well have been a clause providing that the Aeginetans should be autonomous so long as they paid their tribute to Athens. It was at least a strange interpretation of autonomy that the Athenian Assembly should, by its bare fiat, deny to Aeginetans the right to import desirable woollens from their Megarian neighbours.

These grievances were real enough, but more powerful was the Corinthian veiled threat which followed, that if Sparta would not fight for her allies, they must look elsewhere for a leader. Thucydides takes occasion to put into the mouth of the Corinthians a brilliant contrast between Lacedaemon and Athens, which illuminates not only the crisis itself but the ten

* F. E. Adcock, "The Breakdown of the Thirty Years' Peace, 445–431 B.C.," *The Cambridge Ancient History*, Vol. 5 (Cambridge: Cambridge University Press, 1940), pp. 186–191.

years of war which followed it. The Corinthians did not go unanswered, for there is no reason to doubt the historian's statement that Athenian envoys, on some pretext or other, were at Sparta at the time. These now gave the Periclean answer that Athens stood by her rights and her Empire, but was ready, as the Peace provided, to submit disputes to arbitration.

Opinion at Sparta was divided. As in every state with a proud military tradition, there was a party unwilling to see its bright sword rust, anxious to cut a straight road through the maze of statesmen's calculations. But the Spartans were cautious legalists, especially while they viewed the grievances of others. On juridical grounds the offer to accept an arbitration placed Athens in the right. The offer might prove illusory, for there was no impartial state considerable enough to be judge in such a cause. But that did not justify its summary refusal. Athens and Corinth were not formally at war before Potidaea, or, if they were, Corinth was the aggressor. Sparta had condoned the Athenian intervention to protect Corcyra by a year of inactivity. And far more cogent were the arguments of the wise king Archidamus that Athens was no ordinary Greek power to be lightly attacked and quickly defeated. The Spartans should think long before they began a war which their children might inherit. Let Sparta test the truth of the Athenian protestations and meanwhile prepare for war if war must come. The answer to these politic considerations was given by the ephor Sthenelaidas who led the war-party. 'Athens was plainly the offender; the Thirty Years Peace was at an end; Sparta must stand by her friends.' This thesis, so manly and so intelligible, prevailed, and the Lacedaemonian Assembly voted that the Truce was at an end and that war was justified.

But the victory of the war-party was not yet complete, not yet even certain. For,

according to Greek practice, Sparta was still far from a declaration of war, and the Peloponnesian League as a whole could only make war if a majority of its members voted for it. So a meeting of the League was summoned and meanwhile the Spartans sent to consult Apollo at Delphi 'whether it would be better for them if they made war.' 'And the god replied, it is said, that "if they made war with all their might they would win, and that he himself would help when summoned or even un-invoked."' It was to take nearly thirty years to prove the god right and meanwhile the news from Potidaea was none too good. Corinthian envoys feverishly frightened or cajoled the Peloponnesian states, and when the conference met they ended the debate with a speech of resolute and resourceful optimism. Thucydides has put together, in their name, a masterly analysis of their advantages as against the Athenian position, the possibilities of attack, the glorious uncertainty of war, the claim to be fighting for Greek freedom against a city that had become a tyrant.

The decision was taken, a majority voted for war and, as it was now October or November, the Lacedaemonians settled down to a winter of diplomatic manœuvring for position.

At this game they found their master. First came an antiquated gambit, the demand that the Athenians should expel the tainted house of the Alcmaeonidae, the family of Pericles. It was a test of Pericles' personal position, which proved too strong to be shaken. The Athenians invited Sparta to clear herself of newer guilt, the killing of Helot suppliants and the death of Pausanias. Thucydides (1, 139) then describes more serious demands, first, the raising of the siege of Potidaea, second, the restoration of autonomy to Aegina, third, the repeal of the Megarian decree. 'There would be no war if they repealed the decree.' This can hardly be the whole truth, for Sparta was bound at least to satisfy Corinth, and the simple repeal of the Megarian decree would hardly do that.

The Athenian answer was to bring justificatory charges against the Megarians and to refuse the other demands. Whereupon Sparta sent three new envoys with the message: 'The Lacedaemonians desire the peace to continue and it would continue, if you leave the Greeks autonomous.' It is often said that this was an ultimatum which struck at the very existence of the Athenian Empire. But legalists might have debated for ever how far the Athenian Empire infringed the autonomy of each of its members. The studied vagueness of the proposal, perhaps due to a change of feeling in the Spartan ephorate, seems devised not so much to close the negotiations as to keep them open, and, to judge from the account of the debate which followed, that was the view of the Athenian Assembly.

This was the crucial debate and at this point Thucydides brings in a speech by Pericles. It is quite possible that he has put together what Pericles said on two occasions, the first at which the Megarian decree was more specifically the point at issue, the second the debate on this vaguer demand.

The attitude of Pericles is that Athens cannot yield to a threat of force, that the Athenians cannot hold their own in fear. They will accept an arbitration but until their case is tried they will neither cease to besiege Potidaea nor to exclude the Megarians from their markets and the harbours they control. This last may be the answer to a hint attributed to a Spartan envoy by Plutarch (*Pericles*, 30) that if the Athenians will not repeal the decree, they may at least disregard it. This unyielding attitude was justified by pertinent criticism of the Corinthian plans for the conduct of the war. Behind the question of formal right or wrong stands the shadow of a military calculation. And one factor in the calculation was the moral effect of confident unwavering acceptance of every

challenge. Pericles prevailed; the Lacedaemonian envoys received their answer and returned, and after that no further embassies were sent.

The issue was only too plain. In the barren field of diplomatic dialectics Pericles had scored a notable success. It was logically impossible for Sparta to accept an arbitration under the Thirty Years Peace which it had already declared to be at an end. It was practically impossible, now that so many questions had been brought in and the Greek world was ranged in two camps. Above all, Sparta could not now recede a step without admitting a diplomatic defeat which would have meant the loss of her leadership of the Peloponnesian League. The break-up of that League would enable the subtle and patient state-craft of Pericles to achieve for Athens all that a war could give to her. The 'violent hatred' conceived by the Corinthians, the fumbling policy of Sparta, following in order to lead, the resolution of Pericles to make no sacrifice of security or prestige for the sake of peace and to face the issue while he could control the event, had combined to make inevitable a war for which an unbiassed study of the ancient evidence can find no single cause which appears sufficient to the modern mind. Neither rivalry in trade, nor prejudice of race, nor the opposition of political ideas, nor a chivalrous sympathy on the part of the Peloponnesians with the subjects of Athens, can be promoted to be more than elements which went to make war possible but not inevitable. The ancient fiction that Pericles 'set Greece in a blaze' from vulgar personal motives rests on a naïve evaluation of the jests of comedy and on a chronological confusion which concentrated in the year 432 the attacks on Pericles' friends which belonged to the past and the attacks on Pericles himself which belonged to the future.

'The truest explanation (ἡ ἀληθεστάτη πρόφασις),' writes Thucydides (1, 23), 'though it appeared least in what was said,

I consider to be the growing power of the Athenians which alarmed the Lacedaemonians and forced them into war.' It has often been pointed out that neither the history of the ten years which preceded nor of the ten years which followed the outbreak of the war justifies this statement. It seems to explain more truly why the war began again in 413 and ended as it did than why it began at all in 431. In the opinion of the present writer, the words were written by Thucydides after the fall of Athens as he looked back to the Archidamian War and saw it darkened by the tragic shadows of the Sicilian Expedition and the Decelean War, after Alcibiades had made Athens more aggressive and

Lysander had made Sparta more determined. But the historian's conception of the whole period as a unity made one by the logic of events is not binding upon us, and we have the right to appeal from the Thucydides of the day after to the Thucydides of the day before. In the earlier stratum of the Thucydidian history on which the preceding narrative is based we have an account of the antecedents of the Archidamian War which is true to fact and true to the Greeks and Greek wars of that time. Angry men at Corinth had not feared fire, clever men at Athens had played with it, a generation of ill-will had lowered the flashpoint and a conflagration was only too easy.

8. THE ECONOMIC CAUSES OF THE WAR*

How did the war come about? Thucydides mentions three causes:
(1) The fear which the Peloponnesians, and especially Sparta, felt at the growing power of Athens;
(2) The affair of Epidamnos and Corcyra, followed by that of Potidaea;
(3) The Megarian decree.
Modern historical criticism has added a fourth:
(4) The rivalry between Corinth and Athens for the trade with the west.
Thucydides' view is that the first was the real and efficient cause; while the second was the immediate, and, to men generally, the obvious cause. The third he hardly admits to have been a cause at all.

Of the fourth possible cause he does not appear to have formed any conception, though he provides the premises upon which this modern conclusion has been founded.

Let it be granted that Thucydides' view has such obvious logical defects that

modern criticism is justified in looking to premises other than those on which his conclusion is founded. It is his premises which are defective. Athens' power had not grown continuously since the time of the foundation of the Delian League. She had been much more powerful in the fifties than she was in the thirties of the century. The Thirty Years' Peace of 446 had been a terrible set-back alike to her resources and to her ambitions, so much so that after that date she had pursued a conspicuously unaggressive policy in strong contrast to her policy in the previous period.

Yet it is probable, to say the least of it, that there is some truth in Thucydides' statement of cause. In what sense had Athens' power increased? In a political sense it seems, as far as the available evidence goes, to have retrograded. Modern criticism, seeing this difficulty, seeks to get over it by saying that the increase had been commercial, and that the real point in dispute was whether Athens should be allowed to absorb the trade of the west, or, at any rate, to get a predominant position in it. Thus the question was really one between Athens and

* G. B. Grundy, *Thucydides and the History of his Age*, Vol. 1 (Oxford, Eng.: Basil Blackwell, 1948), pp. 322–330.

Corinth, for there is not the slightest reason to suppose, that any of the other states of the Peloponnesian League, except perhaps Sikyon, were interested to any appreciable extent in the general trade with the west. This question, it is said, was brought to a head by the alliance between Athens and Corcyra which resulted from the complications about Epidamnos. If Corcyra, the critical strategic point on the western route, fell under the control of Athens, the Corinthian position with regard to Sicilian and Italian trade would be imperilled. Hence the Corinthians roused the league to action upon a question in which the other members of the league had little personal interest. Those who support this theory point to a fact which does undoubtedly tell in its favour, namely, that the narratives of Thucydides shows quite clearly that Corinth had great difficulty in rousing Sparta to action.

There is, however, one feature in the evidence which is very difficult to reconcile with this view. Corinth seems to have won over the other Peloponnesian states to her side before she succeeded in getting the adherence of Sparta. They agreed to the necessity of war with Athens before ever Sparta did. From what is known of the nature of these states, it is reasonable, indeed almost necessary, to assume that the situation created by the affair of Corcyra affected their interests in some way. It is not likely that they were concerned about the fate of Potidaea. Athens had never been aggressive towards any of them save Boeotia; and the security of the states of Peloponnese was amply guaranteed by Spartan interests. They must have been interested in some way in Corinthian trade with the west. It was a trade, indeed, in which the major part of the profits went to Corinth; but, all the same, they must have enjoyed some important indirect advantage from it. Thucydides says nothing explicit about their economic position; but then he says nothing explicit about the more marked economic position of Attica,

though it is of course implied in the statement which he makes with regard to the difficulties caused by the occupation of Dekelea, and the consequent diversion of the corn route. And so it is with the economic position of the Peloponnesian states. There are two purely incidental passages in which their situation with regard to foreign food supply is implied; but even so, the significance of the first of them would not be comprehensible did not the second exist. Speaking of the motives which prompted the Athenians to send an expedition to Sicily in 427, he says: 'They sent their ships on the plea of relationship, but (in reality) because they wished to stop the export of corn to Peloponnese, and to test the possibility of bringing Sicily into subjection.'

In the light of this passage, a previous passage in the Corinthian speech at the second Congress at Sparta acquires considerable significance.

The Corinthians warn their allies in the League that 'the inland states which are not on the highway of trade must bear in mind that if they do not join in with the states of the coast, the export of commodities and the import of such things as come to the continent by sea will be rendered more difficult for them. They must not put a wrong construction upon our words, as though they did not concern them, but must bear in mind that, if they leave the coast powers in the lurch, the danger will eventually come to them. . . .' Read with the passage from the Third Book the meaning becomes quite explicit. 'If you let the Athenians get hold of Corcyra, the route to Sicily, and consequently the Sicilian corn trade, will be in their hands. Of course states like Corinth, which actually carry on that trade, will suffer most; but your turn will come when you are unable to obtain through Corinth that corn which you purchase through your manufactured and home-grown commodities.'

The position of the Greek world at this

time with regard to the corn trade is fairly clear. Of the three districts, the Pontus, Sicily, and Egypt, from which the supply was derived, Athens ultimately controlled the first. She probably regulated it even before the war broke out; she certainly did so later. But there seems to have been a clause in the Thirty Years' Peace of 446 which stipulated for free access to the Athenian market for states of the Peloponnesian League. 'The Megarians alleged,' says Thucydides, 'among other serious grounds of complaint, that they were excluded from the ports in the Athenian Empire and from the Attic market, contrary to the treaty.' He then immediately adds, in a passage of extreme significance, that at the first Congress at Sparta, 'the Corinthians came forward last, after having allowed the other allies to take the lead in inciting the Spartans to action.' . . .

Here again we see the states of the Peloponnesian League displaying the same interest in Megarian trade that they had displayed in Corinthian trade. As has been already pointed out, the whole history of these states renders it to the last degree improbable that their sympathy was disinterested. It cannot be attributed to a feeling of *esprit de corps* among members of the league, for the league was essentially one which had been forced upon them by Sparta. It cannot have been because they feared Athens was trying to force Megara into the same relations with regard to her as had existed in the fifties of the century. That was a matter which was important to Sparta, to whom the blocking of the Isthmus would have meant a dangerous decrease of that influence which she had for her own safety to exercise in Northern Greece, and to Boeotia and Corinth, as neighbours of the Megarid. The attitude of the members of the Peloponnesian League is only explicable on the assumption that the real significance of the decrees was that they excluded Megara from participation in the Pontus corn trade; and that the measure which Athens

had already meted out to Megara might in the future be meted out to them also.

The words already quoted from the speech of the Corinthians at the second Congress at Sparta become of still more significance from the fact that the Megarian decree was already in operation at the time to which Thucydides ascribes the words.

As regards the second source of supply, Sicily, the position has been indicated in what has already been said. Athens had made a determined effort in the fifties to get control of the near end of the route thither. The treaty of 446 left her merely in possession of Naupaktos. From that time until the complications about Corcyra arose the route was open to general competition. But if Corcyra fell into the hands of Athens she would control it, and would be able to close it, if she so wished. Hence the significance of the operations in North-West Greece in the earlier half of the Ten Year's War.

In truth, the position of the Peloponnesian states was very critical.

But it may be said, 'Why, if such was the case, did Sparta hold back?' It is in the first place probable that Sparta, possessed of the rich plains of Lakonia and Messenia, was by no means so badly situated with regard to food supply as the other states of Peloponnese. In any case the ruling minority could never be seriously affected by the question. But it is also possible that the chief cause of her reluctance to enter upon war was the influence of Archidamos, who doubted the effectiveness of Spartan resources when used against the military position which Athens held in consequence of her having not merely the command of the sea, but a great fortified centre which could be supplied from the sea.

The third source of supply, Egypt, was in itself important, but by nature and circumstances not so easily available as the other two. It was, in the first place, in possession of a great power, not, like the Pontus corn region, partitioned among small principalities, nor like Sicily, under the control of Greek city states. But to the Peloponnesians the voyage to Egypt presented difficulties both actual and possible. In those days of navigation the most popular route thither was naturally along the south coast of Asia Minor, by Cyprus, and down the Syrian shore. This is the route which the Athenians used during the war. Another route went from Kythera to Crete, and thence across the open Levant to the mouths of the Nile. This was being used by the Peloponnesians during the Ten Years' War, and was obviously of considerable importance to them, as is implied by what Thucydides says with regard to Nikias' capture of Kythera. But the voyage over the open Levant was not the kind of navigation which the trader of those days attempted, if he could possibly avoid its necessity; and, as a means of communication with Egypt, the Cretan route must have been somewhat ineffective by reason of its very danger.

The position of the Peloponnesian states in the period preceding the Peloponnesian War becomes thus quite clear. They were threatened with the possibility of being cut off from the two most accessible sources of food supply.

With Athens the case was, of course, different. It does not seem likely, in view of Perikles' policy since 446 and his experience before that date, that he had any idea of renewing on the part of Athens that attempt to corner the world's corn supply which had failed so disastrously in the fifties. Nor can Athens have been so profoundly interested in the corn trade of Sicily as the Peloponnesian states were. She had the Pontus trade to fall back upon. But her general trade interests in Sicily were considerable, and she could not let Corcyra fall into Corinthian hands. All the other matters in dispute were no more than secondary to that disputed question. The demands made upon Potidaea were a mere precaution in view of the bad relations with its mother-city

Corinth. When the demands were refused, Athens as an imperial state had to enforce them. The Megarian decrees were probably issued to bring to an end a state of disturbed peace far more dangerous to Athens, with a number of discontented allies on her hands, than a state of actual war. The war must come; it was better that it should come soon.

In recent works on Greek history the view has been taken that it was the trading party at Athens which forced the Peloponnesian War, and showed itself most keen in its prosecution. It has even been suggested that this party forced Perikles' hand in the matter of the Megarian decrees, and that Thucydides has deliberately suppressed this fact. Why he should have suppressed such a fact, had it been a fact, it is difficult to conceive. His admiration for Perikles, his obvious belief that the war brought ruin to that Periklean democracy of which he admired so many elements, would have led him to dissociate his hero from a responsibility for the beginning of that course of events which was to lead to such disaster. Yet he is emphatic in his assertion that Perikles was an out-and-out supporter of a war policy.

The motives of parties at Athens must be judged in the light of the situation before the war began. That was a very complicated one. To the Athenian the possibility of Corcyra falling into the hands of Corinth had offered the prospect of Athens being cut off from Sicily and its trade, in which she had large interests. So far there was a general trade interest involved which she would naturally be loath to lose. But Sicily was an all-important resource to her in case she were cut off at some future time from the Pontus; and her connection with that region through the narrow waters of the Hellespont and Bosphoros was in the very nature of things most precarious. The question whether she should turn to the Pontus or to Sicily for her food supply had been, up to 446, a disputed one in

Athenian politics. She could face the risk in the Hellespont and Bosphoros so long as she had access to Sicily.

To the Peloponnesians the possession of Corcyra by Athens would mean that that power would control the two most available sources of foreign corn which the world of that day provided, and the Megarian decree showed the kind of use which Athens would be capable of making of such a situation. The Peloponnesian states were convinced that Athens had become a great political, because a great economic, danger to them, and saw that she must remain so, as long as she remained an imperial power. Their determination was to destroy the Athenian empire, a determination which was evidently known at Athens before the war began, and which determined the attitude of parties there towards it, both while as yet it was in prospect, and after it began.

Under Themistokles the economic difficulties of the semi-employed or unemployed population of Attica had been solved by employment on board the fleet. The expenses of that system, which was in existence for a few years only, he had intended to supply by encouraging the settlement of skilled metic traders in the country, and so increasing its commercial wealth, and with that its power of giving employment in the state service.

Under Aristides and Kimon employment on board the fleet was still the remedy, but the financial support was supplied by the tribute.

Under Perikles the indigent ultra-democrat became the controlling element in the policy of the state. He looked to the tribute as his main means of support in the public service. Commercial expansion might do something, but the tribute was the main thing; and consequently he was prepared to stake all on the maintenance of the empire. He would even expand it, not so much for commercial purposes, as for the sake of increasing the tribute income. This is clearly shown in Thucydides' account of the reasons which made the Sicilian Expedition so popular. He says nothing of commercial expansion. The attraction was that the expedition offered the prospect of pay for the present, and an inexhaustible source of pay for the future. The alleged commercial causes of the Peloponnesian War must therefore be understood in a limited sense.

The two main factors in the position of the Athenian state were:

(1) The necessity of importing corn from abroad;
(2) The necessity of providing for the unemployed.

Hence, in view of the precarious nature of the connection with the Pontus, Athens could not see any power in the position of being able to cut her communications with Sicily; nor could she for one moment contemplate the possibility of the destruction of her empire.

Under ultra-democracy Athens was far more of a socialistic or communistic, than of a commercial state.

9. In Defense of Thucydides*

It might reasonably be argued that this question is one of those historical problems which form excellent subjects for the writing of essays, but which are far too

* G. Dickins, "The True Cause of the Peloponnesian War," *Classical Quarterly*, 5 (1911), pp. 238–248. Used by permission of the Clarendon Press, Oxford.

complex to admit of a decisive answer, and consequently are much better left alone. No one man is responsible for a war between great powers, and the motives which influence the vast number of people, whose consent is necessary, can rarely, if ever, be identical. It is therefore comparatively easy to argue against any given motive which is asserted to be the one and only reason. Certainly the writer would make no effort to rake up the ashes of this controversy, were it not that in Dr. Grundy's recent work on Thucydides a new and ingenious theory is put forward concerning the *vera causa* of the Peloponnesian War.

The whole of Dr. Grundy's valuable publication is coloured by his theory that the acquisition of the means of subsistence was the root-principle of the policy of Greek States, a theory which there is no room here to examine in detail. In so far as it applies to the Peloponnesian War, it may be stated thus: Athens was compelled to interfere in the north-west, owing to the necessity of opening out new sources of corn-supply and of providing for her unemployed. The Peloponnese was bound to resist any such project, firstly, because Corinth did not want to see her trade ruined; secondly, because the inland communities were afraid of a blockade and the loss of their imported corn; and, thirdly, because the allies were able to bring pressure upon Sparta.

In Dr. Grundy, then, another critic is raised up in judgment upon Thucydides. The prevalent English opinion on this point is well illustrated in the favourable reception of Mr. Cornford's book, in the general tendency of most Oxford lecturers on the subject, and in the new articles on the Peloponnesian War and on Greek History in the *Encyclopaedia Britannica*. Thucydides' judgment of a purely imperial cause is generally rejected, and the secret of the outbreak is found in the relations of Athens and Corinth rather than of Athens and Sparta. Professor Bury's defence of Thucydides in his Harvard Lectures is almost the only recent presentation of the other point of view.

It is, then, perhaps excusable for some champion, however unworthy, to make another stand on behalf of the deliberate judgment of Thucydides.

Διότι δ' ἔλυσαν (τὰς σπονδὰς) τὰς

αἰτίας προύγραψα πρῶτον καὶ τὰς διαφοράς, τοῦ μή τινα ζητῆσαί ποτε ἐξ ὅτου τοσοῦτος πόλεμος τοῖς ῞Ελλησι κατέστη. τὴν μὲν γὰρ ἀληθεστάτην πρόφασιν, ἀφανεστάτην δὲ λόγῳ, τοὺς 'Αθηναίους ἡγοῦμαι μεγάλους γιγνομένους καὶ φόβον παρέχοντας τοῖς Λακεδαιμονίοις ἀναγκάσαι ἐς τὸ πολεμεῖν· αἱ δ' ἐς τὸ φανερὸν λεγομέναι αἰτίαι αἵδ' ἦσαν ἑκατέρων, ἀφ' ὧν λύσαντες τὰς σπονδὰς ἐς τὸν πόλεμον κατέστησαν. [To the question why they broke the treaty, I answer by placing first an account of their grounds for complaint and points of difference, that no one may ever have to ask the immediate cause which plunged the Hellenes into a war of such magnitude. The real cause I consider to be the one which was formally most kept out of sight. The growth of the power of Athens, and the alarm which this inspired in Lacedaemon, made war inevitable. Still it is well to give the grounds alleged by either side, which led to the dissolution of the treaty and the breaking out of the war. (Translated by Crawley)] . . . and so to a discussion of the 'incidents' of Epidamnus and Potidaea.

Fortunately his meaning is perfectly plain. The αἰτίαι [aitiai = grounds for complaint], or rather the λεγομέναι αἰτίαι ἀφ' ὧν [alleged grounds by which] the truce was broken, were αἵδε, i.e., Epidamnus and Potidea, but the ἀληθεστάτη πρόφασις ἀφανεστάτη δὲ λόγῳ [real cause most kept out of sight] was the fear inspired in the Spartans by the growth of the Athenian power.

The rejection of his deliberate judgment on the cause of the war would probably not have pained Thucydides so much as the salves applied by the critics to his injured reputation. 'Thucydides is quite wrong,' implies Mr. Cornford, 'but you must not blame him because he is writing drama rather than history.' 'Thucydides is wrong,' says Dr. Grundy, 'but excusably so, since he is writing after the end of the war, when the original causes have been obscured by the new developments which arose very soon after the war began.' And here we might very well raise the point, 'What is the value of your commercial or economic *vera causa*, if it had effect only for the first three or four years of the war, while you admit that the question of political supremacy was paramount for the rest of a twenty-seven year struggle? Surely that question of supremacy must have lain hid (ἀφανεστάτη δὲ λόγῳ) all the time.'

But, if the war arose for commercial or economic reasons, all this defence of Thucydides' reasoning is very thin white-wash. It is not once only that he gives his opinion, but at least six times in the first book. Certainly Thucydides, as Dr. Grundy's book illustrates, is now beginning to meet the fate of Homer. The χωρίζοντες [splitters, scholars who divide the *History* into earlier and later passages] have got him firmly in their grip, and doubtless it is easy to prove that all these passages belong to later redactions. But, for all that, Thucydides must stand or fall by his own judgments, and if, writing soon after the end of the war, he stated over and over again as his convinced opinion that the cause of the war was the imperial jealousy of Athens and Sparta and nothing else, then if we refuse to believe him, we must admit that he has made about as grave a blunder as he could make. He wrote his history from contemporary notes, and he must have written down some motive as the cause in 431. He can find no excuse in forgetting the events of 431, for he had his diary. His judgment is a considered judgment, written perhaps after 404, but written after full deliberation and with complete knowledge of all the facts, and his credit as a historian must rest upon it.

Here we meet with a more insidious objection. Thucydides may have been writing not to combat any view of commercial or economic rivalry between Corinth and Athens, but simply to answer the accusation of Aristophanes and con-temporary gossip, that Pericles brought on the war for his own advantage and for personal reasons. Commercial causes, it is agreed, were not separated from political in ancient times, and the imperial struggle between Sparta and Athens would be held to cover the commercial jealousy of Athens and Corinth. But whether the Piraeus traders drove Pericles to war, or whether his motive was the necessity of feeding and employing the unemployed, in neither case can we give Thucydides much credit for discernment in attributing the outbreak to Spartan fear of Athenian expansion. And again, if it was Athenian aggression in the north-west arising out of Attico-Corinthian rivalry that caused the war, it is a bad blunder on Thucydides' part to speak of Spartan fear of Athens as the real cause, and thereby to imply that the true aggression came from the Peloponnese.

It is impossible really to confuse the issue or to effect a compromise. Either Thucydides is wrong or his modern English critics are mistaken, and perhaps a brief re-examination of the problem will be permitted in the hope of throwing a little new light on the question.

The main arguments brought against Thucydides are the following:

1. Why should Sparta be driven to war from fear of Attic expansion in 431, when Athens was really much weaker than she had been a quarter of a century before?

2. The rivalry between Athens and Corinth was far greater than that between Athens and Sparta.

3. Corinth had most to gain from the declaration of war, and Sparta practically nothing.

4. Sparta showed great reluctance to fight at all, and in the early years of the war little energy or initiative.

5. Heavy pressure was brought to bear upon Sparta by the inland Peloponnesian states in fear for their food supply.

6. Corinth forced Sparta to fight by threats of secession.

The attack is formidable, and can be countered only by a careful examination of party politics in Sparta.

Not enough attention has been paid to the fact that at any rate after 550 we have clear evidence of two main parties in Sparta. About that year Sparta came to a very grave turning-point in her policy. Hitherto an absorbing and conquering state, which had amalgamated all Laconia, Messenia, Cynuria, and Southern Arcadia, she was induced by the resistance of Tegea to exchange her policy of conquest for one of alliance and hegemony. Tegea was the first member of the Peloponnesian League. The change is contemporaneous with two other important developments. Spartan art, hitherto a luxurious and flourishing plant, stops abruptly as the Lycurgan ἀγωγή [agoge = training or education] is reintroduced with great severity, and the power of the ephors is established on a firmer and more predominant basis. It is impossible to avoid connecting these three contemporaneous events with a single line of policy—that of the great ephor Cheilon. The reintroduction of the ἀγωγή, with the consequently greater exclusiveness of Sparta, and greater emphasis on the democratic character of the régime; the probable initiation of the Thalamae cult in the interest of the ephors, as opposed to the royal monopoly of Delphi; the abandonment of conquest, partly no doubt already owing to questions of population, but mainly because conquest tended to aggrandize the kings; and, finally, the known increase of the ephors' power at this time— all show clearly that 550 marks the rising of the ephorate to power as an equipoise to the kings, and the beginning of that division of interests between ephors and kings, that was to become a commonplace of Spartan politics.

The reign of Cleomenes shows the two parties in full opposition, and also throws a light on the unscrupulousness of the ephors. When Cleomenes desires to attack Athens in 506, they combine with Demaratus and the Corinthians to restrain him; when he spares Argos, they attack him for his want of energy; when he consults for pan-Hellenic unity by taking hostages from Aegina, they again raise up an antagonist in the shape of Demaratus; and when he finally intrigues for the overthrow of their power with the Arcadians and helots, they accuse him of treachery and procure his ruin. Thus their policy is not constructive but destructive, anti-royal rather than anti-imperialist.

Exactly the same attacks are made on Pausanias. He is accused of medism—a ridiculous charge that led to an acquittal, and his humiliation at the hands of the allies is willingly accepted in Sparta. He, too, is driven by constant opposition into a plot to overthrow not Sparta but the incubus on the Spartan constitution, and is driven to exile and death. Leonidas is abandoned at Thermopylae, and throughout the Persian wars Sparta takes an indecisive line, not because of treachery to the Greek cause, but because of the party struggles between kings and ephors. For the ephors were not always supreme. Cleomenes frequently got his own way, and in 494 was acquitted on trial. Pausanias also was acquitted on trial, and in 478, in spite of the withdrawal of Leotychidas from the war in the preceding year, he induced the assembly to put him at the head of a fleet, and led the Greek forces to victory in Cyprus and Byzantium.

Thus we may legitimately assume the existence of two parties in Sparta from 520 to 478, a royal progressive imperial party, anxious for conquest, for hegemony, and even tampering with ideas of emancipation, along with an anti-royal party, headed by the ephors, ready to be inconsistent as long as it got its way, and violently opposed to any ideas of emancipation or relaxation of the strict democratic Lycurgan regime.

Even after the fall of Pausanias the imperialist party in Sparta continued to have power. Diodorus recounts how the reception of the news of the repudiation of Spartan hegemony led to anger and demands for war with Athens, and from that moment an anti-Athenian party came into existence. The ephors who hailed the humiliation of Pausanias with delight were forced in their own defence to preach the doctrine of dual hegemony. They were willing to sacrifice empire to their political exigencies, and to accept an equality of Athens by sea and Sparta by land. Thus in 477, when the war-party was crying for armed intervention to prevent the fortification of Athens, the ephors permitted themselves to be hoodwinked by Themistocles; but later, finding in that statesman an ally or correspondent of Pausanias, they joined in the hue and cry that drove him into Persia. A little later we find Spartan aid promised to Thasos in 465, and an Attic invasion projected for the following year. But a curious *volte-face* has taken place, for it is the ephors who must have made the promise in Sparta's name, and consequently the ephors who are now identified with the war-party.

This sudden change of front is in no way surprising when we remember that the ephors had no constructive but only an anti-royal policy, proved by their unscrupulous struggle with Cleomenes and Pausanias. The warlike Agiadae were no longer predominant. In 468 Archidamus the Eurypontid succeeded Leotychidas, and both as the elder and the far more capable monarch became the representative of Spartan royalty for the next forty years. Archidamus was consistently for peace. He refused to lead the expedition in 457 and 445, and he preached peace in 431. Consequently the ephors were bound to become imperialists, and they effected the change with great celerity. In 462 it was Archidamus, Cimon's friend, who summoned him to Sparta's help at Ithome. The party which drove him out with contumely in the following year and threw down the gauntlet to Athens can only

have been that of the ephors. It was the ephors who punished Pleistoanax in 445 for not destroying Athens, and Sthenelaidas, the ephor, who insisted on war in 431. But Archidamus, who spoke against war in 431, who refused to hold command in 457 and 445, must have been the cause of the rejection of the Lesbian proposals a little before the war and the Persian proposals in 456.

We have dealt at some length with the events of the Pentecontaetia, because it is essential to this question to be perfectly clear on the point that there were two parties in Sparta, a war-party and a peace-party, whose power varied according as Archidamus or one of the ephors was the most persuasive and influential politician of the year.

The ephors were supreme in 465, Archidamus in 462, the ephors in 461, the ephors in 457, Archidamus in 456, the ephors in 446, Archidamus in 440, Archidamus a little before the war, but the ephors in 432-1.

With this fact ever before our eyes we can turn to the objections brought against the theory of Thucydides.

1. Why should Sparta be driven to war in 431 from fear of Attic expansion, when Athens was really far weaker than she had been from 460 to 450?

It is true that Athens was weaker in 431 than she had been in 460, but this argument is not an adequate statement of the facts. For, in the first place, the Athenian expansion of the sixties had actually driven Sparta to war. Few would deny that the war which broke out in 461 was due to Spartan fear of Attic expansion, and that war went on until more by Athenian disasters than by Spartan valour it came to a successful end in 445. Sparta, in the shape of ephors, did not desire the annihilation of Athens, but her strict adherence to the *status quo* of 477, to the dual hegemony, and to a purely maritime empire. Attic expansion in the sixties had made her fear that the balance of power was threatened. The peace of 445 fulfilled, or nearly fulfilled, Spartan desires, and forced a re-acceptance of the *status quo*.

But if Athens was weaker in 431 than she had been in 460, she was far stronger than she had been in 445. Since the peace she had repaired her treasury and fleet, had put down all disaffection in her league, and was on the point of stretching out her arms to Sicily. The *status quo* was threatened again in 431 very much as it had been in 461, and the expansion of 445 to 435 was analogous to that of 477 to 461.

At this point it may be advisable to consider the question of Potidaea, since it has been held that its important position in the pages of Thucydides is hardly justified, and that his inclusion of it as an important factor in the outbreak of the war is unsatisfactory.

When Thucydides speaks of αἰτίαι and διαφοραί [*aitrai* and *diaphorai* = complaints and differences], he calls Potidaea and Epidamnus αἰτίαι, and considers the smaller grievances, the Megarian decree, the treatment of Aegina, etc., as διαφοραί. Potidaea was subsequent to Corcyra, and therefore not so immediately important from the point of view of the imperial relations of Athens and Sparta, but it is fitly included among the proximate causes of the war, since the treatment of Potidaea must have influenced the votes of many of the smaller Greek states. It was a violent interference with the natural Greek right of autonomy, and whether in its execution it displayed Athenian weakness or strength, it its conception it showed clearly the autocratic and individualistic character of Athenian rule. It may not have impelled Sparta to war as much as the Corcyrean affair did, but it operated far more powerfully on the minor states of the Peloponnesian league, and caused the further exasperation of Corinth.

2. Attico-Corinthian rivalry was greater than Attico-Spartan.

So far from this being true, an anti-Athenian party had existed, as we have seen, in Sparta since 480, and had been since 468 identified with the ephors. It had already brought about war with Athens once, and only Archidamus and the frail bulwark of the Thirty Years' Peace were restraining it. Once let Athens break the letter of the agreement, and the war-party would be supreme. To this is due the importance of the academic question in the Corinthian and Corcyrean debate, as to whether a defensive alliance with Corcyra would break the truce or not, unimportant surely except for its effect on Sparta.

As for Attico-Corinthian rivalry, its bitterness dates from after, not before, the Corcyrean alliance. Herodotus gives quite a false picture of the relations of Athens and Corinth at the time of the Persian wars, and himself elsewhere admits that they were friendly. There had been war in 459, because Athens threatened the north-west trade, but the arrangements of 445 had been satisfactory, and so far from showing rancour, Corinth had stood up for Athens as recently as 440. Corinthian jealousy of Athens dates from the renewal of Attic projects in the west— *i.e.*, from 434—and was neither of long-standing or in the least hereditary. Thus it was not the case that Attic jealousy of Corinthian commerce forced Pericles' hand in the matter; on the contrary, we shall have to admit that that jealousy only arose out of Pericles' action.

3. Corinth had more to gain from the war than Sparta, who could gain nothing from it.

No one can deny that after the alliance of Athens and Corcyra was was a matter of supreme importance to Corinth, but to say that Sparta had nothing to gain from it is to judge from after events. The Spartans, as Thucydides shows, had every hope of success in the war. They did not realize their own powerlessness, and they thought a few years' invasion would reduce Athens to terms. Moreover, the object of the war from their point of view was not so much to gain anything definite as to check Attic expansion. The Attic-Corcyrean alliance meant:

A. Practically an Athenian corner in ships.
B. A death-blow to Corinthian trade.
C. The ultimate extension of Attic influence over Italy and Sicily.

A. was comparatively unimportant by itself, but B. was of supreme importance to Sparta, for if Corinthian trade was ruined, the only financial resource of the Peloponnesian league would be removed. With Athens predominant over Corinth, or even only possessed of her western trade, the funds and the fleet of the Peloponnesian Leagure would be reduced to nil, and Sparta half crippled before the war began. C. If Athens were to be allowed to control the west as she controlled the east, the Peloponnese would be isolated. A part of her corn-supply, all her ship-building wood, and many sources of commerce would be in Attic hands, and, most important of all, the Attic monopoly of trade would make her so wealthy, so influential, and so strong, that Sparta would be defeated before a blow was struck. These were the imperial and political reasons that made the Corcyrean question of such vital importance to Sparta from the very first.

4. Sparta showed great reluctance to fight at all and little energy in the first years of the war.

We have already seen the most important reason for this reluctance in the condition of Spartan parties. Archidamus and the peace party were a strong brake on the wheel of the imperialist policy, and only the cumulative effects of Corcyra, Potidaea, and Megara were able to overcome their resistance. Moreover, Sparta was bound to wait a little to see develop-

ments. The alliance with Corcyra was not a formal breach of the peace, and Sparta was scrupulous in such matters. Only after the affairs of Potidaea and Megara were Athenian intentions perfectly clear. The operations were all in the north-west, because that was the important, and in fact the essential, spot. If Athens could be driven out of the north-west, all would be well. The Corinthians believed in direct attack, and after some hesitation the Spartans followed them, but not with enthusiasm, because Sparta had only one strategy for war, and believed in no other. Invasion with the ravaging of crops was the one Spartan military method, and the unexpected indifference of Athens to this form of warfare paralyzed the Spartan War Office from the first. It took them some years to devise some other plan of attack. As to the frequent efforts to bring the war to an end and to offer terms, it must always be remembered that Sparta was fighting for the restitution of the *status quo*, and if she could get that, she would much sooner stop the war, which was expensive both in money and men. Her imperialists, like Lysander, were still in the schoolroom.

5. The next argument is the especial discovery of Dr. Grundy, that Corinth persuaded the smaller states to vote for war because their corn-supply was threatened.

The reply to this argument is that it goes too far. Dr. Grundy has over-estimated the population of the Peloponnese. It is impossible in a short space to deal at all fully with Dr. Grundy's figures, but one may perhaps be permitted to question very strongly the principles put forward in his note on p. 231 of his book. He suggests there that if the whole cultivable area of Greece were cultivated at the present day, imported corn would be unnecessary. A larger area was cultivable in ancient times, and a great amount of imported corn was necessary. Therefore, he concludes, the ancient population was much larger than the modern. But does this follow?

In the first place, although doubtless the *cultivable* area is smaller now than in antiquity, it is very dubious if the *cultivated* area is smaller. Although the towns of modern Greece are smaller than those of ancient Helllas, there are probably far more villages at the present day, and therefore a greater part of the country is within reach. The blessings of peace, which meant not only that you do not lose your crops through war, but that you can cultivate lands much farther away from your settlement, must have affected the cultivated area, and if, as Dr. Grundy argues rather unfortunately in another place (p. 91), it paid the ancient Greek better to grow something else and to get his corn from abroad, we have still further reason for reducing the land under corn in antiquity. Moreover, rotation of crops and the introduction of Indian corn have revolutionized the possibilities of agriculture, and it is therefore impossible to base any figures of population on the very dubious comparison between the area cultivated in ancient and modern times. On any reasonable estimate of the population—e.g., of Laconia—there can be no doubt that the ancient population was smaller than the modern. The decisive figure is the 35,000 helots sent to Plataea. They were sent not to fight but to be out of the way of mischief while Sparta was empty. They represent, then, the greater part of the able-bodied helot population. In that case there cannot have been more than 200,000 helots, who with 80,000 perioeci, and certainly not more than 30,000 Spartiates, fail to equal the 350,000 modern inhabitants of the same area.

Within a smaller population, we have no reason to consider the problem of food-supply acute in the Peloponnese. The quotation from Herodotus in regard to the corn-ships of 480 refers to Aegina and the Peloponnese—*i.e.* to the neigh-bouring part of Peloponnese, the barren Acte from Corinth to Troezen. Most of Argolis is, in fact, an indifferent country for crops. But neither Aegina nor Argolis was concerned in the matter of an Athenian blockade. Achaea, Elis, Arcadia, Laconia, and Messenia have ample cultivable land, and even if on Dr. Grundy's theory it had been found more profitable as a rule to substitute vines and olives for corn, yet a corn-crop only takes a year to grow, and if the danger of blockade were imminent, corn could speedily be grown all over Peloponnese. But Dr. Grundy over-estimates the possibilities of blockade. The history of the war itself is sufficient to show that an Athenian blockade of Peloponnese was impossible. The theory that the Peloponnesians gravely proposed to import corn overland from a point north of Corcyra, through modern Albania and Aetolia to Oeniadae, and thence by sea to Cyllene is hardly credible. Not only would it be impossible physically and financially to import corn on mule-back through a wild stretch of barren country, but the Athenian privateers from Naupactus and Cephallenia would have stopped it at the end of its long journey. Doubtless a possible rise in corn may have contributed to the annoyance of the smaller Peloponnesian states, but it was the hard political facts of Megara and Potidaea and not an economic theory that united them. It was autonomy, not food, for which Greece was fighting.

There is a tendency to-day among historians to give far too much weight to commercial or economic motives in dealing with ancient states. Such motives are rarely mentioned by ancient writers, and naturally so, because even if subsidiary, they were never ἀληθέσταται προφάσεις [*alethestatai: prophaseis* = truest causes], simply because they were not understood by the mass of the people. Even in Athens, the political influence of the Piraeus traders cannot have been as great as Mr. Cornford would have us believe, and the idea that Sparta could be persuaded to fight for the commerce of Corinth or the corn-supply of Arcadia is preposterous.

6. The answer to this argument, and the final explanation of the cause of the war by the critics of Thucydides, is that Corinth threatened to secede to Argos if Sparta would not fight, and so Sparta was driven into action.

History does not bear out the view that Sparta's hand could be forced in this way. Neither the Corinthian war nor the Mantinean campaign suggests that Argos and Corinth could ever have made a united stand against Sparta. Argos was a far more dangerous ally to Corinth than Sparta could ever be, and for good or evil the fate of the two latter was bound up together. It is the imperial danger, not the economic, that the Corinthian advocates harp upon. The Corinthian speech is that of impassioned pleaders because their interests were bound up with the war, but there is no trace in the speech of Sthenelaidas that the threat of secession has made the slightest impression, or was, in fact, anything more than a rhetorical flourish.

Our conclusion, then, on the whole matter is that the criticism of Thucydides has failed, and that his ἀληθεστάτη πρόφασις still holds. The position of affairs after 440 was an enriched and growing Athens on the one side, watched on the other by a jealous Sparta with a war-party always on the *qui vive*.

To this powder-magazine comes the spark of the Corintho-Corcyrean difference. What was Pericles to do? He had not yet begun to save for war, because he did not anticipate it so soon, though he knew, as all Greece did, that it was inevitable in the end. If he let Corcyra go, he was losing 200 ships (Corcyra would never have fought Corinth without Attic help), and he would have lost his bridge to the west. If he accepted, he made war certain, as soon as Sparta realized the position; but he would have his bridge to the west, and

he thought Athens was impregnable. She was to be on the defensive throughout, and Sparta was at last to admit that she could do nothing. Then the Peloponnesian League would break up, as it had done in 473 and 464, and as it actually did in 421. Athens would be left mistress of the Greek world.

This explains Pericles' acceptance of the alliance. Sparta's hesitation for a year or two is easily understood. The truce was not yet technically broken, and she did not yet know what use Athens was going to make of her position. Potidaea and Megara showed that, The treatment of Potidaea was essential to guard against a weak spot in Athens' armour; the treatment of Megara was a warning to the world that while Sparta was helpless, Athens could deal with Spartan allies as she liked. And so, with the Athenian cards on the table, Archidamus had to give way, and πολλῷ πλείους voted for war in the Spartan assembly because they saw that the Corcyrean alliance was building for Athens a bridge to the treasures of the west. The *status quo* was altered, and Potidaea and Megara showed them how Athens intended to use her supremacy. Sparta had fought in 461 because Athens was growing too powerful. She found that the snake was scotched, not killed, and that the Corcyrean alliance would mean beginning the work of destruction all over again. The imperial importance of this alliance was recognized in Sparta from the first. The peace party vainly tried to patch up a compromise before the war by intervening at Corinth, and at the last moment Archidamus tried to stem the tide of popular passion; but no one who reads the account of the debate in Sparta can fail to see that the overwhelming feeling of the audience was in favour of war not against the commercial foe of Corinth, who might secede from the League, but against the imperial menace of Athens, which was threatening to isolate the Peloponnese. 'Our aim in Sicily,' said

Alcibiades later, 'is τῇ Πελοποννήσῳ . . . ἐπιχειρήσειν, κομίσαντες ξύμπασαν μὲν τὴν ἐκεῖθεν προσγενομένην δύναμιν τῶν Ἑλλήνων, πολλοὺς δὲ βαρβάρους μισθωσάμενοι καὶ Ἴβηρας καὶ ἄλλους τῶν ἐκεῖ ὁμολογουμένως νῦν βαρβάρων μαχιμωτάτυς τριήρεις τε πρὸς ταῖς ἡμετέραις πολλὰς ναυπηγησάμενοι, ἐχούσης τῆς Ἰταλίας ξύλα ἄφθονα, αἷς τὴν Πελοπόννησον πέριξ πολιορκοῦντες καὶ τῷ πέζῳ ἅμα ἐκ γῆς ἐφορμαῖς τῶν πόλεων τὰς μέν βίᾳ λαβόντες, τὰς δ᾽ ἐντειχισάμενοι. ῥᾳδίως ἠλπίζομεν καταπολεμήσειν καὶ μετὰ ταῦτα καὶ τοῦ ξύμπαντος Ἑλληνικοῦ ἄρξειν᾽ [to attack Peloponnese, bringing with us the entire force of the Hellenes lately acquired in those parts, and taking a number of barbarians into our pay, such as the Iberians and others in those countries, confessedly the most warlike known, and building numerous galleys in addition to those we have already, timber being plentiful in Italy; and with this fleet blockading Peloponnese from the sea and assailing it with our armies by land, taking some of the cities by storm, drawing works of circumvallation round others, we hoped without difficulty to affect its reduction, and after this to rule the whole of the Hellenic name. (Translated by Crawley.)] The plans are those of a later date, but there was more than one Alcibiades living in 431 to whom such ideas had already occurred, and the Peloponnesians who had the fate of Potidaea, Megara, and Aegina before their eyes, may well have been excused if they even exaggerated the dangers of the Athenian empire.

The Unpopularity of the Athenian Empire

IT IS A COMMONPLACE that the Greeks were jealous of their independence, lovers of the liberty of the *polis* to a fault. On this assumption it is axiomatic that the subject-states of the Athenian Empire must have chafed under Athenian control and been eager to rebel at the first opportunity. This view is not dispelled by a casual reading of Thucydides, our major source, for he makes it clear that the Empire was a tyranny and generally unpopular to all Greeks. The interpretation of Thucydides was rarely challenged until quite recently, but within the last decade a lively controversy has developed. Was the Empire a tyranny? Did its subjects universally long for freedom? Is the account of Thucydides to be trusted? Was the Empire truly unpopular? These are the questions which continue to be debated and which are discussed in this chapter.

1. THE BIRTH AND GROWTH OF THE ATHENIAN EMPIRE*

The way in which Athens came to be placed in the circumstances under which her power grew was this. After the Medes had returned from Europe, defeated by sea and land by the Hellenes, and after those of them who had fled with their ships to Mycale had been destroyed, Leotychides, King of the Lacedæmonians, the commander of the Hellenes at Mycale, departed home with the allies from Peloponnese. But the Athenians and the allies from Ionia and Hellespont, who had now revolted from the king, remained and laid siege to Sestos, which was still held by the Medes. After wintering before it, they became masters of the place on its evacuation by the barbarians; and after this they sailed away from Hellespont to their respective cities. Meanwhile the Athenian people, after the departure of the barbarian from their country, at once proceeded to carry over their children and wives, and such property as they had left, from the places where they had deposited them, and prepared to re-build their city and their walls. For only isolated portions of the circumference had been left standing, and most of the houses were in ruins; though a few remained, in which the Persian grandees had taken up their quarters.

Perceiving what they were going to do, the Lacedæmonians sent an embassy to Athens. They would have themselves pre-

* Thucydides, 1. 89–90, 93–100, 114–117, translated by Richard Crawley.

ferred to see neither her nor any other city in possession of a wall; though here they acted principally at the instigation of their allies, who were alarmed at the strength of her newly acquired navy, and the valour which she had displayed in the war with the Medes. They begged her not only to abstain from building walls for herself, but also to join them in throwing down the walls that still held together of the ultra-Peloponnesian cities. The real meaning of their advice, the suspicion that it contained against the Athenians, was not proclaimed; it was urged that so the barbarian, in the event of a third invasion, would not have any strong place, such as he now had in Thebes, for his base of operations; and that Peloponnese would suffice for all as a base both for retreat and offence. After the Lacedæmonians had thus spoken, they were, on the advice of Themistocles, immediately dismissed by the Athenians, with the answer that ambassadors should be sent to Sparta to discuss the question. Themistocles told the Athenians to send him off with all speed to Lacedæmon, but not to despatch his colleagues as soon as they had selected them, but to wait until they had raised their wall to the height from which defence was possible. Meanwhile the whole population in the city was to labour at the wall, the Athenians, their wives and their children, sparing no edifice, private or public, which might be of any use to the work, but throwing all down. After giving these instructions, and adding that he would be responsible for all other matters there, he departed.

* * *

In this way the Athenians walled their city in a little while. To this day the building shows signs of the haste of its execution; the foundations are laid of stones of all kinds, and in some places not wrought or fitted, but placed just in the order in which they were brought by the different hands; and many columns, too, from tombs and sculptured stones were put in with the rest. For the bounds of the city were extended at every point of the circumference; and so they laid hands on everything without exception in their haste. Themistocles also persuaded them to finish the walls of Piræus, which had been begun before, in his year of office as archon; being influenced alike by the fineness of a locality that has three natural harbours, and by the great start which the Athenians would gain in the acquisition of power by becoming a naval people. For he first ventured to tell them to stick to the sea and forthwith began to lay the foundations of the empire. It was by his advice, too, that they built the walls of that thickness which can still be discerned round Piræus, the stones being brought up by two waggons meeting each other. Between the walls thus formed there was neither rubble nor mortar, but great stones hewn square and fitted together, cramped to each other on the outside with iron and lead. About half the height that he intended was finished. His idea was by their size and thickness to keep off the attacks of an enemy; he thought that they might be adequately defended by a small garrison of invalids, and the rest be freed for service in the fleet. For the fleet claimed most of his attention. He saw, as I think, that the approach by sea was easier for the king's army than that by land: he also thought Piræus more valuable than the upper city; indeed, he was always advising the Athenians, if a day should come when they were hard pressed by land, to go down into Piræus, and defy the world with their fleet. Thus, therefore, the Athenians completed their wall, and commenced their other buildings immediately after the retreat of the Mede.

Meanwhile Pausanias, son of Cleombrotus, was sent out from Lacedæmon as commander-in-chief of the Hellenes, with twenty ships from Peloponnese. With him sailed the Athenians with thirty ships, and a number of the other allies. They made an expedition against Cyprus and subdued most of the island, and afterwards against

Byzantium, which was in the hands of the Medes, and compelled it to surrender. This event took place while the Spartans were still supreme. But the violence of Pausanias had already begun to be disagreeable to the Hellenes, particularly to the Ionians and the newly liberated populations. These resorted to the Athenians and requested them as their kinsmen to become their leaders, and to stop any attempt at violence on the part of Pausanias. The Athenians accepted their overtures, and determined to put down any attempt of the kind and to settle everything else as their interests might seem to demand. In the meantime the Lacedæmonians recalled Pausanias for an investigation of the reports which had reached them. Manifold and grave accusations had been brought against him by Hellenes arriving in Sparta; and, to all appearance, there had been in him more of the mimicry of a despot than of the attitude of a general. As it happened, his recall came just at the time when the hatred which he had inspired had induced the allies to desert him, the soldiers from Peloponnese excepted, and to range themselves by the side of the Athenians. On his arrival at Lacedæmon, he was censured for his private acts of oppression, but was acquitted on the heaviest counts and pronounced not guilty; it must be known that the charge of Medism formed one of the principal, and to all appearance one of the best-founded articles against him. The Lacedæmonians did not, however, restore him to his command, but sent out Dorkis and certain others with a small force; who found the allies no longer inclined to concede to them the supremacy. Perceiving this they departed, and the Lacedæmonians did not send out any to succeed them. They feared for those who went out a deterioration similar to that observable in Pausanias; besides, they desired to be rid of the Median war, and were satisfied of the competency of the Athenians for the position, and of their friendship at the time towards themselves.

The Athenians having thus succeeded to the supremacy by the voluntary act of the allies through their hatred of Pausanias, fixed which cities were to contribute money against the barbarian, which ships; their professed object being to retaliate for their sufferings by ravaging the king's country. Now was the time that the office of 'Treasurers for Hellas' was first instituted by the Athenians. These officers received the tribute, as the money contributed was called. The tribute was first fixed at four hundred and sixty talents. The common treasury was at Delos, and the congresses were held in the temple. Their supremacy commenced with independent allies who acted on the resolutions of a common congress. It was marked by the following undertakings in war and in administration during the interval between the Median and the present war, against the barbarian, against their own rebel allies, and against the Peloponnesian powers which would come in contact with them on various occasions. My excuse for relating these events, and for venturing on this digression, is that this passage of history has been omitted by all my predecessors, who have confined themselves either to Hellenic history before the Median war, or to the Median war itself. Hellanicus, it is true, did touch on these events in his Athenian history; but he is somewhat concise and not accurate in his dates. Besides, the history of these events contains an explanation of the growth of the Athenian empire.

First the Athenians besieged and captured Eion on the Strymon from the Medes, and made slaves of the inhabitants, being under the command of Cimon, son of Miltiades. Next they enslaved Scyros the island in the Ægean, containing a Dolopian population, and colonised it themselves. This was followed by a war against Carystus, in which the rest of Eubœa remained neutral, and which was ended by surrender on conditions. After this Naxos left the confederacy, and a war ensued, and she had to return after a siege; this was the first instance of the engagement being broken by the subjugation of an allied city, a precedent which was followed by that of the rest in the order which circumstances prescribed. Of all the causes of defection, that connected with arrears of tribute and vessels, and with failure of service, was the chief; for the Athenians were very severe and exacting, and made themselves offensive by applying the screw of necessity to men who were not used to and in fact not disposed for any continuous labour. In some other respects the Athenians were not the old popular rulers they had been at first; and if they had more than their fair share of service, it was correspondingly easy for them to reduce any that tried to leave the confederacy. For this the allies had themselves to blame; the wish to get off service making most of them arrange to pay their share of the expense in money instead of in ships, and so to avoid having to leave their homes. Thus while Athens was increasing her navy with the funds which they contributed, a revolt always found them without resources of experience for war.

Next we come to the actions by land and by sea at the river Eurymedon, between the Athenians with their allies, and the Medes, when the Athenians won both battles on the same day under the conduct of Cimon, son of Miltiades, and captured and destroyed the whole Phœnician fleet, consisting of two hundred vessels. Some time afterwards occurred the defection of the Thasians, caused by disagreements about the marts on the opposite coast of Thrace, and about the mine in their possession. Sailing with a fleet to Thasos, the Athenians defeated them at sea and effected a landing on the island. About the same time they sent ten thousand settlers of their own citizens and the allies to settle the place then called Ennea Hodoi or Nine Ways, now Amphipolis. They succeeded in gaining possession of Ennea Hodoi from the Edonians, but on advancing into the interior of Thrace were cut off in Drabescus, a town of the Edonians, by the assembled Thracians, who regarded the settlement of the place Ennea Hodoi as an act of hostility. Meanwhile the Thasians being defeated in the field and suffering siege, appealed to Lacedæmon, and desired her to assist them by an invasion of Attica. Without informing Athens she promised and intended to do so, but was prevented by the occurrence of the earthquake, accompanied by the secession of the Helots and the Thuriats and Æthæans of the Periœci to Ithome. Most of the Helots were the descendants of the old Messenians that were enslaved in the famous war; and so all of them came to be called Messenians. So the Lacedæmonians being engaged in a war with the rebels in Ithome, the Thasians in the third year of the siege obtained terms from the Athenians by razing their walls, delivering up their ships, and arranging to pay the monies demanded at once, and tribute in future; giving up their possessions on the continent together with the mine.

* * *

[*Thucydides next gives a summary of the "First Peloponnesian War" (459–445 B.C.).*]

Three years afterwards a truce was made between the Peloponnesians and Athenians for five years. Released from Hellenic war, the Athenians made an expedition to Cyprus with two hundred vessels of their own and their allies, under the command of Cimon. Sixty of these were detached to Egypt at the instance of Amyrtæus, the king in the marshes; the rest laid siege to Kitium, from which, however, they were compelled to retire by the death of Cimon and by scarcity of provisions. Sailing off Salamis in Cyprus, they fought with the Phœnicians, Cyprians, and Cilicians by land and sea, and being victorious on both elements departed home, and with them the returned squadron from Egypt. After this the Lacedæmonians marched out on a sacred war, and becoming masters of the temple at Delphi, placed it in the hands of the Delphians. Immediately after their retreat, the Athenians marched out, became masters of the temple, and placed it in the hands of the Phocians.

Some time after this, Orchomenus, Chæronea, and some other places in Bœotia, being in the hands of the Bœotian exiles, the Athenians marched against the above-mentioned hostile places with a thousand Athenian heavy infantry and the allied contingents, under the command of Tolmides, son of Tolmæus. They took Chæronea, and made slaves of the inhabitants, and leaving a garrison, commenced their return. On their road they were attacked at Coronæa, by the Bœotian exiles from Orchomenus, with some Locrians and Eubœan exiles, and others who were of the same way of thinking, were defeated in battle, and some killed, others taken captive. The Athenians evacuated all Bœotia by a treaty providing for the recovery of the men; and the exiled Bœotians returned, and with all the rest regained their independence.

This was soon afterwards followed by the revolt of Eubœa from Athens. Pericles had already crossed over with an army of Athenians to the island, when news was brought to him that Megara had revolted, that the Peloponnesians were on the point of invading Attica, and that the Athenian garrison had been cut off by the Megarians, with the exception of a few who had taken refuge in Nisæa. The Megarians had introduced the Corinthians, Sicyonians, and Epidaurians into the town before they revolted. Meanwhile Pericles brought his army back in all haste from Eubœa. After this the Peloponnesians marched into Attica as far as Eleusis and Thrius, ravaging the country under the conduct of King Pleistoanax, the son of Pausanias, and without advancing further returned home. The Athenians then crossed over again to Eubœa under the command of Pericles, and subdued the whole of the island: all

but Histiæa was settled by convention; the Histiæans they expelled from their homes, and occupied their territory themselves.

Not long after their return from Eubœa, they made a truce with the Lacedæmonians and their allies for thirty years, giving up the posts which they occupied in Peloponnese, Nisæa, Pegæ, Trœzen, and Achaia. In the sixth year of the truce, war broke out between the Samians and Milesians about Priene. Worsted in the war, the Milesians came to Athens with loud complaints against the Samians. In this they were joined by certain private persons from Samos itself, who wished to revolutionise the government. Accordingly the Athenians sailed to Samos with forty ships and set up a democracy; took hostages from the Samians, fifty boys and as many men, lodged them in Lemnos, and after leaving a garrison in the island returned home. But some of the Samians had not remained in the island, but had fled to the continent. Making an agreement with the most powerful of those in the city, and an alliance with Pissuthnes, son of Hystaspes, the then satrap of Sardis, they got together a force of seven hundred mercenaries, and under cover of night crossed over to Samos. Their first step was to rise on the commons, most of whom they secured, their next to steal their hostages from Lemnos; after which they revolted, gave up the Athenian garrison left with them and its commanders to Pissuthnes, and instantly prepared for an expedition against Miletus. The Byzantines also revolted with them.

As soon as the Athenians heard the news, they sailed with sixty ships against Samos. Sixteen of these went to Caria to look out for the Phœnician fleet, and to Chios and Lesbos carrying round orders for reinforcements, and so never engaged; but forty-four ships under the command of Pericles with nine colleagues gave battle, off the island of Tragia, to seventy Samian vessels, of which twenty were transports, as they were sailing from Miletus. Victory remained with the Athenians. Reinforced afterwards by forty ships from Athens, and twenty-five Chian and Lesbian vessels, the Athenians landed, and having the superiority by land invested the city with three walls; it was also invested from the sea. Meanwhile Pericles took sixty ships from the blockading squadron, and departed in haste for Caunus and Caria, intelligence having been brought in of the approach of the Phœnician fleet to the aid of the Samians; indeed Stesagoras and others had left the island with five ships to bring them. But in the meantime the Samians made a sudden sally, and fell on the camp, which they found unfortified. Destroying the look-out vessels, and engaging and defeating such as were being launched to meet them, they remained masters of their own seas for fourteen days, and carried in and carried out what they pleased. But on the arrival of Pericles, they were once more shut up. Fresh reinforcements afterwards arrived—forty ships from Athens with Thucydides, Hagnon, and Phormio; twenty with Tlepolemus and Anticles, and thirty vessels from Chios and Lesbos. After a brief attempt at fighting, the Samians, unable to hold out, were reduced after a nine months' siege, and surrendered on conditions; they razed their walls, gave hostages, delivered up their ships, and arranged to pay the expenses of the war by instalments. The Byzantines also agreed to be subject as before.

2. The Class Struggle in the Athenian Empire*

To speak next of the allies, and in reference to the point that emissaries from Athens come out, and, according to common opinion, calumniate and vent their hatred upon the better sort of people, this is done on the principle that the ruler cannot help being hated by those whom he rules; but that if wealth and respectability are to wield power in the subject cities the empire of the Athenian People has but a short lease of existence. This explains why the better people are punished with infamy, robbed of their money, driven from their homes, and put to death, while the baser sort are promoted to honour. On the other hand, the better Athenians protect the better class in the allied cities. And why? Because they recognise that it is to the interest of their own class at all times to protect the best element in the cities. It may be urged that if it comes to strength and power the real strength of Athens lies in the capacity of her allies to contribute their money quota. But to the democratic mind it appears a higher advantage still for the individual Athenian to get hold of the wealth of the allies, leaving them only enough to live upon and to cultivate their estates, but powerless to harbour treacherous designs.

Again, it is looked upon as a mistaken policy on the part of the Athenian democracy to compel her allies to voyage to Athens in order to have their cases tried. On the other hand, it is easy to reckon up what a number of advantages the Athenian People derives from the practice impugned. In the first place, there is the steady receipt of salaries throughout the year derived from the court fees. Next, it enables them to manage the affairs of the allied states while seated at home without the expense of naval expeditions. Thirdly, they thus preserve the partisans of the democracy, and ruin her opponents in the law courts. Whereas, supposing the several allied states tried their cases at home, being inspired by hostility to Athens, they would destroy those of their own citizens whose friendship to the Athenian People was most marked. But besides all this the democracy derives the following advantages

* Pseudo-Xenophon, *The Constitution of the Athenians*, 1, 3 (abridged). Translated by H. G. Dakyns.

from hearing the cases of her allies in Athens. In the first place, the one per cent levied in Piraeus is increased to the profit of the state; again, the owner of a lodging-house does better, and so, too, the owner of a pair of beasts, or of slaves to be let out on hire; again, heralds and criers are a class of people who fare better owing to the sojourn of foreigners at Athens. Further still, supposing the allies had not to resort to Athens for the hearing of cases, only the official representative of the imperial state would be held in honour, such as the general, or trierarch, or ambassador. Whereas now every single individual among the allies is forced to pay flattery to the People of Athens because he knows that he must betake himself to Athens and win or lose his case at the bar, not of any stray set of judges, but of the sovereign People itself, such being the law and custom at Athens. He is compelled to behave as a suppliant in the courts of justice, and when some juryman comes into court, to grasp his hand. For this reason, therefore, the allies find themselves more and more in the position of slaves to the people of Athens.

Furthermore, owing to the possession of property beyond the limits of Attica, and the exercise of magistracies which take them into regions beyond the frontier, they and their attendants have insensibly acquired the art of navigation. A man who is perpetually voyaging is forced to handle the oar, he and his domestic alike, and to learn the terms familiar in seamanship. Hence a stock of skilful mariners is produced, bred upon a wide experience of voyaging and practice. They have learned their business, some in piloting a small craft, others a merchant vessel, while others have been drafted off from these for service on a ship-of-war. So that the majority of them are able to row the moment they set foot on board a vessel, having been in a state of preliminary practice all their lives.

* * *

There is another point in which it is sometimes felt that the Athenians are ill advised, in their adoption, namely, of the less respectable party, in a state divided by faction. But if so, they do it advisedly. If they chose the more respectable, they would be adopting those whose views and interests differ from their own, for there is no state in which the best element is friendly to the people. It is the worst element which in every state favours the democracy—on the principle that like favours like. It is simple enough then. The Athenians choose what is most akin to themselves. Also on every occasion on which they have attempted to side with the better classes, it has not fared well with them, but within a short interval the democratic party has been enslaved, as for instance in Bœotia; or, as when they chose the aristocrats of the Milesians, and within a short time these revolted and cut the people to pieces; or, as when they chose the Lacedæmonians as against the Messenians, and within a short time the Lacedæmonians subjugated the Messenians and went to war against Athens.

3. THE REVOLT AT MITYLENE*

In 428 the chief city of Lesbos, Mitylene, revolted from Athens. The causes of this rebellion and the Athenian treatment of the rebels have been the center of much of the debate on the nature of the Athenian Empire.

The next summer the Peloponnesians sent off the forty-two ships for Mitylene, under Alcidas, their high admiral, and themselves and their allies invaded Attica, their object being to distract the Athenians by a double movement, and thus to make it less easy for them to act against the fleet sailing to Mitylene. The commander in this invasion was Cleomenes, in the place of King Pausanias, son of Pleistoanax, his nephew, who was still a minor. Not content with laying waste whatever had shot up in the parts which they had before devastated, the invaders now extended their ravages to lands passed over in their previous incursions; so that this invasion was more severely felt by the Athenians than any except the second; the enemy staying on and on until they had overrun most of the country, in the expectation of hearing from Lesbos of something having been achieved by their fleet, which they thought must now have got over. However, as they did not obtain any of the results expected, and their provisions began to run short, they retreated and dispersed to their different cities.

In the meantime the Mitylenians, finding their provisions failing, while the fleet from Peloponnese was loitering on the way instead of appearing at Mitylene, were compelled to come to terms with the Athenians in the following manner. Salæthus having himself ceased to expect the fleet to arrive, now armed the commons with heavy armour, which they had not before possessed, with the intention of making a sortie against the Athenians. The commons, however, no sooner found themselves possessed of arms than they refused any longer to obey their officers; and forming in knots together, told the authorities to bring out in public the provisions and divide them amongst them all, or they would themselves come to terms with the Athenians and deliver up the city.

The government, aware of their inability to prevent this, and of the danger they would be in, if left out of the capitulation, publicly agreed with Paches and the army to surrender Mitylene at discretion and to admit the troops into the town; upon the understanding that the Mitylenians should be allowed to send an embassy to Athens to plead their cause, and that Paches should not imprison, make slaves of, or put to death any of the citizens until its return. Such were the terms of the capitulation; in spite of which the chief authors of the negotiation with Lacedæmon were so completely overcome by terror when the army entered, that they went and seated themselves by the altars, from which they were raised up by Paches under promise that he would do them no wrong, and lodged by him in Tenedos, until he should learn the pleasure of the Athenians concerning them. Paches also sent some galleys and seized Antissa, and took such other military measures as he thought advisable.

* * *

Arrived at Mitylene, Paches reduced Pyrrha and Eresus; and finding the Lacedæmonian, Salæthus, in hiding in the town, sent him off to Athens, together with the Mitylenians that he had placed

* Thucydides, 3. 25–28, 35–51, translated by Richard Crawley.

in Tenedos, and any other persons that he thought concerned in the revolt. He also sent back the greater part of his forces, remaining with the rest to settle Mitylene and the rest of Lesbos as he thought best.

Upon the arrival of the prisoners with Salæthus, the Athenians at once put the latter to death, although he offered, among other things, to procure the withdrawal of the Peloponnesians from Platæa, which was still under siege; and after deliberating as to what they should do with the former, in the fury of the moment determined to put to death not only the prisoners at Athens, but the whole adult male population of Mitylene, and to make slaves of the women and children. It was remarked that Mitylene had revolted without being, like the rest, subjected to the empire; and what above all swelled the wrath of the Athenians was the fact of the Peloponnesian fleet having ventured over to Ionia to her support, a fact which was held to argue a long-meditated rebellion. They accordingly sent a galley to communicate the decree to Paches, commanding him to lose no time in despatching the Mitylenians. The morrow brought repentance with it and reflexion on the horrid cruelty of a decree, which condemned a whole city to the fate merited only by the guilty. This was no sooner perceived by the Mitylenian ambassadors at Athens and their Athenian supporters, than they moved the authorities to put the question again to the vote; which they the more easily consented to do, as they themselves plainly saw that most of the citizens wished some one to give them an opportunity for reconsidering the matter. An assembly was therefore at once called, and after much expression of opinion upon both sides, Cleon, son of Cleænetus, the same who had carried the former motion of putting the Mitylenians to death, the most violent man at Athens, and at that time by far the most powerful with the commons, came forward again and spoke as follows:

'I have often before now been convinced that a democracy is incapable of empire, and never more so than by your present change of mind in the matter of Mitylene. Fears or plots being unknown to you in your daily relations with each other, you feel just the same with regard to your allies, and never reflect that the mistakes into which you may be led by listening to their appeals, or by giving way to your own compassion, are full of danger to yourselves, and bring you no thanks for your weakness from your allies; entirely forgetting that your empire is a despotism and your subjects disaffected conspirators, whose obedience is insured not by your suicidal concessions, but by the superiority given you by your own strength and not their loyalty. The most alarming feature in the case is the constant change of measures with which we appear to be threatened, and our seeming ignorance of the fact that bad laws which are never changed are better for a city than good ones that have no authority; that unlearned loyalty is more serviceable than quick-witted insubordination; and that ordinary men usually manage public affairs better than their more gifted fellows. The latter are always wanting to appear wiser than the laws, and to overrule every proposition brought forward, thinking that they cannot show their wit in more important matters, and by such behaviour too often ruin their country; while those who mistrust their own cleverness are content to be less learned than the laws, and less able to pick holes in the speech of a good speaker; and being fair judges rather than rival athletes, generally conduct affairs successfully. These we ought to imitate, instead of being led on by cleverness and intellectual rivalry to advise your people against our real opinions.

'For myself, I adhere to my former opinion, and wonder at those who have proposed to reopen the case of the Mitylenians, and who are thus causing a delay which is all in favour of the guilty, by making the sufferer proceed against the offender with the edge of his anger blunted; although where vengeance follows most closely upon the wrong, it best equals it and most amply requites it. I wonder also who will be the man who will maintain the contrary, and will pretend to show that the crimes of the Mitylenians are of service to us, and our misfortunes injurious to the allies. Such a man must plainly either have such confidence in his rhetoric as to adventure to prove that what has been once for all decided is still undetermined, or be bribed to try to delude us by elaborate sophisms. In such contests the state gives the rewards to others, and takes the dangers for herself. The persons to blame are you who are so foolish as to institute these contests; who go to see an oration as you would to see a sight, take your facts on hearsay, judge of the practicability of a project by the wit of its advocates, and trust for the truth as to past events not to the fact which you saw more than to the clever strictures which you heard; the easy victims of newfangled arguments, unwilling to follow received conclusions; slaves to every new paradox, despisers of the commonplace; the first wish of every man being that he could speak himself, the next to rival those who can speak by seeming to be quite up with their ideas by applauding every hit almost before it is made, and by being as quick in catching an argument as you are slow in foreseeing its consequences; asking, if I may so say, for something different from the conditions under which we live, and yet comprehending inadequately those very conditions; very slaves to the pleasure of the ear, and more like the audience of a rhetorician than the council of a city.

'In order to keep you from this, I proceed to show that no one state has ever injured you as much as Mitylene. I can make allowance for those who revolt because they cannot bear our empire, or who have been forced to do so by the enemy. But for those who possessed an island with fortifications; who could fear our enemies only by sea, and there had their own force of galleys to protect them; who were independent and held in the highest honour by you—to act as these have done, this is not revolt—revolt implies oppression; it is deliberate and wanton aggression; an attempt to ruin us by siding with our bitterest enemies; a worse offence than a war undertaken on their own account in the acquisition of power. The fate of those of their neighbours who had already rebelled and had been subdued, was no lesson to them; their own prosperity could not dissuade them from affronting danger; but blindly confident in the future, and full of hopes beyond their power though not beyond their ambition, they declared war and made their decision to prefer might to right, their attack being determined not by provocation but by the moment which seemed propitious. The truth is that great good fortune coming suddenly and unexpectedly tends to make a people insolent: in most cases it is safer for mankind to have success in reason than out of reason; and it is easier for them, one may say, to stave off adversity than to preserve prosperity. Our mistake has been to distinguish the Mitylenians as we have done: had they been long ago treated like the rest, they never would have so far forgotten themselves, human nature being as surely made arrogant by consideration, as it is awed by firmness. Let them now therefore be punished as their crime requires, and do not, while you condemn the aristocracy, absolve the people. This is certain, that all attacked you without distinction, although they might have come over to us, and been now again in possession of their city. But no, they thought it safer to throw in their lot with the aristocracy and so joined their rebellion! Consider therefore! if you subject to the same punishment the ally who is forced to rebel by the enemy, and him who does so by his own free choice, which of them, think you, is there that will not rebel upon the slightest pretext; when the reward of success is freedom, and the penalty of failure nothing so very terrible? We meanwhile shall have to risk our money and our lives against one state after another; and if successful, shall receive a ruined town from which we can no longer draw the revenue upon which our strength depends; while if unsuccessful, we shall have an enemy the more upon our hands, and shall spend the time that might be employed in combating our existing foes in warring with our own allies.

'No hope, therefore, that rhetoric may instil or money purchase, of the mercy due to human infirmity must be held out to the Mitylenians. Their offence was not involuntary, but of malice and deliberate; and mercy is only for unwilling offenders. I therefore now as before persist against your reversing your first decision, or giving way to the three failings most fatal to empire—pity, sentiment, and indulgence. Compassion is due to those who can reciprocate the feeling, not to those who will never pity us in return, but are our natural and necessary foes: the orators who charm us with sentiment may find other less important arenas for their talents, in the place of one where the city pays a heavy penalty for a momentary pleasure, themselves receiving fine acknowledgments for their fine phrases; while indulgence should be shown towards those who will be our friends in future, instead of towards men who will remain just what they were, and as much our enemies as before. To sum up shortly, I say that if you follow my advice you will do what is just towards the Mitylenians, and at the same time expedient; while by a different decision you will not oblige them so much as pass sentence upon yourselves. For if they were right in rebelling, you must be wrong in ruling. However, if, right or wrong, you determine to rule, you must carry out your principle and punish the Mitylenians as your interest requires; or else you must give up your empire and cultivate honesty without danger. Make up your minds, therefore, to give them like for like; and do not let the victims who escaped the plot be more insensible than the conspirators who hatched it; but reflect what they would have done if victorious over you, especially as they were the aggressors. It is they who wrong their neighbour without a cause, that pursue their victim to the death, on account of the danger which they foresee in letting their enemy survive; since the object of a wanton wrong is more dangerous, if he escape, than an enemy who has not this to complain of. Do not, therefore, be traitors to yourselves, but recall as nearly as possible the moment of suffering and the supreme importance which you then attached to their reduction; and now pay them back in their turn, without yielding to present weakness or forgetting the peril that once hung over you. Punish them as they deserve, and teach your other allies by a striking example that the penalty of rebellion is death. Let them once understand this and you will not have so often to neglect your enemies while you are fighting with your own confederates.'

Such were the words of Cleon. After him Diodotus, son of Eucrates, who had also in the previous assembly spoken most strongly against putting the Mitylenians to death, came forward and spoke as follows:

'I do not blame the persons who have reopened the case of the Mitylenians, nor do I approve the protests which we have heard against important questions being frequently debated. I think the two things most opposed to good counsel are haste and passion; haste usually goes hand in hand with folly, passion with coarseness and narrowness of mind. As for the argument that speech ought not to be the exponent of action, the man who uses it must be either senseless or interested:

senseless if he believes it possible to treat of the uncertain future through any other medium; interested if wishing to carry a disgraceful measure and doubting his ability to speak well in a bad cause, he thinks to frighten opponents and hearers by well-aimed calumny. What is still more intolerable is to accuse a speaker of making a display in order to be paid for it. If ignorance only were imputed, an unsuccessful speaker might retire with a reputation for honesty, if not for wisdom; while the charge of dishonesty makes him suspected, if successful, and thought, if defeated, not only a fool but a rogue. The city is no gainer by such a system, since fear deprives it of its advisers; although in truth, if our speakers are to make such assertions, it would be better for the country if they could not speak at all, as we should then make fewer blunders. The good citizen ought to triumph not by frightening his opponents but by beating them fairly in argument; and a wise city without over-distinguishing its best advisers, will nevertheless not deprive them of their due, and far from punishing an unlucky counsellor will not even regard him as disgraced. In this way successful orators would be least tempted to sacrifice their convictions to popularity, in the hope of still higher honours, and unsuccessful speakers to resort to the same popular arts in order to win over the multitude.

'This is not our way; and, besides, the moment that a man is suspected of giving advice, however good, from corrupt motives, we feel such a grudge against him for the gain which after all we are not certain he will receive, that we deprive the city of its certain benefit. Plain good advice has thus come to be no less suspected than bad; and the advocate of the most monstrous measures is not more obliged to use deceit to gain the people, than the best counsellor is to lie in order to be believed. The city and the city only, owing to these refinements, can never be served openly and without disguise; he who does serve it openly being always suspected of serving himself in some secret way in return. Still, considering the magnitude of the interests involved, and the position of affairs, we orators must make it our business to look a little further than you who judge offhand; especially as we, your advisers, are responsible, while you, our audience, are not so. For if those who gave the advice, and those who took it, suffered equally, you would judge more calmly; as it is, you visit the disasters into which the whim of the moment may have led you, upon the single person of your adviser, not upon yourselves, his numerous companions in error.

'However, I have not come forward either to oppose or to accuse in the matter of Mitylene; indeed, the question before us as sensible men is not their guilt, but our interests. Though I prove them ever so guilty, I shall not, therefore, advise their death, unless it be expedient; nor though they should have claims to indulgence, shall I recommend it, unless it be clearly for the good of the country. I consider that we are deliberating for the future more than for the present; and where Cleon is so positive as to the useful deterrent effects that will follow from making rebellion capital, I who consider the interests of the future quite as much as he, as positively maintain the contrary. And I require you not to reject my useful considerations for his specious ones: his speech may have the attraction of seeming the most just in your present temper against Mitylene; but we are not in a court of justice, but in a political assembly; and the question is not justice, but how to make the Mitylenians useful to Athens.

'Now of course communities have enacted the penalty of death for many offences far lighter than this: still hope leads men to venture, and no one ever yet put himself in peril without the inward conviction that he would succeed in his design. Again, was there ever city rebelling that did not believe that it possessed either in itself or in its alliances resources adequate to the enterprise? All, states and individuals, are alike prone to err, and there is no law that will prevent them; or why should men have exhausted the list of punishments in search of enactments to protect them from evil-doers? It is probable that in early times the penalties for the greatest offences were less severe, and that, as these were disregarded, the penalty of death has been by degrees in most cases arrived at, which is itself disregarded in like manner. Either then some means of terror more terrible than this must be discovered, or it must be owned that this restraint is useless; and that as long as poverty gives men the courage of necessity, or plenty fills them with the ambition which belongs to insolence and pride, and the other conditions of life remain each under the thraldom of some fatal and master passion, so long will the impulse never be wanting to drive men into danger. Hope also and cupidity, the one leading and the other following, the one conceiving the attempt, the other suggesting the facility of succeeding, cause the widest ruin, and, although invisible agents, are far stronger than the dangers that are seen. Fortune, too, powerfully helps the delusion, and by the unexpected aid that she sometimes lends, tempts men to venture with inferior means; and this is especially the case with communities, because the stakes played for are the highest, freedom or empire, and, when all are acting together, each man irrationally magnifies his own capacity. In fine, it is impossible to prevent, and only great simplicity can hope to prevent, human nature doing what it has once set its mind upon, by force of law or by any other deterrent force whatsoever.

'We must not, therefore, commit ourselves to a false policy through a belief in the efficacy of the punishment of death, or exclude rebels from the hope of repentance and an early atonement of their error. Consider a moment! At present, if a city that has already revolted perceives that it cannot succeed, it will come to terms while it is still able to refund expenses, and pay tribute afterwards. In the other case, what city think you would not prepare better than is now done, and hold out to the last against its besiegers, if it is all one whether it surrender late or soon? And how can it be otherwise than hurtful to us to be put to the expense of a siege, because surrender is out of the question; and if we take the city, to receive a ruined town from which we can no longer draw the revenue which forms our real strength against the enemy? We must not, therefore, sit as strict judges of the offenders to our own prejudice, but rather see how by moderate chastisements we may be enabled to benefit in future by the revenue-producing powers of our dependencies; and we must make up our minds to look for our protection not to legal terrors but to careful administration. At present we do exactly the opposite. When a free community, held in subjection by force, rises, as is only natural, and asserts its independence, it is no sooner reduced than we fancy ourselves obliged to punish it severely; although the right course with freemen is not to chastise them rigorously when they do rise, but rigorously to watch them before they rise, and to prevent their ever entertaining the idea, and, the insurrection suppressed, to make as few responsible for it as possible.

'Only consider what a blunder you would commit in doing as Cleon recommends. As things are at present, in all the cities the people is your friend, and either does not revolt with the oligarchy, or, if forced to do so, becomes at once the enemy of the insurgents; so that in the war with the hostile city you have the masses on your side. But if you butcher the people of Mitylene, who had nothing to do with the revolt, and who, as soon as they got arms, of their own motion surrendered the town, first you will commit the crime of killing your benefactors; and next you will play directly into the hands of the higher classes, who when they induce their cities to rise, will immediately have the people on their side, through your having announced in advance the same punishment for those who are guilty and for those who are not. On the contrary, even if they were guilty, you ought to seem not to notice it, in order to avoid alienating the only class still friendly to us. In short, I consider it far more useful for the preservation of our empire voluntarily to put up with injustice, than to put to death, however justly, those whom it is our interest to keep alive. As for Cleon's idea that in punishment the claims of justice and expediency can both be satisfied, facts do not confirm the possibility of such a combination.

'Confess, therefore, that this is the wisest course, and without conceding too much either to pity or to indulgence, by neither of which motives do I any more than Cleon wish you to be influenced, upon the plain merits of the case before you, be persuaded by me to try calmly those of the Mitylenians whom Paches sent off as guilty, and to leave the rest undisturbed. This is at once best for the future, and most terrible to your enemies at the present moment; inasmuch as good policy against an adversary is superior to the blind attacks of brute force.'

Such were the words of Diodotus. The two opinions thus expressed were the ones that most directly contradicted each other; and the Athenians, notwithstanding their change of feeling, now proceeded to a division, in which the show of hands was almost equal, although the motion of Diodotus carried the day. Another galley was at once sent off in haste, for fear that the first might reach Lesbos in the interval,

and the city be found destroyed; the first ship having about a day and a night's start. Wine and barley-cakes were provided for the vessel by the Mitylenian ambassadors, and great promises made if they arrived in time; which caused the men to use such diligence upon the voyage that they took their meals of barley-cakes kneaded with oil and wine as they rowed, and only slept by turns while the others were at the oar. Luckily they met with no contrary wind, and the first ship making no haste upon so horrid an errand, while the second pressed on in the manner described, the first arrived so little before them, that Paches had only just had time to read the decree, and to prepare to execute the sentence, when the second put into port and prevented the massacre. The danger of Mitylene had indeed been great.

The other party whom Paches had sent off as the prime movers in the rebellion, were upon Cleon's motion put to death by the Athenians, the number being rather more than a thousand. The Athenians also demolished the walls of the Mitylenians, and took possession of their ships. Afterwards tribute was not imposed upon the Lesbians; but all their land, except that of the Methymnians, was divided into three thousand allotments, three hundred of which were reserved as sacred for the gods, and the rest assigned by lot to Athenian shareholders, who were sent out to the island. With these the Lesbians agreed to pay a rent of two minæ a year for each allotment, and cultivated the land themselves. The Athenians also took possession of the towns on the continent belonging to the Mitylenians, which thus became for the future subject to Athens. Such were the events that took place at Lesbos.

4. Civil War at Corcyra*

Much of the debate on the popularity of the Empire depends upon an understanding of domestic political struggles within the states composing the Athenian League. The best statement of the nature of these struggles is provided by Thucydides in his account of the revolution which took place in 427 at Corcyra, an island off the western coast of the Greek mainland which was an ally of Athens. Encouraged by the presence of a Spartan fleet, the Corcyrean oligarchs undertook a rebellion. At first the Spartan navy was unopposed and Spartan troops ravaged the countryside.

Meanwhile the commons in Corcyra, being still in great fear of the fleet attacking them, came to a parley with the suppliants and their friends, in order to save the town; and prevailed upon some of them to go on board the ships, of which they still manned thirty, against the expected attack. But the Peloponnesians after ravaging the country until midday sailed away, and towards nightfall were informed by beacon signals of the approach of sixty Athenian vessels from Leucas, under the command of Eurymedon, son of Thucles; which had been sent off by the Athenians upon the news of the revolution and of the fleet with Alcidas being about to sail for Corcyra.

The Peloponnesians accordingly at once set off in haste by night for home, coasting along shore; and hauling their ships across the Isthmus of Leucas, in order not to be seen doubling it, so departed. The Corcyræans, made aware of the approach of the Athenian fleet and of the departure of the enemy, brought the Messenians from outside the walls into the town, and ordered the fleet which they had manned to sail round into the Hyllaic harbour; and while it was so doing, slew such of their enemies as they laid hands on, dispatching afterwards as they landed them, those whom they had persuaded to go on board the ships. Next they went to the sanctuary of Hera and persuaded about fifty men to take their trial, and condemned them all to death. The mass of the suppliants who had refused to do so, on seeing what was taking place, slew each other there in the consecrated ground; while some hanged themselves upon the trees, and others destroyed themselves as they were severally able. During seven days that Eurymedon stayed with his sixty ships, the Corcyræans were engaged in butchering those of their fellow-citizens whom they regarded as their enemies: and although the crime imputed was that of attempting to put down the democracy, some were slain also for private hatred, others by their debtors because of the monies owed to them. Death thus raged in every shape; and, as usually happens at such times, there was no length to which violence did not go; sons were killed by their fathers, and suppliants dragged from the altar or slain upon it; while some were even walled up in the temple of Dionysus and died there.

So bloody was the march of the revolution, and the impression which it made was the greater as it was one of the first to occur. Later on, one may say, the whole Hellenic world was convulsed; struggles being everywhere made by the popular chiefs to bring in the Athenians, and by the oligarchs to introduce the Lacedæ-monians. In peace there would have been neither the pretext nor the wish to make such an invitation; but in war, with an alliance always at the command of either faction for the hurt of their adversaries and their own corresponding advantage, oppor-tunities for bringing in the foreigner were

* Thucydides, 3. 80–84, translated by Richard Crawley.

never wanting to the revolutionary parties. The sufferings which revolution entailed upon the cities were many and terrible, such as have occurred and always will occur, as long as the nature of mankind remains the same; though in a severer or milder form, and varying in their symptoms, according to the variety of the particular cases. In peace and prosperity states and individuals have better sentiments, because they do not find themselves suddenly confronted with imperious necessities; but war takes away the easy supply of daily wants, and so proves a rough master, that brings most men's characters to a level with their fortunes. Revolution thus ran its course from city to city, and the places which it arrived at last, from having heard what had been done before carried to a still greater excess the refinement of their inventions, as manifested in the cunning of their enterprises and the atrocity of their reprisals. Words had to change their ordinary meaning and to take that which was now given them. Reckless audacity came to be considered the courage of a loyal ally; prudent hesitation, specious cowardice; moderation was held to be a cloak for unmanliness; ability to see all sides of a question inaptness to act on any. Frantic violence became the attribute of manliness; cautious plotting, a justifiable means of self-defence. The advocate of extreme measures was always trustworthy; his opponent a man to be suspected. To succeed in a plot was to have a shrewd head, to divine a plot a still shrewder; but to try to provide against having to do either was to break up your party and to be afraid of your adversaries. In fine, to forestall an intending criminal, or to suggest the idea of a crime where it was wanting, was equally commended, until even blood became a weaker tie than party, from the superior readiness of those united by the latter to dare everything without reserve; for such associations had not in view the blessings derivable from established institutions but were formed by ambition for their overthrow; and the confidence of their members in each other rested less on any religious sanction than upon complicity in crime. The fair proposals of an adversary were met with jealous precautions by the stronger of the two, and not with a generous confidence. Revenge also was held of more account than self-preservation. Oaths of reconciliation, being only proffered on either side to meet an immediate difficulty, only held good so long as no other weapon was at hand; but when opportunity offered, he who first ventured to seize it and to take his enemy off his guard, thought this perfidious vengeance sweeter than an open one, since, considerations of safety apart, success by treachery won him the palm of superior intelligence. Indeed it is generally the case that men are readier to call rogues clever than simpletons honest, and are as ashamed of being the second as they are proud of being the first. The cause of all these evils was the lust for power arising from greed and ambition; and from these passions proceeded the violence of parties once engaged in contention. The leaders in the cities, each provided with the fairest professions, on the one side with the cry of political equality of the people, on the other of a moderate aristocracy, sought prizes for themselves in those public interests which they pretended to cherish, and, recoiling from no means in their struggles for ascendancy, engaged in the direct excesses; in their acts of vengeance they went to even greater lengths, not stopping at what justice or the good of the state demanded, but making the party caprice of the moment their only standard, and invoking with equal readiness the condemnation of an unjust verdict or the authority of the strong arm to glut the animosities of the hour. Thus religion was in honour with neither party; but the use of fair phrases to arrive at guilty ends was in high reputation. Meanwhile the moderate part of the citizens perished between the two, either for not joining in the quarrel, or because envy would not suffer them to escape.

Thus every form of iniquity took root in the Hellenic countries by reason of the troubles. The ancient simplicity into which honour so largely entered was laughed down and disappeared; and society became divided into camps in which no man trusted his fellow. To put an end to this, there was neither promise to be depended upon, nor oath that could command respect; but all parties dwelling rather in their calculation upon the hopelessness of a permanent state of things, were more intent upon self-defence than capable of confidence. In this contest the blunter wits were most successful: Apprehensive of their own deficiencies and of the cleverness of their antagonists, they feared to be worsted in debate and to be surprised by the combinations of their more versatile opponents, and so at once boldly had recourse to action: while their adversaries, arrogantly thinking that they should know in time, and that it was unnecessary to secure by action what policy afforded, often fell victims to their want of precaution.

Meanwhile Corcyra gave the first example of most of the crimes alluded to; of the reprisals exacted by the governed who had never experienced equitable treatment or indeed aught but insolence from their rulers—when their hour came; of the iniquitous resolves of those who desired to get rid of their accustomed poverty, and ardently coveted their neighbours' goods; and lastly, of the savage and pitiless excesses into which men who had begun the struggle not in a class but in a party spirit, were hurried by their ungovernable passions. In the confusion into which life was now thrown in the cities, human nature, always rebelling against the law and now its master, gladly showed itself ungoverned in passion, above respect for justice, and the enemy of all superiority; since revenge would not have been set above religion, and gain above justice, had it not been for the fatal power of envy. Indeed men too often take upon themselves in the prosecution of their revenge to set the example of doing away with those general laws to which all alike can look for salvation in adversity, instead of allowing them to subsist against the day of danger when their aid may be required.

5. The Consequence of the Sicilian Disaster*

The failure of the Athenian attempt to conquer Sicily and the terrible loss of men and ships which it entailed had a great effect on the attitude of the subject states to Athens. Thucydides describes their response to the great defeat of 413.

Such were the events in Sicily. When the news was brought to Athens, for a long while they disbelieved even the most respectable of the soldiers who had themselves escaped from the scene of action and clearly reported the matter, a destruction so complete not being thought credible. When the conviction was forced upon them, they were angry with the orators

who had joined in promoting the expedition, just as if they had not themselves voted it, and were enraged also with the reciters of oracles and soothsayers, and all other omen-mongers of the time who had encouraged them to hope that they should conquer Sicily. Already distressed at all points and in all quarters, after what had now happened, they were seized by a fear and consternation quite without example. It was grievous enough for the state and for every man in his proper

* Thucydides, 8. 1–2, translated by Richard Crawley.

person to lose so many heavy infantry, cavalry, and able-bodied troops, and to see none left to replace them; but when they saw, also, that they had not sufficient ships in their docks, or money in the treasury, or crews for the ships, they began to despair of salvation. They thought that their enemies in Sicily would immediately sail with their fleet against Piræus, inflamed by so signal a victory; while their adversaries at home, redoubling all their preparations, would vigorously attack them by sea and land at once, aided by their own revolted confederates. Nevertheless, with such means as they had, it was determined to resist to the last, and to provide timber and money, and to equip a fleet as they best could, to take steps to secure their confederates and above all Eubœa, to reform things in the city upon a more economical footing, and to elect a board of elders to advise upon the state of affairs as occasion should arise. In short, as is the way of a democracy, in the panic of the moment they were ready to be as prudent as possible.

These resolves were at once carried into effect. Summer was now over. The winter ensuing saw all Hellas stirring under the impression of the great Athenian disaster in Sicily. Neutrals now felt that even if uninvited they ought no longer to stand aloof from the war, but should volunteer to march against the Athenians, who, as they severally reflected, would probably have come against them if the Sicilian campaign had succeeded. Besides, they considered that the war would now be short, and that it would be creditable for them to take part in it. Meanwhile the allies of the Lacedæmonians felt all more anxious than ever to see a speedy end to their heavy labours. But above all, the subjects of the Athenians showed a readiness to revolt even beyond their ability, judging the circumstances with passion, and refusing even to hear of the Athenians being able to last out the coming summer. Beyond all this, Lacedæmon was encouraged by the near prospect of being joined in great force in the spring by her allies in Sicily, lately forced by events to acquire their navy. With these reasons for confidence in every quarter, the Lacedæmonians now resolved to throw themselves without reserve into the war considering that, once it was happily terminated, they would be finally delivered from such dangers as that which would have threatened them from Athens, if she had become mistress of Sicily, and that the overthrow of the Athenians would leave them in quiet enjoyment of the supremacy over all Hellas.

6. PHRYNICHUS' VIEW OF OLIGARCHY, DEMOCRACY, AND EMPIRE*

In 411 B.C. the Athenians were hard-pressed. Some of their subjects had rebelled; others were on the point of rebellion. Sparta was in league with Persia and able to match Athenian sea-power. Alcibiades, the brilliant but treacherous Athenian politician, had been exiled by the democracy and was intriguing at the court of the Persian satrap Tissaphernes. He promised the Athenians that if they overthrew the democracy and established an oligarchy Persia would break their Spartan alliance and come over to the Athenians.

The design was first mooted in the camp, and afterwards from thence reached

*Thucydides, 8. 48. Translated by Richard Crawley.

the city. Some persons crossed over from Samos and had an interview with Alcibiades, who immediately offered to make first Tissaphernes, and afterwards the king, their friend, if they would give up the democracy, and made it possible for the king to trust them. The higher class, who also suffered most severely from the war, now conceived great hopes of getting the government into their own hands, and of triumphing over the enemy. Upon their return to Samos the emissaries formed their partisans into a club, and openly told the mass of the armament that the king would be their friend, and would provide them with money, if Alcibiades were restored, and the democracy abolished. The multitude, if at first irritated by these intrigues, were nevertheless kept quiet by the advantageous prospect of the pay from the king; and the oligarchical conspirators, after making this communication to the people, now re-examined the proposals of Alcibiades among themselves, with most of their associates. Unlike the rest, who thought them advantageous and trustworthy, Phrynichus, who was still general, by no means approved of the proposals. Alcibiades, he rightly thought, cared no more for an oligarchy than for a democracy, and only sought to change the institutions of his country in order to get himself recalled by his associates; while for themselves their one object should be to avoid civil discord. It was not the king's interest, when the Peloponnesians were now their equals at sea, and in possession of some of the chief cities in his empire, to go out of his way to side with the Athenians whom he did not trust, when he might make friends of the Peloponnesians who had never injured him. And as for the allied states to whom oligarchy was now offered, because the democracy was to be put down at Athens, he well knew that this would not make the rebels come in any the sooner, or confirm the loyal in their allegiance; as the allies would never prefer servitude with an oligarchy or democracy to freedom with the constitution which they actually enjoyed, to whichever type it belonged. Besides, the cities thought that the so-called better classes would prove just as oppressive as the commons, as being those who originated, proposed, and for the most part benefited from the acts of the commons injurious to the confederates. Indeed, if it depended on the better classes, the confederates would be put to death without trial and with violence; while the commons were their refuge and the chastiser of these men. This he positively knew that the cities had learned by experience, and that such was their opinion. The propositions of Alcibiades, and the intrigues now in progress, could therefore never meet with his approval.

7. THE CHARACTER OF THE ATHENIAN EMPIRE*

Was the Athenian empire a selfish despotism, detested by the subjects whom it oppressed and exploited? The ancient sources, and modern scholars, are almost unanimous that it was, and the few voices (such as those of Grote, Freeman, Greenidge and Marsh) raised in opposition to this harsh verdict—which will here be called "the traditional view"—have not succeeded in modifying or even explaining its dominance. Characteristic of the attitude of many historians is the severe judgment of Last, who, contrasting Athens as the "tyrant city" with Rome as "communis nostra patria," can see nothing more significant in Athenian imperial government than that "warning which gives some slight value to even the worst of failures".

The real basis of the traditional view, with which that view must stand or fall, is the belief that the Athenian empire was hated by its subjects—a belief for which there is explicit and weighty support in the sources (above all Thucydides), but which

* G. E. M. de Ste. Croix, "The Character of the Athenian Empire," Historia, 3 (1954–55), pp. 1–6, 9–11, 16, 31, 36–40.

nevertheless is demonstrably false. The first section of this paper will therefore be devoted to showing that whether or not the Athenian empire was politically oppressive or economically predatory, the general mass of the population of the allied (or subject) states, far from being hostile to Athens, actually welcomed her dominance and wished to remain within the empire, even—and perhaps more particularly—during the last thirty years of the fifth century, when the ὕβρις [hybris] of Athens, which bulks so large in the traditional view, is supposed to have been at its height.

THE ALLEGED UNPOPULARITY OF THE EMPIRE

By far the most important witness for the prosecution, in any arraignment of Athenian imperialism, is of course Thucydides; but it is precisely Thucydides who, under cross-examination, can be made to yield the most valuable pieces of detailed evidence of the falsity of his own generalisations. Before we examine his evidence, it will be well to make clear the conception of his speeches upon which some of the interpretations given here are based. Whatever Thucydides may have meant by the much discussed expression τὰ δέοντα, whatever purpose he may originally have intended the speeches to serve, there can surely be no doubt that some of the speeches in fact represent what the speakers would have said if they had expressed *with perfect frankness* the sentiments which the historian himself attributed to them, and hence may sometimes depart very far from what was actually said, above all because political and diplomatic speeches are seldom entirely candid.

Now Thucydides harps constantly on the unpopularity of imperial Athens, at least during the Peloponnesian War. He makes no less than eight of his speakers accuse the Athenians of "enslaving" their allies or of wishing to "enslave" other states, and he also uses the same expression in his own person. His Corinthian envoys at Sparta, summarising the historian's own view in a couple of words, call Athens the "tyrant city". Thucydides even represents the Athenians themselves as fully conscious that their rule was a tyranny: he makes not only Cleon but also Pericles admit that the empire had this character. It must be allowed that in such political contexts both "enslavement" and "tyranny"—δουλεία and τυραννίς [douleia and tyrannis], and their cognates— are often used in a highly technical sense: any infringement of the ἐλευθερία [eleutheria = freedom or liberty] of a city, however slight, might be described as "enslavement"; and terms such as τύραννος πόλις [tyrannos polis = tyrant city] do not necessarily imply (as the corresponding English expressions would) that Athens was an oppressive or unpopular ruler. However, it will hardly be denied that Thycydides regarded the dominance of Athens over her allies as indeed oppressive and unpopular. The speech he puts into the mouths of the Athenians at Sparta in 432 admits that their rule is "much detested by the Hellenes" and that Athens has become "hateful to most people". At the outbreak of the war, says Thucydides, "people in general were strongly in favour of Sparta, especially as she professed herself the liberator of Hellas. Every individual and every city was eager to help her by word and deed, to the extent of feeling that personal participation was necessary if her cause were not to suffer. So general was the indignation felt against Athens, some desiring to be liberated from her rule, others dreading to pass under it". In the winter of 413–12, when the news of the Athenian disaster in Sicily had become known, Thucydides would have us believe that all Hellas was astir, neutrals feeling that they ought to attack Athens spontaneously, and the subjects of Athens showing themselves ready to revolt "even beyond their capacity to do so", feeling passionately on the subject and refusing even to hear of the Athenians' being able to last out the summer.

This is what Thucydides wanted his readers to believe. It is undoubtedly the conception he himself honestly held. Nevertheless, his own detailed narrative proves that it is certainly false. Thucydides was such a remarkably objective historian that he himself provided sufficient material for his own refutation. The news columns in Thucydides, so to speak, contradict the editorial Thucydides, and the editor himself does not always speak with the same voice.

In the "Mytilenean Debate" at Athens in 427, Thucydides makes Diodotus tell the assembled Athenians that in all the cities the demos is their friend, and either does not join the Few, the ὀλίγοι [oligoi], when they revolt, or, if constrained to do so, at once turns on the rebels, so that in fighting the refractory state the Athenians have the mass of the citizens (τὸ πλῆθος [to plethos]) on their side. (The precise meaning of these expression—δῆμος, πλῆθος, ὀλίγοι [demos, plethos, oligoi] and the like —will be considered in the third section of this paper.) It is impossible to explain away the whole passage on the ground that Diodotus is just saying the kind of thing that might be expected to appeal to an Athenian audience. Not only do we have Thucydides' general statement that throughout the Greek world, after the Corcyraean revolution of 427, the leaders of the popular parties tried to bring in the Athenians, as οἱ ὀλίγοι the Spartans; there is a great deal of evidence relating to individual cities, which we must now consider. Of course, the mere fact that a city did not revolt from Athens does not of itself necessarily imply fidelity: considerations of expediency, short-term or long-term, may often have been decisive—the fear of immediate Athenian counter-action, or the belief that Athens would ultimately become supreme. But that does not alter the fact that in almost every case in which we do have detailed information about the attitude of an allied city, we find only the Few hostile; scarcely ever is there reason to think that the demos was not mainly loyal. The evidence falls into two groups: for the 450s and 440s B.C. it is largely epigraphic, for the period of the Peloponnesian War it is mainly literary. We shall begin with the later period, for which the evidence is much more abundant.

The revolt of Lesbos in 428–7, in which Mytilene was the ringleader, is particularly interesting, because it is only at the very end of Thucydides' account that we gain any inkling of the real situation. At first, Thucydides implies that the Mytileneans were wholehearted and that only a few factious citizens, who were proxenoi of Athens, cared to inform the Athenians of the preparations for revolt. We hear much of the determined resistance of the Mytileneans and of their appeal to Sparta, and we may well be astonished when we suddenly discover from Thucydides that "the Mytileneans" who had organised and conducted the revolt were not the main body of the Mytileneans at all, but only the governing oligarchy, for no sooner had the Spartan commander Salaethus distributed hoplite equipment to the formerly light-armed demos, with the intention of making a *sortie en masse* against the besieging Athenian force, than the demos immediately mutinied and the government had to surrender to Athens.

In describing the activities of Brasidas in the "Thraceward region" in 424–3, Thucydides occasionally gives us a glimpse of the internal situation in the cities. First, it is worth mentioning that in recording the northward march of Brasidas through Thessaly, Thucydides says that the mass of the population there had always been friendly to Athens, and that Brasidas would never have been allowed to pass if ἰσονομία [isonomia] instead of the traditional δυναστεία [dynasteia] had existed in

Thessaly. When Brasidas arrived in the "Thraceward district", probably in September 424, there seem to have been few if any Athenian garrisons there, for Thucydides mentions none, except that at Amphipolis, and represents the Athenians as sending out garrisons at the end of that year, "as far as they could at such short notice and in winter." Brasidas made his first attempt on Acanthus. The inhabitants were divided, the common people being faithful to Athens; but eventually the citizens gave way and opened their gates, influenced not only by an able speech from Brasidas, a judicious blend of threats and promises, but also by "fear for their fruit", for it was just before vintage, and Brasidas had threatened to ravage. When the Spartan invited the surrender of Amphipolis, he at first found little support within that town. However, the combined effect of his military success in occupying the surrounding country, the advantageous terms he offered, and the efforts of his partisans within, was sufficient to procure the surrender of the city.

Thucydides declares now categorically that there was general enthusiasm for revolt among the Athenian subject cities of the district, which sent secret messages to Brasidas, begging him to come to them, each wishing to lead the way in revolting. They had the additional inducement, as Thucydides points out, of the recent Athenian defeat at Delium. On the face of it, Thucydides' account is plausible enough. There is good reason to suppose, however, that when he speaks of the "cities" that were subject to Athens, he is thinking merely of the propertied classes. When Brasidas marched into the peninsula of Acte, most of the towns (which were insignificant) naturally surrendered at once, but Sane and Dium, small as they were, and surrounded by cities now in alliance with Brasidas, held out, even when their lands were ravaged. Turning his attention to the Sithonian peninsula, Brasidas captured Torone, though it was

held by an Athenian garrison (probably just arrived); but this was done only through the treachery of a few, to the dismay of the majority, some ·of whom joined the Athenian garrison when it shut itself up in the fort of Lecythus, only to be driven out to Pallene. A Spartan commander was subsequently put in charge of the town. In 423, after Scione had revolted spontaneously, its neighbour Mende was betrayed to Brasidas by a few. Later, when the Athenian army arrived, there were disturbances at Mende, and soon the common people fell upon the mixed Scionean and Peloponnesian garrison of seven hundred. After plundering the town, which had not made terms of surrender, the Athenians wisely told the Mendeans that they could keep their civic rights and themselves deal with their own traitors. In the case of Acanthus, Sane, Dium, Torone and Mende, then, we have positive evidence that the bulk of the citizens were loyal to Athens, in circumstances which were anything but propitious. In Aristophanes' *Peace*, produced in 421, it is οἱ παχεῖς καὶ πλούσιοι [*hoi pacheis kai plousioi* = the rich] whom the Athenians are said to have pursued with charges of favouring Brasidas. It would be simpleminded to suppose that this happened just because the richest citizens were the most worth despoiling. It may be that some of the other towns went over to Brasidas with the free consent of the demos, but only in regard to Scione, and possibly Argilus (whose citizens apparently hoped to gain control over Amphipolis by backing Brasidas) does the narrative of Thucydides provide any grounds for this assumption; and even at Scione, which did not revolt until 423, some at first "disapproved of what was being done".

* * *

We can now go back to the 450s and 440s B.C., a period for which, as mentioned above, the evidence on the questions under discussion is predominantly epigraphic.

The revolt of Erythrae, from 454 or earlier to 452, was almost certainly due to the seizure of power by a Persian-backed tyranny. Miletus was also in revolt from at least 454 until 452/1; but during this period she was apparently under the control of a close oligarchy or tyranny, which seems to have driven out an important section of the citizen body (perhaps with Persian support), and was sentenced in its turn to perpetual and hereditary outlawry about 452, when the exiles returned and the city was brought back into the Athenian empire. The probable absence of Colophon from the tribute quota-lists of the second assessment period (450/49 to 447/6), and the Athenian decree relating to that city of (probably) 446, certainly point to a revolt about 450; but the known Persian associations of this inland city, the fact that it was handed over to the Persian Itamenes in 430 by one of two parties in a στάσις (presumably of the usual character—oligarchs against democrats), and the Colophonian oath to preserve democracy—perhaps newly introduced, or at any rate restored—in the treaty made with Athens in 446 or thereabouts, strongly suggest that the revolt was the work of oligarchs receiving Persian support. The revolt of Euboea in 446 may well have been mainly the work of the Hippobotae, the aristocrats of Chalcis, for the Athenians drove them out on the reduction of the island and probably gave their lands to cleruchs, but inflicted no punishment beyond the taking of hostages, as far as we know, on the other Euboeans, except that they expelled the Hestiaeans (who had massacred the crew of an Athenian ship) and settled an Athenian colony on their lands. The revolt of Samos in 440/39, after certain Samians who "wished to revolutionise the constitution" had induced the Athenians to set up a democracy, was certainly brought about by exiled oligarchs, who allied themselves with the Persian satrap Pissuthnes, employed a force of seven hundred

mercenaries, and worked in conjunction with the δυνατώτατοι [dynatotatoi = most powerful] remaining in the city. Here again there is no evidence of general hostility to Athens among the Samians, although once the oligarchs had got a firm grip on the city, and had captured and expelled the democratic leaders, they put up a stout resistance to Athens and were no doubt able to enforce the adherence of a considerable number of the common folk.

It is significant that in this early period, whenever we do have information about the circumstances of a revolt, we find good reason for attributing it to oligarchs or tyrants, who could evidently rely on Persian assistance wherever the situation of the city permitted. This is precisely the state of affairs we have already seen to exist later, during the Peloponnesian War. In some cases, both early and late, the bare fact of a revolt is recorded, without detail. Some of these revolts may have been wholehearted, but we certainly cannot assume so just because we have no evidence. Surely the reverse is true: surely we may assume that the situation we find in virtually all the towns for which we do have sufficient information existed in most of the remainder. The mere fact of the coming to power of an oligarchy in an allied city immediately upon a revolt from Athens, as evidently at Eretria in 411, tends to confirm that the democratic party in that city was pro-Athenian.

It is not difficult to find other examples of loyalty to Athens on the part of her allies, or pro-Athenian movements inside cities in revolt. When the Athenian armament in Sicily was at its last gasp, the division under Demosthenes being on the very point of surrender, the Syracusans made a proclamation offering freedom to any of the islanders (the Athenian allies) who were willing to come over to them. Further resistance was now quite hopeless, and nothing could have restrained the allies from deserting except the strongest sense of loyalty. Yet Thucydides tells us that "not many cities went over". The majority remained, to undergo a fate which they must have well known could only be death or enslavement. In 428 Methymna refused to follow the rest of the Lesbian cities in their revolt. In 430 there was a στάσις [stasis = revolution] at Colophon: one faction called in the Persians and expelled the other, which removed to Notium but itself split into two factions, one of which gained control of the new settlement by employing mercenaries and allied itself with the medising citizens remaining in Colophon. In 427 the defeated party, no doubt democratic in character, called in the Athenians, who founded a new colony at Notium for the exiled Colophonians. The capture of Selymbria and Byzantium by the Athenians in 408-7 was brought about in each case by the treachery of a faction inside the city.

In the light of all the evidence which has been cited above, we can understand and accept Plato's explanation of the long life of the Athenian empire: the Athenians, he says, kept their ἀρχή [arche = empire] for seventy years "because they had friends in each of the cities".

An overwhelming body of evidence has now been produced to show that the mass of the citizens in the allied or subject states were loyal to Athens throughout the whole period of the empire, until the final collapse in the Ionian War, and could on occasion give proof of a deep devotion to the imperial city, which can only be compared with the similar devotion of contemporary oligarchs to Sparta. This judgment holds, whatever the character of Athenian imperialism may have been and whatever verdict we ourselves may wish to pass upon it. The evidence is all the more impressive in that it comes mainly from Thucydides, who, whenever he is generalising, or interpreting the facts rather than stating them, depicts the subjects of Athens as groaning under her tyrannous rule. A subsidiary conclusion of

no small importance which has emerged from this survey is that Thucydides, generally (and rightly) considered the most trustworthy of all ancient historians, is guilty of serious misrepresentation in his judgments on the Athenian empire. He was quite entitled to disapprove of the later empire, and to express this disapproval. What we may reasonably object to is his representing that the majority of its subjects detested it. At the same time, it must be laid to Thucydides' credit that we are able to convict him of this distortion precisely because he himself is scrupulously accurate in presenting the detailed evidence. The partiality of Thucydides could scarcely have been exposed but for the honesty of Thucydides.

THE POLITICAL OUTLOOK OF THUCYDIDES

Our subject is the Athenian empire and not its great historian; but as certain criticisms have been made of Thucydides in the first and second sections of this article, it is only right that an explanation should be offered of the reasons for the defects in his History which have been pointed out above. Why did Thucydides, who was an exceptionally truthful man and anything but a superficial observer, so deceive himself about the attitude of the Greeks towards the Athenian empire? There can only be one answer: political and social influences, at the end of the fifth century exceptionally powerful, drove the historian to look at the whole Greek world in terms of that relatively small section of the Athenian citizen body to which he himself belonged, so that when he wrote of the detestation of Athens, or the longing for revolt, felt by οἱ πολλοί [hoi polloi = the many] or οἱ Ἕλληνες πάντες, or αἱ πόλεις ὑπήκοοι, or οἱ ξύμμαχοι, or πᾶς καὶ ἰδιώτης καὶ πόλις [hoi Hellenes pantes = all the Greeks, hai poleis hypekooi = the subject states, hoi xymmachoi = the allies, pas kai idiotes kai *polis*=every individual and every state], he was thinking only of the upper classes, of that comparatively small body of what is sometimes called "educated opinion". This point of view he quite honestly conceived as that of the Greeks in general. It is a perfectly natural and very common failing, and it is entirely characteristic of the Greek and Roman historians, most of whom, if they did not actually belong to the governing class of their day, had thoroughly acquired its outlook. When we are studying Thucydides, then, we must never forget that we are studying a member—if an exceptionally intelligent and gifted member—of the Athenian propertied class.

* * *

What was Thucydides' attitude to the Athenian empire? This is a question to which almost everyone gives a different answer. The principal reason for this is that the historian's attitude to the empire was thoroughly ambivalent, that he could habitually entertain quite different feelings towards it at one and the same time, now one and now another coming uppermost. On the one hand he was much impressed by the greatness and brilliance of imperial Athens, in which, as a patriotic Athenian, he must have felt a deep pride. In inter-state politics he was a realist, calmly accepting the fact that in the relations between Greek cities force and not justice was in practice the supreme arbiter. He was not shocked by the calculated and restrained exercise of state power, which he regarded as an inevitable and in some ways a desirable feature of the contemporary scene. On the other hand, sharing as he did the outlook of the allied ὀλίγοι, he felt that Athens had abused her power—not as much as another imperial city in her position might easily have been tempted to abuse it, but enough to provoke general hatred and a longing to be quit of her rule. In the Melian Dialogue, with enigmatic impartiality, he gives the Athenians an unanswerable case, according

to the prevailing practice of inter-state relations, based ultimately on the appeal to force, in the name of expediency; but he has chosen for this highly generalised debate a setting which could not fail to arouse in his readers, knowing of the massacre that was to come, the strongest prejudice against the Athenian speakers.

One thing Thucydides does not say, explicitly or implicitly, although the statement is often attributed to him: he does not say that the Athenian radical democrats believed that "Might is Right". When the Athenian envoys at Sparta say, αἰεὶ καθεστῶτος τὸν ἥσσω ὑπὸ τοῦ δυνατωτέρου κατείργεσθαι, they are simply saying, "It has always been the rule for the weaker to be subject to the stronger". They are merely recognising a natural tendency, a "law of human nature", not trying to adduce a moral justification. The theory that the interest of the stronger is τὸ δίκαιον [*to dikaion*=justice], that Might is Right, does not seem to make its appearance in surviving literature until the time of Plato, who puts it into the mouths of Callicles, not an historical character, and Thrasymachus, a sophist whom there is not the slightest reason to connect with the radical democrats. Did any fifth century Greek seriously maintain that Might is Right, or is this merely a clever distortion of the realist position actually held by the Athenian radicals? It is easy to imagine how this distortion could come about. The oligarchs had been accustomed to maintain that under the old regime, where they had been masters, Right rather than Might had prevailed. When the democrats exposed this pretence, the obvious counter-attack was to twist the democratic admission that force did govern into the claim that force ought to govern.

WHY THE MANY WERE FRIENDLY TO ATHENS

It is part of the traditional view of the Athenian empire that the common people of Athens, under the influence of the "demagogues", drove the allies hard, while the "best people" did what they could to protect them. Of course oligarchs like Thucydides the son of Melesias, and perhaps Antiphon, would pose as defenders of the allies, by way of showing their opposition to the whole policy of the democrats. But the traditional view cannot be allowed to stand here either. Apart from the other evidence, there is a very striking and important passage in the last book of Thucydides, which seldom receives the attention it deserves. The whole passage (which would presumably have been worked up into a set speech if the History had ever been finished) describes the point of view of Phrynichus, the Athenian oligarch, in 411. Phrynichus realised, says Thucydides, that the setting up of an oligarchy at Athens would not have the effect of making the allies, many of whom were then in revolt, any better disposed towards Athens. He admitted "that the allies expected the upper classes (of Athens) to prove just as troublesome to themselves as the demos, as being those who devised the acts injurious to the allies, proposed them to the demos, and gained most of the benefit from them; and that as far as the upper classes were concerned, they (the allies) might come to a violent end without trial, whereas the demos was their refuge and the chastiser of these men". This is a very remarkable statement, all the more valuable in that it is put by Thucydides (without contradiction) into the mouth of an oligarch, who could have no possible reason for making an admission so damaging to his own party if it were not true. It gives us two pieces of information: that most of the perquisites of empire went to the Athenian upper classes; and that the Athenian demos was more just and merciful towards the allies than were its "betters".

Humble folk in the allied cities who were oppressed by their own ὀλίγοι would have had no hesitation in trying to obtain redress from Athens, either in the form of assistance for a *coup d'état* or by recourse to recognised judicial procedure. The power to transfer certain cases to Athens, especially serious criminal cases, was one of the most important features of the government of the empire. The Old Oligarch shows how the process operated to the advantage of the common people both at Athens and in the allied states. He says outright that the Athenians persecute the χρηστοί, ... τοὺς δὲ πονηροὺς αὔξουσιν [rich . . . and assist the poor], and again that in the law courts τοὺς μὲν τοῦ δήμου σώζουσιν, τοὺς δ' ἐναντίους ἀπολλύουσιν [they preserve the men of the *demos* but destroy their opponents]. He explains that by compelling the allies to sail to Athens for judicial decisions the Athenians not only derive financial benefit (which he probably exaggerates); they can govern the allied states, supporting the popular side and making short work of their opponents, without having to go overseas; and thus the allies are obliged not merely to pay respect to visiting generals, trierarchs and ambassadors (who would at least be gentlemen) but also to curry favour with the Athenian demos itself and lick its boots, thus becoming "slaves of the Athenian demos". He adds the information that if the allies were allowed to try their cases at home, they in their turn, detesting Athens as they do, would make short work of the pro-Athenian parties in their midst—by which he means democratic agitators and suchlike. If you want real εὐνομία [eunomia], he says, you must have the laws made for the demos by the δεξιώτατοι [dexiotatoi=the wealthy], and then the χρηστοί [chrestoi= good] will chastise the πονηροί [poneroi= bad] and not allow μαινομένους ἀνθρώπους [mainomenous anthropous=madmen] any voice at all. The Old Oligarch reflects with satisfaction that in such a desirable state of affairs the demos would rapidly fall into δουλεία. These passages give us an interesting glimpse of the attitude of many influential members of the propertied classes in the fifth century, against whose interests the Athenians were working when they claimed overriding powers in respect of certain judicial cases. We are able for a moment to foresee what would happen when Athenian control was removed—what actually did happen after the "liberation" of the allies by Sparta, when (as at Athens itself under the "Thirty") there were "many massacres", and "the slaughter of countless numbers of the popular party".

We need not be surprised, then, that the masses in the cities of the Athenian empire welcomed political subordination to Athens as the price of escape from the tyranny of their own oligarchs. This is not the place to consider whether they received other benefits from Athenian rule; protection against their own oligarchs is enough for our present purposes. Athens undoubtedly gave much support to the Many in the allied states against their own Few, who of course (with the sympathy of the Few at Athens, including Thucydides) regarded the resulting democratisation as the direct consequence of Athenian tyranny. Almost all our literary sources, imbued with oligarchical prejudice, present this point of view only. Active Athenian support of the Many must certainly have increased after 461, and may perhaps have become intensified again after the death of Pericles; but in the absence of confirmatory detailed evidence there is no reason to suppose that the Athenians became to any marked extent increasingly "oppressive", except in the peculiar oligarchical sense, during the second half of the fifth century.

We may accept the statement of Isocrates that the Athenians did not set up "opposition governments" unjustifiably in the allied states, and thus stir up factional strife. On the contrary, it was the boast of the Athenian democrats that they had suppressed στάσις. To borrow a phrase from a modern politician, Athens

did not "export revolution", at any rate to states which were not already well supplied with that commodity. The way Isocrates puts it, in another speech, is that "our fathers tried to induce (ἔπειθον) the allies to establish in their cities the same form of government as they themselves preserved with loving care". This may not be so very far from the truth. At any rate, it is a grave error to take the introduction of a democracy on the Athenian model as a necessary indication of Athenian "bullying". Would not the Many in an oligarchical state be only too delighted to copy, even in minute details, the famous constitution of democratic Athens? Might they not even be glad to have an Athenian garrison on hand while they were learning to work their new constitution? We know that the democrats at Corcyra in c. 410, having reason to suspect that their δυνατώτατοι were about to hand the city over to Sparta, obtained a garrison from the Athenians. And the Athenian garrison at Lesbian Methymna, as already mentioned, had probably been supplied at the request of the party in power. At Erythrae the well known inscription shows the Athenians installing a garrison whose commander is given the task of supervising the selection by lot of the vital Council. But there is not the slightest warrant for inferring from this that Erythrae required to be "held down" by an armed force; and as for what have been referred to as the "important political functions" of the garrison commander, these were limited (in the surviving portion of the decree) to supervising a choice by lot, and therefore amounted to no more than ensuring that there was *no* jiggery-pokery. Democracies cannot easily be created overnight; it may take a long time to learn how to work one. Clever oligarchs, skilled in the hereditary art of government, would know just how to take advantage of the inefficiency of a new democratic regime, and they could probably rely in most cases on getting power back into their own hands before very long, unless the popular government received assistance as well as advice from the parent democracy. If the city could not afford to pay its councillors and dicasts (and probably very few cities could), the Many would find it very difficult to prevent the Few from regaining domination of the Council and the courts, upon which so much would depend. If it came to fighting, a small body of determined hoplites could be relied upon to deal with a much larger number of unpractised light-armed—and if the odds were too great, mercenaries could be hired. The Athenians, therefore, must have received many requests for assistance from the democratic parties in other states, and of course their intervention was regarded by the oligarchs—themselves quite prepared to call in the Spartans, if not the Persians— as an intolerable infringement of αὐτονομία and ἐλευθερία [autonomia and eleutheria = autonomy and freedom]. If the Athenian ἡγεμονία [hegemonia = leadership] changed by degrees into an ἀρχή, (ἀρχή) the responsibility would seem to lie partly with the Many in the allied states, who often welcomed and even invited inter-

vention. It may well be embassies bearing appeals of this sort, δῆμος to δῆμος, which Aristophanes has in mind when he sneers in the Acharnians at allied ambassadors who come to Athens with fine, complimentary phrases, flattering the Athenians in order to gain their own ends; he adds an encomium of himself as τοὺς δήμους ἐν ταῖς πόλεσιν δείξας, ὡς δημοκρατοῦντα [having shown the peoples in the cities the nature of democratic government].

No attempts has been made here to present a complete defence of the Athenian empire, or to give a "balanced judgment" upon it. There is no doubt that the Athenians did derive considerable profits for themselves out of the empire, and to some extent exploit their allies. But if, as we have seen, the empire remained popular with the Many, then its benefits, from their point of view, must have outweighed the evils. The more abuses we find in Athenian imperialism (and of course abuses were not lacking), the more virtues, from the point of view of the Many, we must at the same time discover, or else we shall be further than ever from being able to account for the popularity of the empire.

8. THE POPULARITY OF THE ATHENIAN EMPIRE*

The question of the popularity of the Athenian Empire among its subjects is an important one, both for our understanding of the history of the fifth century and for our estimate of the reliability, judgment, and even the integrity of Thucydides. The historian clearly portrays the Empire as a tyranny, hated by the majority of the subjects; he puts such sentiments into the mouths of the Athenian envoys to Sparta in 432 and attributes them to Perikles and Kleon when they are addressing the Athenian *demos*. He states much the same

on his own in describing the feelings of the Greeks against Athens at the beginning of the war and their readiness to revolt after the failure of the Sicilian expedition. Although it has been noticed that these latter statements seem to be rather exaggerated generalizations in the light of what happened later, it has usually been assumed that Thucydides' judgment was the common one among the Athenians as well as the other Greeks and that the unpopularity of the Empire was a fact recognized during its existence.

Grote did question Thucydides' judgment to the extent that he claimed that the general feeling towards Athens among

* Donald W. Bradeen, "The Popularity of the Athenian Empire," *Historia*, 9 (1960), pp. 257–269.

her subjects was one of "neither attachment nor hatred, but simple indifference and acquiescence in her supremacy." He thought that most of the trouble for Athens was stirred up by oligarchs playing upon "the general political instinct of the Greek mind—desire of separate autonomy;" he did not deny the existence of this feeling in all classes of the allies, yet he believed that it was often outweighed by the practical advantages of the Empire and thought that often the mass of the people in the allied cities were actively pro-Athenian. But Grote's position, in that he could not really bring himself to reject Thucydides' opinion completely, was basically ³inconsistent and won few followers; in general Thucydides' view of the unpopularity of the Empire has prevailed.

Recently, however, Grote's arguments have been revived and pushed to their logical extreme by A. H. M. Jones and G. E. M. de Ste. Croix. The latter's position, in sum, is that the Empire remained popular with "the mass of citizens in the allied or subject states," who "were loyal to Athens throughout the whole period of the empire, until the final collapse in the Ionian War;" a corollary to this is that Thucydides "is guilty of serious misrepresentation in his judgment on the Athenian Empire." The reason for this misrepresentation de Ste. Croix finds in Thucydides' oligarchic political outlook and his sympathy for the anti-Athenian Few among the allies. This is an intriguing thesis and the article is both interesting and impressive as it ranges far beyond this basic position by defending not only the Athenians and their Empire but also the demagogues and even the subjugation of Melos. In a way much of its appeal comes from the fact that de Ste. Croix sets out to prove his case against Thucydides primarily with evidence from Thucydides himself; as he puts it, "the news columns in Thucydides, so to speak, contradict the editorial Thucydides, and

the editor himself does not always speak with the same voice." Now the attraction here stems from the fact that most of us ancient historians have a sympathy for Athens and her Empire; no matter how impartial we try to be, our whole training as classicists, and possibly our political bent as well, incline us that way. We want to justify Athens' treatment of her subjects, but in the way of such a justification stands the judgment of Thucydides, for whose work we have a great respect. But now if we can prove from Thucydides himself that his judgment is wrong, then the obstacle is removed, and if it be true that the majority of the subjects approved of the Empire, then here is our justification. It is tempting to seize upon this and de Ste. Croix already has some converts. Perhaps most important of all is the fact that a recent textbook in its summary of the Empire presents de Ste. Croix' conclusions without qualification. This certainly calls for a re-examination of the evidence and de Ste. Croix' handling of it. I hope to show that his argument is based upon three general assumptions which are questionable, to say the least; that there are several serious omissions in the presentation of the case; and that what appears to be a mass of corroborative evidence consists for the most part of ambiguous situations interpreted from de Ste. Croix' point of view.

First we should discuss the basic assumptions underlying de Ste. Croix' case; the first two of these may best be analyzed together. One seems to be that Thucydides was a partisan oligarch who allowed his political convictions to distort his picture of the entire situation; the second is that the speeches in his history can be lumped with his expressed personal opinions as the "editorial" Thucydides. Objections may be raised to the former on two counts. The first objection, less important in that it is probably more semantic than real, is to calling Thucydides an oligarch. Undoubtedly he would have been one had he been involved in Athenian politics in 412, but so were many men who had been "democrats" twenty years before. The main question is whether their political thinking had changed in the meantime or had the nature of Athenian democracy. At any rate, the real basis of the belief that Thucydides was an oligarch is his judgment on the Constitution of the 5000, and de Ste. Croix himself has made such an inference suspect by his excellent analysis of that government as a true μετρία ξύγκρασις. Nevertheless there is no doubt that Thucydides was an aristocrat and that he disapproved of the "radical" democracy. But, arguments about names aside, the main objection to de Ste. Croix' assumption is rather this: Was Thucydides the kind of man who would allow political views to distort seriously his historical judgment? This may seem to be only a matter of opinion, but it certainly is difficult to see behind the history an author who was either of the two things implied in this assumption. For on this basis he must have been either a fool who, with many times the evidence we have now, could not see the "truth" which we can now discover, primarily from the evidence he gives us, or else a completely dishonest man who deliberately painted a false picture. De Ste. Croix obviously thinks of him as the former, for he calls him "an exceptionally truthful man and anything but a superficial observer" who deceived himself because ". . . political and social influences, at the end of the fifth century exceptionally powerful, drove the historian to look at the whole Greek world in terms of that relatively small section of the Athenian citizen body to which he himself belonged . . ." It may again be only a matter of opinion, I but cannot conceive that Thucydides, with the experience he must have had with the differences of opinion among the classes at Athens, was so blind as to think that the oligarchs' beliefs were those of "all the Greeks" or "every state and private citizen."

But be that as it may, if we consider this assumption in the light of the second, I think that the alternatives between which we must choose will be seen to be different. The second assumption is that the speeches are part of the "editorial" Thucydides, or, to put it bluntly, that they were completely his own and, so to speak, made from whole cloth. De Ste. Croix does not say this in so many words, but he does state that they "represent what the speakers would have said if they had expressed *with perfect frankness* the sentiments which the historian himself attributed to them." But if these speeches are "editorial," we must surely add that the sentiments which Thucydides attributes to the speakers are his own. So de Ste. Croix regards them, except when they happen to agree with his thesis. Now this raises the question of the much disputed passage in I, 22, 1, in which Thucydides discusses the composition of the speeches. Complete agreement will never be reached on this subject, but whatever is meant there by τὰ δέοντα, it can hardly indicate that the historian gave the speakers his own political views, since he states immediately thereafter that he kept as closely as possible to the general meaning of what was actually said —an avowal which has been more or less ignored in much of the recent discussion of the passage but cannot be dismissed. This was Thucydides' announced intention, and it was certainly easier in some cases than in others to abide by it. The speeches easiest for him to report accurately were those delivered in Athens before his exile, and it is in two of these, by Perikles and Kleon, that the Empire is described as a tyranny which cannot be safely given up because of the hatred of the unwilling subjects. One cannot insist that Thucydides must have been present on these occasions, but it can hardly be denied that he must have known how the politicians spoke of the Empire before the *demos*. Granted this, the treatment of the Empire in these speeches can be explained in two ways. The first possibility is that the politicians did not recognize the unpopularity of the Empire but Thucydides deliberately misrepresented their attitude; this is very unlikely for an "exceptionally truthful man" who has announced that he would keep as closely as possible to what was actually said. The alternative is that the unpopularity of the Empire was recognized publicly by the orators and the *demos*, as we should expect from the tone of fifth century decrees which seem neither to mince words nor to make any pretense about the position of the allies. In this case we certainly should believe that this unpopularity existed, since these people were definitely not the type to present the views of oligarchs as those of all the subjects. Such are the alternatives with which we are left after analyzing the two assumptions together. I do not see how anyone can seriously doubt that the second represents the true situation; if one wishes to deny it, I should think that this would necessitate a frontal attack upon the integrity of Thucydides.

The third assumption which I wish to re-examine is that in almost every subject city the *demos*, in a political sense, represented the majority and was, more or less by definition, pro-Athenian. De Ste. Croix states that "it would be perverse in the extreme to pretend" otherwise, but I am not so sure, in these days of "People's Democracy." The one time when we have definite figures, the *demos* at Samos, in a political sense, seems to number 300 in 412/11. Of course this means very little, as the situation was complicated by the presence of Athenian troops and ships, but this is a condition which, in a lesser degree, we cannot ignore at any period of the Empire. We must certainly take into account the ever-present threat of the Athenian fleet and the amount of military and civil control which the Athenians exercised over her allies. This definitely was not negligible. Aristotle may well be exaggerating when he speaks of seven hundred Athenian officials abroad in the fifth century, but even back near the middle of the century we have epigraphic proof of the presence of *phrourarchoi*, *episkopoi*, and *archontes* in the allied cities. It would be naive to think that these would not use their influence wherever possible to encourage pro-Athenian democratic elements, whether these had the support of the majority of the citizens or not. It seems to me quite conceivable that in most cases the majority was not sympathetic with Athens or even with a democracy, at least in the sense of rule by an urban *demos*. In fact, many of the subject states could not have had an urban *demos* of the type which Athens had, and we surely must make a distinction here between agricultural towns and commercial cities. Certainly in the Chalkidike, for instance, most of the population was rural, with that traditional rural conservatism which would have been satisfied with the oligarchic constitution of their ancestors, whether they were under a democracy or not.

It is customary to think of a violent political antagonism between the rich (oligarchs) and the poor (democrats), but this was something which was brought on and fostered by the Peloponnesian War. Aristotle does, it is true, conceive of the basic difference between oligarchy and democracy as one of wealth, not numbers, but this was after the split caused by the war had been widened by the economic difficulties of the first half of the fourth century. Even then the poor were not always dissatisfied and ready to overthrow an oligarchy, since Aristotle states that they were quite willing to remain quiet as long as the government did them no violence, judicially or economically. Such, I think, must have been the normal situation in most of the subject states, although this certainly could have been changed later by the propaganda during the war. Even in cities where there were nominal democracies, it is unlikely that real control was in the hands of the poor, since this presupposes the ability of the state to pay salaries on a large scale.

There was little chance, then, in the smaller cities of the Empire, for a democracy of the Athenian type, but what of the larger commercial cities, like Chios, Miletos, Mytilene, or Samos, which as centers of trade and usually possessing their own fleets, would have had a class equivalent to the *thetes* at Athens? Here, if anywhere, we should expect to find a pro-Athenian *demos*, eager for democracy. De Ste. Croix thinks that he can see one at Mytilene in Thucydides' account of the revolt of 428/7: towards the end, when that city was besieged by the Athenians and the Spartan commander gave shields and spears to the *demos* for a last-ditch sally, these men refused to obey and demanded that food should be brought out and shared equally or they would negotiate with the Athenians; this forced the government to surrender the city. Now this was the act of men driven by hunger and despair, not by any love for or loyalty to Athens. Diodotos presents it in this latter light when he has a case to plead, and so does de Ste. Croix, but this is not proving Thucydides' judgment wrong by the "news columns" in Thucydides, but by a distortion of them. I suggest that the important aspect of the situation at Mytilene is not the fact that the *demos* acted as it did in 428/7, but rather that the government was an oligarchy to the end and that the *demos* acquiesced in this, and in the revolt, so long. To me there can be only one reason for this—the people preferred autonomy under an oligarchy to the closer subjugation to Athens which a democracy would bring with it. For surely the setting up of a democracy would be possible only through the armed intervention of Athens, which would entail an Athenian garrison and probable loss of the fleet. It is true that de Ste. Croix denies the existence of an autonomous group of allies, either *de jure* or *de facto*. The question is debatable, but whether he be

right or wrong, it is sufficient for our purposes here to note that the Mytileneans had, besides their oligarchic government, two things which would set them apart from most of the other allies—freedom from tribute and a fleet of their own; these could easily be equated with autonomy, at least in the popular mind. Now it is among the rowers in this fleet that one would expect to find the democratic Athenian sympathizers, but such was apparently not the case, since the Athenians threw into prison the crews of the ten Mytilenean ships at Athens when they suspected the revolt. And certainly long before this, if there had been any real desire for a democracy among the Mytilenean *demos*, the Athenians could have found a chance to support them against their oligarchs. Although the editors of *The Athenian Tribute Lists* have shown that the Athenians certainly did not impose democracy, one can hardly deny that they would have been sympathetic with a real "grass-roots" movement in any subject state. Therefore, it seems, the people of Mytilene did not have a desire for democracy and were so far from being pro-Athenian that they supported their own oligarchy; one of the main reasons for this must have been their preference for what at least seemed to them to be autonomy.

Much the same may be said of the *demos* in other large cities of the Empire, particularly Samos, Miletos, and Chios. As far as we know, the last of these was under an oligarchy during the whole fifth century, and it is worth noting that, had there been any strong feeling or support for a democracy, the Athenians had an excellent chance to take advantage of it when in 424 they forced Chios to tear down her new wall on suspicion of a revolt. The political history of Miletos is obscure; she seems definitely to have had an oligarchy after her revolt in the 450's, and although she may well have had a democracy at a later date, this is one of the few places in which de Ste. Croix can find no sign of pro-Athenian sympathies during the Ionian War. The Milesians' readiness to revolt and their perseverance in revolting do not indicate the presence of any large pro-Athenian democratic element. As for Samos, it is instructive to analyze the political situation there during and after the revolt in 440/39. The Athenians, as a result of Samos' war with Miletos, set up a democracy at the instigation of an unspecified number of private citizens who wished to change the constitution. This government, however, did not last long, as the oligarchs' mercenaries and Persian help offset the Athenian garrison. The re-established oligarchy seems to have been able to trust its fleet during the siege, put up a stout resistance, but finally was forced by weight of numbers to surrender. It is often assumed that at this time Athens again set up a democracy, but there is no certain evidence for this. It is not mentioned by Thucydides, who gives other terms of the settlement. Since Samos certainly had an oligarchy in 412, either the democracy was never restored, as seems likely, or possibly it was replaced peacefully; any real *stasis* would certainly have echoes in our sources. In either case, it is hard to see a pro-democratic, pro-Athenian *demos*, and the original Samian democrats in 440 must have been a rather unrepresentative group.

But now we come to another point. We have analyzed above in Mytilene the first and most impressive piece in what de Ste. Croix calls "an overwhelming body of evidence . . . that the mass of citizens in the allied or subject states were loyal to Athens." The rest of this evidence consists mainly of an analysis of the revolts of the 'fifties and 'forties, of Brasidas' campaign in Thrace, and of the campaigns in Ionia after the defeat of the Sicilian expedition. But these are ambiguous situations and what de Ste. Croix offers is not evidence but a reinterpretation of what must have happened, granting always that his analysis

of the political situation is right, Thucydides' wrong. But I submit that this is not legitimate evidence, since Thucydides' account is reasonable in itself and agrees in general with his conclusions. There is really no need to analyze in detail all of this "evidence;" one could write an expanded account of it on the basis that Thucydides was right which would not only be consistent but would also be likely to be far nearer the truth, since it would be backed by the main source for the period and also would take into account the military situation and the presence of Athenian garrisons. These were far more numerous than de Ste. Croix cares to admit, and one of the weaknesses of his case is that he continually ignores them. For instance, although it seems quite clear from Thucydides that the Athenian general Eukles and his garrison played a major role in the initial resistance to Brasidas at Amphipolis, de Ste. Croix does not even mention him in his account of this resistance and its collapse. The fact is that neither the Thracian nor Ionian campaigns, carried on during the course of the war, are really fair tests of Athens' popularity, for there were always extraordinary military pressures which distorted the situation. A garrison within a city, or the approach of a fleet, could insure in most cases the support of the majority, whose main interest was to be on the winning side, not necessarily of the war as a whole but of the local struggle at the moment. Furthermore, the propaganda during the war, as Thucydides points out in his analysis of the Corcyrean revolution, stressed Athens and democracy, Sparta and oligarchy, and this had certainly complicated matters, especially by 412. As for the evidence for the revolts of the earlier period, most of which is epigraphic and quite ambiguous, it seems to show that most of the uprisings were led by oligarchs, who were therefore obviously anti-Athenian, as we might expect, but it proves nothing as to whether the majority of the citizens supported the revolts or not. We have no way of telling whether the democrats who appear during or after the revolts are really representative of the majority or are only a few who took advantage of the situation to get in power as pro-Athenians; the latter seems definitely to have been the case in Samos in 440.

It has been stated above that the situation in the Chalkidike in 424 and that in Ionia in 412 were not fair tests of Athens' popularity because of the military action at the time. However, there are two occasions when we can see how the subject states acted when there was no actual war and the balance of military power definitely favored Athens. Neither of these, incidentally, is mentioned by de Ste. Croix. The first is the revolt of the Thracian Chalkidians in 433/2. Now it is true that this was instigated by Perdikkas and that the actual revolt did not take place until they were joined by the Potidaians, who had the backing of Korinth and the promise of a Peloponnesian invasion of Attika if Athens attacked them. But nevertheless these Chalkidians took a desperate chance in acting when they did. They were exposed to Athenian sea power, and that they fully realized this is made clear by their abandonment of their cities near the coast. They were certainly not coerced or frightened into the revolt, since Perdikkas was not a military threat, at least if they remained loyal to Athens. We can judge what was thought of his power from the fact that the Athenians sent against him 30 ships and only 1000 hoplites. The only motive which could have led the Chalkidians on was a desire for freedom, and I cannot see how their governments, whether they were democracies or oligarchies, could have taken this step against such great odds without the support of a large majority of their people.

An even clearer example of the attitude toward Athens of the people in an allied city, when acting as free agents, is that of Amphipolis after the Peace of Nikias.

Although by the terms of that treaty this town was to be returned to the Athenians, the inhabitants opposed this stoutly. At first the Spartan commander, Klearidas, cooperated by refusing to act against the city's will, but later he was forced to withdraw his garrison along with all the Peloponnesian troops in Thrace. But even then the city refused to return to the Athenian alliance, in the face of Athens' might and with no hope of help from Sparta; it was resisting an attack of Athenians, Macedonians, and Thracians as late as 414.

It seems to me that these actions of the Chalkidians and the Amphipolitans, the situation being what it was in both cases, is the best evidence for the feelings towards Athens of the peoples in the subject and allied states, and for their desire for freedom above all else. It corroborates the opinion which Thucydides attributes to Phrynichos, who, while discussing the effects of a promise of oligarchy to the subject states in 412, says that the allies do not wish to be subject with either an oligarchy or a democracy but prefer to be free with whichever form of government they might get. De Ste. Croix does not discuss this passage, although he accepts as true without hesitation, and puts great stress upon, the next statement in the paragraph, which speaks of the allies' distrust of the Athenian oligarchs. But in this context these two statements are complementary and cannot be separated so arbitrarily, since the first, in a way, explains the second; that is, the oligarchs are not trusted because they are identified as the prime movers of the oppression of the cities and will infringe even more upon that freedom which these cities want above all.

This statement of Phrynichos, which agrees well with Thucydides' own views, would appear to sum up admirably the attitude of the subject and allied states. To most of these Greeks freedom was the most important of blessings, and this was the basis of the opposition to Athens. As Grote saw long ago, it was an emotional, not a rational, opposition. We may now think that the majority in the cities must have been far better off under a democracy, guided by Athenian overseers and protected by Athenian garrisons, that the imposition of Athenian coinage over the whole Empire was an economic blessing which they should have recognized, that Athenian juries must have acted more justly in trying allies than many of their own courts, and that the tribute was little to pay for the advantages which the Empire offered. We may even be right in this from a rational, historical point of view, but this is no reason to rewrite the history of Thucydides. For to the subject citizens, the carrying of the tribute and "first fruits" to Athens each spring, the forced appearances before a foreign court, the prohibition against coining their own silver, and the presence of Athenian garrisons and overseers were all signs of their loss of freedom and autonomy. When the chance came to try to win these back, they usually took it, whatever material advantages they threw away by so doing.

SECTION XII

Demosthenes *vs.* Philip of Macedon

THE FOURTH CENTURY witnessed the attrition of the power and prosperity of the Greek city-states. Constant warfare, poverty and civil strife increased disunity. Sparta and Thebes attempted to achieve hegemony but, like Athens, each failed. After the Battle of Mantinea in 362 B.C., as Xenophon says, "there was more confusion and disorder in Greece than before." Into the power vacuum stepped Philip of Macedon, who embarked upon a vigorous, ingenious, and ultimately successful campaign to put Greece under Macedonian control. In this effort he was most vigorously opposed by the Athenian politician and orator Demosthenes. He advocated a policy of Athenian patriotism and panhellenic resistance to Macedon. His efforts produced the coalition which opposed Philip and which was finally smashed at Chaeronea in 338 B.C. Demosthenes and his policy remain the subject of much debate. Was he a sincere patriot or a self-seeking politician? Was his policy a good one? Was it practical, given the "degenerate" nature of the Athens of his time? Was he a man of narrow vision or a defender of liberty and autonomy at any cost?

1. THE PUBLIC CAREER OF DEMOSTHENES*

His first entering into public business was much about the time of the Phocian war, as himself affirms, and may be collected from his Philippic orations. For of these, some were made after that action was over, and the earliest of them refer to its concluding events. It is certain that he engaged in the accusation of Midias when he was but two-and-thirty years old, having as yet no interest or reputation as a politician. And this it was, I consider, that

induced him to withdraw the action, and accept a sum of money as a compromise. For of himself—

"He was no easy or good-natured man,"

but of a determined disposition, and resolute to see himself righted; however, finding it a hard matter and above his strength to deal with Midias, a man so well secured on all sides with money, eloquence, and friends, he yielded to the entreaties of those who interceded for him. But had he seen any hopes or possibility of prevailing, I cannot believe

---

* Plutarch, *Demosthenes*, 12–31, translated by John Dryden.

412

that three thousand drachmas could have taken off the edge of his revenge. The object which he chose for himself in the commonwealth was noble and just, the defence of the Grecians against Philip; and in this he behaved himself so worthily that he soon grew famous, and excited attention everywhere for his eloquence and courage in speaking. He was admired through all Greece, the King of Persia courted him, and by Philip himself he was more esteemed than all the other orators. His very enemies were forced to confess that they had to do with a man of mark; for such a character even Æschines and Hyperides give him, where they accuse and speak against him.

So that I cannot imagine what ground Theopompus had to say that Demosthenes was of a fickle, unsettled disposition, and could not long continue firm either to the same men or the same affairs; whereas the contrary is most apparent, for the same party and post in politics which he held from the beginning, to these he kept constant to the end; and was so far from leaving them while he lived that he chose rather to forsake his life than his purpose. He was never heard to apologise for shifting sides like Demades, who would say he often spoke against himself, but never against the city; nor as Melanopus, who, being generally against Callistratus, but being often bribed off with money, was wont to tell the people, "The man indeed is my enemy, but we must submit for the good of our country;" nor again as Nicodemus, the Messenian, who having first appeared on Cassander's side, and afterwards taken part with Demetrius, said the two things were not in themselves contrary, it being always most advisable to obey the conqueror. We have nothing of this kind to say against Demosthenes, as one who would turn aside or prevaricate, either in word or deed. There could not have been less variation in his public acts if they had all been played, so to say from first to last, from the same score.

Panætius, the philosopher, said that most of his orations are so written as if they were to prove this one conclusion, that what is honest and virtuous is for itself only to be chosen; as that of the Crown, that against Aristocrates, that for the Immunities, and the Philippics; in all which he persuades his fellow-citizens to pursue not that which seems most pleasant, easy, or profitable; but declares, over and over again, that they ought in the first place to prefer that which is just and honourable before their own safety and preservation. So that if he had kept his hands clean, if his courage for the wars had been answerable to the generosity of his principles, and the dignity of his orations, he might deservedly have his name placed, not in the number of such orators as Mœrocles, Polyeuctus, and Hyperides, but in the highest rank with Cimon, Thucydides, and Pericles.

Certainly amongst those who were contemporary with him, Phocion, though he appeared on the less commendable side in the commonwealth, and was counted as one of the Macedonian party, nevertheless, by his courage and his honesty, procured himself a name not inferior to these of Ephialtes, Aristides, and Cimon. But Demosthenes, being neither fit to be relied on for courage in arms, as Demetrius says, nor on all sides inaccessible to bribery (for how invincible soever he was against the gifts of Philip and the Macedonians, yet elsewhere he lay open to assault, and was overpowered by the gold which came down from Susa and Ecbatana), was therefore esteemed better able to recommend than to imitate the virtues of past times. And yet (excepting only Phocion), even in his life and manners, he far surpassed the other orators of his time. None of them addressed the people so boldly; he attacked the faults, and opposed himself to the unreasonable desires of the multitude, as may be seen in his orations. Theopompus writes, that the Athenians having by name selected Demosthenes, and called upon him to accuse a certain person, he refused to do it; upon which the assembly being all in an uproar, he rose up and said, "Your counsellor, whether you will or no, O ye men of Athens, you shall always have me; but a sycophant or false accuser, though you would have me, I shall never be." And his conduct in the case of Antiphon was perfectly aristocratical; whom, after he had been acquitted in the assembly, he took and brought before the court of Areopagus, and, setting at naught the displeasure of the people, convicted him there of having promised Philip to burn the arsenal; whereupon the man was condemned by that court, and suffered for it. He accused, also, Theoris, the priestess, amongst other misdemeanours, of having instructed and taught the slaves to deceive and cheat their masters, for which the sentence of death was passed upon her, and she was executed.

The oration which Apollodorus made use of, and by it carried the cause against Timotheus, the general, in an action of debt, it is said was written for him by Demosthenes; as also those against Phormion and Stephanus, in which latter case he was thought to have acted dishonourably, for the speech which Phormion used against Apollodorus was also of his making; he, as it were, having simply furnished two adversaries out of the same shop with weapons to wound one another. Of his orations addressed to the public assemblies, that against Androtion, and those against Timocrates and Aristocrates, were written for others, before he had come forward himself as a politician. They were composed, it seems, when the was but seven or eight and twenty years old. That against Aristogiton, and that for the Immunities, he spoke himself, at the request, as he says, of Ctesippus, the son of Chabrias, but, as some say, out of courtship to the young man's mother. Though, in fact, he did not marry her, for his wife was a woman of Samos, as Demetrius, the Magnesian, writes, in his

book on Persons of the same Name. It is not certain whether his oration against Æschines, for Misconduct as Ambassador, was ever spoken; although Idomeneus says that Æschines wanted only thirty voices to condemn him. But this seems not to be correct, at least so far as may be conjectured from both their orations concerning the Crown; for in these, neither of them speaks clearly or directly of it, as a cause that ever came to trial. But let others decide this controversy.

It was evident, even in time of peace, what course Demosthenes would steer in the commonwealth; for whatever was done by the Macedonian, he criticised and found fault with, and upon all occasions was stirring up the people of Athens, and inflaming them against him. Therefore, in the court of Philip, no man was so much talked of, or of so great account as he; and when he came thither, one of the ten ambassadors who were sent into Macedonia, though all had audience given them, yet his speech was answered with most care and exactness. But in other respects, Philip entertained him not so honourably as the rest, neither did he show him the same kindness and civility with which he applied himself to the party of Æschines and Philocrates. So that, when the others commended Philip for his able speaking, his beautiful person, nay, and also for his good companionship in drinking, Demosthenes could not refrain from cavilling at these praises; the first, he said, was a quality which might well enough become a rhetorician, the second a woman, and the last was only the property of a sponge; no one of them was the proper commendation of a prince.

But when things came at last to war, Philip on the one side being not able to live in peace, and the Athenians, on the other side, being stirred up by Demosthenes, the first action he put them upon was the reducing of Eubœa, which, by the treachery of the tyrants, was brought under subjection to Philip. And on his proposition, the decree was voted, and they crossed over thither and chased the Macedonians out of the island. The next was the relief of the Byzantines and Perinthians, whom the Macedonians at that time were attacking. He persuaded the people to lay aside their enmity against these cities, to forget the offences committed by them in the Confederate War, and to send them such succours as eventually saved and secured them. Not long after, he undertook an embassy through the states of Greece, which he solicited and so far incensed against Philip that, a few only excepted, he brought them all into a general league. So that, besides the forces composed of the citizens themselves, there was an army consisting of fifteen thousand foot and two thousand horse, and the money to pay these strangers was levied and brought in with great cheerfulness. On which occasion it was, says Theophrastus, on the allies requesting that their contributions for the war might be ascertained and stated, Crobylus, the orator, made use of the saying, "War can't be fed at so much a day." Now was all Greece up in arms, and in great expectation what would be the event. The Eubœans, the Achæans, the Corinthians, the Megarians, the Leucadians, and Corcyræans, their people and their cities, were all joined together in a league. But the hardest task was yet behind, left for Demosthenes, to draw the Thebans into this confederacy with the rest. Their country bordered next upon Attica, they had great forces for the war, and at that time they were accounted the best soldiers of all Greece, but it was no easy matter to make them break with Philip, who, by many good offices, had so lately obliged them in the Phocian war; especially considering how the subjects of dispute and variance between the two cities were continually renewed and exasperated by petty quarrels, arising out of the proximity of their frontiers.

But after Philip, being now grown high and puffed up with his good success at Amphissa, on a sudden surprised Elatea and possessed himself of Phocis, and the Athenians were in a great consternation, none durst venture to rise up to speak, no one knew what to say, all were at a loss, and the whole assembly in silence and perplexity, in this extremity of affairs Demosthenes was the only man who appeared, his counsel to them being alliance with the Thebans. And having in other ways encouraged the people, and, as his manner was, raised their spirits up with hopes, he, with some others, was sent ambassador to Thebes. To oppose him, as Marsyas says, Philip also sent thither his envoys, Amyntas and Clearchus, two Macedonians, besides Daochus, a Thessalian, and Thrasydæus. Now the Thebans, in their consultations, were well enough aware what suited best with their own interest, but every one had before his eyes the terrors of war, and their losses in the Phocian troubles were still recent: but such was the force and power of the orator, fanning up, as Theopompus says, their courage, and firing their emulation, that, casting away every thought of prudence, fear, or obligation, in a sort of divine possession, they chose the path of honour, to which his words invited them. And this success, thus accomplished by an orator, was thought to be so glorious and of such consequence, that Philip immediately sent heralds to treat and petition for a peace: all Greece was aroused, and up in arms to help. And the commanders-in-chief, not only of Attica, but of Bœotia, applied themselves to Demosthenes, and observed his directions. He managed all the assemblies of the Thebans, no less than those of the Athenians; he was beloved both by the one and by the other, and exercised the same supreme authority with both; and that not by unfair means, or without just cause, as Theopompus professes, but indeed it was no more than was due to his merit.

But there was, it would seem, some divinely ordered fortune, commissioned, in the revolution of things, to put a period at this time to the liberty of Greece, which opposed and thwarted all their actions, and by many signs foretold what should happen. Such were the sad predictions uttered by the Pythian priestess, and this old oracle cited out of the Sibyl's verses:

"The battle on Thermodon that shall be
 Safe at a distance I desire to see,
 Far, like an eagle, watching in the air,
 Conquered shall weep, and conqueror perish
  there."

This Thermodon, they say, is a little rivulet here in our country in Chæronea, running into the Cephisus. But we know of none that is so called at the present time; and can only conjecture that the streamlet which is now called Hæmon, and runs by the Temple of Hercules, where the Grecians were encamped, might perhaps in those days be called Thermodon, and after the fight, being filled with blood and dead bodies, upon this occasion, as we guess, might change its old name for that which it now bears. Yet Duris says that this Thermodon was no river, but that some of the soldiers, as they were pitching their tents and digging trenches about them, found a small stone statue, which, by the inscription, appeared to be the figure of Thermodon, carrying a wounded Amazon in his arms; and that there was another oracle current about it, as follows:

"The battle on Thermodon that shall be,
 Fail not, black raven, to attend and see;
 The flesh of men shall there abound for
  thee."

In fine, it is not easy to determine what is the truth. But of Demosthenes it is said that he had such great confidence in the Grecian forces, and was so excited by the sight of the courage and resolution of so many brave men ready to engage the enemy, that he would by no means endure they should give any heed to oracles, or hearken to prophecies, but gave out that he suspected even the prophetess herself, as if she had been tampered with to speak in favour of Philip. The Thebans he put in mind of Epaminondas, the Athenians of Pericles, who always took their own measures and governed their actions by reason, looking upon things of this kind as mere pretexts for cowardice. Thus far, therefore, Demosthenes acquitted himself like a brave man. But in the fight he did nothing honourable, nor was his performance answerable to his speeches. For he fled, deserting his place disgracefully, and throwing away his arms, not ashamed, as Pytheas observed, to belie the inscription written on his shield, in letters of gold, "With good fortune."

In the meantime Philip, in the first moment of victory, was so transported with joy, that he grew extravagant, and going out after he had drunk largely to visit the dead bodies, he chanted the first words of the decree that had been passed on the motion of Demosthenes—

"The motion of Demosthenes, Demosthenes's
  son,"

dividing it metrically into feet, and marking the beats.

But when he came to himself, and had well considered the danger he was lately under, he could not forbear from shuddering at the wonderful ability and power of an orator who had made him hazard his life and empire on the issue of a few brief hours. The frame of it also reached even to the court of Persia, and the king sent letters to his lieutenants commanding them to supply Demosthenes with money, and to pay every attention to him, as the only man of all the Grecians who was able to give Philip occupation and find employment for his forces near home, in the troubles of Greece. This afterwards came to the knowledge of Alexander, by certain letters of Demosthenes which he found at Sardis, and by other papers of the Persian officers, stating the large sums which had been given him.

At this time, however, upon the ill-success which now happened to the Grecians, those of the contrary faction in the commonwealth fell foul upon Demosthenes and took the opportunity to frame several informations and indictments against him. But the people not only acquitted him of these accusations, but continued towards him their former respect, and still invited him, as a man that meant well, to take a part in public affairs. Insomuch that when the bones of those who had been slain at Chæronea were brought home to be solemnly interred, Demosthenes was the man they chose to make the funeral oration. They did not show, under the misfortunes which befell them, a base or ignoble mind, as Theopompus writes in his exaggerated style, but on the contrary, by the honour and respect paid to their counsellor, they made it appear that they were no way dissatisfied with the counsels he had given them. The speech, therefore, was spoken by Demosthenes. But the subsequent decrees he would not allow to be passed in his own name, but made use of those of his friends, one after another, looking upon his own as unfortunate and inauspicious; till at length he took courage again after the death of Philip, who did not long outlive his victory at Chæronea. And this, it seems, was that which was foretold in the last verse of the oracle—

"Conquered shall weep, and conqueror perish there."

Demosthenes had secret intelligence of the death of Philip, and laying hold of this opportunity to prepossess the people with courage and better hopes for the future, he came into the assembly with a cheerful countenance, pretending to have had a dream that presaged some great good fortune for Athens; and, not long after, arrived the messengers who brought the news of Philip's death. No sooner had the people received it, but immediately they offered sacrifice to the gods, and decreed that Pausanias should be presented with a crown. Demosthenes appeared publicly in a rich dress, with a chaplet on his head, though it were but the seventh day since the death of his daughter, as is said by Æschines, who upbraids him upon this account, and rails at him as one void of natural affection towards his children. Whereas, indeed, he rather betrays himself to be of a poor, low spirit, and effeminate mind, if he really means to make wailings and lamentation the only signs of a gentle and affectionate nature, and to condemn those who bear such accidents with more temper and less passion. For my own part, I cannot say that the behaviour of the Athenians on this occasion was wise or honourable, to crown themselves with garlands and to sacrifice to the gods for the death of a prince who, in the midst of his success and victories, when they were a conquered people, had used them with so much clemency and humanity. For besides provoking fortune, it was a base thing, and unworthy in itself, to make him a citizen of Athens, and pay him honours while he lived, and yet as soon as he fell by another's hand, to set no bounds to their jollity, to insult over him dead, and to sing triumphant songs of victory, as if by their own valour they had vanquished him. I must at the same time commend the behaviour of Demosthenes, who, leaving tears and lamentations and domestic sorrows to the women, made it his business to attend to the interests of the commonwealth. And I think it the duty of him who would be accounted to have a soul truly valiant, and fit for government, that, standing always firm to the common good, and letting private griefs and troubles find their compensation in public blessings, he should maintain the dignity of his character and station, much more than actors who represent the persons of kings and tyrants, who, we see, when they either laugh or weep on the stage, follow, not their own private inclinations, but the course consistent with the subject and with their position. And if, moreover, when our neighbour is in misfortune, it is not our duty to forbear offering any consolation, but rather to say whatever may tend to cheer him, and to invite his attention to any agreeable objects, just as we tell people who are troubled with sore eyes to withdraw their sight from bright and offensive colours to green, and those of a softer mixture, from whence can a man seek, in his own case, better arguments of consolation for afflictions in his family, than from the prosperity of his country, by making public and domestic chances count, so to say, together, and the better fortune of the state obscure and conceal the less happy circumstances of the individual. I have been induced to say so much, because I have known many readers melted by Æschines's language into a soft and unmanly tenderness.

But now to turn to my narrative. The cities of Greece were inspirited once more by the efforts of Demosthenes to form a league together. The Thebans, whom he had provided with arms, set upon their garrison, and slew many of them; the Athenians made preparations to join their forces with them; Demosthenes ruled supreme in the popular assembly, and wrote letters to the Persian officers who commanded under the king in Asia, inciting them to make war upon the Macedonian, calling him child and simpleton. But as soon as Alexander had settled matters in his own country and came in person with his army into Bœotia, down fell the courage of the Athenians, and Demosthenes was hushed; the Thebans, deserted by them, fought by themselves, and lost their city. After which, the people of Athens, all in distress and great perplexity, resolved to send ambassadors to Alexander, and amongst others, made choice of Demosthenes for one: but his heart failing him for fear of the king's anger, he returned back from Cithæron, and left the embassy. In the meantime, Alexander sent to Athens, requiring ten

of their orators to be delivered up to him, as Idomeneus and Duris have reported, but as the most and best historians say, he demanded these eight only,—Demosthenes, Polyeuctus, Ephialtes, Lycurgus, Mœrocles, Demon, Callisthenes, and Charidemus. It was upon this occasion that Demosthenes related to them the fable in which the sheep are said to deliver up their dogs to the wolves; himself and those who with him contended for the people's safety being, in his comparison, the dogs that defended the flock, and Alexander "the Macedonian arch-wolf." He further told them, "As we see corn-masters sell their whole stock by a few grains of wheat which they carry about with them in a dish, as a sample of the rest, so you by delivering up us, who are but a few, do at the same time unawares surrender up yourselves all together with us;" so we find it related in the history of Aristobulus, the Cassandrian. The Athenians were deliberating, and at a loss what to do, when Demades, having agreed with the persons whom Alexander had demanded, for five talents, undertook to go ambassador, and to intercede with the king for them; and, whether it was that he relied on his friendship and kindness, or that he hoped to find him satiated, as a lion glutted with slaughter, he certainly went, and prevailed with him both to pardon the men, and to be reconciled to the city.

So he and his friends, when Alexander went away, were great men, and Demosthenes was quite put aside. Yet when Agis, the Spartan, made his insurrection, he also for a short time attempted a movement in his favour; but he soon shrunk back again, as the Athenians would not take any part in it, and, Agis being slain, the Lacedæmonians were vanquished. During this time it was that the indictment against Ctesiphon, concerning the crown, was brought to trial. The action was commenced a little before the battle in Chæronea, when Chærondas was archon, but it was not proceeded with till about ten years after, Aristophon being then archon. Never was any public cause more celebrated than this, alike for the fame of the orators, and for the generous courage of the judges, who, though at that time the accusers of Demosthenes were in the height of power, and supported by all the favour of the Macedonians, yet would not give judgment against him, but acquitted him so honourably, that Æschines did not obtain the fifth part of their suffrages on his side, so that, immediately after, he left the city, and spent the rest of his life in teaching rhetoric about the island of Rhodes, and upon the continent in Ionia.

It was not long after that Harpalus fled from Alexander, and came to Athens out of Asia; knowing himself guilty of many misdeeds into which his love of luxury had led him, and fearing the king, who was now grown terrible even to his best friends. Yet this man had no sooner addressed himself to the people, and delivered up his goods, his ships, and himself to their disposal, but the other orators of the town had their eyes quickly fixed upon his money, and came in to his assistance, persuading the Athenians to receive and protect their supplicant. Demosthenes at first gave advice to chase him out of the country, and to beware lest they involve their city in a war upon an unnecessary and unjust occasion. But some few days after, as they were taking an account of the treasure, Harpalus, perceiving how much he was pleased with a cup of Persian manufacture, and how curiously he surveyed the sculpture and fashion of it, desired him to poise it in his hand, and consider the weight of the gold. Demosthenes, being amazed to feel how heavy it was, asked him what weight it *came to*. "To you," said Harpalus, smiling, "it shall *come with* twenty talents." And presently after, when night drew on, he sent him the cup with so many talents. Harpalus, it seems, was a person of singular skill to discern a man's covetousness by the air of his countenance, and

the look and movements of his eyes. For Demosthenes could not resist the temptation, but admitting the present, like an armed garrison, into the citadel of his house, he surrendered himself up to the interest of Harpalus. The next day, he came into the assembly with his neck swathed about with wool and rollers, and when they called on him to rise up and speak, he made signs as it he had lost his voice. But the wits, turning the matter to ridicule, said that certainly the orator had been seized that night with no other than a silver quinsy. And soon after, the people, becoming aware of the bribery, grew angry, and would not suffer him to speak, or make an apology for himself but ran him down with noise; and one man stood up, and cried out, "What, ye men of Athens, will you not hear the cup-bearer?" So at length they banished Harpalus out of the city; and fearing lest they should be called to account for the treasure which the orators had purloined, they made a strict inquiry, going from house to house; only Callicles, the son of Arrhenidas, who was newly married, they would not suffer to be searched, out of respects, as Theopompus writes, to the bride, who was within.

Demosthenes resisted the inquisition, and proposed a decree to refer the business to the court of Areopagus, and to punish those whom that court should find guilty. But being himself one of the first whom the court condemned, when he came to the bar, he was fined fifty talents, and committed to prison; where, out of shame of the crime for which he was condemned, and through the weakness of his body, growing incapable of supporting the confinement, he made his escape, by the carelessness of some and by the contrivance of others of the citizens. We are told, at least, that he had not fled far from the city when, finding that he was pursued by some of those who had been his adversaries he endeavoured to hide himself. But when they called him by his name, and coming up nearer to him, desired he would accept from them some money which they had brought from home as a provision for his journey, and to that purpose only had followed him, when they entreated him to take courage, and to bear up against his misfortune, he burst out into much greater lamentation, saying, "But how is it possible to support myself under so heavy an affliction, since I leave a city in which I have such enemies, as in any other it is not easy to find friends." He did not show much fortitude in his banishment, spending his time for the most part in Ægina and Trœzen, and, with tears in his eyes, looking towards the country of Attica. And there remain upon record some sayings of his, little resembling those sentiments of generosity and bravery which he used to express when he had the management of the commonwealth. For, as he was departing out of the city, it is reported, he lifted up his hands towards the Acropolis, and said, "O Lady Minerva, how is it that thou takest delight in three such fierce untractable beasts, the owl, the snake, and the people?" The young men that came to visit and converse with him, he deterred from meddling with state affairs, telling them, that if at first two ways had been proposed to him, the one leading to the speaker's stand and the assembly, the other going direct to destruction, and he could have forseen the many evils which attend those who deal in public business, such as fears, envies, calumnies, and contentions, he would certainly have taken that which led straight on to his death.

But now happened the death of Alexander, while Demosthenes was in this banishment which we have been speaking of. And the Grecians were once again up in arms, encouraged by the brave attempts of Leosthenes who was then drawing a circumvallation about Antipater, whom he held close besieged in Lamia. Pytheas, therefore, the orator, and Callimedon, called the Crab, fled from Athens, and taking sides with Antipater, went about with his friends and ambassadors to keep the Grecians from revolting and taking part with the Athenians. But, on the other side, Demosthenes, associating himself with the ambassadors that came from Athens, used his utmost endeavours and gave them his best assistance in persuading the cities to fall unanimously upon the Macedonians, and to drive them out of Greece. Phylarchus says that in Arcadia there happened a reencounter between Pytheas and Demosthenes, which came at last to down-right railing, while the one pleaded for the Macedonians, and the other for the Grecians. Pytheas said, that as we always suppose there is some disease in the family to which they bring asses' milk, so wherever there comes an embassy from Athens that city must needs be indisposed. And Demosthenes answered him, retorting the comparison: "Asses' milk is brought to restore health and the Athenians come for the safety and recovery of the sick." With this conduct the people of Athens were so well pleased that they decreed the recall of Demosthenes from banishment. The decree was brought in by Demon the Pæanian, cousin to Demosthenes. So they sent him a ship to Ægina, and he landed at the port of Piræus, where he was met and joyfully received by all the citizens, not so much as an archon or a priest staying behind. And Demetrius, the Magnesian, says that he lifted up his hands towards heaven, and blessed this day of his happy return, as far more honourable than that of Alcibiades; since he was recalled by his countrymen, not through any force or constraint put upon them, but by their own good-will and free inclinations. There remained only his pecuniary fine, which, according to law, could not be remitted by the people. But they found out a way to elude the law. It was a custom with them to allow a certain quantity of silver to those who were to furnish and adorn the altar for the sacrifice of Jupiter Soter. This office, for that turn, they bestowed on Demosthenes, and for the performance of it ordered him fifty talents, the very sum in which he was condemned.

Yet it was no long time that he enjoyed his country after his return, the attempts of the Greeks being soon all utterly defeated. For the battle of Cranon happened in Metagitnion, in Boëdromion the garrison entered into Munychia, and in the Pyanepsion following died Demosthenes after this manner.

Upon the report that Antipater and Craterus were coming to Athens, Demosthenes with his party took their opportunity to escape privily out of the city; but sentence of death was, upon the motion of Demades, passed upon them by the people. They dispersed themselves, flying some to one place, some to another; and Antipater sent about his soldiers into all quarters to apprehend them. Archias was their captain, and was thence called the exile-hunter. He was a Thurian born, and is reported to have been an actor of tragedies, and they say that Polus, of Ægina, the best actor of his time, was his scholar; but Hermippus reckons Archias among the disciples of Lacritus, the orator, and Demetrius says he spent some time with Anaximenes. This Archias finding Hyperides the orator, Aritonicus of Marathon, and Himeræus, the brother of Demetrius the Phalerian, in Ægina, took them by force out of the temple of Æcus, whither they were fled for safety, and sent them to Antipater, then at Cleonæ, where they were all put to death; and Hyperides, they say, had his tongue cut out.

Demosthenes, he heard, had taken sanctuary at the temple of Neptune in Calauria and, crossing over thither in some light vessels, as soon as he had landed himself, and the Thracian spearmen that came with him, he endeavoured to persuade Demosthenes to accompany him to Antipater, as if he should meet with no hard usage from him. But Demosthenes, in his sleep the night before, had a strange dream. It seemed to him that he

was acting a tragedy, and contended with Archias for the victory; and though he acquitted himself well, and gave good satisfaction to the spectators, yet for want of better furniture and provision for the stage, he lost the day. And so, while Archias was discoursing to him with many expressions of kindness, he sate still in the same posture, and looking up steadfastly upon him, "O Archias," said he, "I am as little affected by your promises now as I used formerly to be by your acting." Archias at this beginning to grow angry and to threaten him, "Now," said Demosthenes, "you speak like the genuine Macedonian oracle; before you were but acting a part. Therefore forbear only a little, while I write a word or two home to my family." Having thus spoken, he withdrew into the temple and taking a scroll as if he meant to write, he put the reed into his mouth, and biting it as he was wont to do when he was thoughtful or writing, he held it there some time. Then he bowed down his head and covered it. The soldiers that stood at the door, supposing all this to proceed from want of courage and fear of death, in derision called him effeminate, and faint-hearted, and coward. And Archias drawing near, desired him to rise up, and repeating the same kind of thing he had spoken before, he once more promised to make his peace with Antipater. But Demosthenes, perceiving that now the poison had pierced, and seized his vitals, uncovered his head, and fixing his eyes upon Archias, "Now," said he, "as soon as you please, you may commence the part of Creon in the tragedy, and cast out this body of mine unburied. But, O gracious Neptune, I, for my part while I am yet alive will rise up and depart out of this sacred place; though Antipater and the Macedonians have not left so much as thy temple unpolluted." After he had thus spoken and desired to be held up, because already he began to tremble and stagger, as he was going forward, and passing by the altar, he fell down, and with a groan gave up the ghost.

Ariston says that he took the poison out of a reed, as we have shown before. But Pappus, a certain historian whose history was recovered by Hermippus, says, that as he fell near the altar, there was found in his scroll this beginning only of a letter, and nothing more, "Demosthenes to Antipater." And that when his sudden death was much wondered at, the Thracians who guarded the doors reported that he took the poison into his hand out of a rag, and put it in his mouth, and that they imagined it had been gold which he swallowed, but the maid that served him, being examined by the followers of Archias, affirmed that he had worn it in a bracelet for a long time, as an amulet. And Eratosthenes also says that he kept the poison in a hollow ring, and that that ring was the bracelet which he wore about his arm. There are various other statements made by the many authors who have related the story, but there is no need to enter into their discrepancies; yet I must not omit what is said by Demochares the relation of Demosthenes, who is of opinion it was not by the help of poison that he met with so sudden and so easy a death, but that by the singular favour and providence of the gods he was thus rescued from the cruelty of the Macedonians. He died on the sixteenth of Pyanepsion, the most sad and solemn day of the Thesmophoria, which the women observe by fasting in the temple of the goddess.

Soon after his death, the people of Athens bestowed on him such honours as he had deserved. They erected his statue of brass; they decreed that the eldest of his family should be maintained in the Prytaneum; and on the base of his statue was engraven the famous inscription—

"Had you for Greece been strong, as wise you were,
The Macedonian had not conquered her."

For it is simply ridiculous to say, as some have related, that Demosthenes made these verses himself in Calauria, as he was about to take the poison.

A little before he went to Athens, the following incident was said to have happened. A soldier, being summoned to appear before his superior officer, and answer to an accusation brought against him, put that little gold which he had into the hands of Demosthenes's statue. The fingers of this statue were folded one within another, and near it grew a small plane-tree, from which many leaves, either accidently blown thither by the wind, or placed so on purpose by the man himself, falling together and lying round about the gold, concealed it for a long time. In the end, the soldier returned and found his treasure entire, and the fame of this incident was spread abroad. And many ingenious persons of the city competed with each other, on this occasion, to vindicate the integrity of Demosthenes in several epigrams which they made on the subject.

As for Demades, he did not long enjoy the new honours he now came in for, divine vengeance for the death of Demosthenes pursuing him into Macedonia, where he was justly put to death by those whom he had basely flattered. They were weary of him before, but at this time the guilt he lay under was manifest and undeniable. For some of his letters were intercepted, in which he had encouraged Perdiccas to fall upon Macedonia, and to save the Grecians, who, he said, hung only by an old rotten thread, meaning Antipater. Of this he was accused by Dinarchus, the Corinthian, and Cassander was so enraged, that he first slew his son in his bosom, and then gave orders to execute him; who might now at last, by his own extreme misfortunes, learn the lesson that traitors who made sale of their country sell themselves first; a truth which Demosthenes had often foretold him, and he would never believe. Thus, Sosius, you have the life of Demosthenes from such accounts as we have either read of heard concerning him.

2. Demosthenes *vs.* Philip*

In 341 B.C. Demosthenes delivered his *Third Philippic*, in which his over-all policy is described. It is usually considered the greatest of his speeches.

Many speeches are made, men of Athens, at almost every meeting of the Assembly, with reference to the aggressions which Philip has been committing, ever since he concluded the Peace, not only against yourselves but against all other peoples; and I am sure that all would agree, however little they may act on their belief, that our aim, both in speech and in action, should be to cause him to cease from his insolence and to pay the penalty for it. And yet I see that in fact the treacherous sacrifice of our interests has gone on, until what seems an ill-omened saying may, I fear, be really true—that if all who came forward desired to propose, and you desired to carry, the measures which would make your position as pitiful as it could possibly be, it could not (so I believe), be made worse than it is now. It may be that there are many reasons for this, and that our affairs did not reach their present condition from any one or two causes. But if you examine the matter aright, you will find that the chief responsibility rests with those whose aim is to win your favour, not to propose what is best. Some of them, men of Athens, so long as they can maintain the conditions which bring them reputation and influence, take no thought for the future [and therefore think that you also should take none]; while others, by accusing and slandering those who are actively at work are simply trying to make the city spend its energies in punishing the members of its own body, and so leave Philip free to say and do what he likes. Such political methods as these, familiar to you as they are, are the real causes of the evil. And I beg you, men of Athens, if I tell you certain truths outspokenly, to let no resentment on your part fall upon me on this account. Consider the matter in this light. In every other sphere of life, you believe that the right of free speech ought to be so universally shared by all who are in the city, that you have extended it both to foreigners and to slaves; and one may see many a servant in Athens speaking his mind with greater liberty than is granted to citizens in some other states: but from the sphere of political counsel you have utterly banished this liberty. The result is that in your meetings you give yourselves airs and enjoy their flattery, listening to nothing but what is meant to please you, while in the world of facts and events, you are in the last extremity of peril. If then you are still in this mood to-day, I do not know what I can say; but if you are willing to listen while I tell you, without flattery, what your interest requires, I am prepared to speak. For though our position is very bad indeed, and much has been sacrificed, it is still possible, even now, if you will do your duty, to set all right once more. It is a strange thing, perhaps, that I am about to say, but it is true. The worst feature in the past is that in which lies our best hope for the future. And what is this? It is that you are in your present plight because you do not do any part of your duty, small or great; for of course, if you were doing all that you should do, and were still in this evil case, you could not even hope for any improvement. As it is, Philip has conquered your indolence and your indifference; but he has not conquered

* Demosthenes, *Third Philippic*, in *The Public Orations of Demosthenes*, translated by A. W. Pickard-Cambridge (Oxford, 1912), Vol. 2, pp. 27–46. Used by permission of the Clarendon Press, Oxford.

Athens. You have not been vanquished—
you have never even stirred.

[Now if it was admitted by us all that
Philip was at war with Athens, and was
transgressing the Peace, a speaker would
have to do nothing but to advise you as to
the safest and easiest method of resistance
to him. But since there are some who are
in so extraordinary a frame of mind that,
though he is capturing cities, though
many of your possessions are in his hands,
and though he is committing aggressions
against all men, they still tolerate certain
speakers, who constantly assert at your
meetings that it is some of *us* who are
provoking the war, it is necessary to be
on our guard and come to a right understanding on the matter. For there is a
danger lest any one who proposes or
advises resistance should find himself
accused of having brought about the war.]

[Well, I say this first of all, and lay it
down as a principle, that if it is open to us
to deliberate whether we should remain
at peace of should go to war . . .]

Now if it is possible for the city to
remain at peace—if the decision rests
with us (that I may make this my starting-
point)—then, I say that we ought to do
so, and I call upon any one who says that
it is so to move his motion, and to act and
not to defraud us. But if another with
weapons in his hands and a large force
about him holds out to you the *name* of
peace, while his own acts are acts of war,
what course remains open to us but that of
resistance? though if you wish to profess
peace in the same manner as he, I have no
quarrel with you. But if any man's
conception of peace is that it is a state in
which Philip can master all that intervenes
till at last he comes to attack ourselves,
such a conception, in the first place, is
madness; and, in the second place, this
peace that he speaks of is a peace which
you are to observe towards Philip, while
he does not observe it towards you: and
this it is—this power to carry on war
against you, without being met by any

hostilities on your part—that Philip is
purchasing with all the money that he is
spending.

Indeed, if we intend to wait till the
time comes when he admits that he is at
war with us, we are surely the most
innocent persons in the world. Why, even
if he comes to Attica itself, to the very
Peiraeus, he will never make such an
admission, if we are to judge by his
dealings with others. For, to take one
instance, he told the Olynthians, when he
was five miles from the city, that there
were only two alternatives—either they
must cease to live in Olynthus, or he to
live in Macedonia: but during the whole
time before that, whenever any one
accused him of any such sentiments, he
was indignant and sent envoys to answer
the charge. Again, he marched into the
Phocians' country, as though visiting his
allies: it was by Phocian envoys that he
was escorted on the march; and most
people in Athens contended strongly that
his crossing the Pass would bring no good
to Thebes. Worse still, he has lately
seized Pherae and still holds it, though he
went to Thessaly as a friend and an ally.
And, latest of all, he told those unhappy
citizens of Oreus that he had sent his
soldiers to visit them and to make kind
inquiries; he had heard that they were sick,
and suffering from faction, and it was right
for an ally and a true friend to be present
at such a time. Now if, instead of giving
them warning and using open force, he
deliberately chose to deceive these men,
who could have done him no harm, though
they might have taken precautions against
suffering any themselves, do you imagine
that he will make a formal declaration of
war upon you before he commences
hostilities, and that, so long as you are
content to be deceived? Impossible! For
so long as you, though you are the injured
party, make no complaint against him,
but accuse some of your own body, he
would be the most fatuous man on earth
if *he* were to interrupt your strife and

contentions with one another—to bid you turn upon himself, and so to cut away the ground from the arguments by which his hirelings put you off, when they tell you that *he* is not at war with Athens.

In God's name, is there a man in his senses who would judge by words, and not by facts, whether another was at peace or at war with him? Of course there is not. Why, from the very first, when the Peace had only just been made, before those who are now in the Chersonese had been sent out, Philip was taking Serrhium and Doriscus, and expelling the soldiers who were in the castle of Serrhium and the Sacred Mountain, where they had been placed by your general. But what was he doing, in acting thus? For he had sworn to a Peace. And let no one ask, 'What do these things amount to? What do they matter to Athens?' For whether these acts were trifles which could have no interest for you is another matter; but the principles of religion and justice, whether a man transgress them in small things or great, have always the same force. What? When he is sending mercenaries into the Chersonese, which the king and all the Hellenes have acknowledged to be yours; when he openly avows that he is going to the rescue, and states in it his letter, what is it that he is doing? He tells you, indeed, that he is not making war upon you. But so far am I from admitting that one who acts in this manner is observing the Peace which he made with you, that I hold that in grasping at Megara, in setting up tyrants in Euboea, in advancing against Thrace at the present moment, in pursuing his machinations in the Peloponnese, and in carrying out his entire policy with the help of his army, he is violating the Peace and is making war against you;—unless you mean to say that even to bring up engines to besiege you is no breach of the Peace, until they are actually planted against your walls. But you will not say this; for the man who is taking the steps and contriving the means which will lead to my capture is at war with me, even though he has not yet thrown a missile or shot an arrow. Now what are the things which would imperil your safety, if anything should happen? The alienation of the Hellespont, the placing of Megara and Euboea in the power of the enemy, and the attraction of Peloponnesian sympathy to his cause. Can I then say that one who is erecting such engines of war as these against the city is at peace with you? Far from it! For from the very day when he annihilated the Phocians—from that very day, I say, I date the beginning of his hostilities against you. And for your part, I think that you will be wise if you resist him at once; but that if you let him be, you will find that, when you wish to resist, resistance itself is impossible. Indeed, so widely do I differ, men of Athens, from all your other advisers, that I do not think there is any room for discussion to-day in regard to the Chersonese or Byzantium. We *must* go to their defence, and take every care that they do not suffer [and we must send all that they need to the soldiers who are at present there]. But we *have* to take counsel for the good of all the Hellenes, in view of the grave peril in which they stand. And I wish to tell you on what grounds I am so alarmed at the situation, in order that if my reasoning is correct, you may share my conclusions, and exercise some forethought for yourselves at least, if you are actually unwilling to do so for the Hellenes as a whole; but that if you think that I am talking nonsense, and am out of my senses, you may both now and hereafter decline to attend to me as though I were a sane man.

The rise of Philip to greatness from such small and humble beginnings; the mistrustful and quarrelsome attitude of the Hellenes towards one another; the fact that his growth out of what he was into what he is was a far more extraordinary thing than would be his subjugation of all that remains, when he has already secured so much;—all this and all similar themes, upon which I might speak at length, I will pass over. But I see that all men, beginning with yourselves, have conceded to him the very thing which he has been at issue in every Hellenic war during the whole of the past. And what is this? It is the right to act as he pleases—to mutilate and to strip the Hellenic peoples, one by one, to attack and to enslave their cities. For seventy-three years you were the leading people of Hellas, and the Spartans for thirty years save one; and in these last times, after the battle of Leuctra, the Thebans too acquired some power: yet neither to you nor to Thebes nor to Sparta was such a right ever conceded by the Hellenes, as the right to do whatever you pleased. Far from it! First of all it was your own behaviour—or rather that of the Athenians of that day—which some thought immoderate; and all, even those who had no grievance against Athens, felt bound to join the injured parties, and to make war upon you. Then, in their turn, the Spartans, when they had acquired an empire and succeeded to a supremacy like your own, attempted to go beyond all bounds and to disturb the established order to an unjustifiable extent; and once more, all, even those who had no grievance against them, had recourse to war. Why mention the others? For we ourselves and the Spartans, though we could originally allege no injury done by the one people to the other, nevertheless felt bound to go to war on account of the wrongs which we saw the rest suffering. And yet all the offences of the Spartans in those thirty years of power, and of your ancestors in their seventy years, were less, men of Athens, that the wrongs inflicted upon the Greeks by Philip, in the thirteen years, not yet completed, during which he has been to the fore. Less do I say? They are not a fraction of them. [A few words will easily prove this.] I say nothing of Olynthus, and Methone, and Apollonia, and thirty-two cities in the Thracian region, all annihilated by him with such savagery,

that a visitor to the spot would find it difficult to tell that they had ever been inhabited. I remain silent in regard to the extirpation of the great Phocian race. But what is the condition of Thessaly? Has he not robbed their very cities of their governments, and set up tetrarchies, that they may be enslaved, not merely by whole cities, but by whole tribes at a time? Are not the cities of Euboea even now ruled by tyrants, and that in an island that is neighbour to Thebes and Athens? Does he not write expressly in his letters, 'I am at peace with those who choose to obey me'? And what he thus writes he does not fail to act upon; for he is gone to invade the Hellespont; he previously went to attack Ambracia; the great city of Elis in the Peloponnese is his; he has recently intrigued against Megara; and neither Hellas nor the world beyond it is large enough to contain the man's ambition. But though all of us, the Hellenes, see and hear these things, we send no representatives to one another to discuss the matter; we show no indignation; we are in so evil a mood, so deep have the lines been dug which sever city from city, that up to this very day we are unable to act as either our interest or our duty require. We cannot unite; we can form no combination for mutual support or friendship; but we look on while the man grows greater, because every one has made up his mind (as it seems to me) to profit by the time during which his neighbour is being ruined, and no one cares or acts for the safety of the Hellenes. For we all know that Philip is like the recurrence or the attack of a fever or other illness, in his descent upon those who fancy themselves for the present well out of his reach. And further, you must surely realize that all the wrongs that the Hellenes suffered from the Spartans or ourselves they at least suffered at the hands of true-born sons of Hellas; and (one might conceive) it was as though a lawful son, born to a great estate, managed his affairs in some wrong or improper way;—

his conduct would in itself deserve blame and denunciation, but at least it could not be said that he was not one of the family, or was not the heir to the property. But had it been a slave or a supposititious son that was thus ruining and spoiling an inheritance to which he had no title, why, good Heavens! how infinitely more scandalous and reprehensible all would have declared it to be. And yet they show no such feeling in regard to Philip, although not only is he no Hellene, not only has he no kinship with Hellenes, but he is not even a barbarian from a country that one could acknowledge with credit;—he is a pestilent Macedonian, from whose country it used not to be possible to buy even a slave of any value.

And in spite of this, is there any degree of insolence to which he does not proceed? Not content with annihilating cities, does he not manage the Pythian games, the common meeting of the Hellenes, and send his slaves to preside over the competition in his absence? [Is he not master of Thermopylae, and of the passes which lead into Hellenic territory? Does he not hold that district with garrisons and mercenaries? Has he not taken the precedence in consulting the oracle, and thrust aside ourselves and the Thessalians and Dorians and the rest of the Amphictyons, though the right is not one which is given even to all of the Hellenes?] Does he not write to the Thessalians to prescribe the constitution under which they are to live? Does he not send one body of mercenaries to Porthmus, to expel the popular party of Eretria, and another to Oreus, to set up Philistides as tyrant? And yet the Hellenes see these things and endure them, gazing (it seems to me) as they would gaze at a hailstorm—each people praying that it may not come their way, but no one trying to prevent it. Nor is it only his outrages upon Hellas that go unresisted. No one resists even the aggressions which are committed against himself. Ambracia and Leucas belong to the Corinthians—he has attacked them: Naupactus to the Achaeans—he has sworn to hand it over to the Aetolians: Echinus to the Thebans—he has taken it from them, and is now marching against their allies the Byzantines—is it not so? And of our own possessions, to pass by all the rest, is not Cardia, the greatest city in the Chersonese, in his hands? Thus are we treated; and we are all hesitating and torpid, with our eyes upon our neighbours, distrusting one another, rather than the man whose victims we all are. But if he treats us collectively in this outrageous fashion, what do you think he will do, when he has become master of each of us separately?

What then is the cause of these things? For as it was not without reason and just cause that the Hellenes in old days were so prompt for freedom, so it is not without reason or cause that they are now so prompt to be slaves. There was a spirit, men of Athens, a spirit in the minds of the people in those days, which is absent to-day—the spirit which vanquished the wealth of Persia, which led Hellas in the path of freedom, and never gave way in face of battle by sea or by land; a spirit whose extinction to-day has brought universal ruin and turned Hellas upside down. What was this spirit? [It was nothing subtle nor clever.] It meant that men who took money from those who aimed at dominion or at the ruin of Hellas were execrated by all; that it was then a very grave thing to be convicted of bribery; that the punishment for the guilty man was the heaviest that could be inflicted; that for him there could be no plea for mercy, nor hope of pardon. No orator, no general, would then sell the critical opportunity whenever it arose—the opportunity so often offered to men by fortune, even when they are careless and their foes are on their guard. They did not barter away the harmony between people and people, not their own mistrust of the tyrant and the foreigner, nor any of these

high sentiments. Where are such sentiments now? They have been sold in the
market and are gone; and those have been
imported in their stead, through which the
nation lies ruined and plague-stricken—
the envy of the man who has received his
hire; the amusement which accompanies
his avowal; [the pardon granted; to; those;
whose; guilt; is proved;] the hatred of one
who censures the crime; and all the
appurtenances of corruption. For as to
ships, numerical strength, unstinting
abundance of funds and all other material
of war, and all the things by which the
strength of cities is estimated, every
people can command these in greater
plenty and on a larger scale by far than
in old days. But all these resources are
rendered unserviceable, ineffectual un-
profitable, by those who traffic in them.

That these things are so to-day, you
doubtless see, and need no testimony of
mine: and that in times gone by the
opposite was true, I will prove to you, not
by any words of my own but by the record
inscribed by your ancestors on a pillar of
bronze, and placed on the Acropolis [not
to be a lesson to themselves—they needed
no such record to put them in a right mind
—but to be a reminder and an example to
you of the zeal that you ought to display
in such a cause]. What then is the record?
'Arthmius, son of Pythonax, of Zeleia, is
an outlaw, and is the enemy of the Athenian
people and their allies, he and his house.'
Then follows the reason for which this
step was taken—'because he brought the
gold from the Medes into the Peloponnese.' Such is the record. Consider, in
Heaven's name, what must have been the
mind of the Athenians of that day, when
they did this, and their conception of their
position. They set up a record, that
because a man of Zeleia, Arthmius by
name, a slave of the King of Persia (for
Zeleia is in Asia), as part of his service to
the king, had brought gold, not to Athens,
but to the Peloponnese, he should be an
enemy of Athens and her allies, he and his

house, and that they should be outlaws.
And this outlawry is no such disfranchise-
ment as we ordinarily mean by the word.
For what would it matter to a man of
Zeleia, that he might have no share in the
public life of Athens? But there is a clause
in the Law of Murder, dealing with those
in connexion with whose death the law
does not allow a prosecution for murder
[but the slaying of them is to be a holy
act]: 'And let him die an outlaw,' it runs.
The meaning, accordingly, is this—that
the slayer of such a man is to be pure
from all guilt. They thought, therefore,
that the safety of all the Hellenes was a
matter which concerned themselves—
apart from this belief, it could not have
mattered to them whether any one bought
or corrupted men in the Peloponnese; and
whenever they detected such offenders,
they carried their punishment and their
vengeance so far as to pillory their names
for ever. As the natural consequence, the
Hellenes were a terror to the foreigner,
not the foreigner to the Hellenes. It is not
so now. Such is not your attitude in these
or in other matters. But what is it? [You
know it yourselves; for why should I
accuse you explicitly on every point? And
that of the rest of the Hellenes is like your
own, and no better; and so I say that the
present situation demands our utmost
earnestness and good counsel.] And what
counsel? Do you bid me tell you, and will
you not be angry if I do so?

[He reads from the document.]

Now there is an ingenuous argument,
which is used by those who would reassure
the city, to the effect that, after all, Philip
is not yet in the position once held by the
Spartans, who ruled everywhere over sea
and land, with the king for their ally, and
nothing to withstand them; and that, none
the less, Athens defended herself even
against them, and was not swept away.
Since that time the progress in every
direction, one may say, has been great,
and has made the world to-day very

different from what it was then; but I believe that in no respect has there been greater progress or development than in the art of war. In the first place, I am told that in those days the Spartans and all our other enemies would invade us for four or five months—during, that is, the actual summer—and would damage Attica with infantry and citizen-troops, and then return home again. And so old-fashioned were the men of that day—nay rather, such true citizens—that no one ever purchased any object from another for money, but their warfare was of a legitimate and open kind. But now, as I am sure you see, most of our losses are the result of treachery, and no issue is decided by open conflict or battle; while you are told that it is not because he leads a column of heavy infantry that Philip can march wherever he chooses, but because he has attached to himself a force of light infantry, cavalry, archers, mercenaries, and similar troops. And whenever, with such advantages, he falls upon a State which is disordered within, and in their distrust of one another no one goes out in defence of its territory, he brings up his engines and besieges them. I pass over the fact that summer and winter are alike to him—that there is no close season during which he suspends operations. But if you all know these things and take due account of them, you surely must not let the war pass into Attica, nor be dashed from your seat through looking back to the simplicity of those old hostilities with Sparta. You must guard against him, at the greatest possible distance, both by political measures and by preparations; you must prevent his stirring from home, instead of grappling with him at close quarters in a struggle to the death. For, men of Athens, we have many natural advantages for a war, if we are willing to do our duty. There is the character of his country, much of which we can harry and damage, and a thousand other things. But for a pitched battle he is in better training than we.

Nor have you only to recognize these facts, and to resist him by actual operations of war. You must also by reasoned judgement and of set purpose come to execrate those who address you in his interest, remembering that it is impossible to master the enemies of the city, until you punish those who are serving them in the city itself. And this, before God and every Heavenly Power—this you will not be able to do; for you have reached such a pitch of folly or distraction of—I know not what to call it; for often has the fear actually entered my mind, that some more than mortal power may be driving our fortunes to ruin—that to enjoy their abuse, or their malice, or their jests, or whatever your motive may chance to be, you call upon men to speak who are hirelings, and some of whom would not even deny it; and you laugh to hear their abuse of others. And terrible as this is, there is yet worse to be told. For you have actually made political life safer for these men, than for those who uphold your own cause. And yet observe what calamities the willingness to listen to such men lays up in store. I will mention facts known to you all.

In Olynthus, among those who were engaged in public affairs, there was one party who were on the side of Philip, and served his interests in everything; and another whose aim was their city's real good, and the preservation of their fellow citizens from bondage. Which were the destroyers of their country? which betrayed the cavalry, through whose betrayal Olynthus perished? Those whose sympathies were with Philip's cause; those who, while the city still existed brought such dishonest and slanderous charges against the speakers whose advice was for the best, that, in the case of Apollonides at least, the people of Olynthus was even induced to banish the accused.

Nor is this instance of the unmixed evil wrought by these practices in the case of the Olynthians an exceptional one, or without parallel elsewhere. For in Eretria, when Plutarchus and the mercenaries had been got rid of, and the people had control of the city and of Porthmus, one party wished to entrust the State to you, the other to entrust it to Philip. And through listening mainly, or rather entirely, to the latter, these poor luckless Eretrians were at last persuaded to banish the advocates of their own interests. For, as you know, Philip, their ally, sent Hipponicus with a thousand mercenaries, stripped Porthmus of its walls, and set up three tyrants—Hipparchus, Automedon, and Cleitarchus; and since then he has already twice expelled them from the country when they wished to recover their position [sending on the first occasion the mercenaries commanded by Eurylochus, on the second, those under Parmenio].

And why go through the mass of the instances? Enough to mention how in Oreus Philip had, as his agents, Philistides, Menippus, Socrates, Thoas, and Agapaeus —the very men who are now in possession of the city—and every one knew the fact; while a certain Euphraeus, who once lived here in Athens, acted in the interests of freedom, to save his country from bondage. To describe the insults and the contumely with which he met would require a long story; but a year before the capture of the town he laid an information of treason against Philistides and his party, having perceived the nature of their plans. A number of men joined forces, with Philip for their paymaster and director, and haled Euphraeus off to prison as a disturber of the peace. Seeing this, the democratic party in Oreus, instead of coming to the rescue of Euphraeus, and beating the other party to death, displayed no anger at all against them, and agreed with a malicious pleasure that Euphraeus deserved his fate. After this the conspirators worked with all the freedom they desired for the capture of the city, and made arrangements for the execution of the scheme; while any of the democratic party, who perceived what was

going on, maintained a panic-stricken silence, remembering the fate of Euphraeus. So wretched was their condition, that though this dreadful calamity was confronting them, no one dared open his lips, until all was ready and the enemy was advancing up to the walls. Then the one party set about the defence, the other about the betrayal of the city. And when the city has been captured in this base and shameful manner, the successful party governed despotically: and of those who had been their own protectors, and had been ready to treat Euphraeus with all possible harshness, they expelled some and murdered others; while the good Euphraeus killed himself, thus testifying to the righteousness and purity of his motives in opposing Philip on behalf of his countrymen.

How for what reason, you may be wondering, were the peoples of Olynthus and Eretria and Oreus more agreeably disposed towards Philip's advocates than towards their own? The reason was the same as it is with you—that those who speak for your true good can never, even if they would, speak to win popularity with you; they are constrained to inquire how the State may be saved: while their opponents, in the very act of seeking popularity, are co-operating with Philip. The one party said, 'You must pay taxes;' the other, 'There is no need to do so.' The one said, 'Go to war, and do not trust him;' the other, 'Remain at peace,'—until they were in the toils. And—not to mention each separately—I believe that the same thing was true of all. The one side said what would enable them to win favour; the other, what would secure the safety of their State. And at last the main body of the people accepted much that they proposed—not now from any such desire for gratification, nor from ignorance, but as a concession to circumstances, thinking that their cause was now wholly lost. It is this fate, I solemnly assure you, that I dread for you, when the time comes that you make your reckoning, and realize that there is no longer anything that can be done. May you never find yourselves, men of Athens, in such a position! Yet in any case, it were better to die ten thousand deaths, than to do anything out of servility towards Philip [or to sacrifice any of those who speak for your good]. A noble recompense did the people in Oreus receive, for entrusting themselves to Philip's friends, and thrusting Euphraeus aside! and a noble recompense the democracy of Eretria, for driving away your envoys, and surrendering to Cleitarchus! They are slaves, scourged and butchered! A noble clemency did he show to the Olynthians, who elected Lasthenes to command the cavalry, and banished Apollonides! It is folly, and it is cowardice, to cherish hopes like these, to give way to evil counsels, to refuse to do anything that you should do, to listen to the advocates of the enemy's cause, and to fancy that you dwell in so great a city that, whatever happens, you will not suffer any harm. Aye, and it is shameful to exclaim after the event, 'Why, who would have expected this? Of course, we ought to have done, or not to have done, such and such things!' The Olynthians could tell you of many things, to have foreseen which in time would have saved them from destruction. So too could the people of Oreus, and the Phocians, and every other people that has been destroyed. But how does that help them now? So long as the vessel is safe, be it great or small, so long must the sailor and the pilot and every man in his place exert himself and take care that no one may capsize it by design or by accident: but when the seas have overwhelmed it, all their efforts are in vain. So it is, men of Athens, with us. While we are still safe, with our great city, our vast resources, our noble name, what are we to do? Perhaps some one sitting here has long been wishing to ask this question. Aye, and I will answer it, and will move my motion; and you shall carry it, if you wish.

We ourselves, in the first place, must conduct the resistance and make preparation for it—with ships, that is, and money, and soldiers. For though all but ourselves give way and become slaves, we at least must contend for freedom. And when we have made all these preparations ourselves, and let them be seen, then let us call upon the other states for aid, and send envoys to carry our message [in all directions—to the Peloponnese, to Rhodes, to Chios, to the king; for it is not unimportant for his interests either that Philip should be prevented from subjugating the world]; that so, if you persuade them, you may have partners to share the danger and the expense, in case of need; and if you do not, you may at least delay the march of events. For since the war is with a single man, and not against the strength of a united state, even delay is not without its value, any more than were those embassies of protest which last year went round the Peloponnese, when I and Polyeuctus, that best of men, and Hegesippus and the other envoys went on our tour, and forced him to halt, so that he neither went to attack Acarnania, nor set out for the Peloponnese. But I do not mean that we should call upon the other states, if we are not willing to take any of the necessary steps ourselves. It is folly to sacrifice what is our own, and then pretend to be anxious for the interests of others—to neglect the present, and alarm others in regard to the future. I do not propose this. I say that we must send money to the forces in the Chersonese, and do all that they ask of us; that we must make preparation ourselves, while we summon, convene, instruct, and warn the rest of the Hellenes. That is the policy for a city with a reputation such as yours. But if you fancy that the people of Chalcis or of Megara will save Hellas, while you run away from the task, you are mistaken. They may well be content if they can each save themselves. The task is yours. It is the prerogative that your forefathers won, and through many a great peril bequeathed to you. But if each of you is to sit and consult his inclinations, looking for some way by which he may escape any personal action, the first consequence will be that you will never find any one who will act; and the second, I fear, that the day will come when we shall be forced to do, at one and the same time, all the things we wish to avoid.

This then is my proposal, and this I move. If the proposal is carried out, I think that even now the state of our affairs may be remedied. But if any one has a better proposal to make, let him make it, and give us his advice. And I pray to all the gods that whatever be the decision that you are about to make, it may be for your good.

3. THE DEBATE OVER DEMOSTHENES*

The man with whom these pages are concerned can no longer be counted among those figures of antiquity whose high reputation in the learned world remains undisputed; it may even seem that I ought to give some excuse for selecting him as my subject. No one who hopes for the unanimous applause of his readers ever does well to take a politician for his hero, especially a politician uncrowned with victory. History is always ready to acknowledge the greatness of a poet or philosopher, no matter how awkwardly he may have fitted his times; but it habitually judges the practicing statesman by his success, not by his intentions. The task of history is to understand the accomplished facts that confront it; and this understanding can all too easily take the form of an apology for those facts, with only a shrug of the shoulders for the side that loses.

But Demosthenes, we may object, was no mere stepchild of *Tyche* stirring our deeper sympathy by his undeserved fate alone. Nevertheless, the classicism of earlier centuries, which venerated him as the unhappy last champion of Greek liberty, has given way to a new type of historical thought arising with the nineteenth century, the effect of which has been sobering. We have now learned that in the time of Demosthenes there was an underlying law of development leading

the Greeks away from the old limited city-state to the world empire of Alexander and the world culture of Hellenism. Seen in this vast new perspective, the figure of Demosthenes dwindles to a tiny obstacle in the path of an irresistible historical process. It now seems purely accidental that the tradition preserved so many of his admired speeches while allowing the systematic historical works of the period to disappear, thus giving posterity a permanently distorted picture of this epoch, with the true proportions quite upset. But this very calamity has been made a virtue. What Herodotus and Thucydides did for the fifth century, the modern historian has had to do for the fourth. And has he not shown true historical discernment in unmasking Demosthenes' eloquence as empty verbosity despite its two-thousand-year renown, and in making himself pleader for the actual historical forces that overcame Demosthenes' resistance to the march of events?

This has been pretty nearly the *communis opinio* of nineteenth-century historians. It was, of course, natural enough that Johann Gustav Droysen, the discoverer of the post-Alexandrian Hellenism, should have been little interested in Demosthenes; for his enthusiasm for Alexander as the true hero and pioneer of the new age made everything else lapse into insignificance. The situation is different when we come to the great historical works of the positivistic period at the close of the century,

* Werner Jaeger, *Demosthenes* (Berkeley: University of California Press, 1938), pp. 1–5.

especially the *Griechische Geschichte* of Karl Julius Beloch. Beloch may be regarded as the most consistent representative of this group, not only because his work is rich in the virtues of matter-of-factness, as is well known, but also because his description of Greek development is dominated by the same theoretical bias by which the entire historical thinking of our times has been determined more or less consciously. We have all grown up in this way of looking at things. The fact that Greek political life took the form of a number of autonomous city-states, was, for the national unitarianism of the nineteenth century, a historical scandal. There was a strong feeling that in the end, at any rate, this "particularism" must somehow have terminated in a larger national unity, as in the small states of Germany and Italy in the nineteenth century. The rôle of unifier which had there fallen to the military powers of Prussia and Savoy, seemed to have been played in Hellas by the kingdom of Macedonia. On this false analogy the whole of Greek history was now boldly reconstructed as a necessary process of development leading quite naturally to a single goal: unification of the Greek nation under Macedonian leadership. That which Demosthenes and most of his contemporaries had looked upon as the death of Greek political liberty, was now all at once regarded as the fulfillment of all the promises with which Fate had blessed the cradle of the Greek people. As a matter of fact, this amounted to judging Greek history by an altogether alien standard; and Demosthenes fell a victim to this misunderstanding. Indeed, a complete revaluation of all historical facts and personages now set in. In general, positivistic scholars have a better developed sense for political, military, and economic factors than they have for the human personality, and this was here operative. Otherwise how could it have happened that just at the time when Demosthenes' stock went down, that of men like Isocrates and Aeschines went up? —a situation which even the most rudimentary sensibility would find psychologically false! Perhaps it is now no longer so difficult to recognize the unhistoricity of the standard that Beloch and others of the same school applied to the events of Demosthenes' period. But when a man has made it his endeavor to obtain a general view of this sort and has at last succeeded, he will find infinite difficulty in escaping its spell when he comes to deal with particulars. For the distortion will extend to the very minutiae of historical judgment. If the standard of measurement is artificial, the findings must likewise be artificial, especially if, as with Beloch, they involve an emotional overtone; in this way the historian becomes little better than a writer of *Tendenzliteratur*, pursuing his prey in every nook and cranny with all the inherent pertinacity and obstinacy of the scholar.

Naturally there have still been defenders of Demosthenes even after this great reversal of historical opinion. Arnold Schaefer's work, the first volume of which appeared in 1856, was prepared with the utmost philological care and is still of fundamental importance for all special problems. It was virtually untouched by Droysen's novel views; the very title, *Demosthenes und seine Zeit*, indicated that Demosthenes would here be made the point of orientation for the history of the entire fourth century. In this work Schaefer attempted to create a detailed historical picture suffused with that hero worship which classicism had devoted to the great orator of liberty, so as to keep the ideal well fortified against the latest onslaughts. But unfortunately this lovable German scholar was the son of a land not yet politically conscious; he had no eye for the dynamics of political life. Accordingly his enormous zeal remained ineffectual when he came to the critical point of judging Demosthenes' politics, and, to tell the truth, his moralizing orthodoxy is often hard to endure. George Grote's version is another thing altogether. But Grote was a banker and a member of Parliament; he views the struggle of the Athenian democracy against the Macedonian empire too much from the standpoint natural to a man of his strong liberal principles, and therefore fails to do full justice either to the opposition party or even to Demosthenes himself. For, as we shall try to prove, Demosthenes' political development was much too complex, and its center of gravity too peculiarly situated, for it to be branded with any partisan label.

If I feel that the time has come for a new evaluation of Demosthenes, that does not mean that we should go back to Schaefer and Grote. Mere reaction is never right, and this would be no more than reaction. Demostheses can never again be made the focal point of a whole century during which the pendulum swung violently from the sturdy regionalism of a long-established folk to a universalism sweeping away all national barriers. But the fact that history decided against Demosthenes does not diminish our interest in the spirit which made him resist the forces of his time. And what man of understanding would esteem him the less because he was

not an Alexander? Thus the history of Demosthenes becomes something more than the biography of any mere party man. For it embodies vicariously a destiny of universal significance: the downfall of the polis or city-state, which had been the typical form of the Greek state throughout its classical period. It had now become inevitable that the old highly developed unity of Greek life as manifested in the polis should be dissolved in the cosmopolitanism of the world empire. The fruit was ripe and ready to fall. This process may seem quite "organic" to the modern historian; but for those to whom it was part and parcel of their daily life—those in whom the spirit of Greek history was still alive—it was an act of unheard-of violence against the moral and spiritual nature of the older Greek civilization. Of this fearful crisis Demosthenes' struggle is one aspect; Plato's attempt to renew the state is another. To overlook the importance of Plato's endeavor as a factor in history on the mere ground that his ideal state could not be realized, is certainly no more false than to deny the historical greatness of Demosthenes' death struggle to maintain the actual polis, simply because sober reason shows us that it was hopeless.

4. THE FUTILITY OF THE POLICY OF DEMOSTHENES*

In Hellas the thought of a national struggle against the Persian power was never forgotten; it was for the Greeks what the struggle against the infidels was for western Christendom centuries later. Even Sparta for a time had sought to clothe its rule and greed with this mask; Jason of Pherae saw a justification for the tyranny which he had established in the national struggle for which he prepared. The clearer the weakness and internal

disorder of the gigantic empire became, the easier and more profitable appeared the task of its destruction, the more general and confident became the expectation that it would happen and must happen. Plato and his school might try to find and realize the ideal state; Isocrates, from whom a still brighter and more popular operation emanated, always came back to this: that the struggle against Persia must be begun, such a war would be a festive procession rather than a military campaign. How could one bear the disgrace that these barbarians wished

* Johann Gustav Droysen, *Geschichte des Hellenismus* (Gotha, 1877), Vol. 1, pp. 31–34, translated by Donald Kagan.

to be the guardians of peace in Hellas while Hellas was in a position to accomplish deeds which were worthy, which were bidden by the gods? And Aristotle said the Greeks could rule the world if they were united in a single state.

The one thought lay quite close to the other, the union of Hellas and the struggle against Persia, and as a combined operation; one should not be allowed to wait until the other was accomplished. But how might such thoughts be realized?

King Philip of Macedon undertook it. He had to do it, one may say, if he wanted to restore and secure the confused kingship of his house. The policy of Athens, Sparta, Olynthus, Thebes, the Thessalian rulers had always fostered quarrels in the royal family, supported usurpations by princely chieftains of the land, and induced the barbarians to launch incursions and raids against Macedonia. If they all had no other legal claim for their proceedings than the weakness of the Macedonian monarchy, only the establishment of a sufficient power was required to prove that right against them. And they had no claim on the consideration of the Macedonian monarchy since for so long they had pursued their own interests against it.

Philip's success was based on the secure foundation which he knew how to give to his power, on the movement of his policy, going forward step-by-step in the face of the Greek states, now alert, now sleeping, but always self-seeking in its means or ends. Above all it rested on the unity, the secrecy, the speed and consequence of his undertakings which were for so long considered impossible by those who were to meet them, until it was no longer possible to elude or to withstand him. While Thessaly sank into disorder with the murder of Alexander, while the Athenians turned all their attention to the Social War, the Thebans to the Sacred War which compelled the partition of Phocis, the Spartans tried to preserve some influence in the Peloponnese, Philip

pushed his borders so far to the south and east that he held the pass to Thrace with Amphipolis, the gold mines with Mount Pangaeus, the Thermaic Gulf and access to the sea with the coast of Macedonia, the road to Thessaly with Methone. Then the Thessalians called upon him for help against a very serious threat from the Phocians. He came. He had a difficult position in the face of the well-led military force of the temple robbers. First he threw them back by moving up reinforcements; he stood at the pass of Thermopylae he placed a Macedonian garrison at Pagasae, and with this he was master of the Thessalian harbor and the road to Euboea. Now the Athenians opened their eyes. Under Demosthenes' leadership they began the struggle against the power which so it appeared, stretched its hand out for the command of Hellas.

No one will doubt the patriotism of Demosthenes and his zeal for the honor and might of Athens, and with the fullest right is he admired as the greatest orator of all time. Whether he was great in the same measure as a statesman, whether he was the statesman of the national policy of Greece, is another question. If the decision in this struggle had been victory over Macedonia what would the further fate of the Greek world have been? At best the establishment of Athenian authority in the same way as the one which had just collapsed a second time: either an alliance on the basis of the autonomy of the allies which would not have been able to check the barbarians in the North, nor to defy the barbarians in the East, nor to take upon itself the defense of the declining Hellenism of the West. Or else it might be an Athenian domination over subject territories, as Samos, Lemnos, Imbros, and Scyros were already, in part in the form of cleruchies, or, as in a looser form Tenedos, Proconnesus, the Chersonese, and Delos were in the possession of Athens. To the extent that the Athenians extended their dominion, they would have encountered greater jealousy, a stronger opposition from rival states; they would only have increased the already deeply corroded split and disunity of the Hellenic world; they would have welcomed any assistance, even from the Persians, the Thracians or Illyrian barbarians, tyrants, wherever it could be found, in order to hold their own. Or would Athens only have warded off the incalculable changes which the power of Macedonia threatened to bring to Hellas, only have preserved conditions as they were? They were so miserable and shameful and were becoming more untenable and explosive the longer they were left in that carelessness and crippling of the petty existence in which one member after another of the Greek world was withering away. If the Athenian patriots believed or pretended they were leading the struggle against Philip in the name of freedom, autonomy, Hellenic culture, national honor, none of these benefits would be secured by the victory of Athens or preserved by the renewed dominion of the Athenian demos over allies or subject territories, by the threadbare and exhausted democracy, its sycophants, demagogues, and mercenaries. It was an error of Demosthenes, who perhaps deserves respect for his heart, certainly not for his wisdom, if he could believe that with that babbling, unwarlike,

banausic citizenry of Athens—even if he could carry it along to glorious decisions with the power of his rhetoric, even if he could galvanize it to action for a moment— he could still make a great policy, still carry through a long and difficult struggle. It was a still more serious error if he could believe that he could halt the growing power of King Philip by means of an alliance with Thebes, Megalopolis, Argos, and other such states tossed together in a moment of danger. Even if a treaty was obtained from him he would return with redoubled force while the Hellenic alliances came to an end with the first defeat. Demosthenes must have known what it meant that he himself, who recommended political projects, was not the military hero who carried them out, that he must entrust them, and with them the fate of the state, to generals like the willful Chares and the dissolute Charidemus. He must have known that even in Athens just as he won influence the rich, the indolent, the self-seeking would find themselves together against him, that his personal enemies, supported by them, would use every trick and delaying tactic provided by the constitution to cross his plans, plans whose value was summed up by an Athenian after the battle of Chaeronea with the bitter words: "if we had not lost, we would have been lost."

5. THE CHARACTER OF DEMOSTHENES*

The question how far Demosthenes was justified in the policy which he pursued has been discussed in the preceding chapters in relation to each of the principal crises of the struggle in which he played so large a part. His vindication of himself in the Speech on the Crown is more convincing than any discussion at the

* A. W. Pickard-Cambridge, *Demosthenes* (New York and London: G. P. Putnam's Sons, 1914), pp. 489–497. Used by permission of Putnam's & Coward-McCann.

present day can possibly be, and very little more need be said.

The claim of Demosthenes to be ranked among the heroic men of the past rests above all on the constancy and sincerity with which he defended the noblest cause known to the Greeks—that of Hellenic liberty; and only those who have failed to recognise that most of what was best in the Greek, and, above all, in the Athenian character sprang from and was bound up with political liberty, can seriously censure his choice. If any cause was, to a Greek, worth fighting for to the death, that for which Demosthenes fought and died was pre-eminently so. Polybius indeed, writing two centuries later, declared that the "crop of traitors" in the Greek cities, whom Demosthenes so vehemently denounced, deserved no such name, and that they were pursuing the true interest of their several countries in submitting to Philip and Alexander, and finding in subjection to a common master that freedom from strife with one another which they had failed to find so long as they were autonomous. Yet such a solution of their political problems can hardly be called an honourable one; nor did these States ever bring forth fruits comparable to those achievements by which the Athenians, when they were most fully inspired by the spirit of freedom, won the admiration of humanity.

Moreover, it is plain that the test by which Polybius tried the policy of the statesmen of the fourth century was simply that of success. Demosthenes' policy, he said, led to the disaster of Chæroneia, whereas the Arcadians and Messenians enjoyed the blessings of peace. If success is the true and only test of statesmanship, Polybius was doubtless right. But if political liberty had proved itself so precious that without it the whole of life would have seemed to be lived on a lower plane, success was an altogether unworthy criterion by which to judge the actions of those who were dominated by such a sentiment. Demosthenes was convinced that such was the persuasion of the Athenians, if not of all other Greek peoples, and that by struggling to the end for the freedom of Athens, and causing the Athenians to struggle for the freedom of the Hellenes, he was fulfilling their noblest instincts.

If, however, success is seriously taken to be the proper criterion of merit, it must not be forgotten that the policy of Demosthenes very nearly did succeed. Philip was actually discomfited before Byzantium; and the defeat of Chæroneia was due to nothing which it was in Demosthenes' power to provide against, nor even to the inferiority of the forces which he had brought together, but simply to bad generalship. Whether, supposing that Philip had been defeated at Chæroneia, the struggle would have been at an end, no one can say; and it is idle to speculate upon such questions; but at least the defenders of Hellenic liberty came near enough to success to justify their attempt, even from the narrow standpoint assumed by Polybius and by some modern critics. Nor is it without significance that Aristotle (who had no special liking for Demosthenes), when he desires to illustrate a common form of fallacy, finds a conspicuous illustration in the statement that the policy of Demostheses was responsible for all the evils that befell his country.

The principal causes of the failure of Demosthenes' plans have long been plain to us—the unsteadiness of the Athenian people; the lack of generals comparable in ability to the statesmen of the time; the disunion of the Greek States. For the second of these causes, no blame attaches to Demosthenes, and it is not certain that he could have been aware of the inferiority of the Athenian commanders until they were put to the test. The disunion of the States he strove hard to overcome, and to a very remarkable extent he succeeded. The alliance of Thebes and Athens was a thing of which the most sanguine prophet could never have dreamed a few years before.

But ought Demosthenes to have recognised that his fellow-countrymen were no longer equal to the strain to which he desired to subject them? Is he to be blamed for taking too generous a view of their character? Certainly he was not unaware of their defects. No one ever pointed out more candidly than he, how far they fell short of the traditional ideal of Athenian citizenship, or realised more clearly their unwillingness to sacrifice pleasure and ease, and to undertake great personal risks for the sake of the national honour. The fickle and spasmodic nature of their patriotism, their liability to be carried about by alternate gusts of courage and alarm, were constantly before him. Yet even so, incapable of sustained effort and prolonged sacrifices as the Athenians were, it was a nobler thing to attempt to revive in them the spirit which they had lost, than to acquiesce in their degeneracy and levity, and to "despair of the Republic." Nor must it be forgotten that in this attempt also Demosthenes came nearly enough within reach of success to justify his policy in the judgment of any large-minded critic.

Demosthenes' ideal and his determination to maintain it, as the ideal not of himself alone but of his nation, stand in no need of vindication; and he well deserves our admiration for the courage with which, in pursuit of this ideal, he contended against those desires and prejudices of his fellow-countrymen which were inconsistent with it. In three important points at least, his policy ran directly counter to popular sentiment—in his demand that the festival-money should be given up for purposes of war; in his far-sighted desire to bring about an alliance with Thebes; and in his attempt to obtain the co-operation of the Persian King against Philip. Yet all these aims he pursued without faltering in face of attack and misrepresentation; and there can be little doubt that he was wise, as well as courageous, in so doing.

The question whether liberty and pre-eminence are political ideals which possess a universal value and need no justification is too large to discuss here. There are many who believe (as Plato and Aristotle probably believed) that these are secondary in importance to the good life of the individual in a peaceful society, and to whom militarism and imperialism are consequently abominable. There is something to be said for this view. But it must not be forgotten that in the Athens of Demosthenes' day it was a view which had

not made its way into the region of practical politics, but was peculiar to philosophic circles. There is no evidence that it was desire for the good life, or for the refined enjoyment of art, literature, and philosophy, that made the majority of the Athenians unwilling to fight; or that any higher motives than business, pleasure, and love of ease were the cause of their reluctance. Nor is it an absurd contention that the life of the individual is itself greatly ennobled by membership of an imperial nation. It may at least be doubted whether more than a handful of Athenians thought otherwise; and if so, it is a mistake to judge Demosthenes by a standard which is out of relation to the political life of his times.

The faults which sullied the character of Demosthenes as a public man are not only conspicuous, but are such as tend in many ways to alienate the sympathies of the modern world from him. The worst, perhaps, was an indifference to truth, which, while it was not incompatible with the larger sincerity manifested in his constancy to the supreme objects of his life, led him to deal very unfairly with his opponents, to falsify history, and to repudiate his own share in transactions which were perfectly proper, but which had come in time to be viewed with disfavour by the majority of the Athenians. Doubtless some of the blame for this should be assigned to the People itself; and Demosthenes' attempts to deceive the People in regard to the past are in some degree excusable when we consider that if he had spoken or admitted the whole truth, his policy in regard to the present and future would certainly have been imperilled. It may be that absolute truthfulness is not possible for the leader of a democracy. But it is difficult not to feel that the misrepresentations of which Demosthenes was guilty sometimes went beyond anything that such considerations can justify; that one who could lament over the calamities of the Phocians, which he had done nothing to prevent, and could ascribe them to the man who (if any one had done so) had helped to mitigate them deserves the severest reprobation; and that his scandalous inventions in regard to his rival's history and morals are utterly atrocious. There was also a certain *intransigeance*—amounting at times almost to ferocity—in his absolute refusal to consider even the most reasonable offers which Philip might make, and in the steps which he took to exacerbate the relations between Athens and the King of Macedon. No doubt he was whole-heartedly convinced that even if a compact, as favourable to Athens as possible, were made with Philip, it would mean at best that Athens would be sure only of the second place in the Hellenic world; and that whatever compact were made, it would only be observed by Philip until such time as he desired to break it. Yet Demosthenes, however sincere and patriotic he may have been, is sometimes repellent in the hatred which he displays, and at times this hatred led him to make false charges and to commit acts of cruelty which admit of no justification.

In his money-dealings he did not always observe the standard of correctness which a modern statesman is expected, as a matter of course, to observe. There is not, however, an iota of evidence that will stand criticism to show that he profited personally by any of the transactions that were alleged against him; and the worst of these transactions, the appropriation of Harpalus' treasure, was probably dictated, just as his receipt of the gold from Persia had been, by public spirit so intense as to render him unscrupulous about means.

Judged by the standard of his times, he is almost beyond reproach. It is not unworthy of notice that within a few months of condemning Demosthenes for taking some of Harpalus' money, the People themselves took all that was left of it to pay the cost of the Lamian War. No one now asserts that the policy of Demosthenes was in the smallest degree influenced by considerations of gain or of gratitude for presents received. It is doubtful whether this could be said of some of the orators who opposed him.

To the enumeration of his faults as a statesman, it must be added that he seems to have been a man of an unsociable and unfriendly temperament, and a bitter and relentless enemy; in all that we learn about him from the ancients or from his own writings, there is no hint of any intimate friendship or domestic affection. So wholly was he identified with political aims, that he almost seems to have had no private life. He was, moreover, deficient in humour and in gentlemanly feeling; and both these faults reveal an unattractive narrowness of imagination.

But against these faults, public and private, is to be set a devotion to a great ideal, absorbing the whole man; a capacity for work unrivalled in the history of great statesmen; a thoroughness in all that he did, which cared for every detail, and left nothing to chance; a gift of language, penetrated and transformed into eloquence of the very highest order by the passion for a great cause; and a courage which rose superior to all physical weakness, and was not daunted by failure or danger. The greatness of his character in these respects more than redeems its unloveliness.

6. The Athens of Demosthenes*

To a large extent an evaluation of Demosthenes' policy depends on an estimate of the Athenian state and its people in his time. It has been usual to consider it greatly inferior to the Athens of Pericles, and incompetent to carry through the program advocated by its greatest orator. In the following essay A. H. M. Jones questions the accuracy of the usual view.

Demosthenes' aims and policy have often been discussed, but his biographers have rarely paid much attention to the Athenians to whom he spoke. We are left with the general impression that, in contrast with the patriotic orator, they were an idle, cowardly, pleasure-loving crew, who would not fight or pay their taxes, but preferred to draw their dole at home, paying—or rather failing to pay—mercenaries to fight their battles. Is this estimate just? It is the picture which appears to emerge from Demosthenes' speeches, which, with those of contemporary orators, afford almost all the evidence available. This evidence I propose to examine afresh.

'Pay war tax' (εἰσφέρετε) and 'serve yourselves in the army' (αὐτοὶ στρατεύεσθε) are the two key-notes of Demosthenes' appeals to the people. Let us first examine the war tax. It is a highly technical and controversial subject, and I hope that you will excuse me if I am somewhat dogmatic. The questions which I wish to answer are: Was it, as is generally believed, a progressive tax? How many people paid it, and what was the limit of exemption? How much money was actually raised?

The *eisphora* was a war tax, raised by decree of the people as occasion demanded, and took the form of a capital levy. For this purpose a census of property was held in 378/7 B.C., in which according to Polybius 'the total assessment' (τὸ σύμπαν τίμημα) of Attica was valued at 5,750

talents; Demosthenes speaks of 'the assessment of the country' (τὸ τίμημα . . . τῆς χώρας) as being in his day 6,000 talents, and reckons levies as percentages of this sum—1 per cent, will bring in 60 talents, 2 per cent. 120 talents and so forth. Now Polybius clearly thought that the 'assessment' represented the total capital (land, houses and other property) of the country—he ignores the fact that it excludes properties below the exemption limit—and represented its real value. Demosthenes, however, in one passage of his first speech against Aphobus uses 'assessment' in another sense: 'three talents is the assessment of fifteen talents,' he says (πεντεκαίδεκα ταλάντων γὰρ τρία τάλαντα τίμημα), and he implies that for smaller fortunes the proportion was less than one-fifth. On this passage, together with an obscure citation in Pollux, has been built the theory that the 'assessment' was not the real value of a man's property, but the taxable value, and that the taxable value was a higher proportion of the real value for the rich than for the poor, so that the *eisphora* was the only known progressive tax of antiquity.

This theory involves very serious difficulties. In the first place it seems very perverse that even the richest should be assessed at one-fifth of their capital; the natural course would have been to assess them at the whole, and scale down the assessment of the poorer classes only. In the second place the theory conflicts with a contemporary inscription, a lease in which the tenant is to pay 54 drachmae a year rent and the *eisphorae*, if any, 'according to the assessment, viz. 7

* A. H. M. Jones, "The Athens of Demosthenes" (Cambridge: Cambridge University Press, 1952).

minae' (κατὰ τὸ τίμημα καθ' ἑπτὰ μνᾶς); the rent works out at about 8 per cent, if 7 minae is the real value of the property, but is absurd if the real value is five or more times that sum. It also makes the 'total assessment' of Attica absurd. Six thousand talents is perhaps rather a low sum, but it excludes, we must remember, thousands of small properties below the exemption limit, and, as frequent allusions in the orators show, concealment of wealth and under-assessment were the rule rather than the exception. On the other hand it is quite impossible that the value of Athenian property assessable for tax can have been not merely five times 6,000 talents, but much more. 'Assessment' is then used in two senses—to denote the real value in the inscription and in the phrase 'the assessment of the country' and as Demosthenes uses it in the first speech against Aphobus. And moreover the tax was levied on the assessment in the first sense of real value, or Demosthenes' calculation that a 1 per cent. levy will yield 60 talents is nonsense. Demosthenes must be using the word in an untechnical way in the passage in which he states that the 'assessment' of 15 talents is 3 talents for the largest fortunes.

Now Demosthenes alludes several times to this 1:5 ratio, but in all the other passages he uses different phraseology: 'they expected me to pay this tax' (ταύτην ἠξίουν εἰσφέρειν τὴτ εἰσφοράν), he says, or 'to pay 500 drachmae per 25 minae' (κατὰ τὰς πέντε καὶ εἴκοσι μνᾶς πεντακοσίας δραχμὰς εἰσφέρειν), as if his guardians put him down to pay one-fifth of his fortune as tax. Of course tax was never levied at this fantastic rate—actually during the ten years of his minority Demosthenes paid 18 minae on the 15 talents at which he was assessed. What do Demosthenes' phrases mean? Mr. Meiggs has recently suggested that the one-fifth is a ceiling, the highest sum which the richest class could be asked to pay as the total of all their tax payments during their lifetime; for the poorer

categories of taxpayers this ceiling would be lower. *Eisphora* was then levied as a given percentage of the real value of all taxable properties, and was not a progressive tax: but if successive levies came to a total of say a twentieth (the actual figures are unknown) of their capital, men of the poorest class could claim exemption, while men of the richest class would go on paying till a fifth of their capital was exhausted.

The theory is attractive in that it gives a meaning to Demosthenes' phraseology and tallies with Greek ways of thinking: they tended to regard a man's fortune as a static sum, ignoring income, and to set off against it the total of his payments on trierarchies, liturgies and war tax. But to put such a system into practice would have involved calculations of great complexity; for in fact fortunes were not static, but rose and fell by inheritances and investment of surplus income on the one hand, and payment of dowries and sales of assets on the other. I find it hard to believe that so complicated a system could have worked and I submit an alternative explanation of Demosthenes' words, which was suggested to me by my former pupil, Mr. de Ste Croix. In one passage Demosthenes states that his guardians made him president (ἡγεμών) of his symmory not on a small valuation but on so high a one as to pay 500 drachmae on 25 minae. Now the presidents with the second and third men (δεύτεροι and τρίτοι) of the symmories later constituted the Three Hundred, who advanced the tax to the State (οἱ προεισφέροντες), subsequently recovering it from the other members of their symmories. May it not be that this system existed from the beginning of the symmories, and that it was liability for this prepayment of tax (προεισφορά) which was scaled up to one-fifth of the payer's fortune according to his wealth?

There are difficulties in this view also. There were in 357 arrears amounting to about 14 talents on the 300-odd talents which had been demanded in the previous twenty years. Some of these arrears may have been due from members of the Three Hundred: it is perhaps significant that of the individual debtors mentioned by Demosthenes two are known to have been trierarchs, and must therefore have been fairly wealthy men, who might have been enrolled in the Three Hundred. But at any rate half of the total arrears was made up out of quite small sums, scarcely any according to Demosthenes over 1 mina; which implies 400 or 500 debtors. How did all these taxpayers still owe money to the treasury if their tax had been advanced by the Three Hundred? They might still owe money to members of the Three Hundred, but not to the State.

Two answers are possible. It may be that the 'prepayment' was a device designed for use in emergencies only, and was rarely or not at all employed in the twenty years in question. Or again the original function of the Three Hundred may have been not to prepay but to guarantee or underwrite the tax of their symmories; this is perhaps suggested by the use of 'pay' ($\epsilon i\sigma\phi\epsilon\rho\epsilon\iota\nu$) and not 'prepay' ($\pi\rho o\epsilon\iota\sigma\phi\epsilon\rho\epsilon\iota\nu$) in connection with the Three Hundred in the earliest reference to them. In that case the guarantee may well never have been enforced, for there was little enthusiasm to collect the tax when once the emergency which had demanded it was past.

The second difficulty is that when in 362 an emergency levy was raised to finance a naval expedition, the people decreed that the members of the council should nominate on behalf of their demes persons who were members of the deme or owned land in it to advance the levy of the State. Here the Three Hundred are entirely ignored, and it has generally been assumed that they did not yet exist. It was, on the usual view, the emergency of 362 which first called for a 'prepayment' and the procedure described above was a first experiment, which led to the establishment of the standing body of Three Hundred.

One objection to this view is that, in a speech delivered a few years before, Isaeus alludes to the Three Hundred as an established institution connected with the *eisphora*. A second is that about 376 (that is directly after the establishment of the symmory system) Demosthenes was made president of his symmory, though a child of 7, because of his wealth: the post of president, that is, was not executive but carried financial responsibility from the first. It seems a necessary inference that the Three Hundred comprising the presidents, second and third men of the 100 symmories were from the beginning financially responsible for the tax due from their groups, either by prepaying or by underwriting it. Indeed this would seem to be the whole point of the symmory system.

It was not then because the Three Hundred did not yet exist that the people in 362 decreed that persons be nominated *ad hoc* in each deme to prepay the tax. It may be that a 'prepayment' had been levied very recently, and that the Three Hundred had claimed that their hands were already full; if there had been a levy in the previous year they could, since the 'prepayment' was a liturgy, have legally claimed exemption. Or alternatively it may be that the symmory system through long disuse had become so disorganized that when a sudden emergency arose it had to be abandoned and *ad hoc* measures adopted. In favour of this view it may be noted that the emergency legislation ignores not only the Three Hundred but, it would seem, the whole symmory system: for it is implied that the collection was made not by symmories but by demes. It may even be that this levy was not a normal *eisphora*, but a special tax on some other basis, substituted for it either because the capacity of the war taxpayers was temporarily exhausted or because the machinery for assessing and collecting a war tax was seriously out of gear. The speaker uses the words $\pi\rho o\epsilon\iota\sigma\phi\epsilon\rho\epsilon\iota\nu$ and $\pi\rho o\epsilon\iota\sigma\phi o\rho\acute{a}$, but these may not be technical terms but mean merely 'to prepay a levy.' On the other hand he alludes to the magistrates who were in charge of the levy as 'the collectors of the military fund' (οἱ τὰ στρατιωτικὰ εἰσπρτάττοντες), which suggests a special military levy rather than a regular war tax.

The object of this long argument has been to prove that the *eisphora* was not a progressive tax, that is, that all liable to it paid the same proportion of their capital, whether they were rich or poor. Now for my second question, How many citizens paid? That the number was large is implied by Demosthenes' language in several passages; he speaks for instance of the mass of the people (τῷ πλήθει τῷ ὑμετέρῳ) as being exhausted by payment of war tax. A rather more precise answer is, I think, possible. There were, it is generally agreed, 100 war tax symmories as against 20 trierarchic symmories. The 20 trierarchic symmories, which were modelled on those of the *eisphora*, comprised 1,200 persons, at 60 per symmory. The 100 war tax symmories on the same basis will have included 6,000 persons. What was the exemption limit? Demosthenes several times alludes to 25 minae as a basic assessment unit—'to pay 500 drachmae per 25 minae' (κατὰ τὰς πέντε καὶ εἴκοσι μνᾶς πεντακοσίας δραχμὰς εἰσφέρειν) and, on one occasion, even more significantly assumes it as such—'you assessed me to pay 5 minae' (πέντε μνᾶς συνετάξατ' εἰσφέρειν), meaning to pay one-fifth. This suggests that 25 minae was the minimum taxable capital. This would accord with what other figures we have. In 322 B.C. Antipater, limiting the franchise to citizens owning over 2,000 drachmae (or 20 minae), found that there were 9,000 who qualified. If there were 9,000 persons who owned more than 20 minae each, there might well be about 6,000 who owned more than 25 minae.

Finally, how much war tax was actually levied? In his speech against Androtion

Demosthenes tells us that the levies between 377 and 357 totalled perhaps 300 talents or a little more; this works out at 0.25 per cent. per annum on the assessment of 6,000 talents. Demosthenes during his ten years' minority (376–366) paid 18 minae on his assessment of 15 talents, which works out at about 0.2 per cent. per annum. This is on capital, of course, but reckoning income as 10 per cent. of capital, which is about right taking land and money together, levies during this period, which was full of wars, represented only a 2 to 2½ per cent. income tax, or in modern terms 5d. to 6d. in the pound. We may therefore with some justification be amused when Xenophon speaks of the Athenians during this very time as 'worn out by levies of war tax' (ἀποκναιόμενοι χρημάτων εἰσφοραῖς). But taxation is a matter of habit—our great-grandfathers were outraged by an extra penny in the pound—and the Athenians never could form the habit of paying war tax since it was an occasional payment and, when it came, relatively heavy—Demosthenes speaks of 1 per cent. and even 2 per cent. as normal, and these are equivalent to an income tax of 2s. and 2s. in the pound. And before we blame the Athenians too loudly we should remember that there was no personal allowance, wife's allowance or children's allowance to soften the blow to the poor man with a large family. Demosthenes is probably justified in invoking the jurors' sympathy for 'the farmers who pinch and scrape', but owing to the cost of bringing up their children and domestic expenses and other public demands have fallen into arrears of war tax. It must have meant much pinching to bring up a family on a farm worth 25 minae. One litigant, indeed, states that 'my father left me and my brother property of only 45 minae each, and it is not easy to live on that.' On the basis of the single fourth-century figure that we possess for the price of land, a farm worth 25 minae would have comprised about 7 acres—

without stock, implements, house or furniture. If let at the rate of 8 per cent. which seems to have been normal, it would have brought in a rent of 200 drachmae a year; and bare food for a single man, without counting clothes, shoes or any extras, cost 180 drachmae. The proprietor of such a holding normally of course worked it himself with the aid of his family, and would make a larger income than the rental value, but even so little enough to feed a family.

An ill-adjusted system of war tax meant then that while the rich got off relatively very lightly, the mass of poor taxpayers were really embarrassed by even an occasional small levy, and were very reluctant to vote one. Actually very little was raised. How then did Athens pay for her wars? For the answer one may turn to Isocrates' pane-gyric on Timotheus. Timotheus' great merit, it appears, was that he was a very cheap general. He received only 13 talents from the treasury for his great campaign round the Peloponnese in which he won Corcyra in 375. Apollodorus gives a vivid picture of his financial straits two years later, when he had to mortgage his estates and borrow right and left to keep his sixty ships together, and Iphicrates, his suc-cessor, had to hire out his rowers as agri-cultural labourers in the intervals between operations. For the campaign which re-sulted in the capture of Samos in 365 Tim-otheus received no public funds, and he financed the capture of Potidaea and other Thraceward cities in the following year from the contributions of the local allies.

These facts affect Demosthenes' second slogan, hoplite service. The Athenians cannot be accused of cowardice. They turned out for campaigns in the good old fifth-century style in Boeotia, Euboea, the Peloponnese and even as far afield as Thessaly. In 369 they raised a levy *en masse* in support of Sparta against Thebes; 6,000 fought at Mantinea in 362; 5,000 foot and 400 horse at Thermopylae in 352. For Chaeronea there was a levy *en*

masse, and 5,000 foot and 500 horse fought in the Lamian war. The Athenians did not object to fighting. What they were afraid of may be deduced from the scheme for a small standing army which Demos-thenes put forward in the *First Philippic*. The Athenian element is to serve for a fixed period, not a long one at that, by a regular system of reliefs; and the State, he insists, must make financial provision for paying them a ration allowance at the meagre rate of 2 obols a day—by way of comparison ephebes (young men doing their military training in Attica) were allowed 4 obols a day for their food under Lycurgus' regime, and even public slaves got 3 obols a day. They will make up the balance, Demosthenes euphemistically hopes, 'from the war.'

In two other passages Demosthenes implies that hoplites were normally ex-pected to keep themselves. In the *de Falsa Legatione* he estimates the cost of the expedition to Thermopylae at 200 talents, 'if you count the private expenditure of those who served,' and in the *First Olynthiac* he asserts that 'if you had to serve abroad yourselves for only thirty days, and take what you would need on service from the produce of the country— while no enemy was in the country, I mean—those of you who are farmers would I think suffer a heavier loss than all you have spent on the war up to date.'

What the Athenian hoplite dreaded, then, was being shipped off to Macedonia and left there to starve for an indefinite period, while the farm or the business at home went to rack and ruin. Things were very different from the good old days of the fifth century, when a hoplite got 2 drachmae a day. And it must be remem-bered that many hoplites were quite poor men; the qualification is generally, and probably correctly, believed to have been property of the value of 2,000 drachmae— roughly 5 acres and a cow. Demosthenes in the *Meidias* is quite apologetic for intro-ducing to the jury a poor hoplite witness—

'he is poor may be, but not a rascal' (πένης μὲν ἴσως ἐστὶν, οὐ πονηρὸς δέ γε)—a curious remark in a speech devoted to abuse of the rich man Meidias. Lysias' client Mantitheus, when his deme assembled for the muster, found that many of his poorer fellow hoplites could not raise their journey money and organized a subscription to supply each with 30 drachmae.

The same considerations applied *a fortiori* to naval service, which Demosthenes also frequently urged on the citizens, since it was thetes who served in the fleet. It may be noted that at this period Athens could not rely on volunteers to row her triremes, but conscription was regularly employed. If one reads Apollodorus' speech against Polycles one realises why. Gone were the days of a drachma a day; for two months only did the men get any pay, for the remaining year and five months only rations, and even the ration money was often short, and failed altogether for the return voyage. For a man with a wife and family to keep this meant disaster, and it is little wonder if, as Apollodorus says, whenever a trireme put back to Athens in the middle of the year, large numbers deserted and the rest refused to sail again unless they were given something to provide for their families (εἰς διοίκησιν τῶν οἰκείων).

Lack of public funds naturally increased the expenses of trierarchs also. In 373 Timotheus made his sixty trierarchs each advance 7 minae to feed their crews: he being a rich man was able to cover this advance by mortgages on his estates, but other trierarchs were less fortunate; Apollodorus had to borrow freely from his father's correspondents overseas. The main vice of the trierarchy, however, was the faulty working of the symmory system. Trierarchic symmories were introduced in 357 B.C. because the trierarchy or syntrierarchy, whereby one or two men were responsible for the upkeep of a trireme for one year, was found too heavy a

burden on some of the persons liable. But no rules seem to have been laid down for sharing the expenses within the symmory and the general practice was that all members paid an equal share. This resulted, as Demosthenes explains in the *Meidias* and the *de Corona*, in the richest members, who could well afford to be sole trierarchs two or three times over, paying one-sixteenth of a trierarchy, while the same amount was paid by the poorer members of the 1,200 who could ill afford it. Demosthenes' first scheme of reform, set out in the speech on the symmories, was ill conceived; he proposed, it is true, to make payments proportional to property, but he also suggested spreading the burden yet wider over the whole body of war taxpayers. The result would have been to make the trierarchy a supplementary war tax, with all its unfairness. Later Demosthenes grasped the real point, and threw the whole burden of the trierarchy on the 300 richest citizens in proportion to their means, so that some performed two trierarchies.

You have no doubt been long waiting for me to mention the *theoricon*, which occupies a larger space in Demosthenes' commentators than in his speeches, and was of greater political than financial importance—as Demosthenes himself says, 'The sum of money about which you are debating is small, but the habit of mind which goes with it is important.' The fund consisted of the annual surplus of regular revenue over peace-time expenses (τὰ περιόντα χρήματα τῆς διοικήσεως)—in war time the surplus went by law to the war fund (τά στρατιωτικά)—and was used for making distributions to the citizens at the rate of 2 obols a head on some festival days. According to Demosthenes even the well-to-do drew it; let us then suppose that of the 21,000 citizens as many as 18,000 actually took the money. The cost would then be 1 talent per day.

The number of distributions varied according to the state of the fund. One lexicographer mentions a drachma as the total in 395–394 B.C.; this is three distributions were made, probably for the three days of the Dionysia. Another lexicographer speaks of payments for the Dionysia and the Panathenaea—six days in all. Hypereides mentions a man who impersonated his son who was abroad, and was fined a talent for the sake of 5 drachmae; this sum he may well have drawn over several years. But assuming that 5 drachmae represents a year's takings, that is that distributions were made on as many as fifteen days, the annual expenditure would be 15 talents, or one-quarter of a 1 per cent. *eisphora*.

The only evidence that large sums were involved in an anecdote in Plutarch, that when the Athenians were eager to launch a fleet to assist the rebels against Alexander, Demades quenched their ardour by stating that the money would have to come from a sum which he had reserved for a distribution at the rate of 50 drachmae a head for the feast of the Choes. If this anecdote has any historical basis, I am inclined to link it with another, according to which Lycurgus (very uncharacteristically) distributed the confiscated estate of one Diphilus to the people at the rate of 50 drachmae (or some say 1 mina) a head. The incident will presumably have taken place in 331, when King Agis was taking the field, and Demades and Lycurgus seem to have been working together to keep Athens out of the war. This payment of 50 drachmae was then not a normal theoric distribution, but a special bonus, arising from a windfall to the treasury.

Be that as it may, all the evidence shows that in the middle of the fourth century the *theoricon* must have been financially very small beer, and Demosthenes was rather foolish to make himself and his policy unpopular by trying to transfer it to the war fund even in peace time. When the revenue was as low as 130 talents a year, it was no doubt irritating to see even half a dozen talents squandered, and Demos-

thenes fell into Eubulus' trap. Later, when the revenue had rise to 400 talents, he changed his mind, and in the *Fourth Philippic* he argues—somewhat sophistically—in favour of the *theoricon*. Politically the *theoricon* was, as Demandes put it, 'the glue of the democracy' (ἡ κάλλα τῆς δημοκρανίας), because all classes found it useful. The poor, which would include not only the thetes but a substantial proportion of the hoplites, naturally found even so tiny a dole very acceptable, since it enabled them to enjoy their festivals with a clear conscience. To the rich it was a valuable political weapon for the policy of peace or appeasement which they favoured. Eubulus could threaten not only *eisphorae*, which affected only 6,000 voters, but the transfer of the *theoricon* to the war fund, which affected all the citizens, if the assembly would not vote for the Peace of Philocrates. Meidias could say, 'Do you expect me to pay war tax for you while you receive distributions? A large part of the *Fourth Philippic* is devoted to combating the argument of the well-to-do citizens that they cannot be expected to pay war tax and perform trierarchies if the poor draw their dole.

It is somewhat paradoxical that the leaders of the peace party should have been a group of the very wealthy men who, owing to the inefficiency of the Athenian financial machine, contributed least in proportion to their means to war expenses. But, this being so, this very inefficiency played into their hands, for war inflicted disproportionate hardship on every other class. Even the well-to-do, the less wealthy of the 1,200 members of the trierarchic symmories, bore an unfair proportion of naval expenses. The more modest war taxpayers were hard pressed to pay their share of the levy. The humble hoplites and the thetes looked forward with dread to being called up for prolonged unpaid foreign service in the army and the fleet, and moreover had to sacrifice their theoric doles. It was these last who really suffered the most by war, yet it was they who, if roused to action, voted for war. On Alexander's death, Diodorus tells us, the men of property (οἱ κτηματικοί) urged that Athens stay quiet, and it was the masses (τὰ πλήθη) who responded to the appeals of the orators of the war party, and declared the Lamian war, in which Athens played so prominent and so creditable a part.

It is understandable that the masses should have required some rousing to vote for war, when it meant such hardship for them. What is less easy to understand is why, once involved in war, they did not vote levies of tax which would have provided them with adequate pay for hoplite and naval service. The war taxpayers numbered only about 6,000, well under a third of the total citizen body of 21,000 and one might have expected the majority of the assembly to vote eagerly for a tax which they would not have to pay. In this connection it is worth noting the language that Demosthenes uses. He never urges the poor to soak the rich; on the contrary he appeals to the assembly to pay tax themselves. In every passage save one the war taxpayers are alluded to in the second person, and the one exception is significant. It is in the speech on the symmories, where Demosthenes is curbing a war-like assembly and deprecating a levy; here he says, 'Suppose *you* want *us* to pay an 8⅓ per cent. tax?' The inference seems to be that, contrary to general belief, the average assembly was attended mainly by the relatively well-to-do citizens, so the war taxpayers were, if not in a majority, a substantial part of the audience, and that it was only at moments of crisis—the speech on the symmories was delivered to combat a war scare that the Persian king was about to attack Athens—that the poorer classes came in force and might outvote those who would have to pay the tax.

If this was so in the assembly, it was even more markedly so in the law courts, where so many political issues were ultimately decided by way of the indictment for illegal proceedings (γραφὴ παρανόμων). We generally picture the law courts as manned by the very poor, eager to earn their 3 obols, but the language of Demosthenes and his contemporaries is hardly consistent with this view. The *Meidias*, with its constant appeal to prejudice against wealth, might seem at first sight to support it. But Meidias is represented as very rich, and moreover ostentatious, a bully and a shirker of his public obligations, and it is noteworthy that Demosthenes finds it necessary to apologise for introducing a really poor witness, the arbitrator Strato, who is a hoplite. The speech might well have been delivered to an audience of well-to-do propertied persons (οἱ εὔποροι or οἱ τὰς οὐσίας ἔχοντες are phrases of commendation in other speeches), who would probably dislike an insolent rich man (πλούσιος is consistently a term of abuse) more than would the very poor. In the *Androtion* and the *Timocrates* Demosthenes depicts the woes of the humbler payers of war tax in a way which he evidently expects to excite the sympathy of his audience—a really poor audience would not have felt very indignant at Androtion's distraining his victims' single maidservants when they had none themselves. The *Leptines* is a very strange speech to deliver to a poor audience. Not a word is said about the effect of the law on the masses, in their capacity of either audiences to the spectacles produced by the choregi or of dancers in the choruses. Leptines' plea was that his law would relieve the (comparatively) poor from the burden of liturgies by abolishing the exemptions of the rich, and Demosthenes tries to prove that the quashing of the law will not adversely affect the class who had to undertake liturgies: his speech must have been addressed to a jury drawn mainly from that class. Even more revealing is a remark in Deinarchus' speech against Demosthenes, where he appeals to any jurors who were members of the Three Hundred when Demosthenes passed his trierarchic law to tell their neighbours how he was bribed to amend it. Such an appeal would have been ridiculous unless members of the Three Hundred, the richest men in Athens, frequently sat on juries.

Upon reflection this is not unnatural. The greatest political issues and the fate of statesmen were decided in the courts. Would it not be prudent for leading politicians to get their supporters to enrol in the 6,000 jurors? They were not obliged to empanel themselves every day for minor cases, but could turn out in force when a *cause célèbre* was to be tried. And there was probably little competition for enrolment as a juror; a working man could not keep a family on 3 obols a day—

he could only just feed himself—and he could earn three times as much even by casual unskilled labour. Why the poor did not attend assemblies, where the pay was better—a drachma or even 9 obols—is more difficult to explain. They perhaps found the intricacies of politics as run by the professionals (οἱ πολιτευόμενοι) baffling, and were frustrated by finding every decree they passed taken to the courts and quashed under the indictment for illegal proceedings.

This analysis has, I hope, helped to explain against what heavy odds Demosthenes was battling in his great struggle for Athenian democracy, and at the same time given you a more sympathetic understanding of the Athenian people to whom he spoke.

SECTION XIII

The Deification of Alexander the Great

ALEXANDER THE GREAT has fascinated students ever since the conclusion of his meteoric career in 323 B.C. Some have argued that the chief problem is psychological rather than historical. What sort of a man was Alexander? A mystic? A hard-headed politician? A brutal conqueror? A visionary humanitarian? These views and still others have been held, but, as C. A. Robinson, Jr., has put it: "The chief interest of present-day students of Alexander revolves around these extraordinary ideas: what was his attitude toward universalism, cooperation between peoples, the brotherhood of man (or however you wish to express it); did he really plan world conquest; why did he seek his own deification?" It is with the last of these questions that this chapter deals.

Although the question of Alexander's divinity arises on many occasions in the career of Alexander, three episodes stand out: his visit to the oracle of Zeus-Ammon at the oasis of Siwah in the Lybian desert; the series of events which took place in Bactria-Sogdiana beginning with the murder of Clitus and ending with the execution of Callisthenes; and finally the alleged decree sent to the Greek cities from Susa ordering them to accord Alexander divine honors. These episodes will be treated separately, in chronological order.

A. THE ORACLE OF ZEUS-AMMON

1. THE ACCOUNT OF ARRIAN*

Flavius Arrianus was a provincial governor and general under the Emperor Hadrian in the second century A.D. He was a pupil of the Stoic sage Epictetus and a writer of historical treatises. His *Anabasis* is generally regarded as the most reliable history of Alexander.

After these transactions, Alexander was seized by an ardent desire to visit Ammon in Libya, partly in order to consult the god, because the oracle of Ammon was said to be exact in its information, and Perseus and Heracles were said to have consulted it, the former when he was despatched by

---

* Arrian, *Anabasis*, 3. 3–4, translated by E. J. Chinnock.

449

Polydectes against the Gorgon, and the latter, when he visited Antaeus in Libya and Busiris in Egypt. Alexander was also partly urged by a desire of emulating Perseus and Heracles, from both of whom he traced his descent. He also deduced his pedigree from Ammon, just as the legends traced that of Heracles and Perseus to Zeus. Accordingly he made the expedition to Ammon with the design of learning his own origin more certainly, or at least that he might be able to say that he had learned it. According to Aristobulus, he advanced along the sea-shore to Paraetonium through a country which was a desert, but not destitute of water, a distance of about 187 miles. Thence he turned into the interior, where the oracle of Ammon was located. The route is desert, and most of it is sand and destitute of water. But there was a copious supply of rain for Alexander, a thing which was attributed to the influence of the deity, as was also the following occurrence. Whenever a south wind blows in that district, it heaps up sand upon the route far and wide, rendering the tracks of the road invisible, so that it is impossible to discover where one ought to direct one's course in the sand, just as if one were at sea; for there are no landmarks along the road, neither mountain anywhere, nor tree, nor permanent hills standing erect, by which travellers might be able to form a conjecture of the right course, as sailors do by the stars. Consequently, Alexander's army lost the way, as even the guides were in doubt about the course to take. Ptolemy, son of Lagus, says that two serpents went in front of the army, uttering a voice, and Alexander ordered the guides to follow them, trusting in the divine portent. He says too that they showed the way to the oracle and back again. But Aristobulus, whose account is generally admitted as correct, says that two ravens flew in front of the army, and that these acted as Alexander's guides. I am able to assert with confidence that some divine assistance

was afforded him, for probability also coincides with the supposition; but the discrepancies in the accounts of the various narrators have deprived the story of certainty.

The place where the temple of Ammon is located is entirely surrounded by a desert of far-stretching sand, which is destitute of water. The fertile spot in the midst of this desert is not extensive; for where it stretches into its greatest expanse it is only about five miles broad. It is full of cultivated trees, olives and palms; and it is the only place in those parts which is refreshed with dew. A spring also rises from it, quite unlike all the other springs which issue from the earth. For at midday the water is cold to the taste, and still more so to the touch, as cold as cold can be. But when the sun has sunk into the west, it gets warmer, and from the evening it keeps on growing warmer until midnight, when it reaches its warmest point. After midnight it goes on getting gradually colder: at day-break it is already cold; but at midday it reaches the coldest point. Every day it undergoes these alternate changes in regular succession. In this place also natural salt is procured by digging, and certain of the priests of Ammon convey quantities of it into Egypt. For whenever they set out for Egypt they put it into little boxes plaited out of palm, and carry it as a present to the king, or some other great man. The lumps of this salt are large, some of them being longer than three fingers' breadth; and it is clear like crystal. The Egyptians and others who are respectful to the deity use this salt in their sacrifices, as it is clearer than that which is procured from the sea. Alexander then was struck with wonder at the place, and consulted the oracle of the god. Having heard what was agreeable to his wishes, as he himself said, he set out on the journey back to Egypt by the same route, according to the statement of Aristobulus; but according to that of Ptolemy, son of Lagus, he took another road, leading straight to Memphis.

2. The Account of Plutarch*

This was a long and painful, and, in two respects, a dangerous journey; first, if they should lose their provision of water, as for several days none could be obtained; and, secondly, if a violent south wind should rise upon them, while they were travelling through the wide extent of deep sands, as it is said to have done when Cambyses led his army that way, blowing the sand together in heaps, and raising, as it were, the whole desert like a sea upon them, till fifty thousand were swallowed up and destroyed by it. All these difficulties were weighed and represented to him; but Alexander was not easily to be diverted from anything he was bent upon. For fortune having hitherto seconded him in his designs, made him resolute and firm in his opinions, and the boldness of his temper raised a sort of passion in him for surmounting difficulties; as if it were not enough to be always victorious in the field, unless places and seasons and nature herself submitted to him. In this journey, the relief and assistance the gods afforded him in his distresses were more remarkable, and obtained greater belief than the oracles he received afterwards, which, however, were valued and credited the more on account of those occurrences. For first, plentiful rains that fell preserved them from any fear of perishing by drought, and, allaying the extreme dryness of the sand, which now became moist and firm to travel on, cleared and purified the air. Besides this, when they were out of their way, and were wandering up and down, because the marks which were wont to direct the guides were disordered and lost, they were set right again by some ravens, which flew before them when on their march, and waited for them when they lingered and fell behind; and the greatest miracle, as

Callisthenes tells us, was that if any of the company went astray in the night, they never ceased croaking and making a noise till by that means they had brought them into the right way again. Having passed through the wilderness, they came to the place where the high priest, at the first salutation, bade Alexander welcome from his father Ammon. And being asked by him whether any of his father's murderers had escaped punishment, he charged him to speak with more respect, since his was not a mortal father. Then Alexander, changing his expression, desired to know of him if any of those who murdered Philip were yet unpunished, and further concerning dominion, whether the empire of the world was reserved for him? This, the god answered, he should obtain, and that Philip's death was fully revenged, which gave him so much satisfaction that he made splendid offerings to Jupiter, and gave the priests very rich presents. This is what most authors write concerning the oracles. But Alexander, in a letter to his mother, tells her there were some secret answers, which at his return he would communicate to her only. Others say that the priest, desirous as a piece of courtesy to address him in Greek, "O Paidion," by a slip in pronunciation ended with the s instead of the n, and said "O Paidios," which mistake Alexander was well enough pleased with, and it went for current that the oracle had called him so.

Among the sayings of one Psammon, a philosopher, whom he heard in Egypt, he most approved of this, that all men are governed by God, because in everything, that which is chief and commands is divine. But what he pronounced himself upon this subject was even more like a philosopher, for he said, God was the common father of us all, but more particularly of the best of us. To the barbarians he carried himself very haughtily,

* Plutarch, *Alexander*, 26–28. Translated by John Dryden.

as if he were fully persuaded of his divine birth and parentage; but to the Grecians more moderately, and with less affectation of divinity, except it were one in writing to the Athenians about Samos, when he tells them that he should not himself have bestowed upon them that free and glorious city; "You received it," he says, "from the bounty of him who at that time was called my lord and father," meaning Philip. However, afterwards being wounded with an arrow, and feeling much pain, he turned to those about him, and told them, "This, my friends, is real flowing blood, not Ichor—

"Such as immortal gods are wont to shed."

And another time, when it thundered so much that everybody was afraid, and Anaxarchus, the sophist, asked him if he who was Jupiter's son could do anything like this, "Nay," said Alexander, laughing, "I have no desire to be formidable to my friends, as you would have me, who despised my table for being furnished with fish, and not with the heads of governors of provinces." For in fact it is related as true, that Anaxarchus, seeing a present of small fishes, which the king sent to Hephæstion, had used this expression, in a sort of irony, and disparagement of those who undergo vast labours and encounter great hazards in pursuit of magnificent objects which after all bring them little more pleasure or enjoyment than what others have. From what I have said upon this subject, it is apparent that Alexander in himself was not foolishly affected, or had the vanity to think himself really a god, but merely used his claims to divinity as a means of maintaining among other people the sense of his superiority.

3. THE ACCOUNT OF CURTIUS*

. . . From Memphis the king sailed on the same river to the interior of Egypt, and after arranging matters in such a way as to make no change in the native customs of the Egyptians, he decided to visit the oracle of Jupiter Ammon.

The journey which it was necessary to make was hardly endurable even for those who were lightly equipped and few in number; on earth and in the sky there is scarcity of water; it is a flat waste of barren sands. When the burning sun inflames these, intolerable heat results and the fiery soil scorches the soles of the feet, and one has to contend, not only against the high temperature and dryness of the region, but also the extreme tenaciousness of the coarse sand, through which, as it is very

deep and gives way beneath the step, the feet toil with difficulty. These troubles the Egyptians in fact exaggerated; but yet a great longing plied spurs to the king's purpose of visiting Jupiter, whom he, not content with mortal eminence, either believed, or wished men to believe, to be the founder of his race. Therefore, with those whom he had decided to take with him he went down the river to the Mareotic Lake. Thither envoys from Cyrenê brought gifts, and asked for peace and for a visit to their cities. He accepted the gifts and after concluding friendship with them continued to pursue his intended journey.

And indeed on the first and the following day the toil seemed endurable, since the solitudes to which they had come were not yet so desolate and barren, yet the land was already sterile and moribund. But when plains covered with deep sand disclosed themselves, just as if they had entered a vast sea, they looked in vain for land; not a tree, not a trace of cultivated

* Reprinted by permission of the publishers from *Loeb Classical Library*, Quintus Curtius Rufus, *History of Alexander*, 4. 7. 5–16, 25–32, translated by John C. Rolfe (Cambridge, Mass.: Harvard University Press, 1946).

soil met the eye. The water also, which camels had carried in leather bottles, gave out, and there was none to be found in the dry soil and burning sand. Besides this, the sun had made everything fiery-hot, their mouths were dry and parched, when suddenly—whether that was a gift of the gods or mere chance—the sky was overcast with clouds which hid the sun, a great help to those worn out by the heat, even if water were lacking. But indeed, when storms poured out copious rain also, each man received it in his own way; some, beside themselves with thirst, even began to try to catch it in their open mouths.

Four days were spent in traversing desert wastes. And now they were not far from the abode of the oracle, when a great flock of ravens met the army; flying at a moderate speed before the van, they now lighted on the ground when the line advanced more slowly, now raised themselves on their wings, as if acting as guides and showing the way. At length they arrived at the abode consecrated to the god.

*   *   *

At the time we are describing, as the king drew near, the eldest of the priests called him son, declaring that his father Jupiter gave him that name. Alexander indeed said that he accepted and acknowledged it, forgetful of his human condition. He then asked whether the rule of the whole world was destined for him by the fates. The prophet, equally disposed to flattery, answered that he would be the ruler of all lands. After this the king went on to inquire whether all the murderers of his father had paid the penalty. The priest said that his father could suffer from no man's crime, but that for the crime against Philip all had suffered punishment; he added that Alexander would be invincible till he departed to join the gods. Then, after sacrifice had been offered, gifts were given both to the priests and to the god, and the king's friends also were allowed to consult Jupiter. They asked nothing more than whether the god authorized them to pay divine honours to their king. The prophets replied that this also would be acceptable to Jupiter.

In the light of a genuine and entirely sane appraisal, these unquestionably vague responses of the oracle would have brought ridicule upon its trustworthiness, but Fortune makes those whom she has forced to have confidence in herself alone more eager as a rule for glory than big enough to have room for it. Accordingly, Alexander not only allowed himself to be called the son of Jupiter, but even ordered it, and thus while he wished to increase the renown of his exploits by such a title, he really spoilt it. And the Macedonians, accustomed, it is true, to the rule of a king, but living in the shadow of a greater freedom than the other peoples, opposed his claim to immortality more stubbornly than was expedient either for themselves or for their king.

4. THE ACCOUNT OF DIODORUS*

Having settled his affairs in Egypt, he undertook a journey to the temple of Ammon, to consult with the oracle there. When he was in the midst of his journey, he was met by the ambassadors of Cyrene, presenting him with a crown and other rich gifts, among which were three hundred war-horses, and five of the best chariots, drawn by four horses each. These he accepted, and made a league of peace and amity with them; and then, with those that attended him, went forward in his journey to the temple. When they came to the parched and dry deserts, (for they had taken water along with them), they passed

---

* Diodorus Siculus, 17. 49–51, translated by G. Booth.

through a region which was nothing but heaps of sand. After the fourth day their water was spent, so that they were in an extremity of distress. While they were in this great perplexity, and knew not what to resolve, a sudden and unexpected shower of rain then falling, supplied all their present necessities; which un-expected preservation they imputed to the kindness and providence of the gods.

Having furnished themselves out of a valley with as much water as was sufficient for four days, in that time they passed over this dire and scorching desert; but, in regard there was no visible path, by reason of the great heaps of sand, those who led the way told the king that there were crows, which, by their croaking at the right hand, directed them the way to the temple; which the king taking as a happy omen, and thereupon concluding that his coming was grateful and accep-table to the gods, he went forward on his journey with more cheerfulness. The next place he came to was called the Bitter Pond: having travelled thence a hundred furlongs, he passed by the cities of Ammon, and in one day's journey more came to the grove of the god.

* * *

When Alexander was introduced by the priests into the temple, and saw the god, one of the old prophets addressed himself to him, and said—"God save thee, my son, and this title take along with thee from the god himself." To whom he made answer—"I accept it, my father, and if you will make me lord of the whole world, your son I will ever be called." Upon which the priest approached near the altar; and when the men, (who according to custom lifted up the image), at the uttering of some words as signs for that purpose, moved forward, the priest answered—"That the god would certainly bestow upon him what he had desired." This was very acceptable to Alexander.

But then he further said—"I entreat thee, O God, that thou wouldst let me know what I have yet to inquire, and that is, whether I have executed justice upon all my father's murderers, or whether any have escaped?" At which the oracle cried out—"Express thyself better, for no mortal can kill thy father, but all the murderers of Philip have suffered just punishment."

He added further—"That his wonderful successes and prosperous achievements, were evidences of his divine birth: for, as he was never yet overcome by any, so he should be ever victorious for the time to come."

Alexander, being greatly pleased with these answers, after he had bestowed many rich and stately gifts upon the oracle, returned back on his way for Egypt, where he intended to build a great city. . . .

5. A POLITICAL EXPLANATION*

But this precocious Founder and crafts-man in politics has not forsworn yet all the dreams of his youth. Between creating a city and organizing a province, he is capable of the romantic folly of the expedition to the oracle of Ammon.

What can be said certainly of this folly?

---

* David G. Hogarth, *Philip and Alexander of Macedon* (New York: Charles Scribner's Sons, 1897), pp. 193–199.

Hardly more than that indeed Alexander went to the Ammon Temple. He can have made no general announcement either of what he asked its priests or of what they replied. For the rest, the record of this expedition is shrouded in inconsistency and myth. As Arrian's two best authorities insisted on distinct routes for Alexander's return from the Oasis, we may infer with some confidence that neither chronicler accompanied him. And with almost equal confidence it can be maintained that the expedition was a small affair that assumed little importance at the time, but came to be subject of general gossip at some later period, when recollection of the facts was confused and vague. Whether Alexander, when he started along the coast from Mareotis, was making indeed for Ammon, or not rather for Cyrene—even this must remain uncertain; for his historians dismiss with a mere mention the submission of the greatest Greek colony in Africa, which was made to him on his way. How did those Cyrenian envoys come so aptly to Paraetonium? Their city must have been summoned to surrender, or have been fearful of an attack. Paraetonium, be it remarked, lies a good deal further west than the usual point at which a caravan leaves the coast and strikes across the desert to the oasis of Siwah; and indeed had Alexander had merely Siwah for objective, his natural road had lain not by the north at all, but through the Fayum.

Let the conjecture, then, be hazarded for what it is worth, that if indeed a large force went with the king to Paraetonium, on receipt of the Cyrenian submission the most part of it was sent back; and Alexander seized the occasion to fulfil an old ambition by going to Siwah. He struck inland with a small party, such as alone can traverse so much waterless desert; and since no chronicler of his acts was included in his following, the Alexander of history melts into the Iskender of romance until such time as he reaches Memphis again.

The obvious purpose of Alexander, as Pharaoh, was to pay a visit of ceremony to his official Father, Amen. His added secret object was to ask a particular question as to his own carnal origin. All tradition agrees on this last point. Likely enough, Olympias had worked on a mind already full of romantic Homeric ideas. His father had publicly called him bastard. Was he, then, after all, like one of the Heroes, god-begotten on a mortal woman? It is not impossible that, in this matter, Alexander was doing no more than the behest of his mother; for he himself mostly made scant account of oracles and divinations, unless they chanced to agree with a policy preconceived.

* * *

None of the authorities, however, on whom Arrian relied, knew what passed in the Holy of Holies. Later gossip was better informed—not impossibly by report of Alexander's own loose talk with intimate friends. It is certain, at least, that publicly and officially Alexander remained son of Philip till his death, and found no greater inconsistency in asserting his private belief that Ammon had indeed begotten him, than Queen Hatasu or Amenhotep III, being children respectively of Thothmes I and Thothmes IV, found in depicting on their temple walls at Der el Bahari and Luxor a legend of their miraculous begetting by Amen.

Certain historians, however, have laboured to elevate Alexander's expedition to Siwah into the inception of a great policy. The king, say they, about to proceed to the East, and already desirous of exaltation above his Macedonians and Greeks, deliberately assumed divine character as son of Amen. Misplaced ingenuity! Every king of Egypt had been son of Amen since the growth of Thebes. The last Nectanebo, as well as the first Ptolemy, bear the title on their inscriptions equally with Alexander. In Egypt sonship to Amen was so far from being an exception, that it could not be escaped by a Pharaoh. Outside Egypt it was useless. Who, beyond Pelusium, worshipped Amen, or, beyond Euphrates, even knew his name?

Furthermore, evidence lacks wholly for the divine style, least of all with any express statement of sonship to Ammon, being used officially by Alexander; or for such "divine honours" as Persians paid or Greeks decreed being rendered as to the son of the Egyptian god. The men of the East prostrated themselves to Alexander as to all their princes; and when the

Macedonian demanded the same adoration from men of the West, it was not as son of Ammon, but as Emperor, that there might be no invidious distinction among his subjects.

Moreover, with respect to this matter two things must be distinguished sharply, which usually are confused: a claim, however publicly made, by Alexander to be of divine parentage is one thing; the institution by him of any cult of himself is wholly another. In Greek mythology, it should be borne in mind, the first of these things did not involve the second. Neither was Achilles worshipped in the Greek camp, nor Aeneas in the Trojan, because they had goddesses to their mothers. Alexander himself, although his Macedonian royalty and the manner of his life led him to assert personality in a manner foreign to Greek civic usage, and even to give his name to cities, appears to have introduced no effigy of himself on to his coinage. In his lifetime we never hear of his temples, altars, groves or games, such as not a generation later were dedicated to the living Demetrius. Greek adulation suggested the paying of divine honours to Alexander more than once, but the supposed prompting of these by an Imperial Decree rests on an inference so indirect from a statement historically so worthless that one can only wonder how it has found a place in the creed of a responsible historian.

There is, in short, hardly any question of public policy involved. Alexander went to Siwah purposing little more than to test a romantic belief which he owed to Homer, and in diverse ways to both his parents; and ever afterwards he hugged to himself the belief that the Egyptian Zeus was not only his official but his fleshly father. In moments of confidence and moments of exaltation, such as became more frequent as his imperial position developed, there can be no doubt that he made a boast of this divine origin, and thereby gave a handle to malcontents, and maybe some difficulty to himself in junctures when it was expedient to make appeal to his dynastic feudal position. It was a foolish fancy, no doubt, incompatible with the more advanced thought of his time, but quite consistent with the belief of older fashion that gods were really existent in human form with human passions.

This much may be granted; but it cannot be conceded by historical truth that Alexander seated himself even in imagination on Olympus, as *praesens deus*. He never pretended that his veins distilled ichor, claimed supernatural powers, or affected to be fed by the smoke of altar fires. Had he cherished such delusions or made such pretensions, his earthly success had never been attained. His wildest imagination did no more than set him among the half-divine Heroes: his sober reason claimed that he was godlike man, one of those noblest mortals who in a peculiar sense are sons of the common Father.

6. A MYSTICAL EXPLANATION*

When Alexander with his suite, conducted by the priests sent out to meet him, entered the temple-court, the prophet went to receive him, and, addressing him according to Egyptian ceremonial but certainly in the Greek language, greeted him as 'son of Ammon' in the name of the god. He then led the king alone into the temple of the priests, where Alexander put his question to the oracle in the Holy of Holies. Thereupon the procession with the idol was enacted as described above, and the prophet announced the answer of the god to the king in the Holy of Holies.

* Ulrich Wilcken, *Alexander the Great*, translated by G. C. Richards (New York: Dial Press, 1932), pp. 125–127. By permission of Quelle & Meyer, formerly of Leipzig, now of Heidelberg.

When Alexander returned into the temple-court, and his friends eagerly asked what had happened, he said nothing more than that 'he had heard what was according to his wish'. Some of his friends also used the opportunity to put questions to the god on their own behalf. They too received answers, according to the rite described, by the mediation of the prophet, but outside in the temple-court like ordinary pilgrims. This was what happened in public.

As the answer of Alexander to his friends shows, he kept the oracle to himself and treated it as secret. He might have had his own reasons for doing so. But it might also have been indicated to him by the prophet that the answer was to be kept secret, according to Egyptian ideas, because the god has spoken to his son. At any rate, Alexander kept the secret; for he wrote to his mother Olympias soon afterwards that he had received secret directions, which he would impart to her alone after his return to Macedonia. As this never happened, Alexander took the secret with him to the grave. So we shall never know what question he asked. The existing military and political situation makes it more than probable that the question referred in some way to his future. But how he formulated it, and how far forward it extended, whether it concerned only the impending struggle with Darius, or the actual winning of the sovereignty over Asia, which he had claimed after Issus, or whether ideas going far beyond that, of actual world-wide rule, were already in his mind, as they appeared without disguise in the later years of his life, Ammon alone knew, and we shall never know.

By those words of Alexander to his friends the public doubtless learned that he had received a favourable answer from the god, and the Greek world, which believed in the infallibility of Zeus Ammon, might now perhaps acknowledge that what Alexander did henceforth was done with the consent and blessing of the god. But even if this was the effect, it fell far short of the impression that the previous salutation of Alexander as son of Zeus Ammon was bound to make. To the prophet this salutation had been a matter of course, because he had before him the king of Egypt; from the Egyptian point of view, it was simply a consequence of the recognition that Alexander was also king of the oasis. Alexander may already have been saluted, in the temple of Ptah at Memphis or in other Egyptian temples which he entered, as son of the particular god in question; but whether these salutations made any profound impression on Alexander, whether, indeed, his attention was specially called to these titles, which were wrapped up in traditional phrases and certainly given in Egyptian, whether their meaning was explained to him, is more than doubtful. Here in the oasis, however, the salutation of him as son of the god, which came to him as a complete surprise, could not but make the deepest impression upon him. The god he regarded as Zeus, the great Greek oracular god, and in Greek language, equally intelligible to him and his escort, the prophet had in addressing him described him as son of the god. This meant that he was saluted as son of Zeus! It must have entered his soul like a flash of lightning and caused the deepest emotion. In form the utterance was not an oracle—he consulted the oracle later—but the prophet had saluted him in the sacred spot and in the name of the god. Alexander beheld in this a revelation of the god, a revelation which he took on trust as a confirmation of the special divine protection under which he had long felt himself, and as a recognition of the divine power working in him, which had led him to his unprecedented successes. He could believe in this all the more, since according to Greek conceptions superhuman deeds raised a man into the divine sphere.

All his life long Alexander clung to this mystic faith that he was the son of Zeus Ammon. Thereby he disowned his natural father Philip as little as any Pharaoh had disowned his father, because he was simultaneously son of Ra, and also of other gods besides. Mysticism and reality ran thus on parallel lines. To the end of his life Alexander dutifully recognised Philip as his father, however much his policy might diverge from that of Philip. On the other hand, how deeply he was moved by his divine sonship, is shown by the fact that he decided later that he would be buried in the oasis near his father Ammon.

B. BACTRIA-SOGDIANA

1. The Account of Plutarch*

Not long after this happened, the deplorable end of Clitus, which, to those who barely hear the matter, may seem more inhuman than that of Philotas; but if we consider the story with its circumstance of time, and weigh the cause, we shall find it to have occurred rather through a sort of mischance of the king's, whose anger and over-drinking offered an occasion to the evil genius of Clitus. The king had a present of Grecian fruit brought him from the sea-coast, which was so fresh and beautiful that he was surprised at it, and called Clitus to him to see it, and to give him a share of it. Clitus was then sacrificing, but he immediately left off and came, followed by three sheep, on whom the drink-offering had been already poured preparatory to sacrificing them. Alexander, being informed of this, told his diviners, Aristander and Cleomantis the Lacedæmonian, and asked them what it meant; on whose assuring him it was an ill omen, he commanded them in all haste to offer sacrifices for Clitus's safety, forasmuch as three days before he himself had seen a strange vision in his sleep, of Clitus all in mourning, sitting by Parmenio's sons who were dead. Clitus, however, stayed not to finish his devotions, but came straight to supper with the king, who had sacrificed to Castor and Pollux. And when they had drunk pretty hard, some of the company fell a-singing the verses of one Pranichus, or as others say of Pierion, which were made upon those captains who had been lately worsted by the barbarians, on purpose to disgrace and turn them to ridicule. This gave offence to the older men who were there, and they upbraided both the author and the singer of the verses, though Alexander and the younger men about him were much amused to hear them, and encouraged them to go on, till at last Clitus, who had drunk too much, and was besides of a forward and wilful temper, was so nettled that he could hold no longer, saying it was not well done to expose the Macedonians before the barbarians and their enemies, since though it was their unhappiness to be overcome, yet they were much better men than those who laughed at them. And when Alexander remarked, that Clitus was pleading his own cause, giving cowardice the name of misfortune, Clitus started up: "This cowardice as you are pleased to term it," said he to him, "saved the life of a son of the gods, when in flight from Spithridates's sword; it is by the expense of Macedonian blood, and by these wounds, that you are now raised to such a height as to be able to disown your father Philip, and call yourself the son of Ammon." "Thou base fellow," said Alexander, who was now thoroughly exasperated, "dost thou think to utter these things everywhere of me,

* Plutarch, *Alexander*, 50–55. Translated by John Dryden.

and stir up the Macedonians to sedition, and not be punished for it?" "We are sufficiently punished already," answered Clitus, "if this be the recompense of our toils, and we must esteem theirs a happy lot who have not lived to see their countrymen scourged with Median rods and forced to sue to the Persians to have access to their king." While he talked thus at random, and those near Alexander got up from their seats and began to revile him in turn, the elder men did what they could to compose the disorder. Alexander, in the meantime turning about to Xenodochus, the Pardian, and Artemius, the Colophonian, asked him if they were not of opinion that the Greeks, in comparison with the Macedonians, behaved themselves like so many demigods among wild beasts. But Clitus for all this would not give over, desiring Alexander to speak out if he had anything more to say, or else why did he invite men who were freeborn and accustomed to speak their minds openly without restraint to sup with him. He had better live and converse with barbarians and slaves who would not scruple to bow the knee to his Persian girdle and his white tunic. Which words so provoked Alexander that, not able to suppress his anger any longer, he threw one of the apples that lay upon the table at him, and hit him, and then looked about for his sword. But Aristophanes, one of his lifeguard, had hid that out of the way, and others came about him and besought him, but in vain; for, breaking from them, he called out aloud to his guards in the Macedonian language, which was a certain sign of some great disturbance in him, and commanded a trumpeter to sound, giving him a blow with his clenched fist for not instantly obeying him; though afterwards the same man was commended for disobeying an order which would have put the whole army into tumult and confusion. Clitus still refusing to yield, was with much trouble forced by his friends out of the room. But he came in again immedi-

ately at another door, very irreverently and confidently singing the verses out of Euripides's Andromache,—

"In Greece, alas! how ill things ordered are!"

Upon this, at last, Alexander, snatching a spear from one of the soldiers, met Clitus as he was coming forward and was putting by the curtain that hung before the door, and ran him through the body. He fell at once with a cry and a groan. Upon which the king's anger immediately vanishing, he came perfectly to himself, and when he saw his friends about him all in a profound silence, he pulled the spear out of the dead body, and would have thrust it into his own throat, if the guards had not held his hands, and by main force carried him away into his chamber, where all that night and the next day he wept bitterly, till being quite spent with lamenting and exclaiming, he lay as it were speechless, only fetching deep sighs. His friends apprehending some harm from his silence, broke into the room, but he took no notice of what any of them said, till Aristander putting him in mind of the vision he had seen concerning Clitus, and the prodigy that followed, as if all had come to pass by an unavoidable fatality, he then seemed to moderate his grief. They now brought Callisthenes, the philosopher, who was the near friend of Aristotle, and Anaxarchus of Abdera, to him. Callisthenes used moral language, and gentle and soothing means, hoping to find access for words of reason, and get a hold upon the passion. But Anaxarchus, who had always taken a course of his own in philosophy, and had a name for despising and slighting his contemporaries, as soon as he came in, cried aloud, "Is this the Alexander whom the whole world looks to, lying here weeping like a slave, for fear of the censure and reproach of men, to whom he himself ought to be a law and measure of equity, if he would use the right his conquests have given him as supreme lord and governor of all, and not be the victim of a vain and idle opinion? Do not you know," said he, "that Jupiter is represented to have Justice and Law on each hand of him, to signify that all the actions of a conqueror are lawful and just?" With these and the like speeches, Anaxarchus indeed allayed the king's grief, but withal corrupted his character, rendering him more audacious and lawless than he had been. Nor did he fail these means to insinuate himself into his favour, and to make Callisthenes's company, which at all times, because of his austerity, was not very acceptable, more uneasy and disagreeable to him.

It happened that these two philosophers met at an entertainment where conversation turned on the subject of climate and the temperature of the air. Callisthenes joined with their opinion, who held that those countries were colder, and the winter sharper there than in Greece. Anaxarchus would by no means allow this, but argued against it with some heat. "Surely," said Callisthenes, "you cannot but admit this country to be colder than Greece, for there you used to have but one threadbare cloak to keep out the coldest winter, and here you have three good warm mantles one over another." This piece of raillery irritated Anaxarchus and the other pretenders to learning, and the crowd of flatterers in general could not endure to see Callisthenes so much admired and followed by the youth, and no less esteemed by the older men for his orderly life and his gravity and for being contended with his condition; and confirming what he had professed about the object he had in his journey to Alexander, that it was only to get his countrymen recalled from banishment, and to rebuild and repeople his native town. Besides the envy which his great reputation raised, he also, by his own deportment, gave those who wished him ill opportunity to do him mischief. For when he was invited to public entertainments, he would most times refuse to come, or if he were present at any, he put a constraint upon the company by his austerity and silence, which seemed to intimate his disapproval of what he saw. So that Alexander himself said in application to him,—

"That vain pretence to wisdom I detest,
Where a man's blind to his own interest."

Being with many more invited to sup with the king, he was called upon when the cup came to him, to make an oration extempore in praise of the Macedonians; and he did it with such a flow of eloquence, that all who heard it rose from their seats to clap and applaud him, and threw their garland upon him; only Alexander told him out of Euripides,—

"I wonder not that you have spoke so well,
'Tis easy on good subjects to excel."

"Therefore," said he, "if you will show the force of your eloquence, tell my Macedonians their faults, and dispraise them, that by hearing their errors they may learn to be better for the future." Callisthenes presently obeyed him, retracting all he had said before, and, inveighing against the Macedonians with great freedom, added, that Philip thrived and grew powerful, chiefly by the discord of the Grecians, applying this verse to him,—

"In civil strife e'en villains rise to fame;"

which so offended the Macedonians, that he was odious to them ever after. And Alexander said, that instead of his eloquence, he had only made his ill-will appear in what he had spoken. Hermippus assures us that one Strœbus, a servant whom Callisthenes kept to read to him, gave this account of these passages afterwards to Aristotle; and that when he perceived the king grow more and more averse to him, two of three times, as he was going away, he repeated the verses,—

"Death seiz'd at last on great Patroclus too,
Though he in virtue far exceeded you."

Not without reason, therefore, did Aristotle give this character of Callisthenes, that he was, indeed, a powerful speaker, but had no judgment. He acted certainly a true philosopher's part in positively refusing, as he did, to pay adoration; and by speaking out openly against that which the best and gravest of the Macedonians only repined at in secret, he delivered the Grecians and Alexander himself from a great disgrace, when the practice was given up. But he ruined himself by it, because he went too roughly to work, as if he would have forced the king to that which he should have effected by reason and persuasion. Chares of Mitylene writes, that at a banquet Alexander, after he had drunk, reached the cup to one of his friends, who, on receiving it, rose up towards the domestic altar, and when he had drunk, first adored and then kissed Alexander, and afterwards laid himself down at the table with the rest. Which they all did one after another, till it came to Callisthenes's turn, who took the cup and drank, while the king, who was engaged in conversation with Hephæstion, was not observing, and then came and offered to kiss him. But Demetrius, surnamed Phidon, interposed, saying, "Sir, by no means let him kiss you, for he only of us all has refused to adore you;" upon which the king declined it, and all the concern Callisthenes showed was, that he said aloud, "Then I go away with a kiss less than the rest." The displeasure he incurred by this action procured credit for Hephæstion's declaration that he had broken his word to him in not paying the king the same veneration that others did, as he had faithfully promised to do. And to finish his disgrace, a number of such men as Lysimachus and Hagnon now came in with their asseverations that the sophist went about everywhere boasting of his resistance to arbitrary power, and that the young men all ran after him, and honoured him as the only man among so many thousands who had the courage to preserve his liberty. Therefore when Hermolaus's conspiracy came to be discovered, the charges which his enemies brought against him were the more easily believed, particularly that when the young man asked him what he should do to be the most illustrious person on earth, he told him the readiest way was to kill him who was already so, and that to incite him to commit the deed, he bade him not be awed by the golden couch, but remember Alexander was a man equally infirm and vulnerable as another. However, none of Hermolaus's accomplices, in the utmost extremity, made any mention of Callisthenes's being engaged in the design. Nay, Alexander himself, in the letters which he wrote soon after to Craterus, Attalus, and Alcetas, tells them that the young men who were put to the torture declared they had entered into the conspiracy of themselves, without any others being privy to or guilty of it. But yet afterwards, in a letter to Antipater, he accuses Callisthenes. "The young men," he says, "were stoned to death by the Macedonians, but for the sophist" (meaning Callisthenes), "I will take care to punish him with them too who sent him to me, and who harbour those in their cities who conspire against my life," an unequivocal declaration against Aristotle, in whose house Callisthenes, for his relationship's sake, being his niece Hero's son, had been educated. His death is variously related. Some say he was hanged by Alexander's orders; others, that he died of sickness in prison; but Chares writes he was kept in chains seven months after he was apprehended, on purpose that he might be proceeded against in full council, when Aristotle should be present; and that growing very fat, and contracting a disease of vermin, he there died, about the time that Alexander was wounded in India, in the country of the Malli Oxydracæ, all which came to pass afterwards.

2. THE ACCOUNT OF ARRIAN*

I think Clitus deserving of severe censure for his insolent behaviour to his king, while at the same time I pity Alexander for his mishap, because on that occasion he showed himself the slave of two vices, anger and drunkenness, by neither of which is it seemly for a prudent man to be enslaved. But then on the other hand I think his subsequent behaviour worthy of praise, because directly after he had done the deed he recognized that it was a horrible one. Some of his biographers even say that he propped the pike against the wall with the intention of falling upon it himself, thinking that it was not proper for him to live who had killed his friend when under the influence of wine. Most historians do not mention this, but say that he went off to bed and lay there lamenting, calling Clitus himself by name, and his sister Lanice, daughter of Dropidas who had been his nurse. He exclaimed that having reached man's estate he had certainly bestowed a noble reward on her for her care in rearing him, as she had lived to see her own sons die fighting on his behalf, and he himself had slain her brother with his own hand. He did not cease calling himself the murderer of his friends; and for three days rigidly abstained from food and drink, and paid no attention whatever to his personal appearance. Some of the soothsayers revealed that the avenging wrath of Dionysus had been the cause of his conduct, because he had omitted the sacrifice to that deity. At last with great difficulty he was induced by his companions to touch food and to pay proper attention to his person. He then paid to Dionysus the sacrifice due to him, since he was not at all unwilling that the fatality should be attributed rather to the avenging wrath of the deity than to his own depravity. I think Alexander deserves great praise for this, that he did not obstinately persevere in evil, or still worse become a defender and advocate of the wrong which had been done, but confessed that he had committed a crime, being a man (and therefore liable to err). There are some who say that Anaxarchus the Sophist was summoned into Alexander's presence to give him consolation. Finding him lying down and groaning, he laughed at him, and said that he did not know that the wise men of old for this reason made Justice an assessor of Zeus, because whatever was done by him was justly done; and therefore also that which was done by the Great King ought to be deemed just, in the first place by the king himself, and then by the rest of men. They say that Alexander was then greatly consoled by these remarks. But I assert that Anaxarchus did Alexander a great injury and one still greater than that by which he was then oppressed, if he really thought this to be the opinion of a wise man, that indeed it is proper for a king to come to hasty conclusions and act unjustly, and that whatever is done by a king must be deemed just, no matter how it is done. There is also a current report that Alexander wished men to prostrate themselves before him (as to a god) entertaining the notion that Ammon was his father, rather than Philip; and that he now showed his admiration of the customs of the Persians and Medes by changing the style of his dress, and by the alteration he made in the general etiquette of his court. There were not wanting those who in regard to these matters gave way to his wishes with the design of flattering him; among others being Anaxarchus, one of the philosophers attending his court, and Agis, an Argive who was an epic poet.

But it is said that Callisthenes the Olynthian, who had studied philosophy

* Arrian, *Anabasis*, 4. 9–12. Translated by E. J. Chinnock.

under Aristotle, and was somewhat brusque in his manner, did not approve of this conduct; and so far as this is concerned I quite agree with him. But the following remark of his, if indeed it has been correctly recorded, I do not think at all proper, when he declared that Alexander and his exploits were dependent upon him and his history, and that he had not come to him to acquire reputation from him, but to make him renowned among men; consequently that Alexander's participation in divinity did not depend on the false assertion of Olympias in regard to his procreation, but on what he might report to mankind in his history of the king. There are some writers also who have said that on one occasion Philotas asked him what man he thought to be held in especial honour by the people of Athens; and that he replied, "Harmodius and Aristogeiton; because they slew one of the two despots, and put an end to the despotism." Philotas again asked, "If a man happened now to kill a despot, to which of the Grecian States would you wish him to flee for preservation?" Callisthenes again replied, "If not among others, at any rate among the Athenians an exile would be able to find preservation; for they waged war on behalf of the sons of Heracles against Eurystheus, who at that time was ruling as a despot over Greece." How he resisted Alexander in regard to the ceremony of prostration, the following is the most received account. An arrangement was made between Alexander and the Sophists in conjunction with the most illustrious of the Persians and Medes who were in attendance upon him, that this topic should be mentioned at a wine-party. Anaxarchus commenced the discussion by saying that Alexander would much more justly be deemed a god than either Dionysus or Heracles, not only on account of the very numerous and mightly exploits which he had performed, but also because Dionysus was only a Theban, in no way related to Macedonians; and Heracles was

an Argive, not at all related to them, except in regard to Alexander's pedigree; for he was a descendant of Heracles. He added that the Macedonians might with greater justice gratify their king with divine honours, for there was no doubt about this, that when he departed from men they would honour him as a god. How much more just then would it be to reward him while alive, than after his death, when it would be no advantage to him to be honoured.

When Anaxarchus had uttered these remarks and others of a similar kind, those who were privy to the plan applauded his speech, and wished at once to begin the ceremony of prostration. Most of the Macedonians, however, were vexed at the speech and kept silence. But Callisthenes interposed and said, "O Anaxarchus, I openly declare that there is no honour which Alexander is unworthy to receive, provided that it is consistent with his being human; but men have made distinctions between those honours which are due to men and those due to gods, in many different ways, as for instance by the building of temples and by the erection of statues. Moreover for the gods sacred inclosures are selected, to them sacrifice is offered, and to them libations are made. Hymns also are composed in honour of the gods, and eulogies for men. But the greatest distinction is made by the custom of prostration. For it is the practice that men should be kissed by those who salute them; but because the deity is located somewhere above, it is not lawful even to touch him, and this is the reason no doubt why he is honoured by prostration. Bands of choral dancers are also appointed for the gods, and paeans are sung in their honour. And this is not at all wonderful, seeing that certain honours are specially assigned to some of the gods and certain others to other gods, and, by Zeus, quite different ones again are assigned to heroes, which are very distinct from those paid to the deity. It is not therefore reasonable to confound all these distinctions without discrimination, exalting men to a rank above their condition by extravagant accumulation of honours, and debasing the gods, as far as lies in human power, to an unseemly level, by paying them honours only equal to those paid to men." He said that Alexander would not endure the affront, if some private individual were to be thrust into his royal honours by an unjust vote, either by show of hands or by ballot. Much more justly then would the gods be indignant at those mortals who usurp divine honours or suffer themselves to be thrust into them by others. "Alexander not only seems to be, but is in reality beyond any competition the bravest of brave men, of kings the most kingly, and of generals the most worthy to command an army. O Anaxarchus, it was your duty rather than any other man's to become the special advocate of these arguments now adduced by me, and the opponent of those contrary to them, seeing that you associate with him for the purpose of imparting philosophy and instruction. Therefore it was unseemly to begin this discussion, when you ought to have remembered that you are not associating with and giving advice to Cambyses or Xerxes, but to the son of Philip, who derives his origin from Heracles and Aeacus, whose ancestors came into Macedonia from Argos, and have continued to rule the Macedonians, not by force, but by law. Not even to Heracles himself while still alive were divine honours paid by the Greeks; and even after his death they were withheld until a decree had been published by the oracle of the god at Delphi that men should honour Heracles as a god. But if, because the discussion is held in the land of foreigners, we ought to adopt the sentiments of foreigners, I for my part demand, O Alexander, that you should think of Greece, for whose sake the whole of this expedition was undertaken by you, that you might join Asia to Greece. Therefore make up your mind whether you will return thither and compel the Greeks, who are men most devoted to freedom, to pay you the honour of prostration, or whether you will keep aloof from Greeks, and inflict this dishonour on the Macedonians alone, or thirdly whether you will make a difference altogether as to the honours to be paid you, so as to be honoured by the Greeks and Macedonians as a human being and after the manner of the Greeks, and by foreigners alone after the foreign fashion. But if it is said that Cyrus, son of Cambyses, was the first man to whom the honour of prostration was paid and that afterwards this degrading ceremony continued in vogue among the Persians and Medes, we ought to bear in mind that the Scythians, men poor but independent, chastened that Cyrus; that other Scythians again chastened Darius, as the Athenians and Lacedaemonians did Xerxes, as Clearchus and Xenophon with their 10,000 followers did Artaxerxes; and finally, that Alexander, though not honoured with prostration, has chastened this Darius."

By making these and other remarks of a similar kind, Callisthenes greatly annoyed Alexander, but spoke the exact sentiments of the Macedonians. When the king perceived this, he sent to prevent the Macedonians from making any further mention of the ceremony of prostration. But after the discussion silence ensued; and then the most honourable of the Persians arose in due order and prostrated their bodies before him. But when one of the Persians seemed to have performed the ceremony in an awkward way, Leonnatus, one of the Companions, laughed at his posture as mean. Alexander at the time was angry with him for this, but was afterwards reconciled to him. The following account has also been given: Alexander drank from a golden goblet the health of the circle of guests, and handed it first to those with whom he had concerted the ceremony of prostration. The first who drank from the goblet rose up and performed the act of prostration, and received a kiss from him. This ceremony proceeded from one to another in due order. But when the pledging of health came to the turn of Callisthenes, he rose up and drank from the goblet, and drew near, wishing to kiss the king without performing the act of prostration. Alexander happened then to be conversing with Hephaestion, and consequently did not observe whether Callisthenes performed the ceremony completely or not. But when Callisthenes was approaching to kiss him, Demetrius, son of Pythonax, one of the Companions, said that he was doing so without having prostrated himself. So the king would not permit him to kiss him; whereupon the philosopher said, "I am going away only with the loss of a kiss." I by no means approve of any of these proceedings, which manifested both the insolence of Alexander on the present occasion and the churlish nature of Callisthenes. But I think that, so far as regards himself, it would have been quite sufficient if he had expressed himself discreetly, magnifying as much as possible the exploits of the king, with whom no one thought it a dishonour to associate. Therefore I consider that not without reason Callisthenes became odious to Alexander on account of the unseasonable freedom of speech in which he indulged, as well as from the egregious fatuity of his conduct. I surmise that this was the reason why such easy credit was given to those who accused him of participating in the conspiracy formed against Alexander by his pages, and to those also who affirmed that they had been incited to engage in the conspiracy by him alone. . . .

3. THE ACCOUNT OF CURTIUS*

And now, when all was ready in advance, thinking that the time was then ripe for what he had long perversely planned, he began to consider how he might usurp divine honours. He wished, not only to be called, but to be believed to be the son of Jupiter, as if he could rule men's minds as well as their tongues, and he ordered the Macedonians to pay their respect to him in the Persian fashion and to salute him by prostrating themselves on the ground. In his desire for such things he did not lack pernicious adulation, the constant evil of kings, whose power is more frequently overthrown by flattery than by foes. And this was not the fault of the Macedonians—for none of them could endure to impair any jot of his native customs—but of the Greeks, who had debased their profession of the liberal arts by evil habits:—Agis, an Argive, the composer of the worst of poems next after Choerilus, and Cleo, from Sicily, the latter indeed a flatterer, from a defect not only in his own nature, but also in his nation, and other sweepings of their own cities; these were mingled by the king even with his nearest friends and the leaders of his greatest armies. These at that time were opening Heaven to him, boasting that Hercules and Father Liber and Castor with Pollux would give place to the new deity.

Therefore on a festal day he ordered a banquet to be prepared with all magnificence, to which not only Macedonians and Greeks, the chief of his friends, but also nobles of the enemy were invited. When the king had taken his place at table with these, after feasting for a little while he left the banquet. Cleo, as had been prearranged, began the conversation by expressing admiration for the king's glorious deeds. Then he enumerated their obligations to him; these, he said, could

* Reprinted by permission of the publishers from *Loeb Classical Library*, Quintus Curtius Rufus, *History of Alexander*, 8. 5. 5–24, translated by John C. Rolfe (Cambridge, Mass.: Harvard University Press, 1946).

be requited in only one way, namely, since they knew that he was a god, by admitting it and paying for such great favours by the slight expense of incense. The Persians indeed were not only loyal but also wise in worshipping their kings among the gods; for the majesty of the empire was the protector of its safety. Not even Hercules and Father Liber had been acknowledged as gods until they had overcome the jealousy of those who lived with them: future generations believed only so much about each man as his own time had vouched for. But if the rest of the company were in doubt, he himself would prostrate himself on the ground when the king entered the banquet. The rest ought to do the same, and especially those endowed with wisdom; for it was by those that a precedent in worshipping the king ought to be shown.

Quite clearly this speech was directed against Callisthenes. The austerity of the man and his ready freedom of speech were odious to the king, as if he alone were delaying the Macedonians, who were prepared for such obsequiousness. He then, when silence ensued and the rest were looking at him alone, said: "If the king had been present at your talk, surely the words of no one would be needed to reply to you; for he himself would beg that you should not force him to descend to foreign and alien rites, nor would you expose his highly successful exploits to odium by such flattery. But since he is not present, I am replying to you in his behalf that no fruit is at the same time both durable and prematurely ripened, and that you are not giving divine honours to your king, but taking them from him. For there is need of time for a man to be believed to be a god, and it is always thus that future generations requite great men. But I pray for a late immortality for the king, in order that his life may be long and his majesty eternal. Divinity sometimes overtakes a man, it never accompanies him.

"You mentioned Hercules and Father Liber just now as examples of consecration to immortality. Do you believe that they were made gods by the decree of a single banquet? Their mortal nature was removed from sight before Fame transported them to Heaven. Forsooth you and I, Cleo, make gods, from us the king will receive endorsement of his divinity! I should like to try your power; make someone a king, if you can make a god. Is it easier to bestow heaven than empire? May the propitious gods have heard without offence what Cleo said, and suffer things to go on in the same course in which they have flowed up to now. May they allow us to be content with our habits. I am not ashamed of my fatherland, nor do I desire to learn from the vanquished how I ought to do honour to my king. For my part, I admit that they are the victors if we accept from them the laws under which we live."

Callisthenes was heard with favourable ears as a defender of the public liberty. He had forced, not only assent, but also words, especially of the older men, to whom the change of their long-standing customs to those of strangers was distasteful. And the king was not unaware of anything that was said on one side and the other, since he was standing behind the curtains which he had caused to be spread round the couches. Therefore he sent words to Agis and Cleo to put an end to the discussion and to allow only the barbarians, when he entered, to prostrate themselves after their custom, and a little later, as if he had transacted some unusually important business, he returned to the banquet. When the Persians paid reverence to him, Polypercon, who was reclining above the king, in mockery began to urge one of them, who touched the ground with his chin, to strike it harder against the earth, and thus aroused the anger of Alexander, which he had already been unable to contain. Accordingly he said: "You, then, will not adore me? To you alone do we seem to be deserving of ridicule?"

Polypercon replied that the king did not seem to deserve ridicule, nor he himself contempt. Then the king dragged him from his couch, hurled him to the ground, and when he had fallen on his face, said: "Do you not see that you have done the same thing which a little while before you ridiculed in another?" And ordering that he should be put in prison, he broke up the banquet.

4. CONCERN FOR THE PERSIANS*

. . . The idea of a fusion of the nations, which had perhaps suggested itself to him before, developed in his mind, and a few months afterwards, in the spring of 327, found for the time first its visible expression in his marriage with Roxane.

As a corollary of this, immediately after his return to Bactra he attempted to introduce the Persian *proskynesis* among his Macedonians and Greeks. Since primeval times it had been an Oriental practice for the subjects of a king to greet him by throwing themselves on the ground. It probably did not imply a recognition of the king as god; it was merely a sign of the most complete subjection to an absolute ruler. This custom of *proskynesis* as the Greeks called it, which was introduced by Cyrus, the founder of the empire, and applied to the Persians as well as to his other subjects, was always regarded by the Greeks, as soon as they came in contact with it, as something particularly contemptible and quite specially Oriental. The free Greek could abase himself before his god, but never before a man, and thus the observation of the custom may have contributed to the error, which appears as early as Aeschylus, that the Persians worshipped their kings as gods in their lifetime. Alexander certainly knew from his Persian courtiers that the Persians regarded the *proskynesis* simply as an expression of the deepest reverence for their lord. But as he was naturally familiar with the Greek conception, it was a

dangerous undertaking to promote the levelling of his subjects by an attempt to establish among Macedonians and Greeks a custom which the Persians followed in his case as a matter of course.

We must decidedly reject the view that he meant indirectly to force his recognition as a god, for later on he required the obeisance only of the Greeks and not of the Macedonians. His purpose rather was to express the equal position of the Persians with the Macedonians and Greeks by means of this common court ceremonial. It was a step which went far beyond anything he had previously done in this direction. Perhaps he would not have undertaken it, had there not been at his court in his immediate circle individuals who were ready in this matter to go with him through thick and thin. In particular his closest friend, Hephaestion, seems to have been the stage-manager. How conscious they were of the danger of the experiment is shown by the caution with which it was presented. It was agreed that at a symposium the king should drink out of a cup to the friends who were in the plot one after the other, and that each should drain the cup, fall down before him, and then exchange with him the kiss of friendship, also a Persian custom. At first all went according to plan. But when it came to Callisthenes' turn, he, surprised by the suggestion of making the *proskynesis*, omitted it. Alexander had turned to Hephaestion: when his attention was drawn to the omission, he refused to kiss Callisthenes, who thereupon defiantly called out to him: 'Well, I go away the poorer by a kiss.' The evening thus ended with an

* Ulrich Wilcken, *Alexander the Great*, translated by G. C. Richards (New York: Dial Press, 1932), pp. 168–171. By permission of Quelle & Meyer, formerly of Leipzig, now of Heidelberg.

unpleasant incident. But what finally induced Alexander to give up his design was not so much the refusal of Callisthenes as the realisation that on this point his old Macedonians would stubbornly resist him. We do not hear that in later years he again required the *proskynesis* from them. It is to the king's credit that he saw he had been too hasty in his attempt, and did not hesitate to give way. The West was to be spared this Eastern ceremony for many years. It was not till Diocletian that it was introduced along with other Oriental court customs.

It was the more surprising that Callisthenes opposed the king in this matter, as in his book he was unbounded in his glorification of him, and had even most vigorously supported his divine sonship. Nor had the change of his Panhellenic hero into a Great King apparently disturbed his personal relations with Alexander; after the murder of Cleitus he was one of those who sought to comfort the distracted monarch. His resistance to the *proskynesis* did not so much imply a protest against the deification of Alexander, such as is formulated in the language ascribed to him, but is probably to be explained on the ground that he saw in it a barbaric and ridiculous mode of reverence, by which the free Greek was depressed to the level of the barbarians he despised. His tie with Alexander was irremediably broken, and the king hated him, since now he was regarded as head of the opposition.

Soon afterwards a new conspiracy was detected, among the royal pages. This time the reason was not political but purely personal, the wounded honour of young Hermolaus, whom Alexander had caused to be chastised in front of the other pages, because he had shot a wild boar before him at a hunting party. Though the conspiracy was in itself more harmless than the first, it was yet more dangerous; for these pages waited on the king's person and intended to kill him at night when sleeping. If on the night agreed upon Alexander had not stayed till morning in a symposium,—as was said, by the warning of a Syrian prophetess—he would have been lost. The conspiracy was discovered the next day: the pages, as sons of Macedonian nobles, were brought before the military court, and on their confession condemned to death and executed by stoning.

Callisthenes had been tutor to many of them and in close relations with them; in Alexander's mood towards him, the suspicion was natural that he had known of the conspiracy or even instigated it. Alexander had him arrested and an enquiry instituted. As Callisthenes was a Greek, there was no question of trying him by the Macedonian army. Alexander's first thought was to send him before the court of the *Synhedrion* at Corinth. This information is valuable, because it again shows that Alexander still looked on himself as being for the Greeks *Hegemon* of the Hellenic League. But subsequently he abandoned the idea, and after taking Callisthenes with him for months as a prisoner, he had him condemned and executed by a private court in India. It is beyond doubt that Alexander believed in his guilt, for Ptolemy and Aristobulus both maintain that he was the instigator of the plot. Yet his guilt was not judicially proved and is difficult to accept. In the Greek world, which regarded his execution as a judicial murder, Alexander was sorely compromised by his condemnation. The excitement in the Peripatetic School, which counted Callisthenes as one of its adherents, was particularly acute. Theophrastus gave vent to his grief for the tragic end of his friend in a treatise, *Callisthenes*, or *On Mourning*, in which he stated that Alexander did not understand how to make a right use of his good fortune. The Peripatetics thus initiated the unfavourable estimate of Alexander as a tyrant intoxicated by his power and dazzled by his luck, an estimate which was developed ever more incisively in succeeding histories. On the other hand the relation between Alexander and Aristotle, who as uncle and teacher of Callisthenes must have been very closely affected, was in spite of this incident, only temporarily, if at all, disturbed. They continued to correspond and exchange ideas.

5. POLITICAL CONSIDERATIONS*

. . . Up to this time there had been a clear distinction between being the son of a god and being a god; all the mortal sons of Zeus had not been raised to heaven. But by the third century B.C. the distinction had become blurred, and that process was already beginning; some of the chorus of flatterers were hinting that Alexander was a god, just as Callisthenes had hinted it in his story of Mount Climax. Of Alexander's own mind we know little. He never called himself son of Ammon, and to be so called by others roused him to fury, and few ever dared do it; whatever his relationship with Ammon exactly was, it was evidently to him something not for profane tongues. Equally, he never called himself son of Zeus; but he allowed others so to call him. Naturally he did not believe it; he was occasionally sarcastic on the subject, and in public regularly alluded to his father Philip. But as he permitted it, he may have thought that some day it might have its uses.

In the spring of 327 the whole matter came to a head. Alexander had already initiated his policy of fusion, the fusion of the Macedonian and Persian elements in his empire; apart from his Persian satraps, he had, since Darius' death, adopted on State occasions Persian dress and Persian court ceremonial, and had made Chares the historian chamberlain. He now resolved to introduce the Persian custom of prostration (*proskynesis*) for all those approaching the king. To Persians it was only a ceremony; the Achaemenid kings had not been gods, and prostration in Persian eyes did not imply worship. But to Greeks and Macedonians it did imply worship; man did not prostrate himself save to the gods. Alexander knew perfectly how Greeks must interpret prostration, and must therefore have intended to become a god; and as Greeks, Macedonians, and Persians were all involved, it can only mean that he intended to become, officially, the god of his empire; he was doing rather more than feeling his way. His reasons were entirely political; the thing was to him merely a pretence which might form a useful instrument of statecraft and become, he thought, a considerable help to his policy of fusion; also, among other things, he had to settle how the autocrat of Asia, without playing the autocrat, could get a juridical standing in those free Greek cities in whose hands lay his empire's access to the Aegean. What put the idea of becoming a god into his head seems clear enough. It had been put there long before he crossed to Asia, by the two chief political thinkers of his youth, his tutor Aristotle and Isocrates; for Isocrates had said to Philip that, if he conquered Persia, nothing would be left him but to become a god, and Aristotle, not content with telling Alexander that he had no peer, had said, with Alexander in mind, that the supreme ruler when he came would be as a god among men. Whether Callisthenes really had much to do with it, as some believed later, can hardly be said; he may perhaps have been one of the factors which led Alexander to believe that the time was ripe.

Such was the background of Alexander's attempt to introduce *proskynesis*. He had the support of Hephaestion and one or two other Macedonians; and both he and Hephaestion believed that Callisthenes would aid them, as was natural after his

* W. W. Tarn, *Alexander the Great* (Cambridge: Cambridge University Press, 1948), Vol. 1, pp. 78–82.

story of the sea prostrating itself before the king; some indeed asserted that Callisthenes had promised. But when prostration was actually introduced, events took an unexpected course. The Macedonians offered no actual opposition, but their displeasure and even anger were evident; one general did worse than oppose—he laughed. But the first Greek called on, Callisthenes, opposed in good earnest and asked Alexander to confine this Asiatic custom to Asiatics. Alexander had a strong sense of what was possible; he dropped prostration for good and all, and with it the idea of becoming the god of his Empire. But he was furious with Callisthenes. He had counted on his influence as an aid to his policy, and Callisthenes had failed him.

The reason for Callisthenes' change of attitude has been debated ever since, without much result. In the Peripatetic literature drawn on by Plutarch in his *Life* of Alexander he figures as a lover of liberty opposing a tyrant; he was of course the same Callisthenes, the man who, Aristotle said, had no sense. Doubtless, as Aristotle's pupil, he despised barbarians and objected to Persian ceremonial; but the time to think of that was before he wrote about Mount Climax, and hinted that Alexander was a god. To say that he had Panhellenic ideas, and wished to make of Alexander a god for Greeks but not for Persians, is no explanation, for to make Alexander actually a god at all was not his intention; he had merely been playing with fire, with the usual result. One may suppose that he had only meant to write up Alexander in extravagant terms, and suddenly found himself (as he thought) faced with the terrible consequences of what he had done; the god he had helped to make meant to act as such; it was no longer rhetoric but sober earnest. He tried to draw back, too late.

Then came the Pages' conspiracy. One of the royal pages, Hermolaus, had anticipated Alexander at a boar-hunt; he was deprived of his horse and whipped, apparently the usual Macedonian custom. He and some friends thereon conspired to kill Alexander; they were detected and put to death. This act of personal revenge had no political import, but it involved Callisthenes, who had been Hermolaus' tutor. Whether he was formally a party to the conspiracy is uncertain; but he had indulged in some wild talk to the boys on the virtue of killing tyrants, and Ptolemy says the boys confessed that this talk lay at the bottom of the whole business. Alexander put Callisthenes to death, presumably for conspiracy; to relieve him of odium, Chares spread a story that Callisthenes died naturally in prison. The verdict of the historian Timaeus may be recorded: Callisthenes deserved his fate, for he had made of a man a god, and done all in his power to destroy Alexander's soul. How far the verdict is true will probably never be known. But Callisthenes had his revenge; and Alexander paid. He incurred the hostility of Aristotle's school; Theophrastus in a pamphlet lamented Callisthenes' death and branded Alexander as a tyrant, and Demetrius of Phalerum presently carried the school over to Alexander's enemy Cassander; and the two philosophers worked out a doctrine of Chance, which was applied to Alexander. Thus from the Peripatetic school, of which Callisthenes had been a member, arose that debased portrait of Alexander against which Plutarch so passionately protested, and from which history for long could not shake itself free—the portrait of a despot whose achievements were due to luck, and who was ruined at the end by the excess of his own fortune.

6. MILITARY NECESSITY*

Our problem, obviously, is to discover what brought the idea of deification out of Alexander's head at Bactra. Does it seem likely, as Wilcken suggests, that Alexander had the Persians so much on his mind at this time that he was ready to offend the Greeks and Macedonians? Is Tarn's explanation any more satisfying, that western affairs were so much on Alexander's mind at this time that he was willing to risk trouble with his generals in order to obtain "a judicial standing" in far-away Greece? He was having trouble enough with his generals, as it was.

Alexander's motive, whatever it was, must be sought in the immediate background of the days in Bactria-Sogdiana; and it seems equally sensible to suggest that the motivation must have been a strong one. These were days, of course, of extraordinary ideas; but it had also been a period of continuous guerrilla warfare. Moreover, it was a time of continuing opposition to Alexander: the tragedies of Philotas, Parmenio, and Cleitus;[88] the mutiny of the Thessalian cavalry; the resistance of the seer Aristander and Callisthenes to the crossing of the Jaxartes, which barely survives in Arrian and must have been but a part of wider hostility to

Alexander.[89] All this lay in the background. Nor, incidentally, would it be downed; for the Macedonian opposition at the banquet was soon followed by the conspiracy of the Pages, who said, so Arrian quotes Ptolemy and Aristobulus, that "Callisthenes had instigated them to make the daring attempt" against Alexander.[90] Sheer military necessity—the business of getting on with one's generals and immediate circle surely amounts to that— was as present here as at the time of the Thessalian mutiny; and it required as drastic treatment. Mutinous cavalry could be replaced with local cavalry—but what to do with an uncertain officer corps? We have no ancient evidence for this or any other explanation, obviously; but it seems clear that Alexander decided to abandon the comradely relationship with his officers, which had long characterized the Macedonian monarchy, and to put an end to wavering support plots by becoming an autocrat. Or better, to put it in Greek terms, he decided, in this century of religious indifference which had already raised living men to divine status, to become a god.

[89] This is discussed on p. 292, fn. 20 of my paper, "Alexander's Deification," *Am. Jour. Philol.*, LXIV (1943), 286–301.

[90] Arrian IV, 14, 1. Truesdell S. Brown does not advance the study of Alexander when he says that the Pages, "steadily refused to implicate Callisthenes", in "Callisthenes and Alexander," *Am. Jour. Philol.*, LXX (1949), 225–48.

* C. A. Robinson Jr., "The Extraordinary Ideas of Alexander the Great," *American Historical Review*, 62 (1956–57), pp. 340–341.

[88] Cleitus' murder is described in Arrian IV, 8.

C. THE DEIFICATION DECREE

1. THE DECREE RESTORING GREEK EXILES*

Alexander, a little before his death, had ordered all the exiles and outlawed persons

* Diodorus Siculus, 18. 8, translated by G. Booth.

of the Grecian cities to be recalled, as well to advance his own honour and esteem, as to gain the hearts of many in every city by his clemency, who might stand up for his interest against the innovations and defections of the Grecians. At the approach, therefore, of the time of celebrating the Olympiads, he sent away Nicanor, a native of the city Stagira, with a letter concerning the restoration of the banditties of Greece, and commanded it to be proclaimed by the common cryer, who executed the command, and read the letter, in these words—

King Alexander, to the Banditties of the Grecian cities

We were not the cause of your banishment, but will be of the return of you all into your own country, excepting such as are banished for outrageous crimes; of which things we have written to Antipater, requiring him to proceed by force against all such as shall oppose your restoration.

When these orders were proclaimed, the people set up a great shout, testifying their approbation: for those of them that were present at the solemnity readily laid hold on the king's mercy, and returned their thanks with expressions of their joy, and applauses of his grace and favour: for all the banished men were then got together

at the Olympiads, above the number of twenty thousand. Many there were who approved of their restoration as a prudent act; but the Ætolians and Athenians were much offended at it; for the Ætolians expected that the Œnians who were banished out from among them should have undergone due punishment for their crimes: for the king had made a great noise with his threats, that he would not only punish the children of the Œnians, but that he himself would execute justice upon the authors themselves. Whereupon the Athenians would not agree by any means to part with Samos, which they had divided by lot; but, because they were not at present able to cope with Alexander, they judged it more advisable to sit still, and watch till they found a convenient opportunity, which fortune presently offered them: for Alexander dying in a short time afterwards, and leaving no children to succeed him, they grew confident that they should be able not only to regain their liberty, but likewise the sovereignty of all Greece.

2. A BROADER PURPOSE*

From Susa Alexander turned his attention again to affairs in Greece. Since the defeat of Agis and the infliction of punishment on the Spartans he had had neither time nor cause to occupy himself with Hellas. Though after the ending of the Panhellenic war of vengeance he still was *Hegemon* of the Corinthian League, yet through the colossal successes of the last years and through the extension of his empire to India the relation of power between the *Hegemon* and the Greek allies had altered very much to their disadvantage. Conscious of these superhuman and extraordinary achievements, Alexander

now issued from Susa the request that he should be recognised as a god by the Greek allies.

To understand this step we must first remove certain misinterpretations which it has received. It is a widespread error that Alexander, in the interest of the unity of his world-empire, demanded worship as a divinity from all his subjects. There is no indication to point to his having issued this request to the Asiatics as well. The request is attested in the case of the Greeks, and, as we may assume, only in the case of the Greeks of the Corinthian League. This makes it clear also that his request was not addressed to the Macedonians; for Macedonia was outside the league. The idea of a general official cult for the empire was quite alien to Alexander, though his

* Ulrich Wilcken, *Alexander the Great*, translated by G. C. Richards (New York: Dial Press, 1932), pp. 209–215. By permission of Quelle & Meyer, formerly of Leipzig, now of Heidelberg.

successors after his death put his portrait on coins instead of the types of the gods.

Equally erroneous is the conception, formerly widespread but held by some people even to-day, that the idea of apotheosis was Oriental; and this is why they see in the act a sign of the king's growing Orientalism. We may here exclude from consideration the unique divine kingship of Egypt, the effect of which even on Alexander was, as we saw, quite local in its limitations. In the third millennium a worship of the ruler as divine had been developed along with the notion of world-empire in Mesopotamia; but from Hammurabi (about 2000) onwards it had disappeared, and thus—this is the important point—the Achaemenids had never been worshipped as gods by their subjects. In Alexander's day the idea was quite unknown to the Aisatic East and cannot have been borrowed thence.

Modern scholarship has recognised that it is rather a purely Greek idea, which was called into life again by Alexander. With the Greeks the dividing line between gods and men, as their legends and myths bear out, had always been fluid. As Heracles had earned a place among the Olympians by his deeds, so in the bright light of history the mortal who had performed superhuman tasks in the eyes of his contemporaries, had in his lifetime been the recipient of divine honours. Lysander, for instance, when he was at the summit of his power, had been worshipped as a god with altars and paeans by the Samian oligarchs. Clearchus, tyrant of Heracleia, a pupil of Isocrates, had caused himself to be worshipped by his subjects as son of Zeus. Moreover Philip's partisans at Ephesus had set up his statue in the Temple of Artemis, and had thus paid him divine honours. When Philip himself at the marriage feast at Aegae (336) had his own image carried in a procession as the thirteenth along with the twelve chief gods of Macedonia, which made him appear, if not a god, at least as enthroned with the gods, one may conjecture in this the influence of Greek ideas upon the Macedonian court. Nor was it only practice that gave Alexander precedent; theory also played its part. His teacher Aristotle said in his *Politics*, that if there is a man who in ability and political capacity is incomparably superior to all others, such a man is 'as a god among men,' and added that against such there is no law; 'for they are a law to themselves.' And had not Isocrates written to his father Philip in his latest letter that, if he forced the Great King to submission, nothing remained for him but to become a god? Had not Alexander now accomplished infinitely more than Philip?

It was in harmony with purely Greek ideas that after his victorious return from India he claimed divine honours from the Greeks. The idea was all the more familiar to him, because, seven years before, the priest of Ammon had greeted him as son of Zeus. If then he had not committed himself to proclaiming officially in the Greek world this divine sonship, the announcement of which he had accepted with faith, in the sense of the Greek conception, as a divine revelation and a recognition of his superhuman divine force, yet this consciousness of a divine sonship had always remained in his mind. Possessed by it, elevated by his fabulous successes and in expectation of his plans for world-sovereignty, he now took the decisive step of going further than these special revelations, and of requiring divine honours from the Greeks of the Corinthian League. It is a mistaken view of Alexander's character to bar out this inner religious experience and to assume that the demand was a purely political move, the only object of which was to lift him as a god above the stipulations of the Corinthian League and to subject the autonomous Greek cities and their lands to his divine will. Certainly his apotheosis, if accepted, meant a great increase of his personal prestige with the cities of the league, a consummation which could not but be desirable to him; and on the theory of Aristotle his will would then have been raised above the laws. But on the one hand, Alexander had already, as we saw, previously set himself above the provisions of the league treaty, without needing a divine authority, merely on the ground of his growing predominance, and he could continue to do the same. On the other hand the Greeks, though they admitted the apotheosis, did not on that account recognise his will as divine law, but—at any rate in the case of the Athenians— refused him obedience and were determined to resist him to the uttermost even by violence. In the practice of political life they made a distinction between the god whom they worshipped with a cult, and the earthly *Hegemon*, whose rights and duties were fixed in their eyes afterwards as before by the Covenant of the league. It must be mentioned that even later the Hellenistic cult of kings, though as imperial cult it meant more in the several Greek states than Alexander's apotheosis, was never an obstacle to disobedience, and had no influence whatever on the practice of political life.

This distinction between the political and religious spheres, along with the Greek character of the apotheosis, explains to us the fact that the Greeks complied with Alexander's wish without serious scruples. Naturally the members of the anti-Macedonian factions argued against it, but if those political consequences had really been bound up with the apotheosis, the opposition would have been of a different kind, and the speeches in the popular assemblies would not have been as harmless or as ironical in their tone as those that have been handed down to us; nor would a champion of freedom like Demosthenes, after an original protest, have finally advised the Athenian people to recognise the king 'as son of Zeus or as Poseidon too if he wished.' The indifference, which treated the question almost as a bagatelle,

demonstrates that it was a question not of high politics but of religion, which in the opinion of the *illuminati* to whom the old polytheism was no longer possessed of any meaning, had no exciting importance.

We are ill-informed how the affair was managed. That the initiative proceeded from Alexander is certain; but we do not hear in what shape it reached the Greeks. It can scarcely have been a command, but more probably a desire which he either expressed or caused to be expressed to the *Synhedrion*, and which, however formulated, was indubitably equivalent to a demand. The *Synhedrion* may then have communicated the desire to the several members of the league; for actually no uniform league cult was created, but the individual states by popular decree received the king among the gods of their community. What form they chose, whether as god or as son of a god (see Demosthenes), was obviously entirely left to them. The prevailing assumption that at Athens, on the proposal of Demandes, Alexander received his cult as the 'new Dionysus' has recently been proved erroneous.

In the spring of the next year (323) ambassadors from Hellas reached Alexander at Babylon to honour him with golden crowns. They appeared not as envoys to an earthly king, but with wreaths on their heads as 'festal ambassadors' (*Theoroi*) who come to a god, as Arrian states. Hellas had complied with his desire.

The effort to rearrange affairs in Greece called forth as well new orders of Alexander, issued from Susa in the spring of 324. This time they were commands, and he sent them to the *Synhedrion* by Nicanor of Stagira. The one which concerned the local leagues of the Achaeans, Arcadians and Boeotians, is obscure to us, because we have it only in a mutilated form. The other edict was very important. By it Alexander ordered that in the territory of the league all exiles—with the exception of temple-robbers and murderers, usually omitted from amnesties—should return to their homes and be entirely or partially reinstated in their previous properties. The sanction was added, that in case any city refused to receive its exiles back Antipater, the representative of Alexander, was to compel them by force. Politically one must regard this decree as an act of wise statesmanship. Alexander attacked one of the worst cancers of the Greek system of small states and endeavoured to remove it; and one will esteem the decree all the more highly, because under existing political conditions many of the exiles to be restored must have been his political opponents, whom he might hope to reconcile by this act. On the other hand it is obvious that this order, issued by Alexander alone, without any co-operation of the *Synhedrion* was a glaring violation of the Covenant of the league. Though the paragraph in question is not preserved to us, yet according to the spirit of the Covenant it cannot be doubtful that an arrangement like this could only be made by the co-operation of *Hegemon* and *Synhedrion*.

We may emphasise the fact that in the tedious discussions of this edict no trace is anywhere to be found of any reference to the religious importance that Alexander

obtained by apotheosis in the league cities. This last stage of the way to the ignoring of the *Synhedrion* and the forming of an autocratic position is rather to be explained exclusively by Alexander's vastly increased consciousness of power. The decree is not a result of the claim to apotheosis, which, as we have shown, had no political object; on the contrary, both have their roots in the same psychological fact. In the decree speaks the man who was aiming at world-sovereignty and was determined to shake off the inconvenient fetters of the Covenant of the league. To the *Synhedrion*, to which Nicanor handed the original edict, fell merely, it appears, the task of communicating copies of it to all the members of the league. In this last stage of his development Alexander used the *Synhedrion* simply as the place of publication for the expression of his absolute and omnipotent will. It was probably under the impression of the news thus heard from Susa—the mass marriages with Persian women and this edict—that Aristotle sent to Alexander the well-known warning to treat the Hellenes as a *Hegemon* and the barbarians as a despot. Teacher and pupil could no longer understand each other.

3. The Political Motive*

In 324, at Susa, Alexander was faced by a new problem. In old Greece there was a mass of exiles from every city, many of them democrats exiled by Antipater or his governments. Some had taken service as mercenaries with Alexander's satraps while he was in India; when he made the satraps disband their private armies, they had returned to Greece with their arms and without occupation. The position in that overcrowded country had become difficult;

at best the exiles were a focus for every kind of discontent, at worst a possible menace. Alexander saw that, if he were to have the peace in his world (not merely in his Empire, for Greece was not in his Empire) which soon after he was to pray for at Opis, the exiles must be restored to their cities and their cities must receive them. But his difficulty was that the cities were those of the League of Corinth, and as its President he had sworn to the Covenant of the League, which forbade him to interfere in the internal affairs of the cities; yet it was very necessary to interfere. In these circumstances he issued

* W. W. Tarn, *Alexander the Great* (Cambridge: Cambridge University Press, 1948), Vol. 2, pp. 370–373.

to the cities of the League a decree ordering them to receive back their exiles (which he had no constitutional power to issue) and also a request for his own deification (which probably came first); for the Covenant bound Alexander the king but did not, and would not, bind Alexander the god, and he could therefore set it aside without losing his self-respect. To us this may seem a quibble, but no one can say it was a quibble to him, or that his careful observance throughout life of the outer forms of religion meant that they were nothing to him but forms. It has been objected that deification did not actually give him any new powers, but that is not the point; he had all the power he wanted, but he had not the right to use it; and to be a god gave him a juridical standing in the cities which he could not otherwise have got, for there was no place for a king in the constitution of a Greek city. The cities of the League granted his request and deified him, thereby (in form) condoning his breach of the Covenant; for while Alexander was thinking of a way of escape from the Covenant which bound him, the cities and States of the League were thinking primarily of the exiles decree, which hit some of them hard, notably Athens and Aetolia, and was disturbing to them all; and they were hoping to appease Alexander by granting his request for deification, which by comparison seemed to them of little importance. Calling him a god did not mean that they were going to worship him; no cult of him was set up anywhere, and in fact there is no sign that, Egypt apart, anybody ever did worship him till after his death; the first known case is that of Eumenes and his Macedonian troops in the Alexander-tent. His request for deification, then, was a limited *political* measure for a purely political purpose, and nothing else. It is well known that some scholars have long believed this, while others have strenuously denied it; I trust that what I have written in this study will show that the view which I follow

is not only true but inevitable. His deification showed that he meant to stand above parties and factions, for many of the exiles, banished by Antipater or by the governments he supported, were Macedonia's enemies; it also showed that he had no intention of adopting Aristotle's view that such as he were above the law and that he could break the Covenant of the League at his pleasure. That his deification was purely political seems to be further supported by two facts: one is that he never put his own head on his coinage, as he must have done had he been a god in the sense in which many of the kings who followed him were gods; and the other is that his request for deification did not (so far as is known) extend to the Greek cities of Asia Minor, who were his free allies and who were not members of the League of Corinth. There may have been no exiles problem there; but had there been he could have settled it without being their god, for he was not bound to them by any covenant which forbade him to interfere in their internal affairs. His deification, therefore, in 324 B.C., like his preliminary attempt at Bactra, was entirely a political matter, but this time limited to the cities of the League of Corinth; and it only remains to consider two modern objections to this view.

Professor Berve's pupil A. Heuss has put forward the view, if I understand him rightly, that a political *Herrschaft*—say kingship—was always compounded of two independent elements, a political and a religious, and that you cannot abolish the religious element and make the political element do the work of both. He said there was warrant enough for this view in history, but did not say what it was; as I understand the matter, one need go no further than the Macedonian and Epirote monarchies to see that Heuss' view is untenable, and that there were plenty of kings whose kingship had no religious element; indeed I doubt if one could find any king in Alexander's day and in his sphere whose kingship *had* any religious element, putting aside Egypt and the little priest-kings of Asia Minor. Heuss makes a point that the deified kings (he includes Alexander) never mention their divine powers in their letters to the cities, where one would expect it. Why one should expect it I cannot imagine, seeing that they never mention their temporal powers either, any more than is ever done by kings or presidents to-day.

The other objection is one made in 1931 by Wilcken in his *Alexander der Grosse*. After discarding offhand the view that Alexander's deification in 324 was a political measure (though he had taken the scene at Bactra to be a political measure) he said (p. 201) that both the decree for the recall of the exiles and Alexander's request to the Greek cities of the League for deification had their roots in Alexander's psychology, and that that psychology was not only an outcome of his amazing success but was connected with, or conditioned by, his desire and plans for world-dominion; for he had been conscious for years that he *was* the son of Zeus-Ammon (p. 198) and history will go wrong if it neglects this inner religious experience. It must have given full weight to Alexander's inner religious experience (Ammon), fuller, possibly, than, even if not quite in the same way as, my predecessors; but this can have nothing to do with his deification in 324. There are several things to be said about Wilcken's view; the first and most obvious is that he has refuted it himself by his repeated statement that, as was indeed the fact, Alexander's request for deification in 324 was confined to the Greek cities of the League of Corinth, who were not even his subjects; what has that to do with the psychology of world-rule? The second is

that, before it is possible to talk of Alexander's plans for world-dominion, some one has got to refute my demonstration (App. 24), based on evidence, that his supposed plans in that behalf are a late invention; this has never been done, and I greatly doubt if it can be. As to Alexander's psychology in the matter of deification, I should be sorry to claim exact knowledge; but I have been considering it throughout this study, and as there is no reputable evidence that he ever called himself the son of any god, let alone a god, or that he even alluded to the descent of his line from Zeus, it is only fair to suppose that he did not believe that he was a god or even the son of one; and if those about him called him a son of Zeus, or even intimated that he ought to be a god, that has no bearing on his own thoughts or beliefs. Wilcken made one other point: his deification in 324 cannot have been political, or the Greek cities would never have granted it in the casual way they did. Certainly the cities did not take it to be a political move; but the only sign of casualness, I think, is the contemptuous remark attributed to Demosthenes, which is none too certain. I have already explained why the cities granted deification; but, quite apart from that, no city could afford to refuse. There was a great struggle at Athens over the proposal, but Demosthenes finally gave in, and those who desired appeasement and peace carried the day; Sparta, bled white at Megalopolis, was helpless; and probably most of the cities, great and small, acted as they did largely through fear of Alexander, for the moment that that fear was removed by his death they tore up the Covenant of the League of Corinth and started war against Macedonia, led by Athens, who punished Demades for having moved the proposal that Alexander should be a god.

4. Did Alexander Request Deification?*

Divine pretensions were always, in the ancient world, a heaven-sent subject for a clever epigram; Agesilaus had already made this clear; and almost every Greek capable of an epigram, it seems, was credited with one at Alexander's expense. The Spartan Damis said, with devastating irony, "As Alexander wants to be a god, let him be one." At Athens there was a crop of epigrammatists. Diogenes (probably not alive at the time) is reported to have said, "when the Athenians voted Alexander to be Dionysus, you had better make *me* Sarapis." Pytheas, rebuked for presumption in speaking, as a young man, against the honouring of Alexander, said "But I am older than the man whom you are voting to be a god"; older, in fact, than the eternal. Lycurgus said, "What sort of a god can this be when the first thing that you would have to do on leaving his temple would be to purify yourself." Demades, who proposed that Alexander should be recognized as a thirteenth god, is reported, in Valerius Maximus' Latin translation, to have said to his opponents, "Videte ne, dum caelum custoditis, terram amittatis." Demosthenes, on principle opposed to the granting of divine honours to Alexander, spoke at least once in a different tone, saying, "Recognize him as the son of Zeus. Recognize him as son of Poseidon too, if he would like it," though it is hard to see in this highly satirical remark any genuine support for the proposal.

Our knowledge of these witticisms comes from a wide variety of sources, all except Dinarchus and Hyperides, late and derivative. Since Callisthenes concluded his account of Alexander between 330 and 328 B.C., and since the Greek and Mace-

donian *entourage* of Alexander had probably been referring to him, however mockingly, as "son of Zeus" since the visit to Ammon in 332/1 B.C., one might assume that in mainland Greece these various epigrams were made over a wide period of time, in the last eight or nine years of Alexander's life. Only one of them is given a historical context, though even that has not an exact date. Both Plutarch in the *Moralia* and Aelian, undoubtedly drawing on a common source, state that the Spartan epigram of Damis was made in response to a request emanating from Alexander himself, that he should be voted a god. The consensus of historians, therefore, has ascribed all these epigrams (except that of Diogenes, which is regarded as unhistorical) to a single occasion, and has seen the occasion in the receipt of a request sent by Alexander to the League of Corinth in 324 B.C. from Susa, at the time when he ordered the restoration of the political exiles to the Greek member states of the League of Corinth.

For this last instruction, which was sent by Nicanor and read to the assembled Greeks at Olympia, there is abundant evidence, literary and epigraphic. For the sending of a request for divine honours, if we except the common source of the passages in Plutarch's *Moralia* and in Aelian, referred to already, there is no evidence at all. Arrian is silent; but his silence is not fatal, for there is a lacuna in his text and he says nothing, either, of the dispatch ordering the recall of the political exiles. Plutarch is silent, in his life of Alexander, but then he is silent too about the recall of the exiles. But, more serious, Diodorus and Q. Curtius, both of whom mention the order for the recall of the exiles, make no mention at all of any request for consecration.

There are, however, two pieces of evidence which may be relevant. The first

* J. P. V. D. Balsdon, "The 'Divinity' of Alexander the Great," *Historia*, 1 (1950), pp. 383–388.

is the behaviour of Demosthenes at Athens. To make him depart from his attitude of opposition on principle to according divine honours to Alexander, some great constraint must have been required, such constraint (it is suggested) as would be found in a request from Alexander himself. Yet, how strong is this, as evidence? Timaeus contrasted Demosthenes with Callisthenes, as opposing extravagant honours to Alexander. Dinarchus accused him of being quite inconsistent, sometimes speaking one way and sometimes the other. And Demosthenes' actual proposal, as given by Hyperides, was as ironical as it was complimentary.

A second piece of indirect evidence has been found in Arrian. Arrian mentioned the arrival of embassies from Greece to Alexander in 324 B.C. In 323 B.C. he mentioned embassies again, bringing golden crowns from the Greek cities and this statement has inscriptional support, showing that the crowns were voted after and on account of the receipt of the instruction for the recall of the exiles. But in 323 B.C. the envoys came, Arrian says, and crowned Alexander, "ὡς θεωροὶ δῆθεν ἐς τιμὴν θεοῦ ἀφιγμένοι." There is nothing in the offer of a golden crown to indicate recognition of divinity; and "ὡς θεωροὶ δῆθεν" is not the same as a statement that they came actually ὡς θεωροὶ rather than πρέσβεις; moreover, the passage is one which in general should not be pressed too hard, for it is that very rare thing in Arrian, a piece of fine writing. The envoys were "as if they had come on a sacred embassy to honour a god," he says; he continues, "τῷ δὲ οὐ πόρρω ἄρα ἡ τελευτὴ ἦν."

Even if the passage is stressed, however, it does not suggest that the initiative had come from Alexander himself.

This is the evidence; and D. G. Hogarth in 1887 claimed that it failed to warrant the assumption that Alexander sent any instruction or request for the recognition of his divinity to the states of mainland Greece in 324 B.C. Many scholars accepted Hogarth's conclusion; others believe that it was demolished by Eduard Meyer. But all that Meyer did was to claim that Demosthenes could not have acted as he did except under strong compulsion; and that is not enough to prove Hogarth wrong. Hogarth could only be proved wrong if it could be established that certain facts of the history of 324/3 B.C. are unintelligible, or all but unintelligible, except on the hypothesis of such a request sent by Alexander in 324; and this, I imagine, is what Tarn would claim.

Tarn thinks that in ordering the restoration of the exiles to the Greek cities, Alexander was overstepping his constitutional rights as ἡγεμών of the Corinthian League since he had not, as ἡγεμών, the right to interfere in the internal affairs of the individual cities. He therefore required a higher status in the League than he possessed already; indeed he required an overriding status. Recognition as a god would give him this status.

To this suggestion there are a number of strong objections.

First we have at least two inscriptions, one referring to the restoration of the exiles at Tegea, the second to the restoration of the exiles at Samos. The first appears to refer to Alexander simply as βασιλεὺς Ἀλέξανδρος the second refers to him as Ἀλέξανδρος. There is no suggestion at all of a divine title.

Secondly, on Tarn's hypothesis, the request for consecration was made in order to prevent any doubts about the constitutional legality of the exiles decree. Tarn writes in one passage, "The exiles decree was therefore accompanied, or possibly even preceded, by a request to the cities of the League for his deification"; in another, "A decree . . . to cities of the League to receive back their exiles and also a request for his own deification (which probably came first)." Why the "possibly" and the "probably?" Surely it *must* on Tarn's hypothesis have come first.

Thirdly, imagination really boggles at the picture that seems to be envisaged. It was a "request," required in order to sanction a "decree." Yet the decree was issued before it could be known whether the "request" was granted. And what sort of a request was it? "Calling him a god did not mean that they were going to worship him," Tarn states. Not in any way at all? Not even with "hero's honours?" What was he to get, then? An array of titles, different in each different city? At Athens, "Son of Zeus, Son of Poseidon, Thirteenth God?" Would such a conglomeration of titles make him a god of the Corinthian League; which was the only place where, on Tarn's hypothesis, he needed to be a god? "His request for deification was a limited *political* measure, for a purely political purpose and nothing else," but "certainly the cities did not take it to be a political move." It looks, in fact, rather like trickery. If the Greeks said, "But you are not empowered to command the recall of the exiles," he would be able to say, "Ah, you ought to have thought of that before you voted me a god." Is this really the kind of behaviour which fits at all with Tarn's, or indeed with any historian's, picture of Alexander?

No, we need not think that at Susa on his way back from India Alexander was troubled about constitutional niceties within the Corinthian League. As concerned the exiles, his instruction would be enough; and it was. He read it first to his own assembled troops before the instruction itself was dispatched to Greece. This indicated no particular *punctilio*. In every Greek city he has had his partisans, and with the return of the exiles their numbers would be greatly increased. Within the cities there was the same rift between pro-Macedonians and anti-Macedonians as there was in the Greek cities of the early second century B.C. between pro-Romans and anti-Romans. As long as Alexander was in the far East, his opponents in Greece could hope; he might always be killed. But now he was on his way West again. This was the moment for his supporters to do everything that they could to ingratiate themselves with him, to compromise their opponents. The question of divine honours was an excellent one on which to force the issue. There is no reason at all why, with such slender evidence to support the hypothesis, one should see in this the maladroit hand of Alexander himself.